Guide to North American Steam Locomotives

RAILROAD REFERENCE

COMPILED BY GEORGE H. DRURY

Editor: Bob Hayden   Copy Editor: Terrence Spohn   Layout: Sabine Beaupré   Cover Design: Mark Watson

On the cover: Norfolk & Western 1218, a class A 2-6-6-4 built by N&W at Roanoke, Virginia, in 1943, and Nickel Plate 587, a USRA light 2-8-2 built by Baldwin in 1918 for the Lake Erie & Western, pose for photographers on July 21, 1989, at Asheville, North Carolina, during the convention of the National Railway Historical Society. Photo by Mason Y. Cooper.

KALMBACH BOOKS

DEDICATION

This volume is dedicated to the memory of David P. Morgan, Editor of *Trains Magazine* from 1953 to 1987. Shortly before his death he wrote that he envied me this project; the tasks of research and writing would have been both richer and easier with his counsel.

Library of Congress Cataloging-in-Publication Data

Drury, George H.
    Guide to North American steam locomotives / George H. Drury.
         p.   cm. — (Railroad reference series; no. 8)
    Includes index.
    ISBN 0-89024-206-2
    1. Locomotives—United States. 2. Locomotives—Canada. 3. Locomotives—
Mexico. I. Title. II. Series
TJ603.2.D78 1993   93-41472
625.2'61'097—dc20   CIP

To order additional copies of this book or other Kalmbach books, call toll free at (800) 533-6644.

INTRODUCTION

The steam locomotive is the most fascinating machine yet devised. It was the first piece of industrial technology that was on public display: Steam locomotives came right into every town, and all their working parts were open to view. The men who ran them were visible and accessible, whether inspecting and oiling the machinery during a stop or seated in the cab. The romance of the locomotive was almost unbearable. The engineer's seat was at a throne-like height above ordinary people, and the train was a link to exotic places (at the very least, the next town).

The romance has been explored and explained by others. What lies behind the romance is the development of a technology. Steam locomotives were the machinery of transportation factories, and each factory — each railroad — had its own ideas about the machinery it needed; and rarely did two of them agree about the proper design. This book explores those designs and explains how they developed.

Locomotive development until 1900

The first locomotives, like Stephenson's *Rocket* of 1829, were contraptions. They had boilers, cylinders, and wheels, but each pioneering builder had his own ideas about placement of the components. By 1840 the conventions had been established: horizontal firetube boiler with firebox at the rear and smokebox and stack at the front, horizontal cylinders ahead of the driving wheels and usually outside the frames, a cab to shelter the engineer and the fireman at the rear, and, behind the cab, a car carrying fuel and water — the tender.

The typical locomotive of the 1860s and 1870s was a 4-4-0 weighing about 30 tons. It had a deep, narrow firebox (about 33 inches wide) set between the driving axles, and a low-mounted, tapered boiler. Slide valves actuated by Stephenson valve gear routed saturated steam to the cylinders. It was a simple machine, sufficient for most duties. Other types in common use, usually for freight service, were the Ten-Wheeler (4-6-0), essentially a 4-4-0 with a third pair of drivers, and the Mogul (2-6-0). Locomotives were little changed from the designs of 1850, because there had been little need for change. Train length and weight were limited by the strength of couplers, draft gears, and underframes. Primitive braking systems and the lack of signals kept trains speeds low. During that period there was considerable experimentation with various aspects of locomotive design. The net effect of most of it was to prove what wouldn't work.

Until about 1880 railroads generally bought locomotives designed by the builders. Then different lines began to need specialized locomotives, first choosing from designs offered by the builders, then

1895	1896	1897	1898	1899	1900	1901	1902	1903	1904
CB&Q 2-4-2 Steel under-frames for cars					CB&Q 2-6-2 Oil as fuel Steel cars	2-8-0 with wide firebox Alco formed	MP 4-6-2 Vauclain balanced compound	AT&SF 2-10-2 C&O 0-8-0	B&O 0-6-6-0 Stoker PRR test plant

TIME LINE: Significant innovations in steam locomotive technology

developing their own. The result was that Alco and Baldwin could build identical 2-8-0s for Boston & Maine, but those 2-8-0s would differ greatly from 2-8-0s built for the Pennsylvania Railroad and the Denver & Rio Grande.

In the 15 years before 1900 railroad technology made several major advances. The Master Car Builders Association adopted the Janney automatic knuckle coupler in 1887 and the Westinghouse automatic air brake in 1889. Automatic block signals were coming into use. Steel was replacing wood for car underframes and, within a few years, for entire cars.

Faster, stronger, more powerful locomotives were needed. Increased tractive effort could be achieved by increasing the weight on the drive wheels, but few railroads had track that could support high axle loads. For most railroads a heavier locomotive required more wheels to spread the weight. In turn, a larger locomotive needed greater steaming capacity — a larger firebox.

Wide fireboxes and trailing trucks

By 1890 locomotive fireboxes were located above the frames instead of between them, making possible an increase in width of approximately 8 inches. A firebox above the frames could also be longer, but the length was limited by how far a fireman could fling coal with a shovel.

One development of a regional nature that was a step toward increased steaming capacity was the Wootten firebox, shallow and wide for the best combustion of slow-burning anthracite. It was introduced on the Philadelphia & Reading Railroad in 1877. Its width,

7 to 8 feet, required that it be located entirely above the drivers. The width also required that the engineer's cab be placed ahead of the firebox astride the boiler, resulting in the Camelback or Mother Hubbard configuration.

A firebox entirely above the drivers was practical on low-drivered locomotives but not on high-drivered passenger locomotives — it would raise the center of gravity too high. The solution was to place the firebox entirely behind the drive wheels.

Baldwin introduced the 2-4-2 at the Columbian Exposition in Chicago in 1893. A medium-size trailing wheel instead of a third driving axle allowed a deeper firebox. In 1895 Baldwin built an experimental 2-4-2 for the Chicago, Burlington & Quincy. Number 590 had 84¼" drivers and a wide firebox over the trailing wheels. Most 2-4-2s and 4-4-2s built during the 1890s were characterized by a non-swiveling trailing axle and a narrow firebox. The trailing truck evolved gradually, beginning with provision for lateral movement. The 2-4-2, intended for fast, light passenger trains, was unstable at high speeds and was quickly superseded by the 4-4-2, but the 2-4-2 wheel arrangement found a niche in logging and industrial service as a tank engine, essentially an 0-4-0 with guiding wheels fore and aft (and also in thousands of Lionel "Scout" electric train sets, which are beyond the scope of this book).

Development from 1900 to 1918

By 1900 the elements of larger steam locomotives were ready for combination: the wide firebox and the swiveling trailing truck. That year the Chicago, Burlington & Quincy built the first four 2-6-2s at its

1905	1906	1907	1908	1909	1910	1911	1912	1913	1914
Superheater NP 2-8-2 with wide firebox	GN 2-6-6-2	Erie 0-8-8-0	Flexible stay-bolt Power reverse	SP 2-8-8-2	Alco 4-6-2 No. 50000	PRR simple 2-8-8-2 C&O 4-8-2		Booster engine	

Burlington, Iowa, shops. The 2-6-2 appeared in passenger and freight versions, differing in driver size, but the type tended to be rear-heavy. The four-wheel lead truck of the 4-6-2 provided more stability at passenger-train speeds; the 2-8-2, which combined the deep firebox of the 2-6-2 and the four coupled axles of the 2-8-0, had better weight distribution. The 4-6-2 and the 2-8-2 soon became the most common passenger and freight locomotive types on North America's railroads. On some railroads they were the limit of motive power development.

Adding a driving axle to the 4-6-2 and the 2-8-2 produced the 4-8-2 and the 2-10-2 for passenger and freight service, respectively. The 4-8-2 proved to be as good for freight service as it was for passenger trains. The 2-10-2 was usually a ponderous machine, pressing the limits of piston thrust and rod weight. It could pull almost anything, but not very fast.

Development after 1920

Locomotive development in the mid-1920s took two directions. The American Locomotive Company advocated three-cylinder locomotives. Splitting the power output of the boiler three ways instead of two meant pistons and rods could be lighter. The extra weight of the third cylinder almost always required a four-wheel lead truck; 4-6-2, 4-8-2, 4-10-2, and 4-12-2 were the common wheel arrangements. The third cylinder and main rod were located between the frames, making maintenance difficult, but where three-cylinder power was the rule, not the exception, it performed well — witness Union Pacific's 90 4-12-2s.

The other and ultimately more significant trend in locomotive development was Lima's Super-Power concept. The basic premise was that a large firebox supported by a four-wheel trailing truck was necessary to provide sufficient steam at speed. The first Super-Power wheel arrangement was the 2-8-4, quickly followed by the 2-10-4. The 4-6-4 was a natural development for passenger service. The 4-8-4 was initially a passenger engine, but like the 4-8-2 it was just as useful for freight, and can be considered the ultimate modern locomotive type.

Articulated locomotives

The compound articulated locomotive, designed by Anatole Mallet, appeared in 1903. The rear engine received steam from the boiler and exhausted it to the cylinders of the front engine. The first type built, the 0-6-6-0, was unstable for road service but sufficient for pusher and hump-yard work. The 2-6-6-2 was more successful, producing about the same output as a 2-10-2 but better able to negotiate curves and remain to stable at freight-train speeds. The last of that type were built in 1949. The 0-8-8-0, first built in 1907, had the same characteristics as the 0-6-6-0. The 2-8-8-2 appeared in 1909, and it was built until 1950.

In the mid-1920s the simple articulated appeared, with all four cylinders receiving steam directly from the boiler. The four-wheel trailing truck was first applied to an articulated in 1928, creating the 2-8-8-4. The 2-6-6-4 appeared in 1935 and the 4-6-6-4 in 1936, both designed for fast freight service. The latter received wide acceptance and was the best articulated locomotive design.

1915	1916	1917	1918	1919	1920	1921	1922	1923	1924
Cast trailing truck Reading 4-4-4		USRA control began Dec. 26	Virginian 2-10-10-2		USRA control ended March 1		NYC H-10 2-8-2	One-piece engine bed	C&O simple 2-8-8-2 Lima 2-8-4

Other types

Locomotive development includes a number of types that were built for only one or two railroads. Some were experimental, and some were built in large quantities (a few types were experimental *and* built in quantity). Among the wheel arrangements are 4-10-2, 4-12-2, 2-10-10-2, 2-6-6-6, 4-8-8-2 (2-8-8-4 if you start counting wheels at the smokebox; 4-8-8-2 if you start at the headlight), and 4-8-8-4. In the 1930s and 1940s the Pennsylvania Railroad invested heavily in nonarticulated duplex-drive locomotives of several types — 6-4-4-6, 4-4-4-4, 4-4-6-4, and 4-6-4-4 — plus a 6-8-6 steam turbine locomotive. Baltimore & Ohio had a single duplex-drive 4-4-4-4. None of the duplex-drives could be judged a success. Four railroads experimented with steam turbines, in most cases as the prime mover of a steam turbine-electric locomotive.

About the information in the book — and beyond

Entire books have been written about single classes of locomotives; any book that attempts to explain the locomotives of an entire continent in 448 8¼" by 5½" pages will emphasize breadth over depth. Constraints of time and space meant some topics, even a few railroads, had to remain unexplored. Some railroads and locomotives got less ink than others — information just wasn't available. Over the years much has been made of some landmark locomotives; I have tried to bring some balance to the topic. I welcome corrections and additions.

For those who want further information on specific railroads I have cited what I think is the best book. Many of those books are out of print. Dealers specializing in out-of-print railroad books advertise in *Trains Magazine*; your local public library may be able to obtain such books through interlibrary networks. The two best sources of steam locomotive rosters are issues of *Railroad Magazine* from the mid-1930s to the mid-1950s and the twice-yearly *Bulletin* of the Railway & Locomotive Historical Society (the title of the magazine changed to *Railroad History* with issue No. 127).

For further reading on steam locomotive development as a whole, I suggest:

The Steam Locomotive in America, by Alfred W. Bruce, published in 1952 by W. W. Norton & Company — a technical history of the steam locomotive.

The Evolution of the Steam Locomotive, by Frank M. Swengel, published in 1967 by Midwest Rail Publications, P. O. Box 578, Davenport, IA 52805 (LCC 67-29846) — organized chronologically and without an index, but containing a remarkable amount of information and insight.

Model Railroader Cyclopedia, Volume 1 — Steam Locomotives, by Linn H. Westcott, published in 1960 by Kalmbach Publishing Co., 21027 Crossroads Circle, P. O. Box 1612, Waukesha, WI 53187 (ISBN 0-89024-001-9) — HO scale drawings of more than 125 steam locomotives copiously illustrated with black-and-white photos, plus good explanations of many facets of the steam locomotive.

Steam's Finest Hour, by David P. Morgan, published in 1990 (second editon) by Kalmbach Publishing Co., 21027 Crossroads Circle, P. O. Box 1612, Waukesha, WI 53187 (ISBN 0-89024-002-7) — an explo-

1925	1926	1927	1928	1929	1930	1931	1932	1933	1934
T&P 2-10-4 SP and UP 4-10-2s	UP 4-12-2	NYC 4-6-4 Last Camelbacks built	NP 4-8-4 Erie 2-8-4 with 70" drivers Last 4-4-0 built	Shelter required for Camelback firemen		Last 2-10-2 built		D&S 2-10-0 only engine delivered	Welded boiler

ration of the best locomotives built after the mid-1920s, with photos and specifications for each.

Articulated Steam Locomotives of North America, by Robert A. LeMassena, published in 1979 by Sundance Publications, 250 Broadway, Denver, CO 80203 (ISBN 0-913582-26-3) — a history of all the articulateds.

Acknowledgments

I couldn't have compiled the book alone. A number of entries were written by others who knew their subjects far better than I: Forrest W. Beckum, Jr., Charles B. Castner, John Gruber, John S. Ingles, E. W. King, Jr., Charles Kratz, Albert M. Langley, Jr., Dale Roberts, Bill Schafer, and Jim Scribbins. I was glad to have their assistance.

Andrew McBride spent many hours keyboarding rosters, giving me a head start on writing about those railroads. William D. Edson and Henry A. Rentschler cheerfully and quickly answered several vexing questions. Throughout the project Bob Hayden and Terry Spohn not only contributed clarity to what I wrote but offered ideas and encouragement. I thank them all.

George H. Drury

Waukesha, Wisconsin
September 1993

CLASSIFICATION, NOMENCLATURE, AND NUMBERING

As locomotives developed there arose a need for a classification system, and number and arrangement of wheels worked out to be the best way to do it. The Whyte system that was eventually settled on seems obvious, but it was preceded by others. Baldwin Locomotives Works, for example, classified its locomotives with a numeral denoting the total number of wheels under the locomotive, a fraction indicating trailing and lead trucks ($\frac{1}{4}$ for trailing truck and lead truck; $\frac{1}{3}$ for trailing truck but no lead truck), and a letter giving the number of driving axles (B for 1, C for 2, D for 3, etc.). A Pacific was classed 12-$\frac{1}{4}$-D, for example.

A clearer, easier system was developed by Frederick Methven Whyte, a New York Central mechanical engineer. Numerals represented the number of wheels in each group, starting at the front end: lead truck, drivers, trailing truck. For articulated locomotives a numeral was used for each group of drivers. The numerals were separated by hyphens.

Most wheel arrangements were given names derived from the first user of that wheel arrangment. The derivations are explained in the entries for the individual types.

Type	Name	
0-4-0	Four-wheel switcher	OO
0-6-0	Six-wheel switcher	OOO
0-8-0	Eight-wheel switcher	OOOO

1935	1936	1937	1938	1939	1940	1941	1942	1943	1944
P&WV 2-6-6-4	UP 4-6-6-4	B&O duplex-	ICC requires	Electro-Motive		UP 4-8-8-4	PRR 4-4-4-4		PRR turbine
	CP 4-4-4	drive 4-4-4-4	power	FT No. 103		C&O 2-6-6-6			
		Last 4-4-2 built	reverse						
			GE turbine						

7

0-10-2	Union	∠OOOOOo
2-4-2	Columbia	∠oOOo
2-6-0	Mogul	∠oOOO
2-6-2	Prairie	∠oOOOo
2-8-0	Consolidation	∠oOOOO
2-8-2	Mikado	∠oOOOOo
2-8-4	Berkshire	∠oOOOOoo
2-10-0	Decapod	∠oOOOOO
2-10-2	Santa Fe	∠oOOOOOo
2-10-4	Texas	∠oOOOOOoo
2-6-6-6	Allegheny	∠oOOO OOOooo
2-8-8-4	Yellowstone	∠oOOOO OOOooo
4-4-0	American, Eight-Wheeler	∠ooOO
4-4-2	Atlantic	∠ooOOo
4-4-4	Jubilee	∠ooOOoo
4-6-0	Ten-Wheeler	∠ooOOO
4-6-2	Pacific	∠ooOOOo
4-6-4	Hudson	∠ooOOOoo
4-8-0	Twelve-Wheeler	∠ooOOOO
4-8-2	Mountain	∠ooOOOOo
4-8-4	Northern	∠ooOOOOoo
4-10-0	Mastodon	∠ooOOOOO
4-10-2	Southern Pacific, Overland	∠ooOOOOOo
4-12-2	Union Pacific	∠ooOOOOOOo
4-6-6-4	Challenger	∠ooOOO OOOoo
4-8-8-4	Big Boy	∠ooOOOO OOOoo

Some railroads chose their own names for wheel arrangements, either officially or unofficially. New York Central, which constantly reminded passengers that it was the Water Level Route, designated its 4-8-2s Mohawks, not Mountains, and its 4-8-4s were Niagaras, not Northerns.

The 4-8-4 had more names than any other type. Memories of the War Between The States were still fresh in 1930 when Nashville, Chattanooga & St. Louis ("The Dixie Line") chose Dixie instead of Northern for its 4-8-4s; Richmond, Fredericksburg & Potomac called its 4-8-4s Generals and Governors and named them individually for Confederate generals and Virginia governors. Local rivalry may be responsible for 2-8-4s being known as Limas on the Boston & Maine — they were Berkshires on the parallel Boston & Albany. During World War II anti-Japanese sentiment caused some railroads to rename their Mikados to MacArthurs.

Occasionally railroads renamed enlarged or improved versions of a wheel arrangement. The New Haven, for example, introduced its 3-cylinder 4-8-2s as the New Haven type, and the Atlantics built for Milwaukee Road's *Hiawatha* were dubbed the Milwaukee type. Such names seldom stuck.

Railroad classes

Railroads needed a convenient way to refer to groups of similar locomotives. Most roads eventually assigned a letter more or less arbitrarily to each wheel arrangement, usually with a number to note successive groups or different sizes of a type, and sometimes with a letter after the number to indicate variations. For example,

1945	1946	1947	1948	1949	1950	1951	1952	1953	1954
		Last 4-6-6-4 C&O turbines	Last 4-6-2, 4-6-4, 4-8-2, Alco steam locomotive	Last 2-8-4, 2-10-4, Lima, Baldwin steam locomotives	Last 4-8-4			Last steam locomotive built by N&W	N&W turbine

Louisville & Nashville's classification was:

0-4-0	A	2-6-0	F	4-6-2	K
0-6-0	B	4-6-0	G	4-8-2	L
0-8-0	C	2-8-0	H	2-8-4	M
4-4-0	D	2-8-2	J		

Other roads chose a letter or two to abbreviate the common name of the type. One of the hazards is that several names start with the same letter. Southern Pacific showed some ingenuity:

0-6-0	S	Six-wheel switcher	2-10-2	F	Freight
0-8-0	SE	Eight-wheel switcher	4-4-0	E	Eight-Wheeler
2-6-0	M	Mogul	4-4-2	A	Atlantic
2-6-2	Pr	Prairie	4-6-0	T	Ten-Wheeler
2-8-0	C	Consolidation	4-6-2	P	Pacific
2-8-2	Mk	Mikado	4-8-0	TW	Twelve-Wheeler
2-8-4	B	Berkshire	4-8-2	Mt	Mountain
2-10-0	D	Decapod			
4-8-4	GS	Golden State or General Service			
2-6-6-2	MM	Mallet Mogul			
2-8-8-2	MC	Mallet Consolidation			
4-8-8-2	AC	Articulated Consolidation (cab-forward)			

Occasionally railroads assigned the same letter to two types. On the Milwaukee Road, for instance, classes F1 through F5 were 4-6-2s and F6 and F7 were 4-6-4s. The Pennsylvania's 2-10-4s came on the scene long after the experimental 2-6-2s had been scrapped and were assigned the same letter, J. The converse was sometimes the case. Canadian National assigned letters F, G, H, and I to 4-6-0s

of different driver sizes. Other roads — Santa Fe, for example — skipped letters entirely and simply referred to locomotives by number groups: the 1950 class, the 3700 class.

Some railroads used an s in their locomotive classifications to indicate superheating. Well-known examples are Southern Railway Ps-4 and Pennsylvania Railroad K4s Pacifics.

There were many ways to designate subclasses and sub-subclasses: numbers, letters (both lower-case and small capitals), and even fractions. In the text and the rosters I stay as close as possible to what was painted on the locomotives.

Numbering

In the beginning, or at least when numbers replaced names, railroads numbered their locomotives in sequence as they acquired them. When all the locomotives were 4-4-0s of about the same size it didn't make much difference. As different types of locomotives developed and locomotive fleets grew in size, many railroads found it useful to assign numbers so that engines that were alike had adjacent numbers, so that all the 80s were 2-6-0s and all the 90s 2-8-0s, or all the passenger engines were 300s and all the freight engines 400s. Some railroads used different number series for divisions or subsidiaries. A few railroads continued the older practice, and some reassigned numbers when old locomotives were scrapped, as if the supply of numbers was limited. (In the case of the Pennsylvania Railroad it was. In 1920 PRR had nearly 8,000 engines, and PRR was reluctant to use five-digit engine numbers.)

UNDERSTANDING THE NUMBERS

Throughout this book I use the locomotive designs of the United States Railroad Administration (USRA, see page 405) as a standard for comparison, much as ornithologist Roger Tory Peterson uses the robin in *A Field Guide to the Birds*. The important dimensions aren't height, width, and length but driver diameter, cylinder size, weight, and tractive effort.

USRA Locomotive Types

Type	Driver diameter (inches)	Cylinders (inches)	Total weight (pounds)	Weight on drivers (pounds)	Tractive effort (pounds)
0-6-0	51	21 × 28	163,000	163,000	39,100
0-8-0	51	25 × 28	214,000	214,000	51,000
2-8-2 (light)	63	26 × 30	292,000	220,000	54,700
2-8-2 (heavy)	63	27 × 32	320,000	239,000	60,000
2-10-2 (light)	57	27 × 32	352,000	276,000	69,600
2-10-2 (heavy)	57	30 × 32	380,000	293,000	73,800
2-6-6-2	57	23, 35 × 32	448,000	358,000	80,000
2-8-8-2	57	25, 39 × 32	531,000	474,000	101,300C 121,600S
4-6-2 (light)	73	25 × 28	277,000	162,000	40,700
4-6-2 (heavy)	79	27 × 28	306,000	197,000	43,900
4-8-2 (light)	69	27 × 30	327,000	224,000	53,900
4-8-2 (heavy)	69	28 × 30	352,000	243,000	58,200

Driver diameter: A rule of thumb was that maximum safe speed in miles per hour equaled driver diameter in inches, a speed equivalent to 336 driver revolutions per minute. Alfred W. Bruce said the maximum horsepower output was generally reached at 300 rpm for modern freight locomotives and 360 rpm for passenger locomotives, the difference being a matter of counterbalancing. A switcher with 51" drivers moved 13 feet 4 inches with one revolution of the drivers; a Milwaukee Road *Hiawatha* Atlantic with 84" drivers moved 22 feet, so at 60 mph (88 feet per second) its drivers made 4 revolutions per second or 240 rpm.

Cylinder diameter and piston stroke: The greater the diameter of the cylinder, the greater the piston thrust for a given boiler pressure. Piston stroke equals twice the distance of the crankpin from the center of the drive wheel. A long stroke means greater force at the rim; a short stroke reduces piston travel and wear.

Boiler pressure: It is possible to increase the force on the piston by either increasing the boiler pressure or increasing the cylinder diameter. Increasing the boiler pressure — within limits a matter of setting the safety valves — increases stress on the boiler and aggravates problems such as foaming and rusting.

Grate area: A large fire gives off more heat than a small fire. The amount of steam produced by the boiler depends on the size of the fire — the larger the grate, the larger the fire. Slow-burning coal, such as anthracite, required a larger grate than bituminous for the same size locomotive.

Total weight is a rough indicator of the size and capacity of a locomotive. The heavier of two locomotives of the same type is likely to be the more powerful.

Weight on drivers is a more accurate indicator of how much a locomotive can pull — how it can apply its tractive effort.

Factor of adhesion is the ratio of weight on drivers to tractive effort. The ideal is about 4 to 1; much less and a locomotive will be likely to spin its wheels on wet rail or with a heavy load.

Tractive effort (or tractive force) is the force in pounds exerted by a locomotive, measured at the driving wheel. It is a theoretical figure: boiler pressure times the square of the cylinder diameter times the piston stroke divided by driver diameter. Tractive effort isn't drawbar pull — it doesn't include operational factors — but it provides a basis for comparison of locomotives.

Axle loading: The weight of a locomotive can be considered a single mass in the middle of a bridge or several smaller weights pressing down on the rails at a number of points a few feet apart. Light rail and lightly constructed roadbed can support a heavy locomotive if the weight is spread out over more axles — for example, a light 4-8-2 instead of the heavy 4-6-2. USRA locomotives were designed with a maximum load per axle of 54,000 pounds for the "light" locomotives and 60,000 for the "heavy" engines.

THE PARTS OF A STEAM LOCOMOTIVE

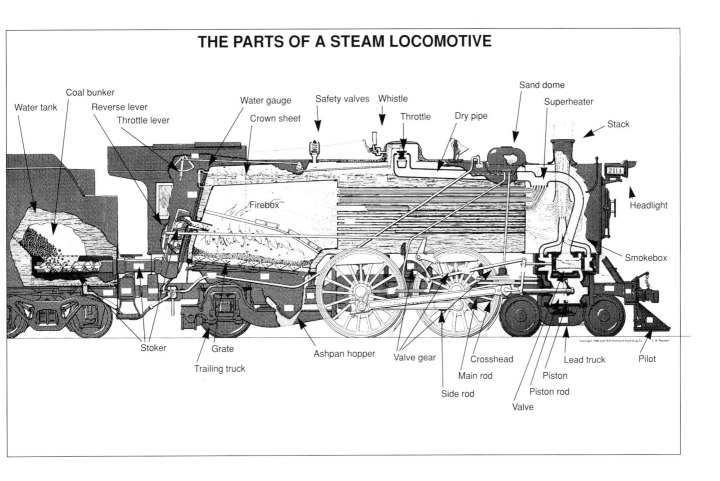

Water tank · Coal bunker · Reverse lever · Throttle lever · Water gauge · Crown sheet · Safety valves · Whistle · Throttle · Dry pipe · Sand dome · Superheater · Stack · Headlight · Smokebox · Firebox

Stoker · Grate · Trailing truck · Ashpan hopper · Valve gear · Crosshead · Main rod · Side rod · Valve · Piston rod · Piston · Lead truck · Pilot

AMERICAN LOCOMOTIVE COMPANY

American Locomotive Company (Alco) was created in 1901, when eight companies merged in order to better compete with the ever-expanding Baldwin Locomotive Works. The components were Brooks Locomotive Works, Cooke Locomotive & Machine Works, Dickson Manufacturing Company, Manchester Locomotive Works, Pittsburgh Locomotive & Car Works, Rhode Island Locomotive Works, Richmond Locomotive Works, and Schenectady Locomotive Works. Two firms joined Alco shortly after it was established, the Locomotive & Machine Company of Montreal in 1902, and Rogers Locomotive Works in 1905.

Brooks Locomotive Works was founded in 1869 by Horatio Brooks, master mechanic of the Erie Railway, who leased Erie's Dunkirk, New York, shops, which were being closed down. By 1882, when the company purchased the facilities from the Erie, Brooks was a major locomotive builder. Several new buildings were constructed shortly after the firm joined Alco. During the 1920s the designation on the builder's plate changed to Dunkirk Works.

Locomotive production at Brooks gave way to war materials between 1915 and 1917. After World War I the Brooks Works, by then Alco's number two plant, developed three-cylinder locomotives. In 1928 Alco elected to consolidate all locomotive production at Schenectady. Brooks, which had produced about 13,000 locomotives, continued to produce heavy machinery for a number of years.

Cooke Locomotive & Machine Works, Paterson, New Jersey, was established about 1800 and entered the locomotive business in 1852 as Danforth, Cooke & Company. In 1865 the company was reorganized as the Danforth Locomotive & Machine Company. In 1871 Charles Danforth retired and John Cooke returned to active management. In 1883, a year after Cooke's death, the firm took his name instead of Danforth's, and built a new plant in 1889.

Despite the modernity of the Cooke facilities, Alco chose not to update them, and instead concentrated production of small locomotives there until 1926, when production ceased.

Dickson Manufacturing Company, founded at Scranton, Pennsylvania, in 1856 by Thomas Dickson, began producing locomotives in 1862. It prospered in the 1880s and 1890s, offering a wide variety of locomotives. In 1901 the company planned to concentrate on locomotives and sold its general machinery division — then the company was sold to Alco, which soon phased out locomotive construction in Scranton. The last of 1,762 locomotives left the Dickson shops in April 1909.

Manchester Locomotive Works, Manchester, New Hampshire, was incorporated in 1854. One of the principals had designed locomotives for Amoskeag Manufacturing Company in Manchester; another had built locomotives at the Lawrence (Massachusetts) Machine Works. The business began to prosper in the late 1860s. Soon after the turn of the century, Manchester found itself limited to small locomotives by the size and age of its buildings, but Alco was unwilling enlarge the plant. Locomotive production ceased in 1913; total production was 1,793 locomotives.

Montreal Locomotive Works was the 1908 reorganization of the Locomotive & Machine Company of Montreal, formed in 1902. MLW continued in operation after Alco stopped building diesel locomotives in 1969 and was acquired by Bombardier Inc. in 1973.

Pittsburgh Locomotive & Car Works was organized in 1865 by, among others, Andrew Carnegie. Its shop in Allegheny City, Pennsylvania, (now part of Pittsburgh) produced its first locomotive in 1867. The plant was upgraded and enlarged several times, enabling Pittsburgh to be one of the earliest builders of large locomotives. Locomotive production at Pittsburgh ceased in 1919.

Rhode Island Locomotive Works, in Providence, Rhode Island, grew out of the Burnside Rifle Company. After the Civil War the demand for weapons disappeared and the company turned to locomotive production. The 1880s were prosperous for the company, but the financial panic of 1893 idled it for several years.

In 1906 Alco began to rebuild Rhode Island's plant for automobile production (it had never been well suited to locomotive manufacture), and the last of 5,995 locomotives was produced in 1908.

Richmond Locomotive Works, Richmond, Virginia, was the largest locomotive builder in the south. Its history goes back to a machine shop opened in 1865. It began building small locomotives in the late 1870s, suffered a fire that destroyed its plant, underwent a change of management, and was reorganized as the Richmond Locomotive & Machine Works in 1887.

Alco enlarged the plant in the early 1900s, and it was soon building locomotives as large as 2-8-8-2s. Locomotive construction was suspended from 1914 to 1918 in favor of war materials, then resumed with less vigor than before the war as Alco began to concentrate its business at Schenectady. Richmond outshopped the last of its nearly 4,500 locomotives in September 1927.

Rogers Locomotive Works began as a machine shop in Paterson, New Jersey, in 1832. It began producing locomotives in 1837 and soon acquired a reputation for solid, modern design. By the early 1860s it was third in production after Baldwin and Norris, and second after Norris shut down in 1866. Its status began to decline in the 1880s. In 1899 the death of the company president threw management back onto the founder's son, Jacob Rogers, who had left the business in 1893. Rogers shut the plant down until he could find new owners, who ran the company only briefly before selling out to Alco in 1905. The plant was obsolete and, amazingly, lacked rail access. Rogers Works produced light locomotives and machinery until 1913. Total production was about 6,300 locomotives.

Schenectady Locomotive Works was founded in 1848 by Edward and Septimus Norris, Philadelphia locomotive builders. The business was not successful until it was reorganized in 1851 by John Ellis, who was soon joined by Walter McQueen. The firm had a stormy history, and it was not until the 1880s that it became a major builder of locomotives. The plant was upgraded in the 1890s and it became the chief works of the American Locomotive Company.

By 1929 all of Alco's U. S. locomotive production had been moved to Schenectady, and soon thereafter the Depression brought U. S. locomotive production almost to zero. Consturction of machinery other than locomotives kept Alco alive through the Depression.

Alco began building diesels in the 1920s, but continued building steam locomotives until 1948. It had more success with diesels than the other two major steam locomotive builders, Baldwin and Lima, but never challenged Electro-Motive's position as number one. American Locomotive Company changed its name to Alco Products, Inc., in 1955, and exited the locomotive business in 1969.

Alco's last domestic steam locomotives were seven Pittsburgh & Lake Erie 2-8-4s produced in 1948. Their tenders were built by Lima because Alco had already shut down its tender plant.

I have tried to cite the specific factory or works of American Locomotive Company for locomotives built after 1902 instead of simply saying "Alco," and I have usually used the premerger name even for postmerger construction — "built by Manchester in 1909" means "built by Alco's Manchester Works in 1909." Where space is tight in the rosters, "Alco" means two, three, or more plants built the locomotives in question.

Recommended reading: *The Diesel Builders, Volume Two, American Locomotive Company and Montreal Locomotive Works*, by John F. Kirkland, published in 1989 by Interurban Press, P. O. Box 6444, Glendale, CA 91205.

ATCHISON, TOPEKA & SANTA FE RAILWAY

By 1901 the Santa Fe's map looked much as it would through most of the 20th century. The main line ran from Chicago to Los Angeles, and Santa Fe rails reached Galveston, Denver, El Paso, Phoenix, San Diego, and Oakland. Still to be added to the map were the line from Coleman, Texas, northwest to Texico (opened in 1912), the Kansas City, Mexico & Orient from Wichita, Kansas, southwest to Presidio, Texas (purchased in 1928), and a cluster of lines in the area between La Junta, Colorado, and Amarillo, Texas (built in the 1920s and 1930s).

Until the turn of the century Santa Fe used 4-4-0s, 4-6-0s, and 2-8-0s, standard for the time. Then the compound locomotive arrived on the scene, and Santa Fe adopted it with enthusiasm. For more than a decade most of the engines the road bought were compounds. An interesting pattern appears: From 1901 to 1903 the road bought 2-6-0s, 2-6-2s, 2-8-0s, 2-8-2s, and 2-10-0s. From 1903 through 1907 the purchase included 0-6-0s, 2-10-2s, 4-4-2s, and 4-6-2s — the Atlantics and the Pacifics concurrently. In 1906 came another large batch of 2-6-2s, followed a year later by a group of 2-8-0s. There was a hiatus in 1908, possibly the effect of the panic of 1907, followed by the resumption of orders for 0-6-0s, 2-10-2s, and 4-6-2s, and the onset of the Mallet era. Another group of 2-8-0s came in 1912.

In 1912 Santa Fe's management changed: John Purcell became assistant to the vice president in charge of the mechanical department. The road seemed to get up, shake itself, and buy large groups of relatively modern and conventional 2-8-2s and 2-10-2s — the last batch of compound 4-6-2s in 1914 is an anomaly. The road then pursued a conventional if conservative course of steam locomotive development, stopping just short of the high-speed simple articulated.

On its eastern lines Santa Fe used bituminous coal from mines in northern Illinois, southern Kansas, southeast Colorado, and northeast New Mexico. West of Albuquerque the road used coal from mines near Gallup. The western coal had a lower heat content, and because it produced sparks, there were restrictions on cars with wood roofs near the engine. The Santa Fe had to haul coal long distances to the western reaches of its system. After oil was discovered in commercial quantities in California, the Union Oil Company experimented with a locomotive owned by a Santa Fe subsidiary. The first attempts at using oil failed, but Santa Fe's shop at San Bernardino finally came up with a device that sprayed oil into the combustion chamber. Santa Fe eventually used oil for steam locomotive fuel almost everywhere on its system.

Santa Fe began dieselizing early, driven by the lack of water along its main line across New Mexico, Arizona, and California's Mojave Desert. The very oldest locomotives were scrapped in the 1920s and 1930s, but the later middle-size locomotives follow a single pattern in their scrapping dates: a few scrapped about 1940; none scrapped during World War II, when the road needed every locomotive it could find; and the rest scrapped in the early 1950s, after dieselization began in earnest. Santa Fe's last revenue steam runs occurred on August 27, 1957. Two locomotives, 2-10-4 5021 and 4-8-4 3780, worked as helpers on eastbound freight trains from Belen to Mountainair, N. M., then returned to Belen, where their fires were extinguished.

Santa Fe classified its locomotives simply by number series instead of letters to indicate type. Occasionally later groups of engines received lower numbers than earlier ones, and locomotives rebuilt to another type often kept their original numbers. The 591 class, for instance, includes 2-6-0s, 0-6-0s, and 0-8-0s. The four 1200-class Pacifics that were rebuilt to Prairies retained their numbers and their 1200-class membership cards. Some railroads seemed to order locomotives in multiples of 5 or 10, Santa Fe did not.

Freight locomotives

Santa Fe was not a major user of the Mogul type. The last new 2-6-0s it purchased were 35 compounds and 15 simple engines built in 1901. The compounds were converted to simple engines between 1918 and 1921. Between 1925 and 1928 seven of that class were rebuilt to 0-6-0s and 43 became 0-8-0s. Santa Fe acquired small groups of Moguls when

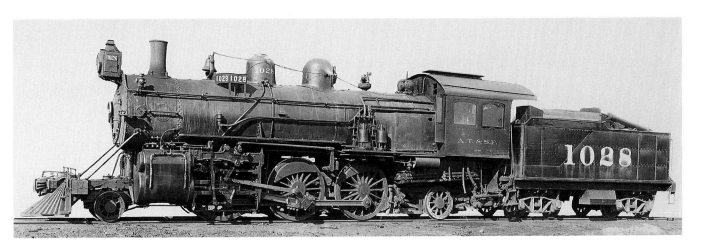

Prairie 1028 was built by Baldwin in 1901 as a four-cylinder Vauclain compound. Topeka Shops converted it to a simple engine in 1914.

it bought the Oklahoma Central and the Kansas City, Mexico & Orient. One of the Orient 2-6-0s lasted until 1951.

Considering its route map, it is appropriate that Santa Fe was a major user of the Prairie type. The first group, the 1000 class, arrived from Baldwin in 1901. They were 79"-drivered Vauclain compounds intended for fast passenger service. They were given 69" drivers and rebuilt as simple locomotives in 1922 and 1923. The nearly identical locomotives of the 1014 class arrived from Baldwin in 1901 and 1902. They soon swapped their 79" drivers for the 69" wheels of the 1200-class Pacifics, and they were simpled between 1912 and 1918. The 103 members of the 1050 class, built in 1902 and 1903, were much the same but had 69" drivers. They were converted to simple engines between 1911 and 1922. In 1906 and 1907 Baldwin delivered the 1800-class Prairies. They were mainline freight power, four-cylinder balanced compounds weighing 243,000 or 248,000 pounds (previous classes weighed 190,000 pounds). The 1800s were simpled in the 1920s. The

2-6-2s were eventually downgraded from mainline work and found a niche in mixed train and local freight service, a steam-era equivalent of the road's homebuilt CF7 diesels.

Three 2-6-2 classes are outside Santa Fe's sequence of motive power development. Schenectady built two tandem compounds in 1902 for pusher service on the grades out of the Illinois River valley at Chillicothe, Illinois. They arrived with outside-bearing trailing trucks but later received inboard-bearing trucks, possibly when they were rebuilt to simple engines in 1918. Between 1929 and 1932 four 1200-class Pacifics were converted to 69"-drivered Prairies. In the process they put on about 28 tons of weight, but the rebuilding and the change to a two-wheel lead truck resulted in a slightly lower percentage of the total weight on the drivers. They had a noticeable gap between the cylin-

ders and the first pair of drivers, and their odd appearance wasn't improved by the application of outside lead truck journals. The reason for the conversion is unknown — but they outlived most of the 1200-class Pacifics by at least a decade. In 1943 Santa Fe bought a 44"-drivered industrial-size 2-6-2 from the Oakland Terminal Railway and sold it a year later to the Modesto & Empire Traction Company.

Nationwide, more 2-8-0s were built than any other type, but Santa Fe's Consolidations were neither numerous nor particularly modern. The 729, 759, 769, and 900 classes were all 57"-drivered simple machines. The 789 and 824 classes were built as Vauclain compounds and rebuilt as simple engines between 1907 and 1910; the 825 class were built as tandem compounds and not simpled until about 1920. The 1950 and 1900 classes, built in 1907 and 1912-1913, respectively, were slightly more modern in appearance and heavier than previous 2-8-0s, but they seem to be an afterthought, purchased between orders for 2-10-2s and 2-8-2s.

The road acquired a handful of low-drivered 2-8-0s from railroads it purchased; some of the ex-New York Central 2-8-0s that came from the Kansas City, Mexico & Orient lasted until the mid-1950s.

Santa Fe's first Mikados came from Baldwin in 1902 and 1903. They were Vauclain compounds with wide fireboxes located partly over the rear drivers. They were converted to simple locomotives in 1908 and

1909, and remained in service almost to the end of steam. A decade of 2-10-2 purchases passed before the next group of Mikados arrived in 1913. These, the 3100 class, had the same 57" drivers and 25" × 32" cylinders as the earlier 885 class as rebuilt and weighed only slightly more, but their fireboxes were behind the rear drivers. The 3129 class followed in 1916: same cylinders and drivers (later changed or re-tired to 58") but 200 pounds boiler pressure instead of 170, and 15,000 pounds heavier. The 3100 and 3129 classes were approximately the size of USRA light Mikados.

Right after the 3129 class came the 3160 class, which had 27" × 32" cylinders, 63" drivers, and at least 20 tons more weight — heavier than a USRA heavy Mike. The 4000-class Mikes continued the evolution. Successive batches within each class were heavier because of additions to the basic design like feedwater heaters, cast trailing trucks, and a second sand dome.

As with the Prairies, there were a few oddities among the Mikes. In 1924 San Bernardino shops took apart two 2-8-8-2s, which had been the largest locomotives in the world in 1909, and used the rear high-pressure engines as the basis for two 2-8-2s that were more or less equivalent to the contemporary 4000 class. In July 1945 the Santa Fe purchased three L1s-class Mikados from the Pennsylvania Railroad, substituted a standard Santa Fe pilot for Pennsy's footboards, repainted and relettered them, used them briefly (by then World War II was over), then set them aside.

Santa Fe thought its big Mikados would solve a problem southwest of Shopton, Iowa (Fort Madison). AT&SF's Chicago-Kansas City route is the shortest and fastest rail route between those cities. Southwest of Shopton the line runs crosswise to the rivers that flow southeast into the Mississippi and Missouri, and consequently has a succession of ascending and descending grades and many curves. The Santa Fe needed a locomotive that could handle unassisted the trains that came into Shopton from Chicago. The line was busy enough that shorter, more frequent trains would produce congestion, and the grades were too frequent and too short for efficient use of helpers.

The Mikes found themselves short of breath west of Shopton with trains they had brought in from Chicago. Santa Fe knew it would have to change engines at Shopton, but to what? The road's 2-10-2s were slow and their long rigid wheelbase wasn't well suited to the curves. Lima had just introduced the 2-8-4 and the Super-Power concept, and Santa Fe was buying its first 4-6-4s and 4-8-4s. A 2-8-4 seemed a logical addition to the shopping list.

Santa Fe's 2-8-4 matched Lima's A-1 in driver size, grate area, and weight, and was a bit less in boiler pressure, cylinder diameter, and tractive effort. Santa Fe was conservative in the matter of components and details, so its new 2-8-4s were basically good 1922 engines with a 1927 wheel arrangement. They received various mechanical improvements in the 1930s, but by 1940 the road recognized that they were not fast-freight locomotives. It tested a 4-8-2 in freight service across northern Missouri. It proved faster and cheaper to run, but the road stuck with the 2-8-4s. In early 1941 Santa Fe tested a four-unit FT over the line. It was faster, cheaper to run, and more powerful — and the

2-8-4s were saved only by World War II. Indeed, Santa Fe added five 2-8-4s to its roster in 1945 to handle a surge of traffic to western ports — Boston & Maine locomotives that had been replaced first by 4-8-2s, then by diesels. In 1949 a drop in oil prices caused Santa Fe to store its remaining coal-burning engines. The 2-8-4s were among those stored, but six were converted to oil and worked in Kansas and Texas until 1953.

Santa Fe had 11 Decapods in four classes. In 1902 the road bought three tandem compound 2-10-0s for pusher service on the 3.5 percent grades of Raton Pass. Number 987 was Baldwin's first tandem compound and the largest, most powerful locomotive in the world at the time. American Locomotive Company's Schenectady works built 987 and 988, somewhat lighter and less powerful. All three were converted to simple locomotives at the San Bernardino shops, 987 and 989 in 1911 and 988 in 1915. When Santa Fe purchased the KCM&O in 1928 it acquired three Russian Decapods that soon went to scrap and five larger Decapods of a standard Baldwin design that remained in service until the early 1950s.

The 1902 Decapods went to work as pushers on Raton Pass. From the summit they returned to the foot of the grade in reverse — slowly. They were long-wheelbase locomotives, and the track was full of curves. In 1903 Santa Fe ordered Decapods with trailing trucks to guide the locomotives when running in reverse. The new wheel arrangement, 2-10-2, was soon named for the railroad. The 900 class had the same dimensions as No. 987; the only difference was the extra axle under the cab. The first group of 2-10-2s, 915-998, comprised 25 oil burners and 45 coal burners. In 1903 the road ordered a single simple 2-10-2, No. 985, and in 1904 ordered 15 more coal burners, 900-914. They were followed by 74 more, 1600-1673, built between 1905 and 1907.

In 1911 the road built ten 2-10-10-2 Mallets, using ten 2-10-2s to make the high-pressure engines and buying ten 2-10-0 frames and boiler-superheater-reheater-feedwater heater units from Baldwin. Within a few years they were back at Topeka shops, where they had been assembled, being taken apart and made into 2-10-2s. The rear units did not get

2-10-2 — SANTA FE

In 1902 the Atchison, Topeka & Santa Fe bought three Decapods for use as pushers over Raton Pass on the Colorado-New Mexico border. They worked well as pushers; the problem was getting them down the grade to assist the next train. There was no way to turn engines at the summit; they had to back down. The relatively long rigid wheelbase of the 2-10-0s didn't take well to the curves of the line, so the Santa Fe ordered its next batch of 10-drivered engines with a rear guiding axle, creating a new wheel arrangement. Santa Fe's first 2-10-2s had a wide firebox over the rear drivers; the purpose of the trailing truck was not to make possible a larger firebox but to guide the locomotive into curves when it was running in reverse.

The first 2-10-2s with a wide firebox behind the drivers were Chicago, Burlington & Quincy 6000-6004, built by Baldwin in 1912. They were large engines, carrying more weight on their drivers than a USRA heavy 2-10-2 and almost as much as Santa Fe's 3800 class. They were built with reinforced frames, and Burlington was

pleased enough with their performance to order 26 more in 1914.

By 1919 the 2-10-2 was the dominant freight engine in the Locomotive Cyclopedia. It was considered the equal of the 2-6-6-2 in pulling power — but in exchange for the complexity of the Mallet the 2-10-2 offered drawbacks of its own. Five coupled axles gave the type a long rigid wheelbase, which could be compensated for by small drivers, one or more pairs of blind (flangeless) drivers, or devices that allowed some of the drivers to move laterally. Small drivers restricted the speed of the locomotive; blind drivers threw the job of guiding the locomotive onto the other drivers, with a resultant increase in tire and flange wear; lateral-motion devices ultimately made ten-coupled locomotives (and high-drivered eight-coupled locomotives) practical.

A larger locomotive that could pull heavier trains required larger cylinders. The large cylinders produced powerful thrust, which required strong (therefore heavy) main rods. Until the early 1920s locomotive bearings and frames were unable to handle the maximum piston thrust of a 2-10-2 — cast-steel frames were still in the future when the 2-10-2 flourished. In addition, the main rods transmitted their power at a point close to the center of gravity of the locomotive, which made the type, like the Prairie, prone to nosing. More than that, the heavy main rod required heavy counterbalancing. It was never possible to completely counterbalance

New York, Ontario & Western 356, built by Alco in 1915, followed the design of the first 2-10-2s in having its firebox over the rear two pairs of 57" drivers. Canadian Government Railways, Boston & Maine, and New Haven rostered similar Santa Fe types. Photo by A. V. Neusser.

Reading 3014 and the other members of the K1sb class were the heaviest 2-10-2s built. The Hodges trailing truck appears dwarfed by the Wootten firebox, but was adequate to carry its 57,000 pound load. Broadbelt collection.

the main rod, because one end moves back and forth and the other end moves in a circle. The small drivers used on most 2-10-2s did not provide enough space for adequate counterbalancing, and at speeds over 30 mph the unbalanced forces tended to destroy both locomotive and track. The Burlington's first 2-10-2s had supplemental counterweights on the axle between the frames; it soon fitted the locomotives with lightweight rods.

Nonetheless, some railroads liked the Santa Fe type. Baltimore & Ohio's second series of 2-10-2s were powerful and faster than most other 2-10-2s. Chicago & Illinois Midland found the 2-10-2 ideal for its coal trains; C&IM 703 and 704, built by Lima in 1931, were among the last of the type built. Between 1940 and 1950 the road bought 10 2-10-2s from the Wabash, and in 1951 and 1952 bought 9 of the type from the Atlantic Coast Line.

Canadian National Railways sent its last 2-10-2, No. 4207, to scrap on December 14, 1961. The locomotive was built by Brooks in 1919 for the Boston & Albany. Duluth, Missabe & Iron Range used its 2-10-2s during 1960, and No. 514, also built by Brooks in 1919, powered an excursion train on September 29, 1962.

Other names: Central (Illinois Central)
Total built: approximately 2,200
First: Atchison, Topeka & Santa Fe 915, 1903
Last and heaviest: Reading 3010-3019, class K1sb, Baldwin 1931, 451,000 pounds
Lightest: Atchison, Topeka & Santa Fe 985, built by Baldwin in 1904, 276,000 pounds
Longest lived: Santa Fe 940, built 1903, donated to city of Bartlesville, Oklahoma, for display, August 1956
Last in service: Duluth, Missabe & Iron Range 514, Brooks 1919, excursion September 29, 1962
Greatest number: Atchison, Topeka & Santa Fe, 342

their old numbers back but became the 3010 class; the front units became the 3020 class.

The weak point of the tandem compound was the piston rod seal between the high-pressure and low-pressure cylinders. Repacking the piston rod required removing the high-pressure cylinders — the job took days and had to be done often. An interim solution was to equip each locomotive with a small crane on each side of the smokebox to assist the task. This was analogous to equipping your car with four built-in jacks to facilitate frequent tire-changing because the tires last only two weeks.

The road experimented by removing the high-pressure cylinders from No. 1600, adding a superheater, and reducing boiler pressure to 140 pounds. The test results have been lost, but the high-pressure cylinders went back onto No. 1600; 32 simple 2-10-2s, 1674-1705, were delivered in 1912 and 1913; and the tandem compound 2-10-2s were rebuilt as simple engines between 1916 and 1923.

In 1919 Santa Fe needed large, heavy, modern freight locomotives. The road's previous 2-10-2s were essentially turn-of-the-century Decapods with trailing axles; Santa Fe's new 2-10-2 evolved from a contemporary heavy Mike. Compare the new 3800 class, the 1674 class (the last of the earlier design), and the USRA heavy 2-10-2:

	3800	1674	USRA
Driver diameter	63"	57"	57"
Cylinders	30" × 32"	28" × 32"	30" × 32"
Boiler pressure	195 pounds	170 pounds	190 pounds
Weight on drivers	309,000 pounds	245,000 pounds	293,000 pounds
Total engine weight	402,000 pounds	293,000 pounds	380,000 pounds
Tractive force	75,700 pounds	63,000 pounds	73,800 pounds

Santa Fe bought 141 of these big 2-10-2s between 1919 and 1927. One of them, No. 3829, was built with a four-wheel trailing truck. That experiment was apparently inconclusive; the road continued to buy 2-10-2s, but it did not make 3829 into a 2-10-2.

In 1930 the road bought a single large 2-10-4 from Baldwin, No. 5000.

It was slightly lighter than the contemporary C&O 2-10-4 but had the same 69" drivers, carried a higher boiler pressure, and could produce a little more tractive force. It was nicknamed "Madame Queen" almost immediately. It had larger cylinders and higher boiler pressure than Chesapeake & Ohio's contemporary 2-10-4; it was more powerful but 32 tons lighter. Madame Queen was placed in service and tested thoroughly, but not until December 1936 did Santa Fe order more of the type: five coal burners and five oil burners. Large as No. 5000 was, the new 2-10-4s were larger. They were 21 tons heavier and had 74" drivers, the largest ever used on ten-coupled engines — larger than could be found on any passenger locomotive of some major railroads. As World War II gathered momentum, Santa Fe ordered 25 more in 1943, all oil burners. They were the last new steam locomotives Santa Fe purchased. In 1956 the Pennsylvania Railroad leased 12 of the 5001 class and used them for a brief season alongside its own J1-class 2-10-4s, which were based on the C&O design. PRR's 2-10-4s were heavier and exerted a bit more tractive force, but Santa Fe's were faster.

Passenger locomotives

Santa Fe bought its last 4-4-0s in 1897 and its last new Ten-Wheelers in 1901, five Vauclain compounds that were converted to simple engines in 1911. Santa Fe's last Ten-Wheeler in service, No. 472, went to scrap in 1939. Three Arizona & California 4-6-0s built in 1903 were scrapped in the mid-1920s, and two 1911 machines acquired along with the Clinton & Oklahoma Western were scrapped almost as soon as they became Santa Fe property in 1929.

Santa Fe's first Atlantic was built by Schenectady in 1889. It was a Camelback with an experimental tubular firebox; its tender rode on a four-wheel truck and a six-wheel truck (foreshadowing the tenders of the last Atlantics to be built at Schenectady). The locomotive was converted to a conventional 4-4-0 in 1892. Ten Atlantics came from Dickson in 1899; they were converted to 4-6-0s in 1904. Santa Fe tried the Atlantic a third time in 1903 — four 73"-drivered Vauclain balanced compounds from Baldwin — and achieved success. Between 1905 and 1910 the road added 168 such locomotives to its roster. Some had 79"

Santa Fe's last Atlantics were the 1480 class. Among the odd features of the "Bull Moose" class were a Jacobs-Shupert firebox, external steam pipes from the steam dome to the cylinders and from the valves to the smokebox, and Walschaerts valve gear mounted backwards (for space reasons) activating inboard valves. Baldwin photo; collection of H. L. Broadbelt.

Pacific 3420, built in 1921, was typical of Santa Fe's last series of Pacifics. Rebuilding by Topeka Shops in 1935 added a train control box and an Elesco feedwater heater on the pilot deck, new main rods, larger disc drivers, a stack extension, and additional train control apparatus atop the boiler. As built, Baldwin photo, collection of H. L. Broadbelt; rebuilt, AT&SF photo.

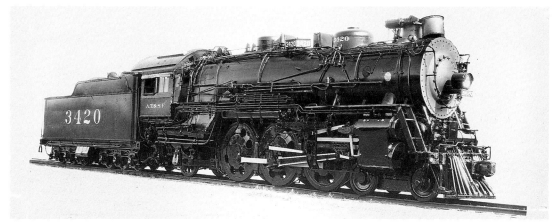

drivers; others, 73"; all had the main rods connected to the first pair of drivers. In the late 1920s the Atlantics were either scrapped, with the boilers used for 0-8-0s, or rebuilt as simple engines which lasted into the 1940s.

The 1480-class deserves special mention. They were the road's first Atlantics with outside valve gear and outside-bearing trailing trucks. They had extended boilers that contained a superheater and reheater; they also had Jacobs-Shupert fireboxes, two steam domes, and outside dry pipes. They were given the nickname "Bull Moose." Their rebuilding included shortening the boiler and frame, and connecting the main rods to the rear drivers. Locomotives 1487 and 1488 remained on the roster until 1953.

Santa Fe's first Pacifics, the 1200 class, came from Baldwin in 1903 with 69" drivers. They soon swapped those wheels for the 79" drivers of the 1014-class Prairies. The 1200s were simple (single-expansion) engines, with inboard piston valves and inboard-bearing trailing trucks. Subsequent Pacifics had 73" drivers; some were four-cylinder balanced compounds and some were simple. Like the Atlantics that preceded them, the compound Pacifics were rebuilt as simple engines. Unlike the Atlantics, most members of each class were rebuilt, except for the 1226 class. The Pacifics grew in size as they evolved, from 216,000 pounds for the 1200 class to 285,000 pounds for the 3500 class.

The 3400 class came from Baldwin between 1919 and 1924. They were only slightly heavier than their immediate predecessors, but they looked bigger and more modern. They were built with 73" drivers, and the upper part of the cab sides slanted inward. Most of the 3400s were rebuilt with 79" drivers and modernized in the early 1940s.

Number 3600 was intended for display at the 1915 Panama Pacific Exposition in San Francisco. It was delivered in 1915, apparently too late for the fair. It looked just like a 3500 but differed in minor dimensions. Like most one-of-a-kinds, it was scrapped early — in 1938.

On many of Santa Fe's routes Pacifics weren't adequate for long passenger trains. The Mountain type was introduced on the Chesapeake & Ohio in 1911 for passenger service on heavy grades, and it quickly achieved acceptance as a heavy passenger and fast freight locomotive. Santa Fe ordered two 4-8-2s from Baldwin in 1917. Compared to their immediate predecessors, the 3500-class Pacifics (which were four-cylinder balanced compounds), the Mountains weighed about 38 percent more and produced 67 percent more tractive force. They had 69" drivers, 4" smaller than the Pacifics. Number 3700 was a coal burner and had Baker valve gear; No. 3701 was an oil burner with Walschaerts valve gear; both had Delta trailing trucks. By the time they were delivered the road had ordered 10 more, 5 oil burners and 5 coal burners, all with Walschaerts valve gear and Hodges trailing trucks, the latter a change from the Rushton trailing truck the Santa Fe had used previously. Successive orders between 1920 and 1924 were also divided between oil and coal. Engine weight was about the same as that of a USRA heavy Mountain, 352,000 pounds, but the first two members of the class weighed 373,700 pounds, and No. 3721 weighed only 338,310 pounds.

The 4-8-2s were generally assigned to western parts of the Santa Fe. They remained top-rank passenger power until schedules were accelerated in the mid-1930s. They were then assigned to secondary trains and eventually to flatland freight service.

Santa Fe's first Hudsons, the 74"-drivered 3450 class, built in 1927, appeared to be little more than an evolutionary development of the 3400-class Pacific. They were about the same size as a New York Central J-1b Hudson, but had somewhat less heating surface. They were rebuilt extensively in the late 1930s with 79" drivers, internal changes that reduced the heating surface slightly but improved boiler circulation, and a great deal of external plumbing. The 3460 class Hudsons were most assuredly not big Pacifics. They were among the largest of the type and looked like Santa Fe's contemporary 3765-class 4-8-4s. They had 84" drivers and were initially assigned to the road's fastest trains between Chicago and La Junta, Colorado — west of La Junta was 4-8-4 territory. The first of the class, No. 3460, was streamlined.

The next development was, logically enough, the 4-8-4. In 1927 Santa Fe purchased a single 4-8-4 (the road's diagram book called it a Heavy

Mountain type), No. 3751 (Baldwin's first 4-8-4 and the 13th built for service in North America), and tested it. Compared with the Mountain type, the new engine could pull 33 percent more while consuming 19 percent less coal. The Northern had 30" × 30" cylinders; the Mountain, 28" × 28". Both worked at 210 pounds; the Northern had 73" drivers, against the Mountain's 69". The Northern weighed 423,000 pounds, and produced a tractive force of 66,000 pounds. Although the locomotive was not quite cutting-edge technology — for example, its boiler pressure, 210 pounds, was lower than other contemporary 4-8-4s — Santa Fe was satisfied with the locomotive and ordered 13 more. The 3751s were built as coal burners but were converted to oil in 1937 and 1938 (later 4-8-4s were built as oil burners). Between 1939 and 1941 they were rebuilt with 80" drivers, new frames, and other improvements. Boiler pressure was increased to 230 pounds. The rebuilds were on a par with the 3765 and 3776 classes. Santa Fe assigned them to through

runs between Kansas City and Los Angeles, 1776 miles.

The 11 4-8-4s of the 3765 class were delivered in 1938. They were considerably larger than the first 4-8-4s: 80" drivers, and locomotive weight just short of 500,000 pounds. They were followed by the 3776 class in 1941. Both classes had nickel steel boilers, most of which were replaced between 1949 and 1952. Santa Fe's last 4-8-4s, the 2900 class, were the heaviest Northerns built — 510,150 pounds — because of wartime restrictions on the use of lightweight materials such as nickel steel and manganese alloys. Most of the 2900s were initially assigned to freight service, but later also pulled passenger trains. As dieselization progressed after World War II most of Santa Fe's 4-8-4s moved to freight duties.

Two 4-8-4s were test beds for poppet-valve experimentation. Number 3764 was built in 1929 with Caprotti poppet valves, which were removed in 1934, and 3752 was given Franklin rotary cam poppet valve

The heaviest 4-8-4s built were the 2900 class — big to begin with, and made heavier by wartime restrictions on materials. Some Santa Fe locomotives had extendible stacks that lifted the smoke above the train and improved the draft in the firebox; No. 2927, shown at Pasadena in 1947, illustrates the up position. The roller-bearing rods are retrofits, as is the Baldwin disc driver replacing the Boxpok type in the No. 4 position. Photo by Stan Kistler.

gear in 1948. Number 3765 was slated for streamlining like Hudson 3460 until it was discovered that the 3765 class was turning out heavier than anticipated; streamlining would have added yet more weight.

The first 4-8-4, 3751, was placed on display at San Bernardino, California, in 1958, and was restored to operation in 1991 by the San Bernardino Railroad Historical Society.

Articulateds

Santa Fe explored two-cylinder, four-cylinder, and four-cylinder-balanced compound locomotives before it turned to four-cylinder articulated compounds: Mallets. Most accounts of these experiments rate them by degree of unsuccessfulness. Santa Fe's experience is all the more amazing compared with what other railroads were doing. Almost alone among western railroads, AT&SF never had a high-speed simple articulated. The memories of the Mallets must have been strong indeed.

The first Mallets were a pair of 2-8-8-2 freight engines and a pair of 4-4-6-2 passenger engines. The 2-8-8-2s were considered the best (or least unsuccessful) of Santa Fe's Mallets. They were dismantled in 1924 to create two 2-8-2s. The 4-4-6-2s were possibly the worst. The front (low-pressure) engine tended to slip, quickly using all the steam in the receiver pipe from the high-pressure engine, rendering itself useless, and throwing all the load on the high-pressure engine. They were rebuilt to 4-6-2s in 1915 and had long, useful lives.

The next Mallets were 2-6-6-2s. Topeka Shops built the first from a

Prairie Mallet 3322, built by Baldwin in 1911, was one of four of its class built with accordion-jointed boilers. The first and third domes are sand domes; the second and fourth are steam domes. Collection of John B. McCall.

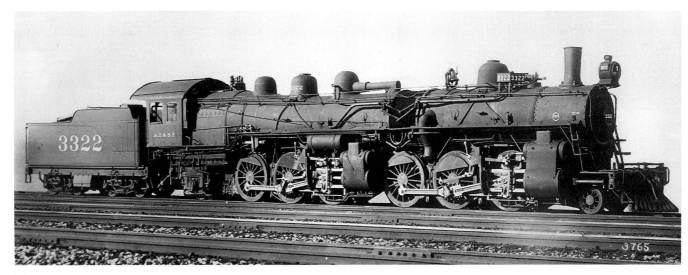

pair of 2-6-2s, and the rest came from Baldwin. They all had 69" drivers and long slender boilers, and looked as though the drawing for the standard 2-6-2 had been copied twice and taped together. Most had rigid boilers; a few had jointed boilers. The 2-6-6-2s worked primarily on the main freight route southwest from Kansas across Oklahoma and New Mexico to Belen, N. M., bypassing the grades of Raton Pass. They lasted longer than AT&SF's other Mallets.

The jointed boilers were an effort to correct the inherent instability of the Mallet. The front engine was free to swing sideways to permit the locomotive to go around curves; it could also move vertically so the wheels could follow vertical curves — humps and dips — and moving vertically was incompatible with supporting the front end of the boiler. Obviously a compromise was necessary, and the Mallet worked well at low speeds. (The eventual solution used on high-speed 4-6-6-4s was to restrict the vertical movement of the front engine completely and let vertical curves in the track be handled by the vertical movement of the axles in the frames.) The Santa Fe decided to have each engine support a separate boiler and join the two boilers with a flexible coupling. The rear boiler comprised the firebox, the boiler proper, and the superheater. The front section contained two separate firetube sections — a reheater (to reheat steam as it passed from the high-pressure cylinders to the low-pressure cylinders) and a feedwater heater — and a smokebox. The joint between the two boiler sections was either a ball-and-socket joint with several packing rings around the joint and spring-loaded bolts holding the sections together, or an accordion joint consisting of 60 steel rings riveted or bolted together at their inner and outer edges alternately.

The joint section was an area where hot gases, smoke, and cinders swirled around between the boiler tubes and the reheater tubes; there was a similar open area between the reheater tubes and the feedwater heater tubes. Steam moved between the two sections in pipes that carried the exhaust of the rear high-pressure cylinders to the reheater, but those connections were movable, as were other steam, water, and air lines between the two engines. The jointed boiler was potential lifetime employment for a steamfitter.

About the same time Topeka Shops and Baldwin teamed up to create 10 2-10-10-2s from 10 existing 2-10-2s and 10 new front units. They were unique in that when they were dismantled, each became two locomotives (the others became just one plus spare parts). Then Topeka assembled four 2-8-8-0s from four 2-8-0s for the rear sections and four new front sections from Baldwin. They too were quickly restored to what they had been before.

During World War II the road purchased eight 2-8-8-2s from Norfolk & Western for helper service on Raton Pass. Santa Fe was sufficiently impressed with their steaming ability to contemplate using the boilers on new 4-8-4s, but instead scrapped one and sold the rest to the Virginian Railway.

Switchers

Santa Fe bought its last new switcher in 1913. Thereafter it converted Consolidations and Moguls into switchers, occasionally using boilers from Atlantics. None of the resulting engines could be considered modern; few of the 0-8-0s and none of the 0-6-0s, for instance, had outside valve gear. Santa Fe chose to put its money into the locomotives that made money — long-haul, over-the-road power — and either build switchers out of the materials at hand or use locomotives that had been superseded in mainline service.

Proposed locomotives

"If you think the elephant preposterous,
You've probably never seen a rhinosterous." — Ogden Nash

Santa Fe had some of the wildest articulateds on the rails, but wilder ones yet existed in its files. Before the 4-4-6-2 passenger Mallets were built, the road received proposals from Baldwin for a 2-4-4-2 and from Alco for a 4-4-4-2. Both were compounds, of course; both had 73" drivers. The Alco proposal called for no lateral motion in either the lead truck or the trailing axle, because the wheelbases of the two engine units were so short. In 1908 Santa Fe considered a 2-8-8-2 with the forward (low-pressure) unit backwards, like Canadian Pacific's 0-6-6-0s.

In 1913 the road asked Baldwin to design a quadruplex 2-8-8-8-8-2. The jointed boiler was to have three engine units under it, a cab for the engineer in front, and a cab for the fireman on the rear. The fourth engine was to be under the tender. The design also covered a quintuplex, which would have two engine units under a jointed tender, and a 2-10-10-10-10-10-2 was theoretically possible. The Erie's experience with its triplexes was that they ran out of steam embarrassingly fast. Even if a boiler could have supplied steam to eight or ten cylinders, the couplers, draft gear, and center sills of the freight cars behind the locomotive could not have withstood the drawbar pull.

In 1926 the Santa Fe entertained Baldwin proposals for three-cylinder simple engines, a 4-8-2 and a 4-8-4, but stayed with conventional two-cylinder designs. In 1930 the road proposed, or at least sketched, a 2-8-10-2 compound Mallet with 69" drivers. Perhaps the design came from a young man in the motive power office who wasn't around when compounds and articulateds afflicted the railroad two decades previous; perhaps it came from a veteran who thought that maybe they'd would work better this time. Later came a proposal for a cab-forward, oil-fired, duplex-drive 6-4-4-4.

Historical and technical societies:

Santa Fe Railway Historical Society, P. O. Box 92887, Long Beach, CA 90809-2887

Santa Fe Modelers Organization, 1704 Valley Ridge, Norman, OK 73072

Recommended reading:

Iron Horses of the Santa Fe Trail, by E. D. Worley, published in 1965 by the Southwest Railroad Historical Society, P. O. Box 26369, Dallas, TX 75226-0369 (LCC 63-22759)

"Thirty years of 4-8-4's," by Lloyd E. Stagner, in *Trains Magazine*, February 1987, pages 24-40

"Prairie Mallets," by John B. McCall, in *Trains Magazine*, February 1987, pages 42-49

"Missouri Berkshires," by Lloyd E. Stagner, in *Trains Magazine*, February 1987, pages 50-55

Published rosters: *Railway & Locomotive Historical Society Bulletin*, No. 75

AT&SF STEAM LOCOMOTIVES BUILT SINCE 1900

Type	Class	Numbers	Qty	Builder	Built	Retired	Notes
0-6-0	591	591-604	7	AT&SF	1926-1928	1947-1952	Rebuilt from 2-6-0
0-6-0	2000	2000-2038	39	Baldwin	1906	1931-1951	
0-6-0	2039	2039-2092	54	Baldwin	1911-1913	1931-1951	
0-6-0	2100	2100-2109	10	AT&SF	1904	1932-1950	
0-6-0	2110	2110-2121	12	Baldwin	1905-1906	1930-1951	
0-6-0	2122	2122-2131	10	AT&SF	1906-1907	1930-1950	
0-6-0	2147	2147-2149	3	Cooke	1903	1947-1948	
0-6-0	2500	2500-2503	4	Pittsburgh	1909	1933-1934	Ex-KCM&O
0-8-0	566	566-615	35	AT&SF	1926-1928	1951-1954	Rebuilt from 2-6-0
0-8-0	591	594-605	8	AT&SF	1921-1928	1947-1954	Rebuilt from 2-6-0
0-8-0	649	656	1	AT&SF	1926	1934	Rebuilt from 2-8-0
0-8-0	729	729-757	15	AT&SF	1929-1933	1947-1955	Rebuilt from 2-8-0
0-8-0	769	770-787	5	AT&SF	1929-1934	1948-1954	Rebuilt from 2-8-0
0-8-0	789	797,803,822	3	AT&SF	1924-1931	1950-1952	Rebuilt from 2-8-0
0-8-0	824	824	1	AT&SF	1937	1950	Rebuilt from 2-8-0
0-8-0	825	825-864	35	AT&SF	1922-1937	1947-1955	Rebuilt from 2-8-0
0-8-0	2150	2150-2154	5	AT&SF	1902	1931-1933	2-8-0
0-8-0	2535	2535	1	AT&SF	19032	1952	
							Rebuilt from ex-KCM&O 2-8-0
2-6-0	566	566-590	25	Baldwin	1901		Converted to 0-8-0
2-6-0	591	591-605	15	Baldwin	1901		Converted to 0-6-0 and 0-8-0
2-6-0	566	606-615	10	Baldwin	1901		Converted to 0-8-0
2-6-0	865	865-869	5	Baldwin	1906	1927-1929	Ex-OklahomaCentral
2-6-0	2526	2526-2534	9	Cke, Pitt	1907	1934-1951	Ex-KCM&O
2-6-2	564	564-565	2	Schen	1902	1936, 1947	Tandem compound
2-6-2	1000	1000-1013	14	Baldwin	1901	1941-1954	Vauclain compound
2-6-2	1014	1014-1039	26	Baldwin	1901-1902	1937-1955	Vauclain compound
2-6-2	1050	1050-1152	103	Baldwin	1902-1903	1940-1955	Vauclain compound
2-6-2	1200	1207-1215	4	Baldwin	1903	1950-1952	Rebuilt from 4-6-2
2-6-2	1800	1800-1887	88	Baldwin	1903	1940-1955	Balanced compound
2-6-2	2447	2447	1	Baldwin	1923	Sold 1944	Ex-Oakland Terminal
2-8-0	729	729-758	30	Baldwin	1900	1932-1949	15 rebuilt to 0-8-0
2-8-0	759	759-768	10	Baldwin	1900	1939-1954	
2-8-0	769	769-788	20	Richmond	1900	1939-1954	5 rebuilt to 0-8-0
2-8-0	789	789-823	35	Baldwin	1901-1902	1938-1954	3 rebuilt to 0-8-0
2-8-0	824	824	1	Baldwin	1901		Rebuilt to 0-8-0

AT&SF STEAM LOCOMOTIVES BUILT SINCE 1900 (continued)

Type	Class	Numbers	Qty	Builder	Built	Retired	Notes
2-8-0	825	825-864	40	RI, Pitt	1902	1949-1955	35 rebuilt to 0-8-0
2-8-0	870	870-874	5	Baldwin	1905	1937-1948	Ex-StLRM&P
2-8-0	875	875-876	2	Baldwin	1905	1929	Ex-New Mexico Central
2-8-0	990	990-999	10	AT&SF	1900-1901	1939-1948	
2-8-0	1900	1900-1919	20	Baldwin	1912-1913	1940-1955	
2-8-0	1950	1950-1991	42	Baldwin	1907	1940-1955	
2-8-0	2439	2439-2441	3	Brooks	1904	1940-1951	Ex-SFP&P
2-8-0	2442	2442-2444	3	Brooks	1906	1939-1940	Ex-SFP&
2-8-0	2504	2504-2505	2	Schen	1903	1933-1934	Ex-KCM&O, NYC
2-8-0	2506	2506	1	Schen	1903	sold 1946	Ex-KCM&O, NYC
2-8-0	2507	2507-2525	19	Schen	1906-1910	1952-1955	Ex-KCM&O, NYC
2-8-0	2535	2535-2549	15	Pittsburgh	1909-1910	1947-1954	Ex-KCM&O
2-8-0	2550	2550-2551	2	Cooke	1906	1939, 1953	Ex-KCM&O
2-8-0	2552	2552-2553	2	Cooke	1905	1955, 1952	Ex-KCM&O
2-8-0	2559	2559-2564	6	Brooks	1901-1903	1930-1934	
							Ex-KCM&O,StL&H, NYC
2-8-2	882	882-884	3	BLW, PRR	1916-1917	1947	Ex-Pennsylvania Railroad
2-8-2	885	885-899	15	Baldwin	1902-1903	1949-1954	
2-8-2	1798	1798, 1799	2	AT&SF	1924	1950, 1952	Ex-2-8-8-2
2-8-2	3100	3100-3128	29	Baldwin	1913	1949-1955	
2-8-2	3129	3129-3158	30	Baldwin	1916	1948-1954	
2-8-2	3160	3160-3287	128	Baldwin	1917-1920	1950-1956	
2-8-2	4000	4000-4100	101	Baldwin	1921-1926	1950-1956	
2-8-4	4101	4101-4115	15	Baldwin	1927	1954-1955	
2-8-4	4193	4193-4199	7	Lima	1928	1949, 1954	Ex-Boston & Maine
2-10-0	987	987	1	Baldwin	1902	1933	
2-10-0	988	988-989	2	Schen	1902	1938	
2-10-0	2554	2554-2556	3	Baldwin	1918	1930, 1934	Ex-KCM&O
2-10-0	2565	2565-2569	5	Baldwin	1925	1953-1955	Ex-KCM&O
2-10-2	900	900-984	85	Baldwin	1903-1904	1938-1956	
2-10-2	985	985	1	Baldwin	1904	1936	
2-10-2	1600	1600-1673	74	Baldwin	1905-1907	1939-1956	
2-10-2	1674	1674-1705	32	Baldwin	1912-1913	1940-1956	
2-10-2	3010	3010-3019	10	AT&SF	1915-1917	1939-1952	Ex-3000 class (rear)
2-10-2	3020	3020-3029	10	AT&SF	1915-1918	1940-1952	Ex-3000 class (front)
2-10-2	3800	3800-3940	140	Baldwin	1919-1927		
2-10-4	3800	3829	1	Baldwin	1919	1955	
2-10-4	5000	5000	1	Baldwin	1930		
2-10-4	5001	5001-5010	10	Baldwin	1938	1959	
2-10-4	5011	5011-5035	25	Baldwin	1944	1959	
2-6-6-2	1157	1157	1	AT&SF	1910	1924	Jointed boiler
2-6-6-2	1158	1158-1159	2	Baldwin	1910	1929, 1927	Jointed boiler
2-6-6-2	1160	1160-1169	10	Baldwin	1910	1928-1933	Rigid boiler
2-6-6-2	1170	1170-1197	28	Baldwin	1910	1928-1934	Rigid boiler
2-6-6-2	3300	3300-3323	24	Baldwin	1911	1927-1934	
							20 rigid boiler, 4 jointed boiler
2-8-0-0	3296	3296-3299	4	AT&SF	1911	R1923	Rebuilt from and to 2-8-0
2-8-8-2	1790	1790-1797	8	Alco	1919		Ex-Norfolk & Western
2-8-8-2	1798	1798-1799	2	Baldwin	1909	R1924	
2-10-10-2							
	3000	3000-3009	10	BLW-ATSF	1911	1915-1918	
							Rebuilt from and to 2-10-2
4-4-2	256	256-259	4	Baldwin	1903	1925-1927	Vauclain compound
4-4-2	507	507-541	35	Baldwin	1904	1925-1943	Balanced compound
4-4-2	542	542-559	18	Baldwin	1904	1924-1947	Balanced compound
4-4-2	1400	1400-1451	52	Baldwin	1905-1907	1926-1929	Balanced compound
4-4-2	1452	1452-1478	27	Baldwin	1909-1910	1924-1953	Balanced compound
4-4-2	1480	1480-1502	23	Baldwin	1910	1926-1953	Balanced compound
4-4-2	1550	1550-1561	12	Baldwin	1905-1906	1925-1930	Built as 1450-1461
4-6-0	468	468-497	30	RI	1900	1926-1939	
4-6-0	498	498-502	5	Baldwin	1901	1929-1938	
4-6-2	1200	1200-1225	26	Baldwin	1903	1939-1950	Simple
4-6-2	1226	1226-1266	41	Baldwin	1905-1906	1932-1950	Balanced compound
4-6-2	1270	1270-1289	20	Baldwin	1909-1910	1940-1951	Simple
4-6-2	1290	1290-1296	7	Baldwin	1907	1939-1952	Simple
4-6-2	1297	1297-1308	12	Baldwin	1910-1911	1935-1950	Simple
4-6-2	1309	1309-1336	28	Baldwin	1911	1940-1952	Balanced compound
4-6-2	1337	1337-1388	52	Baldwin	1912-1913	1938-1954	Balanced compound
4-6-2	1398	1398, 1399	2	AT&SF	1915	1949, 1950	Rebuilt from 4-4-6-2
4-6-2	3400	3400-3449	50	Baldwin	1919-1924	1950-1955	
4-6-2	3500	3500-3534	35	Baldwin	1914	1940-1955	Balanced compound
4-6-2	3600	3600	1	Baldwin	1915	1938	
4-6-4	3450	3450-3459	10	Baldwin	1927	1952-1956	Rebuilt 1936-1939
4-6-4	3460	3460-3465	6	Baldwin	1937	1956	3460 streamlined
4-8-2	3700	3700-3750	51	Baldwin	1918-1924	1950-1955	
4-8-4	3751	3751-3764	14	Baldwin	1927-1929	1956-1959	
4-8-4	3765	3765-3775	11	Baldwin	1938	1959	
4-8-4	3776	3776-3785	10	Baldwin	1941	1956-1959	
4-8-4	2900	2900-2929	30	Baldwin	1943-1944	1959	
4-4-6-2	1398	1398-1399	2	Baldwin	1909	R1915	Rebuilt to 4-6-2

ATLANTA & WEST POINT RAIL ROAD
WESTERN RAILWAY OF ALABAMA
GEORGIA RAILROAD

The Atlanta & West Point and the Western of Alabama together were known as the West Point Route. They were affiliated with the Georgia Railroad, which was not a corporation but instead an organization that operated the railroad properties of the Georgia Railroad & Banking Co. for the Louisville & Nashville and the Atlantic Coast Line. Ownership of the three railroads was convoluted and involved not only ACL and L&N but Central of Georgia. It is sufficient to consider all of them part of the Atlantic Coast Line family.

The West Point Route was a trunk line, part of the principal Washington-Atlanta-New Orleans passenger route: Southern Railway between Washington and Atlanta; West Point Route, Atlanta-Montgomery; and Louisville & Nashville, Montgomery-New Orleans (through trains via Atlanta and Birmingham, Southern Railway all the way, were a streamliner-era development). A&WP's line extended 87 miles southwest from Atlanta to West Point, Georgia, on the Alabama state line; WofA ran from there through Montgomery, 88 miles, to Selma, Ala., 50 miles beyond Montgomery. Neither road had any branches. Locomotives of the two railroads ran through between Atlanta and Montgomery.

The main line of the Georgia Railroad ran from Augusta, Ga., where it connected with Atlantic Coast Line, Southern, Charleston & Western Carolina, and Georgia & Florida, 171 miles west to Atlanta, climbing steadily all the way. Several branches brought the total mileage to 329.

All three roads dieselized quickly in the early 1950s. Western of Alabama bought four Baldwin VO-1000 diesel switchers in 1944, but there were no further diesel purchases until 1948, when the three roads began purchasing cab units from EMD. A&WP completed its diesel roster with GP7s in 1952; the other two roads finished with GP9s in 1954.

The locomotive numbers of the three railroads are as confusing as their corporate affiliations. A simple roster or list is inadequate; a four-dimensional matrix might not be sufficient. Locomotives were sometimes numbered in the sequence in which they were delivered and sometimes in blocks by type. General renumberings in the early part of the 20th century endeavored to bring order out of chaos but resulted only in a different sort of chaos. Rebuildings of locomotives often — but not always — included renumbering, usually to the next available number in the series for that class. In addition, there were renumberings without rebuildings, usually to avoid duplication of numbers on the three railroads. Western of Alabama locomotives were numbered in the 100s and 300s; Atlanta & West Point locomotives in the 200s and 400s; the Georgia Railroad used numbers from 101 to 805.

Consider Georgia Railroad 4-6-0 17/151/160/216: built as 17 in 1911; renumbered 151 in 1916 in a general renumbering; again renumbered to avoid conflict with WofA Pacific 151, which was running on the Georgia Railroad; and rebuilt in 1940 as 216. The seven Pacifics owned by the three roads carried 15 different combinations of road name and number.

Freight locomotives

The West Point Route acquired a group of Ten-Wheelers for freight service between 1903 and 1912, WofA 125-131 and A&WP 225-231. They had 61" drivers and weighed 180,800 pounds. Through the years they were rebuilt with piston valves and Baker or Southern valve gear.

Soon after the 20th century began, the Georgia Railroad adopted the Ten-Wheeler as its standard locomotive, replacing earlier Americans and Moguls. The road acquired a fleet of 38 dual-service 4-6-0s with 20" × 26" cylinders, 66" drivers, and engine weights ranging from 165,000 to 173,000 pounds. They were eventually rebuilt with piston valves and Walschaerts valve gear; a few received 67" or 72" drivers.

Georgia Railroad's first Mikados, 300-302, arrived from Lima in 1915. They were built to a standard Harriman design — 27" × 30" cylinders, 63" drivers, 280,000 pounds — and were part of a group built for Illinois Central, Central of Georgia, and the Georgia Railroad (IC controlled CofG). A second batch of Harriman 2-8-2s was built by Lima in 1918: Georgia 303, Western of Alabama 350 and 351, and Atlanta & West Point 400 and 401.

Atlanta & West Point 427, shown north of Newnan, Georgia, in 1949, is a copy of a USRA light Mikado. At first glance the air pumps appear to be upside down; they are New York Air Brake pumps (Westinghouse equipment is more common), which have the steam cylinders below and the air cylinders above. Photo by R. D. Sharpless.

Georgia 253 was built by Rogers in 1907 as Western of Alabama 150. Rebuildings changed the cylinders, valve gear, trailing truck, domes, tender — little remains from 1907 in this mid-1940s photo. Photo by D. W. Salter.

A&WP 430 and identical twin Western Railway of Alabama 380, built by Baldwin in 1944, were thoroughly modern copies of the USRA heavy Mikado of 1918. Among the improvements are dual air pumps mounted on the pilot, Elesco coil-type feedwater heater, Boxpok drivers, cast trailing truck, and a large 12-wheel tender. BLW photo.

Georgia 320-326, WofA 375-378, and A&WP 425-427, built by Lima in 1923 and 1925, were copies of the USRA light Mikado. Just before World War II the Georgia Railroad purchased two Mikes from the New York Central; four more came from the Clinchfield in 1943. The last two Mikes purchased by the West Point Route were WofA 380 and A&WP 430, built by Baldwin in 1944. They were essentially updated USRA heavy 2-8-2s, a testimonial to the soundness of the 1918 USRA design.

Passenger locomotives

The West Point Route had a number of 72"-drivered Ten-Wheelers built just before and after the turn of the century, and two with 78" drivers which were rebuilt in 1923 and 1924 with 72" wheels. Like the freight engines, the passenger Ten-Wheelers were later modernized with piston valves and Southern or Baker valve gear.

In 1907 WofA and A&WP took delivery of a pair of Rogers Pacifics (WofA 150 and A&WP 250), light machines (231,700 pounds) with 72" drivers, 23" × 28" cylinders, slide valves, and inside-journal trailing trucks. Another such locomotive, WofA 151, came from Richmond in 1910; Walschaerts valve gear had replaced Stephenson gear, but otherwise the design was the same. A&WP received two light Pacifics, 280 and 281, from Brooks in 1913.

The West Point Route rebuilt the three early Pacifics in 1922 and 1923 with piston valves and Walschaerts valve gear. WofA 150 was renumbered 152, 151 kept its number, and A&WP 250 was renumbered 251. Two of them were sold to the Georgia Railroad in 1934: A&WP 251 became Georgia 251, and WofA 151 became Georgia 252. The third early Pacific, WofA 152 became Georgia 253 in 1936.

Georgia Railroad also rebuilt the Pacifics; the most noticeable changes were outside-journal trailing trucks and, as you might expect, new numbers but not all the way around: 251 (née A&WP 250) became 254 in 1937 (and got Southern valve gear); 252 (née WofA 151) became 255 in 1938; 253 kept its number. In 1940 A&WP 281, one of the two Brooks Pacifics, became Georgia 281.

In 1926 the West Point Route bought a pair of 4-6-2s from Lima that were copies of USRA heavy Pacifics except for Delta trailing trucks and 73" drivers instead of 79": WofA 190 and A&WP 290. The latter is still active in excursion service, carrying the number it was built with.

Western of Alabama bought two light 4-8-2s, 180 and 181, from Richmond in 1920; they were nearly identical to 4-8-2s Richmond built for Central of Georgia about the same time. In 1936 three more Mountains, 185-187, came to the road from the Florida East Coast. During World War II 180 and 181 were assigned to the Georgia Railroad in exchange for Pacifics 254 and 255.

Switchers

The West Point Route 0-6-0s all had the same dimensions — 19" × 24" cylinders and 52" drivers — though they were built over a period of 10 years. Georgia's 0-6-0s had drivers an inch smaller and cylinders an inch larger and were therefore slightly more powerful.

The USRA assigned a pair of Pittsburgh-built 0-8-0s to the West Point Route in 1918, WofA 115 and A&WP 215, and two Baldwin 0-8-0s to the Georgia Railroad in 1919. In 1943 three 0-8-0s came south from the Detroit Terminal Railroad: A&WP 219, which had 53" drivers; and A&WP 218 and Georgia Railroad 805, which had 58" drivers.

The three roads had just one Consolidation among them, WofA 120, a low-drivered locomotive purchased from the Birmingham Southern in 1943 and used as a switcher; and one 20th century Mogul, A&WP 210, bought new in 1912 and used for switching and transfer work at Atlanta.

Recommended reading:

Steam Locomotives and History: Georgia Railroad and West Point Route, by Richard E. Prince, published in 1962 by Richard E. Prince (LCC 62-11515)

Published rosters:

Railroad Magazine: December 1939, page 112; July 1952, page 106
Trains Magazine: June 1943, page 13 (WofA and A&WP)

A&WP-WofA-GA STEAM LOCOMOTIVES BUILT SINCE 1900

Type	Class	Numbers	Qty	Builder	Built	Retired	Notes
Atlanta & West Point							
0-6-0		25	1	Rogers	1900		
0-6-0	E	200-202	3	Richmond	1912-1913	1950	
0-8-0	G	215	1	Richmond	1912	1954	
0-8-0	G	218, 219	2	Schenectady	1923, 1925	1954, 1951	Ex-Detroit Terminal
2-6-0	B	210	1	Richmond	1912	1954	
2-8-2	F	400, 401	2	Lima	1918	1952, 1951	
2-8-2	F	425-427	3	Lima	1923, 1925	1954	
2-8-2	F	430	1	Baldwin	1944	1954	
4-6-0	A	225-231	7	Rogers	1903-1912	1936-1954	
4-6-0	A	260	1	Rogers	1906	1954	Rebuilt to 261, 1923
4-6-0	A	275	1	Rogers	1900	1947	
4-6-2	P	250	1	Rogers	1907	to GA 251	Rebuilt to 251, 1923
4-6-2	P	280, 281	2	Brooks	1913	1953	281 to GA 281
4-6-2	P	290	1	Lima	1926		
Western Railway of Alabama							
0-6-0	E	100-104	6	Rogers	1903-1907	1939-1950	
0-6-0	E	105	1	Cooke	1910	1947	
0-8-0	G	115	1	Pittsburgh	1918	1954	
2-8-0	C	120	1	Richmond	1913	1951	Ex-Birmingham Southern
2-8-2	F	350, 351	2	Lima	1918	1954, 1952	
2-8-2	F	375-378	4	Lima	1923, 1925	1952-1954	
2-8-2	F	380	1	Baldwin	1944	1954	
4-6-0	A	125-128	4	Rogers	1903-1907	1938-1952	
4-6-0	A	129-131	3	Richmond	1911-1912	1945-1952	
4-6-0	A	171	1	Rogers	1903	1938	Rebuilt to 173 in 1924
4-6-0	A	175	1	Rogers	1900	1952	
4-6-0	A	160	1	Rogers	1906	1953	Rebuilt to 161 in 1924
4-6-2	P	150	1	Rogers	1907	to GA 253	Rebuilt to 152 in 1922
4-6-2	P	151	1	Richmond	1910	to GA 252	
4-6-2	P	190	1	Lima	1926	1954	
4-6-2	P	190	1	Lima	1926	1954	
4-8-2	M	180, 181	2	Richmond	1920	1954, 1952	
4-8-2	M	185-187	3	Schenectady	1924	1954	Ex-Florida East Coast
Georgia Railroad							
0-6-0	E	701-709	9	Baldwin	1902-1912	1949-1951	
0-8-0	G	801, 802	2	Baldwin	1919	1954, 1953	
0-8-0	G	805	1	Schenectady	1922	1953	Ex-Detroit Terminal
2-6-0	B	423-429	5	Baldwin	1901-1903	1922-1935	
2-6-0	B	451-456	6	Baldwin	1903-1904	1935, 1949	
2-8-2	F	300-303	4	Lima	1915-1918	1953-1954	
2-8-2	F	305, 306	2	Brooks	1907	1953	Ex-New York Central
2-8-2	F	320-326	7	Lima	1923-1925	1952-1954	
2-8-2	F	500-503	4	Baldwin	1919		Ex-Clinchfield; renumbered 331-334 in 1948
4-6-0	A	101-222	38	Baldwin	1905-1912	1926-1954	
4-6-2	P	251	1	Rogers	1907	1953	Ex-A&WP 251; rebuilt to 254 in 1937
4-6-2	P	252	1	Richmond	1910	1954	Ex-WofA 151; rebuilt to 255 in 1938
4-6-2	P	253	1	Rogers	1907	1953	Ex-WofA 150
4-6-2	P	281	1	Brooks	1913	1954	Ex-A&WP 281

ATLANTIC COAST LINE RAILROAD

In 1900 the Atlantic Coast Line Railroad reached from Richmond and Norfolk, Virginia, to Augusta, Georgia, and Charleston, South Carolina. In 1902 it acquired the Plant System — the Savannah, Florida & Western Railway and its subsidiaries — which had a network of lines in southeast Georgia and north Florida and a long branch northwest to Montgomery, Alabama. That same year it gained control of Louisville & Nashville, which in turn controlled the Nashville, Chattanooga & St. Louis. ACL quickly became one of the three strong railroads of the South (the others were Southern Railway and L&N) and the dominant Northeast-to-Florida route for both passengers and freight.

The Atlanta, Birmingham & Coast Railroad was completed (as the Atlanta, Birmingham & Atlantic) from Brunswick and Waycross, Ga., to Atlanta and Birmingham between 1908 and 1910. It was in financial difficulty even before it was completed. ACL saw the line as a strategic asset, offering access to Atlanta and Birmingham and connections with the L&N and the NC&StL. ACL acquired control of the road in 1926 and merged it at the end of 1945. The AB&C brought with it an exceptionally ragtag assortment of secondhand locomotives.

The Coast Line was notable for using the Pacific, traditionally a passenger locomotive, in both passenger and freight service. The main line lay along the coastal plain between Richmond and Jacksonville, almost a water-level route. When ACL's freight trains outgrew the 4-4-0s that pulled them, the road turned to 4-6-0s instead of 2-8-0s, choosing the stability of a four-wheel lead truck over the pulling power of eight drivers. As trains grew heavier and faster, ACL progressed to the Pacific, which was equally suited to hauling Florida-bound vacationers and northbound citrus fruit (by 1939 14 percent of ACL's freight revenue came from oranges and grapefruit). ACL was the only road in the United States that used the Pacific extensively for freight.

Much of ACL's traffic was interchanged with the Florida East Coast at Jacksonville. ACL's own lines fanned out to the Gulf of Mexico at Tampa, St. Petersburg, Naples, and Port Everglades. Until the lines were rebuilt in later years, ACL's heavy power, such as the larger Pacifics, couldn't operate in much of the territory beyond Jacksonville. The former Alabama Midland Railway (ex-Plant System) from Bainbridge, Ala., northwest to Montgomery crossed the tail of the Appalachians and ran crosswise to the rivers. The line required heavier locomotives for freight trains. AB&C's lines to Atlanta and Birmingham had the same crossgrain profile and the same need for heavy freight power.

In 1938 ACL bought a dozen 4-8-4s for mainline passenger service and neighboring Seaboard Air Line bought diesels. ACL bought a pair of Electro-Motive passenger units in 1939 and quickly ordered more, then turned its attention to freight: 24 two-unit FTs and 12 two-unit F2s by 1946 — dieselization was under way. By 1952 diesels were handling 99 percent of ACL's trains; a few steam locomotives remained on the roster for seasonal peaks and lines that could not take the weight of a diesel. At the end of 1954 six steam locomotives were on the roster, five of them built before 1920; a year later there were none.

Passenger and dual-service locomotives

In the early 1890s Atlantic Coast Line was in the market for a fast passenger locomotive with more steaming capacity than its 4-4-0s. ACL's officials viewed the 2-4-2 that Baldwin built for the World's Columbian Exposition and thought the large firebox supported by a trailing axle might be the answer. Baldwin designed a new locomotive type, the 4-4-2, for the Atlantic Coast Line and named it for the railroad. ACL bought 10 Atlantics between 1894 and 1900 (plus a pair of 2-4-2s, just to test the type) but soon decided they were too light, relegated them to local trains, and scrapped them in 1934. ACL left its name on the type but turned to Ten-Wheelers for mainline duties.

Baldwin delivered five Ten-Wheelers in 1898 for freight service. They were successful, and ACL ordered more, some with 64" drivers for freight service and others with 69" drivers for passenger duty. The type acquired the nickname "Copper Head" for a decorative copper flange on the stack. ACL continued to order the same basic Ten-Wheeler — 19" × 26" cylinders (later 20" × 26"), 185 pounds pressure, equally spaced drive wheels, 140,000 to 160,000 pounds — until 1910. The last batches were built with piston valves and Walschaerts valve gear, and many early Copper Heads were eventually superheated and fitted with Modern steam chests, which were bolt-on replacement piston valves. Copper Head classes included K, K-4, K-5, K-6, K-14, and K-15.

In 1922 ACL and Baldwin designed a new Ten-Wheeler, class K-16, 34,000 pounds heavier than the newest Copper Heads. It was intended for routes which couldn't handle the Pacifics, but ACL had begun to improve its track and roadbed, and there was little need for it.

ACL acquired three 4-6-2s with the Plant System. They were built by Rhode Island in 1893 as cross-compounds for Milwaukee Road, which soon turned them back. Rhode Island rebuilt them as simple locomotives for Plant System. ACL rebuilt them as 4-6-0rs in 1912.

The first of ACL's own Pacifics arrived from Baldwin in 1911: 15 class P engines with 73" drivers and slide valves. Eventually they were superheated and equipped with Modern steam chests, and reclassified P-S. The P-1 class was delivered in 1912, essentially the same size as the P class but superheated and equipped with piston valves. The P-2 class was delivered in 1913 for freight service: again the same engine but with 64" drivers. ACL decided the P-2 wasn't what it wanted, but the locomotives remained on the roster until dieselization. The P-3 class of 1914 was a 69"-drivered version of the same engine intended for dual service; it set the pattern for future 4-6-2s. The 27 members of the P-4 class, delivered between 1916 and 1918, had inch-larger cylinders than the P-3s and were slightly heavier.

In 1919 and 1920 ACL received 70 USRA light Pacifics built by Alco's Brooks and Richmond plants — unusual for ACL, which was a loyal Baldwin customer. The P-5-A 4-6-2s were larger, heavier, and more powerful than any of ACL's own designs and became ACL's standard passenger locomotive. After the war ACL and Baldwin modified the design with 69" drivers to create a slightly heavier dual-service machine

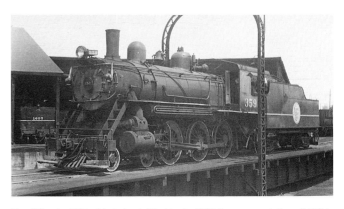

Ten-Wheeler 359, at Lakeland, Florida, in 1946, is representative of ACL's Copper Heads, even though the ornamental copper flange on the stack is long gone. When it was superheated it was equipped with Modern steam chests. Photo by George W. Pettengill.

Pacific 403 is a P-2, built in 1913 with 64" drivers for freight service. The odd-shaped cab is typical of ACL's early Pacifics. Photo by George W. Pettengill.

that would be better suited for freight, and ACL purchased 165 of them between 1922 and 1926.

Merger of the Atlanta, Birmingham & Coast added 13 Pacifics to ACL's roster: 11 ex-Florida East Coast engines that were lighter than any of ACL's own Pacifics, and 2 ex-Great Northern engines that were somewhat heavier than the P-4.

In 1938 ACL took delivery of a dozen class R-1 4-8-4s from Baldwin. They had cast-steel engine beds, 80" disc drivers, roller bearings on the lead trucks and drivers, tenders riding on 8-wheel trucks, and a two-tone gray-and-black paint scheme. When they entered service the road soon discovered that the reciprocating machinery had been over-counterbalanced and at high speeds the locomotives pounded the rails and threw the track out of alignment. The condition was never completely corrected. After the war ACL began dieselizing its mainline passenger trains and assigned the 4-8-4s to freight service.

A wartime increase in traffic to the west coast of Florida caused ACL to purchase five 4-8-2s from the Delaware, Lackawanna & Western in 1943. They were used primarily between Tampa and Albany, Georgia. Two more 4-8-2s, former Florida East Coast engines, came from the AB&C in 1946.

Freight locomotives

When ACL absorbed the Plant System it got four 2-8-0s that Baldwin had built for the Alabama Midland in 1901. ACL bought ten more Consolidations from Baldwin in 1903, three in 1905, and four in 1911. They were all assigned to the Montgomery route until they were replaced by Mikados and dispersed around the system as switchers. ACL received 20 Mikados from Baldwin in 1911. They were light locomotives (233,450 pounds) with 56½" drivers and slide valves. The M-2s of 1919 were purchased for coal trains on the line to Montgomery. They were an order of magnitude bigger than the M class, weighing as much as a USRA light Mike and exerting somewhat more tractive effort.

In 1925 ACL bought 20 Santa Fe type locomotives for use on the Montgomery route. They were large engines, 12 tons heavier than the USRA 2-10-2, and they introduced the automatic stoker and the Van-

4-6-2 — PACIFIC

Deciding which locomotive was the first Pacific is, like several other firsts, a matter of judgment and opinion. In 1886 George S. Strong of the Lehigh Valley designed a double-firebox Camelback 4-6-2 which was soon rebuilt as a 4-6-0. In 1887 Schenectady Locomotive Works built a 4-6-2 for the Chicago, Milwaukee & St. Paul — it looked like a nice, well-proportioned 4-6-0 that had somehow picked up a little wheel under its cab. The CM&StP acquired three cross-compound 4-6-2s from Rhode Island in 1893, also of the Ten-Wheeler-with-trailing-axle type. The Milwaukee Road returned them to the builder in short order and they were converted to simple engines and sold to the Plant System. Not until they became the property of Atlantic Coast Line were they rebuilt to Ten-Wheelers. Robert Grimshaw's *Locomotive Catechism* of 1893 referred to these locomotives as the St. Paul type. The first true Pacifics, with trailing trucks obviously necessary to support a firebox behind the drive wheels, were built by Baldwin in 1901 for New Zealand.

The first real Pacifics for North America were built by Brooks for Missouri Pacific and its St. Louis, Iron Mountain & Southern sub-

Among the first 4-6-2s was Chicago, Milwaukee & St. Paul 796, whose trailing axle appears unnecessary. Milwaukee Road photo.

sidiary in 1902. The type caught on fast. The Pacific offered greater steaming capacity than the Ten-Wheeler, more pulling power than the Atlantic, and greater stability at speed than the Prairie. The proportions of the Pacific — dimensions of the boiler and firebox, driver size, piston thrust — seemed to balance well naturally.

Chesapeake & Ohio bought Pacifics in 1902; Chicago & Alton, Northern Pacific, and Santa Fe in 1903; Union Pacific, Southern Pacific, Frisco, and New York Central in 1904. Within a decade the 4-6-2 was the standard passenger locomotive. Only three passenger-carrying roads of any significance lacked Pacifics: New York, Ontario & Western; St. Louis Southwestern; and Western Pacifi. All three moved directly from the 4-6-0 to the 4-8-2. Many railroads found the Pacific adequate for passenger work until they dieselized.

By 1930 the type had been superseded by the Hudson and the Northern, and the 4-6-2s built after 1930 constitute exceptions to the rule. Boston & Maine's 10 heavy Pacifics of 1934 and 1937 were Lima's low-cost response to a Baldwin proposal for a 4-6-4. Reading's 10 homebuilt Pacifics of 1948 were ordered by a management that viewed the diesel as suitable only for switching service and chose to remain with steam for over-the-road work (though by 1948 the road had 10 two-unit FTs on the roster and had more freight cab units on order from EMD and Alco). Pacifics were all that Reading's predominantly local and short-distance passenger trains required, and it may have made more sense to use steam locomotives from the company shops for low-return passenger business and put store-bought diesels on money-making freight trains. Canadian Pacific's lightweight G5 Pacifics of 1944-1948 were what the road's conservative management bought to replace ancient 4-6-0s in secondary and branchline service, but shortly after the last G5s were delivered CPR took its first steps toward dieselization.

First: Missouri Pacific and St. Louis, Iron Mountain & Southern; Brooks, 1902.

Last: Canadian Pacific G5 1301, Canadian Locomotive Company, August 1948

Last in service: National Railways of Mexico still had a number of Pacifics in service, some of them former Mexican Railway three-cylinder engines, in the early 1960s.

Greatest number: Pennsylvania Railroad, 696 (425 were class K4s)

Heaviest: Chicago, St. Paul, Minneapolis & Omaha E-3 600-602 (347,000 pounds)

Lightest: Little River 110 (117,300 pounds)

Recommended reading: "A Pacific primer," by David P. Morgan, in *Trains Magazine*, September 1988, pages 32-41

The earliest domestic Pacifics were like Northern Pacific 2080, built by Alco's Schenectady Works in 1903: long, straight boiler, inboard piston valves, and inboard-bearing trailing truck. Photo by R. V. Nixon.

Many consider the Pacific reached its zenith, at least in terms of appearance, in Southern Railway's green-and-gold Ps-4 class, built by Schenectady, Richmond, and Baldwin between 1923 and 1929. It was a development of the USRA heavy Pacific. One example is on display in the Smithsonian Institution's National Museum of American History in Washington. BLW photo.

The ultimate development of dual-service power on the Atlantic Coast Line was the R-1-class 4-8-4, built by Baldwin in 1938. In appearance the R-1s were very much the modern Baldwin locomotive.

Baldwin and ACL modified the USRA light Pacific into a dual-service locomotive with 69" drivers. Number 1719 was delivered in 1925.

derbilt tender to ACL.

AB&C had 17 2-8-2s in three classes: four small engines built by Baldwin between 1912 and 1915 (ACL scrapped two almost immediately); 11 ex-New York Central engines, 10 of which had been rebuilt from 2-8-0s between 1912 and 1915; and two heavy Baldwin products of 1910 (scrapped soon after ACL acquired them). The road had three light 2-10-2s built by Baldwin in 1917. They had 57" drivers; ACL applied oversize tires, which increased the diameter to 63".

Switchers

ACL's standard switcher was its E-4 class, a low-slung, slide-valve 0-6-0 that looked older than it was. It was followed by the E-10, which had a higher boiler and a firebox above the frames instead of between them, but still with slide valves, Stephenson gear, and main rods connected to the second axle. There were only two E-11s: superheated, piston valves, and Southern valve gear. The E-12s had the main rods connected to the rear axle and Walschaerts valve gear. The USRA assigned 10 0-6-0s to ACL, which classified them E-9-S. The E-13 looked like a USRA 0-6-0 but lacked the superheater; the road reverted to slide

valves for the E-7 class of 1924 (ACL reused classes that had been vacated; in addition, four E-7s were Baldwin plant switchers built in 1917 and 1918 and bought by ACL in 1921). The 0-8-0s are easier to understand — 35 Baldwin copies of the USRA design.

Historical and technical society: Atlantic Coast Line and Seaboard Air Line Railroads Historical Society, P. O. Box 325, Valrico, FL 33594-0325

Recommended reading: *Atlantic Coast Line Railroad Steam Locomotives, Ships and History*, by Richard E. Prince, published in 1966 by Richard E. Prince (LCC 66-25851)
Published rosters: *Railroad Magazine*: December 1938, page 113; March 1947, page 119

ACL STEAM LOCOMOTIVES BUILT SINCE 1900

Type	Class	Numbers	Qty	Builder	Built	Retired	Notes
0-6-0	E	117	1	Baldwin	1900	1929	
0-6-0	E-3	118-120	3	Baldwin	1901	1934	
0-6-0	E-3	124-125	2	Baldwin	1903	1936	
0-6-0	E-4	126-190	65	Baldwin	1904-1910	1935-1952	
0-6-0	E-5	121-123	3	Richmond	1901	1929	Ex-SF&W
0-6-0	E-7	1151-1158	8	Baldwin	1917-1924	1950-1952	
0-6-0	E-9-S	1136-1145	10	Cooke	1918-1919	1951-1952	
0-6-0	E-10	1100-1125	26	Baldwin	1912-1913	1948-1952	
0-6-0	E-11	1126, 1127	2	Baldwin	1916	1951, 1952	
0-6-0	E-12	1128-1135	8	Baldwin	1917	1952	
0-6-0	E-13	1146-1150	5	Baldwin	1920	1950-1952	
0-6-0	AS-1	7023-7028	3	Baldwin	1907	1946-1952	Ex-AB&C
0-8-0	E-14	1200-1234	35	Baldwin	1923-1926	1952	
0-8-0	AS-2	7033-7035	3	AB&C	1939-1942	1952	
							Ex-AB&C, rebuilt from 4-6-0
2-8-0	L	700-713	14	Baldwin	1901, 1903	1939-1942	
2-8-0	L-1	714-716	3	Baldwin	1905	1951-1955	
2-8-0	L-2	717-720	4	Baldwin	1911	1951-1955	
2-8-2	M	800-819	20	Baldwin	1911	1950-1952	
2-8-2	M-2	820-836	17	Baldwin	1918-1923	1952	
2-8-2	AK-1	7205-7213	4	Baldwin	1912-1915	1946-1951	Ex-AB&C
2-8-2	AK-2	7225-7235	11	Alco	1912-1915	1947-1952	Ex-AB&C, ex-NYC
2-8-2	AK-3	7301, 7302	2	Baldwin	1910	1946, 1947	Ex-AB&C
2-10-0	O	8000-8009	10	BLW, Rich.	1917-1918	1949-1952	
2-10-2	Q-1	2000-2019	20	Baldwin	1925	1951-1952	
2-10-2	AF-1	7401-7403	3	Baldwin	1917	1951-1952	Ex-AB&C
4-4-2	I-3	98, 99	2	Baldwin	1900	1934	
4-6-0	K	322-327	6	Richmond	1900	1934	
4-6-0	K	328-351	24	Baldwin	1901-1903	1934-1935	
4-6-0	K-4	212-222	11	Baldwin	1903	1934	
4-6-0	K-5	233-244	12	Baldwin	1907	1936-1939	
4-6-0	K-5	910-1005	96	Baldwin	1906-1907	1935-1954	
4-6-0	K-6	223-232	10	Baldwin	1905	1935-1942	
4-6-0	K-6	351-399	49	Baldwin	1904-1906	1935-1950	
4-6-0	K-6	900-909	10	Baldwin	1906	1935-1947	
4-6-0	K-9	206-210	5	RI	1900	1934-1942	Ex-SF&W
4-6-0	K-9	211	1	Baldwin	1902	1934	
4-6-0	K-14	245-254	10	Baldwin	1910	1947-1950	
4-6-0	K-14	1006-1011	6	Baldwin	1910	1947-1951	
4-6-0	K-15	1012-1044	34	Baldwin	1912-1933	1947-1955	
4-6-0	K-16	1045	1	Baldwin	1922	1952	
4-6-0	AW-1	7060	1	Baldwin	1907	1949	Ex-AB&C
4-6-0	AW-2	7064	1	Baldwin	1907	1949	Ex-AB&C
4-6-0	AW-3	7101-7113	6	Baldwin	1906-1907	1950-1952	Ex-AB&C
4-6-0	AW-4	7115-7124	9	Baldwin	1906-1907	1946-1952	Ex-AB&C
4-6-2	P	260-274	15	Baldwin	1911	1939-1944	
4-6-2	P-1	275-286	12	Baldwin	1912	1939-1944	
4-6-2	P-2	400-410	11	Baldwin	1913	1950-1952	
4-6-2	P-3	411-455	45	Baldwin	1914-1916	1947-1952	
4-6-2	P-4	456-482	27	Baldwin	1917-1918	1949-1952	
4-6-2	P-5-A	1500-1569	70	Brks, Rich	1919-1920	1949-1952	
4-6-2	P-5-B	1600-1764	165	Baldwin	1922-1926	1950-1953	
4-6-2	AJ-1	7071-7086	11	Schen	1911-1913	1946-1955	Ex-AB&C, ex-FEC
4-6-2	AJ-2	7153, 7175	2	Lima	1914	1949, 1950	Ex-AB&C, ex-GN
4-8-0	AS-3	7034	1	Baldwin	1906	1949	Ex-AB&C, ex-N&W
4-8-2	J-1	1401-1405	5	Brooks	1924	1951-1952	Ex-DL&W
4-8-2	AM-1	7351, 7372	2	Schen	1924	1951	Ex-AB&C, ex-FEC
4-8-4	R-1	1800-1811	12	Baldwin	1938	1951-1952	

BALDWIN LOCOMOTIVE WORKS

Baldwin was the largest, longest-lived, and most successful of the steam locomotive builders. It was started in Philadelphia in 1831 by Matthias W. Baldwin, a jeweler, and produced its first locomotive in 1832. By 1861 Baldwin had produced 1,000 locomotives; seven years later the total was 2,000. By the late 1800s Baldwin was producing almost 700 locomotives a year and had 30 to 40 percent of the domestic market. It was one of the largest machinery manufacturers in the United States, and in 1907 employed 18,499 men. Baldwin Locomotive Works was incorporated in 1909 as successor to M. W. Baldwin.

In 1903 the company began building a new plant in Eddystone, on the Delaware River about 12 miles southwest of Philadelphia. The original plant on Broad Street in Philadelphia remained in use for another 22 years; the move to Eddystone was completed in June 1928.

During the 1920s, when Lima was advocating Super-Power and Alco was beating the drums for three-cylinder locomotives, Baldwin built and sent out on a demonstration tour a three-cylinder compound 4-10-2 with a watertube firebox. It was much admired but brought home no orders. Later Baldwin pushed the duplex-drive concept and found only the Pennsylvania Railroad had any interest in the idea.

During the Depression Baldwin purchased several machinery firms, among them the Whitcomb Locomotive Works of Rochelle, Illinois, and the Milwaukee Locomotive Manufacturing Company, both builders of small gasoline and diesel locomotives. The cost of diversification and the construction of the new plant at Eddystone combined to put Baldwin into bankruptcy in 1935. World War II brought a brief return to prosperity, but the decline resumed after the war. It merged with Lima-Hamilton, successor to Lima Locomotive Works, in November 1950 to form Baldwin-Lima-Hamilton Corporation.

Baldwin began producing diesel switchers in the late 1930s and started building road diesels in 1945. Baldwin's diesel market share never exceeded 13 percent, and it ceased building common-carrier-size locomotives in 1956.

Baldwin built its last domestic steam locomotives in 1949, ten Chesapeake & Ohio 2-6-6-2s that were updated versions of a 1910 design.
Recommended reading: *The Locomotives That Baldwin Built*, by Fred Westing, publishing in 1966 by Superior Publishing Co.

SAMUEL MATTHEWS VAUCLAIN (1856-1940) was the son of a Pennsylvania Railroad roundhouse foreman who had helped Matthias W. Baldwin assemble *Old Ironsides*, the first locomotive of the Philadelphia, Germantown & Norristown Railroad. The younger Vauclain had his first locomotive ride at age 4, and at age 16 he began an apprenticeship in the PRR shops. In 1883 the railroad sent Vauclain to Philadelphia to inspect an order of locomotives Baldwin was building. Soon afterward he accepted a job as general foreman of Baldwin's Seventeenth Street shop, which built tenders, then became superintendent of the locomotive erecting shop. In 1886 he was made general superintendent of Baldwin Locomotive Works.

Vauclain undertook a thorough reorganization and mechanization of the shop. He was made a partner in the firm in 1896, vice president in 1911, senior vice president in 1917, and president in 1919. On March 28, 1929, he was elevated to chairman of the board, an honorary position that constituted semi-retirement.

Vauclain introduced the four-cylinder compound in 1889. He put Baldwin on a double shift to reduce the time expensive machinery lay idle, and he advocated electric power for those machines. He worked long hours and rarely spent much time with his family (three sons and three daughters). He died February 4, 1940, at the age of 83, outliving his wife and two of his children.
Recommended reading: *Steaming Up!* by Samuel M. Vauclain and Earl Chapin May, published in 1973 (a reprint of the 1930 edition) by Golden West Books, P. O. Box 80250, San Marino, CA 91108 (ISBN 0-87095-044-4)

BALTIMORE & OHIO RAILROAD

The Baltimore & Ohio was America's first railroad, and by 1900 its main line extended from Philadelphia through Baltimore and Washington to Cumberland, Maryland. There it split, one route going to Chicago via Pittsburgh and Akron and the other to St. Louis via Cincinnati. A secondary line, B&O's original route, ran from Grafton, West Virginia, on the St. Louis line through Wheeling, W. Va., and Newark, Ohio, to Chicago Junction (later Willard), Ohio, on the Chicago line.

B&O's expansion in the 1880s (to Cincinnati and St. Louis in one direction and to Philadelphia in the other, plus a Pittsburgh-Akron-Chicago Junction connection) cost money, and both traffic and revenue dropped in the 1890s. B&O entered a three-year receivership in 1896. It came under the control of the Pennsylvania Railroad and the leadership of Leonor F. Loree in 1901. Loree undertook a number of line improvement programs that gave the B&O double track and easier grades and curves in many areas.

Pennsy control ended in 1906, and Daniel Willard became president of the B&O in 1910. In the next two decades B&O fleshed out its map by acquiring railroads: the Coal & Coke Railroad from Elkins to Charleston, W. Va.; portions of the Cincinnati, Hamilton & Dayton and the Cincinnati, Indianapolis & Western; the Chicago & Alton; the Buffalo, Rochester & Pittsburgh; and the Buffalo & Susquehanna.

The Baltimore & Ohio was never a wealthy road; it generally had to work longer and harder than its competitors. On almost any list of New York-Chicago passenger railroads it was behind the Pennsylvania and New York Central. NYC's route was 53 miles longer than Pennsy's but it didn't climb over mountains; B&O's route was longer than NYC's by the same amount and had mountains, too — and its trains left from Jersey City, not Manhattan. B&O's New York-Washington traffic never approached Pennsy's. Its fast-freight route between the Midwest and the East Coast relied on the Western Maryland and the Reading to bypass Washington, Baltimore, and Philadelphia. Coal was the largest single commodity B&O carried, but it didn't have the coal volume of its neighbors.

In 1924 B&O bought one of the first diesel switchers that Alco, GE, and Ingersoll-Rand built. In 1935 it bought an 1800-h.p. boxcab passenger diesel, which outperformed a pair of specially designed lightweight steam locomotives. It was followed by ten two-unit passenger dieselsbetween 1937 and 1940, and in 1942 and 1943 by six four-unit FTs for freight. At the same time B&O was buying diesel switchers.

B&O continued to buy, build, and rebuild steam locomotives after World War II, and was one of the last railroads to dieselize completely. The recession of the late 1950s hastened complete dieselization because traffic declined — B&O was able to move all its traffic with diesel power. B&O operated a farewell-to-steam excursion between Cleveland and Holloway, Ohio, on May 17, 1958, behind Q-4b 421 (renumbered from 4434 in B&O's renumbering program of the 1950s). A few steam locomotives remained on the road's roster at the beginning of 1960.

Freight locomotives

B&O's freight trains outgrew the 2-6-0 wheel arrangement before the turn of the century, but the road bought two batches of 10 each in 1911 and 1917 for switching and transfer service in Chicago. These Moguls looked like chunky, close-coupled 0-6-0s that had acquired lead trucks. B&O's first Consolidations came in 1873; the last in 1910. At the turn of the century compound locomotives were in vogue. B&O bought two classes of them, 39 E-18s and 111 Camelback E-19s.

Between 1902 and 1904, after the B&O came under the control of the Pennsylvania Railroad, the road received 197 class E-24 Consolidations that were duplicates of Pennsy's H6 class. They were followed between 1905 and 1910 by 414 E-27-class Consolidations.

In 1911 and 1912 Baldwin converted two E-27s into 2-8-2s. The two Q-odd class engines, 4160 and 4161, remained in service until 1949. At the same time Baldwin built 220 Mikes from scratch — class Q-1 and various subclasses.

B&O's next 2-8-2s were 100 USRA light Mikados in class Q-3 (Q-2

Baltimore & Ohio 2500 was the first of the E-27 class, which ultimately numbered 414 locomotives. Note that the firebox is over the rear pair of drivers. Collection of C. W. Witbeck.

The 63" drivers of S-1 No. 6208 are larger than customary for 2-10-2s. They made B&O's "Big Sixes" fast freight power, not drag locomotives. Hundman Collection.

was assigned to the Mikes acquired with the Cincinnati, Indianapolis & Western), of which the first, No. 4500, was the first USRA locomotive. Between 1920 and 1922 Baldwin built 135 Q-4 Mikados. All three classes had 64" drivers. The Q-1s had 24" × 32" cylinders; the Q-3s, 26" × 30"; and the Q-4, 26" × 32". Boiler pressure was 205 pounds for the Q-1, 200 for the Q-3, and 220 for the Q-4. The Q-1s were in the 280,000-pound range; the Q-3s were about 6 tons heavier; and the Q-4s weighed 327,000 pounds.

B&O's heavy grades required more than 2-8-2s. The road bought two groups of 2-10-2s. Baldwin built 31 S-class engines in 1914. They had 58" drivers and weighed 410,000 pounds. The second batch, 125 S-1s, came from Baldwin and Lima between 1923 and 1926. They had the same 30" × 32" cylinders of the first group but operated at 220 pounds pressure instead of 205. They had 64" drivers, which permitted better counterbalancing and thus higher speeds. Most 2-10-2s were low-speed engines that could pull anything, given enough time. B&O's S-1s were an exception: They were powerful and fast.

During World War II B&O needed to move freight between Pittsburgh and Chicago faster than its Mikados could do it. In 1941 and 1942 the road rebuilt four Q-4 Mikados with 70" drivers. They were suc-

cessful, but rather than build more of that type, B&O decided to create 4-8-2s — the four-wheel lead truck would be better for fast running. Between 1942 and 1948 Mount Clare shops built 40 T-3-class 4-8-2s. All had 70" drivers and cast-steel engine beds with integral cylinders. The boilers came from old Mikados and Pacifics; they were lengthened at the forward end, resulting in a boiler that looks too small at the front. Some had roller bearings on all axles, others had none; some had Vanderbilt tenders, others had rectangular tenders. They weighed 375,000 pounds. In 1947 B&O bought 13 Mountains from the Boston & Maine. These T-4s, built between 1935 and 1940, had 73" drivers and weighed 417,800 pounds.

Articulated locomotives

The B&O was built early, and its crossings of the Alleghenies were steep and crooked. Helpers were standard on trains over Sand Patch Grade between Cumberland, Md., and Connellsville, Pa., and over a succession of grades on the line west from Cumberland to Grafton and Parkersburg, W. Va. In 1904 John E. Muhlfeld, B&O's superintendent of motive power, saw that the articulated locomotive patented by Anatole Mallet in 1885 had potential for work on heavy grades. Alco's Schenectady works built America's first Mallet in 1904, an 0-6-6-0. Under its

During World War II B&O needed fast freight locomotives. Baltimore's Mount Clare Shops used the boilers of old Pacifics and Mikados as the starting point for 40 class T-3 Mountains like No. 5586. Photo by Don Wood.

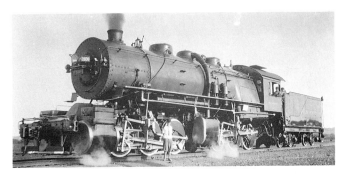

Old Maude, No. 2400, North America's first Mallet, was shined up for presentation at the Fair of the Iron Horse, B&O's centenary celebration in 1927. Photo by Donald A. Somerville.

boiler were two engines — frames, drive wheels, cylinders, and rods. The rear one was stationary with respect to the boiler, but the front engine was hinged at its rear end; a sliding bearing let it support the front of the boiler. The rear engine used steam at boiler pressure, 235 pounds, in 20" × 32" cylinders; the front unit used the steam a second time in 32" × 32" cylinders. Its tractive force, 71,500 pounds, was almost twice what a contemporary E-24 Consolidation could produce. Number 2400 was exhibited at the St. Louis World's Fair of 1904, then went to work as a pusher on Sand Patch, then as a hump engine at Willard, Ohio. Long before it was scrapped in 1938 it was nicknamed "Old Maude." (It's either that or "Queen Mary" for ancient one-of-a-kinds.)

In 1911 Baldwin added a front engine to an E-24 Consolidation, creating a 2-6-8-0. It lasted for six years before returning to its original configuration. B&O returned to Schenectady for 30 0-8-8-0s, built between 1911 and 1913. The new locomotives were an order of magnitude bigger than Old Maude: 26" and 41" cylinders, 56" drivers, and 105,000 pounds tractive force. They proved slow and complicated.

B&O then turned to the 2-8-8-0, taking delivery of 60 from Baldwin in 1916 and 1917. They had the same size cylinders as the 0-8-8-0s and drivers 2" larger. Another 26 similar machines came in 1919 and 1920. Between 1927 and 1940 B&O converted 64 of the 86 2-8-8-0s to simple articulateds, with high-pressure cylinders on both engines.

In 1922 B&O bought 16 2-8-8-2s from the Seaboard Air Line and converted them to 2-8-8-0s. They differed from B&O's previous 2-8-8-0s in having 63" drivers. B&O bought another group of articulateds from the Seaboard in 1947, 10 high-speed, 69"-drivered 2-6-6-4s. The 2-6-6-4s were good engines and well liked by crews.

The last articulateds built for B&O were 30 simple 2-8-8-4s, class EM-1, built by Baldwin in 1944 and 1945. They were truly modern locomotives — and they weren't what B&O wanted. The EM-1s probably would not have been built but for the restrictions on diesels imposed by the War Production Board.

Passenger locomotives

B&O bought its last Ten-Wheelers in 1901, nine class B-17 and 35 class B-19 Vauclain compounds from Baldwin and 35 class B-18 cross-compounds from Rhode Island. The B-17 had 78" drive wheels; the other two classes had 68" drivers. All three classes were converted to simple engines within a few years. They were intended for first-class passenger service on the mountainous parts of the B&O.

Atlantics replaced 4-4-0s on routes with easier grades. The first, a half-dozen A-class Vauclain compounds, arrived in 1900. They were converted to simple locomotives and reclassified A-1 in 1904. Twenty A-2 Atlantics, duplicates of Pennsylvania Railroad's E3a class, came from Schenectady in 1903. They were followed by 25 A-3s from Baldwin in 1910. B&O inherited from the Buffalo, Rochester & Pittsburgh ten Atlantics that were soon scrapped, and three from the Buffalo & Susquehanna, two of which remained in service until 1948 on a portion of the line that had been isolated from the rest of the B&O by floods in 1942.

The Pacific was B&O's ultimate passenger locomotive. Its Hudsons were experimental, as were the first Mountain types, and B&O's later Mountain types were intended for flatland freight service. B&O's first Pacifics came from Schenectady in 1906, 35 P-class locomotives numbered 2100-2134, then 5000-5034 (1918), then 5150-5184 (1926). They had 74" drivers, inboard piston valves, and Stephenson valve gear.

They were followed by class P-1, 41 locomotives from Baldwin in 1911 — most were P-1a, actually, and classification gets confusing here, with class P-1 converted to P1aa, P-1 and P-1a converted to P-1ba, and at least 30 converted from Mikados. Generally the P-1 was the mainstay of B&O passenger service.

In 1912 B&O took control of the Cincinnati, Hamilton & Dayton Rail-

P-7e 5314, formerly *President Lincoln*, is typical of the rebuilt President class. B&O photo.

road and in 1917 began renumbering its equipment into B&O series. The road had five Pacifics built by Schenectady in 1910. B&O classified them P-2 and numbered them 2175-2179, then 5090-5094 (1919), then 5095-5099 (1924).

B&O acquired several batches of Pacifics in the Teens: 30 P-3s from Baldwin in 1913; 10 P-4s from Baldwin in 1917, with 76" drivers like the P-3s and Vanderbilt tenders; 30 P-5s, USRA light Pacifics, 20 from Baldwin and 10 from Alco's Brooks works in 1919; and 15 P-6s from Baldwin in 1922 — they had a USRA appearance modified with cast trailing truck, Vanderbilt tender, and two air compressors.

In 1927 B&O received 20 P-7 Pacifics from Baldwin for Washington-New York service (previously, Reading locomotives handled the trains east of Philadelphia). They were painted olive green and trimmed in red and gold, and were named for the first 21 presidents of the United States (one represented both John Adams and John Quincy Adams). They were essentially copies of the USRA heavy Pacific.

Some of the P-7s underwent extensive rebuilding in later years, receiving various combinations of improvements such as cast engine beds, roller bearings, feedwater heaters, 12-wheel tenders, semi-water-tube fireboxes, and streamlining.

In an effort to eliminate helpers on passenger trains west of Cumberland, Md., B&O built a pair of 4-8-2s in 1925 and 1926, using the boilers of two 2-10-2s. The two class T Mountains worked passenger trains until 1953 but were never duplicated. B&O made several other excursions beyond the Pacific type for passenger service, all one-of-a-kind experimental locomotives described below.

Switchers

B&O's best-known switchers were four C-16-class saddle-tank, oil-burning 0-4-0s built by Baldwin in 1912 for service along the Baltimore waterfront — "Dockside" or "Little Joe" to model railroaders. Two were converted to coal-burning 0-4-0s of conventional configuration in 1926.

The 0-6-0s built for B&O in the 20th century comprised a group of 40 built in 1901 and 1903 by Richmond and Baldwin, 5 Camelbacks built in 1906 by Baldwin for service on Staten Island, and 40 USRA six-wheel

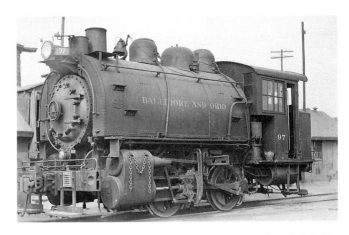

The C-16 class is familiar to model railroaders — in the 1940s and 1950s Varney's "Dockside" was a staple of HO scale. Photo by W. R. Hicks.

switchers. B&O acquired a number of 0-6-0s when it purchased other railroads.

B&O never bought an 0-8-0, but converted great quantities of 2-8-0s to 0-8-0s by removing the lead truck and replacing the pilot with footboards. A large number were created in the years just before the turn of the century. The road converted 22 nearly new E-24 Consolidations to switchers in 1905, and two more in 1912, but converted them all back to 2-8-0s by 1915. In 1923 B&O once again needed heavy switchers, and in the ensuing six years converted 86 E-24s to class L-1 and L-1a 0-8-0s — some for the second time — and 115 E-27s to class L-2 0-8-0s. The locomotives kept their original drive wheels, 56" and 57" for the L-1s and 63" for the L-2s. The larger-than-customary drive wheels resulted not in racy-looking switchers but engines that appeared embarrassed at having lost their lead trucks.

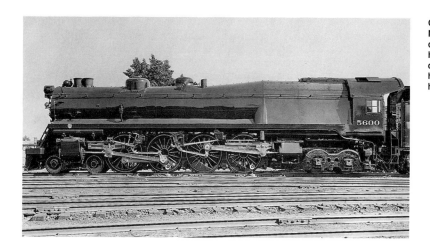

George H. Emerson's final watertube-firebox experiment was No. 5600, a duplex-drive 4-4-4-4. The location of the rear cylinders made them vulnerable to dirt and cinders. Add them to the humped firebox, an air reservoir tucked in above the forward cylinders, a double stack, and backward valve gear and you have an engine that is not quite Picasso-esque but seems to have too many parts in the wrong places. B&O photo.

The construction of two 4-8-2s in 1925 and 1926 left a pair of 2-10-2 frames sitting on the shop floor at Mount Clare. B&O built new boilers and tenders, creating a pair of 0-10-0s for hump service. They were about the same size as 0-10-0s built for the Duluth, Missabe & Northern in 1928, but much more powerful.

Experimental locomotives

George H. Emerson became B&O's chief of motive power and equipment in 1920. He hatched many ideas during his tenure, and one of his pets was the watertube firebox, which he said could save the road a million dollars in staybolt costs alone. In 1927 Mount Clare Shops in Baltimore applied watertube fireboxes to 2-8-0 2504 and 2-8-2 4045. The Consolidation had no other major improvements; the Mikado was given a stoker and a feedwater heater. The Mike's firebox was rebuilt in 1933, and at the same time the locomotive was given separate inlet and exhaust valves. The Consolidation survived until 1949; the Mike to

1951, outlasting all the other watertube firebox experiments. Two more 2-8-0s were rebuilt in 1928 and 1929; one was reboilered again in 1933, but the other lasted until 1948. About the same time Mount Clare built a Pacific with a watertube firebox: 5320, *President Cleveland*, class P-9. It had Caprotti poppet valves; they lasted about a year. A conventional firebox replaced the watertube affair in 1945.

In 1930 Baldwin built two 4-8-2s, class T-1, No. 5510, and T-2 5550; and two 2-6-6-2s, KK-1 7400, and KK-2 7450. The T-1 and the KK-1 had watertube fireboxes; the T-2 and the KK-2 had conventional fireboxes. Emerson's plan was to compare the two pairs of engines. In 1931 No. 5550 was given a watertube firebox and No. 7400 was converted to a 4-4-6-2 to make it a passenger engine. The conversion was not successful and the original wheel arrangement was restored in 1933.

In 1933 Mount Clare converted a Pacific to a Hudson with a watertube firebox. The next year B&O ordered a pair of lightweight passen-

GEORGE H. EMERSON (1869-1950) was born in St. Paul, Minnesota. He began his railroad career in 1880 as a water boy on a wood train on the Willmar Division of the Great Northern, and in 1882 became a boilermaker apprentice in GN's shops in St. Paul. He was successively boilermaker, fireman, engineer, locomotive foreman, general shop foreman, master mechanic, superintendent of motive power, assistant general manager, and general manager of the Great Northern. From October 1917 to January 1920 he was in command of the Russian Railway Service Corps in Siberia.

Samuel Vauclain of Baldwin Locomotive Works recommended Emerson to Daniel Willard, president of the Baltimore & Ohio, and in March 1920 Emerson became chief of motive power and equipment. He retired from the B&O in December 1941.

His obituary in the B&O company magazine mentioned his role in the design of the *Abraham Lincoln* and *Royal Blue* streamliners and the purchase of B&O's first road diesel but curiously made no reference to his extensive work in steam locomotive design, centering on the watertube firebox.

B&O's innovations in freight and passenger car design during his tenure included air conditioned passenger cars, bay-window cabooses, experimental aluminum and lightweight steel freight and passenger cars, and the wagon-top boxcar, which had continuous side and roof sheets.

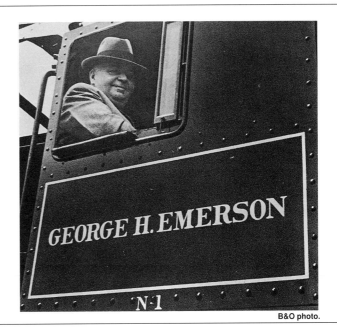

B&O photo.

ger trains and built two 84"-drivered lightweight steam locomotives to pull them, 4-4-4 No. 1, *Lady Baltimore*, and 4-6-4, No. 2, *Lord Baltimore*. They were sleek-looking, and they were fast once they got a train started, but they were slippery. B&O flogged off both to the Alton, which eventually returned them. In 1935 and 1936 Mount Clare built two more watertube-firebox Hudsons from scratch.

Mount Clare put a number of Emerson's ideas together in 1937 with locomotive 5600, a rigid-frame, duplex-drive 4-4-4-4 named *George H. Emerson*. The front pair of cylinders, located in the usual place, drove the first two pairs of 76" drivers; the rear cylinders, underneath the watertube firebox, drove the rear two pairs of drivers. It spent a lot of time in the shop.

Undeterred, Emerson proposed and Mount Clare began construction of a 4-8-4 that was to have had a four-cylinder geared engine on each driving axle, 16 cylinders in all. One four-cylinder engine was built and tested, but by then 24-cylinder locomotives — Electro-Motive diesels — were pulling B&O's premier passenger trains and were proving more reliable than anything with a firebox of any kind.

Locomotives acquired through purchase of other railroads

Staten Island Rapid Transit Railway's steam locomotives were never numbered into the B&O series. Until electrification in 1925, passenger trains were pulled by 2-4-4Ts and Camelback 4-4-0s. SIRT's roster included a 2-8-0 and two 0-6-0s, all Camelbacks, and parent B&O had five Camelback 0-6-0s specifically built for service on Staten Island.

B&O acquired control of the Cincinnati, Hamilton & Dayton in 1912. Its only modern locomotives were five light Pacifics. The Cincinnati, Indianapolis & Western, acquired in 1927, had four modern Pacifics, eight Mikados, and five six-wheel switchers that were about the size of USRA 0-6-0s. B&O bought two West Virginia railroads, the Coal & Coke Railroad in 1917 and the Morgantown & Kingwood Railroad in 1920. Both roads were powered primarily by low-drivered 2-8-0s.

When B&O took over the Buffalo, Rochester & Pittsburgh Railway at the beginning of 1932 it moved the BR&P locomotives around its system — not the case with other roads it acquired. The Buffalo & Susquehanna brought with it three low-drivered Atlantics and 42 Consolidations, all with Stephenson valve gear and inboard piston valves. They lasted surprisingly long — some 2-8-0s into the late 1950s — because the line was isolated from the rest of the B&O after 1942.

B&O bought the Chicago & Alton in 1931. Its locomotives were given B&O classifications and numbered in B&O series, but they didn't migrate to the B&O proper and remained with the Alton when B&O let go of the road in 1943. They are not listed in the roster below.

Historical and technical society: Baltimore & Ohio Railroad Historical Society, P. O. Box 13578, Baltimore, MD 21203-3578

Recommended reading: *B&O Power*, by Lawrence W. Sagle, published in 1964 by Alvin F. Staufer (LCC 64-23526)

Published rosters:

Railroad Magazine: June 1934, page 90; July 1934, page 82; November 1948, page 112, December 1948, page 80; December 1953, page 70; October 1957, page 58 (renumbering of the 1950s; steam locomotives on pages 66 and 68)

B&O STEAM LOCOMOTIVES BUILT SINCE 1900

Type	Class	Numbers	Qty	Builder	Built	Retired	Notes
0-4-0	C-13	76, 77	2	Baldwin	1902	-1948	
0-4-0T	C-16	96-99	4	Baldwin	1912	1944-1951	
0-6-0	D-7	1137-1176	40	Richmond, Baldwin	1901, 1903-1948		
0-6-0	D-12	1197	1	Richmond	1925	1953	Ex-Curtis Bay RR
0-6-0	D-23	1180-1184	5	Baldwin	1906	-1947	Camelback
0-6-0	D-29	91-94	4	Pittsburgh	1900-1901	-1930	Ex-CH&D
0-6-0	D-30	350-369	20	Baldwin	1919-1956		USRA
0-6-0	D-30	370-389	20	Alco	1919-1956		USRA
0-6-0	D-35	330-332	3	Cooke	1902-1928		Ex-CI&W
0-6-0	D-36	333-335	3	Brooks	1905-1934		Ex-CI&W
0-6-0	D-37	336-338	3	Brooks	1901-1934		Ex-CI&W
0-6-0	D-38	339-343	5	Lima	1916	-1934	Ex-CI&W
0-6-0	D-44	390-394	5	Brooks	1904	-1954	Ex-BR&P
0-8-0	L-1, L-1a	1000-1085	86	B&O	1923-1929	-1959	Ex-E-24 2-8-0
0-8-0	L-2–L-2c	600-714	115	B&O	1924-1941	-1959	Ex-E-27 2-8-0
0-8-0	L-4, L-4a	772-789	18	Brooks	1918, 1923	1956-1958	Ex-BR&P
0-10-0	U	950, 951	2	B&O	1926, 1927	1953	
0-6-6-0	DD-1	7000	1	Schenectady	1904	1938	
0-8-8-0	LL-1	7020-7049	30	Schenectady	1911	-1950	
2-6-0	K-16	901-910	10	Baldwin	1911	-1949	
2-6-0	K-17	2441-2450	10	Lima	1917	-1954	
2-8-0	E-18	1900-1938	39	Baldwin	1900	-1936	Compound
2-8-0	E-19	1939, 1940	2	Baldwin	1900		Compound
2-8-0	E-19	1771-1779, 1800-1899	109		1900-1901	-1935	Compound
2-8-0	E-19a	1959-1965	7	Baldwin	1903	-1935	Simple
2-8-0	E-23	1955-1958	4	Schenectady	1902	-1925	
2-8-0	E-24	2200-2397	197	Rich,Pitt,Rog	1902-1904	-1956	
2-8-0	E-27	2500-2913	414	Schen, Rich	1905-1910	-1959	
2-8-0	E-29	1706-1721	16	Brooks	1905	-1937	Ex-CH&D
2-8-0	E-30	1722-1736	15	Baldwin	1905	-1937	Ex-CH&D
2-8-0	E-31	2914-2913	20	Brooks	1910	-1954	
2-8-0	E-32	1737-1740	4	Baldwin	1904-1905	1939	Ex-Coal & Coke
2-8-0	E-33	2934-2945	12	Baldwin	1903-1906	1950	Ex-Coal & Coke
2-8-0	E-34	2946-2949	4	Baldwin	1912-1913	1950	Ex-Coal & Coke
2-8-0	E-35	2950, 2951	2	Baldwin	1914	-1950	Ex-Coal & Coke
2-8-0	E-36	2952, 2953	2	Baldwin	1916	-1950	Ex-Coal & Coke
2-8-0	E-37	413	1	Baldwin	1906	-1936	Ex-M&K

B&O STEAM LOCOMOTIVES BUILT SINCE 1900 (continued)

Type	Class	Numbers	Qty	Builder	Built	Retired	Notes
2-8-0	E-38	414	1	Baldwin	1918	-1939	Ex-M&K
2-8-0	E-39	415, 416	2	Baldwin	1903	-1947	Ex-M&K
2-8-0	E-40	417-422	6	Baldwin	1907, 1909	-1938	Ex-M&K
2-8-0	E-41	425-434	10	Baldwin	1916	-1950	Ex-CI&W
2-8-0	E-43	436	1	Baldwin	1900	1929	Ex-CI&W
2-8-0	E-44	437, 438	2	Alco	1901	-1929	Ex-CI&W
2-8-0	E-45	439	1	Alco	1905	1934	Ex-CI&W
2-8-0	E-52–58	3010-3096	83	BLW, Brks	1901-1909	-1950	Ex-BR&P
2-8-0	E-60, 60a	3100-3142	42	Brks, Pitt	1904-1908	-1957	Ex-B&S
2-8-2	Q-odd	4160, 4161	2	Baldwin	1911, 1912	1949	Rebuilt from 2-8-0
2-8-2	Q-1	4000-4159	160	Baldwin	1911	-1956	
2-8-2	Q-1b	4170-4219	50	Baldwin	1912	-1956	
2-8-2	Q-2	4162-4169	8	Lima	1916	-1950	Ex-CI&W
2-8-2	Q-3	4500-4599	100	Baldwin	1918	-1959	
2-8-2	Q-4	4400-4634	135	Baldwin	1920-1923	-1959	
2-8-2	Q-4d	4635-4662	3		1941-1942		
2-8-2	Q-10	4700-4747	48	Brooks	1912-1917		Ex-BR&P
2-10-0	Y	6500-6507	8	Brooks	1907, 1909	-1951	Ex-BR&P
2-10-2	S	6000-6030	31	Baldwin	1914	-1953	
2-10-2	S-1	6100-6224	125	BLW, Lima	1923-1926	-1959	
2-6-6-2	KK-1	7400	1	Baldwin	1930	1953	Watertube firebox
2-6-6-2	KK-2	7450	1	Baldwin	1930	1953	
2-6-6-2	KK-4	7500-7554	55	Schen, Brks	1914-1923		Ex-BR&P
2-6-6-4	KB-1	7700-7709	10	Baldwin	1935, 1937	1953	Ex-SAL
2-8-8-0	EL-1	7100-7114	15	Baldwin	1916	-1954	
2-8-8-0	EL-2	7200-7214	15	Baldwin	1916	-1952	
2-8-8-0	EL-3	7115-7144	30	Baldwin	1917	-1952	
2-8-8-0	EL-4	7020-7049	11	B&O	1919-1923	-1950	Ex-class LL-1
2-8-8-0	EL-5	7145-7170	26	Baldwin	1919-1920	-1954	
2-8-8-0	EL-6	7300-7315	16	Richmond	1917-191	-1954	Ex-SAL 2-8-8-2
2-8-8-2	EE-2, 2a	7316-7324	9	Brooks	1918, 1923		Ex-BR&P
2-8-8-4	EM-1	7600-7629	30	Baldwin	1944-1945	-1960	
4-4-0	G-18	630	1	Baldwin	1903	1936	Ex-M&K
4-4-0	H-12	717, 718	2	Baldwin	1905	-1929	Ex-Coal & Coke
4-4-0	M-3	862, 863	2	Baldwin	1906	-1936	Ex-Coal & Coke
4-4-0	M-4	864	1	Baldwin	1912	-1934	Ex-Coal & Coke
4-4-0	M-5	865-867	3	Brooks	1904	-1930	Ex-CI&W
4-4-0	M-6a, -6	868, 869	2	Alco	1904, 1906	1929, 193	0Ex-CI&W
4-4-2	A (A-1)	1450-1455	6	Baldwin	1900-1901	-1929	Vauclain compound

Type	Class	Numbers	Qty	Builder	Built	Retired	Notes
4-4-2	A-2	1456-1475	20	Schenectady	1903	-1933, 1947	
4-4-2	A-3	1424-1449	25	Baldwin	1910	1944	
4-4-2	A-6	1487, 1488	2	Brooks	1901	-1937	Ex-BR&P
4-4-2	A-7	1489-1491	4	Brooks	1903	-1936	Ex-BR&P
4-4-2	A-8, A-8a	1492-1496	5	Brooks	1906, 1909	-1937	Ex-BR&P
4-4-2	A-9	1484, 1485	2	Schenectady	1904	-1948	Ex-B&S
4-4-2	A-10	1486	1	Brooks	1906	1936	Ex-B&S
4-4-4	J-1	1, 5330	1	B&O	1943	1949	Lady Baltimore
4-6-0	B-17	1328-1336	9	Baldwin	1901	-1935	Vauclaincompound
4-6-0	B-18	2000-2034	35	Rhode Island	1901	-195x	
4-6-0	B-19	2035-2069	35	Baldwin	1901	-1934	Vauclain compound
4-6-0	B-55	163	1	Baldwin	1906	1947	Ex-M&K
4-6-0	B-56	164	1	Baldwin	1909	1946	Ex-M&K
4-6-0	B-57	165-170	6	Schenectady	1916	-1938	Ex-CI&W
4-6-0	B-58	171-180	10	Baldwin	1916	-1953	Ex-CI&W
4-6-2	P	5000-5034	35	Schenectady	1906	-1950	
4-6-2	P-2	5095-5099	5	Schenectady	1910	-1948	Ex-CH&D
4-6-2	P-3	5100-5129	30	Baldwin	1913	-1952	
4-6-2	P-4	5130-5139	10	Baldwin	1917	-1953	Vanderbilt tenders
4-6-2	P-5	5200-5219	20	Baldwin	1919	-1956	USRA light
4-6-2	P-5	5220-5229	10	Schenectady	1919	-1956	USRA light
4-6-2	P-6	5230-5244	15	Baldwin	1922	-1949	Vanderbilt tenders
4-6-2	P-7	5300-5319	20	Baldwin	1927	-1958	Presidents
4-6-2	P-8	5196-5199	4	Alco	1924	-1952	Ex-CI&W
4-6-2	P-9	5320	1	B&O	1928		
4-6-2	P-17	5140-5148	9	Brooks	1912-1913	-1953	Ex-BR&P
4-6-2	P-18	5185-5192	9	Brooks	1918	-1953	Ex-BR&P
4-6-2	P-19	5260-5264	5	Brooks	1923	-1953	Ex-BR&P
4-6-4	V-1	5047	1	B&O	1933	1950	
4-6-4	V-2	2 (5340)	1	B&O	1935	1949	Lord Baltimore
4-6-4	V-3	5350	1	B&O	1935	1950	
4-6-4	V-4	5360	1	B&O	1936	1950	
4-8-2	T	5500, 5501	2	B&O	1925, 1926	1953	
4-8-2	T-1	5510	1	Baldwin	1930	1951	
4-8-2	T-2	5550	1	Baldwin	1930	1952	
4-8-2	T-3	5555-5594	40	B&O	1943-1948	-1960	
4-8-2	T-4	5650-5662	13	Baldwin	1935-1940	-1958	Ex-B&M
4-4-4-4	N-1	5600	1	B&O	1937	1950	George H.Emerson

BANGOR & AROOSTOOK RAILROAD

The Bangor & Aroostook was incorporated in 1891 to build north from Brownville, Maine, into Aroostook County, the northernmost part of the state. In 1892 the road acquired two smaller railroads that connected it to the Maine Central. By the turn of the century it extended north to Van Buren on the Canadian border, and in 1905 south to tidewater at Searsport.

The principal mission of the BAR was to gather potatoes, lumber, and paper, move them south, and deliver them to the Maine Central at Northern Maine Junction west of Bangor. The road crossed no mountain ranges; its worst grades were between Millinocket and Brownville, where the line crossed the watershed between the Penobscot and Piscataquis rivers. Pushers were necessary on the longest trains during the potato-shipping season. Passenger service consisted of no more than two or three trains a day on the main line between Bangor and Van Buren, 236 miles, and connecting local and mixed trains on the branches. (Most of Aroostook County's population, about 91,000 today, is concentrated in the eastern portion of the county along the Canadian border.)

In July 1946 an Electro-Motive F3 demonstrator worked on BAR freight and passenger trains. The three-unit diesel could pull almost twice as much freight as the road's 4-8-2s; two units on a passenger train consumed about one gallon of fuel per mile, a fraction of what an equivalent oil-burning steam locomotive would — and no water. The figures gave management something to think about, and BAR was one of the first roads to dieselize.

By 1949 BAR was dieselized except for winter-season traffic peaks. The road worked out an agreement whereby it would lease new diesels to the Pennsylvania Railroad from May to November for use at the ore docks at Erie, Pa.; the diesels would return to Maine for the winter. The last run of a BAR steam locomotive occurred on July 22, 1951, when Pacific 251 made a round trip from Derby to Greenville on trains 9 and 12.

Freight locomotives

BAR acquired eight 4-4-0s built between 1864 and 1888, some of them secondhand, when it leased the Bangor & Piscataquis in 1892, and between 1893 and 1907 the road purchased an assortment of 4-4-0s, 2-6-0s, 4-6-0s, and 0-6-0s from Manchester Locomotive Works (later Alco's Manchester Works).

In 1907 the road bought three Consolidations from Rhode Island Locomotive Works. They had been built for the Pittsburgh, Binghamton & Eastern. (The PB&E was proposed in 1907 to build from Clearfield, Pennsylvania, to Binghamton, New York. It was abandoned in 1914 with approximately equal numbers of financial reorganizations and actual miles of track in its history.) BAR must have been satisfied with those 2-8-0s, because it bought 16 more of the same dimensions (57" drivers, 23" × 30" cylinders) from Schenectady between 1914 and 1924.

During 1929 and 1930 seven 4-8-2s from Alco replaced the Consolidations in through freight service. The larger firebox, 63" drivers, and four-wheel lead truck gave them more capacity for sustained speed than the 2-8-0s, but they were still small engines, weighing 315,300 pounds and exerting a tractive force of 49,200 pounds — 6 tons lighter than a USRA light 4-8-2 and almost 5,000 pounds less tractive effort. Their main rods were connected to the third drivers, a characteristic shared with other low-drivered 4-8-2s. Two more 4-8-2s arrived from Alco in 1935. In 1937 Alco delivered five Consolidations for freight service on the north end of the railroad. The 2-8-0 was hardly hot, new technology, but none of the steam locomotives that were would fit the job and the railroad.

BAR purchased its last two new steam locomotives in 1945, 4-8-2 No. 109 and 2-8-0 No. 405, essentially one more of each of its previous orders. In 1946 it went shopping in the used-locomotive market and came home with two Boston & Maine 2-8-0s, four B&M 0-8-0s, and five 16-year-old 4-8-2s from the New York, Ontario & Western. The NYO&W 4-8-2s were near-duplicates of New York Central's L-2 Mohawks. They

Built in 1929, Bangor & Aroostook No. 100 was the first of the road's 4-8-2s. The 63" drivers and main rods connected to the third drivers indicate the engine was designed for freight service. A booster on the trailing truck materially assisted its starting tractive effort. Alco photo.

Consolidation No. 404 was built by Alco in 1937. The wheel arrangement may have been outdated, but the locomotive was nonetheless modern to the point of having a front-end throttle. It had the same cylinder and driver-size specifications as BAR's 4-8-2s. Alco photo.

had 69" drivers and weighed 360,000 pounds. B&M and NYO&W had begun dieselization — and BAR was about to.

Passenger locomotives

The C-1 and F-1 Ten-Wheelers were the mainstay of BAR passenger service until 1927, when five Pacifics arrived. They were small Pacifics, weighing 237,000 pounds (40,000 pounds less than a USRA light Pacific); 69" drivers gave them pulling power instead of great speed. Their horizontal-bar pilots and outside lead truck journals gave them a Canadian National Railways look.

Switchers

Six 0-6-0s were scrapped in the mid-1930s, not long after three 0-8-0s arrived from Alco in 1928 and 1931. BAR bought four 0-8-0s from the Boston & Maine in February 1946, just before management decided to dieselize.

Recommended reading: *Bangor & Aroostook*, by Jerry Angier and Herb Cleaves, published in 1986 by Flying Yankee Enterprises, P. O. Box 595, Littleton, MA 0460 (ISBN 0-9615574-3-5)

Published rosters:
Railway & Locomotive Historical Society Bulletin, No. 53, page 42
Railroad Magazine: February 1935, page 88; January 1950, page 104

BAR STEAM LOCOMOTIVES BUILT SINCE 1900

Type	Class	Numbers	Qty	Builder	Built	Retired	Notes
0-6-0	M	310, 311	2	Manchester	1900-1901	Sold 1917, 1916	
0-6-0	P	320-325	6	Manchester	1905-1908	1935-1937	
0-8-0	SA	330	1	Alco	1928	1951	
0-8-0	S-1A	340, 341	2	Alco	1931	1953	
0-8-0	S-2A	335-338	4	Alco	1922	1949-1950	Ex-B&M
2-8-0	GA	170-172	3	Rhode Island	1907	1949-1951	
2-8-0	G	180-195	16	Schenectady	1914-1924	1947-1951	
2-8-0	G-1A	196, 197	2	Baldwin, Alco	1913	1950, 1947	Ex-B&M
2-8-0	G-2	400-405	6	Alco	1937, 1945	1951-1956	
4-4-0	K-1	214-216	3	BAR	1915	1923-1924	Rebuilt from 2-6-0
4-6-0	C-1	240-243	4	Manchester	1902	1928-1951	
4-6-0	D-1	54-78	25	Manchester	1901-1907	1927-1952	
4-6-0	D-2a	82-87	6	Manchester	1907	1935-1951	
4-6-0	D-3	90-95	6	Manchester	1911	1951-1952	
4-6-0	Ea	140-142	3	Rhode Island	1906	1947-1951	
4-6-0	F-1	234, 235	2	Manchester	1907	1926	
4-6-2	F	250-254	5	Schenectady	1927	1945-1953	
4-8-2	M	100-109	10	Alco	1929-1945	1950-1953	
4-8-2	M-1	120-124	5	Alco	1929	1948-1949	Ex-NYO&W

BESSEMER & LAKE ERIE RAILROAD

By 1900 the Bessemer & Lake Erie had grown from a local coal hauler to a heavy-duty railroad connecting Lake Erie shipping at Conneaut, Ohio, with the Carnegie steel mills in Pittsburgh. It was under the control of Carnegie Steel, and in 1901 Carnegie became part of United States Steel. The road's principal job was to move iron ore from the docks at Conneaut to the steel mills in Pittsburgh. The route had a sawtooth profile, starting with a 12-mile climb away from Lake Erie with grades ranging up to 1 percent. A grade of 1 percent is not especially severe, but iron ore is heavy, and it moves in trainload lots. The 144-mile line from Conneaut to North Bessemer, Pa. crosses five summits and there was little level track.

Trainloads of iron ore require powerful locomotives and solid track, and the Bessemer had both. By the mid-Teens the 2-6-6-2 and the 2-10-2 had both matured into heavy road freight engines of approximately equal pulling power. The Mallet spread the power output through two sets of cylinders and rods, which could be lighter than those of a 2-10-2. The lighter machinery and articulation made the Mallet easier on the track than the 2-10-2; on the debit side were the cost of maintaining of a second set of cylinders and rods and the Mallet's unstable riding characteristics.

B&LE chose the simplicity of the 2-10-2 and later the 2-10-4 and made sure its track could handle them. The road had standardized on 100-pound rail for its main line by 1900, then chose 130-pound rail in 1917, 152-pound in 1939, and 155-pound (the heaviest produced) in 1948. In 1953, after the steel mills stopped producing 155-pound rail and Electro-Motive delivered new locomotives that weighed only 62,000 pounds per axle, the Bessemer adopted 140-pound rail as standard.

B&LE bought a Westinghouse diesel switcher in 1936. A few Baldwin switchers arrived in 1949, then a tidal wave of Electro-Motive F7s in 1950 and 1951. Dieselization was complete in early 1953.

B&LE's 47 2-10-4s were copies of Burlington's 2-10-4s and were put to the same use — hauling heavy trains of minerals. B&LE photo.

Freight locomotives

The Bessemer had a large fleet of 2-8-0s with 54" drivers. The differences among the classes of Consolidations were primarily weight and cylinder dimensions: 173,000 to 182,000 pounds and 22" × 28" for the C1s, 202,000 to 213,000 pounds and 22" × 30" for the C2s, 251,000 to 261,000 pounds and 24" × 32" for the C3s, and 268,000 pounds and 26" × 30" for the C4s. When C3As 150 and 151 were built in 1900 they were the heaviest, most powerful locomotives in the world.

In 1916 B&LE turned to the Santa Fe type. Its Baldwin-built 2-10-2s constituted a major leap in locomotive design from the 2-8-0. They had 60" drivers and 30" × 32" cylinders and weighed 404,000 pounds. At first glance they resembled Erie's contemporary 2-10-2s, even to inadequate-looking Vanderbilt tenders, but Erie's locomotives had 63" drivers and 31" × 32" cylinders.

In 1919 B&LE was allotted five USRA heavy 2-10-2s. They had 57" drivers and were about 25,000 pounds lighter than Bessemer's own 2-10-2s, and they exerted about 12,000 pounds less tractive effort. The USRA engines were scrapped before the older Santa Fes of Bessemer's own design.

Baldwin built its first 2-10-4s in 1927 to haul coal for the Chicago, Burlington & Quincy. They had 64" drivers, 31" × 32" cylinders, about 524,000 pounds engine weight, and 353,000 pounds on the drivers. The Bessemer bought a single copy of the Burlington locomotive in 1929, and nine more in 1930. By 1944 B&LE had amassed a fleet of 47 2-10-4s, all but 10 of them built by Baldwin. By 1951 many of the 2-10-4s were out of work, replaced by diesels. B&LE sold 18 of them to the Duluth, Missabe & Iron Range, another U. S. Steel railroad.

Passenger locomotives

B&LE was never a major passenger carrier. At its maximum Bessemer's passenger service consisted of two or three local trains running the length of the main line plus connecting branchline trains. The road used Ten-Wheelers and Americans on its passenger trains until 1913, when it took delivery of four light Pacifics from Alco's Schenectady Works.

Switchers

Seven six-wheel switchers built in 1909 and 1911 lasted until dieselization. The four S3A-class 0-6-0s of 1909 were heavy, weighing 184,400 pounds; the S2Ds of 1911 were nearly 60,000 pounds lighter. Alco built a dozen heavy, modern 0-8-0s for the B&LE between 1936 and 1943. They had 57" drivers and 25" × 30" cylinders, and weighed about 280,000 pounds (by comparison, the USRA 0-8-0's specifications were 51" drivers, 25" × 28" cylinders, and 214,000 pounds).

Published rosters: *Railroad Magazine*: May 1938, page 68; July 1938, page 79 (corrections); October 1951, page 97

The last locomotive type added to the Bessemer's roster was the eight-wheel switcher, 12 heavy examples of which were built by Alco between 1936 and 1943. They were useful not only for switching but for way freights. Photo by Irvine G. Milheim Jr.

B&LE STEAM LOCOMOTIVES BUILT SINCE 1900

Type	Class	Numbers	Qty	Builder	Built	Retired	Notes
0-6-0	S2B	232, 233	2	Brooks	1900	1936	
0-6-0	S2D	227-229	3	Baldwin	1911	1950-1952	
0-6-0	S3A	234-237	4	Baldwin	1909	1948-1950	
0-8-0	S4A-S4E	251-262	12	Alco	1936-1943	1953-1954	
2-8-0	C1B	85-90	6	Pittsburgh	1900-1901	1927-1936	
2-8-0	C1B	95-114	20	Pittsburgh	1902-1903	1927-1936	
2-8-0	C1C	93, 94	2	Brooks	1901	1936	
2-8-0	C1D	84	1	Baldwin	1900	1926	
2-8-0	C1D	91, 92	2	Baldwin	1901	1926	
2-8-0	C1E, C1F	125-145	21	Pittsburgh	1907, 1909	1929-1930	
2-8-0	C2A	115-124	10	Pittsburgh	1905	1936	

Type	Class	Numbers	Qty	Builder	Built	Retired	Notes
2-8-0	C2B-C2D	325-362	38	Pittsburgh	1911, 1913	1936-1954	
2-8-0	C3A	150-153	4	Pittsburgh	1900-1902	1936-1943	
2-8-0	C3B, C3D	154-157	4	Baldwin	1909, 1911	1951-1954	
2-8-0	C4A	158, 159	2	Baldwin	1913	1953, 1951	
2-10-2	D1A	501-520	20	Baldwin	1916	1948-1951	
2-10-2	D2A	521-525	5	Baldwin	1919	1947	
2-10-4	H1A-H1G	601-647	10	Baldwin	1929-1944	1952-1954	
					621-631, 635, 637, 638, 641, 645-647 to DM&IR			
4-4-0	E5A	15	1	Cooke	1900	1936	
4-4-0	E5B, E5C	16-19	4	Pittsburgh	1905, 1908	1936-1944	
					16 and 19 to Union Ralroad			
4-4-0	E5D	10, 11	2	Pittsburgh	1909	1944	
4-6-2	P1A	901-904	4	Schenectady	1913	1953	

BOOSTERS

While it takes far more tractive force to start a train than to keep it moving, paradoxically it requires less steam. A steam locomotive that could generate enough steam to haul a load at 40 or 50 mph had plenty of extra steam available at low speeds. The booster engine was devised to convert some of that steam to additional tractive force for starting a train.

The booster was a small two-cylinder steam engine usually mounted on the trailing truck, geared to one axle through an idler gear that could be moved in and out of mesh. It was a low-speed device, usable up to about 15 mph.

Locomotives without a trailing truck could be fitted with a tender booster, which was a two-cylinder engine geared to one axle of a tender truck; power was transmitted to the other axle through side rods.

The device with the pipes under the rear of the Lima articulated trailing truck (doubtless intended for the first 2-8-4) is a Franklin Locomotive Booster. It drove only the rear axle of the truck. Lima photo.

BOSTON & MAINE RAILROAD

The Boston & Maine of the mid-1880s consisted of a main line from Boston to Portland, Maine, and a few branches from that route, primarily in Massachusetts. In 1884 B&M began acquiring neighboring railroads, primarily through lease: Eastern Railroad (Boston to Portland), 1884; Worcester, Nashua & Rochester, 1886; Boston & Lowell, 1887; Connecticut River, 1893; Concord & Montreal, 1895; and Fitchburg, 1900.

At the turn of the century B&M reached from Boston northeast to Portland, northwest through New Hampshire and Vermont to Lake Champlain and the Canadian border, and west to the Hudson and Mohawk rivers; and from Springfield, Mass., north along the Connecticut River. Tying the main routes together was a spider web of branch lines. Except for the Grand Trunk and Maine Central routes across the north end of the state, New Hampshire was B&M's own territory, and traffic to and from Maine had to go via B&M or cross the Canadian border.

Boston & Maine's principal freight route was from the Hudson River at Mechanicville, N. Y., east to Ayer, Mass., thence southeast to Boston and northeast to Portland. More freight moved into New England than out, and the imbalance increased throughout the twentieth century as heavy industry moved out of the Northeast.

The primary passenger routes were from Boston northeast to Portland and northwest to connections with the Rutland, Central Vermont, and Canadian Pacific for Montreal. B&M operated a busy suburban service on the lines out of Boston, with commuter territory extending 50 to 60 miles from the city.

For the most part, B&M fought no major battles with topography. The exception was the line from Mechanicville to Boston. Eastbound freights faced almost 50 miles of ascending grade averaging about 0.3 percent from the Hudson River to the summit in the middle of the Hoosac Tunnel and 40 miles of grades up to 1 percent from the Connecticut River to Gardner, at the summit of the divide between the Merrimac and Connecticut rivers. Westbound trains ascended fairly steadily from Boston to Fitchburg, then had an unabated grade of just over 1 percent for 12 miles to Gardner; farther west was a grade averaging nearly 0.4 percent for more than 30 miles from the Connecticut River to the Hoosac Tunnel.

Rationalizations and abandonments in the 1920s and 1930s eliminated many redundant lines, but B&M still had a high proportion of light-rail branches. Its largest locomotives, the P-4s, T-1s, and R-1s, were restricted to main lines: Boston to Portland; Boston to White River Junction, Vermont; Boston to Troy and Mechanicville, N. Y.; Worcester-Gardner, Mass.; Worcester-Ayer-Lowell Junction, Mass.; and Springfield, Mass.-White River Junction — but those lines constituted about 40 percent of Boston & Maine's mileage and carried most of its traffic.

Steam operation ended in 1956. The last steam locomotives to see regular use were Moguls and P-2 Pacifics; P-4-a 3713 made a ceremonial last run to Portland on April 22, 1956.

Freight locomotives

Boston & Maine is perhaps best remembered for the 137 Moguls of the B-15 class. They were built by Manchester and Schenectady between 1903 and 1910. Their 63" drivers gave them a measure of speed, and they weighed a little over 70 tons, which meant they could go anywhere on the railroad. Many of the class received superheaters and piston valves and survived into the 1950s in branchline and commuter service.

B&M's primary freight power for the first two decades of the twentieth century was the Consolidation. The largest of the 2-8-0s was class K-8, a 221,200-pound machine with 63" drivers and 24" × 28" cylinders. Between 1911 and 1916 — after the road had turned to locomotives with trailing trucks for mainline passenger service — Baldwin, Schenectady, and Brooks built 135 such locomotives for the B&M. Their immediate predecessors, the K-7s, were 170,000-pound 2-8-0s built from 1905 to 1910. Most were scrapped during the 1930s, but a few survived

Boston & Maine Moguls 662 (later 1389) and 1366 were built by Alco's Manchester Works in 1903. Number 662 illustrates the appearance as built; No. 1366 was photographed in 1945 and shows the difference four decades can make: cross-compound air pump, steel cab, centered headlight, piston-valve conversion steam chests, and cast tender trucks. The large turbogenerator is for train lighting; the cluster of cables at the top of the smokebox is for lighting the train when the engine is running in reverse. Photo of 1366 by Homer Newlon.

into the 1950s in commuter service and others were sold to Vermont short lines.

The drag-freight philosophy continued with the receipt of 20 2-10-2s in 1920 and 10 more in 1923. (B&M skipped over the Mikado in its motive power development but during World War II briefly leased 2-8-2s from Erie, Lackawanna, and Maine Central.) The Santa Fes were fat, ponderous machines, notable for vestibule cabs and inboard-bearing trailing trucks. Their advent required a program of bridge-strengthening and clearance-widening on the railroad.

By the mid-1920s freight customers were demanding speed. B&M watched with interest the trial of Lima's A-1 on the Boston & Albany in 1925 and observed B&A's success with 45 2-8-4s of that design. B&M purchased 25 2-8-4s of its own from Lima in 1928 and 1929, practically duplicates of the B&A engines except for boiler pressure (240 pounds, 20 pounds greater), cylinders ($27\frac{1}{2}" \times 30"$, $\frac{1}{2}"$ smaller), and feedwater heater. The B&A engines, like Lima's prototype, had Elesco feedwater heaters; the B&M engines had Coffin feedwater heaters mounted on the smokebox front. Classed T-1-a and T-1-b, they were known on the B&M as Limas, not Berkshires. They weighed 406,800 pounds, much more than the 2-10-2s, and required another program of bridge strengthening.

Lima's Super Power concept was based on a large firebox. To accommodate the firebox, the locomotive frame ended behind the rear driver. Pulling and pushing forces were transmitted through the trailing truck. The rear of the firebox was supported by the truck, and as the truck swiveled, twisting forces were placed on the firebox, which wasn't designed for such stress. Backing on a curve put considerable lateral force on the trailing truck, and it was derailment-prone. Lima later turned to a conventional four-wheel trailing truck.

In addition B&M's 2-8-4s were slippery. B&M reduced the cylinder diameter by half an inch and modified the springing to put more weight on the drivers, alleviating the problem to some extent. When the first 4-8-2s arrived in the mid-1930s there was a proposal to convert some of the 2-8-4s to high-drivered 2-6-4s for mixed traffic. Investigation showed

2-6-0 — MOGUL

The 2-6-0 first appeared about 1852 as a rigid-frame locomotive. The invention in 1864 of the equalizing lever connecting the lead truck to the lead pair of drivers gave the type the three-point suspension that made the 4-4-0 work so well. The first of the type with a swiveling lead truck were built for the Louisville & Nashville by Baldwin; they were converted to 4-6-0s in the 1870s.

The Mogul offered about 50 percent more tractive effort than the 4-4-0 and found favor as a heavy freight engine, but it was soon superseded by the 2-8-0, which appeared in 1866. The 2-6-0 was relegated to lighter duties, and few were built after 1920.

The late Moguls are a diverse lot. In 1913 Lima built four good-sized Moguls for Chicago & Western Indiana in 1913 — 165,000 pounds, 63" drivers. They appear to have been used primarily for switching in and around Dearborn Station in Chicago, which C&WI owned, and for commuter trains.

In 1917 Lima built ten 2-6-0s for Baltimore & Ohio. They were short, close-coupled engines, looking like high-mounted 0-6-0s with lead trucks. They had 52" drivers and weighed 182,300 pounds.

Green Bay & Western bought 8 Moguls between 1914 and 1920. All were in the 135,000-140,000-pound range, slightly less than a Boston & Maine B-15.

The 2-6-0 disappeared from some railroads early; other roads, like Boston & Maine, kept Moguls on the roster until the end of steam. It's interesting that railroads generally favored either the Mogul or the Ten-Wheeler for light work but not both.

Last built and heaviest: Southern Pacific M-21, 520-529, SP Houston Shops, 1928-1929, 215,230 pounds

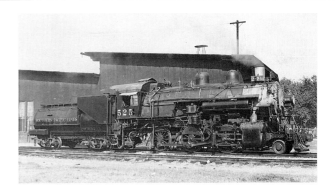

Southern Pacific's M-21 class were the heaviest Moguls and the last built. Espee's Houston Shops built them in 1928 and 1929, using frames from a group of compound, cylindrical-firebox 2-6-0s. After ten years on the Texas & New Orleans (SP's lines east of El Paso, Texas) they were transferred to the Southern Pacific of Mexico, where they served briefly before moving to SP's Pacific Lines (lines west of El Paso) and then quickly back to the T&NO. They were scrapped between 1950 and 1954. Number 525 is shown at Lafayette, Louisiana, in 1946. Note the unusual position of the air pump on the right side of the engine, balancing a Worthington Type BL feedwater heater on the left. — Photo by H. K. Vollrath.

Greatest number: Canadian National, 469
Last in service: Canadian National 674, July 10, 1959 (built for Grand Trunk in 1899)

that such an engine would have axle loadings too high for most B&M routes.

The T-1s were never totally satisfactory. As World War II came to an end, traffic eased in the East and increased in the West. By then B&M had received the first of its freight diesels and sold ten 2-8-4s to Southern Pacific and seven to Santa Fe.

Before B&M bought its 2-8-4s, Baldwin had proposed a light 4-8-4 of approximately the same size as the USRA light 4-8-2. Nothing came of that proposal. As the B&M accelerated its freight schedules, though, it was limited by the 63" drivers of the T-1s. It needed a faster locomotive that could also handle heavy summer-season passenger trains.

The distinguishing feature of B&M's T-1 was the horseshoe-shaped Coffin feedwater heater mounted on the front of the smokebox. B&M locomotives normally carried their headlight at the center of the smokebox door, but positioned there on the 2-8-4 it would prevent the door from being opened all the way; it was mounted instead on a platform above the pilot deck. The boiler of the 2-8-4 all but filled B&M's clearance diagram, and the pilot deck proved to be the only place for the bell, too. Lima Locomotive Works photo, collection of Allen County Hi•torical Society.

Baldwin proposed a heavy 4-8-4 in 1931, but B&M didn't want to upgrade its track and bridges again. Baldwin then proposed an efficient 73"-drivered 4-8-2 — and delivered five of them, class R-1-a, in early 1935. The 416,000-pound engines were distinguished by fireboxes with 79 square feet of grate area — at the limit of two-wheel trailing trucks (and weight limitations precluded trailing truck boosters). Four-wheel trailers would have allowed a larger firebox, but the weight would exceed the railroad's limits. Like the newly arrived P-4-a Pacifics, the R-1s had Coffin feedwater heater concealed in their smokeboxes. B&M reordered three times for a total of 18 4-8-2s, the last five arriving in 1941. Also like the P-4s, the R-1s carried names that were chosen from contest entries. The first 13 of the class were sold to the Baltimore & Ohio in 1947; B&M kept the five R-1-d engines as a hedge against shortages of diesel power.

Passenger locomotives

B&M's last Americans, the 77 members of the A-41 class, were built between 1900 and 1911. Meanwhile, B&M purchased its first Atlantics in 1902 and had 41 of them by 1909 (plus one built in 1895 for the Concord & Montreal). The first Pacifics came in 1910, and the most numerous class, 70 P-2s, were built by Schenectady from 1911 to 1916. The P-1s and P-2s were relatively light machines (236,700 pounds and 247,700 pounds, respectively). The 10 P-3s of 1923 were somewhat heavier (267,800 pounds, still less than a USRA light Pacific) and had booster-equipped trailing trucks and drop-equalizer tender trucks. They had the same driver diameter, 73", as their predecessors, but the 24" x 28" cylinders were 2" larger.

The P-4s constituted a quantum leap for B&M. The road needed larger passenger power, and Baldwin proposed a 4-6-4, but Lima suggested that a 4-6-2 could meet B&M's requirements at a lower price. Lima delivered five 4-6-2s in late 1934, class P-4-a, and five more in early 1937, class P-4-b. Weight on the 80" drivers was just short of 70,000 pounds, and total weight of the locomotive was 339,200 pounds. Trailer boosters gave a total starting tractive force of 52,800 pounds. The P-4-a class had smoke lifters and a modest shroud along the top of the boiler, extending from the sand dome back to the cab; all ten were named. The P-4s were intended for fast merchandise trains as well as passenger duties.

B&M purchased four Pacifics from the Delaware, Lackawanna & Western in 1943 and classed them as P-5.

Oddities

B&M had its share of oddities. Four oil-burning 2-6-6-2s were purchased in 1910 to work through the 4¾-mile Hoosac Tunnel. The tunnel electrification opened within 6 months, and B&M sold the Mallets to the Maine Central. In 1922 two 0-8-8-0s arrived from Alco at Schenectady to work the hump yard at Mechanicville. They were sold to the Bingham & Garfield in Utah in 1929.

When B&M leased the Fitchburg Railroad in 1900 it acquired 18 brand-new 4-8-0s, which remained on the roster until 1926. The road got a similar quarter-century of use out of a handful of 0-4-4Ts and 2-6-4Ts built in the 1890s for suburban service. K-8-b No. 2648, a 2-8-0, was built in 1913 with a McClellon watertube boiler, which it carried until 1920.

Historical and technical society: Boston & Maine Railroad Historical Society, P. O. Box 2936, Middlesex-Essex GMF, Woburn, MA 01888-9998.

Recommended reading: *Minuteman Steam*, by Harry A. Frye, published in 1982 by the Boston & Maine Railroad Historical Society, P. O. Box 2936, Middlesex-Essex GMF, Woburn, MA 01888-9998. (ISBN: 0-916578-05-4; LCC: 82-071735).

Published rosters

Railway & Locomotive Historical Society Bulletin: No. 26 (1849 and 1856), No. 28 (Eastern Railroad), No. 29 (Northern Railroad), No. 31 (Boston & Lowell), No. 32 (Connecticut & Passumpsic), Nos. 34 and 35 (Concord & Montreal), No. 37 (Fitchburg), No. 38 (Vermont & Massachusetts).

Railroad Magazine: April 1933, page 88; January 1946, page 100; October 1956, page 54 (last 13 steam locomotives in service).

The ultimate development of Boston & Maine steam power was the five 4-8-2s of the R-1-d class, 4113-4117, distinguished from earlier 4-8-2s by their pedestal tenders. Red-and-white italic lettering was applied to R-1s, P-3s, P-4s, and P-5s in the 1940s. Photo by F. H. Donahue.

B&M STEAM LOCOMOTIVES BUILT SINCE 1900

Type Notes	Class	Numbers	Qty	Builder	Built	Retired
0-6-0	G-9-b	160-185	18	Manchester	1899-1901	1926-1927
0-6-0	G-10	200-309	110	Manchester	1903-1910	1927-1949
0-6-0	G-9-c	190-199	10	Baldwin	1902-1903	1926-1928
0-6-0	G-11	400-429	30	Manchester	1911, 1913	1947-1953
0-6-0	G-11-b	430-452	23	Brooks	1916	1953-1955
0-6-0	G-11-c	830-832,	4	Schenectady	1917-1920	1952-1953
						Ex-Portland Terminal, 1951
0-8-0	H-1-a	600, 601	2	Schenectady	1916	
						To Portland Terminal, 1935
0-8-0	H-2-a	610-631	22	Schenectady	1922	1946-1955
						4 to BAR, 1 to MEC, 1946
0-8-0	H-3	640-654	15	Baldwin	1927, 1929	1951-1953
0-8-8-0	M-2-a	800, 801	2	Schenectady	1922	
						To Bingham & Garfield, 1929
2-6-0	B-15	1360	137	Manch, Schen	1903-1910	1927-1955
2-8-0	K-5	2310-2343	34	Schenectady	1901-1902	1926-1936
2-8-0	K-6	2350-2359	10	Schenectady	1901-1902	1928-1936
						Simpled 1910-1919
2-8-0	K-7	2360-2429	66	Schenectady	1905-1911	1928-1955
2-8-0	K-8	2600-2734	135	BLW,Sch,Brks.	1911-1916	1937-1954
						2 to BAR 1946
2-8-4	T-1	4000-4024	25	Lima	1928-1929	1948-1955
						10 to SP, 7 to AT&SF, 1945

B&M STEAM LOCOMOTIVES BUILT SINCE 1900 (continued)

Type	Class	Numbers	Qty	Builder	Built	Retired	Notes
2-10-2	S-1-a	3000-3019	20	Schenectady	1920	1946-1949	
				11 rebuilt to S-1-c, 1940; 8 to MEC, 1936-1947			
2-10-2	S-1-b	3020-3029	10	Schenectady	1923	1940-1948	
2-6-6-2	M-1	3000-3003	4	Schenectady	1910	To MEC 1911-1912	
4-4-0	A-40-b	944-949	6	Manchester	1900	1926-1927	
							Ex-Fitchburg
4-4-0	A-41	950-1029	77	Manc., BLW	1900-1911	1926-1947	
4-4-0	A-45	1133-1136	4	Schenectady	1900	1926-1935	
							Ex-Fitchburg
4-4-0	A-46	1170-1173	4	Baldwin	1900	1926-1929	
4-4-2	J-1	3204-3244	41	Schen, Manch	1902-1909	1927-1952	
4-6-0	C-15-c	2020-2025	6	Rhode Island	1900	1927-1928	
4-6-0	C-17	2060-2064	5	Rhode Island	1900	1927-1928	

Type	Class	Numbers	Qty	Builder	Built	Retired	Notes
4-6-0	C-20		4	Baldwin	1900	1928	
							Ex-Fitchburg
4-6-0	C-21	2100-2129	26	Schenectady	1904-1906	1935-1937	
4-6-2	P-1	3600-3611	12	Schenectady	1910	1938-1952	
4-6-2	P-2	3620-3689	70	Schenectady	1911-1916	-1956	
4-6-2	P-3-a	3700-3709	10	Schenectady	1923	1952-1955	
4-6-2	P-4	3710-3719	10	Lima	1934, 1937	1953-1954	
4-6-2	P-5-a	3696-3699	4	Brooks	1924	1951-1952	
							Ex-Lackawanna
4-8-0	L-1-a	2900-2909	10	Schenectady	1899	1926	
						Ex-Fitchburg, simpled 1904	
4-8-0	L-1-b	2910-2917	8	Rhode Island	1900	1926	
						Ex-Fitchburg, simpled 1904	
4-8-2	R-1	4100-4117	18	Baldwin	1935-1941	1955-1956	
						4100-4112 to B&O, 1947	

CAMELBACK LOCOMOTIVES

Bituminous or soft coal, the most common form of the mineral, fueled most modern North American steam locomotives. Anthracite, or hard coal, which is found primarily in eastern Pennsylvania, burns slowly and almost without smoke and was considered the best coal for home heating. For such use it was cleaned and graded so the pieces were all the same size. The leftover pieces were called culm.

Culm was an ideal fuel for railroads that served the anthracite mines of eastern Pennsylvania. It was readily available and cheap, but it had one drawback: it burned slowly. The only way it could produce enough heat was to be burned in a wide, shallow fire. The narrow, deep firebox of 19th century locomotives wasn't suitable for culm; it required a grate with two to three times the usual area. Since the distance a fireman could fling coal through the firedoor was limited, the firebox had to be wider, not longer. John E. Wootten (1822-1898), general manager of the Philadelphia & Reading, introduced such a firebox in 1877.

The disadvantage of the wide Wootten firebox was that it restricted the view forward and left little room at the rear of the locomotive for a cab. The solution was to build a cab for the engineer straddling the boiler just ahead of the firebox. The fireman remained at the rear of the locomotive on an unprotected deck. Communication between the two men was all but impossible. Perched on the right running board, the engineer's cab had almost no room for control levers and handles, and it was a bad place to be when a side or main rod broke.

Some early Camelbacks were built with a roof over the front of the tender to protect the fireman, but photographs of the roof in service are rare — it may have hindered filling the tender with coal. In later years most Camelbacks had a small hood projecting to the rear offering minimal protection from the weather, but many offered no protection at all. Firing a locomotive was not easy in the best of circumstances; feeding a wide firebox through two firedoors while standing on a deck plate that bridged two vehicles bouncing in opposite directions in a blizzard or a cloudburst must have been absolute hell.

Railroad books and magazines occasionally refer to various Interstate Commerce Commission regulations outlawing Camelbacks or mandating protection for the fireman. I have been unable to find documentation of such regulations in either *Railway Age*, the trade magazine, or the *Locomotive Cyclopedia*. The last Camelbacks were built in 1927 for the Lehigh & New England.

By 1915 railroads began to use conventional cabs on locomotives with Wootten fireboxes. Some cabs had the lower front corners cut away for the rear corners of the firebox; others were mounted entirely behind the backhead. Some railroads convertedCamelbacks to rear-cab locomotives, depending on such factors as traffic levels, the need for locomotives, and the age and condition of the Camelbacks.

The wide firebox was also useful for low-grade bituminous coal, accounting for Camelbacks on such roads as Chicago & Eastern Illinois and Union Pacific. Other terms applied to the type are center-cab and Mother Hubbard.

Central of New Jersey 4-6-0 774 was generally considered the last operating Camelback on a common carrier railroad; it made its final run in 1954. Colorado Fuel & Iron used former Reading 0-4-0 1189 at its Birdsboro, Pa., plant until 1962. It is now on the roster of the Strasburg Railroad, a tourist carrier at Strasburg, Pa.

Central of New Jersey 610 carried an unusual rear cab that offered the fireman almost as much protection as on a conventional locomotive. Photo by Wayne Brumbaugh.

CANADIAN LOCOMOTIVE COMPANY

Canadian Locomotive Company dates from 1850, when a predecessor machinery works was founded at Kingston, Ontario. It produced its first locomotive, Grand Trunk Railway No. 88, in 1856. It was the pre-eminent locomotive builder in Canada in the years before 1887; between 1887 and 1904 it was the only locomotive builder other than the railroads themselves. In 1900 the company, by then the Scottish-owned Canadian Locomotive & Engine Company, shut down. That year a group of Kingston industrialists bought and reorganized it as Canadian Locomotive Company. Production resumed, and by 1905 CLC was producing 45 locomotives a year. In 1911 the company was purchased by a Toronto banker and a group of British financiers. During World War I CLC converted some of its facilities to munitions production and built its first locomotives for export: 50 2-10-0s for Russia and 40 2-8-0s for the British Army to use in France.

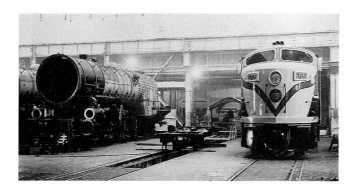

In 1923 CLC built Canadian National Railways' first 4-8-2, and in 1924 it built the largest locomotives in the British Empire — five 2-10-2s for CN. In 1928 it constructed the first of CN's 4-8-4s and North America's first large road diesel, CN 9000.

Again in World War II CLC turned to munitions work, then during the postwar years built large numbers of steam locomotives for export. In 1950 Fairbanks-Morse acquired CLC. The Kingston plant produced FM-design diesels until about 1956.

Canadian Locomotive Company continued to build steam locomotives even as it was assembling diesels. Side by side on the erection floor are a broad gauge Pacific for India and a C-Liner for Canadian National. CLC photo.

CANADIAN NATIONAL RAILWAYS

Canadian National Railways came into being during World War I and the years immediately afterward. Canada's population in 1901 was 5,371,000 — about the same as that of Chicago and its inner suburbs today, but those 5 million people were spread from the northeastern tip of Nova Scotia's Cape Breton Island to Prince Rupert, British Columbia. Immigration caused a great increase in Canada's population during the ensuing decade. Canada's railroads were able to keep pace with the population increase, but the increase in population was insufficient to support the railroads. When World War I cut off the supply of capital from England, the railroads other than Canadian Pacific found themselves in financial difficulty. They were a diverse lot: the Intercolonial, the National Transcontinental, the Canadian Northern, the Grand Trunk Pacific, and the Grand Trunk.

One of CN's early tasks was to combine the widely differing motive power rosters of its predecessors. Canadian Northern was powered almost exclusively by Ten-Wheelers and Consolidations; its roster included four Pacifics and a single Mikado, a Duluth, Winnipeg & Pacific machine with 49" drivers. Grand Trunk Pacific's roster was similar. Grand Trunk had large numbers of Moguls and relatively few Ten-Wheelers plus 186 Consolidations, 105 Pacifics, and 168 Mikados. Canadian Government Railways (which had taken over the Intercolonial and the National Transcontinental) ran heavy to Consolidations, Mikados, and Pacifics; 20 Santa Fes were the largest locomotives on its roster. Six-wheel switchers came to CN from all its components; eight-wheel switchers came from Grand Trunk (27), Canadian Government Railways (7), and Canadian Northern (1).

For new mainline power, Canadian National took the opposite approach from Chesapeake & Ohio, which rostered a wide variety of wheel arrangements for different regions and different services. After an initial group of 4-8-2s, CN practically standardized on the 4-8-4, rostering 160 of its own plus 43 for U. S. subsidiary Grand Trunk Western.

CN dieselized relatively late. The last steam run from Vancouver was on October 6, 1957, and the last Montreal-Toronto steam run was April 17, 1959. The last scheduled steam run on the system was on April 25, 1960, from The Pas to Winnipeg, Manitoba. CN continued to operate steam-powered excursion trains through the 1960s. Central Vermont operated steam locomotives until the spring of 1957, and the last regular operation of steam on Grand Trunk Western was on March 27, 1960.

Freight locomotives

CN came into existence late enough so that it bought only a few small locomotives. It built four 2-8-0s in 1926 and 20 more in 1931, splitting them half and half in each case between its Point St. Charles shops in Montreal and Transcona shops in Winnipeg.

In 1924 CN received 75 2-8-2s for mainline freight trains and five 2-10-2s for transfer service in Toronto. Point St. Charles turned out one Mikado in 1930, and CN bought five from Canadian Locomotive Company in 1936. In 1929 and 1930 CLC built 33 2-10-2s for CN. They had two distinctions: they were the largest locomotives in the British Empire, and they introduced the Vanderbilt tender to Canada.

Passenger and dual-service locomotives

Canadian National Railways' first new steam locomotives were delivered in 1923, 16 4-8-2s that were the first of a long line of dual-service Mountains and Northerns. The next year 21 more 4-8-2s arrived.

Northern Pacific bought the first 4-8-4s in 1927. Canadian National followed almost immediately with 40 of the type, designating them the Confederation type rather than Northern. They were light machines by American standards, ideal for routes inherited from railroads that couldn't afford heavy rail and rock ballast. They weighed 378,000 pounds, not much more than Canadian Pacific's contemporary Hudsons, and carried 57,500 pounds per driving axle, little more than a USRA light Mikado. By comparison, total weight of Northern Pacific's class A 4-8-4 was 426,000 pounds, with 65,000 pounds on each driving axle. NP's last 4-8-4s, the A-5s, tipped the scales at 508,500 pounds.

The 75 Mikados built for Canadian National in 1923 and 1924 were noteworthy in having Belpaire boilers. At 314,800 pounds they were medium-weight 2-8-2s, about halfway between the USRA light and heavy Mikados. When built, they were equipped with Worthington feedwater heaters; the device has been removed from No. 3554, shown in July 1957, accounting for the empty space ahead of the air pump. In November 1954 CN changed the position of its herald from a 9-degree tilt to horizontal. Rail Photo Service photo by H. W. Pontin.

With their light axle loadings, CN's 4-8-4s could roam over most of the CN system, though they usually remained east of the prairies. Most of the locomotives CN assigned to western Canada were oil burners, and none of the 4-8-4s was converted to oil fuel. CN's Mountains and Northerns had 73" drivers, except for the U-4s, which had 77" drivers and were streamlined. For its last new steam engines, delivered in 1944, CN reverted to the Mountain type — 20 semi-streamlined 4-8-2s for fast passenger service.

Almost the sole exception to the 4-8-2 and 4-8-4 for mainline work was a group of five 80"-drivered Hudsons built by Montreal in 1930 for Montreal-Toronto passenger service.

Switchers

Between 1919 and 1925 CN continued Canadian Government Railways' program of converting 2-8-0s into 0-8-0s. Then CN built 45 0-8-0s between 1927 and 1931 and bought 10 each from CLC and Montreal in

Canadian National 6157 is a member of class U-2-c, one of 20 built by Montreal in 1929. Details shared with CN's first Northerns of 1927 are the outside-journal lead truck and the banjo frame or outside cradle — frame members outside the ashpan aft of the drivers. The vestibule cab and triangular number indicator are CN trademarks. Rail Photo Service photo by James Adams.

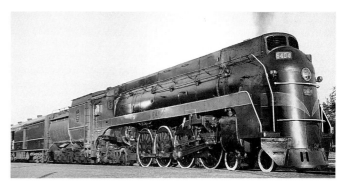

The streamlining of Canadian National's five U-4-a class 4-8-4s, built by Montreal in 1936, was based on wind tunnel tests. The primary concern of the designers was to keep smoke from swirling around the cab and obscuring the engineer's view. Lima built six U-4-b look-alikes for Grand Trunk Western in 1938. Photo by Don Wood.

1929. Between 1923 and 1929 Grand Trunk Western bought 52 from all three major U. S. builders, and in 1936 and 1937 removed the lead trucks from seven Mikados to create 0-8-2 transfer locomotives.

Experiments

Canadian National was not an experimenter or an innovator except for one item: smoke lifters and deflectors. The most commonly applied smoke lifters were vertical plates alongside the smokebox, but CN tried a variety of cowls around the stack and did considerable research that led to the streamlined 4-8-4s (which nonetheless had non-streamlined Vanderbilt tenders).

Historical and technical society: CN Lines Special Interest Group, 2488 Paige Janette Drive, Harvey, LA 70058.

Recommended reading:

Canadian National Steam Power, by Anthony Clegg and Ray Corley, published in 1969 by Trains & Trolleys, Box 1434, Station B, Montreal 110, PQ, Canada.

"How to Streamline a Steam Locomotive," by N. W. Emmott, in *Trains Magazine*, March 1973, page 35.

Published rosters:

Railroad Magazine: September 1937, page 82; October 1937, page 124; November 1937, page 77; December 1937, page 77; November 1947, page 124; December 1947, page 114; October 1953, page 38; June 1957, page 68 (renumbering); July 1966, page 53 (Grand Trunk Pacific); July 1966, page 57 (Canadian Northern); August 1966, page 50 (Intercolonial and Canadian Government Railways).

Trains Magazine: March 1974, page 24 (Duluth, Winnipeg & Pacific).

CN STEAM LOCOMOTIVES BUILT SINCE 1900

Type	Class	Numbers	Qty	Builder	Built	Built for	Retired
0-6-0	O-2-a	7000, 7001	2	Pittsburgh	1904	CNor	1930, 1931
0-6-0	O-3-a	7002-7005	4	CFdry	1907	CNor	1931, 1939
0-6-0	O-4-a	7006	1	Baldwin	1906	CNor	1930
0-6-0	O-7-a, -b	7009-7030	22	Montreal	1910-1911	CNor	1931-1954
0-6-0	O-10-a, -b	7031-7065	35	CLC	1912-1914	CNor	1932-1958
0-6-0	O-11-a	7066	1	Schenectady	1910	DW&P	1936
0-6-0	O-14-a-d	7067-7081	15	CLC	1902-1908	CGR	1923-1952
0-6-0	O-9-a	7124-7217	93		1903, 1907	GT	1932-1957
		Built by Grand Trunk Railway, Schenectady, Baldwin, Lima, Montreal, and CLC					
0-6-0	O-9-a	7218, 7219	2	Baldwin	1905, 1913	D&TSL	1935
0-6-0	O-5-a	7300, 7301	2	Pittsburgh	1907	CNor	1954, 1939
0-6-0	O-13-a	7302-7304	3	CLC	1918	CNor	1956, 1958
0-6-0	O-15	7305-7318	14	CLC	1904-1913	CGR	1939-1957
0-6-0	O-12	7319-7423	105		1914-1920	CGR, CNor	1950-1961
		Built by CLC, Canada Foundry, Montreal					
0-6-0	O-18	7424-7521	98	GT, Lima, CLC	1919-1923	GT, GTW	1954-1961
0-6-0	O-19-a	7522-7531	10	Cooke, Schen.	1919	GTW, GT (NE)	1955-1961
0-6-0	O-20-a	7532-7541	10	Montreal	1911	GTP	1954-1961
0-6-0	O-19-b	7542, 7543	2	Montreal	1928, 1929		1955, 1966
		Purchased from National Harbours Board, Vancouver, in 1953					
0-8-0	P-2-a	8010-8014	5	CGR, CN	1918-1925		1931-1938
0-8-0	P-3-	8015...8087	12	CGR, CNr	1918-1925		1928-1932
						Converted from 2-8-0s	
0-8-0	P-4	8200-8226	27		1920, 1923	GT	1955-1957
		Built by CLC, GT, and Lima					
0-8-0	P-5-a	8296-8299	4	Schenectady	1923	CV	1855-1961
		Acquired from Central Vermont 1942					
0-8-0	P-5-	8300-8329	30	Schen, Lima	1923-1927	GTW	1955-1961
0-8-0	P-5-d	8330-8339	10	CN Shops	1927-1928		1957-1961
0-8-0	P-5-e	8340-8349	10	Baldwin	1927	GTW	1955-1961
0-8-0	P-5-f	8350-8369	20	CLC, MLW	1929		1955-1961
0-8-0	P-5-g	8370-8381	12	Baldwin	1929	GTW	1960-1961
0-8-0	P-5-h	8282-8416	35	CN Shops	1930-1931		1954-1961
0-8-0	P-5-j	8417-8422	6	Brooks	1914-1923		1954-1960
		Acquired from Buffalo Creek Railroad 1947.					
0-8-2	S-1	3515-3523	7		1936-1937	GTW	
		Converted from 2-8-2s of the same numbers by GTW shops.					
2-6-0	C-3-a	401	1	Montreal	1910-1911		1940
		Built for Quebec & Saguenay					1940
2-6-0	C-3-a,b,c	402-407	6	Montreal	1910-1911	CGR	1954
2-6-0	C-5-b	409-420	12	MLW, CLC	1909-1914	1932-1955	
		Acquired from McArthur Co. (contractors)					
2-6-0	C-7-a	423-428	6	Montreal	1911	GTP	1939-1954
2-6-0	C-3-a	429 (1)	1	Montreal	1910	AQ&W	1935
2-6-0	E-13-a	429 (2)	1	Montreal	1928	QRL&P	1953
2-6-0	D-3-a	476	1	Montreal	1905	CNor	1925
2-6-0	D-11-a	483	1	Baldwin	1902	CNor	1925
2-6-0	D-12-a	484-486	3	Dickson	1902	DW&P	1925
2-6-0	E-7-a, b	661-864	204		1898-1908	GT	1927-1959
		Built by Baldwin, Schenectady, Dickson, Brooks, Montreal, CLC, and GT					
2-6-0	E-8-a, -b	865-889	25	CLC	1909	GTP	1935-1941
2-6-0	E-9-a	890-901	12	Brooks	1906	GT	1934
2-6-0	E-10-a	902-926	25	CLC	1910	GT	1930-1960
		16 of class renumbered 80-94, 96 in 1951					
2-6-0	E-11-a	927, 928	2	Baldwin	1907	D&TSL	1929
2-8-0	L-4-a	1800 (2)	1			AQ&W	1930
2-8-0	L-5-a	1800 (1)-18023		Rhode Island	1906	DW&P	1925-1934
2-8-0	L-6-a	1803, 1804	2	Schenectady	1910	DW&P	1925, 1933
2-8-0	M4	1805-1956	151		1898-1910	CGR	1922-1954
		Built by Richmond, Baldwin, Dickson, CLC, and Manchester					
2-8-0	M-8-a	1981-1984	4	Schenectady	1905	CV	1957
		Reassigned to Duluth, Winnipeg & Pacific in 1928					
2-8-0	M-1	2010-2064	55	CLC	1907-1908	CNor	1935-1955
2-8-0	M-2-a	2065-2089	25	CFdry	1907-1908	CNor	1927-1941
2-8-0	M-3-a	2090-2124	35	Montreal	1907-1909	CNor	1941-1961
2-8-0	M-3-c	2125-2129	5	Brooks	1911	DW&P	1958-1960
2-8-0	M-3-d, -e	2130-2179	50	CLC	1912-1913	CNor	1951-1961
2-8-0	M-5-a--d	2180-2200	21		1912-1916	CGR	1948-1961
		Built by CLC, Montreal, Canada Foundry					
2-8-0	N-3	2334-2384	51	MLW, CLC	1913-1916	CGR	1954-1961
2-8-0	N-1-b	2385-2399	15	CFdry	1913-1914	CGR	1952-1958
2-8-0	N-1-a--c	2400-2454	55	CFdry	1912-1918	CNor	1955-1960
2-8-0	N-2-a	2455-2464	10	Brooks	1916-1917	DW&P	1957-1959
2-8-0	N-2-b	2465-2514	50	Montreal	1918	CNor	1954-1961
2-8-0	N-4	2515-2686	172		1906-1911	GT	1952-1961
		Built by Montreal, Schenectady, and Brooks					
2-8-0	N-5-a, -b	2687-2746	60	MLWI, CLC	1911-1912	GTP	1955-1961
2-8-0	N-5-c, -d	2747, 2748	2	CN	1926		1960, 1958
2-8-0	N-5-d	2749-2768	20	CN	1931		1954-1961
2-8-0	N-4-g	2800, 2801	2	Pt. St. Ch.	1926		1959
2-8-0	N-4-h	2810-2819	10	Schenectady	1906	CV	1954-1961

Type	Class	Numbers	Qty	Builder	Built	Built for	Retired
2-8-2	R-1-a	3000	1	Cooke	1914	DW&P	1939
2-8-2	S-1	3198-3524	327		1913-1926	CGR, GT, CN	1953-1961
		Built by CN, CLC, MLW, Schenectady, and Baldwin					
2-8-2	S-2	3525-3599	75	MLW, CLC	1923-1924	CN	1957-1961
2-8-2	S-3	3700-3757	58	Schenectady	1918-1924	GT, GTW	1952-1961
2-8-2	S-4-b	3800-3805	6	CN, CLC	1930, 1936	CN	1957
2-10-2	T-1	4000-4019	45	Brooks, MLW	1916-1920	CGR, CN	1952-1961
2-10-2	T-2-a	4100-4104	5	CLC	1924	CN	1955, 1957
2-10-2	T-3-a	4200-4209	10	Brooks	1919		1955-1961
		Purchased from Boston & Albany 1928					
2-10-2	T-4	4300-4332	33	CLC	1929-1930	CN	1957-1959
4-4-0	A-20-a	120-122	3	CLC	1904, 1906	CNor	1925
4-4-0	A-24-a	123, 124	2	CLC	1904, 1906	CNor	1922, 1931
4-4-0	B-26-a	325-399	75	MLW, CFdry	1908-1909	CNor, GTP	1925-1941
4-6-0	F-1-a, -b	1000-1011	12	Montreal	1909-1912	CGR	1926-
4-6-0	F-2-a	1012	1	Pittsburgh	1905	CGR	1958
4-6-0	F-3-a	1013, 1014 (1)	2	Montreal	1909	QOR	1931
4-6-0	F-4-a	1015 (1)	1	Montreal	1911	AQ&W	1931
4-6-0	F-1-c	1014-1018 (2)	5	Montreal	1909-1911	Temis.	1954-1957
4-6-0	G-3-a	1027-1030	4	CLC	1907	CNor	1925-1934
4-6-0	G-4-a	1031	1	Baldwin	1907	CNor	1920
4-6-0	G-6-a	1034-1038	5	CFdry	1905	CNor	1925-1926
4-6-0	G-8-a	1042	1	Baldwin	1901	CNor	1933
4-6-0	G-10-a, -b	1048-1082	35	CLC	1902-1903	CNor	1927-1947
4-6-0	G-11-a	1083-1102	20	CFdry	1906	CNor	1927-1934
4-6-0	G-12-a	1103, 1104	2	Schenectady	1904	CNor	1923, 1925
4-6-0	G-13-a	1105-1108	4	Cooke	1901	CNorR	1925
4-6-0	G-14-a	1109	1	Baldwin	1901	CNor	1933
4-6-0	G-15-a	1110	1	CLC	1902	CNor	1925
4-6-0	G-16-a	1111-1160	50	Montreal	1912-1913	CNor	1943-1961
4-6-0	G-17-a	1161-1165	5	Montreal	1913	CNor	1954-1957
4-6-0	G-21-a	1178	1	Schenectady	1907	AQ&W	1937
4-6-0	H-1-a, -b	1200, 1201	2	Montreal		QOR	1929, 1930
4-6-0	H-2-c	1206	1	Baldwin	1904	CNor	1919
4-6-0	H-2-a	1202-1205	4	Montreal	1907	QM&S	1930-1931
4-6-0	H-3-a	1207, 1208	2	Brooks	1903	CNor	1955, 1954
4-6-0	H-3-a, -b	1209-18, 20	11	Montreal	1904, 1906	CNor	1935-1950
4-6-0	H-4-a, -b	1221-1245	25	CLC	1906-1907	CNor	1930-1956
4-6-0	H-5-a	1246-1260	15	CFdry	1907	CNor	1929-1944
4-6-0	H-6-a—e	1261-1346	86	Brooks, MLW	1902-1911	CNor	1932-1959
4-6-0	H-6-f	1347-1351	5	Baldwin	1911	DW&P	1957-1961
4-6-0	H-7-a	1352, 1353	2	Rogers	1906	DW&P	1927
4-6-0	H-6-g	1354-1409	66	Montreal	1912-1913	CNor	1954-1961
4-6-0	H-8-a	1410-1412	3	CLC	1911	CGR	1936-1937
4-6-0	H-10-a	1423-1452	30	MLW, CLC	1910	GTP	1947-1961
4-6-0	I-3	1509-1529	21		1899-1907	CGR	1925-1928
		Built by Canadian Locomotive Company, Intercolonial Railway, and Manchester					
4-6-0	I-4	1530-1535	6	CLC	1903-1904	CGR	1925-1930
4-6-0	I-5	1536-1542	7	Dickson	1901	CGR	1925-1936
4-6-0	I-6-b	1547-1577	31		1898-1905	CGR	1931-1939
		Built by Baldwin, Schenectady, GT, and Montreal					
4-6-0	I-7	1578-1588	11		1901-1905	GT	1931-1945
		Built by Schenectady, GT, and Montreal					
4-6-0	I-8-a	1589-1628	40		1906-1908	GT	1931-1945
		Built by Baldwin, Schenectady, GT, and Montreal					
4-6-2	J-1-a	5000-5003	4	Montreal	1913	CNor	1957-1961
4-6-2	J-3-a, -b	5030-5079	50	BLW, MLW	1912-1913	GT	1955-1961
4-6-2	J-4	5080-5099	20	MLW, CLC	1914-1918	CGR	1958-1961
4-6-2	J-4-e, -f	5125-5156	32	Montreal	1920	CN	1955-1961
4-6-2	J-7-a, -b	5250-5294	45	Montreal	1918-1919	CGR	1957-1961
4-6-2	J-7-c	5295-5304	10	Montreal	1920	CN	1959-1961
4-6-2	K-1	5500-5542	43	CLC, MLW	1905-1911	CGR	1939-1957
4-6-2	K-2	5543-5556	14	Montreal	1913-1916	CGR	1954-1961
4-6-2	K-3	5557-5611	55		1910-1913	GT	1954-1962
		Built by Grand Trunk, Montreal, and Baldwin					
4-6-2	K-3-g	5612-5626	15	Montreal	1911	GTP	1957-1961
4-6-2	K-4	5627-5634	8	Alco, BLW	1924, 1929	GTW	1960-1961
4-6-4T	X-10-a	45-50	6	Montreal	1914	GT	1956-1961
4-6-4	K-5-a	5700-5704	5	Montreal	1930	CN	1960-1967
4-8-2	U-1-a, -b	6000-6036	37	CLC	1923-1924	CN	1951-1961
4-8-2	U-1-c	6037-6041	5	Baldwin	1925	GTW	1955-1961
4-8-2	U-1-d, -e	6042-6058	17	CLC, MLW	1929-1930	CN	1952-1961
4-8-2	U-1-f	6060-6079	20	Montreal	1944	CN	1960-1962
4-8-4	U-2	6100-6189	90	CLC, MLW	1927-1940	CN	1948-1961
4-8-4	U-2-g, -h	6200-6264	65	Montreal	1942-1944	CN	1960-1961
4-8-4	U-3	6300-6336	37	Alco	1927, 1942	GTW	1959-1961
4-8-4	U-4-a	6400-6404	5	Montreal	1936	CN	1960-1961
4-8-4	U-4-b	6405-6410	6	Lima	1938	GTW	1960-1961

CANADIAN PACIFIC RAILWAY

Canadian Pacific entered the twentieth century with a virtual monopoly on railroading in Canada west of North Bay, Ontario. The main line led through Winnipeg, Regina, and Calgary to Vancouver. Branches ran from Regina to Prince Albert, from Calgary to Edmonton, from Dunmore west through Crows Nest Pass into the Kootenays, and from the U. S. border at North Portal to the main line near Moose Jaw. CP's lines in eastern Canada were largely in place, but branches were still being extended. Yet to come were construction of a line from Toronto north to Sudbury and acquisition of the Quebec Central and Dominion Atlantic Railways.

CP's expansion meant more locomotives were needed. The hot item in locomotives at the turn of the century was the compound. Railroads differed in their enthusiasm for compounds; CP was definitely pro-compound, rostering cross-compounds and Vauclain compounds of several wheel arrangements.

Enthusiastic as it was about compound locomotives, CP took interest in another development that could enhance locomotive efficiency: the superheater. In 1901 and 1903 CP installed Schmidt superheaters in three Ten-Wheelers — the first such application outside Prussia. CP soon noted that superheating avoided much of the complexity of compound locomotives. It purchased its last compounds, a group of 2-8-0s, in 1903.

The expansion of the railroad and the growth of the motive power fleet called for enlarged shop facilities. In 1902 CP began construction of Angus Shops, named for Richard B. Angus, one of the original directors of the company.

In February 1904 Henry H. Vaughan became superintendent of motive power for lines east of Winnipeg, and at the end of 1905 he was promoted to assistant to the vice president in charge of motive power for the whole railroad. Vaughan continued the work on superheating, developing his own type of superheater. In 1904 the railroad purchased 41 2-8-0s fitted with Schmidt and Cole superheaters, and in 1905 ten 4-6-0s were built with the Vaughan-Horsey superheater. Comparisons with compound locomotives showed a significant reduction in coal consumption for superheated locomotives.

The superheater had the effect of making CP's compounds, even relatively new ones, obsolete (they were soon rebuilt to superheated simple engines). The road needed a versatile, multipurpose engine and developed the class D10 Ten-Wheeler, of which it acquired 502 examples between 1907 and 1913. The D10s had 63"-drivers and 21" × 28" or 22" × 28" cylinders; they were built by Montreal, Canadian Locomotive Company, Richmond, Schenectady, and CP's Angus Shops. A number of D10s remained in service as late as 1960.

With the outbreak of World War I in 1914, locomotive development came to a halt and the shops turned to war work. Henry H. Vaughan, who was responsible for CP's motive power development, was forced out. In 1921 Angus Shops all but ceased building new steam locomotives in order to free facilities for repairs to existing equipment.

CP's best-known chief of motive power and rolling stock was Henry Blaine Bowen, who served in that capacity from 1928 to 1949. He is remembered especially for the Hudsons he designed.

CP began purchasing diesel switchers in the 1930s. In 1949 Canadian Pacific dieselized two districts, the Esquimalt & Nanaimo Railway on Vancouver Island and the route from Montreal to Wells River, Vermont. CP dieselized several other districts, then in 1953 shifted to a policy of dieselization by train run. In the late 1950s the pace of dieselization increased, and steam was gradually confined to Manitoba and Quebec. In 1959 only a few local passenger trains out of Montreal remained behind steam. Steam was kept available for standby service until 1962, but the last steam-hauled train was a Canadian Railroad Historical Association train operated on November 6, 1960. A few locomotives provided steam for CP's passenger car yard in Montreal while the facility's stationary boilers were being repaired in the winter of 1960-1961.

Between 1881 and 1949 Canadian Pacific acquired 3,257 steam locomotives, 502 of which were D-10 Ten-Wheelers like No. 1004, which is shown leading a freight at Wroxeter, Ontario, in July 1957. Photo by Don Wood.

The Selkirks of 1938 were unique on two counts for ten-coupled steam locomotives: they were streamlined and they were built for passenger service. Rail Photo Service photo by G. C. Corey.

Freight locomotives

CP introduced a 220,000-pound 2-8-0 in 1909, at the time the heaviest freight locomotive in Canada. Even while the railroad was acquiring such machines in quantity, it developed a 2-8-2 of the same hauling capacity but with a larger firebox and greater steaming capacity. During World War I CP designed a larger 2-8-2 and a 2-10-2, and construction of these locomotives began immediately after the war: 105 2-8-2s (Class P2) and 15 2-10-2s.

One of Bowen's first locomotive designs was a 2-8-4 based on the P2 Mikado. During the design process it became a 2-10-4 with the boiler of the 4-8-4 designed by Bowen's predecessor. Twenty such machines were built by Montreal in 1929. They were assigned to work in the Rockies west of Calgary. In 1938 ten more 2-10-4s appeared, semistreamlined for passenger service between Calgary and Revelstoke. The name Selkirk was applied to the type at that time. The final six Selkirks came in 1949, just months before CP dieselized its lines in Vermont.

For service east of the Rockies, CP purchased 69 P2-class 2-8-2s from 1940 to 1948 and rebuilt 65 Consolidations into P1n-class 2-8-2s between 1946 and 1949.

Passenger locomotives

CP chose the Pacific type for passenger service. Between 1906 and 1914 it received 39 class G1 and 166 class G2 Pacifics. The two classes were nearly identical except for driver size: 75" for the G1 and 70" for the G2.

In 1914 Angus Shops built two 4-8-2s, first of that type in Canada, as a response to the increased weight of passenger trains made up of steel cars. At the end of World War I, the road reverted to the Pacific type, producing two classes, G3 and G4, successors to the G1 and G2 and, like them, differing primarily in driver diameter.

In 1928 Angus Shops built a pair of 4-8-4s. They arrived just as their designer, Charles H. Temple, retired and Bowen took over. The 4-8-4s were too heavy for service on much of the CP system and spent most of their careers on Montreal-Toronto night trains. Canadian Pacific settled instead on the Hudson for heavy passenger service.

The first ten of Bowen's Hudsons arrived from Montreal Locomotive Works in late 1929, followed by another ten a year later. They had 75" drivers and 22" × 30" cylinders. In working order they weighed 360,000 pounds, with 194,000 pounds on the drivers. CP's lines could carry heavier axle loadings than Canadian National's lines, and CP was able to get about the same amount of locomotive on three driving axles as CN had on four in its U-2 class Northerns.

The introduction of lightweight passenger trains in 1934 — Burlington's *Zephyr* and Union Pacific's M-10000 — did not go unnoticed in Canada. CP's response was a quartet of four-car streamlined trains for Montreal-Quebec, Toronto-Detroit, and Calgary-Edmonton service. To power the trains, Montreal Locomotive Works outshopped five F2a-class streamlined 4-4-4s in 1936. The type was named Jubilee, to commemorate the 50th anniversary of CP's transcontinental service. The new locomotives had 80" drivers, and the main rods were connected to the forward drivers, like Milwaukee Road's *Hiawatha* Atlantic.

In 1937 and 1938 CP received 20 more 4-4-4s classed F1a. They had 75" drivers and main rods connected to the rear drivers. Their streamlining differed from that of the earlier Jubilees primarily in the shape of the pilot. Intended for fast local trains that never materialized, they wound up on secondary local passenger trains.

Also in 1937 CP received 30 more Hudsons. They were mechanically the same as the Hudsons of 1929 and 1930 but were streamlined like the second Jubilees. They were assigned to long-distance passenger runs such as Toronto-Fort William, Ont. (811 miles), and Winnipeg-Calgary (832 miles). CP quickly ordered 10 more, delivered in 1938.

When Hudson 2850, first of the newest group of 4-6-4s, was assigned to the train carrying King George VI and Queen Elizabeth of England across Canada in 1939, it was decorated with royal crowns on the skirting above the cylinders. The engine was displayed at the 1939 New York World's Fair and kept the crowns upon returning to work between Fort William and Winnipeg. Crowns were eventually applied to all the streamlined 4-6-4s, and they became known as Royal Hudsons. Five oil-burning Hudsons, the last of the type, were built in 1940 to work

Canadian Pacific had the second-largest fleet of Hudsons, 65 in all, of which 45 were streamlined like No. 2841, shown at Toronto in 1958. Note the crown at the front of the running board skirt; these were the Royal Hudsons. Just below the teardrop-shaped classification light is a bulge in the boiler jacket concealing an Elesco feedwater heater. The feedwater heater pump appears below the numbers on the running board; the air pump is carried in the same position on the right side of the locomotive. Photo by John A. Rehor.

between Revelstoke and Vancouver.

Other power

Between 1909 and 1911 Canadian Pacific acquired the only articulateds built in Canada for domestic service, six 0-6-6-0s for helper service in the Rockies and the Selkirks. The first five were compounds; the sixth was one of the first two simple articulateds in the world (a Pennsylvania 2-8-8-2 was under construction at the same time). The articulateds differed from customary practice in that the front engine was backwards — cylinders to the rear, just in front of the cylinders of the rear engine. They were converted to 2-10-0s in 1917.

In 1910 CP built three 4-6-4Ts for Montreal suburban service and in

4-4-4 — JUBILEE

Inspired by a Bavarian design, the Philadelphia & Reading built four 4-4-4s in 1915. The name Reading was given to the wheel arrangement, but it soon became a name for a non-existent type. The locomotives had an experimental four-point suspension system that didn't work out. They were rebuilt to Atlantics in 1916 and lasted until 1952.

In 1934 Baltimore & Ohio built a lightweight 4-4-4 numbered 1 and named *Lady Baltimore*. No. 1 had a water-tube boiler and 84" drivers and weighed 217,800 pounds. Less than half of that weight, 98,900 pounds, was on the drivers. Tractive force was 28,000 pounds, giving a factor of adhesion of 3.53 — making Lady Baltimore was a very slippery engine. After a brief stint on the Alton, which B&O owned then, she worked on a Cleveland-Holloway, Ohio, local passenger train for a while and was scrapped in 1949.

Canadian Pacific's two groups of 4-4-4s were introduced in 1936 and 1937. The F2a locomotives, introduced in 1936, had their main rods connected to the forward pair of 80" drivers. The type was named Jubilee, to commemorate the 50th anniversary of CPR's transcontinental passenger service. The F1a class, built in 1937

The F2a Jubilees were equipped with Boxpok drivers, rare on CPR, and their main rods were connected to the first pair of drivers. The streamlined shroud is deceptive; the top of the boiler is about even with the handrail. No. 3000, first of the class, is shown at Glencoe, Ontario, in July 1957. Photo by Don Wood.

and 1938, had main rods connected to the rear pair of their 75" drivers. They were somewhat shorter and, including the tender, weighed almost 17 tons less in working order. CPR's 4-4-4s worked for 20 years. Most members of the two classes were scrapped in 1957 and 1958.

Other names: Reading, Baltimore
Total built: 30
First: Reading 110-113, 1915.
Last: Canadian Pacific class F1a, Nos. 2910-2929, built November 1937-March 1938.
Longest-lived and last in service: Canadian Pacific F1a 2928, removed from roster March 1963.
Greatest number: Canadian Pacific, 25 (20 F1a, 5 F2a).
Heaviest: Canadian Pacific F2a, 263,000 pounds.
Lightest: Baltimore & Ohio 1, 217,800 pounds.

1912, two 0-6-4Ts for passenger terminal switching at Montreal and Toronto. In the next two years Angus Shops produced a group of new 0-8-0s (most of the road's eight-wheel switchers had been rebuilt from 2-8-0s) and a trio of 0-10-0s.

After the first group of 2-10-4s appeared, Angus Shops began construction of an experimental 2-10-4 with a multi-pressure boiler. Number 8000 emerged in May 1931. It had two conventionally located cylinders working at 250 pounds driving the third axle and a third cylinder between the frames working at 850 pounds driving the second axle. It was a bi-pressure simple locomotive — CP had long since had its fling with compounds. In addition, the multipressure boiler had a closed 1600-pound-pressure system used for heat transfer within the boiler. The locomotive was retired in 1936 and scrapped in 1940.

Canadian Pacific was alone in the attention it paid to power for secondary trains. Other railroads assigned older locomotives to secondary trains as they were replaced by new ones. During the late 1930s and the 1940s CP recognized that the D10 Ten-Wheelers and the G1 and G2 Pacifics were wearing out. Between 1938 and 1948 CP purchased 122 G3-class Pacifics, all but the last 10 built by Canadian Locomotive Company. In 1944 CP designed and built 2 G5 Pacifics, modernized versions of the G2 and prototypes of 100 more built between 1945 and 1948 by Montreal and Canadian Locomotive Company.

Recommended reading:
Canadian Pacific Steam Locomotives, by Omer Lavallée, published in 1985 by Railfare Enterprises Limited, Box 33, West Hill, Ontario, Canada M1E 4R4 (ISBN 0-919130-34-8).
"New Ones Out of Old Ones" (2-8-0 to 2-8-2), in *Trains Magazine*, May 1947, page 60.
"2-10-4 to Revelstoke," by David P. Morgan, in *Trains Magazine*, September 1950, page 16.
"Destined to Die Young" (G-5 Pacifics) by F. H. Howard, in *Trains Magazine*, February 1954, page 51.
"Hudson Royalty," by James A. Brown and Omer Lavallée, in *Trains Magazine*, August 1969, page 20.

"The Case of the Lonely Canadian 4-8-4's," by R. N. Gridgeman, in *Trains Magazine*, January 1976, page 20.

Published rosters:
Railway & Locomotive Historical Society Bulletin, No. 83, entire issue.
Railroad Magazine: February 1933, page 129; September 1947, page 32; September 1953, page 32; March 1954, page 16; May 1966, page 40 (1929 roster).

CP STEAM LOCOMOTIVES BUILT SINCE 1900)

Type	Class	Numbers	Qty	Builder	Built	Retired	Notes
0-6-0	U2e	6045-6050	6	CP	1904	-1935	
0-6-0	U2f	6058-6062	5	CP	1900	-1930	
0-6-0	U3a	6101-6130	30	CP	1901-1904	1930-1940	
0-6-0	U3b	6140-6142	3	Schenectady	1902	1933	
0-6-0	U3c	6143-6208	66	CP	1905-1910	1930-1950	
0-6-0	U3d	6209-6259	51	CP	1911-1912	1935-1955	
0-6-0	U3e	6260-6304	45	CP	1912-1913	1950-1958	
0-6-4T	T3a	5996, 5997	2	CP	1912	1930, 1951	
0-8-0	V5a	6600-6609	10	CP	1930-1931	1956-1957	
0-8-0	V2c	6876	1	Canada Foundry	1904	1946	
0-8-0	V3a	6900-6903	4	CP	1906-1911	1937-1946	
0-8-0	V3c	6904-6913	10	CP	1913	1949-1966	
0-8-0	V4a	6920-6949	30	CP, MLW	1907-1910	1943-1964	
0-8-0	V5a	6960-6968	9	CP	1930-1931	1957-1965	
0-10-0	W1a	6950-6952	3	CP	1914	1954-1957	
Type	Class	Numbers	Qty	Builder	Built	Retired	Notes
0-6-6-0	R1	5750-5755	6	CP	1909, 1911	R1916-1917	
						Rebuilt to 2-10-0s 5750-5755	
2-8-0	M1e	3232-3245	14	CLC	1899-1900	1921-1941	
2-8-0	M2a	3250-3258	9	CP	1900-1901	1928-1945	
2-8-0	M2b	3259	1	CP	1901	1930	
2-8-0	M2c	3260-3271	12	Richmond	1900	1923-1946	
2-8-0	M2d	3272-3281	10	CLC	1900	1930-1946	
2-8-0	M2e	3282-3295	14	CLC	1901-1903	1928-1937	
2-8-0	M2f	3296-3305	10	Canada Foundry	1904-1905	1929-1936	
2-8-0	M3b	3350-3391	42	Schenectady	1901-1902	1930-1960	
2-8-0	M4a-h	3400-3565	166		1904-1910	1935-1961	

Built by Montreal, Canadian Locomotive Co., Schenectady, CP, and Baldwin

CP STEAM LOCOMOTIVES BUILT SINCE 1900 (continued)

Type	Class	Numbers	Qty	Builder	Built	Retired	Notes
2-8-0	N2	3600-3760	161		1909-1914	1954-1963	
		Built as N3 (3800-3960) by Montreal, Canadian Locomotive Co., Canada Foundry, and CP					
2-8-0	N4	3952-3956	5	Montreal, CLC	1913-1921	1955-1958	
		Ex-Algoma Eastern 52-56, acquired with the road, 1931; second 3952-3956					
2-8-2	P1a	5000-5019	20	CP	1912	1957-1965	
						To P1d, 5100-5119 1926-1930	
2-8-2	P1b	5020-5094	65	MLW	1913		
						1957-1964 to P1e, 5120-5194, 1926-1930	
2-8-2	P1n	5200-5264	65		1910-1914	1957-1964	
		Built by Montreal, Canadian Locomotive Co., and Canada Foundry					
2-8-2	P2	5300-5473	174	CP, MLW, CLC	1919-1948	1956-1965	
2-10-0	R2	5750-5755	6	CP	1916-1917	1956-1960	Ex-0-6-6-0
2-10-0	R3	5756-5790	35	CP	1917-1919	1952-1965	
2-10-2	S2a	5800-5814	15	CP	1919-1920	1954-1959	
2-10-4	T1a	5900-5919	20	Montreal	1929	1956	
2-10-4	T1b	5920-5929	10	Montreal	1938	1957	
2-10-4	T1c	5930-5935	6	Montreal	1949	1959	
2-10-4	T4a	8000	1	Montreal	1931	1940	
4-4-4	F1a	2910-2929	20	CLC	1937-1938	1957-1961	
4-4-4	F2a	3000-3004	5	Montreal	1936	1957-1958	
4-6-0	D4g	417-492	76	CP, Montreal	1912-1915	1939-1966	

Type	Class	Numbers	Qty	Builder	Built	Retired	Notes
4-6-0	D6	500-559	60		1902-1904	1930-1955	
		Built by Schenectady, North British Locomotive Co. (Glasgow, Scotland), and Sächsische Maschinenbau A. G. (Chemnitz, Germany)					
4-6-0	D9c	560-597	28	Schenectady	1903	1939-1955	
4-6-0	D10	600-1111			1905-1913	1938-1965	
		Built by Richmond, Montreal, Canadian Locomotive Co., CP, and Schenectady					
4-6-2	G1	2200-2238	39	CP, Montreal	1906-1914	1940-1961	
4-6-2	G2	2500-2665	166	CP, Montreal, Schenectady	1906-1914	1940-1961	
4-6-2	G3	2300-2472	173	CP, MLW, CLC	1919-1948	1941-1966	
4-6-2	G4	2700-2717	18	CP	1919-1921	1954-1965	
4-6-2	G5	1200-1301	102	CP, MLW, CLC	1944-1948	1959-1964	
4-6-4T	T2a	5991-5993	3	CP	1910, 1912	1935	
4-6-4	H1a	2800-2809	10	Montreal	1929	1957-1959	
4-6-4	H1b	2810-2819	10	Montreal	1930	1957-1962	
4-6-4	H1c	2820-2849	30	Montreal	1937	1956-1966	
4-6-4	H1d	2850-2859	10	Montreal	1938	1958-1965	
4-6-4	H1e	2860-2864	5	Montreal	1940	1957-1961	
4-8-2	I1a	2900, 2901	2	CP	1914	1945, 1944	
		Built as classes H1a and H1b respectively and reclassified in 1929					
4-8-4	K1a	3100, 3101	2	CP	1928		
Shay	S1a, c	5901, 5903	2	Lima	1900, 1903	1914, 1913	

CENTRAL OF GEORGIA RAILWAY

At the turn of the century the Central of Georgia's routes sprawled across Georgia and much of eastern Alabama. From hubs at Macon and Columbus, Ga., lines reached to Atlanta, Savannah, Augusta, and Athens, Ga.; Chattanooga, Tennessee; and Birmingham, Montgomery, Andalusia, and Florala, Ala. The CofG was part of several passenger and freight routes between the Midwest and Florida, most of which funneled into the Atlantic Coast Line at Albany, Ga. In 1907 the road came under the control of E. H. Harriman, who sold his interest in the CofG to the Illinois Central (which he controlled) in 1909. The road reorganized in 1948 after 16 years of receivership, free of IC control and also without its previous long-standing financial interest in the Western Railway of Alabama.

By the end of World War II CofG had replaced its oldest 2-8-0s with diesel switchers from Electro-Motive, Alco, and Baldwin. A dozen EMD passenger diesels took over mainline passenger trains between 1946 and 1950. CofG received its only freight cab units, eight F3s, in 1947 and 1948; freight trains were dieselized with hood units in the early 1950s. Dieselization was complete on May 1, 1953.

Freight locomotives

Rogers built CofG's last three freight Ten-Wheelers in 1904. Their 61" drivers made them freight locomotives, but they were lighter than the passenger 4-6-0s Rogers had just delivered. The CofG turned to the 2-8-0 for freight service.

CofG's oldest Consolidations were 10 machines built by Baldwin in 1887 for the Columbus & Western Railway, a CofG subsidiary between Columbus and Birmingham. Larger 2-8-0s displaced them into switching service, and all but one were gone by 1930. Cooke built 22 Consolidations between 1901 and 1903. They had 55" drivers, weighed 193,400 pounds, and were intended for the Columbus-Birmingham route, which crossed the south end of the Appalachians. The next group of Consolidations came from Baldwin in 1904 and 1905 for faster, lighter freight trains elsewhere on the CofG. They had smaller cylinders and higher drivers (57") and weighed 161,830 pounds. Two years later 25 more light 2-8-0s arrived from Baldwin along with 25 heavy 2-8-0s. Both groups (later classified C-3 and C-4) had 57" drivers. The C-3s had 20" × 28" cylinders and weighed 163,390 pounds; the C-4s had 22" × 30" cylinders and weighed 203,100 pounds. In 1912 CofG bought 10 2-8-0s from its parent, Illinois Central. Although the IC engines weighed about as much as the C-4 class and had the same size cylinders, their 63" drivers made the engines faster but less powerful than the C-4s. In 1919 CofG rebuilt one into a 2-8-2, then rebuilt another in 1921. Pleased with the results, CofG sent the remaining eight to Alco's Richmond Works for conversion.

The first Mikados on CofG's roster were 15 built to a Harriman design by Baldwin in 1912, virtual duplicates of engines that IC had acquired the year before. They were superheated and had piston valves, Walschaerts valve gear, 63" drivers, and outside-bearing trailing trucks. Lima built four to the same design in 1915 and six more in 1916, the latter as part of an Illinois Central order. (Ten of those IC Mikes came to CofG secondhand in 1921.) The Lima 2-8-2s of 1923 were built along with Mikes for IC and Georgia Railroad. Ten 2-8-2s from Baldwin in 1926 gave CofG a total of 67 Harriman Mikes, all the same design.

In 1919 the road received 10 Mallets from Alco's Richmond Works. The compound 2-6-6-2s were 10,000 pounds lighter than the USRA 2-6-6-2, but had larger cylinders which gave them 8,000 pounds more tractive effort. They went to work as pushers on a grade out of Sylacauga, Ala., but proved too much locomotive for the railroad. In 1926 Central of Georgia traded them to Illinois Central for seven 2-10-2s. That same year CofG acquired ten new 2-10-2s from Baldwin, copies of the USRA heavy Santa Fe. On the CofG as on the Illinois Central they were known as the Central type and were initially given the classification CT. The 2-10-2s were much better suited to CofG's Birmingham route than the Mallets and could be used on other lines as well. In 1942 CofG bought two USRA heavy 2-10-2s from the Chicago & Eastern Illinois to handle a surge of wartime traffic.

Passenger locomotives

Not until after 1900 did CofG consider the Ten-Wheeler a passenger locomotive. Rogers delivered six 69"-drivered 4-6-0s in 1902 and five more in 1904. Some were eventually rebuilt with piston valves and Walschaerts valve gear.

The first Pacifics came from Baldwin in 1905 and 1906. They were typical early Pacifics, with slide valves and inboard-bearing trailing trucks. They had 68" drivers and weighed only 192,000 pounds, but could exert one third more tractive effort than the Ten-Wheelers. Ten heavier Pacifics arrived from Baldwin in 1912. They had 69" drivers and outside-journal trailing trucks and were built with superheaters; but at 239,500 pounds they were still light Pacifics.

The Central of Georgia needed new passenger locomotives after World War I and chose the Mountain type. Traffic between the Midwest and Florida had increased and steel cars had replaced wood; Pacifics were no longer able to handle the trains. The Pacifics bumped from mainline service by the 4-8-2s were assigned to secondary trains, replacing still older locomotives worn out by heavy wartime traffic. Between 1919 and 1926 Alco's Richmond Works and Baldwin delivered 32 4-8-2s to the CofG. All had the same dimensions; there were only minor evolutionary differences between successive groups. The first

Mikado 1846 (later 646) was built by Lima in 1923. The Harriman influence is evident in the straight boiler and the deep-arched cab roof. Lima photo.

Differences in details — pilot, smokebox front, Elesco coil-type feedwater heater, short tender — obscure the similarity between Central of Georgia's 4-8-4s (nicknamed "Big Apples") and Southern Pacific's GS-6 class. Photo by S. F. Lowe.

group was 481-490, then 491-497, 476-480, 471-475, and finally 466-470 (post-1925 numbers), with ascending builder numbers and ascending road numbers in each group.

At the beginning of World War II CofG had extra freight and passenger locomotives, but traffic to and from military posts on the railroad, primarily Fort Benning at Columbus, soon put them to work. Next the Florida trains outgrew the 4-8-2s. Because of wartime restrictions on new designs CofG ordered near-duplicates of Southern Pacific's GS-6 class 4-8-4. CofG's engines lacked the skyline casings and had Elesco coil-type feedwater heaters instead of the Worthington SA units of the SP engines. Turntable lengths dictated short eight-wheel tenders.

Switchers

Few of CofG's early 0-6-0s lasted until the 1925 renumbering. Thereafter the only switchers on the roster were a dozen 0-6-0s built by Baldwin in 1904 and 1906. Some were eventually rebuilt with superheaters and piston valves. Two other switchers deserve mention: In 1913 Alco's Rogers Works delivered two 0-4-0s intended for light duty. CofG sold them to the United Verde Copper Company of Jerome, Arizona, in 1918.

Recommended reading:

Central of Georgia Railway and Connecting Lines, by Richard E. Prince, published in 1976 by Richard E. Prince

Central of Georgia Railway Album, by W. Forrest Beckum, Jr. and Albert M. Langley, Jr., published in 1986 by Union Station Publishing, 785 Murrah Road, North Augusta, South Carolina 29841 (ISBN 0-9615257-1-1)

Published rosters: *Railroad Magazine*: December 1932, page 135; June 1948, page 116

CofG STEAM LOCOMOTIVES BUILT SINCE 1900

Type	Class	Numbers 1925	Pre-1925	Qty	Builder	Built	Retired	Notes
0-4-0			1191, 1192	2	Rogers	1913	Sold 1918	
0-6-0	S-1	50-61	1150-1161	12	Baldwin	1904-1906	1950-1953	
2-8-0	C-1	111-132	1011-1032	22	Cooke	1901-1903	1935-1946	
2-8-0	C-2	150-187	1050-1087	38	Baldwin	1904-1905	1934-1947	
2-8-0	C-3	200-224	1200-1224	25	Baldwin	1906-1907	1935-1953	
2-8-0	C-4	500-524	1700-1724	25	Baldwin	1906-1907	1950-1953	

CofG STEAM LOCOMOTIVES BUILT SINCE 1900

Type	Class	Numbers 1925	Pre-1925	Qty	Builder	Built	Retired	Notes
2-8-0			1751-1760	10	Brooks	1903		Rebuilt to 2-8-2s 1771-1780
2-8-2		571-580	1771-1780	10	Richmond	1919-1923		
2-8-2	MK	601-615	1801-1815	15	Baldwin	1912	1939-1952	
2-8-2	MK	616-627	1816-1827	10	Lima	1915-1916	1948-1952	
2-8-2	MK	628-637	1828-1837	10	Lima	1916	1948-1953	Ex-Illinois Central
2-8-2	MK	638-657	1838-1857	20	Lima	1923	1948-1953	
2-8-2	MK	658-667	1858-1867	10	Baldwin	1925	1952-1953	
2-10-2	J-1	701-710		10	Baldwin	1926	1950-1953	
2-10-2	J-2	711, 712		2	Baldwin	1918	1950	Ex-Chicago &Eastern Ilinois
2-10-2	J-3	771-777		7	Schen	1916-1918	1947-1943	Ex-Illinois Central 2601-2607
2-6-6-2	ML	790-799	1901-1910	10	Richmond	1919		To Illinois Central in 1926
4-6-0	T	400-410	1600-1610	11	Rogers	1902-1904	1935-1944	
4-6-0	T	297-299	1397-1399	3	Rogers	1904	1934	
4-6-2	P-1	414-428	1614-1628	15	Baldwin	1905-1906	1939-1952	
4-6-2	P-2	431-440	1651-1660	10	Baldwin	1912-1913	1935-1952	
4-6-2	P-2	441-444	1661-1664	4	Lima	1916	1950-1952	
4-8-2	MT	471-497	1671-1697	27	Richmond	1919-1925	1948-1953	
4-8-2	MT	466-470		5	Baldwin	1926	1951-1953	
4-8-4	K	451-458		8	Lima	1943	1953	

CENTRAL RAILROAD OF NEW JERSEY

The Central Railroad of New Jersey had an odd combination of routes. One line ran west from Jersey City through Bound Brook and High Bridge, N. J., to Easton and Allentown, Pennsylvania, then north through the anthracite-mining area to Wilkes-Barre and Scranton. The Jersey City-Allentown route was continued west to Harrisburg by the Reading; as far west as Bound Brook the Allentown route was part of the New York-Philadelphia-Washington route of the Reading and Baltimore & Ohio. The other line ran southwest through the unpopulated middle of southern New Jersey; it was connected to the rest of the CNJ by the New York & Long Branch, which CNJ and the Pennsylvania Railroad owned jointly. In 1901 the Reading acquired control of the CNJ, and the Baltimore & Ohio acquired control of the Reading. The CNJ essentially became the New York terminal railroad for the Reading and the B&O.

CNJ was an anthracite carrier, and anthracite culm was readily available for fuel — which meant Camelback locomotives. Its first non-Camel-back locomotives in the modern era arrived in 1918: Pacifics, Mikados, and six-wheel switchers — 10 USRA 0-6-0s built by Cooke and 6 stock Baldwin 0-6-0s. Pacifics, Mikes, and six- and eight-wheel switchers continued to arrive from the builders until 1930. No new locomotives were purchased for the commuter service, because CNJ planned to electrify.

In 1924 Alco, General Electric, and Ingersoll-Rand teamed up to build five 60-ton, 300-h.p. diesel switchers. CNJ purchased the first of them for its Bronx terminal — CNJ 1000 is considered the first commercially successful diesel locomotive. No more diesels arrived until the late 1930s, when CNJ began buying switchers. Cab diesels from Baldwin and EMD replaced steam on most mainline freights in 1947, and at the same time CNJ received six double-end passenger diesels from Baldwin, the only ones in North America — and a reminder of CNJ's double-end suburban tank locomotives. By April 1953 all but a few commuter trains were dieselized. Ten-Wheeler 774 made a ceremonial last run, and on July 1, 1954, CNJ announced it was totally dieselized.

Mikado 875, a 1922 Brooks product, was derived from the USRA light Mikado. The most noticeable modification of the USRA design is the wide firebox for burning anthracite. The paired single-stage air pumps aft of the Elesco feedwater pump are uncommon; it was more usual to use one or two cross-compound pumps. Photo by Donald W. Furler.

Freight locomotives

Until 1918 CNJ's most modern freight locomotives were the I5 and I4 2-8-0s of 1903-1906, and their immediate predecessors, a large group of 4-8-0s built by Brooks between 1899 and 1901. The Twelve-Wheelers and the I5 Consolidations had 55" drivers; the I4 Consolidations, which were newer than the I5s, had 61" drivers. They were drag freight locomotives. The Ten-Wheelers, which had 69" drivers, were used on fast freights.

The USRA assigned 10 light Mikados to the CNJ in 1918, setting the pattern for all of CNJ's 2-8-2s. Between 1920 and 1925 the road bought 56 more Mikes of the same dimensions, but with wider fireboxes. The later batches were built with Delta trailing trucks and Elesco feedwater heaters. A few were equipped with enormous 50-foot tenders.

Passenger locomotives

Central of New Jersey had four 4-4-0s built in the 20th century. Three of them, Brooks products of 1903, were the heaviest Americans, weighing 173,600 pounds (110 pounds more than Reading 400-419, not statistically significant). The fourth was an inspection engine on which the conventional cab at the rear was extended forward to the stack, creating a passenger-car-like body. Chairs were arranged on either side of the hump down the middle that was the boiler. Superintendents and presidents rode up front and inspected the line (it can't have been pleasant in July and August); the engineer could either look over their heads or lean out the window. A parallel role of the inspection engine was to haul one or two business cars.

Like its parent, the Reading, Central of New Jersey experimented with high-drivered Vauclain compound Atlantics, and in 1901 received six of them from Brooks. They weighed 191,000 pounds and had huge 85" drivers. In 1902 CNJ bought 3 light Atlantics (152,100 pounds) for trains to Atlantic City — the heavier 4-4-2s were restricted because of bridges on the route. They were, of course, Camelbacks, and they had 84¼" drivers. Rebuilding of both groups about 1910 added weight and reduced the driver size to 79". The six Atlantics of the P7 and P8 classes were built by the Reading in 1912: Camelback, 79" drivers, and 220,000 pounds engine weight. They looked old-fashioned compared to Pennsylvania Railroad's first E6 Atlantic of 1910.

CNJ's 111 20th-century Ten-Wheelers were built over a period of 18 years and were essentially the same locomotive, allowing for minor evolution: 69" drivers, 200- to 220-pound boiler pressure, cylinders increasing from 19" × 26" to 23" × 28", and total weight increasing from 175,000 pounds to 225,000 pounds. The Atlantics pulled the fast trains, the Consolidations and Twelve-Wheelers dragged the coal, and the Ten-Wheelers did all the jobs that were left over — and did them until the mid-1950s.

CNJ's first Pacifics were the six G-1s of 1918, 820-825. They had 79" drivers and looked like Reading's early Pacifics, but they had bigger boilers. They were intended for Jersey City-Philadelphia trains operated jointly with the Reading and the B&O. In 1918 the USRA allowed B&O passenger trains to use the Pennsylvania Railroad's station in New York, and the arrangement remained in effect until 1926. After B&O trains returned to CNJ's terminal in Jersey City, B&O locomotives

Built by Brooks in 1905, Central Railroad of New Jersey 852 and its two sisters were the heaviest 4-4-0s constructed.

began working through between Washington and Jersey City. In 1923 Baldwin delivered another five Pacifics that were almost the same, except for Delta trailing trucks. They were classified G-2 and numbered 826-830.

Five more Pacifics arrived from Baldwin in 1928, G-3s 831-835. They sported the 79" drivers of the previous classes, but had narrow fireboxes for burning soft coal and were equipped with stokers and Elesco feedwater heaters. Three were painted blue for the *Blue Comet* train of 1929. The five G-4 Pacifics of 1930 were similar to the G-3s except for having 74" drivers and welded tenders. They were intended for CNJ's lines in Pennsylvania, which had more grades and curves than the New Jersey routes.

Suburban tank engines

Short-distance passenger trains originated and terminated at several points that lacked turntables. The CNJ had simply run the 4-4-0s on these trains in both directions, adding a pilot and a headlight to the tender, but the flanges of the rear drivers wore quickly, because they bore the entire job of leading the locomotive into curves when running in reverse. In 1902 and 1903 Baldwin designed and built 20 2-6-2 tank engines. Their 63" drivers gave them a measure of speed, and two-wheel trucks fore and aft guided them into curves equally well in both directions. They carried coal in a small bunker behind the cab and

No locomotive more typified the Central of New Jersey than the Camelback Ten-Wheeler. Both 782 and 788 were built by Baldwin in 1918, relatively late for 4-6-0s and among the last Camelbacks built. Both locomotives have "triple-balanced wheels," in which the usual single counterweight is replaced by two located 120 degrees from the crankpin (the net counterbalancing effect was exactly the same). Photo of 782 by H. F. Harvey; photo of 788 by Robert P. Morris.

water in rectangular tanks on each side of the boiler. In 1912 CNJ bought five similar locomotives from the Long Island Rail Road.

When suburban trains were equipped with steel coaches heavier locomotives became necessary. Baldwin built five 63-drivered 4-6-4Ts with wide fireboxes for anthracite coal and Elesco feedwater heaters. They carried fuel behind the cab and water in a tank that wrapped around the coal bunker and under the cab.

Switchers

Between 1901 and 1915 CNJ bought or built 101 0-6-0s and 25 0-8-0s, all Camelbacks. The sudden surge of traffic moving to the port of New York during World War I resulted in the addition of 16 0-6-0s to CNJ's roster, 10 USRA machines and 6 of the type Baldwin built and kept in stock for industries and contractors. The modernization of CNJ's roster during the 1920s included 5 large 0-6-0s and 30 0-8-0s.

Historical and technical society: Anthracite Railroads Historical Society, P. O. Box 519, Lansdale, PA 19446-0519

Recommended reading: *Locomotives of the Jersey Central*, by Warren B Crater, published in 1978 by Railroadians of America, 270 West Colfax Avenue, Roselle Park, NJ 07204

Published rosters: *Railroad Magazine*: June 1935, page 135; August 1951, page 109; January 1968, page 52 (1930 roster)

CNJ STEAM LOCOMOTIVES BUILT SINCE 1900

Type	Class 1919	Class 1945	Numbers	Qty	Builder	Built	Retired	Notes
0-4-0T	A1	4S22	840	1	Baldwin	1907	1954	
0-6-0	B2	6S23	50-100	51	Brooks, BLW	1902-1905	1930-1951	Camelback
0-6-0	B3	6S31	1-8	8	Brooks	1901	1934-1952	Camelback
0-6-0	B3a	6S31	9-23	15	Brooks	1902-1906	1934-1954	Camelback
0-6-0	B3b	6S31	24-33	10	CNJ	1910	1947-1954	Camelback
0-6-0	B4	6S34	34-49	16	CNJ	1912-1915	1945-1954	Camelback
0-6-0	B5	6S38	135-140	6	Baldwin	1918	1950-1952	
0-6-0	B6s	6S39	101-110	10	Cooke	1918	1954-1955	USRA
0-6-0	B7s	6S46	111-115	5	Schenectady	1923	1953-1955	
0-8-0	E1	8S53	270-294	25	Schen, BLW	1912-1918	1948-1954	Camelback
0-8-0	E2s	8S53	295-304	10	Schenectady	1923	1951-1955	
0-8-0	E3s	8S61	305-314	10	Baldwin	1927	1952-1955	
0-8-0	E4s	8S64	315-319	5	Baldwin	1929	1955	
0-8-0	E4as	8S64	320-324	5	Baldwin	1930	1955	
2-6-2T	J1	SU23	200-219	20	Baldwin	1902-1903	1935-1945	
2-6-2T	J1	SU23	220-224	5	Baldwin	1904	1945	Ex-Long Island
4-6-4T	H1s	SU31	225-230	5	Baldwin	1923	1947-1950	
2-8-0	I5	C44	650-665	16	Brooks	1903, 1905	1934-1940	Camelback
2-8-0	I4		675-684	10	Brooks	1906	1948-1953	Camelback
2-8-2	M1s	M63	850-859	10	Brooks	1918	1947	USRA
2-8-2	M2s	M63	860-870	11	Brooks	1920	1947-1952	
2-8-2	M2as	M63	871-895	25	Brooks	1922	1947-1955	
2-8-2	M3s	M63	896-915	20	Schenectady	1923	1947-1952	
2-8-2	M3as	M63	916-935	20	Baldwin	1925	1951-1955	
4-4-0	D9s		557-559	3	Brooks	1905	1934	Camelback
4-4-0	Insp		900	1	Baldwin	1903	1937	Renumbered 999 in 1923
4-4-2	P1a		572-574	3	Baldwin	1902	1928-1930	Camelback
4-4-2	P6s	A28	590-595	6	Brooks	1901-1902	1946-1947	Camelback
4-4-2	P7s		803-805	3	Reading	1912	1935-1937	Camelback
4-4-2	P8		800-802	3	Reading	1912	1938-1940	Camelback
4-6-0	L3	T26	600-630	31	Brooks	1902	1934-1950	Camelback
4-6-0	L3s	T34	631-635	5	Baldwin	1902	1946-1950	Camelback,
4-6-0	L5	T28	150-166	17	Brooks	1900-1901	1934-1952	Camelback
4-6-0	L5a		167, 168	2	Brooks	1902	1936	Camelback
4-6-0	L5b	T32	169-174	6	Brooks	1903	1936-1953	Camelback
4-6-0	L5c	T32	175-184	10	Brooks	1906	1934-1953	Camelback
4-6-0	L6as		750-759	10	Baldwin	1910	1953-1954	Camelback
4-6-0	L7s	T38	760-769	10	Baldwin	1912	1948-1954	Camelback
4-6-0	L7as	T38	770-779	10	Baldwin	1913-1914	1950-1956	Camelback
4-6-0	L8s	T40	780-789	10	Baldwin	1918	1950-1954	Camelback
4-6-2	G1s	P43	820-825	6	Baldwin	1918	1948-1954	
4-6-2	G2s	P43	826-830	5	Baldwin	1923	1953-1955	
4-6-2	G3s	P47	831-835	5	Baldwin	1928	1950-1955	
4-6-2	G4s	P52	810-814	5	Baldwin	1930	1954-1955	
4-8-0	K1	TW40	430-480	51	Brooks	1899-1901	1934-1948	Camelback

CENTRAL VERMONT RAILWAY

In 1898, after several decades of financial ups and downs, the Central Vermont came under control of the Grand Trunk Railway. Its map looked much as it does today. a main line from the north end of Lake Champlain southeast across Vermont to the Connecticut River at White River Junction, south along the river to the Massachusetts border (partly on Boston & Maine rails), then southeast again to tidewater at New London, Connecticut — plus a few minor branches and (then but not now) a steamship line from New London to New York.

CV interchanged a considerable amount of traffic to and from Boston with the Boston & Maine at White River Junction. Traffic also moved to and from the B&M along the Connecticut River, so that the CV south of East Northfield, Massachusetts, was branchline in character.

Most CV steam power was equipped with feedwater heaters. The 2-10-4s were built with Elesco units, while the 4-8-2s had Coffin feedwater heaters concealed in their smokeboxes. Smaller locomotives were retrofitted with feedwater heaters, usually Elesco, but many 2-8-0s carried Coffin feedwater heaters on their smokebox fronts, and a few 4-6-0s carried them over the smokebox, like a horse collar.

CV was the last railroad in New England to dieselize. Steam remained active in early 1957, when the New Haven and the Boston & Maine were replacing their first-generation diesels. The last run of a CV steam locomotive was April 4, 1957 — 4-8-2 No. 602 on a freight train — and on May 20 that year two CN 4-8-4s took extra sections of the *Montrealer* from White River Junction to Montreal.

Freight locomotives

Central Vermont's standard freight engine until 1928 was the 2-8-0. Six were delivered by Alco in 1915 and 1916. In 1923, the year CV's parent, Grand Trunk, became part of Canadian National Railways, 16 more arrived, all owned by CN and leased to CV.

CV is best known for ten 2-10-4s built by Alco at Schenectady in 1928. At 419,000 pounds they were the lightest 2-10-4s built for service in North America. Even so, they were restricted to CV's main line north

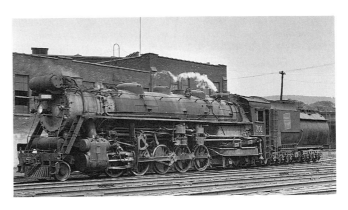

Central Vermont's biggest locomotives — and the heaviest in New England — were ten 2-10-4s built in 1928. Cab, tender, frame, feedwater heater, and number indicator all show the influence of owner Canadian National Railways. Rail Photo Service photo by H. W. Pontin.

of Brattleboro, Vermont. Their 60" drivers, which limited them to 35 mph, and their modest grate area (84.4 square feet — Pennsy's J1 had 121.7 square feet) indicated they were drag-freight engines, really 2-10-2s with another axle to spread the weight. But they looked impressive, and they survived into the mid-1950s (the last was scrapped in 1959), long after steam had disappeared from neighboring railroads.

Passenger locomotives

CV's first modern locomotives were three Pacifics delivered by Baldwin in 1912. In 1915 and 1916 CV received four Ten-Wheelers — a regression of a sort. From April 1925 to July 1927 CV leased five ex-Grand Trunk 4-6-2s from parent CN until the delivery in 1927 of four racy 4-8-2s intended for CV's leg of such Boston-Montreal and New York-Montreal trains as the *Montrealer* and the *Ambassador*. Like the 1923 locomotives, they were owned by CNR and leased to CV. They were about the same size as Florida East Coast's 400-series 4-8-2s.

Switchers

CV took delivery of three 0-6-0s from Lima in 1912. In 1923 it acquired eight 0-8-0s, built by Alco at Schenectady. They were owned by CN and leased to CV.

Historical and technical society: Central Vermont Railway Historical Society, 5806 Edith Court, Virginia Beach, VA 23464.

Recommended reading: *Canadian National Steam Power*, by Anthony Clegg and Ray Corley, published in 1969 by Trains & Trolleys, Box 1434, Station B, Montreal 110, PQ, Canada.

Published rosters: *Railroad Magazine*: December 1935, page 88; August 1947, page 117

CV STEAM LOCOMOTIVES BUILT SINCE 1900

Type	Class	Numbers	Qty	Builder	Built	Scrapped	Notes
0-6-0	O-9-a	387-389	3	Lima	1912	1952-1954	
0-8-0	P-1-a	500-507	8	Schenectady	1923	1956-1959	
2-8-0	M-2-a	400-408	9	Schenectady	1905	1944-1954	4 to Canadian National, 1942
2-8-0	N-4-h	409-418	10	Schenectady	1906	1957-1961	4 to Canadian National, 1928
2-8-0	M-3-a	450-455	6	Schenectady	1916	1955-1960	All to Canadian National, 1928 Ex-420-425
2-8-0	N-5-a	460-475	16	Schenectady	1923	1955-1960	
2-10-4	T-3-a	700-709	10	Schenectady	1928	1954-1959	
4-6-0	I-6	211-217	3	Schenectady	1904, 1906	1928-1941	
4-6-0	I-7-a	218-221	4	Schenectady	1915-1916	1943-1955	
4-6-2	K-3-b	230-232	3	Baldwin	1912	1952-1954	
4-8-2	U-1-a	600-603	4	Schenectady	1927	1956-1959	

CHESAPEAKE & OHIO RAILWAY

At the beginning of the 20th century the Chesapeake & Ohio extended from Newport News, Virginia, west through Richmond and the coalfields of West Virginia to Cincinnati, Ohio. C&O reached Washington, D. C., and Louisville, Kentucky, by trackage rights on Southern and Louisville & Nashville, respectively. The road was affiliated with the New York Central and had close ties with NYC's Big Four (Cleveland, Cincinnati, Chicago & St. Louis) subsidiary.

C&O was a major coal hauler, and the Midwest was becoming a better market for coal than the East. In 1903 the C&O and four other roads acquired joint ownership of the Hocking Valley Railroad, which extended from Galipolis, Ohio, on the Ohio River, north-northwest across Ohio to Toledo; by 1911 C&O had acquired control of the HV. C&O gained a second outlet to the Great Lakes in 1910 with the purchase of the Chicago, Cincinnati & Louisville Railroad, a line from Cincinnati northwest to Hammond, Indiana. The Cincinnati-Chicago line never achieved better than stepchild status; the Hocking Valley

was to be C&O's primary outlet to the Great Lakes. In 1917 the Hocking Valley was connected to the C&O proper by trackage rights on the Norfolk & Western and a new bridge across the Ohio River near Portsmouth, Ohio. C&O built its own line parallel to the N&W in the 1920s and merged the Hocking Valley in 1930.

In 1923 C&O came under the control of the Van Sweringen brothers of Cleveland, who also controlled the Nickel Plate, the Erie, the Pere Marquette, and the Hocking Valley. The railroads had a joint mechanical advisory committee, and their later locomotives share many design features.

C&O believed in tailoring its locomotives to specific routes and services. A Washington-Cincinnati passenger train might have a Pacific from Washington to Charlottesville (115 miles), a 4-8-4 over the mountains from Charlottesville to Hinton (169 miles), and a 4-6-4 from Hinton to Cincinnati (308 miles) — and the two-car local from Cincinnati to Hammond, Indiana, was usually pulled by an Atlantic. Another

C&O's 2-10-4s proved the validity of Lima's Super-Power concept: T-1 3032 could pull the same train as a 2-8-8-2 — and do it faster. Photo by W. G. Fancher.

part of C&O's motive-power philosophy was the avoidance of double-heading. C&O was the diametric opposite of the Pennsylvania Railroad, which had hundreds of K4-class Pacifics on all types of passenger trains across its system, and often doubleheaded them.

The steepest part of the main line was the 80 miles from Clifton Forge west to Hinton, with a 1.14 percent ruling grade westbound and a 0.57 percent ruling grade eastbound. Freight bypassed the mountains west of Charlottesville on a line that paralleled the James River from Richmond to Clifton Forge.

C&O purchased its last new steam locomotives in 1949, then dieselized quickly between 1949 and 1956.

Before C&O adopted a new number scheme in 1924, some of its locomotives were renumbered five or six times. The 1924 numbers are used here in both text and roster. C&O occasionally reused class letters, usually for locomotives acquired through merger.

Freight locomotives

C&O received its first 2-8-0s in 1881. By 1900 the road's state-of-the-art 2-8-0 was the G-6. It had 56" drivers and a long, narrow firebox above the frames, and it weighed 186,500 pounds, fairly heavy for the time. The G-7 of 1903 was an improvement on the design, with a wide firebox above the drivers and inboard piston valves. Alco's Richmond Works built 180 of them; Baldwin built 25. In 1916 Pittsburgh built six more G-7 Consolidations, which had larger cylinders, superheaters, and Walschaerts valve gear — and by then C&O was adding those improvements to the earlier G-7s. The two G-8s had larger boilers than the G-7s and apparently warranted neither duplication nor immediate scrapping. The 50 G-9s were duplicates of the G-7s except for Walschaerts valve gear.

C&O acquired numerous groups of Consolidations by merger. It reused old, long-vacated classes for Hocking Valley and Pere Marquette engines; most of those engines remained in service until dieselization. The small 2-8-0s acquired with short lines were generally of little use and were sold or scrapped soon after acquisition, sometimes before C&O numbers were painted on the cab.

About 1910 C&O needed bigger, faster locomotives. It bought 4-8-2s for passenger service and and 2-6-6-2s for freight on the mountainous portion of the main line and asked Alco to design a 2-8-2 for freight service east and west of the Alleghenies. Alco's Richmond Works delivered a single Mikado at the end of 1911, about six months after C&O received the first 4-8-2s. The class K-1 2-8-2 was basically the same as the J-1 4-8-2 except for a two-wheel lead truck and 56" drivers instead of 63"; many components were the same. It was 3' shorter and weighed 7,000 pounds less, but carried 3,000 pounds more on its drivers. After testing the 2-8-2, C&O ordered 49 more, which were delivered in 1912; six more arrived in 1914. In 1912 and 1913 Richmond built 11 near-duplicates for the Hocking Valley, which by then was under C&O control. In 1930 the HV engines came to C&O as class K (later K-1). In the mid-1920s C&O altered their appearance by moving the air pumps to the front of the smokebox and giving them smaller cabs; the distinctive inboard-bearing trailing truck and outboard ashpan hoppers remained.

By the early 1920s the K-1s had been overtaken by technology. C&O ordered two batches of up-to-date 2-8-2s from Richmond, 50 K-2s and 50 K-3s. The K-2s had boosters and weighed 358,000 pounds; the K-3s lacked boosters but had larger fireboxes and longer piston stroke and weighed 355,000 pounds. (C&O considered the K-2 a "light" Mikado and the K-3 a "heavy" Mikado; even though the K-2 was heavier than the K-3.) Both were heavy when compared to USRA Mikes — or to the USRA light 2-10-2. Richmond built 50 more Mikes in 1923 and 1924, a slightly heavier version of the K-3 that was classed K-3A.

The K-5, K-6, and K-8 Mikes were Pere Marquette engines. The K-5s were updated copies of the USRA light Mikado, and the K-8s were USRA light Mikados that came to the Pere Marquette in 1920 secondhand from Indiana Harbor Belt, Wabash, and New York Central. The K-6 class consisted of five former Erie 2-8-2s that Pere Marquette had purchased in 1929. The K-7 class was vacant and may have been intended for three 2-8-2s that were scrapped within a year of the C&O-Pere Marquette merger. C&O used the M class for a handful of small 2-8-2s that were acquired with short lines and sold or scrapped soon afterward.

C&O bought no 2-10-2s of its own, but acquired 34 of the type secondhand. In 1920 and 1922 the Hocking Valley bought 16 nearly new 2-10-2s from the Lehigh Valley. They had wide fireboxes for burning a mixture of anthracite and bituminous coal, inboard-bearing trailing trucks, and outboard ashpan hoppers. When C&O merged Hocking Valley in 1930 C&O sold six (two to the Pere Marquette) and kept ten, which it used principally between Clifton Forge and Washington. C&O gave some of them its characteristic pumps-on-the-smokebox look.

During World War II the road ran short of locomotives and in 1945 bought seven 2-10-2s from Chicago & Eastern Illinois. C&EI 2000, 2001, and 2003-2005 became class B-2; C&EI 4000 and 4001 (built as Wabash 2513 and 2509) became class B-3. The Pere Marquette merger brought two groups of 2-10-2s to C&O's roster: two ex-Hocking Valley, ex-Lehigh Valley engines that went right into class B-1 with their old stablemates, and 15 smaller 2-10-2s.

C&O assigned its second group of simple 2-8-8-2s to coal trains moving from Russell, Ky., to Columbus, Ohio. There the trains were split up and Hocking Valley 2-10-2s and 2-6-6-2s forwarded them to Toledo. As soon as the entire Russell-Toledo line was C&O property, though, the road wanted a locomotive that could take coal trains the entire distance, eliminating an engine change, and do the job faster. C&O tested an Erie Berkshire and decided the concept was good, but it wanted something bigger and heavier — and it got a 2-10-4 with 69" drivers. With booster cut in the 2-10-4 equalled the tractive effort of the 2-8-8-2, though crews were skeptical at first. The T-1s introduced the four-wheel trailing truck and the outside-journal lead truck to the C&O. They didn't look like C&O power: the air pumps were tucked away behind shields on the pilot beam, a big rectangular tender replaced the long Vanderbilt tanks C&O had been using for a decade, and the smokebox door was round (but not much larger than the oval door C&O had been squeezing between the airpumps). The road was pleased with their performance and considered buying more to use on the main line, but instead stretched the 2-10-4 into the 2-6-6-6, just as the 2-8-4 had been stretched into the 2-10-4. The T-1s remained on the Russell-

The first 2-6-6-2 on the road's roster was No. 751 (later 1301) photographed outside Alco's Schenectady Works. It was the first articulated to have a full-size trailing truck supporting a firebox entirely behind the drivers. The outside dry pipe from the steam dome to the high-pressure cylinders was replaced by an inside pipe on later C&O 2-6-6-2s. Alco photo.

Toledo run until they were replaced by 2-6-6-6s in 1948. A few were moved east to tidewater Virginia, but were scrapped soon afterward.

In the early 1940s C&O noticed that the Mikados that powered freight trains on the flatter parts of the system were no longer the best, biggest, heaviest power that money could buy. The Erie, Nickel Plate, and Pere Marquette, which for some years had been under the same control, all made good use of the 2-8-4 for fast freight service, and C&O chose that type, assisted by the War Production Board, which specified use of an existing locomotive design. C&O based its 2-8-4 on the Nickel Plate and Pere Marquette engines, and Alco delivered 40 in late 1943 and early 1944. Like the other Van Sweringen Berkshires they had 69″ drivers, and their 26″ × 34″ cylinders were identical to those of Pere Marquette's 2-8-4s. C&O classed them K-4 and named the type Kanawha, after the river that paralleled the main line; the crews called them "Big Mikes." They went to work in Newport News-Clifton Forge and Hinton-

Cincinnati freight service and Clifton Forge-Hinton and Ashland-Louisville passenger service. Lima delivered 10 more in 1945 and another 10 in 1947; Alco built the final 30 of the class in 1947.

Pere Marquette's Berkshires joined the C&O roster in 1947, but because of equipment trust provisions most were not relettered and numbered for C&O. As the former PM lines became dieselized a few 2-8-4s were moved to lines in Ohio and West Virginia, but most of the PM 2-8-4s were stored, some not to be scrapped until 1961.

Articulateds

In 1910 C&O's standard coal train power was a G-7 or G-9 Consoli-

Baldwin's last steam locomotives for U. S. service were ten compound 2-6-6-2s built in 1949 to the same basic design as C&O's first engine of that type, built in 1910. Photo by Gene L. Huddleston.

Chesapeake & Ohio's 2-8-8-2s were the first nonexperimental simple articulateds. Number 1541 and 2-10-4 3016 lead a long coal train north through Linworth, Ohio. The number of appliances and the amount of piping on 1541 borders on the incredible. Photo by Richard E. Dill.

dation, good for about 30 loaded steel hopper cars; it required a pusher over the steepest part of the line. In considering larger locomotives, the road calculated that a 2-8-2 could pull another seven or eight cars — but a 2-6-6-2 could pull 20 more cars and not need a pusher. Alco's Schenectady Works built such a locomotive in 1910. It differed in two respects from contemporary Mallets: it had a combustion chamber ahead of the firebox and an outside-bearing radial trailing truck. As it did with its first 2-8-2, C&O tested the locomotive and quickly ordered 24 more. The first was classified H-1; the successors were sufficiently improved that they constituted a separate class, H-2. In the late 1920s the H-1 and H-2s were shouldered aside by 2-8-8-2s, 2-10-4s, and newer 2-6-6-2s; they were all scrapped by 1935.

In 1911 C&O purchased a single 2-6-6-2 from the Chicago & Alton. Designated H-3, it was smaller, lighter, and of an older design than the H-1 and H-2. The reason for its purchase is a mystery (as was C&A's purchase of three of them in the first place), but C&O kept the locomotive in service until the late 1920s.

Chesapeake & Ohio liked its big 2-6-6-2s. Between 1912 and 1918 Alco's Schenectady and Richmond plants built 150 H-4s, which were 35,000 pounds heavier than the H-2s. In 1927 C&O rebuilt H-4 No. 1470 to a simple articulated. Its tractive effort was just halfway between that of an H-4 in normal, compound mode and an H-4 operating as a simple engine. The rebuild wasn't worth duplicating but neither did it warrant immediate scrapping. In 1919 the USRA allocated 20 2-6-6-2s — 15 from Schenectady and 5 from Baldwin — to the C&O. These USRA articulateds, class H-5, were 13,000 pounds heavier than C&O's own design, had high-pressure cylinders an inch larger, and had 540 square feet more heating surface. Each of C&O's 2-6-6-2 designs had less heating surface than the previous one. (Generally, the more flues or tubes, the greater the heating surface, the greater the fuel efficiency, and the greater the number of joints that can eventually leak. Fuel efficiency may not have been important; coal was cheap and plentiful where C&O ran its 2-6-6-2s.) C&O returned to its own design for 45 H-6 2-6-6-2s between 1920 and 1923.

Even before the last of the H-6s were delivered C&O wanted something larger, but tight tunnels kept the road from using what was then the next size larger, the compound 2-8-8-2. The huge low-pressure cylinders of 2-8-8-2s were the focus of the clearance problem, so the road designed a simple 2-8-8-2. The boiler was as large as clearances allowed, limiting stack, sand dome, and steam dome size. The firebox was over the rear two pairs of 57" drivers and a full-size cast trailing truck (other contemporary 2-8-8-2s had inboard-bearing trailing trucks that served mainly to guide the locomotive when backing). The boiler diameter was great enough that the air pumps had to be hung on the front of the smokebox on either side of a tiny oval door; an Elesco feedwater heater was mounted above them. The resulting front-end arrangement quickly became the standard C&O "face."

Alco delivered 25 H-7s in 1923 and 1924, the first large group of simple articulateds anywhere. C&O named them the Chesapeake type (a name that was quickly filed away with other forgotten wheel arrangement names like Calumet and St. Paul) and put them to work between Clifton Forge and Hinton. Baldwin delivered 20 more, class H-7-A, in 1926 for service between Russell and Columbus. The 2-8-8-2s were displaced from the Ohio line in 1930 by 2-10-4s, and after the 2-6-6-6s began arriving from Lima they were out of work. They were too large for the branch lines. C&O scrapped one in 1943, sold three to the Richmond, Fredericksburg & Potomac for hump duty that same year, and sold 30 to Union Pacific in 1945. C&O found work for the rest in hump yard and helper service; they were scrapped in 1952.

C&O's quest for ever-heavier locomotives culminated in the Allegheny, class H-8. In the late 1930s the articulated underwent a transformation on most roads from a drag engine to a fast freight hauler — from compound 2-8-8-2 to simple 4-6-6-4. At the beginning of World War II the H-7s were nearly 20 years old, and C&O had a decade of experience with its 2-10-4s, which were just as powerful and much faster. The road considered additional 2-10-4s to replace the 2-8-8-2s between Clifton Forge and Hinton, but Lima instead proposed a six-coupled articulated with high drivers (67") and a huge firebox that required a six-wheel trailing truck. Total engine weight was 771,300 pounds, and the axle loading was the highest in the world (84,650 pounds per driving axle, average; the first driving axle carried 86,700 pounds). The tender was large enough to require an eight-wheel truck at the rear. Lima delivered the first 10 Alleghenies in 1941 and by the end of 1944 C&O had 45 of them. The last 15 came from Lima in late 1948. They were used primarily on coal trains and were quite successful, but rarely had a chance to show their speed and horsepower.

After World War II C&O had to replace the 2-6-6-2s that worked the mine branches, and decided to replace them in kind — with a compound 2-6-6-2 that was an updated H-1 of 1910. In 1949 it ordered 25 2-6-6-2s from Baldwin, but soon found itself in a financial bind because of a long miners strike and trimmed the order to 10 — the last steam locomotives Baldwin built for service in the United States.

Passenger locomotives

C&O's only Americans and Ten-Wheelers built in the 20th century were former Chicago, Cincinnati & Louisville and Hocking Valley engines acquired with those roads. C&O stored the HV 4-4-0s for several years and retired them in 1935 (the last of C&O's own 4-4-0s had been scrapped in 1929). The Ten-Wheelers had longer lives, and one of the CC&L 4-6-0s, No. 377, has been preserved.

In 1902 C&O took delivery of three Atlantics and two Pacifics from Alco's Schenectady Works. Between 1903 and 1907 the road received 16 more Atlantics from Schenectady and Richmond, and one final 4-4-2 was delivered by Pittsburgh in 1916. The two Pacifics and all but the last Atlantic were standard turn-of-the-century engines with inside piston valves, Stephenson valve gear, 72" drivers, and inboard-bearing trailing trucks; the last Atlantic (No. 80, later 278) was superheated and had Walschaerts gear, 73" drivers, and outboard valves instead. In the early 1920s C&O rebuilt the earlier Atlantics to match No. 80. A few Atlantics

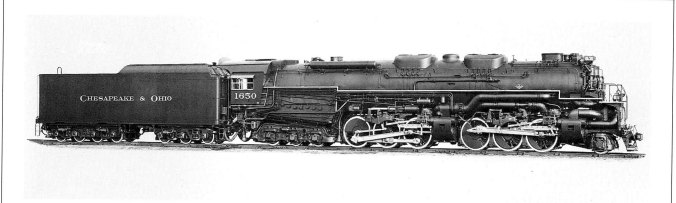

2-6-6-6 — ALLEGHENY

In 1929 Lima Locomotive Works proposed a two-cylinder 2-12-6 freight locomotive that would be the equivalent of contemporary 2-8-8-2s. It had huge cylinders set out ahead of the lead truck and large firebox supported by a six-wheel trailing truck that carried drawbar forces. The design remained simply a proposal.

In 1930 C&O bought 2-10-4s to replace 2-8-8-2s because it believed a high-drivered articulated was impossible. The 2-10-4s turned out to be excellent engines, and the road contemplated buying more in the late 1930s to replace 2-8-8-2s on its main line. By then the high-drivered simple articulated was a reality — neighbor Norfolk & Western's 70"-drivered class A 2-6-6-4, for example. C&O decided it wanted more than a 2-10-4. Even if cast frames and improvements in main rods made six coupled axles possible, the curves of C&O's main line wouldn't have been compatible

Chesapeake & Ohio named the 2-6-6-6 the Allegheny type for the mountain range its main line crossed. Lima photo.

with an updated version of that 2-12-6. The resulting engine was a divided 2-12-6: a 2-6-6-6 with 67" drivers. Lima built 60 for C&O between 1941 and 1948 and 8, virtual copies of the C&O engines, for the Virginian Railway in 1945. Virginian's 2-6-6-6s were retired in 1955 and scrapped in January 1960. A few C&O Alleghenies remained in service until June or July 1956.

Other names: Blue Ridge (Virginian)
First: Chesapeake & Ohio 1600, December 1941
Last: C&O 1659, December 1948
Greatest number: C&O, 60
Heaviest: C&O 1600-1644, 778,000 pounds (the heaviest reciprocating steam locomotives ever built)
Lightest: C&O 1645-1659, 751,830 pounds

were retired in the late 1930's; 13 remained on the roster until 1949.

The 1902 Pacifics followed Missouri Pacific's first 4-6-2, the first real North American Pacific, by only a few weeks. Between 1903 and 1911 C&O received 25 Pacifics of the same design, mostly from Richmond. Between 1915 and 1924 the road rebuilt and upgraded them, just as it had the Atlantics. The F-16 Pacifics of 1913 were considerably larger than the F-15s, weighing 290,000 pounds, half again as much. A year later Richmond delivered the F-17 class, which were even heavier and had 69" drivers; they were considered the most powerful 4-6-2s at the time, and they were intended to supplant the three 4-8-2s on the mountainous section of the main line. Nine years later Richmond delivered five almost identical Pacifics, class F-18. The F-19s came in 1926: They had 74" drivers and were C&O's first Pacifics to have air pumps mounted on the front of the smokebox, but were lighter than the previous two classes. In the early 1930s the F-16, F-17, and F-18 classes were rebuilt with 74" drivers and had their air pumps moved to the smokebox. In 1947 C&O purchased four Pacifics from the Richmond, Fredericksburg & Potomac. They were RF&P's heaviest, about the same size as the F-19s. That same year C&O acquired two groups of light Pacifics when it merged the Pere Marquette. Neither group remained in C&O service long; few were relettered and renumbered for C&O.

By 1910 traffic had increased to the point that passenger trains required doubleheaded Pacifics over the Alleghenies. C&O wanted to avoid doubleheading, and conferred with American Locomotive Company to develop a new locomotive type that combined the eight drivers of the Mikado and the four-wheel lead truck of the Pacific. Alco's Richmond Works built two 4-8-2s for C&O in 1911, and the wheel arrangement was christened the Mountain type. A third came in 1912. They differed from most later 4-8-2s in having drivers only 62" in diameter and main rods connected to the third axle. C&O found the drive wheels too small for passenger-train speeds and went back to heavy Pacifics. During World War I, though, the road returned to the Mountain type with five USRA heavy 4-8-2s, three built by Brooks in 1918 and two by Baldwin in 1919. Two more were delivered by Richmond in 1923.

In the early 1930s C&O upgraded its through passenger trains, extending service north through Columbus and Toledo to Detroit on the former Hocking Valley line. The road needed a more powerful locomotive than the rebuilt Pacifics and Mountains and, pleased with its 2-10-4s, turned to a 4-8-4 that shared many of their design traits. Lima built five in 1935; C&O called them Greenbriers and named each for a Virginia statesman. Two more were delivered in 1942. They were 30,000 pounds heavier and introduced a new C&O face: headlight mounted just above the pilot beam, oval number plate at the center of the smokebox door, and illuminated number boards at the top of the smokebox. The first five Greenbriers were soon given the same appearance.

C&O ordered five more 4-8-4s, delivered in mid-1948. Diesels took over passenger duties in 1951, and the older 4-8-4s, which were due for major repairs, were stored and scrapped. The J-3-A class was placed in freight service east of Clifton Forge for a year, then stored. Three were taken from storage in 1955 because of a surge in freight traffic; they worked between Russell, Kentucky, and Hinton. At the same time C&O leased 10 4-8-4s from Richmond, Fredericksburg & Potomac and found itself with two locomotives of the same type numbered 614. C&O renumbered its own 614 to 611, the original 611 having been scrapped. That locomotive is still in existence, restored to its original number.

At the beginning of the 1940s C&O passenger trains were outgrowing the Pacifics even on the flatter sections of the line. The road ordered eight 4-6-4s from Baldwin. They had boilers almost identical to those used on Nickel Plate and Pere Marquette 2-8-4s, 78" drivers, and roller bearings on all axles. In addition, No. 300, the first of the series, sported roller-bearing side and main rods. These L-2s were the heaviest Hudsons built until five more Hudsons, the L-2-A class, were delivered by Baldwin in 1948. These were 3,500 pounds heavier, the heaviest Hudsons of all. (They were ordered with streamlined shrouds, which would have made them even heavier.) The L-2s were assigned primarily to passenger trains between Hinton and Cincinnati.

Between the two groups of L-2 Hudsons came the L-1 class. (When the first L-2s were built, the L-1 class was used for an electric shop

C&O had the first Mountain type and the heaviest Hudson, but the F-19 Pacific epitomizes Chesapeake & Ohio passenger power. Number 491 displays the C&O "flying pumps" face, with (top to bottom) Elesco feedwater heater, bell, paired cross-compound air pumps, low-mounted headlight, and slatted pilot. Photo by Lucius Beebe.

locomotive.) The Newport News and Louisville sections of the new *Chessie* needed fast, streamlined locomotives, nothing as elaborate as the turbines planned for the main Washington-Cincinnati run of the train, but something more than a Pacific. C&O elected to convert the F-19 Pacifics into streamlined Hudsons. The boilers were rebuilt, and the locomotives were given new frames, poppet valves, and roller bearings all around. Feedwater heaters were swapped with the F-17 class, and four of the five received stainless steel shrouding to match the Budd-built cars of the *Chessie*. The *Chessie* never entered service, and the L-1s went to work on ordinary trains, primarily from Charlottesville east to Washington and Newport News.

Switchers

In the early part of the 20th century the C&O wasn't a major user of switchers. It was primarily a coal carrier, and in those days coal wasn't a specialized commodity that required sorting, classification, and switching. It was simply assembled into long trains and sent on its way. Later, as industries required different grades and types of coal, C&O's switcher fleet grew. Just as C&O's road locomotives were often the heaviest of their type, the switchers were also big. C&O's only conventional 0-6-0s built after 1900 were ten assigned to the Covington & Cincinnati Elevated Railroad & Transfer & Bridge Company.

In 1903 C&O acquired an 0-8-0 to switch the yard at Clifton Forge. The 0-6-0s that worked there couldn't handle the trains brought in by the 2-8-0s, and a grade made matters worse. Richmond delivered another C-8 in 1906, and a duplicate joined the roster when C&O took over the rail operations of Island Creek Coal Company. The next switchers C&O acquired were 15 heavy 0-10-0s built by Richmond in 1919 and 1921.

C&O's first modern switchers were ten 0-8-0s delivered by Lima in 1925. They were classified C-15 and numbered 100-109; they were slightly heavier than USRA 0-8-0s. The 1930 merger of the Hocking Valley added ten identical 0-8-0s, HV 100-109. C&O renumbered them 70-79 and classified them C-14. In the early 1940s the C-15s became C-14s, and in 1948 they were renumbered 60-69 to avoid conflict with Pere Marquette E7s 101-108. In 1929 Baldwin delivered 15 0-8-0s that were a little heavier than the C15s. They were classified C-15-A and numbered 110-124; in the early 1940s they were reclassified C-15.

The largest group of 0-8-0s was the C-16 class, which came from Alco, Lima, and Baldwin between 1930 and 1948. Most of those built by Alco, including 15 Pere Marquette engines identical to those of parent C&O, were delivered with large road tenders that were swapped on delivery for the smaller tenders of existing Mikados and Mallets. In 1949, seven months after the last C-16s arrived from Baldwin, C&O ordered 124 diesel switchers. Two neighbor railroads that were staying with steam seized the chance to buy almost-new switchers cheap: Norfolk & Western bought the 30 Baldwin C-16s for less than half what C&O had paid for them ($94,215 apiece), and the Virginian Railway bought the Lima C-16As of 1942 and 1943 for about $25,000 each (their scrap value was between $5,000 and $6,000).

Oddities and experimental locomotives

Between 1903 and 1908 C&O bought eight four-truck Shays to work steep branches in West Virginia; there were ultimately 16 of the machines on the roster. They were disposed of between 1923 and 1928. A single three-truck Shay was acquired secondhand in 1913 and sold in 1921. The Shays were classed with the switchers. In 1949 C&O purchased three fireless 0-6-0s to switch chemical plants at Charleston, W. Va. They were still in service in 1965.

The C&O was the last major eastern railroad to field a streamlined passenger train, but it planned to compensate for its tardiness with a luxurious domeliner that would run between Washington and Cincinnati on a daytime schedule: the *Chessie*. The Baltimore & Ohio got word of it, streamlined four Pacifics and ten passenger cars, and in January 1947 sent the *Cincinnatian* out to capture the daytime Washington-Cincinnati business — which proved almost nonexistent.

A train as modern as the *Chessie* required a modern locomotive. C&O, Baldwin, and Westinghouse teamed up to design a steam-turbine-electric. The resulting locomotives — C&O got three — were 106 feet long and weighed 856,000 pounds (Union Pacific's Big Boys tipped the scales at 772,000 pounds). The wheel arrangement was 4-8-0-4-8-4; it is

more understandable in diesel notation as 2-C1+2-C1-B (the fourth axle of each group of four was an idler, and the trailing truck was powered). They carried their coal up front, ahead of the cab; behind the cab was a large boiler, relatively conventional in design but mounted firebox-forward. At the rear of the locomotive, over the trailing truck, were the turbine and the generator. Water was carried in a 48' tender. The turbine was rated at 6000 horsepower, and C&O called them "the world's largest single-unit passenger locomotives."

The first turbine was delivered in 1947 and the other two in 1948. They were extremely complicated and had insatiable appetites for both coal and maintenance. They were scrapped in 1950.

Historical and technical society: Chesapeake & Ohio Historical Society, P. O. Box 79, Clifton Forge, VA 24422

Recommended reading: *C&O Power*, by Philip Shuster, Eugene L. Huddleston, and Alvin F. Staufer, published in 1965 by Alvin F. Staufer, LCC 65-26713

Published rosters:

Railroad Magazine: October 1944, page 60; May 1948, page 120; December 1966, page 58 (1926 roster)

Trains Magazine: November 1949, page 29

C&O STEAM LOCOMOTIVES BUILT SINCE 1900

Type	Class	Numbers	Qty	Builder	Built	Retired	Notes
0-6-0	C-3	15	1	Baldwin	1900	1951	Ex-QSL 1
0-6-0T	C-5	13	1	Brooks	1905	1934	Ex-HV 119
0-6-0	C-6	125-129	4	Brooks	1907	1934, 1951	Ex-HV 125-129
0-6-0	C-7	25-34	10	Richmond	1905-1906	1930-1952	C&CER&T&B
0-6-0F	C-8	35-37	3	Porter	1949		Fireless
0-6-0	C-13	35	1	Brooks	1906	1929	Ex-AC&I
0-8-0	C-8	80-82	3	Richmond	1903-1911	1929-1931	
0-8-0	C-9	40-49	10	Pittsburgh	1918		Ex-PM 1300-1309
0-8-0	C-10	50-59	10	Baldwin	1921		Ex-PM 1330-1339
0-8-0	C-11	360-369	10	Lima	1920		Ex-PM 1401-1410
0-8-0	C-13	340-359	20	Cooke	1923		Ex-PM 1310-1329
0-8-0	C-14	90	1	Baldwin	1910		
0-8-0	C-14	60-69	10	Lima	1925	1949-1952	Ex-C&O 100-109
0-8-0	C-14	70-79	10	Lima	1926	1950-1953	Ex-HV 100-109
0-8-0	C-15	110-124	15	Baldwin	1929	1952-1953	Ex-class C-15A
0-8-0	C-16	175-239	65	Alco	1930	1954-1957	
0-8-0	C-16	380-394	15	Alco	1930	1953	Ex-PM 240-254
0-8-0	C-16-A	240-254	15	Lima	1942-1943		To VGN, 1950
0-8-0	C-16	255-284	30	Baldwin	1948		To N&W, 1950
0-10-0	C-12	130-144	15	Richmond	1919-1923	-1956	
2-6-0	E-5	427, 428	2	Baldwin	1908	1935, 1946	
2-6-0	E-6	425, 426	2	Richmond	1907, 1908	-1930	Ex-Virginia Air Line
2-8-0	G-1	725-749	24	Brooks	1911	-1951	Ex-Island Creek Coal
2-8-0	G-2	750-774	25	Rich, Brks	1910, 1911	1949-1951	Ex-PM 901-925
2-8-0	G-3	150-159	10	Brooks	1910	1934-1949	Ex-PM 601-625
2-8-0	G-4	160-169	10	Brooks	1910	1935-1951	Ex-HV 150-159
2-8-0	G-5	170-179	10	Richmond	1911	1935-	Ex-HV 160-169

C&O STEAM LOCOMOTIVES BUILT SINCE 1900 (continued)

Type	Class	Numbers	Qty	Builder	Built	Retired	Notes
2-8-0	G-6	351-425	75	Richmond	1899-1901	-1935	
2-8-0	G-7	790-994	205	Rich., BLW	1903-1907	-1961	
2-8-0	G-7	996-1001	6	Pittsburgh	1916		
2-8-0	G-8	710, 711	2	Richmond	1907	1952	
2-8-0	G-9	1010-1059	50	Richmond	1909	-1961	
2-8-0	G-10	680-689	10	Baldwin	1900	1930	Ex-HV 212-224
2-8-0	G-11	1060-1081	22	Baldwin	1903-1909	-1934	Ex-CC&L 201-222
2-8-0	G-12	299	1	Richmond	1907	1924	Ex-White Oak 99
2-8-0	G-12	1080-1082	3	Baldwin	1906-1907	1935	Ex-HV 280-282
2-8-0	G-14	785, 786	2	Brooks	1907	1930	Ex-AC&I 15, 16
2-8-0	G-15	1085	1	Pittsburgh	1916	1951	Ex-AC&I 17
2-8-0	G-17	1095-1098	4			1929-1935	Ex-SV&E; nee B&O
2-8-2	K	1089-1099	11	Richmond	1912-1913	1935-1952	Ex-HV 180-190
2-8-2	K-1	1100-1155	56	Richmond	1911-1914	1935-1953	
2-8-2	K-2	1160-1209	50	RIchmond	1924		
2-8-2	K-3	1210-1259	50	Richmond	1924		
2-8-2	K-3-A	2300-2349	50	Richmond	1925-1926		
2-8-2	K-5	1060-1069	10	Schen	1927	1952	Ex-PM 1041-1050
2-8-2	K-6	1070-1074	5	BLW, Schen.	1911-1913	1949	Ex-PM1095-1099
2-8-2	K-8	2350-2379	30	Lima, Schen.	1918-1919	1949-1951	
							Ex-PM 1011-1040
2-8-4	K-4	2700-2789	90	Alco, Lima	1943-1947		
2-8-4	N-1	2650-2661	12	Lima	1941		Ex-PM 1216-1227
2-8-4	N-2	2670-2681	12	Lima	1944		Ex-PM 1228-1239
2-8-4	N-3	2685-2699	15	Lima	1937		Ex-PM 1201-1215
2-10-2	B-1	2950-2959	10	Baldwin	1919		
							Ex-HV 130-139, nee LV 4060-4069
2-10-2	B-1	2960, 2961	2	Baldwin	1919	1952	
							Ex-PM 1198, 1199; ex-HV 141, 143; nee LV 4071, 4073
2-10-2	B-2	2000-2005	5	Baldwin	1918	1951	Ex-C&EI 2000-2005
2-10-2	B-3	4000, 4001	2	Alco	1917	1949	
							Ex-C&EI 4000, 4001; nee Wabash 2513, 2509
2-10-2	B-4	2975-2989	15	Brooks	1918	1949-1952	
							Ex-PM 1101-1115
2-10-4	T-1	3000-3039	40	Lima	1930	1952-1953	
2-6-6-2	H-1	1301	1	Schen	1910	1930	
2-6-6-2	H-2	1302-1325	24	Richmond	1911	1935	
2-6-6-2	H-3	1300	1	Brooks	1910		Ex-Chicago & Alton
2-6-6-2	H-3	1275-1299	25	Schen,Rich	1917-1918	1935-1952	Ex-HV 200-224
2-6-6-2	H-4	1325-1474	150	Rich,Schen	1912-1918	1930-1955	
2-6-6-2	H-5	1520-1539	20	Schen,BLW	1919	1952	USRA
2-6-6-2	H-6	1475-1519	45	Rich,Schen	1920-1923	1952-1957	
2-6-6-2	H-6	1300-1309	10	Baldwin	1949	-1957	
2-6-6-6	H-8	1600-1659	60	Lima	1941-1948		
2-8-8-2	H-7	1540-1565	25	Alco	1923-1924	1952	
2-8-8-2	H-7-A	1570-1589	20	Baldwin	1926	1952	
4-4-0	A-5	230-232	3	Baldwin	1903-1904	1925-1929	Ex-CC&L
4-4-0	A-8	210, 211	2	Manch	1900	1926-1929	Ex-CC&L
4-4-0	A-14	83	1	Brooks	1905	1935	Ex-HV 83
4-4-0	A-15	84, 85	2	Brooks	1907	1935	Ex-HV 84, 85
4-4-2	A-16	275-294	20	Alco	1902-1916	1936-1949	
4-6-0	F-7	370, 371	2	Manch	1900	1926-1929	
							Ex-CC&L 101, 102
4-6-0	F-11	375-387	13	Baldwin	1902-1904	1925-1952	
							Ex-CC&L 103-115
4-6-0	F-12	86-88	3	Brooks	1910	1935	Ex-HV 86-88
4-6-0	F-13	89-92	4	Brks,Rich	1912, 1913	1931-1949	Ex-HV 89-92
4-6-2	F-12	405-409	5	Baldwin	1914	1948-1949	Ex-PM 725-729
4-6-2	F-14	410-421	12	Brooks	1920	1949	Ex-PM 711-722
4-6-2	F-15	430-456	27	Alco	1902-1911	1936-1952	
4-6-2	F-16	460-467	8	Baldwin	1913	1951-1952	
4-6-2	F-17	470-475	6	Richmond	1914	1951-1952	
4-6-2	F-18	480-485	6	Richmond	1923	1952	
4-6-2	F-19	490-494	5	Richmond	1926		Rebuilt to 4-6-4
4-6-2	F-20	486-489	4	Baldwin	1927	1952	Ex-RF&P 325-328
4-6-4	L-2	300-307	8	Baldwin	1941-1942	1955	
4-6-4	L-1	490-494	5	C&O	1946-1947	1953-1955	
4-6-4	L-2-A	310-314	5	Baldwin	1948	1955	
4-8-2	J-1	540-542	3	Richmond	1911-1912	1951-1952	
4-8-2	J-2	543-549	7	Alco, BLW	1918-1923	1951-1952	
4-8-4	J-3	600-606	7	Lima	1935, 1942	1953	
4-8-4	J-3-A	610-614	5	Lima	1948		
4-8-0-4-8-4							
	M-1	500-502	3	Baldwin	1947-1948	1950	
Shay	C-10	16	1	Lima	1911	Sold 1921	3-truck
Shay	C-9	1-15, 20	16	Lima	1903-	1923	4-truck

CHICAGO & ILLINOIS MIDLAND

In 1905 the Illinois Midland Coal Company, which was jointly owned by Peabody Coal Company and Samuel Insull's Chicago Edison and Commonwealth Electric companies, purchased the Pawnee Railroad, a short line connecting the town of Pawnee, south of Springfield, Ill., with nearby trunk-line railroads. The coal company was acquiring land in the area and saw the short line as a ready-made means to transport coal. It reincorporated the road and renamed it the Chicago & Illinois Midland Railway. In 1926 the C&IM purchased the Springfield-Peoria line of the defunct Chicago, Peoria & St. Louis, acquired trackage rights on Illinois Central to connect that route with the existing line, and settled down to a career of moving coal north to a barge loading facility on the Illinois River at Havana.

C&IM was one of the last all-steam Class 1 railroads, but by the early 1950s replacement parts were becoming hard to find. Electro-Motive saw the situation as ripe for dieselization and arranged the loan of a pair of Milwaukee Road SD9s. In 1954 C&IM decided to dieselize gradually, starting with a pair of switchers delivered in early 1955. Soon the road ordered more switchers and a group of SD9s. Dieselization turned out to be extremely quick. The first SD9 was delivered on November 17, 1955, and C&IM's last steam-powered road train ran only five days later. Steam switchers remained in service until December 5, 1955. The railroad with a reputation for buying and refurbishing used steam locomotives suddenly had a fleet of diesels all built the same year.

Freight locomotives

In 1904 the Pawnee Railroad bought a pair of 2-8-0s from Alco's Brooks Works to replace a pair of old 4-4-0s, and in 1906 received a third 2-8-0. The first 2-8-0, No. 2, had been built for a Peabody subsidiary but had been assigned to the C&IM. When that subsidiary was sold to the Iron Mountain, the 2-8-0 went with it, and the C&IM acquired its fourth 2-8-0, part of a group of locomotives built for the Buffalo & Susquehanna but not delivered because of financial problems.

Brooks delivered two low-drivered Mikados to the C&IM in 1914, and two of the 2-8-0s were assigned to passenger service, replacing a pair of secondhand 4-4-0s of uncertain ancestry. Two more 2-8-2s of the

C&IM 23 (later 523), class E-2, was built by Alco's Brooks Works in 1918. Its 51" drivers suited it well for coal-mine switching and short hauls of heavy trains. Note the Southern valve gear. Alco photo.

C&IM 701, one of four 2-10-2s turned out by Lima in 1931, has a mile of hopper cars moving southbound at good speed across the prairie at Kelsey, Illinois, in 1954. Photo by Philip R. Hastings.

4-4-0 — AMERICAN

The earliest locomotives had four wheels (the minimum possible) with one axle or both driven. The 2-2-0 and 0-2-2 wheel arrangements proved unsuitable; the 0-4-0 used all its weight for adhesion but was unstable at any kind of over-the-road speed. In 1832, as a development of the 2-2-0 with two rigid axles, John B. Jervis introduced the 4-2-0. A significant feature of its design was three-point suspension: the four-wheel swiveling truck at the front and the two drivers. The single driving axle limited the type's pulling power, and it was succeeded by the 4-4-0.

The 4-4-0 was introduced in 1836 by Henry R. Campbell, an associate of Matthias W. Baldwin. It also had three-point suspension: the center pin of the lead truck and the fulcrums of the equalizers between the drivers. The main rods were connected to the front drivers, leaving plenty of space for access to the Stephenson valve gear, which was between the frames. The first 4-4-0s had deep, narrow fireboxes between the frames and the driver axles; later Americans had fireboxes above the frames. Although some were built with Wootten fireboxes, few had wide, bituminous-burning fireboxes above the drivers. The type was adaptable to almost any driver size and service; it was stable, well balanced, and easy on track.

As railroads spread rapidly in the mid-1800s it was the 4-4-0 that powered them. The famous Civil War locomotive chase of April 12, 1862, Andrews' Raid, was between two 4-4-0s, Western & Atlantic's *Texas* and *General*. (During that incident the stability of the 4-4-0 becomes all the more remarkable considering the condition of the track — it certainly wasn't 130-pound welded rail on rock ballast — and the fact that the *Texas* was running in reverse.) After the war the American was the locomotive that won the West. The two engines that touched pilots at Promontory, Utah, on May 10, 1869, were 4-4-0s, Central Pacific's *Jupiter* and Union Pacific's 119.

Virginia & Truckee 12, painted and lettered to represent Central Pacific *Jupiter* at the Chicago Railroad Fair of 1949, is a typical 1870-era 4-4-0, except for the air pump ahead of the cab. Collection of Frederick E. Braun.

Boston & Maine 710 (later 1003), built by Manchester in 1909, was one of the last 4-4-0s B&M purchased. B&M had been buying 4-4-2s since 1902 and received its first 4-6-2s in 1910. B&M had an extensive network of rural and suburban branch lines on which 115,000-pound 4-4-0s were sufficient for the traffic. Above the frames is a deep, sloping firebox; slide valves are a clue that No. 710 is not superheated. Alco photo.

Reading 410-419 were built by Baldwin in 1914. They were notable for combining a conventional rear cab with a Wootten firebox and were only 110 pounds lighter than Central of New Jersey 557-559. Even with relatively low drivers (68¹/₂") the placement of the firebox above the drivers results in a high-mounted boiler. Photo by Charles S. Freed.

For almost six decades the 4-4-0 was the standard American locomotive; indeed, the type name often has the word "standard" appended. Few of the type were built after 1900, but some remained in service into the 1940s and even the 1950s. Most railroads had some services for which an American was entirely adequate; some lines had track and bridges that could support nothing heavier than an American. Railroads usually bought big, heavy fast locomotives for the road's most demanding services and bumped older, lighter locomotives to secondary service. The Chicago, Burlington & Quincy modernized 105 4-4-0s for branchline service between 1915 and 1917. They were retired in the late 1920s and early 1930s. Railroads continued to buy 4-4-0s after 1900, even though the *Locomotive Cyclopedia* was full of Santa Fes, Mountains, and Mallets.

Other names: Eight-Wheeler

Last: Chicago & Illinois Midland 502, 1928

Longest lived and last in service: In the 1940s and 1950s, rail enthusiasts were forever turning up back-country short lines still using antique 4-4-0s purchased from neighboring Class 1 railroads half a century before. Because of bridge restrictions Canadian Pacific used three 4-4-0s between Chipman and Norton, New Brunswick, until 1959, when a diesel light enough could be obtained. One of the three, No. 29 (built in 1887) pulled CP's last steam-powered train on November 6, 1960. Another ex-CP 4-4-0 built in 1882 hauls tourists on the Prairie Dog Central out of Winnipeg, Manitoba. Several Virginia & Truckee 4-4-0s built in the 1870s still exist; No. 22, *Inyo*, built in 1875, is in operating condition at the Nevada State Railroad Museum at Carson City.

Heaviest: Central Railroad of New Jersey 557-559, 173,600 pounds

Chicago & Illinois Midland 502, a 1928 Baldwin product, was the last 4-4-0 built for service in the U. S. A thoroughly modern locomotive built to an archaic wheel arrangement, it was exactly what its owner needed. It weighed 118,400 pounds. Photo by Vitaly V. Uzoff.

same dimensions, but with Southern valve gear instead of Walschaerts, arrived from Brooks in 1918.

During World War I the coal business increased, requiring more locomotives. The USRA was using the full capacity of the locomotive builders, so C&IM bought a pair of 30-year-old 2-6-0s from the Burlington for passenger service, releasing the 2-8-0s for freight.

The purchase of the Chicago, Peoria & St. Louis by C&IM included no locomotives — CP&StL's locomotives, even its newest, 11 2-8-0s built in 1913, were fit only for scrapping — so the road purchased a group of ex-Pittsburgh & Lake Erie and Peoria & Eastern 2-8-0s and leased a few locomotives from Illinois Central and Wabash.

New power was high on the priority list. The recently acquired Springfield-Peoria line had heavy grades where the line crossed the Sangamon River, so instead of more Mikados the road ordered a pair of 2-10-2s from Baldwin. They were delivered in 1927 along with two delicate-looking 4-4-0s. At that time the C&IM undertook a renumbering of its locomotives, adding 500 to the numbers of the older ones. Two 2-8-2s were added to the roster in 1928 for general freight service. They had 64" drivers instead of the 51" drivers of the earlier Mikados. Two more 2-10-2s for coal trains arrived from Baldwin in 1929, and four 2-10-2s plus a third 2-8-2 from Lima in 1931.

In 1934 C&IM's traffic increased again, and the road purchased a pair of 51"-drivered Mikados from the Chesapeake & Ohio, former Sewell Valley engines. In 1937 C&IM finally needed full-time switchers at Springfield and Havana, and bought a pair of 0-8-0s from Lima — the last new steam locomotives it bought. Another secondhand 2-8-2 arrived in 1938. By then only two Consolidations remained on the roster: C&IM sold No. 510 to the Midland Terminal and scrapped No. 504.

When C&IM needed more locomotives in 1940 it went shopping in the used-locomotive market and came home with three former Wabash 2-10-2s; it acquired six more between 1942 and 1950. During World War II C&IM needed more switchers and bought two 0-8-0s from the Manufacturers Railway in 1944. In 1945 it bought two heavy 2-8-2s from the Lackawanna, and in 1949 two 0-8-0s from the Kentucky & Indiana Terminal plus a third in 1953. In 1951 C&IM bought two 2-10-2s from the Atlantic Coast Line and immediately went back for seven more. The former Wabash engines were coming due for heavy repairs, and the ACL engines were in good condition and more powerful. The ex-Wabash 2-10-2s had small tenders; C&IM replaced them with large tenders from the New York Central, and when the Wabash engines were scrapped, the large tenders replaced the Vanderbilt tenders of the ACL engines.

Passenger locomotives

In 1926 the road decided to upgrade its passenger service to two daily Springfield-Peoria round trips. It ordered a half dozen steel passenger cars as an add-on to a Chicago South Shore & South Bend order for trailer cars (CSS&SB was another of Insull's holdings) and two 4-4-0s from Baldwin for delivery in 1927. The American type was long since obsolete — 1927 was the year the Hudson and the Northern types made their debuts — but a light, modern, efficient 4-4-0 was all that was necessary for C&IM's two- and three-car trains. A third 4-4-0 arrived in 1928 to serve as a spare, and 2-8-2s 550 and 551, also built in 1928, had steam and signal lines for the rare occasions the passenger trains exceeded the capacity of the Americans.

In the late 1940s ridership dropped to the point that C&IM reduced service to one weekday round trip. Two 4-4-0s were sufficient, one for the train and one as a spare, so C&IM sold No. 501 for scrap. The passenger train made its last run in 1953, and the two remaining 4-4-0s were scrapped soon afterward.

Historical and technical society: Chicago & Illinois Midland Historical Society, P. O. Box 121, Macomb, IL 61455

Recommended reading: *Chicago & Illinois Midland*, by Richard R. Wallin, Paul H. Stringham, and John Szwajkart, published in 1979 by Golden West Books, P. O. Box 8136, San Marino, CA 91108 (ISBN 0-87095-077-0)

Published rosters:
Railroad Magazine, July 1954, page 80
Trains Magazine, August 1955, page 26

C&IM STEAM LOCOMOTIVES BUILT SINCE 1900

Type	Class	Numbers	Qty	Builder	Built	Retired	Notes
0-8-0	D-2	540, 541	2	Lima	1937	1955	
0-8-0	D-3	545, 546	2	Baldwin	1929	1955	Ex-MRS
0-8-0	D-4	547-549	3	Lima	1926	1955	Ex-K&IT
2-8-0		2, 3	2	Brooks	1904	1910, 1920	
2-8-0	B-1	504	1	Brooks	1906	1939	Originally No. 4
2-8-0	C-1	510	1	Brooks	1910	1938	Built for B&S
2-8-0	D-1	519, 520	2	Pittsburgh	1903	1935	Ex-P&LE
2-8-0	F-1	530	1	Brooks	1902	1933	Ex-P&E
2-8-0	F-2	531-533	3	Brooks	1902	1933	Ex-P&E
2-8-0	F-3	534-536	3	Brooks	1902-1903	1933	Ex-P&E
2-8-2	E-1	521, 522	2	Brooks	1914	1940	
2-8-2	E-2	523, 524	2	Brooks	1918	1945, 1944	
2-8-2	E-3	525, 526	2	Lima	1922, 1923	1948	
2-8-2	F-5	560, 561	2	Schen.	1922, 1923	1951	Ex-DL&W
2-10-2	G-1	600, 601	2	Baldwin	1927	1955	
2-10-2	G-2	602-603	2	Baldwin	1929	1955	
2-10-2	G-4	651-659	9	Brooks	1917	1952-1955	Ex-Wabash
2-10-2	H-1	700-703	4	Lima	1931	1955	
2-10-2	H-2	751-759	9	Baldwin	1925-1926	1955	Ex-ACL
4-4-0	A-1	500-502	3	Baldwin	1927-1928	1950-1953	

CHICAGO & NORTH WESTERN RAILWAY

In 1900 the map of the Chicago & North Western looked much as it would for most of the 20th century. The North Western's principal route was west from Chicago through Clinton, Cedar Rapids, and Council Bluffs, Iowa, to Omaha, Nebraska — essentially a Chicago extension of the Union Pacific. Other main lines out of Chicago led north to Milwaukee and northwest through Madison, Wisconsin, to the Twin Cities. Yet to be built were the inland freight route from Chicago to Milwaukee (built in 1906 and still called "the new line" today); the direct line from Milwaukee to Sparta, Wis.; the long line from Nelson, Illinois, south almost to St. Louis; and the extension of the Wyoming line from Casper to Lander. C&NW operated Chicago's most extensive suburban service on its three main lines and several branches.

The North Western acquired control of the Chicago, St. Paul, Minneapolis & Omaha Railway in 1882. The Omaha Road's principal routes extended from Omaha northeast through the Twin Cities to Lake Superior at Duluth, and from the Twin Cities southeast to a connection with the C&NW at Elroy, Wis. The Omaha Road maintained a separate loco-

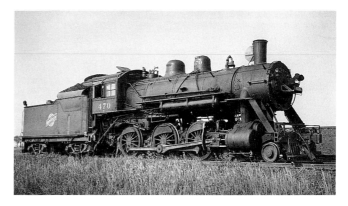

Class R-1 Ten-Wheeler 470 displays the characteristics of that class: firebox above the rear drivers, inboard piston valves, and (invisible but implied) Stephenson valve gear. Photo by Charles H. Ost.

Northern 3008, photographed in 1929, illustrates the H class as delivered, with spoked drivers and banjo frame at the rear. Photo by A. W. Johnson.

Visible in the photo of H-1 No. 3035 are Boxpok drivers and rollers bearings on the lead and trailing trucks. The unobstructed view of the trailing truck is evidence of the new frame. C&NW photo.

motive roster with different class letters and number series. The classification of its Ten-Wheelers and Pacifics was especially untidy, with at least two letters, I and K, for Ten-Wheelers and those same letters plus E for Pacifics. After 1913 Omaha Road locomotives were ordered along with C&NW locomotives, and they used the same classification letters.

Until 1907 C&NW usually did not assign continuous blocks of numbers to groups of locomotives but reused numbers of locomotives that had been retired or scrapped. Photographs show that the 91 Atlantics of the D class, for example, carried random numbers between 152 and 1317. Such a practice confuses historians and can't have made the job of the motive power superintendent any easier. In the roster below, ranges of random numbers are given with an ellipsis (…) instead of a hyphen.

Most C&NW locomotives burned coal, but those assigned to divisions west of the Missouri River were oil burners; in addition the four Pacifics rebuilt for the *400s* were converted to oil. One group of light Pacifics was fitted with special grates for burning lignite, a low-grade coal.

May 10, 1956, saw C&NW's last steam-powered commuter train. A few small steam locomotives remained in service through the summer of 1956, but by fall dieselization was complete.

Freight locomotives

The engines that typify the North Western, the R-1 Ten-Wheelers, were built by Schenectady and Baldwin between 1901 and 1908. They evolved from the R class, built between 1897 and 1900, and had 63" drivers, inboard piston valves, Stephenson valve gear (a few had outboard valves and Walschaerts valve gear), and a firebox over the rear drivers. One of the class, No. 1385, owned by Mid-Continent Railway Museum, is active in excursion service at the museum and occasionally on C&NW's lines.

Between 1909 and 1913 Alco's Schenectady Works and Baldwin built

250 class Z 2-8-0s for the C&NW. They were good-size Consolidations — 238,000 pounds — with 61" drivers and 25" × 32" cylinders. They were superheated; some had Walschaerts valve gear, others had Baker. The Zulus, as they were called, were followed by the 310 Mikados in the J class, built between 1913 and 1923 by Alco's Schenectady, Richmond, and Brooks plants. They had 62" drivers and 27" × 32" cylinders and weighed 304,500 pounds. Details of the Js changed during the period of their construction. The first 192 locomotives had Baker valve gear, and the rest had Young gear; a group of 65 had cast trailing trucks instead of the usual Cole design. The last Js built, 2701-2710, were oil burners for lines in Nebraska and Wyoming. Many J-class Mikes, both C&NW and Omaha Road, were rebuilt into the J-A class, with such improvements as mechanical stokers, 64" Boxpok drivers, and larger tenders; the Omaha Road J-As also received exhaust steam injectors. Mikes that didn't become J-As were given stokers and classed J-S.

The Omaha Road received four heavy USRA 2-8-2s in 1919 and six more slightly modified versions in 1921. They were classed J-2. In 1926 CStPM&O ordered eight more heavy Mikes that were improved versions of the USRA heavy 2-8-2.

In 1927 Alco's Brooks Works delivered a dozen 2-8-4s to the C&NW. They had the same basic dimensions as Lima's A-1, the first of that wheel arrangement, but they had conventional frames and cast trailing trucks. They were assigned to coal trains on the line running south from Nelson to Peoria, Ill.

The Omaha Road took delivery of two 2-10-2s from Baldwin in 1917 for helper service on the grades out of the St. Croix River valley at Hudson, Wis. In 1944 they were transferred to the C&NW in exchange for a pair of 2-8-2s and put to work on the hump at Proviso Yard in Chicago.

Passenger locomotives

Schenectady built six 4-4-2s for the North Western in 1900. They had 81" drivers, inboard piston valves, and non-swiveling trailing wheels. Between 1900 and 1908 C&NW bought 91 such D-class Atlantics. Ten built in 1908 had Young rotary valves and Walschaerts valve gear.

The L-class Pacifics were built by Schenectady in 1910. They were

Omaha Road's E-3 Pacifics were built a year after the class H Northerns and have some of the same details, such as outside-journal lead truck and slant-front cab. C&NW photo.

light, only 181,500 pounds, and had 63" drivers. They were fitted for burning lignite.

Between 1909 and 1923 Alco's Schenectady Works built 168 class E Pacifics for C&NW through and suburban passenger trains and 18 Es for the Omaha Road. They had 75" drivers. The Es evolved as they were built and there were significant differences among them. Early members of the class had 23" × 28" cylinders and a boiler pressure of 200 pounds; later ones, 25" × 28" and 185 pounds. In 1913 Baker valve gear replaced Walschaerts, and in 1921 Young replaced Baker; the last 20 Es, built in 1922 and 1923, had cast trailing trucks. Two of the E class, 1617 and 1620, were streamlined in 1941 for the *Minnesota 400*. Between 1948 and 1953 the E-class Pacifics were renumbered to make way for diesels. The leading 1 was dropped, making the series 500-667; 1600-1602 became 670-672 to avoid conflict with the Omaha's big Pacifics.

The E-1 class, built between 1910 and 1916, had 69" drivers and 22" × 26" cylinders and weighed 233,000 pounds, 16,000 pounds less than the Es. In 1923 Schenectady delivered a dozen E-2 Pacifics, 2901-2912. They had 75" drivers and 26" × 28" cylinders and weighed 295,000 pounds, about halfway between the USRA light and heavy Pacifics. In the early 1930s the C&NW, the Milwaukee Road, and the Burlington decided to accelerate their daytime trains from Chicago to Minneapolis and St. Paul. Burlington ordered a pair of diesel-powered streamlined *Zephyrs*, and the Milwaukee began building streamlined passenger cars and ordered two streamlined Atlantics from Alco for the *Hiawatha*. C&NW's entry in the race to the Twin Cities was the *400* (it would cover approximately 400 miles in 400 minutes), which for its first few years of operation consisted of rebuilt conventional cars pulled by conventional steam locomotives, also rebuilt. In 1934 four E-2s, 2902, 2903, 2907, and 2908, were souped up with 79" drivers and cast steel cylinders. They were converted to oil fuel, boiler pressure was increased from 210 to 225 pounds, and they were reclassified E-2-A. The remaining E-2s received similar improvements in 1935 but remained coal burners and were classified E-2-B. In 1939 the E-2-As were reconverted to coal and all 12 were reclassified E-2.

In 1930 Alco delivered three Pacifics, the world's heaviest, to the Omaha Road: Nos. 600-602, class E-3. They weighed 347,000 pounds — more than many 4-8-2s — and could exert a starting tractive effort of 64,400 pounds with the booster cut in.

The North Western received nine streamlined Hudsons from Alco in 1938. They had 84" drivers, and in most dimensions were similar to Milwaukee Road's contemporary streamlined Hudsons. The major difference was cylinder size: 25" × 29" for C&NW and 23½" × 30" for Milwaukee. The 4-6-4s were painted dark olive green with gold striping and assigned to conventional trains between Chicago & Omaha. Converted to oil in 1947 and 1948, they were C&NW's last new steam locomotives.

North Western's largest locomotives by far were the 35 H-class 4-8-4s built by Baldwin in 1929. During the 1920s traffic on the Chicago-Omaha route increased, and trains began requiring doubleheaded Pacifics and Mikados. The road wanted a dual-service locomotive and chose the 4-8-4 type, introduced by the Northern Pacific in 1927. The Northern that C&NW and Baldwin came up with was immense. It weighed 498,000 pounds, 72,000 more than NP's first 4-8-4s — and almost twice as much

as the J-class 2-8-2s it would replace in freight service. Its 76" drivers were larger than those of most other 4-8-4s, and after the boiler pressure was raised from 250 pounds to 275, its tractive force of 71,800 pounds plus 12,400 with the booster working made it the most powerful 4-8-4 until Norfolk & Western's streamlined J hit the rails. The Hs were so much larger than anything else on the North Western that they were restricted to the Chicago-Omaha main line; only certain tracks in the Chicago passenger terminal could accommodate them, and then only after modifications to the trainshed. Eventually bridges were strengthened elsewhere and the 4-8-4s were allowed as far as Altoona, Wis., or the line to Minneapolis and St. Paul, and from Clyman Junction to Fond du Lac, Wis.

The H class underwent two rebuildings. About 1940 they were given lightweight rods, Boxpok drivers, and roller bearings on all axles. After World War II they again needed major work. Their weak point was the frame aft of the drivers. The cast frame there was outside the trailing truck, creating space for a large ashpan hopper — the same outside cradle or banjo frame was used on the early 4-8-4s of Northern Pacific and Canadian National and on Central Vermont 2-10-4s. For several years the North Western had been patching that part of the frame and it had to decide whether to keep welding and patching, scrap the 4-8-4s in favor of diesels, or rebuild them.

Number 3004 was the guinea pig. It received a new cast nickel-steel frame with integrally cast cylinders, pilot beam, and air reservoirs, plus a new firebox and a host of minor improvements. Reclassified H-1 when it emerged from the 40th Street Shop in Chicago on April 1, 1946, 3004 was a much better engine than it had been in 1929, and it had been an excellent engine then. It was still among the heaviest 4-8-4s, exceeded in weight only by Santa Fe's 2900s, Northern Pacific's A-5's, and Western Maryland's J-1s. C&NW rebuilt 24 of its 4-8-4s between 1946 and 1949, but the decision to dieselize stopped the program.

Switchers

C&NW was assigned 35 USRA 0-6-0s, appropriate since they were reportedly copies of the road's M-2 class, and the Omaha Road received eight. C&NW had only eight 0-8-0s, built in 1927 by Alco's Richmond Works. Assigned to yards in Chicago, they were copies of the USRA 0-8-0, but were somewhat heavier and had much longer tenders. The Omaha Road also had eight 0-8-0s, built by Baldwin in 1928. In 1944 Omaha Road's two 2-10-2s were assigned to hump duty at Proviso Yard. The lead trucks derailed as the locomotives passed over the crest of the hump, so they were removed, making the locomotives into 0-10-2s.

Oddities

Narrow gauge 2-6-0s 278 and 279 were built for a line in southwest Wisconsin between Fennimore, Woodman, and Montford. Both apparently replaced engines of the same numbers. Narrow gauge Twelve-Wheelers 477 and 933 (renumbered in 1905 from 1301 and 1302; originally Fremont, Elkhorn & Missouri Valley 211 and 212) were built by Schenectady in 1902 for service in the Black Hills between Deadwood and Lead, South Dakota.

Historical and technical society: Chicago & North Western Historical Society, P. O. Box 1436, Elmhurst, IL 60126-9998

Recommended reading:
Locomotives of the Chicago and North Western Railway, published in 1938 (supplement issued in 1948) by the Railway & Locomotive Historical Society, P. O. Box 1418, Westford, MA 01886

Chicago and North Western Railway Steam Power, by Charles T. Knudsen, published in 1965 by Knudsen Publications, 3539 N. Lincoln Avenue, Chicago, IL 60613

"Zeppelins they were called but Zeppelins they surely were not: an H of an engine," by Wallace W. Abbey, in *Trains Magazine*, October 1970, page 20

Published rosters:
C&NW: *Railroad Magazine*: December 1934, page 87; August 1948, page 108
CStPM&O:
Railroad Magazine, March 1937, page 72; April 1955, page 41
Railroad History, No. 154, page 40

C&NW STEAM LOCOMOTIVES BUILT SINCE 1900

Type	Class	Numbers	Qty	Builder	Built	Retired	Notes
0-6-0	K	8...1172		Rhode Island	1903		
0-6-0	M	837-856	20	Schenectady	1900	1928-1935	
0-6-0	M-1	1...1052, 574-583, 1297-1317, 1428-1442, 1495-1499, 2000-2104		Alco, BLW	1905-1917		
0-6-0	M-2	2111-2185	75	Schen, Brooks	1916-1923		
0-6-0	M-3	2601-2635		Cooke, Schen	1919		USRA
0-8-0	M-4	2636-2643		Richmond	1927		
0-10-2	J-1	491, 492				1953, 1949	Ex-2-10-2
2-6-0	D-11	278	1	Cooke	1915	1927	Narrow gauge
2-6-0	D-11	279	1	Schenectady	1912	Sold 1927	Narrow gauge
2-8-0	Z	1455-1494, 1700-1910	250	BLW, Schen	1909-1913		
2-8-2	J	2301-2600	300	Alco	1913-1923		
2-8-2	J	2701-2710	10	Brooks	1923		Oil burners
2-8-4	J-4	2801-2812	12	Brooks	1927	1950-1953	
4-4-2	D	152...895, 390-399, 1015-1030, 1080-1101, 1297-1317	91	Schenectady	1900-1908		
4-6-0	Q	1191-1200	10	Rhode Island	1903	1928-1931	
4-6-0	Q	497-506,556-565,1323-1332	30	Rogers	1906	1928-1931	
4-6-0	R	857-886	30	Schenectady	1900	1928-1937	
4-6-0	R-1	18...1042,1066-1079,1125-1169,1323-1428	325	Schen, BLW	1901-1908		
4-6-2	E	1500-1667	168	Schen, Brooks	1909-1923	1937-1956	
4-6-2	E-1	56...944,2201-2226	41	Schenectady	1910-1916		
4-6-2	E-2	2901-2912	12	Schenectady	1923	1954-1957	
4-6-2	L	9...1454	21	Schenectady	1908-1910	1935	
4-8-0	G	477, 933	2	Schenectady	1902	1928, 1925	Narrow gauge
4-6-4	E-4	4001-4009	9	Alco	1938	1953-1956	
4-8-4	H	3001-3035	35	Baldwin	1929	1950-1956	
Chicago, St. Paul, Minneapolis & Omaha locomotives							
0-6-0	F-6	13-16, 24-28	9	Schenectady	1901-1907		
0-6-0	F-10	22, 23	2	Baldwin	1902		
0-6-0	M-1	3,4,9,12,18-21,29-36	16	Schenectady	1909-1912		

Chicago, St. Paul, Minneapolis & Omaha locomotives (continued)

Type	Class	Numbers	Qty	Builder	Built	Retired	Notes
0-6-0	M-1	1, 17, 37, 43, 45					
			5	Baldwin	1913		
0-6-0	M-2	46-54	9	Schenectady	1917		
0-6-0	M-3	75-82	8	Richmond	1921		
0-6-0	M-3	83-86	4	Schenectady	1919		
0-8-0	M-5	60-67	8	Baldwin	1928		
2-8-0	H-3	216, 217	2	Schenectady	1905		
2-8-0	Z	218, 219	2	Schenectady	1913		
2-8-2	J	390-421	32	Schenectady	1913-1916		
2-8-2	J	440, 441	2	Schenectady	1916		Ex-C&NW 2363, 2371
2-8-2	J-2	422-431	10	Schen, Rich	1919, 1921	1950-1954	USRA
2-8-2	J-3	432-439	8	Schenectady	1926	1953-1956	

Type	Class	Numbers	Qty	Builder	Built	Retired	Notes
2-10-2	J-1	491, 492	2	Baldwin	1917		To C&NW
4-4-2	G-3	364-370	7	Schenectady	1906		Same as C&NWclass D
4-6-0	F-1	220	1	Schenectady	1923		
4-6-0	F-2	188, 195, 197, 199, 202, 212, 234					
			7	Schenectady	1921-1924		
4-6-0	I-1	101-106, 222-225, 302-304, 308-363					
			67	Schenectady	1901-1910		Same as C&NW R-1
4-6-0	K-1	107, 108, 110, 112, 125, 183, 184, 201, 203, 204, 236-240, 243-246 ,261, 262					
			21	Schen, Brooks	1911-1913		
4-6-2	I-2	371-387	17	Schenectady	1903-1910		
4-6-2	K-2	388, 389	2	Schenectady	1911		
4-6-2	E	500-517	18	Schenectady	1913-1916		
4-6-2	E-3	600-602	3	Schenectady	1930		

CHICAGO, BURLINGTON & QUINCY RAILROAD

In 1900 most of the Burlington's lines were in the territory between Chicago and Denver. A network of branch lines covering western Illinois, southern Iowa, northern Missouri, and southern Nebraska linked the railroad to the agriculture of the region. Several long lines reached out of CB&Q's principal territory: to Paducah, Kentucky, via the coal fields of southern Illinois; northwest from Lincoln, Nebraska, to Billings, Montana; and northwest from Aurora, Ill., to St. Paul, Minnesota. In 1901 nearly 98 percent of the Burlington's stock was purchased jointly by Great Northern and Northern Pacific, both of which reached from St. Paul to Seattle and Portland; CB&Q gave them a connection to Chicago. In 1908 Burlington acquired control of the Colorado & Southern, which, with its subsidiaries Fort Worth & Denver City and Trinity & Brazos Valley, reached from Wendover, Wyoming, south through Denver to the Gulf of Mexico at Galveston, Texas. Within a few years the Burlington built a line between Billings, Mont., and the north end of the C&S.

The Burlington traversed flat or rolling country for the most part.

The only grades of note were up from river valleys, and they were neither long nor severe. The lines to Billings had heavier grades, but only the branch through the Black Hills to Deadwood, South Dakota, constituted mountain railroading.

In 1898 the Burlington established a locomotive numbering system that would ensure that locomotives of its subsidiaries, such as Hannibal & St. Joseph and Burlington & Missouri River in Nebraska, would have unique numbers. In 1904 the CB&Q merged the subsidiaries and again renumbered the locomotives; post-1904 numbers are used here. The Colorado & Southern and Fort Worth & Denver City had their own numbering and classification systems and the two roads had enough autonomy that their locomotives are described separately on page 134.

Freight locomotives

In 1900 the road's shops at West Burlington, Iowa, built four 2-6-2 freight locomotives following a design by F. A. Delano, the Burlington's superintendent of motive power. These combined the six drivers of the

2-6-0, which the road used extensively in freight and passenger service, with the wide firebox supported by a trailing truck of the Baldwin 2-4-2 delivered in 1895. Their 64" drivers permitted good speed, and generous Belpaire fireboxes made them good steamers. They had 19" × 24" cylinders and weighed 151,220 pounds. The road enlarged the design, boosting cylinder size to 20" × 24", weight to 170,000 pounds, and tractive effort to 25,500 pounds, ordered 50 from Baldwin and 10 from its West Burlington shops, classifying 54 of them R-2. Six of the Baldwin locomotives were built as Vauclain compounds and classed R-2C.

The 50 class R-3 Prairies of 1902 were noticeably larger: 69" drivers, 21" × 26" cylinders, 180,500 pounds total weight, and 28,300 pounds tractive effort. The 150 members of the R-4 class, built by Baldwin in 1904 and 1906 and Brooks in 1905, continued the growth: 22" × 28" cylinders, 208,530 pounds total weight, and 35,000 pounds tractive effort. The R-4s had a conventional firebox instead of the Belpaire firebox used on earlier classes and had inboard piston valves, where previous classes had piston valves directly above the cylinders. The R-5 class had the same dimensions as the R-4s and differed principally in having a larger boiler.

A few Prairies were rebuilt with outboard piston valves and Walschaerts valve gear, but all the R-2s and many R-3s and R-4s were rebuilt into 0-6-0s between 1917 and 1930.

The Burlington had only one group of post-1900 2-8-0s, 100 D-4A and D-4B-class 57"-drivered locomotives built in 1902 by Baldwin and Schenectady. They were intended for slow, heavy freight trains on lines west of the Mississippi River. Most of them were scrapped during the Depression. The Prairie type proved to be better suited to the road's freight trains, and the Mikado was a natural development of the 2-6-2.

Burlington's first 2-8-2s, 60 O-1-class engines, came from Baldwin in 1910. They had the same 64" drivers as the Prairies; they were, naturally, heavier and more powerful — the tractive effort of an O-1 was 49,500 pounds, 40 percent greater than that of the newest 2-6-2s. They were followed almost immediately by 100 O-2 Mikados. They were heavier (310,000 pounds — the O-1s weighed 288,000 pounds) but only a lit-

The CB&Q was a major user of the Prairie type, with 429 of them on its roster. Number 2121, shown at Congress Park, Illinois, in 1939, is an R-5, built in 1907. The inboard piston valves and squared counterweights were already out of date when the locomotive was built. The low tender with curved coal bunker sides and the "mantel-clock" headlight are Burlington trademarks. Photo by J. W. Saunders.

The CB&Q had 278 Mikados on its roster. Number 4978, an O-1A built by Baldwin in 1923, leads a long freight east across the prairie at Somonauk, Illinois, in October 1945. Photo by L. E. Griffith.

2-6-2 — PRAIRIE

Burlington originated the Prairie in 1900 to combine the pulling power of the 2-6-0 with the steaming capacity of the wide firebox. The new type developed in two forms: a fast freight locomotive with drivers between 63" and 69", and a passenger locomotive with 80" drivers.

As a fast freight locomotive 2-6-2s were ordered in large numbers by Burlington, Santa Fe, Milwaukee Road, and Northern Pacific for use across the prairies between the Great Lakes and the Rockies. The passenger version of the Prairie is usually associated with the Lake Shore & Michigan Southern, a New York Central subsidiary.

The type had a few drawbacks. It tended to be rear-heavy, and those that had their main rods connected to the middle drivers were unstable, because those drivers coincided with the center of gravity — or more accurately, the center of yaw. The two-wheel lead truck proved less than satisfactory for high-speed running.

The 4-6-2 appeared in 1902, and the 2-8-2 as a wide-firebox road freight engine in 1905. The four-wheel lead truck of the Pacific made it more stable at speed than the Prairie (the 4-6-2 was generally a well-balanced engine); the 2-8-2 was also well balanced, and the extra length of the boiler and the fourth pair of drivers made it a far more powerful freight locomotive than the Prairie.

After 1910 the 2-6-2 was built primarily as an industrial and logging locomotive, often resembling an 0-6-0 with lead and trailing trucks. Only mainline-size locomotives are included in the statistics below.

Total number built: About 1,250 for common carrier railroads

First: Chicago, Burlington & Quincy 1700-1703, 1900

Last: Chicago, Milwaukee & St. Paul 5620-5644, Brooks, 1909

Last in service: NP had some in service in 1957; McCloud River had a logging-type 2-6-2 active in 1970, though mostly in excursion service

Greatest number: Chicago, Burlington & Quincy, 429

Heaviest: Atchison, Topeka & Santa Fe 1800 class, 248,200 pounds

Lightest: Chicago, Burlington & Quincy 1900-1903, 151,220 pounds

The Prairie developed first as a middleweight, medium-speed freight engine. Northern Pacific 2450, built by Alco in 1907, illustrates the characteristics: main rod connected to rear drivers, firebox behind rear drivers, and inboard piston valves (typical of the era in which most Prairies were built). Photo by R. V. Nixon.

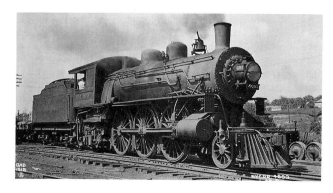

New York Central 4693 is a J-40d class engine, built in 1900 for passenger service on the Lake Shore & Michigan Southern. Those are 81" drivers. Photo by Ivan W. Saunders.

Fat-boilered 2-10-2s 6148 and 6161 lead a freight near Clearmont, Wyoming, in 1942. Both are lignite-burners and have extended smokeboxes. Number 6148 has Worthington BL feedwater heater; 6161 has an Elesco unit. The tank car behind 6148's tender is an auxiliary water car; the hoses and pipes are clearly visible along the side sill of the tender. Photo by W. R. McGee.

tle more powerful. The O-3 Mikados, built by Baldwin between 1915 and 1919, differed only in details from the O-2s. Between 1917 and 1923 Baldwin also built 148 Mikados in the O-1A class. The chief difference between the O-1/O-1As and the O-2/O-3s appears to be the boiler: a tapered boiler on the O-1s and O-1As and a larger straight-top boiler on the O-2s and O-3s. The Mikes were modified over the years with, variously, smaller cabs, cross-compound air pumps, and feedwater heaters — Elesco, Worthington BL, and Coffin.

The USRA assigned 15 heavy Mikados to the Burlington in 1919 — class O-4. They were rebuilt as oil burners and assigned to the western part of the railroad; several eventually went to subsidiaries Colorado & Southern and Fort Worth & Denver.

In 1912, only two years after receiving its first Mikados, the Burlington took delivery of five 2-10-2s for coal trains in southern Illinois. When the M-1s were built they were the world's heaviest nonarticulated locomotives, a distinction they didn't hold long. They weighed 378,700 pounds, only 2,000 pounds less than the USRA heavy 2-10-2 of 1919, and carried 301,800 pounds on their drivers. They were the first 2-10-2s with a wide firebox behind the drivers, and their frames were heavily reinforced. The combination of main and side rods heavy enough to transmit the enormous piston forces and the relatively small 60" drivers required supplemental counterweights on the main driver axle between the frames. Burlington was pleased enough with the performance of the 2-10-2s to purchase 26 more, classified M-2, in 1914. Two of them, 6108 and 6109, were equipped with lightweight alloy-steel reciprocating parts, eliminating the need for the supplemental counterweights, and classified M-2A. The road ran bridge-deflection tests with an M-2A and an M-1: At 40 mph the impact on the rail resulting from unbalanced forces was nearly 40 percent less for the M-2A. Burlington specified lightweight rods for the 45 2-10-2s Baldwin built between 1915 and 1921. Most of the 2-10-2s eventually received feedwater heaters, and the M-2As were given disk main drivers.

The USRA allocated 10 heavy 2-10-2s to the Burlington, which classed them M-3 and numbered them 6300-6309. For much of their life they were leased to the Colorado & Southern, which had five such machines of its own.

In the Teens the Burlington rebuilt and modernized many old 4-4-0s for light duties, creating the A-2 class. A few A-2s became inspection engines, like No. 360. Photo by C. H. Osgood; collection of L. E. Griffith.

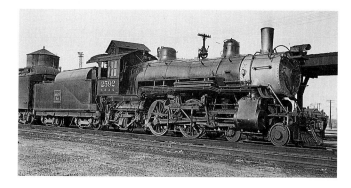

Number 2592, a P-6A, was rebuilt in 1927 from P-2 2544, a Rogers product of 1903. It lasted until 1951. The rebuilding included the replacement of the original 84¼" drivers with 69" wheels. Photo by Robert Graham.

In 1927 Baldwin built its first 2-10-4s for the CB&Q, the first 12 locomotives of the M-4 class. They had 64" drivers and 31" × 32" cylinders and weighed 524,000 pounds. They were assigned to coal trains in southern Illinois. Six more 2-10-4s arrived from Baldwin in 1929. Between 1934 and 1940 Burlington rebuilt the 2-10-4s with an eye to increasing their speed. They were given disk main drivers, better counterbalancing, and roller bearings on all axles, and their cylinder diameter was reduced to 28", reducing the tractive effort from 90,000 to 83,300 pounds.

For fast freight and occasional heavy passenger service, the road took delivery of eight 4-8-4s from Baldwin in 1930. They were numbered 5600-5607 and classed O-5, using the same letter as the 2-8-2s. In 1937 the West Burlington shops built 13 more O-5s, 5608-5620, using boilers furnished by Baldwin. The Baldwin 4-8-4s had 74" spoked drivers and Elesco feedwater heaters; the homebuilt O-5s had the same drivers but Worthington SA feedwater heaters. Burlington's third batch of 4-8-4s, class O-5A, which came from West Burlington shops in 1938 (5621-5625) and 1940 (5626-5635), were characterized by solid pilots, Boxpok drivers, lightweight rods, roller bearings, and vestibule cabs. Later some of the earlier O-5s were given the same improvements and reclassed O-5A. In 1942 the road applied poppet valves to No. 5625. The valves weren't equal to the power they transmitted, and by the time the Burlington decided the experiment was unsuccessful, it was purchasing diesels in quantity. The poppet-valve 4-8-4 was retired early and scrapped in 1954.

Two locomotives made a late transition from freight to passenger service. Between 1958 and 1966 the Burlington operated excursion trains over much of its system with 2-8-2 4960 and 4-8-4 5632.

Articulateds

CB&Q wasn't a major user of articulateds. The only mountainous territory on its map was in the Black Hills of Nebraska and South Dakota; the only other place where Mallets proved useful was the hump yard at Galesburg, Ill.

Three compound 2-6-6-2s, 4000-4002, class T-1, came to the Burlington in 1908. They had been built for the Great Northern, and it is uncertain whether they were delivered directly to the Burlington or worked

Pacific 2861, an S-1, leads a troop train west on the main line at Somonauk, Illinois, in 1945. Photo by L. E. Griffith.

The Hudsons and the Baldwin 4-8-4s looked very much alike. A comparison is possible as Hudson 3005 leads the Exposition Flyer past a freight behind O-5 5601 at Somonauk, Illinois, in September 1944. Photo by L. E. Griffith.

briefly on the GN. Five similar 2-6-6-2s, class T-1A, arrived from Baldwin in 1909. Like the T-1s they had Belpaire fireboxes over the rear two sets of drivers. The T-2 Mallets of 1910 had a rigid two-section boiler like those on Santa Fe's 2-6-6-2s, with a feedwater heater occupying the front half. They had 64" drivers — the T-1s had 55" and the T-1As, 56" — and their fireboxes were aft of the drivers over an outside-journal trailing truck. They were originally set up to burn lignite but were later converted to oil. They proved difficult to maintain and spent most of their lives in the Black Hills, about as remote as possible from Burlington headquarters. Most of the eight T-1s and T-1As found their way to the hump yard at Galesburg, and all but 4001 were rebuilt into 0-8-0s of the F-2 class in 1926 and 1927.

In 1911 Burlington's sole 2-8-8-2, class T-3, arrived from Baldwin. It worked the hump yard at Galesburg before being converted to oil fuel and sent to Alliance, Nebraska.

Passenger locomotives

In 1900 the CB&Q was using 4-4-0s, 4-6-0s, and 2-6-0s in passenger service. The 4-4-0s that were bumped from mainline duties soon after the turn of the century got a reprieve of a decade or more — the road rebuilt

105 between 1915 and 1917 for branchline service with new boilers, new cabs, and in some cases new cylinders. A few were rebuilt with a second cab over the pilot and smokebox for use as inspection engines.

The use of 2-6-0s with 69" and 72" drivers in fast mainline passenger service was unusual, but the Burlington's main lines had few curves, and the two-wheel lead truck proved satisfactory at speed. In 1895 Baldwin built a single high-speed 2-4-2 for the CB&Q. It was a development of the Q's passenger 2-6-0s, but the drivers were higher, 84¼", and in place of the third set of drivers was a trailing axle over which was a wide firebox. There was further innovation behind: a six-wheel, rigid-frame tender characteristic of British practice. The wide firebox proved to be the significant feature of the engine. The wheel arrangement wasn't repeated on the Burlington (Atlantic Coast Line tried two of the type), and No. 590 was rebuilt to a 4-4-2 in 1905.

The Burlington received its first 4-4-2s, the P-1C class, in 1899 and 1900. They were Vauclain compounds that shared driver size and tender configuration with the 2-4-2, but they had narrow fireboxes. Larger conventional tanks soon replaced the six-wheel tenders. The P-1Cs were followed in 1902 by six P-2Cs, also Vauclain compounds with 84¼" drivers, but a wide firebox behind the drivers supported by an outside-frame trailing truck. In 1903 Rogers delivered 25 simple Atlantics, class P-2, essentially the same as the P-2Cs but lighter and more powerful. The Q's last Atlantics were 20 Vauclain balanced compounds delivered in 1904 and 1905. They had low-pressure cylinders in the usual location driving the second set of drivers and a pair of high-pressure cylinders between the frames driving the first set. To provide enough space for the high-pressure main rods, the P-3s had longer boilers and frames, with a noticeable space between the lead truck and drivers.

The P-1Cs were rebuilt to simple engines with 78" drivers between 1913 and 1915. They were reclassed P-1 but kept their numbers. The P-2Cs underwent the same rebuilding as the P-1Cs between 1915 and 1917 and were given a new class, P-5, and new numbers. In the late 1920s the P-3s were rebuilt to classes P-5 and P-6, and a few P-2s were rebuilt to class P-6A. Unlike the Santa Fe's rebuilt balanced-compound Atlantics, Burlington's rebuilds retained the extra length at the front of the engine.

Burlington's first Pacifics were class S-1, delivered by Baldwin and Schenectady between 1906 and 1909. The design was developed from the R-5 Prairie, and the early S-1s had a number of parts that were interchangeable with the 2-6-2s, such as journals and cylinders. The S-1s had 74" drivers and 22" × 28" cylinders, and weighed 234,000 pounds. The S-2s, built almost immediately after the S-1s, weighed about the same but had 69" drivers and 25" × 28" cylinders, giving them 3,500 pounds more tractive effort. They carried a boiler pressure of only 160 pounds.

Within a few years the S-2s were given 74" drivers. S-1 Pacifics 2800-2844 were built with inboard piston valves and Stephenson valve gear, but the other S-1s and the S-2s had the curious combination of inboard valves and Walschaerts gear. When the classes were rebuilt to S-1A and S-2A between 1923 and 1930 they received outboard piston valves and superheaters, and 2800-2844 were fitted with Walschaerts gear. Most of the two classes received feedwater heaters.

Burlington's third class of Pacifics was the S-3, which had the 74" drivers of the S-1 plus 27" × 28" cylinders and a boiler pressure of 180 pounds. It was slightly lighter than the USRA light Pacific but produced

a little more tractive effort. Baldwin delivered 15 in 1915 and 10 in 1918. Five more arrived in 1922, two oil burners for the Fort Worth & Denver and three coal burners with 69" drivers for the Colorado & Southern.

By the 1920s Burlington's long-distance passenger trains needed heavier power. Lima delivered eight 4-8-2s, 7000-7007, in 1922 similar in dimensions to those of the neighboring and competing Rock Island and Union Pacific: 74" drivers, 27" × 30" cylinders, and total weight 364,000 pounds. They had Rushton trailing trucks and eight-wheel tenders. The locomotives were designed to burn lignite and were assigned to Burlington's western lines. Baldwin built 13 more 4-8-2s, class B-1A, in 1925. Six were equipped for burning bituminous coal and seven for lignite. They were built with Worthington BL feedwater heaters, except for 7011, which had an Elesco unit, and had Delta trailing trucks and 12-wheel tenders. The first eight eventually received Worthington feedwater heaters, and some were converted to burn bituminous. Three of the second group became oil burners.

In 1930 the Mountains gave way to 12 4-6-4s from Baldwin, 3000-3011, class S-4. The Hudsons had 78" drivers and 25" × 28" cylinders — the same size cylinders as the S-2 Pacifics, but with 250 pounds of boiler pressure behind them. West Burlington Shops built a thirteenth S4 in 1935 using a boiler supplied by Baldwin.

In 1937 West Burlington fitted 3002 with a stainless steel shroud and roller-bearing side rods to substitute when necessary for the diesels of the *Zephyrs*. The locomotive was renumbered 4000, classed S-4A, and named *Aeolus* (which crews promptly corrupted to Alice the Goon, after a character in the "Popeye" comic strip). In 1938 West Burlington built a duplicate S-4A, 4001, also named *Aeolus*, and rebuilt three S-4s with the same mechanical improvements but no shrouding.

Switchers

Between 1900 and 1913 the Burlington built 130 G-3 0-6-0s in its shops at Aurora, Ill., Havelock, Neb., and West Burlington, Iowa, and Baldwin built 50 more in 1912 and 1913. The G-3s were fairly conventional-looking 0-6-0s, with piston valves (albeit driven by Stephenson valve gear) and main rods connected to the rear drivers. The G-4s were also products of Burlington's shops, old 2-8-0s that had their lead trucks and rear drivers removed. The program lasted long enough that a few latecomers reused numbers of earlier G-4s that had been retired.

The G-6 0-6-0s were also homebuilt. They looked like the G-3s but were heavier and more powerful. The G-7, -8, -9, and -10 classes were rebuilt from 2-6-2s. The amount of rebuilding varied. Some locomotives retained their original Belpaire fireboxes; others got new radial-stay fireboxes. All got lower drivers; some had their driver wheelbases reduced, and others kept the original wheel spacing — the latter were particularly ugly members of a roster that was generally deficient in good-looking locomotives. The G-10s were renumbered; the other three classes kept their original numbers.

The USRA allocated 10 0-6-0s to the Burlington. They were built in 1919 by Alco's Cooke Works; Burlington numbered them 500-509 and classed them G-5, reusing a class that had been applied to a single engine and vacated shortly after 1904. They were considerably more modern looking than Burlington's previous 0-6-0s; the application of Burlington's standard "mantel-clock" headlights was a curiosity. In 1921 Baldwin built 15 0-6-0s that were copies of the USRA design, except that they were not superheated.

The USRA was responsible for Burlington's first 0-8-0s, class F-1, 540-549. They were built by Alco's Brooks Works in 1919 and, like the USRA 0-6-0s, were given standard Burlington headlights. Burlington's second 0-8-0s were rebuilds. By the mid-1920s the T-1 class 2-6-6-2s were assigned to the hump yard at Galesburg, Illinois. They were good steamers but expensive to operate — any economy resulting from using steam twice was more than compensated for by the cost of maintaing the articulated running gear. The Denver shops converted No. 4003 into 0-8-0 550 in 1926. The resulting locomotive was far closer to a new locomotive than a rebuilt one. It had a new mechanism similar to that of the USRA 0-8-0 but using No. 4003's 56" drivers; 4003's boiler had to be shortened about six feet. The road was quite pleased with the result of the conversion, and found that the boiler was more than ample for the 24" × 32" cylinders, so subsequent 2-6-6-2-to-0-8-0 conversions used 25" cylin-

Burlington built O-5A 5633, a handsome 4-8-4, in its West Burlington, Iowa, shops in 1940. With its solid pilot and vestibule cab, it represents the ultimate development of steam freight power on the road. Here one is leading a westbound freight at Eola, Illinois, in 1949. Photo by Henry J. McCord.

ders. Seven of the eight T-1s and T-1As were converted; No. 4001 was scheduled for conversion but was scrapped instead.

The sole member of the F-3 class was No. 5020, an O-1 Mikado that was converted to an 0-8-0 by the simple expedient of removing its lead and trailing trucks. The job was done some time in the late 1920s or early 1930s; No. 5020's retirement in 1939 constitutes an indication that it wasn't a success as a switcher.

Historical and technical society: Burlington Route Historical Society, P. O. Box 456, La Grange, IL

Recommended reading: *Steam Locomotives of the Burlington Route*, by Bernard Corbin and William Kerka, published in 1960 by the authors

Published rosters: *Locomotives of the Chicago, Burlington & Quincy Railroad*, published in 1936 and 1937 (supplement issued in 1948) by the Railway & Locomotive Historical Society, P. O. Box 1418, Westford, MA 01886

CB&Q STEAM LOCOMOTIVES BUILT SINCE 1900

Type	Class	Numbers	Qty	Builder	Built	Retired	Notes
0-6-0	G-3	1400-1579	180	CB&Q, BL BLW	1900-1913	1928-1947	
0-6-0	G-4A	1600-1654	55	CB&Q	1900-1903	1909-1928	Rebuilt from 2-8-0
0-6-0	G-4B,C	1601-1603, 1647, 1651, 1655-1677	28	CB&Q	1904-1921	1926-1939	Rebuilt from 2-8-0
0-6-0	G-5	500-509	10	Cooke	1919	1954	USRA
0-6-0	G-5A	510-524	15	Baldwin	1921	1953-1955	USRA copy
0-6-0	G-6	1678-1699	22	CB&Q	1905-1910	1931-1955	
0-6-0	G-7	1702, 170	32	CB&Q		1931, 1933	Rebuilt from 2-6-2
0-6-0	G-8	1710-1769	70	CB&Q	1917-1929	1938-1951	Rebuilt from 2-6-2
0-6-0	G-9	1805-1848	22	CB&Q	1925-1928	1942-1951	Rebuilt from 2-6-2
0-6-0	G-10	560-594	35	CB&Q	1928-1930	1951-1955	Rebuilt from 2-6-2
0-8-0	F-1	540-549	10	Brooks	1919	1953-1956	USRA
0-8-0	F-2	550-556	7	CB&Q	1926-1927	1946-	Rebuilt from 2-6-6-2
0-8-0	F-3	5020	1	CB&Q		1939	
2-6-0	H-4	1220-1262	43	BLW, Rogers, CB&Q	1899-1900		19 rebuilt to K-10
2-6-2	R-1	1700-1703	4	CB&Q	1900	1929-1930	2 rebuilt to 0-6-0
2-6-2	R-2	1710-1769	60	BLW, CB&Q	1901		All rebuilt to 0-6-0
2-6-2	R-3	1800-1849	50	Baldwin	1902	1928-1930	Many rebuilt to 0-6-0
2-6-2	R-4	1900-1939	40	Baldwin	1904	1928-1953	Few rebuilt to 0-6-0
2-6-2	R-4	1940-1989	50	Brooks	1905	1928-1954	Few rebuilt to 0-6-0
2-6-2	R-4	2000-2049	50	Baldwin	1906	1928-1951	Few rebuilt to 0-6-0
2-6-2	R-5	2050-2224	175	BLW, Brks	1906-1907	1928-1953	
2-8-0	D-4A	3100-3174	75	Schen	1903	1928-1946	
2-8-0	D-4B	3175-3199	25	Baldwin	1903	1928-1932	
2-8-0	D-7	3030, 3031	2	Baldwin	1903	1928	Ex-Iowa & St. Louis
2-8-2	O-1	5000-5059	60	Baldwin	1910-1911	1927-1951	
2-8-2	O-1A	4940-4999	60	Baldwin	1923	1951-1957	
2-8-2	O-1A	5060-5147	88	Baldwin	1917-1922	1953-1957	
2-8-2	O-2	5200-5299	100	Baldwin	1912-1913	1931-1954	
2-8-2	O-3	5300-5359	60	Baldwin	1915-1919	1951-1956	
2-8-2	O-4	5500-5514	15	Baldwin	1919	1954-1957	
2-10-2	M-1	6000-6004	5	Baldwin	1912	1933, 1950	
2-10-2	M-2	6100-6107	8	Baldwin	1914	1951-1953	
2-10-2	M-2A	6108, 6109	2	Baldwin	1914	1952	
2-10-2	M-2	6110-6125	16	Baldwin	1914	1951-1954	
2-10-2	M-2A	6126-6170	45	Baldwin	1915-1921	1951-1954	
2-10-2	M-3	6300-6309	10	Brooks	1919	1953-1954	USRA, leased to C&S
2-10-4	M-4	6310-6327	18	Baldwin	1927, 1929		
2-6-6-2	T-1	4000-4002	3	Baldwin	1908		Rebuilt to F-2, 1926-1927
2-6-6-2	T-1A	4003-4007	5	Baldwin	1909		Rebuilt to F-2, 1926-1927
2-6-6-2	T-2	4100-4109	10	Baldwin	1910	1929-	
2-8-8-2	T-3	4200	1	Baldwin	1911	1934	
4-4-0	A-2	374-478	105	CB&Q	1915-1918	1927-1935	Rebuilt
4-4-0	A-6	479	1	Baldwin	1901	1923	Ex-DRI&NW
4-4-2	P-1C	2500-2504	5	CB&Q	1899-1900	1932-1933	Ex-1591-1595
4-4-2	P-2C	2510-2515	6	Baldwin	1902		Ex-1584-1589
4-4-2	P-2	2520-2527	8	Rogers	1903	1930-	Ex-1576-1583
4-4-2	P-2	2528-2544	17	Rogers	1902-1903	1930	
4-4-2	P-3C	2700-2719	20	Baldwin	1904-1905		Rebuilt to P-5 and P-6
4-4-2	P-4	2599	1	CB&Q	1905	1929	Rebuilt from 2-4-2
4-4-2	P-5	2550-2555	6	CB&Q	1915-1917	1942-1947	Ex-P-2
4-4-2	P-5	2558-2574	14	CB&Q	1924-1927	1942-1954	Ex-P-3
4-4-2	P-6	2580-2585	6	CB&Q	1927-1928	1951-1953	Ex-P-3
4-4-2	P-6A	2590-2597	8	CB&Q	1927-1928	1947-1954	Ex-P-2
4-6-0	K-10	950-968	19	CB&Q	1908-1914	1931-1954	Rebuilt from 2-6-0
4-6-0	K-4	700-723	24	CB&Q	1900-1904	1931-1953	
4-6-0	K-5	800-807	8	CB&Q	1904-1905	1929-1930	
4-6-2	S-1	2800-2869	70	BLW, Schenectady	1906-1909	1933-1955	Most rebuilt to S-1A
4-6-2	S-2	2900-2949	50	Baldwin	1910	1933-1955	Most rebuilt to S-2A
4-6-2	S-3	2950-2974	25	Baldwin	1915, 1918	1951-1958	
4-6-4	S-4	3000-3011	12	Baldwin	1930	1955-	4 rebuilt to S-4A
4-6-4	S-4	3012	1	CB&Q	1935	1955	
4-6-4	S-4A	4001	1	CB&Q	1938		
4-8-2	B-1	7000-7007	8	Lima	1922	1953	
4-8-2	B-1A	7008-7020	13	Baldwin	1925	1953-1955	
4-8-4	O-5	5600-5607	8	Baldwin	1930	1955-	
4-8-4	O-5A	5608-5635	28	CB&Q	1936-1940	1953-	

CHICAGO GREAT WESTERN RAILROAD

The Chicago Great Western began life as the Minnesota & Northwestern Railroad, which completed a line from St. Paul, Minn., to Chicago in 1888. In 1891 the company opened a line southwest from Oelwein, Iowa, to Kansas City, and in 1903 west and southwest from Oelwein to Omaha. During the 1890s it acquired a few secondary lines in southeast Minnesota and northern Iowa, but for the most part it remained a railroad with only main lines, no branches. It acquired the Chicago Great Western name during a reorganization in 1892.

The CGW was never a major passenger carrier. The 2-10-4s the CGW acquired in 1930 for fast, heavy freight trains were unique in the Upper Midwest. Most of the road's competitors used 4-8-4s because they were also useful for heavy passenger trains — CGW's passenger trains never outgrew their light Pacifics.

The CGW explored the possibilities of gas-mechanical and gas-electric cars and diesel locomotives quite early, began dieselizing in earnest in December 1946, and completed the job in 1950. It acquired a reputation for long sets of Electro-Motive F units pulling long, heavy, infrequent freight trains.

The road had to compete hard for freight traffic. Its main routes from Chicago to Kansas City, Omaha, and the Twin Cities were paralleled by five or six other railroads, and on each of those routes at least two of its competitors continued beyond those gateway cities. By the time the CGW was merged by the Chicago & North Western in 1968 there was considerably more rail capacity than necessary between Chicago and the Missouri River, and the C&NW abandoned most of CGW's lines.

Freight locomotives

The ten G-3-class 2-8-0s of 1900 were Vauclain compounds with 55" drivers. They were converted to single-expansion locomotives between 1903 and 1907. The G-2 class 2-8-0s delivered by Rhode Island in 1901 were the same size, about 180,000 pounds, but were cross-compounds. They were simpled and converted to 0-8-0s in 1909 and 1910.

The G-3 Consolidations were the next size larger: 63" drivers, 24" × 30" cylinders, and 222,650 pounds total weight. Between 1927 and 1930 12 of the class were rebuilt with larger fireboxes and 26" cylinders (gaining 18,000 pounds in the process) and reclassed G-4.

CGW discovered the 2-6-2 type in 1902 and within a year had 95 Prairies on its roster in six classes, 63 built by Brooks and 32 by Rhode Island. Among the 2-6-2s there was considerable variation in cylinder size and boiler pressure, the latter ranging from 150 to 225 pounds. The F-1 and F-6 classes were passenger engines, with 73" and 68" drivers, respectively; both classes were rebuilt to Pacifics. The other classes, F-2 through F-5, were freight engines with 63" drivers. The F-2s and F-4s were built as compounds and later simpled; the F-3s were ultimately rebuilt to Pacifics, but half of them became 2-6-6-2s first. A number of F-4s and F-5s were rebuilt with superheaters, piston valves, and Walschaerts valve gear and were reclassed F-7. Most of the F-4s, F-5s, and F-7s were scrapped between 1929 and 1932; the F-7s that weren't scrapped then survived until 1950.

The Great Western received 10 2-8-2s from Baldwin in 1912: class L-1, 700-709. They had 63" drivers and 27" × 30" cylinders, and weighed 283,000 pounds. Baldwin delivered 10 more in 1916. The principal dimensions were the same, but they weighed 2,900 pounds more and were classed L-2.

In 1918 the USRA assigned 10 light Mikados to the CGW. The road numbered them 750-759, well above its own 2-8-2s, and classed them L-3. When CGW returned to Baldwin in 1920 for 10 more 2-8-2s, it specified not USRA copies but returned to its own 1912 design, and 720-729 were classed L-1a. Between 1937 and 1939 Oelwein Shops rebuilt six L-1s with stokers, new frames, and disk main drivers, classing them L-1b and adding 30 to their numbers.

In 1916 Baldwin delivered seven 2-10-2s to the Great Western, class M-1, numbers 800-806. They weighed almost as much as a USRA light 2-10-2 and had cylinders and drivers both 3" larger in diameter, but with

Mikado 716 was built by Baldwin in 1916, and in this builder photo is classed L1a. Baldwin photo.

Chicago Great Western's best-known locomotives were the Texas types built by Lima and Baldwin in 1930 and 1931. Except for details they are duplicates of Texas & Pacific's 2-10-4s. Lima photo.

a boiler pressure of 180 pounds tractive effort was only 43,440 pounds, considerably less than that of any of CGW's Mikados. Five 2-10-2s were scrapped in 1936 and a sixth in 1939; No. 800 hung on until 1950.

In 1929 the road ordered 15 2-10-4s from Lima, and in 1930 6 more from Lima and 15 from Baldwin. They differed from Texas & Pacific's 2-10-4s only in a few details: coal instead of oil fuel, a second sand dome behind the steam dome, and Coffin or Worthington feedwater heaters instead of the Elesco units used by T&P. The T-1 and T-2 classes had conventional trailing-truck boosters, and the T-3 class had Bethlehem Auxiliary Engines driving two axles of the rear tender truck. The 2-10-4s were assigned to the routes from Oelwein to Chicago, St. Paul, and

Kirmeyer, Missouri, across the Missouri River from Leavenworth, Kansas — the Missouri River bridge there couldn't support a Texas type. Soon after the 2-10-4s arrived, Great Western began to place many of its older locomotives in dead storage.

L-1a Mikes 724 and 727 were converted to oil burners in 1940 and assigned to work between Kirmeyer and Kansas City. In 1941 and 1942 wartime traffic caused CGW to pull three L-2 Mikados (710-712) and four Consolidations out of storage and rebuild them.

Great Western took delivery of ten 2-6-6-2 Mallets from Baldwin in 1910. The low-drivered machines proved unsuitable, and by the time CGW sold them to Clinchfield in 1916, 20 2-8-2s had joined CGW's roster. CGW had three more 2-6-6-2s, which it built from three 2-6-2s, much as the Santa Fe did — the front section of the boiler of the homemade Mallets was a feedwater heater. The three were soon taken apart and rebuilt into Pacifics.

Passenger locomotives

Great Western's Ten-Wheelers were a curious lot. The E-3 class, Nos. 235-244, built by Rhode Island in 1900, had 63" drivers, making them dual-service engines. They were sold in 1917, six to the Evansville & Indianapolis and four (along with the ten Baldwin 4-6-0s in the E-1 and E-2 classes) to the Canadian government. The six E-4s of 1901, 170-175, were passenger engines with 68" drivers; the sole E-5, built by Baldwin in 1902, 63". The E-6 and E-7 classes, built by Baldwin in 1909 and 1910, were similar and had 73" drivers. The E-6s went to scrap in 1930 and 1930; the E-7s were rebuilt with stokers and lasted until the end of steam.

In 1910 Great Western began converting the F-6 Prairies to Pacifics in the K-1, K-2, K-3, and K-3a classes. The differences among the classes were primarily in cylinder size and boiler pressure; all kept the 68" drivers they had as Prairies, except the sole K-2, which had 70" drivers for two years before it became a K-3 (and later a K-2a). Superheaters were applied after conversion, necessitating further reclassification. At least one member of each class was subsequently classed K-2a. Most were scrapped between 1929 and 1932. The six that survived through World War II were all in the K-2a class.

The E-7-class Ten-Wheelers were obviously passenger engines with their 73" drivers. Dlsk drivers such as No. 507 received during a visit to Oelwein shops were rare on small locomotives, particularly in full sets. Photo by Henry J. McCord.

Light Pacific 905 has a slightly British look, with its capped stack, curved running board step, and lack of external plumbing. It was built by Brooks in 1903 as a 2-6-2, rebuilt to a Pacific in 1911, and given its British styling in 1924. Photo by C. W. Jernstrom.

Five Pacifics were delivered by Baldwin in 1913, 925-929, class K-5, and three more, 930-932, in 1916. They were about the same size as USRA light Pacifics. The first three, 925-927, were scrapped in 1932; the others remained in service until 1950.

Between 1915 and 1918 CGW rebuilt the three H-2 Mallets, which had been rebuilt from F-3 Prairies, and the other three F-3s into K-6 class Pacifics. They had 63" drivers and weighed 211,200 pounds, less than the E-7 class Ten-Wheelers.

Switchers

Great Western's largest group of switchers was the B-5 class, 15 0-6-0s built by Baldwin in 1915 and 1916. They had 51" drivers and piston valves; engine weight was 156,620 pounds. The road received five USRA six-wheel switchers from Pittsburgh in 1919 and classed them B-6. Two more 0-6-0s, the B-7 class, were delivered by Baldwin in 1922. They were 5,000 pounds lighter than the USRA engines; boiler pressure was 10 pounds lower; cylinder diameter was an inch greater; piston stroke was two inches less; tractive force worked out to about the same. There

may have been an advantage in having drivers the same size as several previous 0-6-0 classes. When CGW leased the St. Paul Bridge & Terminal Railroad in 1934 it acquired B-8-class 0-6-0s 10 and 11 and 2-6-0s 12-16.

In 1908 the road rebuilt G-1-class 2-8-0 No. 303 into an 0-8-0. It was reclassified J-1 but retained its number. In 1910 the entire G-2 class of 2-8-0s was rebuilt into J-2-class 0-8-0s, and were converted from cross-compounds to simple locomotives at the same time. G-1 No. 308 became a J-1 in 1917. Two large 0-8-0s built by Baldwin in 1925 and 1926 were former St. Paul Bridge & Terminal engines. They were chunky-looking machines with large air reservoirs on the pilot beam and Elesco feedwater heaters hung out ahead of the smokebox.

Oddities

CGW's homemade 2-6-6-2s count as oddities, with their Stephenson valve gear and inside piston valves. The shops at Oelwein didn't reserve disk drivers for large, modern locomotives: 4-6-0s and 2-6-2s received them — even though the latter retained their inside-journal spoked trailing trucks. Several of the road's Pacifics received a measure of British

109

styling, primarily concealed piping and flanged stacks, but at least one was painted red and lined in gold for the Twin-Cities-Rochester *Red Bird* of 1925.

CGW STEAM LOCOMOTIVES BUILT SINCE 1900

Published rosters:
Railroad Magazine, July 1939, page 121
Railroad History, No. 154, page 86

Type	Class	Numbers	Qty	Builder	Built	Retired	Notes
0-6-0	B-3	450-454	5	Brooks	1902	1936, 1948	
0-6-0	B-4	455-464	10	Baldwin	1911	1935, 1948	
0-6-0	B-5	465-479	15	Baldwin	1915, 1916	1949-1950	
0-6-0	B-6	480-484	5	Pittsburgh	1919	1949-1950	USRA
0-6-0	B-7	485-487	3	Baldwin	1921	1936, 1950	
0-6-0	B-8	10, 11	2	Alco	1907	1948	Ex-StPB&T
0-8-0	J-1	303, 308	2	CGW	1909, 1917	1932, 1930	Rebuilt from G-1 2-8-0s
0-8-0	J-2	310-319	10	CGW	1910	1930-1932	
0-8-0	J-3	17	1	Baldwin	1925	1950	Ex-StPB&T
0-8-0	J-4	18	1	Baldwin	1926	1950	Ex-StPB&T
2-6-0	D-3	12-16	5	Alco	1914-1917	1948, 1950	Ex-StPB&T
2-6-2	F-1	180-182	3	Brooks	1902		Rebuilt to 4-6-2s 921-923
2-6-2	F-2	221-246	26	Rhode Is.	1902	1929-1930	
2-6-2	F-3	247-252	6	Rhode Is.	1902		247, 248, 250 rebuilt to 2-6-6-2s 650-652 in 1910; 249-251 rebuilt to 4-6-2s 953-955 in 1916-1918
2-6-2	F-4	253-272	20	Brooks	1902	1929-1932, 1950	11 F-4s rebuilt to F-7a, 3 of which lasted until 1950
2-6-2	F-5	273-292	20	Brooks	1903	1929-1932, 1950	10 F-5s rebuilt to F-7b, 6 of which last until 1950
2-6-2	F-6	901-920	20	Brooks	1903		All rebuilt to K-1, K-2, and K-3-class 4-6-2s
2-8-0	G-1	300-309	10	Baldwin	1900		Two rebuilt to J-1, two scrapped in 1930 and 1933, six sold between 1910 and 1916
2-8-0	G-2	310-319	10	Rhode Is.	1901		All rebuilt to J-2
2-8-0	G-3	320-359	30	Baldwin	1909-1910	1930-1950	12 rebuilt to G-4
2-8-0	G-4	600-611	12	CGW	1927-1930	1949-1950	600-611 rebuilt from 356, 330, 346, 322, 344, 359, 328, 332, 336, 337, 325, and 323

Type	Class	Numbers	Qty	Builder	Built	Retired	Notes
2-8-2	L-1	700-709	10	Baldwin	1912	1949-1950	L1 703, 705-709 rebuilt to L-1b 733, 735-739
2-8-2	L-1a	720-729	10	Baldwin	1920	1942-1950	
2-8-2	L-2	710-719	5	Baldwin	1916	1950	L2 710, 712, 716 rebuilt to L-2b 740-742
2-8-2	L-3	750-759	10	Baldwin	1918	1939-1950	USRA
2-10-2	M-1	800-806	7	Baldwin	1916	1936-1950	
2-10-4	T-1	850-864	15	Lima	1930	1948-1950	
2-10-4	T-1	880-882	3	Lima	1931	1948-1950	
2-10-4	T-2	865-873	9	Baldwin	1930	1948-1950	
2-10-4	T-3	874-879	6	Baldwin	1930	1948-1949	
2-10-4	T-3	883-885	3	Lima	1931	1948-1949	
2-6-6-2	H-1	600-609	10	Baldwin	1910		Sold to Clinchfield 1916
2-6-6-2	H-2?	650-652	3	CGW	1910		Rebuilt 1916-1918 to 4-6-2s 950-952
4-6-0	E-3	235-244	10	Rhode Is.	1900		Sold 1917
4-6-0	E-4	170-175	6	Richmond	1901	1914-1921	
4-6-0	E-5	220	1	Baldwin	1902		Sold 1916
4-6-0	E-6	500-503	4	Baldwin	1909	1930-1931	
4-6-0	E-7	504-509	6	Baldwin	1910	1950	
4-6-2	K-1, K-2, K-3	901-920	20	CGW	1910-1917	1932-1950	
4-6-2	K-4	921-923	3	CGW	1911-1912	1932	Rebuilt from 2-6-2s 180-182
4-6-2	K-5	925-932	5	Baldwin	1913, 1916	1932, 1950	
4-6-2	K-6	950-952	3	CGW	1915	1932	Rebuilt from 2-6-6-2s 650-652
4-6-2	K-6	953-955	3	CGW	1916-1918	1932	Rebuilt from 2-6-2s 249, 251, and 252

CHICAGO, INDIANAPOLIS & LOUISVILLE RAILWAY

By 1900 the Chicago, Indianapolis & Louisville had achieved full growth. It consisted of two main lines that crossed at Monon, Indiana: Chicago to Indianapolis, and Michigan City, Ind., to Louisville; plus several branches into coal- and limestone-producing areas west of the Louisville line. The town where the main lines crossed gave the road its nickname, the Monon Route. In 1902 it came under the joint control of the Southern Railway and the Louisville & Nashville. It prospered for a while, but began to decline in the 1920s. Baltimore & Ohio acquired the Monon's principal connection at Indianapolis, the Cincinnati, Indianapolis & Western; and the Monon's two owners preferred other routes from Louisville to Chicago for connecting traffic. The C&IL entered bankruptcy in 1933 and continued to decline to the point where abandonment was imminent.

In 1946 the Monon was reorganized. Its new president, John W. Barriger III, undertook a complete rebuilding of the railroad, and high on his agenda was replacing Monon's steam locomotives with diesels. The last steam locomotive in service was 0-6-0 No. 95, assigned to switching at New Albany, Ind.; it was taken out of service on June 28, 1949.

Most of Monon's steam locomotives were built by Alco's Brooks Works. A general renumbering took place in 1911; those numbers are used in the text and tables below.

Freight locomotives

The Monon's most significant deviation from the usual progression of freight locomotive types was the Twelve-Wheeler: 22 of them between 1898 and 1903. Both classes had 21" × 26" cylinders; the E-1s had 55" drivers, the E-2s, 57". The 4-8-0 was not uncommon at the turn of the century, but it was often a cross-compound locomotive. Monon's were built as simple (single-expansion) locomotives with inboard piston valves. The E-1s were rebuilt in the 1920s with outboard piston valves and Walschaerts valve gear and survived until dieselization; the E-2s were scrapped in 1936 and 1937 without being rebuilt.

The 4-8-0s were followed by several classes of 2-8-0s, mostly 57"-drivered machines weighing from 194,000 to 216,000 pounds. The H-3 class (built after the H-5 and before the H-6) had 63" drivers.

All the Monon's Mikados had 63" drivers. The J-1s, built in 1912, 1918, and 1923, were slightly lighter than the USRA light 2-8-2 but had

Twelve-Wheeler 205 was built by Brooks in 1899. Its inboard valves and narrow Belpaire firebox are typical of Brooks locomotives of the time. It was renumbered 225 in 1911 and rebuilt in 1926 with outboard piston valves, Walschaerts valve gear, a wide radial-stay firebox above the drivers, and an extended smokebox. 205, Alco Historic Photos; 225, collection of Harold K. Vollrath.

Pacific 432 displays the flanged or capped stack and below-center headlight that make up the Monon look. Photo by Richard J. Cook.

28" × 30" cylinders which yielded slightly more tractive effort. Five USRA light 2-8-2s came to the Monon right after the 1918 batch of J-1s. Monon reverted to its own design for the 1923 J-1s, but the J-3s of 1926 were beefed-up copies of the USRA design, 31,000 pounds, with 27" × 32" cylinders. The J-4s, Monon's last steam engines, shared dimensions with the J-3s but were yet heavier.

The largest locomotives on the Monon were eight 2-10-2s, five built by Alco's Schenectady Works in 1914 and three by the Brooks Works in 1916.

Monon's decline in the late 1930s and early 1940s gave it an excess of motive power when other railroads were eager to buy used steam locomotives. Two 2-10-2s were sold to the Tennessee Railroad, one in 1942 and the other in 1945. In 1941 and 1942 Soo Line took eight J-1 2-8-2s; other J-1s went to the Tennessee and the Pittsburgh & West Virginia.

The J-4s were all sold upon dieselization to the Pittsburgh & Shawmut (eight) and the Tennessee, Alabama & Georgia (two).

Passenger locomotives

Monon received two Atlantics in 1901. They were typical Brooks Atlantics of the turn of the century, with 73" drivers, inboard piston valves, and inboard bearing trailing trucks. During the 1920s they were rebuilt with outboard piston valves, Baker valve gear, and cast trailing trucks. They eventually proved too light for steel passenger trains and were scrapped in 1936.

The 69" drivers of the two G-6 Ten-Wheelers of 1900 indicate they were intended for passenger service, but in the early 1920s they were rebuilt along with a number of older 4-6-0s into branchline engines with 51" drivers.

Most of Monon's 4-6-2s were light machines, ranging from 209,000 to 227,000 pounds total weight (the USRA light Pacific weighed 277,000 pounds). The principal difference between the K-1 and K-2 Pacifics, built between 1905 and 1907, was a half inch of cylinder diameter; both had 69" drivers. Rebuilding removed that difference — as rebuilt, both classes had 21½" × 26" cylinders. The K-3s of 1909, K-4s of 1911, and K-5s of 1912 and 1923 had 73" drivers. The K-3s and the K-4s were built with 22" × 28" cylinders; the K-5s, with 23½" × 28" cylinders. During rebuilding the K-4s and K-5s got 23" × 28" cylinders.

The heaviest Pacifics on the roster were the K-6 class, built in 1916. They weighed 285,000 pounds and had 26" × 28" cylinders and 73" drivers. Too heavy for the bridges on the Indianapolis route, they were usually assigned to Chicago-Louisville night trains.

Switchers

Monon's only switchers were 0-6-0s. The three classes built after 1900 exhibit typical growth: 51" drivers and 19" × 24" cylinders for the B-7s of 1902; 51" and 20" × 26" for the B-8s of 1905-1907; and 57" and 23" × 28" for the B-9s, built in 1923.

Proposed locomotives

In 1928 the Monon wanted a pair of engines to use as helpers on the grade north out of the Wabash River valley at Lafayette, Ind. Baldwin proposed a 4-10-4 that would have weighed about 475,000 pounds, as much as a medium-size 2-10-4. Such engines would have required bridges and track to be strengthened and straightened wherever they were used; the J-4 Mikados of 1929 were a wiser choice. (In 1964 the Monon purchased Alco C-628s and experienced roughly the same difficulties it would have had with the 4-10-4s. The road sold them and returned to four-axle diesel power.)

After the Depression Monon's motive power department was intrigued by high-speed simple articulateds. In 1936 Lima proposed a light 2-6-6-6 to the road and in 1940 returned with a 2-6-6-4 proposal, and the road's engineers kept files on the performance of 4-6-6-4s of the Delaware & Hudson and the Clinchfield. Finances precluded the purchase of anything of the kind, and Electro-Motive F3s ultimately proved far better suited to Monon's needs.

Historical and technical society: Monon Railroad Historical-Technical Society, P. O. Box 5303, Lafayette, IN 47903

Recommended reading: *Monon Route*, by George W. Hilton, published in 1978 by Howell-North Books (ISBN 0-8310-7115-X)

Published rosters: *Railroad Magazine*, January 1933, page 130

CI&L STEAM LOCOMOTIVES BUILT SINCE 1900

Type	Class	Numbers	Qty	Builder	Built	Retired	Notes
0-6-0	B-7	25-27	3	Brooks	1902	1937	
0-6-0	B-8	30-36	7	Brooks	1905-1907	1940-1949	
0-6-0	B-9	37-39	3	Brooks	1923	1947	
2-8-0	H-3	250-254	5	Brooks	1910	1936-1946	
2-8-0	H-4	260-265	6	Brooks	1904-1905	1940	
2-8-0	H-5	270-272	3	Brooks	1906	1940-1941	
2-8-0	H-6	280-286	7	Brooks	1911	1941-1948	
2-8-2	J-1	500-533	34	Brooks	1912-1923	1939-1948	
2-8-2	J-2	550-554	5	Schenectady	1918	1947-1949	USRA
2-8-2	J-3	560-565	6	Richmond	1926	1947-1948	
2-8-2	J-4	570-579	10	Schenectady	1929	Sold	
2-10-2	L-1	600-607	8	Schen, Brooks	1914, 1916	1941-1947	
4-4-2	I-1	390, 391	2	Brooks	1901	1936	
4-6-0	G-6	140, 141	2	Brooks	1900	1942, 1948	
4-6-2	K-1	400-403	4	Brooks	1905	1939	
4-6-2	K-2	410-415	6	Brooks	1906-1907	1939-1947	
4-6-2	K-3	420-422	3	Brooks	1909	1941-1947	
4-6-2	K-4	430-432	3	Brooks	1911	1947	
4-6-2	K-5	440-445	6	Brooks	1912, 1923	1946-1948	
4-6-2	K-6	450-452	3	Brooks	1916	1941-1947	
4-8-0	E-1	220-231	12	Brooks	1898-1900	1946-1949	
4-8-0	E-2	240-249	10	Brooks	1902-1903	1936-1937	

CHICAGO, MILWAUKEE, ST. PAUL & PACIFIC RAILROAD

By Jim Scribbins

In 1900 Chicago, Milwaukee & St. Paul's two principal routes were from Chicago through Milwaukee to St. Paul and Minneapolis, and from Chicago to Council Bluffs, Iowa, and Omaha, Nebraska. A branch of the Omaha route reached Sioux City, Iowa, and Sioux Falls, South Dakota. Other important lines extended north through eastern Wisconsin to the Upper Peninsula of Michigan and north through the Wisconsin River valley. The prairies of Minnesota, Iowa, and South Dakota east of the Missouri River were overlaid with numerous secondary and branch lines. CM&StP added a route in 1903 between Lake Michigan and Kansas City. Between 1905 and 1909 the Puget Sound Extension was constructed between the Missouri River in South Dakota and Tacoma, Washington, and a line was built westward from the Missouri River at Chamberlain, S. D., to Rapid City. In 1921, the road leased the Chicago, Terre Haute & Southeastern to reach Indiana coal mines for locomotive fuel, and in 1922 acquired the Chicago, Milwaukee & Gary to link the CTH&SE with the CM&StP. The debt resulting from its post-1900 expansion put CM&StP

Milwaukee Road's 195 Prairies were more modern than most of their contemporaries, sporting piston valves and Walschaerts valve gear. The men posing with CM&StP 2000 are of average height (those are 63" drive wheels) and show how large even a small steam locomotive is. Milwaukee Road photo.

into bankruptcy in 1925, and it emerged in 1928 as the Chicago, Milwaukee, St. Paul & Pacific.

By 1892 the road had begun classifying its locomotives by letter for each wheel arrangement, replacing the practice of distinguishing them only by cylinder size. By 1899 this had been reformed into the system which prevailed until the end of steam — a class letter, with a numeral indicating substantial differences within the same wheel arrangement. For example, G4 through G8 4-6-0s varied in weight and tractive effort. Suffix letters indicated minor differences: 73" drivers on G6a versus 63" on G6f, 69" on G6p, and so on. An "s" designated engines that were superheated after they entered service. CM&StP engine numbers changed often: Some Pacifics carried five different numbers in the years following 1900. The general renumbering of 1912, which remained in effect until 1938, is used in the accompanying roster.

Between 1882 and 1913 nearly seven hundred locomotives were crafted at West Milwaukee shops. Twenty-five years later the second class S-1 4-8-4 was built there. Long before diesels brought standardization and even before the standardization embodied in the USRA

steam locomotives, the Milwaukee Road practiced it. The frames, fireboxes, boilers, cabs, and tenders of the Road's various Pacific classes were identical. The 4-6-2s also had identical tenders. Prairies had the same boilers as the Pacifics. J. F. DeVoy, CM&StP's mechanical engineer, designed a trailing truck used beneath nearly 600 Atlantics, Pacifics, Prairies, and Mikados between 1905 and 1914. Standard Car Truck Company produced it for other railroads as the Barber-DeVoy truck until outside-bearing trucks were introduced circa 1912.

Coal was the standard locomotive fuel until the Idaho forest fires of 1910, when oil was introduced for operations in the Bitter Root Mountains of western Montana. After the Rocky Mountain electrification was opened, oil was used on all steam-operated lines west of Three Forks, Mont. The introduction of the *Hiawatha* in May 1935 brought oil-fired locomotives to the eastern part of the system.

By 1950 diesels were taking over, and the road ceased making major repairs to steam locomotives in 1953. The official last steam trip occurred on January 4, 1955: local freight 91 from LaCrosse, Wis., to St. Paul behind an S2 4-8-4. The confirmed last steam operation was a round trip between Austin, Minn., and LaCrosse, Wis., by Ten-Wheeler 1004 on passenger trains 158 and 157 the night of March 15 and 16, 1957.

Freight locomotives

At the turn of the century, Ten-Wheelers hauled mainline freight. The 4-6-0 appeared in 1881, and over 500 arrived during the next two decades. Simple Ten-Wheelers were class G; Vauclain compounds built between 1892 and 1903 were class B. Between 1915 and 1925 the Bs were simpled and reclassified G6, G7, and G8.

Most freight Ten-Wheelers had 62" drivers. Baldwin built a pair of larger-drivered engines in 1899, predecessors of the B3 and B4 classes, which had 68" and 69" wheels respectively, and were looked upon as general service machines suitable for passenger service. With the arrival of Consolidations and Mikados the Ten-Wheelers were relegated to branchline service. The few compounds not simpled were retired during the late 1920s. Because the Milwaukee had many branch lines, 4-6-0s served to the end of steam.

CM&StP's first Consolidations were four built by Baldwin in 1901: two with 55" drivers, class C1a, and two with 56", class C1b. The road decided upon the 55" version, and Milwaukee Shops built 65 class C1c 2-8-0s between 1904 and 1907. They had the same 55" drivers, 22" × 28" cylinders, and 177,000-pound weight as the Baldwins, but they were rated at 41,890 pounds tractive effort, 2 pounds more than the Baldwins (probably a result of rounding in the calculation). They were numbered downward from 495 to 431; in 1912 they became 7064-7000, again with the oldest having the highest number. Later additions to the C1 class, subclasses d, e, f, and g, were an assortment of 55"- and 57"-drivered 2-8-0s acquired with the Chicago, Terre Haute & Southeastern and the Chicago, Milwaukee & Gary.

Heavier and more powerful C2-class 2-8-0s with 63" drivers and 23" × 30" cylinders were built during 1909 and 1910 by Milwaukee Shops and Baldwin. They were followed in 1912 and 1913 by the C5 class, 15 from Milwaukee Shops and 35 from Brooks. They were slightly heavier than the C2s and had cylinders an inch larger.

The C3 class consisted of five 1909 Rogers engines with 57" drivers

Class L2 Mikado 1884 (later 8084) was a Brooks product of 1912. Its 275,000-pound weight and 50,700-pound tractive effort were quite respectable for the time. Alco photo.

Later L2 Mikados like No. 432, built by Baldwin in 1923, had outside-journal trailing trucks and matched the USRA light 2-8-2 in weight and tractive force. Photo by Stanley H. Mailer.

and 22" × 30" cylinders. CM&StP acquired two small groups of 2-8-0s about the same size with the Idaho & Washington Northern in 1916 and classified them C3 and C3a, at the same time reclassifying the C3s as C3b. The lone C4 came from the Montana Railroad, and eight low-driv-ered C9s came into the fold with Bellingham Bay & British Columbia and the Tacoma Eastern. All but one C9 were gone before 1930. The road's heaviest and most powerful 2-8-0s (240,000 pounds total weight; 50,000 and 53,000 pounds tractive effort) were two groups of Chicago, Terre Haute & Southeastern engines, which became class C7 upon lease of that line in 1921. There were no C6 or C8 classes.

At the same time it was buying 2-8-0s the Milwaukee bought large numbers of 2-6-2s. Brooks delivered 50 Prairies in 1907 for use on the Puget Sound Extension. CM&StP built another 50 at Milwaukee in 1908 and 20 more the next year; Brooks built another 75, for a total of 195 class K1 engines with 63" drivers and 21" × 28" cylinders. They were designed to haul the same size trains between the Twin Cities and Har-lowton, Mont., that Ten-Wheelers hauled between Chicago and the Twin Cities. In practice, the 2-6-2s were used as far west as Alberton, Mont.; triple-heading was necessary on the mountain grades.

The road chose the 2-6-2 because the lignite from Roundup, Mont., it intended to burn in the engines required a large firebox. Although they were intended for service west of the Twin Cities, within a few years the 2-6-2s were assigned throughout the system, serving well in branch-line and local service. Several lasted until the diesel era. Beginning in 1924, many were equipped with superheaters. Slightly smaller cylin-ders and lower boiler pressure gave them a little less tractive effort. Nearly all of the nonsuperheated K1s were retired during 1935-1936.

One more 2-6-2 joined the roster in 1918, a small logging engine acquired with the Puget Sound & Willapa Harbor.

By the time the Puget Sound Extension was completed the 2-6-2s needed assistance over the mountains, so Milwaukee Shops built 20 2-8-2s. Designated L1, the Mikados were basically enlarged K1 Prairies with 24" × 30" cylinders and 63" drivers. They were followed by L2 Mikes of similar dimensions, except for 26" cylinders: 40 from Milwaukee Shops

and 155 from Brooks in 1912, and 25 from Schenectady in 1914. All L2s were built with superheaters, and boasted about 4,000 pounds greater tractive effort than the L1s. So highly regarded were these engines that the road took delivery of 200 more from Baldwin between 1920 and 1923. They had outside-bearing trailing trucks and looked more mod-ern than their prewar brothers, but had the same 54,723-pound trac-tive effort.

In 1918 and 1919 CM&StP received 100 USRA heavy 2-8-2s, the largest group of USRA heavy Mikados assigned to any railroad. Classified L3, with nearly 63,000 pounds tractive effort they were the most powerful road engines until the 4-8-4s arrived. The big Mikes were particularly successful on the main line between Minneapolis and Harlowton, on the routes to the Indiana coalfields, and in iron-ore service in upper Michigan.

Milwaukee's 2-6-0s weren't of any consequence. All were second-hand, and most were acquired through the lease or purchase of other roads. The newest was built in 1906; the last one left the roster in 1934.

Articulateds

Mountain freight called for more power than CM&StP's first 2-8-2s could provide, so the road placed 25 compound 2-6-6-2s from Alco's Schenectady Works in service in 1910 and 1911. Designated class N1 and numbered 5000-5024 (later 9500-9524), they proved successful as helpers, and 16 more, superheated and classed N2, arrived from Sche-nectady during 1912. They were delivered numbered 1650-1654, 5025-5029, and 9105-9110; post-1912 numbers were 9100-9104 and 9600-9610. Both classes had 57" drivers and 70,396 pounds tractive effort.

Eight N1s were oil-burners from the start, assigned to work in the Bitter Roots. After the Harlowton-Avery and Othello-Tacoma portions of the line were electrified, most of the Mallets were converted to oil and assigned to the Idaho division main line and the Elk River and Met-aline Falls branches. Some went to the Coast Division to work the Mor-ton, Everett, and Enumclaw lines. A few N1s remained coal-fired and came east for hump yard, terminal, and ore train service.

The two electrified districts meant articulated locomotives would never develop on the Milwaukee as they did on other western roads. Even so, between January 1929 and December 1931 the Tacoma, Minneapolis, and Milwaukee shops converted 17 N1s to single-expansion engines with superheaters and Coffin feedwater heaters. They were reclassed N3 and numbered 9300-9316 (after 1938, 50-66). The 9300s had increased speed and the greatest tractive effort of any Milwaukee steam power: 82,720 pounds. Later they received new tenders built at Milwaukee which virtually doubled their oil and water capacity. The N1s that were not upgraded were retired between 1927 and 1935, as were all but three N2s.

Dual-Service Locomotives

The nearly 500 Americans on CM&StP's roster at the turn of the century were considered dual-service power. In 1900 Baldwin delivered 25 B3 4-6-0s with 68" drivers, and 16 B4s with 69" drivers. They were Vauclain compounds intended primarily for freight service, but their larger drivers enabled them to be used as passenger engines. Those not scrapped were simpled and became classes G6 and G7 between 1915 and 1927.

In March 1930 the road received a lone Baldwin 4-8-4 which was a stretched version of its new 4-6-4s — and it was referred to as a Modified Mountain. (The road had no 4-8-2s.) Class S1 9700 was specifically acquired to parallel the Hudsons between Minneapolis and Harlowton, 915 miles, and had 74" drivers and 62,136 pounds tractive effort. Since the 4-6-4s proved capable of forwarding the *Olympian* and *Columbian* on their own, by June 1930 No. 9700 was pulling 5,000-ton freight trains on the Chicago-St. Paul and Chicago-Council Bluffs runs. In April 1934 oil-burning equipment was applied to No. 9700 and it was sent to the Idaho Division, where it took over the job of pulling the *Olympian* between the two electrified zones. In 1938 it was renumbered 250.

In February 1938 Milwaukee Shops built its last steam locomotive, 4-8-4 No. 251, a duplicate of No. 250. Constructed as an oil-burner, it spent its entire career on the Idaho division. The two S1s played dual-service roles for a while, then during World War II worked in passenger service full-time.

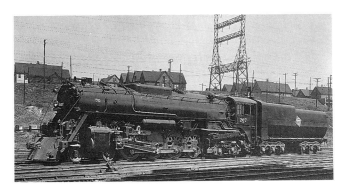

Because of wartime restrictions on new designs, the S3s combined elements of 4-8-4s Alco had recently built for Rock Island and Delaware & Hudson — and the result was a good looking engine. Milwaukee Road photo.

In 1937 and 1938 the road received 30 4-8-4s from Baldwin. Designated S2, they went into time freight service on the Bensenville-St. Paul and Bensenville-Council Bluffs runs. They later operated as far west as Harlowton. Their only passenger assignment was to pull the *Olympian* west of Minneapolis when its consist exceeded 12 cars. Ten additional S2s were acquired in spring of 1940. The S2s were considerably larger than the S1s, and similarities ended with the 74" drivers. The S1s combined 230 pounds of boiler pressure and 28" × 30" cylinders to attain 62,136 pounds of tractive effort; the S2s had 26" × 32" cylinders, 285 pounds boiler pressure, and 70,816 pounds of tractive effort.

In July and September 1944 the road received its final 10 Northerns from Alco. Wartime restrictions prohibited new designs, so they combined a Delaware & Hudson boiler, Rock Island frame, and Union Pacific tender. They were quite different from the S2s in appearance and closer to the two S1s in dimensions and pulling power (74" drivers, 26" × 32" cylinders, 250 pounds pressure, and 62,119 pound tractive effort).

Pacific 826 (earlier 3103, 6703, and 6353) was an F5. Its general appearance was typical of all Milwaukee Road's 4-6-2s. Photo by Jim Scribbins.

Milwaukee's racy F6 4-6-4s were a major step forward from the Pacifics. They had outside-journal lead trucks, cast trailing trucks, and large tenders — but between the Pacifics and the Hudsons the railroad had lavished its resources on electric locomotives. Milwaukee Road photo.

The S3s were true dual-service locomotives; the S2s were primarily freight engines, and clearance and weight restrictions kept them out of Chicago Union Station.

In 1950 four S3s were converted to oil and sent to the Idaho Division, where they pulled passenger trains, including the Olympian Hiawatha, as well as freights. Near the end of their career S3s ran with some regularity between Milwaukee and Savanna, Ill., and rarely all the way to Kansas City — rarely because the Kansas City Division was one of the first lines to receive FT diesels.

Passenger locomotives

The 4-4-2 wheel arrangement was introduced to the railway in 1896, on engines designed to run between Chicago and Milwaukee in 105 minutes with one intermediate stop. Could the locomotive department have forseen what engines of the same wheel arrangement would be doing over the same division 39 years later?

Twenty-eight Vauclain compound 4-4-2s numbered 3100-3127, with 84" drivers and 20,420 pounds tractive effort, came from Baldwin

between 1901 and 1903 to constitute class A2. Also in 1903 the road took delivery of five class A1s, 3013-3017, which were a continuation of the 1896 Atlantic design, simple engines with 79" drivers and 20,197 pounds tractive effort.

Milwaukee Shops got into the act in 1907 and 1908 by constructing five compounds, class A2b, with 22,190 pounds tractive effort and 85" drivers, the largest ever applied to a Milwaukee Road engine. Baldwin built 12 Vauclain compounds with the same dimensions in 1908 and 1909, class A2c, Nos. 3500-3511.

In 1907 Baldwin delivered two Atlantics which drove on the front axle. They were balanced compounds with 85" drivers and 22,200 pounds tractive effort; they were numbered 3133 and 3134. One Atlantic was acquired with the Idaho & Washington Northern. Along with the two balanced compounds, it was simpled, and the three became class A4. In the process the two ex-compounds were changed to drive on the second axle. They ran until 1951 and powered the final trip of local passenger train 8 from Kansas City to Davenport.

The best-known 4-4-2s on the road, and possibly the most celebrated Atlantics anywhere, were the four built for *Hiawatha* service. Numbers 1 and 2 were completed in spring 1935 to pull the original version of the speedliner. They were the first steam locomotives intended to cruise at 100 mph — they could reach 120 — and the first built streamlined. They had 84" drivers, 19" × 28" cylinders, and 30,685 pounds tractive effort, and their main rods were connected to the first pair of drivers. For a while they were referred to as the Milwaukee type.

Engines 3 and 4 were delivered in 1936 and 1937 to pull additional sections of the *Hiawatha* and to work other fast trains between Chicago and Milwaukee. The As were exceptionally successful engines and were displaced only when *Afternoon Hiawathas* exceeded their nine-car capability. Number 3 was retired in 1949, and the others two years later.

Between 1905 and 1907 Milwaukee Shops turned out 33 class G6 Ten-Wheelers, Nos. 2300-2332, and they were followed by 13 more from Brooks two years later, 2700-2712. All had 73" drivers for passenger service, and 25,445 pounds tractive effort. Sixteen of them made it beyond the 1938 renumbering as 1123-1138.

After the *Hiawathas* entered service, the trains on the Wisconsin Valley line between New Lisbon and Wausau, Wis., that connected with them were given improved status as the *Hiawatha, North Woods Service*. Part of the transformation involved streamlining two 4-6-0s with shrouds like those of the Atlantics. They also received air horns but remained hand-fired. Originally Vauclain compound B3s, they were rebuilt to G6s in 1925 and 1926; when they were shrouded, they were designated class G and numbered 10 and 11. In the mid-1940s the Wisconsin Valley line was improved to support Pacifics. In May 1945 Nos. 10 and 11 became the only Milwaukee Road streamliners to be denuded.

The road rostered four 4-6-2s in 1900. They would have been Ten-Wheelers, but were so heavy that the extra wheels were needed to spread their weight; thus they were not regarded as true Pacifics (they were occasionally referred to as the St. Paul type). The first, built by

Otto Kuhler's styling of the *Hiawatha* 4-6-4s of 1938 was striking, even flashy, but lacked the unity and coherence of the Atlantics shown on page 378. Milwaukee Road photo.

Schenectady in 1889, was the most successful and was designated F1, establishing the class letter for future 4-6-2s. It had 68" drivers and 19,490 pounds tractive effort, and weighed 130,600 pounds. It was rebuilt to a 4-6-0 in 1926. The other three, 143,000-pound compounds built by Rhode Island in 1893, were lemons and were sold in March 1900 to the Savannah, Florida & Western (an Atlantic Coast Line predecessor) after being idle much of the seven years CM&StP owned them.

Milwaukee shops built another 4-6-2 in 1905, this time a genuine Pacific designated class F2, with 72" drivers, 23" × 26" cylinders, and 32,470 pounds tractive effort. It was the first locomotive to use the DeVoy lateral-motion trailing truck. Based on experience with No. 851 (renumbered 6050 after 1912), the road ordered 70 larger 4-6-2s, class F3, delivered by Brooks in 1910. They had 79" drivers and 31,870 pounds tractive effort, and weighed 247,300 pounds. Most later received superheaters and other modifications which increased their tractive effort by as much as 3,000 pounds. The first 50 were delivered as 1502-1551 and renumbered almost immediately as 3200-3249, then to 6500-6549 in 1912 and 6120-6169 in 1924. The last 20 were delivered as second 1502-1521 and became 6100-6119 in 1912. The F3s that remained in service in 1938 were renumbered once again to 150-198.

Three F3's received special treatment. Number 6109 was painted orange to head the demonstration tour introducing *Pioneer Limited* roller bearing equipment in 1927. Numbers 151 and 152 were streamlined in 1941 for the *Chippewa* between Milwaukee and Ontonagon, Michigan. Later the pair were re-classed F1. The F3s were among the best of the road's passenger power. They could run 90 mph when worked to the utmost, and the last of them outlived all the Hudsons.

Between 1910 and 1912 Milwaukee Shops built two classes of Pacifics for the western lines, 25 class F4 Pacifics with 69" drivers, 23" × 28" cylinders, and 36,490 pounds tractive effort, and 15 class F5 engines with 69" drivers, 25" × 28" cylinders, and 39,880 pounds tractive effort. Alco's Brooks Works built 50 more F5s during 1912. The F4s were built as saturated engines, but were superheated later. Some were rebuilt to F5s, primarily a matter of larger cylinders. The F5s were built with superheaters and 185 pounds boiler pressure; most were eventually raised to 200 pounds. The F4s and F5s carried a succession of numbers, and in the 1938 renumbering they were placed in the 800 series, F5s below F4s. When the Rocky Mountain, Missoula, and Coast divisions were electrified, most of these Pacifics were transferred to the eastern part of the system and many saw freight duty. All but two F4s and many F5s received 73" drivers which altered their tractive force.

Engines 801 and 812 (by then classified F5an) were streamlined in 1941 to pull the Manilla, Iowa, -Sioux Falls, S. D., section of the *Midwest Hiawatha* and were reclassified F2. After World War II they were transferred to the Wisconsin Valley line where they handled the *Hiawatha, North Woods Service* until summer 1947. Both F2s were retired in 1950.

After the F5s of 1912 there was a gap in Milwaukee Road steam passenger locomotive development. During the Teens the road electrified much of its extension to the Pacific Northwest. It purchased new passenger locomotives, but they were electric; more important, the electrics released steam power for service on the rest of the system. In the 1920s Milwaukee's passenger trains began to outgrow the Pacifics. The road's response to the problem was to beginning fitting its passenger cars with roller bearings, making them easier to start and keep moving.

Chicago, Milwaukee & St. Paul designed the first 4-6-4 in North America, but the 1925 bankruptcy ruled out construction. CM&StP referred to it as the Milwaukee type in internal documents, but the 4-6-4 was named Hudson when New York Central 5200 appeared in 1927 (Milwaukee's 4-6-4s were often referred to as Baltics, a name applied in Europe to 4-6-4 tank engines). When Milwaukee Road emerged from bankruptcy in 1928 it ordered 14 4-6-4s from Baldwin. They were delivered in 1930 for service between Chicago and Minneapolis, but they also ran between Chicago and Omaha, and were tested between Minneapolis and Harlowton opposite the single 4-8-4. In 1931 eight more arrived from Baldwin, and Hudsons became the norm as far west as the Rocky Mountain electrified district. The Pacific class letter designation, F, was used for the new engines, F6s 6400-6413 and F6as 6414-6421. Both groups had 79" drivers, 26" × 28" cylinders, and 45,882 pounds of tractive effort. The F6a class weighed 380,220 pounds, about 5,000 pounds more than the F6s.

The F6a Hudsons usually stayed west of Minneapolis, although some F6s also covered the 915-mile district between Minneapolis and Harlowton. In November 1933 F6a 6415 won industry-wide recognition for running 10 Minneapolis-Harlowton round trips (18,300 miles) in 30 days without any time out for shopping. On July 20, 1934, No. 6402 ran the 85 miles from Chicago to Milwaukee in 67 minutes, 35 seconds. It reached a maximum of 103.5 mph, covered 61 miles at 92.6 mph, and averaged 75.5 mph start-to-stop, a new world record for sustained high-speed steam operation.

For obscure accounting reasons F6as 6414-6418 were Chicago, Terre Haute & Southeastern engines and were so lettered. In the 1938 renumbering Nos. 6400-6421 became 125-138, 142-146, and 139-141. In October 1945, Nos. 132 and 133 were converted to oil fuel and sent to the Idaho division. The F6s and F6as finished their careers in Chicago suburban service.

In 1938, the road was planning more and longer *Hiawatha* trains, making even better steam power imperative. There emerged from Alco that summer six striking Hudsons, Nos. 100-105, class F7. They were streamlined 84"-driver machines, similar in size and concept to Hudsons delivered to Santa Fe and Chicago & North Western about the same time. Unlike the Atlantics they were coal burners. They were assigned to the *Morning Hiawatha*, the *Pioneer Limited*, and *Olympian* between Chicago and Minneapolis. At the beginning of the 1940s the eastbound *Morning Hiawatha* was scheduled to cover the 78.3 miles from Sparta to Portage, Wis., in 58 minutes — 81 mph start-to-stop, the world's fastest regularly scheduled steam-powered train.

After the Chicago-Minneapolis *Hiawathas* were dieselized, the F7s ran to Omaha on the overnight *Arrow* and pulled Chicago-Milwaukee trains, but they weren't well suited to anything but the fastest passenger schedules. They were scrapped between 1949 and 1951, before any of the earlier Hudsons were retired.

Switchers

CM&StP owned a bundle of 0-4-0s built between 1870 and 1893. Many lasted until the late Teens. The 0-6-0s did not come on the property in quantity until the 1890s. Continuing an existing design, Milwaukee Shops built 16 I4s between 1900 and 1902. With 51" wheels, they developed 23,800 pounds tractive effort.

Introduced in 1902, class I5 quickly became the standard CM&StP yard goat. Milwaukee Shops built 172 of them through 1913. They rolled on 51" wheels and had 28,158 pounds tractive effort. Ten I6s built in 1913-14 were Milwaukee Shops' last switchers. They had the standard 51" wheels, but boasted 31,200 pounds tractive effort.

The road owned only two 0-8-0s, 1913 Baldwins acquired with the Chicago, Terre Haute & Southeastern. They were modest-sized engines weighing 171,550 pounds and exerting 34,666 pounds tractive effort. The Southeastern probably used them for switching coal mines. After they became CMStP&P class D1 they were used at Savanna, Ill., and Dubuque, Iowa. Most heavy switching chores were handled by 2-8-0s.

Oddities

For its 3-foot-gauge branch between Bellevue and Cascade, Iowa, the road acquired two secondhand 42"-drivered 2-6-0s with 14,280 pound tractive effort from the Birmingham Rail & Locomotive Company in 1926 and 1928. Classed NM2, they were numbered 3 and 2, and had been built by Baldwin for New York's Catskill & Tannersville in 1908 and 1901. The branch and its locomotives were sold in 1933 to the independent Bellevue & Cascade.

CM&StP owned four Shays built in 1907 and 1908, two of its own and two from the Idaho & Washington Northern. All were off the roster by 1927.

Historical and technical society: Milwaukee Road Historical Association, 5711 Modernaire Street, Madison, Wis. 53711

Recommended reading:

The Hiawatha Story, by Jim Scribbins, published 1970 by Kalmbach Publishing Co., P.O. Box 1612, Waukesha, Wis. 53187 (ISBN 0-89024-018-3)

Milwaukee Road Remembered, by Jim Scribbins, published in 1990 by Kalmbach Publishing Co., P.O. Box 1612, Waukesha, Wis. 53187 (ISBN 0-89024-075-2)

Published rosters:

Railroad History, No. 136, entire issue

Railroad Magazine: October 1932, page 402; November 1939, page 60 (renumbering of 1939); February 1951, page 78; June 1970, page 50 (renumbering of 1939)

CMStP&P STEAM LOCOMOTIVES BUILT SINCE 1900

Type	Class	1912 Nos.	1938 Nos.	Qty	Builder	Built	Retired	Notes
0-6-0	I4a	1137-1159		23	CM&StP	1900-1902	1926-1930	
0-6-0	I5	1160-1165		6	CM&StP	1902-1903	1931-1934	
0-6-0	I5a	1166-1296						
		4500-4534	1400-1522	166	CM&StP	1903-1913	1933-1955	
0-6-0	I5b	1535, 1536		2	BLW	1907-1910	1934	Ex-CM&G
0-6-0	I6s	1297-1306	1525-1534	10	CM&StP	1913-1914	1948-1956	
0-8-0	D1	1400-1401	1550-1551	2	BLW	1913	1952	Ex-CTH&SE
2-6-0	M1	6004, 6005		2	BLW	ca. 1905	1925, 1927	
								Ex-Montana Railroad
2-6-0	M1c	2956, 2957		2	BLW	1901	1930	Ex-CTH&SE
2-6-0	M1d	2958-2964		7	Rogers	1904-1905	1930, 1934	
								Ex-CTH&SE
2-6-0	M1e	2965-2968		4	Brooks	1904-1905	1934	Ex-CM&G
2-6-0	M2	2975-2978		4	Schen	1905-1908	1927, 1934	Ex-CJRy
2-6-0	NM2	2,3		2	BLW	1901, 1908	Sold 1933	
2-6-2	K1	5000-5049	900-912	50	Brooks	1907	1935-1955	
2-6-2	K1	5500-5519	913-918	20	CM&StP	1908	1935-1954	
2-6-2	K1	5520-5569	919-936, 955					
				50	Brooks	1908	1935-1955	
2-6-2	K1	5570-5619	938-950					
			957, 958	50	CM&StP	1908-1909	1935-1955	
2-6-2	K1	5620-5644	951-960	25	Brooks	1909	1935-1955	
2-6-2	K1a	5100		1	BLW	1910	1927	
		Built as Pacific & Eastern 102, acquired with Puget Sound & Willapa Harbor						
2-6-6-2	N1	9500-9524		25	Schen	1910-1911	1927-1935	
								17 rebuilt to N3
2-6-6-2	N2	9100-9104, 9600-9610						
			90-92	16	Schen	1912	1934-35, 1949	
2-6-6-2	N3	9300-9316	50-66	17		1929-1931	1950-1954	
								Rebuilt from N1
2-8-0	C1	7000-7064	1375-1395	65	CM&StP	1904-1907	1934-1949	
2-8-0	C1	7065-7068	1396 (ex-7066)	4	BLW	1901	1934-1940	

Type	Class	1912 Nos.	1938 Nos.	Qty	Builder	Built	Retired	Notes
2-8-0	C1d	7069-7078		10	Rogers	1908-1909	1934-1936	
								Ex-CTH&SE
2-8-0	C1e	7079-7083		5	Brooks	1905	1934	Ex-CM&G
2-8-0	C1f	7084-7087		4	BLW	1907 & 1910	1934	Ex-CM&G
2-8-0	C2	7600-7624	1250-1311	25	CM&StP	1909-1910	1939-1955	
2-8-0	C2	7100-7149	1263-1331	50	BLW	1910	1936-1954	
2-8-0	C3b	7500-7554	1340-1344	5	Rogers	1909	1945-1949	
2-8-0	C3	7555-7560	1345-1347	6	BLW	1907; 1910-11	1934-1951	
								Ex-I&WN
2-8-0	C4	7500		1	BLW	1904	1927	
								Ex-Montana Railroad
2-8-0	C5	7200-7204	1200-1204	5	CM&StP	1912	1951-1954	
2-8-0	C5	7205-7239	1205-1239	35	Brooks	1912	1945-1954	
2-8-0	C5	7240-7249	1240-1249	10	CM&StP	1913	1945-1954	
2-8-0	C7	7700-7716	1350-1366	17	Schen	1910-1918	1950-1953	
								Ex-CTH&SE
2-8-0	C9d	7564		1	BLW	1901	Sold 1926	
								Ex-Bellingham Bay & British Columbia
2-8-0	C9e	7565		1	BLW	1906	1935	
								Ex-Tacoma Eastern
2-8-2	L1	8500-8519	750-769	20	CM&StP	1909	1940-1954	
2-8-2	L2	8000-8039	600-682	40	CM&StP	1912-1913	1930-1955	
2-8-2	L2	8040-8154	612-726	115	Brooks	1912	1934-1954	
2-8-2	L2	8155-8179	661-738	25	Schen	1914	1935-1954	
2-8-2	L2	8200-8299	500-598	100	BLW	1920-1921	1935-1954	
2-8-2	L2	8300-8399	400-499	100	BLW	1922-1923	1950-1956	
2-8-2	L3	8600-8649	300-353	50	Brooks	1918	1938-1955	
2-8-2	L3	8650-8699	311-399	50	Schen	1919	1949-1956	
4-4-0	H7	731,732		2	BLW	1901	1928	
							Ex Davenport, Rock Island & Northwestern	
4-4-0	H8	900-904	40-42	5	Rogers	1904	1934-1951	Ex-CTH&SE
4-4-0	H8	905-908		4	Rogers	1905	1934	Ex-CTH&SE

CMStP&P STEAM LOCOMOTIVES BUILT SINCE 1900 (continued)

Type	Class	1912 Nos.	1938 Nos.	Qty	Builder	Built	Retired	Notes
4-4-2	A		1-4	4	Alco	1935-1937	1949, 1951	Streamlined
4-4-2	A1	3013-3017	28, 29	5	BLW	1903	1934-1940	
4-4-2	A2	3100-3127		28	BLW	1901-1903	1926-1929	Compound
4-4-2	A2b	3128-3132		5	CM&StP	1907-1908	1927-1929	Compound
4-4-2	A2c	3500-3511		12	BLW	1908-1909	1928-1930	Compound
4-4-2	A4as	3135	32	1	BLW	1909	1951	Later B4as
4-4-2	A4s	3133, 3134	30,31	2	BLW	1907	1951	Later B4s
4-6-0	B2	4137-4143		7		1900		Compound, rebuilt to G6
4-6-0	B3	4201-4225		25	BLW	1900		Compound, rebuilt to G6
4-6-0	B4	4301-4382		82	BLW	1900-1903		Compound, rebuilt to G7, G8
4-6-0	G2c	2007		1	BLW	1904	1931	Ex-Tacoma Eastern
4-6-0	G4g	2185		1		1926	1930	Rebuilt from F1 No. 6000
4-6-0	G5s	2250-2264	1185-1198	15		1913-1915	1939-1945	Rebuilt from B1
4-6-0	G5c	2265		1	BLW	1907	1927	Ex-BB&BC 32
4-6-0	G5e	2266-2275		10	BLW	1903	1934	
4-6-0	G6	2300-2332		33	CM&StP	1905-1907	1931-1948	
4-6-0	G6	2700-2712	1123-1133	13	Brooks	1909	1930-1948	
4-6-0	G6	2713-2717		5	BLW	1907-1908	1935	Ex-I&WN
4-6-0	G6	2350-2368	1140-1160	22		1914-1918	1932-1954	Rebuilt from B2
4-6-0	G6	2334-2336		3	BLW	1904-1906	1926,1932	Aacquired with TE; 2334 sold 1926
4-6-0	G6	2372-2393	1161-1182	22		1921-1928	1941-1955	Rebuilt from B2
4-6-0	G6	2751-2775	1100-1122	23		1915-1927	1940-1954	Rebuilt from B3
4-6-0	G	2769,2765	10, 11	2		1926,1925	1951	

Streamlined, classed G, 1936, 1937; destreamlined 1945; renumbered 1111, 1112 in 1948

Type	Class	1912 Nos.	1938 Nos.	Qty	Builder	Built	Retired	Notes
4-6-0	G6	2337-2340		4	Rogers	1905	1934	Ex-CTH&SE
4-6-0	G7	2400-2455	1090-1093	56	CM&StP	1904-1906	1928-1939	
4-6-0	G7	2800-2824	1094-1097	25	CM&StP	1909	1929-1940	
4-6-0	G7	2852-2865	1075-1084	10		1921	1940-1954	Rebuilt from B4
4-6-0	G7	2867-2890	1050-1073	24		1915-1920	1948-1954	Rebuilt from B4
4-6-0	G8	2600-2641	1000-1041	42		1919-1925	1948-1957	Rebuilt from B4
4-6-2	F1	6157, 6160	151, 152	2	Brooks	1910	1954	Built as F3
4-6-2	F2	6050		1	CM&StP	1905	1929	
4-6-2	F2	6301,6320	801, 812	2	Brooks	1912	1950	Built as F5
4-6-2	F3	6100-6169	150-198	70	Brooks	1910	1929-1954	
4-6-2	F4	6200-6219	875-890	20	CM&StP	1910	1934-1954	
4-6-2	F5	6300-6349	800-846	50	Brooks	1912	1935-1954	
4-6-2	F5	6350-6354	825-857	15	CM&StP	1911-1912	1934-1954	
4-6-2	F5	6365-6370	832-855	6		1914-1926	1935-1954	Rebuilt from F4
4-6-4	F6	6400-6413	125-138	14	BLW	1930	1952-1954	
4-6-4	F6a	6414-6421	139-146	8	BLW	1931	1952, 1954	
4-6-4	F7		100-105	6	Alco	1938	1949-1951	Streamlined
4-8-4	S1	9700	250	1	BLW	1930	1954	
4-8-4	S1		251	1	CM&StP	1938	1954	
4-8-4	S2		200-240	40	BLW	1937-1940	1954-1956	No.200 renumbered to 230
4-8-4	S3		260-269	10	Alco	1944	1954, 1956	
Shay	X1	1, 25		2	Lima	1907, 1908	1927	
Shay	X2	I&WN 5, 6		2	Lima	1907	1919	

CHICAGO, ROCK ISLAND & PACIFIC RAILWAY

In 1900 the Rock Island's principal routes extended west from Chicago through Des Moines and Omaha to Denver and southwest through Kansas City to Fort Worth. The road controlled the Burlington, Cedar Rapids & Northern, which had several lines running northwest across Iowa from the Mississippi River. (CRI&P merged the BCR&N in 1902). The Rock Island expanded considerably during the first decade of the 20th century. It acquired or built lines from Memphis west across Arkansas and Oklahoma to Amarillo, Texas; from Liberal, Kansas, southwest to Tucumcari and Santa Rosa, New Mexico; from Kansas City east to St. Louis and north to the Twin Cities; from Little Rock south to Eunice, Louisiana; and (jointly with the Burlington) from Dallas through Houston to Galveston, Texas.

Because of the expansion and the merger of subsidiaries there was a general locomotive renumbering in 1903. Rock Island used several locomotive classification systems, eventually settling on one based on tractive effort. The roster here uses the 1903 numbers and the final classification scheme.

Rock Island became embroiled in the empire building of the early part of the century, and found itself in receivership from 1915 to 1917. When management was returned to the stockholders in 1917 the new board included directors with financial interests in American Locomotive Company. Thereafter Alco built all Rock Island's steam locomotives. The Rock got into financial trouble again and was in bankruptcy from 1933 to 1948. The road wasn't a hard-luck case like the New York, Ontario & Western or the Colorado Midland (at least not until the late 1960s), but neither was it a Santa Fe or a Burlington — and those were its most intense competitors.

In the mid- and late 1920s the Rock converted to oil fuel south and west of Kansas City. Thereafter most orders for locomotives were divided between coal burning and oil burning. The last appearance of steam in revenue service was in July 1953. During floods in April 1954 an 0-8-0 substituted for diesel switchers at Des Moines.

Freight locomotives

Burlington, Cedar Rapids & Northern took delivery of ten 4-6-0s, Nos. 200-209, from Brooks in 1901. They had inside piston valves, Belpaire fireboxes, and 63" drivers, and were BCR&N's heaviest freight engines. They became Rock Island 1490-1499.

In 1901 and 1902 the Rock ordered 91 freight 4-6-0s from Brooks, all 64"-drivered machines with 20" × 28" cylinders. They were numbered 1401-1471 and 1501-1520; No. 1454 was of a different class.

The C-39 class 2-8-0s, 1600-1700, were built by Brooks in 1903 and 1904. They had 63" drivers, 22" × 30" cylinders, and inboard piston valves, and weighed 206,000 pounds (1700 was renumbered 1600 about 1908). They were followed in 1907 by Baldwin-built 1701-1783, which had cylinders an inch greater in diameter, slide valves, and Walschaerts valve gear. Brooks constructed another 164 similar 2-8-0s, 1901-2064, between 1907 and 1910. Locomotives 1901-1910 had slide valves and Walschaerts valve gear; 1911-1930 had slide valves and Stephenson gear; 1931-2064 had outside piston valves and Walschaerts valve gear. After rebuilding and superheating in the 1920s, Nos. 1701-1783 and 1902-2064 were classified C-43. Schenectady-built Consolidations 2100-2144, which had 57" drivers, were transferred from the St. Louis-San Francisco soon after they were delivered in 1907. They were also classed C-43. Acquisition of the Choctaw, Oklahoma & Gulf in 1902 added 90 2-8-0s, including 12 Camelbacks, to the Rock Island roster.

In 1906 Baldwin built an experimental heavy 2-8-0 (232,000 pounds) numbered 1799. It was exhibited at the Jamestown Exposition of 1907 but was too heavy for Rock Island's track and was soon sold to the New York, Susquehanna & Western. The next year Baldwin built another 1799 with the same running gear but a smaller boiler; in fact, it proved too small. Second 1799 was later renumbered 2200.

By 1911 increasing traffic, higher speeds, and steel freight cars called for more steaming capacity than the 2-8-0s had. The Rock Island designed a 2-8-2 with 63" drivers and 28" × 30" cylinders (like its newest 2-8-0s

Consolidation 2110 was built for the Frisco in 1907 and almost immediately transferred to the Rock Island — the two roads were under common control at the time. Photo by Ralph L. Graves.

Handsome Mikado 2518, shown at Eldon, Missouri, in 1936, is a K-60, one of 143 of that class. It has a homemade "loaf of bread" tender. Photo by Wesley Krambeck.

plus a firebox with 63 square feet of grate area and 180-pound boiler pressure. Baldwin delivered 40, numbered 2500-2539, in 1912; Alco's Schenectady Works built 10, numbered 2540-2549, that same year. The Baldwin engines had Baker valve gear; the Alco engines, Walschaerts. Baldwin delivered 25 more in 1913, and Alco delivered another 20 in 1918, for a total of 95 prewar K-60 locomotives.

During World War I the USRA allocated the Rock Island 20 light 2-8-2s. Baldwin built nine, 2300-2308, and Schenectady built 11, numbered 2309-2319, which first went to the Texas & Pacific, where they were found too light. The USRA engines had large grates and were equipped with stokers, so they could produce more steam than the Rock Island's own 2-8-2s; because they were lighter and had shorter tenders they could also go places the K-60 Mikes couldn't.

After the war the road returned to its own design, which gradually evolved: The basic dimensions of the locomotives remained the same, but boiler pressure increased to 190, 200, and eventually 210 pounds, and cast trailing trucks, boosters, and feedwater heaters appeared. Through the years the earlier 2-8-2s were raised to 190 pounds boiler

pressure, increasing their tractive effort by about 3,000 pounds; some were equipped with stokers, and others were converted to oil burners; some were given roller bearings on their driver axles.

The CRI&P was a flatland railroad, contending for the most part with nothing worse than short grades up out of river valleys. The line southwest from Rock Island, Illinois, across Iowa and northern Missouri to St. Joseph and Kansas City ran crosswise to the rivers and was hilly and curvy. The Mikados were originally intended to replace Consolidations on that route, handling trains that the 2-8-0s pulled on other portions of the road. When the 2-8-2s spread to other areas, the Kansas City route again required heavier power (Santa Fe had much the same situation between Fort Madison, Iowa, and Kansas City). In 1918 Rock Island designed a 2-10-2 with 30" × 32" cylinders and 63" drivers and weighing 383,000 pounds, slightly larger than the USRA heavy 2-10-2 that would be on the drawing board later that year (except in the matter of driver size — the USRA engine would have 57" drivers). The first ten of the class arrived from Schenectady in 1918, Brooks built 15 more in 1920, and Schenectady built the final 10 in 1925. The second group had

No railroad in the U. S. had more 4-8-4s on its roster than Rock Island. Number 5020, shown taking on fuel oil at Enid, Oklahoma, in 1948, was built by Alco in 1929. Rebuilding in the late 1930s included 74" drivers, disk main drivers, and increased tender capacity. Photo by Sid Davies, collection of Charles E. Winters.

a few internal improvements, and the third group was built with feedwater heaters: four Worthington BL, three Elesco bundle-type, and three Elesco exhaust steam injectors. Even with 63" drivers, the 2-10-2s had counterbalancing problems and were limited to 30 miles per hour. Disk main drivers applied during the 1930s helped somewhat.

Four years after the last 2-10-2s were delivered, the Rock Island turned to the 4-8-4 type for fast freight trains. Equipped with 69" drivers, they were the first Northerns intended specifically for freight service, but their frames were designed to accept 74" drivers if more speed was required. Alco delivered the first, No. 5000, in February 1929. Within the year 24 more followed, and despite the onset of the Depression, the Rock ordered another 40 for delivery in 1930. Because of their size and weight, the 4-8-4s could operate only between Chicago and Des Moines; Chicago and Dalhart, Texas (93 miles short of the Southern Pacific connection at Tucumcari, N. M.); and Herington, Kansas, and El Reno, Okla. The immediate result of their delivery was storage of the 2-10-2s assigned

to the line between Rock Island and Kansas City; the 4-8-4s speeded up trains significantly in that territory. The 4-8-4s were also assigned to the Rock's heaviest passenger trains.

In the late 1930s the road modernized 10 of the 4-8-4s with roller bearings and thick driver tires that increased wheel diameter to 74", and enlarged their tenders. It undertook a bridge-strengthening program, and by 1940 4-8-4 territory extended to Denver, Tucumcari, and Fort Worth, and from Kansas City to Minneapolis.

Wartime traffic caused the Rock to order 10 oil burning 4-8-4s, 5100-5109, for delivery in 1944. They were built with roller bearings on all axles and 74" Boxpok drivers. The first of that group and the first Electro-Motive FT diesels arrived on the property in the same month, May 1944. In March 1945 World War II was expected to continue through 1946, and the road ordered 10 coal burning 4-8-4s, 5110-5119. The road eventually had 85 Northerns, a count equalled in the U. S. only by Southern Pacific.

Passenger locomotives

Unlike the Burlington, the Rock Island didn't modernize its 4-4-0s. A few survived into the 1930s on branch lines that could not carry larger locomotives. The last two were retired in 1938.

In 1900 Baldwin built a group of Vauclain compound 4-6-0s, five with 78" drivers for passenger service and 17 with 64" drivers for freight. Brooks also built passenger 4-6-0s for the Rock Island in 1902: 1472-1492 with 68" drivers and 1493-1499 with 74" drivers.

The oldest 4-4-2s on the roster were built in 1900 as Burlington, Cedar Rapids & Northern 75-77. They were typical Brooks locomotives with inside piston valves, 74" drivers, and inboard-bearing trailing trucks. They had Belpaire fireboxes, which the BCR&N preferred. Shortly after the Rock Island merged the BCR&N they were renumbered 1001, 1003, and 1002.

Rock Island bought 4-4-2s and 4-6-2s at the same time. In 1901 and 1902 Brooks delivered seven 4-4-2s. They had 79" drivers and were known as the Chautauqua type; they were built as 1301-1307 and soon renumbered 1004-1010. Schenectady delivered 10 more Atlantics, 1011-

Atlantic type 1048 was built by Baldwin in 1905. Note the position of the counterweights on the forward drivers, compensating for the weight of the main rods of the high-pressure cylinders. Baldwin photo.

1020, in 1905, eight with slide valves and two with piston valves. They were built with 73" drivers but later had 74" drivers.

Rock Island sampled Baldwin's balanced-compound principle with a pair of Atlantics, 1048 and 1049, delivered in 1905. They had high-pressure cylinders between the frames driving cranks on the first driving axle and low-pressure cylinders in the usual location driving the rear drivers. They were successful enough that the road took six more, 1042-1047, in 1906.

CRI&P's last two Atlantics, 1040 and 1041, were delivered by Alco's Schenectady Works in 1909. They were four-cylinder balanced simple locomotives. They had four 17" × 26" cylinders, two inside the frames and two outside, all driving the forward pair of 73" drivers. The moving parts were in balance and only small counterbalances were necessary on the drivers. The engines remained in service until 1936 and 1937.

The road's first 4-6-2s, 801-830, were built by Brooks in 1903. They had 69" drivers, inside piston valves, and inboard bearing trailing trucks, and weighed 193,000 pounds. The next group of Pacifics came from Schenectady in 1905 and 1906, 31 engines numbered 831-861. Like the Brooks engines they had 69" drivers, but they combined modernity in the form of outside-frame trailing trucks with a minor bit of antiquity

Number 1041 was a four-cylinder balanced simple locomotive, with all four cylinders driving the first axle. The sign on the side of the smokebox indicates it was pulling a Chicago-Blue Island, Illinois, train via the Rock's Suburban Line. Photo by Robert Graham.

— slide valves on all but four of the engines.

Pacifics 862-894 were built by Schenectady in 1909. They had 73" drivers, piston valves, and Walschaerts valve gear, but were not superheated. They weighed 227,000 pounds, 50,000 pounds less than a USRA light Pacific. The 50 Pacifics delivered by Schenectady in 1910, 895-944, were superheated, but they were set for 180 pounds pressure — the earlier Pacifics worked at 200 pounds — and they had only 45 square feet of grate area, inadequate for the 25" × 28" cylinders. The cylinders were soon reduced to 23" diameter.

Brooks built 30 larger Pacifics in 1913, class P-40, numbers 950-979. Like the previous group they had 73" drivers and 25" × 28" cylinders, but their fireboxes were 40 percent larger. The engines weighed 281,500 pounds and developed a tractive effort of 39,755 pounds (the USRA light Pacific weighed 277,000 pounds and had a tractive effort of 40,700 pounds).

About the time the P-40s arrived Rock Island turned to the 4-8-2 for heavy passenger service. It purchased one more Pacific: No. 999, built by

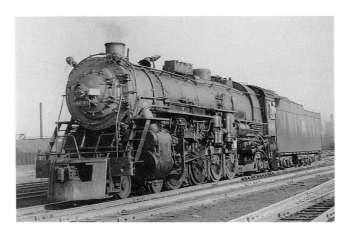

Mountain type 4045, a 1923 Brooks product, was rebuilt about 1940 with light-weight rods, roller bearings on all axles, and large tender, and was converted to a coal burner. Photo by John W. Malven.

Brooks in 1924. The combination of Brooks, mid-1920s, and the top-of-the-series road number is a reliable clue that this was an experimental locomotive. Powering its 74" drivers were 22" × 28" cylinders — three of them. It was almost the equal of a 4-8-2, but having one-third of its moving parts between the frames was against it. Like most one-of-a-kind engines it had a short life. It remained in service until 1934 and was scrapped in 1939.

Schenectady delivered two 4-8-2s numbered 998 and 999 in 1913, only two years after Chesapeake & Ohio originated the type. Their 69" drivers gave them more speed than the early low-drivered examples of the type. They were clearly derived from the 4-6-2, not the 2-8-2. They went to work on the high plains of Kansas and Colorado pulling in one section passenger trains that previously had been split into two. In 1920 they were renumbered 4000 and 4001, and the road ordered ten more

heavier 4-8-2s for the hilly routes from Rock Island to Des Moines and Kansas City. By 1927 the Rock Island had 62 Mountain types in service. Between 1939 and 1942 the 18 newest 4-8-2s were modernized with roller bearings, disk drivers, and lightweight rods.

Switchers

Rock Island's Chicago shops began building 0-6-0s in 1900, and the road bought 60 six-wheel switchers weighing about 140,000 pounds between 1903 and 1907. In 1913 30 0-6-0s weighing 160,000 pounds were delivered by Alco's Richmond Works, and Pittsburgh built 10 USRA 0-6-0s for the Rock Island in 1919.

In 1925 the yards at Armourdale (Kansas City) and Silvis (East Moline, Ill.) required larger power, and Alco delivered 10 copies of the USRA 0-8-0. Many of the road's other heavy switching chores were handled by older road engines; two groups of 2-8-0s were reclassified into the S class for that service.

Oddities and experimental locomotives

The Rock Island did not give its soul to the compound locomotive the way some of its neighbors did. The four-cylinder simple Atlantics of 1909 were unique in North America and remained unchanged through 27 years of service. The three-cylinder Pacific built by Brooks in 1924 was the only locomotive of its kind on the Rock Island, but during the 1920s a number of roads experimented with three-cylinder power.

The loaf-of-bread tenders were unique to the Rock. Faced in the mid-1920s with Vanderbilt tenders that were coming apart between the tank and the frame, the road designed what it officially called a semi-Vanderbilt tender: the original coal or oil bunker and the top of the tank were used unchanged and new sloping tank sides connected the cylindrical portion of the tank with the outside edges of a new frame.

The road experimented with two steam-powered passenger cars. No. 2551, built by Baldwin in 1909, was a coal-burner with its engine concealed in the front truck; and No. 2552, built by American in 1908, was an oil burner whose front truck was essentially a small 2-2-0 engine complete with Walschaerts valve gear. Both cars were converted to unpowered passenger cars in 1917.

Historical and technical society: Rock Island Technical Society, 8746 N. Troost, Kansas City, MO 64155

Published rosters: *Railroad Magazine*: September 1935, page 88; April 1949, page 108; April 1966, page 59 (1912 roster)

Recommended reading: *Rock Island Motive Power 1933-1955*, by Lloyd E. Stagner, published in 1980 by Pruett Publishing Co., 2928 Pearl Street, Boulder, CO 80301 (ISBN 0-87108-537-2)

CRI&P STEAM LOCOMOTIVES BUILT SINCE 1900

Type	Class	Numbers	Qty	Builder	Built	Retired	Notes
0-6-0	S-23	12	1	CRI&P, BLW	1901		
0-6-0	S-23	53, 55	2	Baldwin	1910	1936	
0-6-0	S-23	57-61,65-75,88-99,					
		101-110	38	CRI&P	1900-1903		
0-6-0	S-29	111-130	20	Brooks	1903	1936-1943	
0-6-0	S-29	131-148, 195, 196					
			20	Richmond	1905	1937-1951	
0-6-0	S-25	175-183	9	Baldwin	1901	1934-1936	
0-6-0	S-21	184-194	11	Brooks	1900-1936		
					Ex-Burlington, Cedar Rapids & Northern 10-20		
0-6-0	S-29	220-229	30	Baldwin	1905-1907	1937-1943	
0-6-0	S-33	230-259	30	Richmond	1913	1940-1953	
0-6-0	S-33	275-284	10	Pittsburgh	1919	1953	USRA
0-8-0	S-53	300-309	10	Brooks	1925	1953-1954	
2-6-0	G-24	748-750	3	Baldwin	1901	1935	
2-8-0	S-39	400-499	93	Brooks	1903-1904	1936-1942	Ex-C-39
2-8-0	C-39	1601-1700	100	Brooks	1903-1904	-1952	Most to S-39
2-8-0	C-43	1701-1783	83	Baldwin	1906	1936-1953	
2-8-0		1799 (1)	1	Baldwin	1906		
					Sold to New York, Susquehanna & Western		
2-8-0	C-46	1799 (2)	1	Baldwin	1907	1939	
					Renumbered 2200, then 1784		
2-8-0	C-26	1807-1810	4	Baldwin	1901		
					Ex-Choctaw, Oklahoma & Gulf 207-210		
2-8-0	C-28	1812-1840	29	Baldwin	1899-1901	1933-1941	
					Ex-Choctaw, Oklahoma & Gulf 261-289		
2-8-0	C-31	1852-1878	27	Baldwin	1902	1936-1947	
					Ex-Choctaw, Oklahoma & Gulf 290-316		
2-8-0	C-34	1880-1882	3	Lima	1910	1943-1949	
					Ex-St. Paul & Des Moines 206-208		
2-8-0	S-32	1888-1899	12	Baldwin	1901-1902	1937-1942	
					Ex-Choctaw, Oklahoma & Gulf 150-161, camelback		
2-8-0	C-43	1901-1930	30	Brooks	1907	1936-1952	
2-8-0	C-41	1931-2064	134	Brooks	1909-1910	1937-1952	
2-8-0	C-43	2100-2144	45	Schenectady	1907	1937-1953	
2-8-2	K-55	2300-2319	20	BLW, Schen	1919	1948-1953	USRA
2-8-2	K-60	2500-2642	143	BLW, Schen, Brooks			
					1912-1923	1936-1953	
							4 to Soo Line in 1941
2-8-2	K-60B	2643-2678	36	Brooks	1923	1948-1953	
2-8-2	K-64B	2679-2688	10	Brooks	1926	1952-1953	
2-8-2	K-67B	2689-2713	25	Schenectady	1927	1948-1953	
2-10-2	N-78	3001-3035	35	Schen, Brks	1918-1925	1939-1952	
4-4-0	E-18	674, 677, 682, 683					
			4	Baldwin	1902	1934	
4-4-2	A-23	1001-1003	3	Brooks	1900	-1934	
					Ex-Burlington, Cedar Rapids & Northern 75, 77, 76		
4-4-2	A-24	1004-1010	7	Brooks	1900	-1934	
4-4-2	A-24	1011-1020	10	Schenectady	1905	1935-1937	
4-4-2	A-29	1040, 1041	2	Schenectady	1909	1936, 1937	4-cylinder simple
4-4-2	A-24	1042-1049	8	Baldwin	1905-1906	1935-1942	
							4-cylinder balanced compound
4-6-0	28B	1225-1242	17	Baldwin	1900		Vauclain compound
4-6-0	T-27	1291-1299	9	Baldwin	1902	1934-1936	
4-6-0	T-27	1301-1322	22	Brooks	1902	1934-1935	ex-1472-1493
4-6-0	T-26	1323-1337	15	Brooks	1902-1903	1935	
							1333-1337 were ex-1494-1498
4-6-0	T-23	1340, 1341	2	Baldwin	1900	1934	
4-6-0	D-23	1351-1355	5	Baldwin	1900		
							Vauclain compound, ex-1201-1205
4-6-0	T-28	1401-1471	71	Brooks	1901-1902	1935-1941	
4-6-0	T-28	1472-1488	17	Baldwin	1900	1934-1942	Ex-1226-1242
4-6-0	D-28	1490-1499	10	Brooks	1902		
					Ex-Burlington, Cedar Rapids & Northern 200-209, class 54B		
4-6-0	T-28	1501-1520	20	Brooks	1901-1902	1934-1944	
4-6-0	T-31	1521-1535	15	Schenectady	1905	1936-1949	

CRI&P STEAM LOCOMOTIVES BUILT SINCE 1900

Type	Class	Numbers	Qty	Builder	Built	Retired	Notes
4-6-0	T-31	1550-1587	39	Baldwin	1905	1936-1953	
4-6-2	P-28	801-830	30	Brooks	1903	1935-1936	
4-6-2	P-32	831-861	31	Schenectady	1905	1936-1950	
4-6-2	P-31	862-894	33	Schenectady	1909	1939-1953	
4-6-2	P-33	895-944	50	Schenectady	1910	1939-1953	
4-6-2	P-40	950-979	30	Brooks	1913	1939-1952	

Type	Class	Numbers	Qty	Builder	Built	Retired	Notes
4-6-2	P-46	999	1	Brooks	1924	1939	3 cylinders
4-8-2	M-50	4000-4056	57	Brks, Schen	1913-1927	1939-1953	
							7 to St. Louis Southwestern in 1941
4-8-4	R-67B	5000-5064	65	Schenectady	1929-1930	1951-1953	
4-8-4	R-67B	5100-5119	20	Schenectady	1944, 1946	1953-1955	

CLINCHFIELD RAILROAD

The Clinchfield was built in the 20th century, relatively late in the era of railroad expansion. Its purpose was to tap the coalfields of eastern Tennessee and southwest Virginia and to serve as a north-south bridge route through the Blue Ridge Mountains. The nucleus of the road was the Ohio River & Charleston, which in 1900 had a few miles of track near Johnson City, Tennessee, far from both the Ohio River and Charleston. The South & Western Railway was incorporated in 1905 to begin construction, and was renamed the Carolina, Clinchfield & Ohio Railway in 1908, the year it opened between Johnson City and Marion, North Carolina. In 1909 the road was extended south to Spartanburg, South Carolina, and in 1915 it built north to a connection with Chesapeake & Ohio at Elkhorn City, Kentucky. In 1924 the railroad was leased jointly by the Atlantic Coast Line and the Louisville & Nashville, and the Clinchfield Railroad Company was established (but not incorporated) to operate it. ACL and L&N had little influence on Clinchfield's motive power policy — neither had much experience with mountain railroading.

The Clinchfield was mountain railroading. It ascended from Elkhorn City to Altapass with a sawtooth profile, then made a long, unbroken descent to Marion, followed by another descent to Spartanburg. The line is now part of CSX Transportation.

The Clinchfield's principal business was coal, and it also moved general merchandise and perishables between the Southeast and Midwest.

The road wasn't a major passenger carrier. In 1916 it ran two daily passenger trains each way, one covering the entire 277-mile main line and the other, most of it. Those trains could keep six locomotives busy.

The last steam operation occurred on April 16, 1954, when 4-6-6-4 No. 653 made a round trip from Erwin to Kingsport — well, almost the last. CRR predecessor Ohio River & Charleston acquired a 4-6-0 built in 1882 by the Columbus, Chicago & Indianapolis Central, a predecessor of the Pennsylvania Railroad, and numbered it 5. In 1913 the Carolina, Clinchfield & Ohio sold it to the Black Mountain Railway, a subsidary, and 42 years later in 1955 the Black Mountain sold it to the city of Erwin for display. In 1968 the Clinchfield bought it back, restored it, and put it to work on excursion trains. Because the 4-6-0 was too light to haul more than two steel passenger cars, it was fitted with supplemental controls for diesel helpers. The engine was retired and placed on display at the B&O Railroad Museum at Baltimore in 1979.

Freight locomotives

The largest single group of locomotives ever ordered by the Clinchfield were the 15 H-4-class 2-8-0s built by Baldwin in 1909. They had 57" drivers and weighed 200,000 pounds. They were followed by two groups of 2-8-2s, nine K-1s in 1919 and ten K-2s in 1923. Both classes of Mikados had 63" drivers and 27" × 30" cylinders and exerted a tractive force of 56,000 pounds. They were medium-weight Mikes (307,000 pounds nd 318,000 pounds), falling between the USRA light and heavy 2-8-2s in weight and power. The entire K-1 class was sold in 1943, five to the Charleston & Western Carolina and four to the Georgia Railroad. Both those railroads, like Clinchfield, were affiliates of Atlantic Coast Line.

The Clinchfield had two other Mikados: No. 498, class K-3, purchased from Spanish-American Iron Co., and No. 499, class K-2, purchased in 1917 from the Cambria & Indiana. Both were light 2-8-2s: 498 had 51" drivers, No. 499, 58". Both were assigned to local freight and yard duty.

Articulateds

Of the 114 steam locomotives built after 1900 on Clinchfield's roster, two-thirds of them — 76 — were articulateds. The road's first Mallet, M-1 No. 500, was delivered in 1909, a typical early 2-6-6-2 with 57" drivers, firebox over the rear drivers, outside steam pipe from the steam dome to the high-pressure cylinders, and slide valves on the high-pressure cylinders. It weighed 343,000 pounds. A year later Baldwin delivered ten M-2 class 2-6-6-2s, 550-559. They had larger cylinders with piston valves and weighed 378,000 pounds; their tractive effort of 77,400 pounds was about 7,000 more than that of the M-1. They were rebuilt by Baldwin in 1923 and renumbered 510-519.

In 1916 Clinchfield bought 10 six-year-old 2-6-6-2s from the Chicago Great Western and classed them M-3, retaining their CGW numbers. They matched No. 500 in several dimensions. Their early retirement in 1925 is probably a good indication of their performance.

Clinchfield turned to the 2-8-8-2 in 1919, receiving seven of its own design from Baldwin in March of that year and ten USRA 2-8-8-2s, also from Baldwin, in October and November. The home-designed L-1s weighed 524,000 pounds, had 28" and 42" × 32" cylinders, and worked at a boiler pressure of 200 pounds. The USRA locomotives, class L-2, weighed 541,000 pounds, had 25" and 39" × 32" cylinders, and worked at 240 pounds. The difference in tractive force was 2,000 pounds in favor of the Clinchfield design, but when the road ordered 10 more from Brooks in 1923 it asked for copies of the USRA engine.

At the beginning of World War II the Clinchfield needed locomotives that could pull like the 2-8-8-2s and run like the Mikados. It purchased

Clinchfield 150, a light, low-drivered Pacific seen at Erwin, Tenn., in October 1937, sports an intriguing and uncommon combination of inside valves and outside valve gear. Photo by R. P. Morris.

Mikado 411, a member of the K-4 class, carries its air pumps on the smokebox front and its headlight tucked beneath the smokebox. Photo by R. P. Morris

Clinchfield's most numerous articulateds were 2-8-8-2s. L-3 No. 740 was built by Brooks in 1923. Photo by R. P. Morris.

eight Challengers, single-expansion 4-6-6-4s, from Alco in 1942 and 1943. They were based on Delaware & Hudson's 4-6-6-4 of 1940. In 1947 Alco built four more to the same design. In 1943 the Denver & Rio Grande Western needed additional locomotives to move wartime traffic. D&RGW wanted duplicates of the Baldwin 4-6-6-4s it received in 1937, but the War Production Board diverted six locomotives from a Union Pacific order that Alco was building. The Rio Grande didn't buy them but leased them from the Defense Plant Corporation. By the time traffic levels had returned to normal Rio Grande had begun dieselization in earnest, so they were put up for sale, and Clinchfield bought the six orphans.

Passenger locomotives

Clinchfield predecessor South & Western bought three locomotives in 1905, 4-6-0 No. 1 and 2-8-0s Nos. 51 and 52. The Ten-Wheeler became Clinchfield 99 and was used in passenger, local freight, and work train service. The first new locomotives purchased by the Clinchfield were four G-2-class 4-6-0s, 100-103, built by Baldwin in 1908. They had 63" drivers and weighed 82 tons. They were assigned to passenger service.

Baldwin delivered three Pacifics, 150-152, in 1910. They weighed about 235,000 pounds, and had 69" drivers and inside piston valves driven by Walschaerts valve gear. Two more Pacifics came from Baldwin in 1914, also with 69" drivers but weighing 281,000 pounds. The additional weight and larger cylinders, 25" × 30", gave them a tractive force of 46,200 pounds, quite respectable for a Pacific. They were initially assigned to fast freight service.

Clinchfield's first Challengers, 650-657, were based on Delaware & Hudson's class J 4-6-6-4. Photo by C. W. Witbeck.

Switchers

Clinchfield's only switchers were a pair of 2-8-0s built in 1905 for the South & Western and converted to 0-8-0s in 1917.

Recommended reading: *When Steam Ran the Clinchfield*, by James A. Goforth, published in 1991 by Gem Publishers, P. O. Box 108, Erwin, TN 37650

Published rosters: *Railroad Magazine*: January 1934, page 130; January 1951, page 110

CLINCHFIELD STEAM LOCOMOTIVES BUILT SINCE 1900

Type	Class	Numbers	Qty	Builder	Built	Retired	Notes
2-8-0	H-3	51, 52	2	Baldwin	1905	1938	to 0-8-0, 1917
2-8-0	H-4	300-314	15	Baldwin	1909	1950-1953	
2-8-2	K-1	400-408	9	Baldwin	1919	Sold 1943	
2-8-2	K-2	499	1	Baldwin	1911	1952	Ex-Cambria & Indiana
2-8-2	K-3	498	1	Baldwin	1917		
2-8-2	K-4	410-419	10	Brooks	1923	1952-1955	
2-6-6-2	M-1	500	1	Baldwin	1909	1938	
2-6-6-2	M-2	510-519	10	Baldwin	1923	1951-1952	Rebuilt from 550-559
2-6-6-2	M-2	550-559	10	Baldwin	1910		Rebuilt 1923
2-6-6-2	M-3	600-609	10	Baldwin	1910	1925	Ex-Chicago Great Western

Type	Class	Numbers	Qty	Builder	Built	Retired	Notes
2-8-8-2	L-1	700-706	7	Baldwin	1919	1948-1950	
2-8-8-2	L-2	725-734	10	Baldwin	1919	1950-1952	
2-8-8-2	L-3	735-744	10	Brooks	1923	1951-1952	
4-6-6-4	E-1	650-657	8	Alco	1942-1943	1954	
4-6-6-4	E-2	660-663	4	Alco	1947	1954	
4-6-6-4	E-3	670-675	6	Alco	1943	1953	
4-6-0	G-1	99	1	Baldwin	1905	1938	
4-6-0	G-2	100-103	4	Baldwin	1908	1938	
4-6-2	P-1	150-152	3	Baldwin	1910	1951	
4-6-2	P-2	153, 154	2	Baldwin	1914	1953	

COLORADO & SOUTHERN RAILWAY AND FORT WORTH & DENVER CITY RAILWAY

The Colorado & Southern was formed in 1898 by consolidating several standard gauge and narrow gauge lines in Colorado, Wyoming, and New Mexico that had been part of the Union Pacific system. The standard gauge main line stretched from Wendover, Wyoming, south through Cheyenne and Fort Collins, Denver, and Pueblo, Colorado, to Texline on the Texas-New Mexico state line. There it connected end-to-end with its subsidiary, the Fort Worth & Denver City, which ran southeast through Amarillo and Wichita Falls to Fort Worth and Dallas. In 1905 C&S purchased the Trinity & Brazos Valley Railway, which extended from Fort Worth and Dallas to Houston and Galveston, and sold a half interest to the Rock Island in 1907.

In 1908 the Chicago, Burlington & Quincy acquired control of the C&S. The CB&Q by then was jointly controlled by Great Northern and Northern Pacific, and the C&S and FW&DC would give GN and NP a route from the Pacific Northwest to the Gulf Coast, initially via Alliance, Nebraska, and later on a more direct route via Casper, Wyoming.

Burlington allowed the C&S and FW&DC some autonomy in their affairs, but the locomotives purchased after 1908 were of Burlington design, and from time to time locomotives were moved from parent to subsidiary or vice versa. Generally C&S locomotives were built as coal burners (southern Colorado has extensive coal deposits) and FW&DC locomotives as oil burners. As oil deposits were discovered in Wyoming, locomotives assigned to the north end of the C&S were converted to oil, as were C&S locomotives that were leased to the FW&DC. The FW&DC is notable for equipping very few locomotives with feedwater heaters: only 2-8-2s 464 and 465 and 4-6-2s 551-557. The terrain traversed by the two roads was quite different. FW&DC ran across the plains of Texas, generally following the watercourses; C&S paralleled the Front Range of the Rockies, generally close enough that it ran crosswise to foothills and river valleys.

C&S had several narrow gauge lines from Denver west to Georgetown and Central City and southwest to Leadville and Gunnison. The most modern narrow gauge locomotives were three ex-Denver, Boulder & Western 2-8-0s built in 1898; C&S predecessor Denver, Leadville & Gunnison purchased its last new locomotives, also 2-8-0s, in 1896. In 1938 the C&S considered purchasing the Uintah Railway's two 2-6-6-2s to use on the line to Idaho Springs, but extensive reconstruction of track and bridges would have been required, and operating expenses would have been double those of the 2-8-0s that were handling the twice-weekly train (the line was abandoned in 1941).

In 1899 the C&S adopted a new locomotive numbering system that was to have included FW&DC engines. FW&DC locomotives kept their numbers, though, and in 1906 C&S had to revise its system to accommodate a large number of new locomotives. That same year C&S adopted a classification system proposed by the Interstate Commerce Commission: a letter indicating the number of truck wheels, a digit for the number of driving axles, and additional letters and numbers to indicate different groups of the same type.

Freight locomotives

Colorado & Southern adopted the 2-8-0 for freight service in 1888, and between 1900 and 1907 bought 78 standard gauge Consolidations, more than the sum of all other post-1900 types on its standard gauge roster. In 1900 the C&S asked Baldwin, Cooke, and Rhode Island each to design a new 2-8-0. Baldwin built a low-slung 51"-drivered machine, No. 428, like those it had been building for the road, and the Cooke engine, No. 429, was almost the same. The Rhode Island design had 56" drivers and a higher boiler and weighed 163,360 pounds, about 20,000 pounds more than the Baldwin and Cooke engines. Cylinder diameter and piston stroke were greater (21" × 28"); so was tractive effort. C&S liked the Rhode Island locomotives — it bought five, numbered 451-455, versus one each from Baldwin and Cooke.

In 1903 the Fort Worth & Denver City took delivery of 11 Rhode Island 2-8-0s numbered 201-211 and eventually classed B-4O. They were similar to the C&S locomotives but had cylinders an inch less in diameter and weighed 5,000 pounds less; FW&DC had neither the grades nor the traffic of the C&S.

C&S continued to develop the Consolidation. In 1901 it ordered 10 larger 2-8-0s from Rhode Island. They had cylinders an inch greater in diameter and a larger boiler working at 205 pounds pressure instead of 185 pounds, and they weighed about 30,000 pounds more than the Rhode Island engines delivered the year before. The road was pleased enough with 600-609 that it ordered 15 more (610-624) from Alco's Richmond Works in 1902 and 28 (C&S 625-643 and FW&DC 301-309) from Brooks in 1906. Baldwin delivered Nos. 644-649 in 1907. Classed B-4R1, they differed in the cab and smokebox and had slide valves instead of piston valves. Fort Worth & Denver 310-314 were identical, but were built by Richmond in 1908.

In the 1920s many engines in the B-4R and B-4R1 classes were modernized with new fireboxes, superheaters, outside piston valves, and Walschaerts valve gear. Number 641 achieved fame as the last steam engine in regular service on a Class 1 railroad in the United States, working the isolated Climax-Leadville branch until October 11, 1962.

C&S was intrigued enough by neighbor Santa Fe's experience with compound locomotives to order 12 tandem compound 2-8-0s from Rhode Island in 1903. Like the B-4R class they had 57" drivers, but they had wide fireboxes over the rear drivers. They were successful and were the longest-lived tandem compounds; they were finally converted to simple engines between 1924 and 1926.

In 1907 C&S ordered a group of nine light Consolidations from Baldwin. They had the same running gear as Nos. 644-649 but a much smaller boiler. They were extremely poor steamers and were quickly placed in local freight and switching service. They were scrapped after only 20 to 25 years of service. Rogers, Richmond, and Baldwin built similar

Benjamin Harrison was president of the United States when Denver, Leadville & Gunnison took delivery of 2-8-0 No. 273 in 1890 (C&S renumbered it 70 in 1899). It was still active in 1940 when the photo was taken. It was C&S's only oil-burning narrow gauge engine, and it was one of the last two narrow gauge engines on the roster (69 was the other) when it was sold to the U. S. Army in 1943 for use on the White Pass & Yukon as No. 21. After the war it was shipped to a Seattle scrap dealer and dismantled in 1946 — during Harry Truman's first term as president. Photo by R. H. Kindig.

C&S 2-10-2s 903 and 902 are in command of a freight train at Horse Creek, Wyo., on October 13, 1957. Both are oil burners and are towing auxiliary water tenders; both carry "Burlington Route" heralds on their tenders. An Elesco feedwater heater is atop the smokebox of 903; not visible in this photo is the Worthington BL unit on the left flank of No. 902. Photo by James Lusk.

light 2-8-0s for the Fort Worth & Denver City (250-265) and the Trinity & Brazos Valley (32-46 and 57-59). T&BV 58 and 59 were sold to the FW&DC 1908 as part of the payment for 4-6-0s 106-111. The B-4Qs and B-4Q1s performed little better on the level plains of Texas than they did in Colorado and Wyoming, and all but one were scrapped by 1935.

C&S's first 2-8-2s were delivered by Baldwin in 1911. They were similar to Burlington's O-1 class, but had 57" drivers instead of 64". In the 1920s they were superheated, their boiler pressure was raised from 170 pounds to 200 pounds, and they were fitted with Elesco feedwater heaters. All five were leased to the Burlington from 1933 to 1947.

In 1957 the Burlington sold six class O-4 USRA heavy 2-8-2s to the C&S for use during the sugar-beet harvest seasons. C&S numbered them 804-810 to avoid conflict with diesel numbers (E-4A No. 804 had been scrapped in 1953). Five of them saw service; No. 808 (CB&Q 5509) was cannibalized to keep the others going.

Fort Worth & Denver's first 2-8-2s, 401-410, were also copies of Burlington's O-1 2-8-2, even to the 64" drivers. They were the road's first oil burners and sparked the conversion of most FW&DC locomotives. The USRA allotted five light 2-8-2s to the FW&DC, then because of a surplus of heavy 2-8-2s under construction changed the allocation to heavy

Fort Worth & Denver 556 and Colorado & Southern 373 are the same basic heavy Pacific, but 556 is an oil burner, 373 is a coal burner and has smaller drivers. Baldwin photos.

2-8-2s. They were too long for most of the turntables, but it was heavy 2-8-2s or nothing, so the road accepted them and numbered them 451-455. In 1920 Baldwin delivered 2-8-2s 456-460, copies of Burlington's O-3, and in 1922 another five arrived from Baldwin, heavier and more powerful versions of that design.

C&S turned to the 2-10-2 type for road freight power in 1915 with five Baldwin-built duplicates of Burlington's M-2A class: class E-5A, Nos. 900-904. They worked well, and during their life they received improvements including feedwater heaters, disk main drivers, enlarged tenders, and roller-bearing lead trucks.

In 1918 the USRA allotted five heavy 2-10-2s to the C&S: class E-5B, Nos. 905-909. The C&S preferred them to the Burlington design. They were faster — 63" drivers instead of 60" — and their cast-steel tender frames and trucks were better than the wood tender frames and archbar trucks of the Burlington locomotives. Even so, C&S's last new steam locomotives, E-5Cs 910-914, delivered in 1922, were updated versions of the Burlington design.

Passenger locomotives

The three 1900-vintage Ten-Wheelers in the C-3G class were handsome machines with 63" drivers, but they proved inadequate. C&S didn't attempt to change them but eventually scrapped them in 1925 and 1926 after several years of storage. The next group of 4-6-0s, 323-326 built by Schenectady and 327-329 by Brooks, were more successful. They had 67" drivers and inside piston valves and weighed about 170,000 pounds, 15,000 more than 320-322. In 1919 and 1920 the road rebuilt them with superheaters, outside piston valves, and Walschaerts valve gear. Four of the class were leased to parent Burlington in the 1930s. The two C-3H1 4-6-0s built by Baldwin in 1907 had the same dimensions but were heavier. They received the same improvements as the C-3H class in 1920 and 1921 and were leased to the Burlington in the 1930s.

FW&DC 4-6-0s 101-105 were built by Rhode Island immediately after C&S 320-322. They operated at 180 pounds boiler pressure (the C&S engines worked at 200) and were somewhat more successful than their C&S counterparts. They were fitted with bolt-on piston valve conversions during the 1920s. FW&DC purchased six more Ten-Wheelers in 1902 and 1903. Their 67" drivers made them faster than the previous group of 4-6-0s, but they were lighter and proved to be poor steamers.

About that time the affiliated Trinity & Brazos Valley needed passenger engines but couldn't afford new ones; Fort Worth & Denver City saw that as an opportunity to find a good home for 106-111 and purchased six 4-6-0s that were duplicates of C&S 327-329. FW&DC gave 150-155 superheaters and new cylinders during the 1920s. In 1907 the FW&DC purchased its last two 4-6-0s, 156 and 157, class C-3H1. They were identical to C&S 330 and 331, except for 69" drivers, 2" larger than the C&S engines had. Five engines just like them were built for the Trinity & Brazos Valley that same year.

The T&BV was still short of power in 1907 and purchased five 63"-drivered 4-6-0s from the St. Louis, Brownsville & Mexico. (At the time the president of the StLB&M was also president of the Rock Island, which was half-owner of the T&BV.)

Colorado & Southern ordered 10 4-6-2s from Baldwin in 1910: five for itself numbered 350-354 and five for the FW&DC, 501-505. They were copies of the S-2 Pacifics of parent Burlington, with 69" drivers, superheaters, and the curious combination of Walschaerts valve gear and inside piston valves. C&S's locomotives were rebuilt between 1922 and 1925 with new cylinders and new superheaters, and in 1929 and 1930 they received Elesco feedwater heaters and new tender trucks. FW&DC

501-505 got the same improvements, except for the feedwater heaters.

In early 1918 the USRA allotted five light 4-6-2s to the Fort Worth & Denver City. Later that year the C&S asked the USRA for six heavy Pacifics, three for each of the roads. The agency approved those for FW&DC but not the C&S engines. Meanwhile, parent CB&Q suddenly had a surplus of 4-6-2s and in 1919 leased three brand-new S-3 Pacifics to C&S (when the lease expired a year later, C&S purchased them). The FW&DC recognized that the USRA heavy Pacifics would have been too large for its needs and sought to lease three Burlington 4-6-2s. The USRA granted permission for the FW&DC to purchase three new 4-6-2s of Burlington design, then said "Make it five" — the F-3A1 class, Nos. 551-555, identical to Burlington's S-3 Pacifics but built by Alco's Schenectady Works. Five more arrived from Baldwin in 1922, FW&DC 556 and 557, oil burners with 74" drivers, and C&S 373-375, coal burners with 69" drivers.

Switchers

Between 1906 and 1910 C&S bought 17 0-6-0s to replace an assortment of older 0-6-0s, some built as 0-6-0s and others converted from Moguls. They were built to a Union Pacific design, with 51" drivers and slide valves. The first five, from Cooke, had main rods connected to the second drivers; the others drove on the third drivers.

FW&DC's first 0-6-0s were delivered by Schenectady in 1906. They looked like the 0-6-0s C&S received the same year, but were 12,000 pounds heavier. FW&DC 60-67 and Trinity & Brazos Valley 75 and 76 were identical to C&S 225-231; 68 and 69 were identical to C&S 232-236.

Historical and technical society: Burlington Route Historical Society, P. O. Box 456, La Grange, IL

Recommended reading: *The Colorado Road*, by F. Hol Wagner Jr., published in 1970 by Intermountain Chapter, National Railway Historical Society, P. O. Box 5181, Denver, CO 80217

Published rosters:
Colorado & Southern: *Railroad Magazine*, September 1954, page 40
Fort Worth & Denver City: *Railroad Magazine*, October 1955, page 29

C&S and FW&DC STEAM LOCOMOTIVES BUILT SINCE 1900

Type	Class	Numbers	Qty	Builder	Built	Scrapped	Notes
Colorado & Southern							
0-6-0	A-3E	220-224	5	Cooke	1906	1934-1946	
0-6-0	A-3E1	225-231	7	Schenectady	1907	1934-1947	
0-6-0	A-3E2	232-236	5	Baldwin	1910	1946-1949	
2-8-0	B-4M	422-428	7	Baldwin	1897-1900	1927-1935	
2-8-0	B-4N	429	1	Cooke	1900	1931	
2-8-0	B-4P	451-455	5	Rhode Island	1900	1931-1947	
2-8-0	B-4Q1	700-708	9	Baldwin	1907	1927-1932	
2-8-0	B-4R	600-609	10	Rhode Island	1901	1929-1961	
2-8-0	B-4R	610-624	15	Richmond	1902	1927-1956	
2-8-0	B-4R	625-643	19	Brooks	1906	1927-1962	
2-8-0	B-4R1	644-649	6	Baldwin	1907	1934-1960	
2-8-0	B-4S	520-531	12	Rhode Island	1903	1939-1956	
							Tandem compound
2-8-2	E-4A	800-804	5	Baldwin	1911	1953-1959	
2-8-2	O-4	804 (2)-809	6	Baldwin	1919	1960	
							USRA, ex-CB&Q
2-10-2	E-5A	900-904	5	Baldwin	1915	1956-1961	
2-10-2	E-5B	905-909	5	Baldwin	1919	1954-1960	USRA
2-10-2	E-5C	910-914	5	Baldwin	1922	1955-1960	
4-6-0	C-3G	320-322	3	Rhode Island	1900	1925-1926	
4-6-0	C-3H	323-329	7	Schen, Brooks	1902-1906	1935-1945	
4-6-0	C-3H1	330, 331	2	Baldwin	1907	1950	
4-6-2	F-3A	350-354	5	Baldwin	1910	1947-1951	
4-6-2	F-3B	370-372	3	Baldwin	1918	1953-1960	
							Ex-CB&Q 2970, 2973, 2965
4-6-2	F-3C	373-375	3	Baldwin	1922	1954-1960	
Fort Worth & Denver City							
0-6-0	A-3F	50, 51	2	Schenectady	1906	1952	
0-6-0	A-3E1	60-67	8	Richmond	1907-1908	1934-1948	
0-6-0	A-3E2	68, 69	2	Baldwin	1910	1948	
2-8-0	B-4O	201-211	12	Rhode Island	1903	1934-1960	
2-8-0	B-4Q	250-252	3	Rogers	1906	1940	
2-8-0	B-4Q1	253-267	15	Richmond	1907	1929-1947	
2-8-0	B-4R	301-309	9	Brooks	1906	1934-1955	
2-8-0	B-4R1	310-314	5	Richmond	1908	1953-1960	
2-8-2	E-4A1	401-410	10	Baldwin	1915	1955-1960	
2-8-2	E-4A2	451-455	5	Baldwin	1919	1955-1960	USRA
2-8-2	E-4A3	456-460	5	Baldwin	1920	1956-1960	

Type	Class	Numbers	Qty	Builder	Built	Scrapped	Notes
2-8-2	E-4A4	461-465	5	Baldwin	1922	1955-1956	
4-6-0	C-3F	101-105	5	Rhode Island	1900	1932-1936	
4-6-0	C-3D	106-111	6	Schenectady	1902-1903		Sold to T&BV
4-6-0	C-3H	150-155	6	Brooks	1906	1936-1941	
4-6-0	C-3H1	156, 157	2	Richmond	1907	1929, 1948	
4-6-2	F-3A	501-505	5	Baldwin	1910-1911	1952	
4-6-2	F-3A1	551-555	5	Schenectady	1920	1952-1955	
4-6-2	F-3A2	556, 557	2	Baldwin	1922	1953, 1952	

Trinity & Brazos Valley

Type	Class	Numbers	Qty	Builder	Built	Scrapped	Notes
0-6-0	A-3E1	75, 76	2	Richmond	1907	sold 1917	
2-8-0	B-4Q1	32-46	15	BLW, Richmond	1907		1931-1944
2-8-0	B-4Q1	57-59	3	Baldwin	1907	1931-1935	
4-6-0	C-3D	26-31	6	Schenectady	1902-1903	1928-1935	Ex-FW&DC 106-111
4-6-0	C-3H1	47-51	5	Baldwin	1907	1931-1939	
4-6-0	C-3D	52-56	5	Baldwin	1904	1929-1944	Ex-StLB&M

COMPOUND LOCOMOTIVES

Just what happens inside the cylinder of a locomotive? A valve opens and steam enters the cylinder at boiler pressure. Then the valve closes. The cylinder walls and the cylinder head can't move, but the piston can and does because of the pressure of the steam. As the volume of the cylinder increases, the pressure inside the cylinder decreases — Boyle's Law at work. Another valve opens and the steam is exhausted through the smokebox. The exhaust steam still has plenty of energy left — you can hear it in the explosive "chuff!" Locomotive designers wondered if that energy could be used for something more valuable than noise.

The most logical thing to do with steam exhausted from a cylinder was to pipe it into another cylinder to let it expand further and move another piston. Because the steam was at a lower pressure, it was necessary to use a larger cylinder to develop equal piston thrust. A steam engine that uses the same steam two or more times in a succession of larger cylinders is a compound steam engine.

In 1867 the Erie Railway rebuilt a 4-4-0 into a tandem compound — high- and low-pressure cylinders on the same axis sharing one piston rod. Little is known about the locomotive except that it didn't work well. The first practical compound was a two-cylinder cross-compound tank engine designed by Anatole Mallet in 1875 for the Bayonne & Biarritz Railway in France. (Mallet's later design for an articulated locomotive was a byproduct of his experiments in compounding.)

Cross-compounds

The first practical North American compound locomotives were cross-compounds. They had two cylinders, one on each side just like a conventional locomotive, but they were of different sizes. The diameter of the low-pressure cylinder was about 1.5 times the diameter of the high-pressure cylinder. Steam exhausted from the high-pressure cylinder went to a receiver pipe in the smokebox, then to the low-pressure cylinder. To observers it sounded like the engine was working at half speed because it exhausted only twice per driver revolution.

A valve permitted cross-compounds to be "worked simple" for starting, with steam at boiler pressure in both cylinders. A reducing valve for the low-pressure cylinder ensured that both sides of the engine did approximately the same work. When pressure in the receiver reached a certain point or the engineer turned a valve, the locomotive began working as a compound. The cross-compound locomotive consumed 15 to 20 percent less fuel for the same job, but it was slow and unbalanced. (The cross-compound steam engine survived and found a niche — usually under the left running board — powering the air pump for the brakes.)

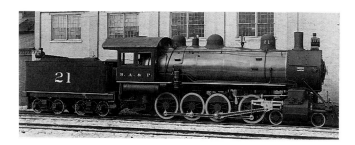

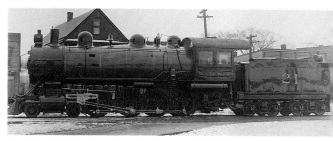

Butte, Anaconda & Pacific 21, photographed at Alco's Schenectady Works in 1903, is a cross-compound. The jacket and insulation of the large low-pressure cylinder on the right side have been trimmed for clearance. Notice that the right side of the locomotive has been specially painted for the photo with flat paint, plus white trim on the tires and running boards, and the glass removed from the cab windows. The second and third drivers are blind — and so close together that there is no room for a flange on either. Right side, C. W. Witbeck collection; left side, Alco History Center.

Vauclain compounds

In 1889 Samuel Vauclain of Baldwin Locomotive Works patented a four-cylinder compound system, and Baldwin built the first of the type, a 4-4-0 for the Baltimore & Ohio. The Vauclain compound had two cylinders on each side: a high-pressure cylinder and a low-pressure cylinder. Usually the small high-pressure cylinder was on top; on low-drivered freight locomotives the low-pressure cylinder was on top for clearance reasons. The diameter of the low-pressure cylinder was about 1.7 times that of the high-pressure cylinder. The two cylinders, a valve chamber, and half the cylinder saddle were cast in a single piece.

A single valve on each side fed steam from the boiler to the high-pressure cylinder and from there to the low-pressure cylinder. The two pistons drove on a common crosshead. The engine could be worked simple — boiler pressure in all four cylinders — for starting. On the whole the design was successful. By 1904, when it was superseded by the balanced compound, Baldwin had built more than 2,000 Vauclain compound locomotives.

Balanced compounds

In 1902 Vauclain revised his design, moving the high-pressure cylinders into the saddle between the frames, still using a single valve for each pair of cylinders. All four cylinders drove the same axle. The low-pressure cylinders were connected to the crankpins of the drive wheels, which were the usual 90 degrees apart. The high-pressure cylinders drove cranks on the axles set at 180 degrees from the crankpins outside. The main rods and pistons on each side were in balance.

Francis J. Cole of American Locomotive Company developed a different balanced compound design. The outside low-pressure cylinders drove on the second axle; the high-pressure cylinders, which were between the frames but set several feet forward on the pilot deck, drove cranks on the first axle. There was a piston valve for each cylinder.

Tandem compounds

Brooks Locomotive Works reintroduced the tandem compound in 1892. The low-pressure cylinders were in the usual place; the high-pressure cylinders were directly ahead of them. The two cylinders shared a common piston rod and a single cylinder head between them. The advantage of the tandem compound was that all the cylinders were accessible, and after Walschaerts valve gear replaced Stephenson, there was no machinery between the frames.

Atlantic City Railroad 1027 is a Vauclain compound built by Baldwin in 1896. The high-pressure and low-pressure cylinder on each side drive on a common crosshead. The piston valve for both cylinders is just inboard of the high-pressure cylinders. Baldwin photo; Collection of H. L. Broadbelt.

Santa Fe 507 is a balanced compound. The high-pressure cylinders are inside the frames; rods from those cylinders are connected to cranks on the first axle. All four cylinders drive on the first axle. The eccentrics for the Stephenson valve gear are on the second driving axle. Note the minimal counterweight on the first driver and its position. Collection of Frederick Westing.

Mallets

American Locomotive Company built America's first Mallet in 1904: Baltimore & Ohio 2400. It consisted of two engines beneath a single boiler. The rear, high-pressure engine was firmly attached to the boiler; the front, low-pressure engine was hinged at its rear to the high-pressure engine. It was what American railroads had been seeking, not so much for economy as for a flexible, double-size locomotive.

The superheater, introduced about 1900, offered an easier route to economy than compounding locomotives. Except for Mallets, compounds disappeared quickly. They were usually rebuilt to superheated simple locomotives. The last non-Mallet compounds were a group of Santa Fe Pacifics built by Baldwin in 1914. The Mallet endured. The last steam locomotives Baldwin built for North American use were Mallets — ten 2-6-6-2s for Chesapeake & Ohio in 1949 — and the Norfolk & Western built its last class Y6b 2-8-8-2 in 1952.

Oddities

The Erie and the Virginian explored the triplex Mallet, essentially a 2-8-8-0 Mallet with a second low-pressure engine under the tender. The boiler of the triplex couldn't generate enough steam for the six cylinders at any speed greater than a walk, and the experiment was a flop, albeit a visually intriguing one.

Delaware & Hudson revived the cross-compound in 1924 when it built an experimental high-pressure 2-8-0. It was followed by two similar 2-8-0s and a triple-expansion 4-8-0. The four were economical of fuel and could drag anything — when they weren't in the shop.

Baldwin's 60,000th locomotive was a three-cylinder 4-10-2 built in 1926. The middle cylinder was high-pressure; the outside cylinders were low-pressure. The locomotive was sent out on a demonstration tour, but the combination of watertube firebox, three-cylinder running gear, and compound working were too exotic for the railroads. The locomotive returned to Philadelphia and was placed on display in the Franklin Institute, where it remains today.

What killed the compound?

Compound engines worked well in stationary power plants and in

Baltimore & Ohio 1705, built by Pittsburgh in 1901, is a tandem compound with high-pressure cylinders ahead of the low-pressure cylinders.

The most successful compound design was the Mallet. New York Central 7106 illustrates the difference in diameter between the high-pressure (rear) and low-pressure (front) cylinders. It was built by Alco in 1920; here in 1946 it was employed in hump switching at Selkirk Yard, near Albany, N. Y. Photo by LaMar M. Kelley.

steamships, where triple-expansion engines were common and quintuple-expansion engines weren't unheard of. In these applications they were low-speed engines, and they ran better when the valves for each stage could be controlled independently — and that task was easier for an engineer who was concerned only with running a stationary engine and did not have to watch for signals, curves, washouts, stations, and cows on the track.

One of the fundamental dilemmas in the design of a steam locomotive concerns the use of exhaust steam to create a draft for the fire. It does that by passing through a nozzle in the smokebox, working on the same principle as an atomizer or spray gun. The more restrictive the nozzle, the better the draft — and the more back pressure in the cylinder. The greater the amount of energy used to create the draft, the less energy will be available to move the train.

Another problem is that of condensation. As steam expands in the cylinder, some of it condenses into water. If the cylinder is hot and the initial steam pressure is high, the problem is almost nonexistent, but if the cylinder is cold and the pressure is low, the water, being incompressible, can damage the piston and cylinder head.

The draft and condensation problems were worse on compound locomotives. By the time steam had pushed the high-pressure piston to the other end of the cylinder, passed through the valves and the pipes to the low-pressure cylinder, and pushed that piston the length of the cylinder, it had very little pressure but a great deal of volume. With little energy left in the steam, exhausting the cylinder took longer, and there was less energy available to create the required draft.

The superheater delivered the efficiency that compounding only promised. It was a simple, no-moving-parts affair, an arrangement of pipes in the smokebox that intercepted steam on its route from steam dome to cylinders and shuttled it back through the firetubes of the boiler, where it absorbed more heat and therefore more energy. You'll find a full discussion of the superheater on page 000.

DELAWARE & HUDSON RAILROAD

The Delaware & Hudson was chartered in 1823 to build a canal to carry coal from Honesdale, Pennsylvania, to Kingston, New York. After the Civil War the D&H expanded northward by acquiring the Albany & Susquehanna Railroad (Albany-Binghamton, N. Y.) and the Rensselaer & Saratoga (Troy-Albany-Whitehall, N. Y.). By 1873 the D&H system extended from Wilkes-Barre, Penna., and Binghamton north to the Canadian border. D&H reached Montreal through acquisition of the Napierville Junction Railway to St. Constant in 1907 and trackage rights on Grand Trunk to Montreal.

Anthracite — the company owned it, mined it, sold it, carried it, and naturally burned it in its locomotives. Locomotives that were assigned to the line from Plattsburgh through the Adirondacks to Lake Placid (abandoned in 1946) burned oil during the summer.

Freight locomotives

The bulk of D&H's freight traffic was coal, and it rolled behind more than 200 2-8-0s. Until 1907 the typical D&H 2-8-0 was a Camelback machine. The first 18 class E-5 locomotives arrived from Alco as Camelbacks in 1906 and 1907, but successive E-5s, delivered from 1907 through 1914, were of conventional single-cab design. Total engine weight was 261,900 pounds. A single E-6-class 2-8-0 came in 1916 and 20 more in 1918. The E-6s had 63" drivers — previous D&H Consolidations had 57" drivers — and weighed 296,000 pounds, a bit more than a USRA light 2-8-2. Between 1926 and 1930 D&H built a dozen class E-5a Consolidations weighing 298,000 pounds.

D&H, like most American railroads, came under the control of the USRA during World War I, but no USRA locomotives were allotted to D&H, because the anthracite used as fuel required a wide firebox. After the war D&H chose not to indulge in such developments as Alco's three-cylinder locomotives and Lima's Super-Power concept. D&H instead stuck with the 2-8-0. A railroad that needs a larger locomotive has two choices: it can add axles to spread the weight or it can rebuild its physical plant to handle more weight on the same number of axles.

Class E-68 (formerly E-5a) 2-8-0 No. 1119 represents Delaware & Hudson's last series of nonexperimental Consolidations, built by Colonie Shops in 1929. The outboard lead truck journal and the outside ashpan hoppers are typical D&H details. D&H photo.

No. 1401, *John B. Jervis*, was the second of D&H's quartet of experimental high-pressure locomotives. The watertube firebox accounts for the shape of the boiler; the pipe over the top of the smokebox in front of the stack carries steam from the high-pressure cylinder on this side to the low-pressure cylinder on the left side. The plumbing behind the stack is for the throttle. Adding to the awkward appearance is the location of the stack well forward of the center line of the cylinders. The locomotive's tractive effort is augmented by a booster engine on the rear truck of the tender. D&H photo.

Pacific 606 shows the effects of rebuilding: recessed headlight, British-looking flanged stack, smoke lifters, sloping plate between the pilot and the smokebox to help lift the smoke, cab sides extending down to the level of the bottom of the tender tank, and a general lack of external piping. Photo by L. W. Bullock.

D&H chose the latter course, systematically upgrading its roadbed, track, and bridges. The usual reason for a trailing truck is to allow a wide firebox; D&H locomotives already had that, in the form of a Wooten firebox above the rear pair of drivers.

D&H modernized its locomotives with superheaters, piston valves, Walschaerts valve gear, and single cabs. The modernization program embraced all classes, and it ran from 1923 to the mid-1930s. The road experimented with tender boosters, poppet valves, feedwater heaters, roller bearings, and outside-bearing engine trucks. The rebuilding program also changed the appearance of locomotives with small cabs, concealed piping, capped stacks, and recessed headlights.

D&H president Loree's search for efficiency culminated in four experimental locomotives built between 1924 and 1933 with high-pressure boilers (350, 400, and 500 pounds) and water-tube fireboxes — three cross-compound 2-8-0s and a triple-expansion, four-cylinder 4-8-0 named for Loree himself. The experimental freight locomotives were complex, and the high steam temperatures required special valve lubricants. Moreover, they were after their time, drag-freight locomotives in an era when railroads were speeding up their freight trains — and Delaware & Hudson was becoming a fast-freight bridge railroad. More significant than the high-pressure quartet was the installation of the world's first fusion-welded boiler on 2-8-0 No. 1219 in 1937.

Between 1910 and 1912 D&H received 13 0-8-8-0s for pusher service from American Locomotive Company. In 1917 it purchased two 2-6-6-0s from the Pittsburgh & West Virginia, converted them to 0-6-6-0s, and put them to work in the hump yard at Oneonta.

Passenger locomotives

Delaware & Hudson was not a major passenger carrier. In 1914 ten Pacifics arrived from Alco to supplant Americans and Ten-Wheelers

Challenger 1531 differs only in details of stack, headlight, and pilot from 4-6-6-4s built for Clinchfield. Photo by William S. Young.

LEONOR FRESNEL LOREE (1858-1940) graduated from Rutgers University in 1877 and entered the Pennsylvania Railroad's engineering department. Between 1881 and 1883 he was engaged in a preliminary survey of the Mexican National Railway (Laredo-Mexico City). He returned to the Pennsylvania and rose to the position of general manager and fourth vice-president, Lines West of Pittsburgh, in 1901.

That same year he became president of the Baltimore & Ohio, which was controlled by the Pennsylvania at that time. In 1904 he introduced the Mallet to America. About that same time he served briefly as head of the Rock Island and the Frisco, which were both part of the Yoakum empire, and in 1906 he was made chairman of the executive committee of the Kansas City Southern, a position he held until 1936. In 1907 Loree became president of the Delaware & Hudson. His emphasis on efficiency profoundly influenced D&H's steam locomotive development.

Loree devised the lap passing siding, organized the first railroad police force, and invented the upper-quadrant semaphore signal. In response to merger proposals in 1925, Loree proposed a fifth eastern trunk line and purchased sizable interests in the Lehigh Valley and the Wabash for the D&H; in 1928 those interests were sold to the Pennsylvania Railroad.

Loree retired from the D&H in 1938 because of failing health and died in 1940.

---

on mainline passenger trains between Albany and Montreal. Three more Pacifics came from Colonie Shops between 1929 and 1930 — experimental locomotives, one with piston valves and two with poppet valves. The only further development of passenger motive power was in the form of dual-service 4-8-4s, which worked primarily on the New York-Montreal trains, the daytime *Laurentian* and the overnight *Montreal Limited.*

Modern power

As anthracite traffic declined, D&H discovered that its strong point was bridge traffic from its connections at Binghamton and Wilkes-Barre to Canadian railroads at the border and to Boston & Maine at Mechanicville, N. Y. Fast freight required more than 2-8-0s. Between 1940 and 1946 Alco built 40 4-6-6-4s for D&H; they were supplemented in 1943 by 15 dual-service 4-8-4s. The Northerns produced less tractive effort than the E-5a and E-6a Consolidations but could move faster.

The Challengers and the Northerns had short lives. They were all scrapped in 1952 and 1953. The last run of a steam locomotive was on the night of July 21, 1953, when 4-8-4 No. 300, the standby engine at Rouses Point, ran to Albany on train 8, then moved to Colonie the next day for scrapping. D&H's dieselization in a way echoed the standardization of the 2-8-0s in that it was accomplished with two models: 1000 h.p. switchers and 1500 and 1600 h.p. road-switchers, all from Alco.

Recommended reading:
Delaware & Hudson, by Jim Shaughnessy, published in 1967 by Howell-North Books, 1050 Parker Street, Berkeley, CA 94710.
"Loree's Locomotives," by David P. Morgan, in *Trains Magazine*, July 1952, page 20.
"Consolidations, Incorporated," by D. W. McLaughlin, in *Trains Magazine*, April 1967, page 38; May 1967, page 20; and June 1967, page 38.
Published rosters: *Railroad Magazine*: November 1936, page 125; April 1947, page 116; April 1959, page 58; June 1963, page 17.

D&H STEAM LOCOMOTIVES ACQUIRED AFTER 1900

Type	Class	Numbers	Qty	Builder	Built	Retired	Notes
0-6-0	B-4	23-56	34	D&H, Dickson	1902-1907	1929-1951	
0-8-0	B-5	81-87	7	D&H	1921-1925	1945-1951	
							Rebuilt from E-4 class 2-8-0s
0-8-0	B-6	91-100	10	D&H	1924-1930	1946-1953	
							Rebuilt from E-3a class 2-8-0s
0-8-0	B-7	151-164	14	D&H	1926-1930	1951-1953	
							Rebuilt from E-5 class 2-8-0s

Type	Class	Numbers	Qty	Builder	Built	Retired	Notes
0-6-6-0	H-1	1500, 1501	2	Schenectady	1910	1935	
							Ex-P&WV 2-6-6-0s 20, 21
0-8-8-0	H	1600-1612	13	Schenectady	1910-1912	1943-1952	
2-8-0	E-2a	738-764	27	Dickson, D&H, Schen			
					1900-1901	1930-1950	
2-8-0	E-2b	765-785	21	Dick, Schen	1901-1902	1930-1950	
2-8-0	E-3	786-803	18	Schenectady	1902		
						Rrebuilt, renumbered, and reclassified	
2-8-0	E-3	804-889	86	Schen, Dick	1903-1906		
						Rebuilt, renumbered, and reclassified	
2-8-0	E-4	1000-1006	7	Schenectady	1899, 1901		
					Rebuilt 1921-1925 to B-5 class 0-8-0 Nos. 81-87		
2-8-0	E-5	1007-1096	90	Schenectady	1906-1914	1942-1953	
2-8-0	E-5a	1111-1122	12	D&H/Schen	1926-1930	1952-1953	
2-8-0	E-6a	1200-1220	21	Schenectady	1916, 1918	1951-1953	

Type	Class	Numbers	Qty	Builder	Built	Retired	Notes
2-8-0	E-7	1400-1402	3	Schenectady	1924-1930	1942	
				Named *Horatio Allen*, *John B. Jervis*, and *James Archbald*			
4-6-0	D-3	500-508	19	Schen, D&H	1903-1905	1939-1952	
4-6-0	D-3	557-561	5	Schen, MLW	1907	1949-1952	
4-6-0	D-3a	521-524	4	Schenectady	1904	1940, 1951	
4-6-0	D-3b	534-559	26	Montreal, D&H, Schenectady			
					1905-1907	1935-1952	
4-6-0	D-3b	590-594,599	6	Schenectady	1911	1942-1946	
						Convertible to oil or soft coal	
4-6-2	P	600-609	10	Schenectady	1914		
4-6-2	P-1	651-653	3	D&H	1929-1931	1951, 1953	
4-8-0	E-7	1403	1	Schenectady	1933	1942	Named *L. F. Loree*
4-8-4	K	300-314	15	Schenectady	1943	1952-1953	
4-6-6-4	J	1500-1539	40	Schenectady	1940-1946	1952-1953	

DELAWARE, LACKAWANNA & WESTERN RAILROAD

The Lackawanna of the first half of the 20th century was a prosperous road and looked it. Its main line extended from Hoboken, New Jersey, northwest through Scranton, Pennsylvania, and Binghamton and Elmira, New York, to Buffalo. Long branches reached north from Binghamton to Utica and to Syracuse and Oswego and southwest from Scranton along the Susquehanna River to Northumberland, Pa. The DL&W was an anthracite carrier and it developed its general merchandise traffic. It operated an extensive suburban passenger service; it had the shortest route from New York to Buffalo, and its long-distance trains were well patronized and carried through cars for points west. In the early years of the 20th century with an eye to speeding up its trains the road undertook several line relocation projects characterized by heavy earthworks and tall concrete viaducts.

Lackawanna's route west crossed the ridges of the Appalachians between the Hudson and Delaware rivers; threaded the Delaware Water Gap; climbed over the Pocono Mountains and descended to the Lackawanna Valley at Scranton, Pa.; climbed over more mountains to the Susquehanna River at Binghamton, N. Y.; followed the Susquehanna, Chemung, and Cohocton rivers for a way; and after a few more grades reached the level country east of Buffalo.

In 1910 DL&W adopted a locomotive classification system consisting of a letter for the type and a number for each successive order for engines. It soon loaded onto the classification system designators for such things as mechanical stokers, power reverses, and brick arches in the firebox. The system became unwieldy and was dropped in 1938. A quirk of the road's numbering system was that even-hundred numbers (200, 300, 1600, etc.) weren't used.

A notable omission from the classification system and the roster was the Atlantic type. The wide firebox that the 4-4-2 wheel arrangement made possible was already present in the form of the Wootten firebox over the 69" drivers of Lackawanna's 4-4-0s and 4-6-0s. By the time the Lackawanna turned to locomotives with trailing trucks, its passenger trains needed six driving axles. Moreover, the Lackawanna was a mountain railroad and the Atlantic wasn't a mountain engine.

Another omission was the articulated. Erie and Delaware & Hudson both used Mallets on the grades out of Scranton. Lackawanna didn't — it was a fast railroad, and Scranton was on the main line (it was on secondary lines of Erie and D&H). Lackawanna seemed to prefer to keep its locomotives as simple as possible, avoiding such fuel-saving gadgetry as compounding and feedwater heaters. If the road had indulged in articulateds — this is pure conjecture — they would have been 1938 Alco 4-6-6-4s numbered 2301-2310.

In 1900 Lackawanna burned anthracite and was one of the principal users of Camelbacks. The hard, clean-burning coal was the heart of an advertising campaign that began in 1901 featuring an auburn-haired maiden named Phoebe Snow, whose "frock stayed white from morn till night upon the Road of Anthracite." (The New York Central, which had a longer route to Buffalo but ran faster, burned sooty, cindery soft coal.) By the Teens, mechanical stokers for industrial use had been developed; they required small-size coal. Anthracite in small sizes became more expensive than soft coal. From the Mikados on, Lackawanna's freight locomotives were designed to burn soft coal. The passenger Pacifics continued to be built with wide fireboxes, though after World War I they burned a mixture of anthracite and bituminous and later straight bituminous (and the advertising department didn't talk about Phoebe's white dress anymore).

The Lackawanna dieselized quickly. The last steam locomotive in service was 0-8-0 No. 232 at Scranton on July 13, 1953.

Freight locomotives

In 1899 the DL&W took delivery of 15 Camelback 4-8-0s from Brooks, followed by five from Dickson in 1900. They were similar to 4-8-0s Brooks had built for the Central Railroad of New Jersey. They were too powerful for their weight (200,000 pounds) and were quite slippery. For 33 more freight locomotives that year, also built by Brooks and Dickson, the road switched to the 2-8-0, which carried slightly more of its weight on the drivers. Over the years these two groups of locomotives, 801-820 and 821-853, were modified by reducing the boiler pressure and the cylinder diameter, and they spent most of their lives in

Mikado 1211, built by Alco's Schenectady Works in 1912, is representative of Lackawanna's first 2-8-2s. The rod running from the cab to the reverse shaft lever was later replaced by a power reverse. The year 1912 is relatively late for inside-journal trailing trucks; outside ashpan hoppers were popular for a period on the anthracite roads. Alco Photo.

The road's late 2-8-2s, exemplified by No. 2131, were among the largest Mikados built. Lackawanna preferred paired single air pumps to cross-compound pumps. Photo by W. R. Osborne.

Lackawanna used three-cylinder 4-8-2s for both passenger and freight service. The freight engines, like No. 2230, shown at Wharton in 1941, were more successful and remained three-cylinder engines until they were scrapped after World War II. You can see the levers for the valve gear on the pilot deck. Photo by W. R. Hicks.

secondary service. Except for two which lasted a few years longer, all the 4-8-0s were scrapped in 1923.

In 1901 Lackawanna asked Schenectady Locomotive Works for a road freight engine. The result was a 57"-drivered 2-8-0 weighing 186,000 pounds (Camelback) or 178,000 pounds (single cab). The road ordered 30 Camelbacks, 855-884, and 30 single-cab locomotives, 740-769. It was pleased with their performance and ordered 30 more, 20 Camelbacks, 885-899 and 301-305, and 10 conventional, 770-779. By 1910 Lackawanna had 91 Camelback 2-8-0s and 100 conventional 2-8-0s, all built to the same specifications (except for firebox and cab): 57" drivers, 21" × 26" cylinders, and total weight of 186,00 to 190,000 pounds.

In 1911 the road designed a larger 2-8-0 for moving heavy freight trains up Dansville Hill between Groveland and Wayland, N. Y. Alco's Schenectady Works built 15 that year, numbers 385-399. They had the same 57" drivers and 200 pound boiler pressure of the earlier 2-8-0s, but their 26" × 30" cylinders and 239,000 pounds gave them about 50 percent more tractive effort.

The 2-8-0s were intended for heavy, slow freight trains, and the road

also needed something faster. In 1903 Schenectady delivered 25 2-6-0s with 63" drivers, 18 Camelbacks (numbered 570-587) and 7 single-cab engines (550-556). Schenectady, Baldwin, and Rogers continued to deliver Moguls, a total of 20 Camelbacks and 46 single-cab engines, until 1911. Ten engines, 501-510, built by Rogers in 1906 and Schenectady in 1908, had 57" drivers and their tractive effort equalled the 2-8-0s built at the same time.

In 1912 Lackawanna opted for its first locomotives with trailing trucks. Alco's Schenectady Works built 15 2-8-2s, 1201-1215, in 1912. They were faster than the 2-8-0s because of their 63"drivers, and their larger, deeper firebox gave them far more steaming capacity. They had inside-bearing trailing trucks and outside ashpan hoppers. Engineers disliked their screw reverse — controlled by a wheel that had to be spun instead the usual lever — and firemen cursed their large, hand-fired fireboxes. Later application of power reverses and mechanical stokers took care of both problems. Mikados 1216-1227, just like the first group,

Some of the Poconos in the 1601-1620 group had Worthington feedwater heaters installed in their smokeboxes, requiring the smokebox to be lengthened. Because the smokebox door was convex, a headlight mounted in the center of the smokebox door would protrude ahead of the coupler, so the headlight was moved to the top of the smokebox front. Number 1608, shown at Port Morris, N. J., exhibits both the raised headlight and the odd enlarged sand dome that was wider at the top than the bottom. Photo by Gordon R. Roth.

were delivered by Schenectady in 1913. Later groups of 2-8-2s, 1228-1237 in 1916, 1238-1252 in 1918, and 1253-1262 in 1920, followed the same design but were slightly heavier and had outside-frame trailing trucks. They were 40,000 to 45,000 pounds lighter than the USRA light Mikado, but their 28" × 30" cylinders gave them about 6,000 to 9,000 pounds more tractive effort.

In the early 1920s Lackawanna purchased 50 heavy Mikados numbered 2101-2150. They were about as much locomotive as could be put on a 2-8-2 running gear with 63" drivers. They had 28" × 32" cylinders, weighed 356,500 pounds, and exerted a tractive force of 67,700 pounds (79,200 pounds with the booster working). They were considerably larger and more powerful than the USRA heavy Mikado — about the same size as a Chesapeake & Ohio K-3 and more powerful, thanks to the booster. When Lackawanna began to dieselize, seven of them were sold to Chicago & Illinois Midland, Alton & Southern, and Montour.

The Mikados DL&W purchased in 1912 were good for long, heavy freight trains, but the line relocations then in progress meant trains could move faster. Lackawanna had just received its first 4-6-2s for passenger service and thought a medium-drivered Pacific could replace the 2-6-0s that were hauling fast merchandise trains. In 1913 Schenectady built seven 4-6-2s numbered 1151-1157 with 69" drivers and a tractive effort of 43,116 pounds, 50 percent more than the Moguls. Lima built 14 more the next year, 1158-1171. Subsequent batches of freight 4-6-2s had 70" drivers: 1172-1883 from Schenectady in 1922 and 1184-1193 from Brooks in 1924. By the time the last freight Pacifics were delivered, the 2100-series Mikados had been delivered and were prov-

Pacific 1133 brakes to a halt at Luzerne, Pa., across the Susquehanna River from Wilkes-Barre, in the late 1940s. The wide firebox of the 4-6-2, the pagoda roof and arched windows of the station, and the Phoebe Snow advertising on the box car combine in a scene that is quintessential Lackawanna. Photo by S. Botsko.

ing almost as fast as the 4-6-2s; delivery of 4-8-4s with 70" drivers in 1929 eliminated any need for freight Pacifics.

In the 1920s Alco pushed the idea of three-cylinder locomotives for heavy freight service. Dividing the power of the locomotive among

American 938 speeds west across the Jersey Meadows with a single coach in tow in November 1938 — white flags on the smokebox indicate the train is an extra, not a regularly scheduled run. The 4-4-0 is one of nine Camelbacks that were rebuilt with single cabs, concealed piping, and a shroud over the turret and pop valves. Photo by J. P. Ahrens.

three cylinders instead of two meant that rods could be lighter, and six power impulses instead of four per revolution of the drivers reduced the amount of surge transmitted to the train. The center main rod, located between the frames, was difficult to lubricate; this drawback was less crucial in slow freight service than in fast passenger service. In 1926 and 1927 Lackawanna purchased 35 three-cylinder 4-8-2s for heavy coal train and pusher service. The four-wheel lead truck was not necessary for speed; instead it carried the weight of the heavy cylinders and the Gresley conjugating valve gear, which was mounted in front of the cylinders and took its motion from extensions of the valve rods of the two outside cylinders. The 4-8-2s had 63" drivers like the 2100-series 2-8-2s; the outside cylinders, which drove the third drivers, were 25" × 32", and the inside cylinder, which drove a crank on the second axle, was 25" × 28". The engines weighed 394,000 pounds and exerted a tractive force of 77,600 pounds.

In 1927 Lackawanna took delivery of the second group of 4-8-4s built in the U. S., 77" drivered machines for passenger service. They were designated the Pocono type. They were successful enough that the road ordered 20 copies with 70" drivers for freight service, Nos. 1601-1620, delivered in 1929. Ten more, 1621-1630, also intended for freight service, arrived from Schenectady in 1932, and a final 20 dual-service locomotives with 74" drivers, 1631-1650, were delivered in 1934, despite the decline in traffic caused by the Depression. The last 20 had roller bearings on all axles and were among the most powerful 4-8-4s built.

Passenger locomotives

Between 1901 and 1911 DL&W purchased 65 Camelback 4-4-0s with 69" drivers for passenger service. The first group, 973-981, continued the existing number series; 18 more, built by Schenectady in 1903 and 1904, filled out the numbers to 999. Successive batches were numbered 958-972, 944-955, 939-943, and 933-938; older 4-4-0s with those numbers were renumbered to make room for the new locomotives in a single block. Baldwin-built 958-972 are among the few classes of Lackawanna locomotives from a builder other than American Locomotive Company or one of its predecessors. Engines 953-955, built in 1905, had experimental superheaters; 954 and 955 had piston valves. All the rest were built with slide valves but were superheated and equipped with piston valves between 1916 and 1921.

The Americans were built for mainline service, but increasing traffic meant longer trains and larger locomotives. The 4-4-0s were moved to suburban trains. In 1911, the year the last 4-4-0s were built, Lackawanna received its first steel passenger cars. By 1923 most of the road's passenger trains consisted of steel cars with electric lighting. The cars were about 25 percent heavier than wood cars of the same capacity, and the axle generators for the lights created additional drag. Between 1923 and 1925 the road rebuilt 10 4-4-0s with new cylinders and Baker valve gear, increasing their tractive effort, but the decision that year to electrify the suburban service meant that most of the 4-4-0s would be out of work, and as other 4-4-0s came due for repair, they were scrapped. The rebuilt Americans remained in service. Nine of the

The final group of Poconos, 1631-1650, built by Alco in 1934, were dual-service locomotives with 74" drivers. Their tractive effort of 76,000 pounds was exceeded by only one other 4-8-4, Norfolk & Western's class J. They had air horns (ahead of the sand dome) instead of whistles. Alco photo.

ten were rebuilt again in 1937 with single cabs, and one, No. 988, was streamstyled with wing-shaped running board skirts.

Before the road bought its 65 4-4-0s it experimented with the 4-6-0 for passenger service. In 1900 Brooks delivered seven heavy Camelback Ten-Wheelers similar to those of the Central Railroad of New Jersey. They had 69" drivers, inside piston valves, and Stephenson valve gear. They were slow engines. Four were rebuilt early with slide valves; in 1919 and 1920 they were superheated and given new cylinders and Walschaerts valve gear. They were the only 4-6-0s scrapped when the suburban service was electrified.

Lackawanna tried the 4-6-0 again in 1905 with five of the type from Schenectady (1008-1012) and four more from Rogers the next year (1013-1016). They were heavier and more powerful than their Brooks predecessors, 1001-1007. They were followed by 20 locomotives, 1017-1036, built by Rogers and Schenectady between 1907 and 1910. They too had 69" drivers but were built with Walschaerts valve gear and piston valves. Ten-Wheelers 1050-1052, built by Rogers in 1907, were similar but had 73" drivers. Nine Ten-Wheelers were rebuilt with single cabs in 1937 and 1938, and No. 1011 was streamstyled.

Between 1912 and 1914 Lackawanna received 14 Pacifics, 1101-1114, with wide fireboxes, single cabs, and 73" drivers, and weighing between 284,000 and 290,000 pounds. Somewhat heavier than the USRA light

Pacific of 1918, they exerted the same tractive effort. All had 25" × 28" cylinders except No. 1110, which was built with 25" × 26" cylinders to see if shorter piston travel resulted in a faster locomotive. Apparently not — the 1914 Pacifics were built with 25" × 28" cylinders.

Five heavier Pacifics — 305,500 pounds — with regular fireboxes for bituminous coal came from Schenectady in 1915 and were placed in service over the Poconos. Number 1131 was built with an experimental watertube firebox, No. 1132 had Baker valve gear applied briefly, and No. 1135 was used as a test lab for feedwater heaters. Schenectady then delivered several groups of Pacifics with 79" drivers: 1126-1130 in 1917, 1120-1125 in 1920, 1115-1119 in 1922, and 1136-1140 in 1923.

In 1936 and 1937 four Pacifics were streamstyled with stainless-steel wing-shaped running-board skirts (they predated the 4-4-0 and 4-6-0 mentioned above), and one of the four, No. 1123, was further decorated with bright green and red paint on the skirts and tender sides.

In 1924 Brooks built five 4-8-2s with 69" drivers to eliminate doubleheading east of Scranton. Numbers 1401-1405 were not particularly fast and remained on premier trains only a year, until the next new power arrived. During World War II, when Lackawanna had a surplus of locomotives, they were sold to Atlantic Coast Line.

Five more 4-8-2s, 1450-1454, arrived from Brooks in 1925. They had 73" drivers and three 25" × 28" cylinders. Two were built with Baker

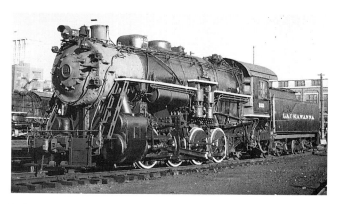

During the Depression Lackawanna kept its shop forces employed converting Pacifics and Mikados into 60 husky 0-8-0s.

valve gear and three with Walschaerts; all five used the Gresley system of levers to control the valve of the center cylinder. The center valve and main rod bearings tended to overheat at high speeds, partly due to the difficulty of reaching them for lubrication. In 1930 and 1931 Lackawanna rebuilt them with new drivers and two 28" × 32" cylinders.

Two years later, in 1927, the road took delivery of five 4-8-4s from Brooks, the second batch of 4-8-4s built in the U. S. They had 77" drivers and, unlike the Northern Pacific 4-8-4s that preceded them, had conventional frames under the firebox.

The last steam passenger locomotives the Lackawanna purchased were five Hudsons with 80" drivers. They were intended to run between Scranton and Buffalo without change. They were fast, powerful engines, designed to pull 16 to 18 cars at 80 mph — but the speed limit on the route was only 70 mph and the trains were rarely more than eight to ten cars. They were replaced by diesels shortly after World War II and relegated to suburban service.

Switchers

Between 1901 and 1911 Lackawanna purchased 125 0-6-0s of the same design, 57 Camelbacks and 68 single-cab engines. They had 51" drivers, slide valves, and main rods connected to the second drivers, and they worked at only 170 pounds pressure.

DL&W turned to 0-8-0s early. In 1906 Dickson delivered five Camelbacks, 151-155, for transfer service between Hoboken and Secaucus. In 1909 the road purchased four single-cab 0-8-0s: 169 and 168 (in that order), both for use at Buffalo, and 184 and 185 for the hump yards at Secaucus and Hampton. Twenty-eight more 0-8-0s similar to 168 and 169 were delivered by Lima and Lackawanna's Scranton shops between 1912 and 1916. They were numbered 156-169 and 170-185 (the previous 184 and 185 became 198 and 199).

In 1928 the road hadn't acquired a new switcher in 12 years, and many of those it had, the 0-6-0s, weren't able to move long strings of loaded coal hoppers, let alone the 70-ton cars that were beginning to appear. Locomotive builders submitted their bids and the road considered them, then considered instead its surplus light Mikados and freight Pacifics. Between 1929 and 1935 the road's Scranton shops used the boilers of the Mikes and Pacifics plus new running gear to build 60 modern, powerful 0-8-0s. They had 58" drivers and 27" × 30" cylinders, weighed 258,000 to 265,500 pounds, and exerted tractive force of 67,300 pounds (the USRA 0-8-0 weighed 214,000 pounds and had a tractive effort of 51,000 pounds).

Historical and technical societies:

Anthracite Railroads Historical Society, P. O. Box 519, Lansdale, PA 19446-0519

Erie Lackawanna Historical Society, 116 Ketcham Road, Hackettstown, NJ 07840

Recommended reading: *The Delaware Lackawanna & Western Railroad in the Twentieth Century, Volume 2*, by Thomas Townsend Taber and Thomas Townsend Taber III, published in 1981 by Thomas Townsend Taber III, 504 South Main Street, Muncy, PA 17756 (ISBN 0-9603398-3-3

Published rosters:

Railroad Magazine: August 1933, page 46; April 1948, page 122
Railway & Locomotive Historical Society Bulletin, No. 72 (entire issue)

DL&W STEAM LOCOMOTIVES BUILT SINCE 1900

Type	Numbers	Qty	Builder	Built	Retired	Notes
0-4-0T	4	1	Rogers	1913		
0-4-0T	7	1	Baldwin	1922	1949	
0-6-0T	8	1	Baldwin	1904	1926	Ex-Brooklyn Dock& Term.
0-6-0	78-84	7	Schenectady	1911	1933-1940	
0-6-0	85-106	21	Cooke	1903, 1905	1926-1932t	
0-6-0	107-112	6	Dickson	1906	1927-1935	
0-6-0	113-146	34	Schenectady	1908	1927-1953	
0-6-0	13-18	6	Dickson	1901	1930-1936	Camelback
0-6-0	19-26	8	Baldwin	1901	1926-1936	Camelback
0-6-0	27-31	5	Schenectady	1908	1932-1941	Camelback
0-6-0	32-43	10	Dickson	1906-1907	1929-1937	Camelback
0-6-0	44-69	6	Cooke	1902, 1906	1926-1937	Camelback
0-8-0	156-161	6	Scranton	1913	1940-1946	
0-8-0	162-167	6	Lima	1912	1937-1949	
0-8-0	168, 169	2	Schenectady	1909, 1910	1939	
0-8-0	170-185	16	DL&W	1914, 1916	1946-1953	
0-8-0	184, 185	2	Schenectady	1910	1937	To 198, 199 in 1916
0-8-0	201-260	60	DL&W	1929-1935	1948-1955	Rebuilt from 4-6-2s and 2-8-2s
0-8-0	151-155	5	Dickson	1906	1937	Camelback
2-6-0	501-506	6	Rogers	1906	1930-1937	
2-6-0	507-510	4	Schenectady	1908	1931-1937	
2-6-0	534-556	23	Schenectady	1903-1911	1929-1947	
2-6-0	557-562	6	Baldwin	1904	1926-1935	
2-6-0	563, 564	2	Rogers	1906	1930, 1942	
2-6-0	565-569	5	Schenectady	1908	1934-1947	
2-6-0	570-587	18	Schenectady	1903	1926-1934	Camelback
2-6-0	588, 589	2	Rogers	1906	1927, 1929	Camelback
2-8-0	350-373	24	Schenectady	1910	1940-1953	
2-8-0	385-399	15	Schenectady	1911	1937, 1940	
2-8-0	724-739	16	Schenectady	1909	1937-1953	
2-8-0	740-779	40	Schen., Dickson	1901-1902	1926-1935	
2-8-0	780-783	4	Rogers	1906	1932, 1936	
2-8-0	784-799	16	Schenectady	1908-1909	1932-1953	
2-8-0	301-305	5	Schenectady	1902	1929-1934	Camelback
2-8-0	306-314	9	Baldwin	1904	1927-1935	Camelback
2-8-0	315-322	8	Schenectady	1905	1927-1935	Camelback
2-8-0	323-346	24	Rogers	1906-1908	1926-1936	Camelback
2-8-0	821-853	33	Dickson, Brks	1900	1923	Camelback
2-8-0	855-899	45	Dickson, Schen	1901, 1902	1923-1935	Camelback
2-8-2	1201-1227	27	Schenectady	1912-1913	1936-1948	
2-8-2	1201-1222 rebuilt to 0-8-0					
2-8-2	1228-1262	35	Schenectady	1916-1920	1946-1953	
2-8-2	2101-2140	40	Schenectady	1922, 1923	1946-1952	
2-8-2	2141-2150	10	Brooks	1924	1946-1950	
4-4-0	933-943	11	Schenectady	1910-1911	1931-1935	Camelback
4-4-0	944-955	12	Schenectady	1905	1929-1937	Camelback
4-4-0	958-972	15	Baldwin	1904	1929-1946	Camelback
4-4-0	973-999	27	Schenectady	1901-1903	1929-1946	Camelback
4-6-0	1001-1007	7	Brooks	1900	1931	Camelback
4-6-0	1008-1012	5	Schenectady	1905	1931-1942	Camelback
4-6-0	1013-1023	11	Rogers	1906-1907	1932-1942	Camelback
4-6-0	1024-1036	13	Schenectady	1908, 1910	1932-1942	Camelback
4-6-0	1050-1052	3	Rogers	1907	1936	Camelback
4-6-2	1101-1114	14	Schenectady	1912-1914	1940-1948	
4-6-2	1115-1130	16	Schenectady	1917-1922	1950-1953	
4-6-2	1131-1135	5	Schenectady	1915	1953	
4-6-2	1136-1140	5	Schenectady	1923	1948-1953	
4-6-2	1151-1157	7	Schenectady	1913		Rebuilt into 0-8-0s
4-6-2	1158-1171	14	Lima	1914		Rebuilt into 0-8-0s
4-6-2	1172-1183	12	Schenectady	1916, 1922		Rebuilt into 0-8-0s
4-6-2	1184-1193	10	Brooks	1924		4 sold to B&M, 6 rebuilt to 0-8-0s
4-6-4	1151-1155	5	Schenectady	1937	1951, 1952	
4-8-0	801-815	15	Brooks	1899	1923	Camelback
4-8-0	816-820	5	Dickson	1900	1923-1929	Camelback
4-8-2	1401-1405	5	Brooks	1924		Sold to ACL, 1943
4-8-2	1450-1454	5	Brooks	1925	1946	Three-cylinder
4-8-2	2201-2235	35	Schenectady	1926-1927	1946-1950	Three-cylinder
4-8-4	1501-1505	5	Brooks	1927	1949	
4-8-4	1601-1620	20	Schenectady	1929	1951	
4-8-4	1621-1630	10	Schenectady	1932	1951, 1952	
4-8-4	1631-1650	20	Schenectady	1934	1951-1953	

DENVER & RIO GRANDE WESTERN RAILROAD

The Denver & Rio Grande was intended to be a narrow gauge railroad from Denver to El Paso, Texas. Construction began in 1870. In 1878 the Rio Grande fought two battles with the Santa Fe, one for occupancy of Raton Pass on the Colorado-New Mexico border and the other for the Royal Gorge of the Arkansas River west of Pueblo, Colo. The Santa Fe got Raton Pass, and the D&RG got Royal Gorge — and found itself with new goals, the mines of southern and western Colorado and a line to Salt Lake City and Ogden, Utah.

The Utah portion of the Rio Grande of recent times was built by the Denver & Rio Grande Western Railway, an affiliate of the D&RG. The rails of the D&RGW and the D&RG were joined in the Utah desert in 1883, forming a 3-foot gauge railroad from Denver to Salt Lake City via Pueblo and Marshall Pass. D&RGW became independent of D&RG in 1886 and became the Rio Grande Western. D&RG gained control again in 1901 and merged the RGW in 1908 to form the Denver & Rio Grande Western Railroad.

In 1881 D&RG began adding a third rail for standard gauge equipment to its main lines. In 1890 the Denver-Ogden main line was converted to standard gauge. By 1906 Alamosa, Salida, and Montrose were the points of demarcation of the narrow gauge network, and thereafter no major narrow gauge lines were converted to standard gauge — they were abandoned or sold.

Rio Grande's slogans were "Scenic line of the world" and "Through the Rockies — not around them." There was no arguing with either, and the latter meant the road didn't have much level track. The main line climbed from Denver (elevation 5,198 feet) to Palmer Lake (7,237 feet) in 52 miles, then took 67 miles to descend to Pueblo (4,672 feet). At Pueblo the line turned west and climbed to Tennessee Pass (10,240 feet), descended steeply along the Eagle River, then followed the Colorado River to Grand Junction (4,583 feet). The descent to Green River, Utah (4,076 feet) was interrupted by several intermediate summits; from Green River the line climbed to Soldier Summit (7,440 feet),

dropped steeply into the Salt Lake basin, where it enjoyed about 90 miles of nearly level track to Salt Lake City (4,233 feet) and Ogden (4,293 feet). The average grade from low point to summit on most of the main line was 0.6 or 0.7 percent, but the west slope of Tennessee Pass had stretches of 3 percent and the west slope of Soldier Summit, 4 percent (reduced to 2 percent by line relocation in 1912 and 1913). The opening of the Dotsero Cutoff cut 175 miles off the Denver-Grand Junction route and replaced the climbs to Palmer Lake and Tennessee Pass with a 4,000-foot ascent from Denver to the Moffat Tunnel — 50 miles of almost continuous 2 percent grade.

The Rio Grande was part of the Gould empire, and it financed the construction of the Western Pacific. For most of the period from 1915 to 1947, when it finally reorganized free of any affiliation with WP and Missouri Pacific, the Rio Grande was in receivership or bankruptcy.

Coal was the Rio Grande's prinicipal commodity: It moved from the mines of southern Colorado to the steel mills of Pueblo and the industries of Denver, and from the mines of southeastern Utah to industries between Provo and Ogden.

The 1908 merger of the Denver & Rio Grande and the Rio Grande Western occasioned a general locomotive renumbering. There was a second renumbering in 1923, and locomotives were reclassified by wheel arrangement and tractive effort. Some locomotives were renumbered twice, some once, some not at all; and some number sequences appeared to be favorites. The series beginning with 1001 was used successively for 4-6-0s built in 1902, 4-6-2s built in 1913, and 2-8-0s built in 1902. D&RG and RGW apparently avoided even-hundred numbers until 1923, and some batches of locomotives were renumbered so that the last became first — Pacifics 1001-1005 became 801-805, and 1006 became 800. The roster in this section shows 1923 numbers and classes. In the text, locomotives are identified by their numbers as built, with subsequent numbers shown in parentheses.

By 1956 D&RGW had only a few standard gauge steam engines in

The Vanderbilt tender of Santa Fe type No. 1401 appears inadequate for what was once the largest two-cylinder locomotive in the world. Some of the 2-10-2s eventually acquired large rectangular tenders. Photo by R. H. Kindig.

The relatively low drivers (63") and main rod connected to the third drivers indicate that Rio Grande 1509 was designed primarily as a freight locomotive. Photo by Wesley Krambeck.

service, primarily switchers and helpers on the Moffat Tunnel route. The last three 2-8-8-2s, 3609, 3612, and 3619, operated until November 1956, when they were hauled to Pueblo for scrapping. The last standard gauge steam run was made by 2-8-0 1151 from Alamosa to South Fork and back on December 26, 1956.

Freight locomotives

Baldwin delivered 15 Consolidations numbered 901-915 (950-964) to the Denver & Rio Grande in 1901, 54"-drivered machines that weighed 183,790 pounds. They were followed in 1902 by 30 Vauclain compound 2-8-0s numbered 1101-1130 (1000-1029), with drivers an inch larger and weighing slightly less. They were converted to simple locomotives a few years later.

In 1906 and 1908 Schenectady delivered 48 Consolidations numbered 1131-1178. They had 57" drivers, piston valves, Stephenson valve gear, and wide fireboxes above the rear drivers. They were the last 2-8-0s built for the D&RG.

Many railroads ended their steam freight locomotive development with the 2-8-2, but Rio Grande barely acknowledged the existence of the type before moving on to something larger, purchasing 14 Mikados numbered 1200-1213 from Baldwin in 1912 for Denver-Pueblo freight service. They weighed 276,000 pounds, somewhat less than a USRA light Mikado, but cylinders an inch larger gave them greater tractive effort. Their 63" drivers gave them enough speed for passenger service, and in the late 1930s and 1940s they often pulled Moffat Tunnel route passenger trains.

Ten 2-10-2s, 1250-1259 (1400-1409), arrived from Brooks in 1916 for helper service on Tennessee Pass and Pueblo-Denver coal trains. Eventually they were assigned to coal trains in Utah. When built they were the largest two-cylinder locomotives in the world, weighing 428,500 pounds, only 20,000 pounds less than a USRA 2-6-6-2. They were built with small Vanderbilt tenders that were replaced in the late 1940s with large rectangular tenders.

The 73" drivers of Rio Grande 1803, a 4-8-4 built by Baldwin in 1937, have the eastbound *Scenic Limited* rolling at good speed through the Arkansas River valley near Buena Vista, Colo., in June 1943. Photo by Otto C. Perry.

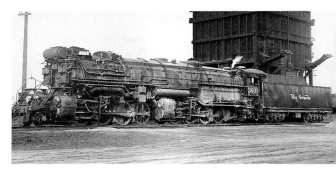

Rio Grande 3609 stands at the coal dock in Grand Junction, Colo., on May 30, 1941. Front and rear cylinders the same size indicate the 1927 Brooks product is a single-expansion articulated. Photo by R. H. Kindig.

Despite the deterioration of the road during the Teens, the USRA allocated no locomotives to the Rio Grande during World War I. The road's nonarticulated freight power consisted of 10 Santa Fes, 14 Mikados, and a lot of Consolidations. In 1922 and 1923 the Grande took delivery of 30 heavy 4-8-2s from Alco's Brooks Works. The first ten, 1501-1510, had 63" drivers and 28" × 30" cylinders and weighed 377,000 pounds, 25,000 more than a USRA heavy Mountain. They were the heaviest 4-8-2s at the time, and their drivers were the smallest since Great Northern's 62"-drivered 4-8-2s of 1914. D&RGW put them to work replacing doubleheaded 2-8-0s on freight trains and doubleheaded Ten-Wheelers on heavy passenger trains between Denver and Salida. The next year brought the M-78 class, 1511-1520, identical except for a booster on the trailing truck, and 10 more M-67s, 1521-1530, duplicates of the first group. The booster-equipped engines were assigned to Grand Junction-Salt Lake City territory, and the new M-67s to Salida-Grand Junction.

Baldwin delivered another 10 dual-service Mountains in 1926, the M-75 class, numbers 1600-1609. They had 67" drivers and three 25" ×

30" cylinders and weighed 419,310 pounds. Again the Rio Grande held honors for the world's heaviest 4-8-2, and the M-75s kept that distinction until it was taken by Illinois Central's homebuilt 4-8-2s of 1942. The M-75s were D&RGW's only three-cylinder locomotives, and they remained three-cylinder locomotives until they were scrapped. Their construction by Baldwin is something of a curiosity. They constitute five-sixths of Baldwin's three-cylinder production; and Brooks, which had built D&RGW's two-cylinder 4-8-2s, was the chief advocate of three-cylinder power.

Four more 4-8-2s came to the Rio Grande in 1945: Norfolk & Western freight Mountains 206-209, built by N&W at Roanoke in 1926. D&RGW classed them M-69 and numbered them 1550-1553. After the crush of wartime traffic abated the four were sold to the Wheeling & Lake Erie

Articulateds

Denver & Rio Grande took delivery of its first articulateds in 1910, 2-6-6-2s 1050-1057 (3300-3307). They took over helper service on Soldier Summit and the west slope of Tennessee Pass, eliminating the

Challenger 3703, built by Baldwin in 1938, displays a clean stack as it leads a long freight across the Utah desert at 60 mph in June 1941. The rising-sun striping on the sandbox behind the headlight was soon replaced by ordinary zebra stripes. Photo by R. H. Kindig.

need to use four or five engines to get even relatively short trains up the grades. In 1913 the road took delivery of 16 larger Mallets, 2-8-8-2s 1060-1075 (3400-3415) from Alco's Schenectady Works. They went to work as road engines between Denver and Grand Junction and later replaced the 2-6-6-2s in helper service over Soldier Summit and Tennessee Pass. Ten years later, in 1923, Alco's Richmond Works delivered 10 copies of the USRA 2-8-8-2 for coal trains on the lines in Utah. They were classed L-107 and numbered 3500-3509. They were followed in 1927 by 10 single-expansion 2-8-8-2s, also from Alco, engines 3600-3609, class L-125. They were the world's largest locomotives at the time they were delivered. Ten more came from Alco in 1930 numbered 3610-3619, class L-127.

During the 1930s D&RGW struggled through a receivership and converted itself into a fast freight route. To speed up freight trains, in 1937 Baldwin delivered 10 simple articulateds, 4-6-6-4s with 70" drivers: class L-105, numbers 3700-3709. They were put into service between Grand Junction and Salt Lake City; the simple 2-8-8-2s that were working there were transferred to the Moffat Tunnel route running directly west from Denver. Five more came from Baldwin in 1942, identical except for Worthington feedwater heaters instead of Elesco. They were the last new steam locomotives Rio Grande bought.

In 1943 the road needed additional locomotives to move wartime traffic. It wanted duplicates of the Baldwin 4-6-6-4s it received in 1937, but the War Production Board diverted six locomotives from a Union Pacific order that Alco was building. Although they were painted and lettered for Rio Grande, the road didn't buy the Challengers but leased them from the Defense Plant Corporation. By the time traffic had returned to normal levels the Grande had begun dieselization in earnest, so Nos. 3800-3805 were put up for sale and Clinchfield bought them.

To handle wartime traffic, D&RGW also bought two Norfolk & Western 2-6-6-2s and 15 N&W Y-2-class 2-8-8-2s in 1943 and 1948.

Passenger locomotives

Ten 63"-drivered Vauclain compound 4-6-0s were delivered by Baldwin in 1902 for passenger service. They were numbered 1001-1010 and renumbered 750-759 in 1908. Alco's Brooks Works sent 30 Ten-Wheelers west for passenger service in 1908, but half were diverted to Western Pacific, which Rio Grande was financing. The others joined the Rio Grande roster as 760-774 (later, engines 760 and 761 traded numbers with 763 and 777 when the latter were given smaller drivers). The series continued in 1909 with 775-793, which were Rio Grande's last Ten-Wheelers. The Baldwin compound 4-6-0s of 1902 were converted to

Franklin & Megantic 2 was photographed without its right running board to show details of its outside frame. Collection of Linwood Moody.

East Broad Top 17, built by Baldwin in 1918, had 48" drivers and weighed 161,000 pounds. It is essentially a scaled-down standard gauge engine; the full-size details such as running board steps, air pumps, and cab look out of scale. Photo by Theodore A. Gay.

NARROW GAUGE LOCOMOTIVES

The narrow gauge era in North America peaked just after 1880, and construction of narrow gauge locomotives began to diminish — the narrow gauge network was shrinking, and the railroads generally had enough locomotives. Until about 1890, most narrow gauge locomotives were simply scaled-down versions of standard gauge engines. The most popular types were 2-6-0, 4-4-0, and 2-8-0. The difficulty of scaling down a standard gauge locomotive was that power output was similarly scaled down, and the most severe limitation was firebox size. A firebox between the frames of a narrow gauge engine couldn't be much wider than a coal shovel; placing the firebox above the frames helped, but it was still limited by the back-to-back spacing of the wheels. Moreover, space between the frames was too restricted for easy maintenance of journals and valve gear.

About 1890 Baldwin began to dominate the shrinking domestic narrow gauge locomotive market. A good part of its business was building locomotives for export, so it had not only experience with different gauges but also facilities to handle narrow gauge engines.

In 1886 Baldwin built a 30" gauge locomotive with the frames outside the drivers; the rods were connected to cranks on the ends of the axles. That same year it built an 0-4-4T for the 2-foot gauge Franklin & Megantic Railroad in Maine, the first domestic outside-frame narrow gauge locomotive.

As the mining industry in Colorado developed, traffic on the Denver & Rio Grande's narrow gauge lines outgrew the road's 2-8-0s, the design of which dated from about 1880. By 1903 locomotive technology had progressed so that Baldwin could build 2-8-2s for D&RG with twice the pulling power of the Consolidations. The locomotives were Vauclain compounds, and they had outside frames. The trailing truck supported a wide firebox entirely behind the drivers, and the wider spacing of the frame rails made the locomotive more stable than an inside-frame model. The Rio Grande acquired 45 new narrow gauge locomotives after 1900, all outside-frame.

Most other narrow gauge locomotives built after 1900 were also 2-8-2s. Baldwin had a standard inside-frame 2-8-2 for 3'6" and meter gauge in its catalog, and it was adaptable to the American "standard" narrow gauge, 3 feet. East Broad Top's six 2-8-2s, built between 1911 and 1920, were of that design, and it was used for White Pass & Yukon locomotives as late as 1947.

The ultimate North American narrow gauge locomotives were Uintah Railway's 2-6-6-2 tank engines, built by Baldwin in 1926 and 1928. They inspired Colorado & Southern and East Tennessee & Western North Carolina to inquire about 2-6-6-2s and D&RGW to propose 2-8-8-2s, but in the late 1920s the future of the narrow gauge lines wasn't sure enough to justify such expensive locomotives.

Recommended reading: *American Narrow Gauge Railroads*, by George W. Hilton, published in 1990 by Stanford University Press, Stanford, CA (ISBN 0-8047-1731-1)

White Pass & Yukon 71, built in 1939, is a modern-looking Mikado. Baldwin photo; Broadbelt Collection.

simple engines in 1909. Like most of the Ten-Wheelers they had 67" drivers; they weighed 261,080 pounds, about 16,000 pounds lighter than a USRA light Pacific, but had a tractive force of 44,594 pounds.

Rio Grande's only Pacifics, 1001-1006 (800-805) were delivered by Baldwin in 1913 for Denver-Grand Junction service on the road's premier trains. They had relatively low drivers for the type, 67", giving them a tractive effort of 44,594 pounds.

The 4-8-2s delivered in 1922 and 1923 were dual-service engines, but their 63" drivers and main rods connected to the third drivers were both characteristic of freight locomotives. The three-cylinder 4-8-2s of 1926 were also nearer freight than passenger in their design.

Baldwin delivered 14 Northerns, Nos. 1700-1713, to Rio Grande in 1929. On most other roads they would have been considered freight engines, but their 70" drivers were the biggest on the road when they were delivered. They were assigned to passenger service and operated without change between Denver and Salt Lake City. Five more 4-8-4s, 1800-1804, came from Baldwin in 1937. They had 73" drivers, roller bearings on all axles, and vestibule cabs.

Switchers

In 1906 Rio Grande received its first switchers, 0-6-0s 831-835 (50-54), from Baldwin, and 20 2-8-0s numbered 1131-1150 from Schenectady. In 1907 two more 0-6-0s, 839 and 840 (58 and 59) came from Baldwin identical to 831-835 (the intervening numbers had been assigned to Rio Grande Western 0-6-0s). The last switchers built for the railroad, 0-6-0s 841-843 (later 60-62), arrived from Alco in 1909. They were part of an order for 15 0-6-0s, 12 of which went to Western Pacific. D&RGW bought no more switchers after 1909, preferring to demote road engines, usually 2-8-0s. In 1937 the shops at Salt Lake City removed the lead truck from 2-8-0 No. 1013 to make it into an 0-8-0. Apparently little was gained from the surgery, because it was not repeated.

Narrow gauge locomotives

Rio Grande's first narrow gauge 2-8-2s were its first narrow gauge engines with outside frames and its only narrow gauge Vauclain compounds — the road's last compounds, class K-27. Baldwin delivered

The K-28 "Sports Model" narrow gauge Mikados carried their air pumps on the smokebox fronts. They were best known for hauling the *San Juan*, the last named narrow gauge passenger train in the U. S., between Alamosa and Durango, Colorado. Photo by Kent Day Coes.

This side view of K-36 No. 482 clearly shows the details of the outside frame. The drivers are between the frames, but the counterweights and crankpins are outside. D&RGW photo.

Nos. 450-464 in 1903. Between 1907 and 1909 they were converted to two-cylinder simple engines with $17'' \times 22''$ cylinders; in a subsequent rebuilding they were equipped with superheaters, piston valves, and Walschaerts valve gear. Curiously they were delivered with slope-back tenders like those used with switchers; they soon received conventional tenders. The K-27s were less forgiving of poorly maintained track than the 2-8-0s they supplanted and soon got the nickname "Mudhens."

After the Mudhens there was a gap of 20 years before the narrow gauge lines received new locomotives (in 1916 the road acquired three heavy outside-frame 2-8-0s built by Baldwin in 1900 and 1903 for the Crystal River Railroad). In 1923 Alco constructed 10 class K-28 Mikados to replace 4-6-0s on Salida-Gunnison and Alamosa-Durango passenger trains. They had 44" drivers, 4" larger than the K-27s, and $18'' \times 22''$ cylinders; their tractive effort of 27,540 pounds was just slightly more than the 27,000 pounds of the Mudhens. They acquired the nickname "Sports Model."

Two years later, Rio Grande acquired its last new narrow gauge steam locomotives, 10 Mikados in the K-36 class, numbers 480-489. Like the K-28s they had 44" drivers, but their $20'' \times 24''$ cylinders gave them a tractive effort of 36,200 pounds; they weighed 187,100 pounds, about 30,000 pounds more than the K-28s and 50,000 more than the K-27s. They were the road's first Baldwin locomotives since 1913.

In 1928 and 1930 the road's Burnham Shops in Denver used the boilers of 10 class C-41 Consolidations in the 1000-1029 series as the basis for the K-37 Mikes, 490-499. They had the same dimensions as the K-36 Mikes but exerted just enough more tractive effort to be classed separately. They were the last narrow gauge steam locomotives the Rio Grande placed in service.

Denver & Salt Lake locomotives

When the D&RGW merged the D&SL in 1947 it added the Mikados, the Mallets, and the remaining Consolidations to its roster; Ten-Wheelers 302 and 303 were assigned D&RGW numbers, but both were scrapped in July 1948. D&SL locomotive development is examined under the entry for that railroad.

Recommended reading: *Locomotives of the Rio Grande*, published in 1980 by Colorado Railroad Museum, P. O. Box 10, Golden, CO 80401 (ISBN 0-918654-25-4)

Published rosters:

Railroad Magazine: February 1937, page 89; December 1942, page 125, January 1943, page 104, and February 1943, page 82 (narrow gauge, in three parts); April 1951, page 106

Railway & Locomotive Historical Society Bulletin, No. 77, page 6

D&RGW STEAM LOCOMOTIVES BUILT SINCE 1900

Type	Class	Numbers	Qty	Builder	Built	Retired	Notes
Standard gauge							
0-6-0	S-23	20-22	3	Schenectady	1900	1928-1936	
0-6-0	S-33	50-54	5	Baldwin	1906	Sold 1942-1943	
0-6-0	S-33	55-59	5	Baldwin	1907	3 sold 1943; 2 scrapped 1952	
0-6-0	S-33	60-62	3	Alco	1908	1944-1952	
2-6-0	G-28	592-597	6	Schenectady	1901	1926-1937	
2-8-0	C-38	900-903	4	Richmond	1900	1936	
2-8-0	C-39	915	1	Baldwin	1912	1937	
2-8-0	C-39	916-925	10	Baldwin	1905	1936-1941	
2-8-0	C-40	930-934	5	Baldwin	1901	1945-1946	
2-8-0	C-40	940-944	5	Richmond	1901	1936	
2-8-0	C-41	950-964	15	Baldwin	1900	1936-1946	
2-8-0	C-41	1000-1029	30	Baldwin	1902	1937-1952	Simpled 1909
2-8-0	C-42	970-973	4	Richmond	1900	1929-1936	
2-8-0	C-43	1031-1039	9	Schenectady	1906-1910	1937-1955	
							Ex-D&SL 111-113, 118-123
2-8-0	C-48	1131-1178	48	Schenectady	1906, 1908	1946-1956	
2-8-0	C-48	1180-1199	20	Schenectady	1906	1949-1956	
2-8-2	K-59	1200-1213	14	Baldwin	1913	1938-1955	
2-8-2	K-63	1220-1227	8	Lima	1915	1948-1956	Ex-D&SL 400-407
2-8-2	K-63	1228, 1229	2	Schenectady	1916	1952, 1956	Ex-D&SL 408, 409

Type	Class	Numbers	Qty	Builder	Built	Retired	Notes
2-10-2	F-81	1400-1409	10	Brooks	1917	1952-1955	
2-6-6-0	L-77	3360-3375	16	Schenectady	1908-1916	1947-1952	
							Ex-D&SL 200-209, 211-216
2-6-6-2	L-62	3300-3307	8	Schenectady	1909	1947-1952	
2-6-6-2	L-76	3350, 3351	2	Schenectady	1916	1952, 1950	Ex-N&W
2-8-8-2	L-96	3400-3415	16	Alco	1913	1944-1951	
2-8-8-2	L-107	3500-3509	10	Richmond	1923	1947-1951	
2-8-8-2	L-109	3550-3564	15	Baldwin, N&W	1918-1924	1947-1951	Ex-N&W
2-8-8-2	L-131	3600-3609	10	Brooks	1927	1955-1956	
2-8-8-2	L-132	3610-3619	10	Schenectady	1930	1955-1956	
4-6-6-4	L-97	3800-3805	6	Alco	1943	To Clinchfield 1947	
4-6-6-4	L-105	3700-3709	10	Baldwin	1938	1951-1956	
4-6-6-4	L-105	3710-3714	5	Baldwin	1942	1951-1956	
4-6-0	33	795	1	Schenectady	1905, 1907	1942, 1948	Ex-D&SL 302
4-6-0	T-24	530-533	4	Schenectady	1901	1927-1928	
4-6-0	T-29	760-793	34	Brooks	1908-1909	1926-1951	
							763, 777 were T-31
4-6-0	T-31	750-759	10	Baldwin	1902	1926-1939	
4-6-2	P-44	800-805	6	Baldwin	1913	1949-1953	
4-8-2	M-67	1501-1510	10	Brooks	1922	1950-1955	
4-8-2	M-78	1511-1520	10	Brooks	1923	1952-1955	
4-8-2	M-67	1521-1530	10	Brooks	1923	1949-1955	
4-8-2	M-69	1550-1553	4	N&W	1926	Sold 1948	Ex-N&W
4-8-2	M-75	1600-1609	10	Baldwin	1926	1941-1949	3-cylinder
4-8-4	M-64	1700-1713	14	Baldwin	1929	1950-1956	
4-8-4	M-68	1800-1804	5	Baldwin	1937	1952-1954	
Shay	Y-33	4, 5	2	Lima	1905, 1906	1926, 1936	Ex-Copper Belt
Narrow gauge							
2-8-0	C-21	360, 361	2	Baldwin	1900	1950, 1951	Ex-Crystal River
2-8-0	C-25	375	1	Baldwin	1903	1949	Ex-Crystal River
2-8-2	K-27	450-464	15	Baldwin	1903	1939-1953	Vauclain compound
2-8-2	K-28	470-479	10	Alco	1923	1946	
2-8-2	K-36	480-489	10	Baldwin	1925	1955 (No. 485)	
2-8-2	K-37	490-499	10	D&RGW	1928, 1930	1950 (496), 1963 (490)	
							Most K-36s and K-37s are still in service

DENVER & SALT LAKE RAILWAY

In 1902 David Moffat incorporated the Denver, Northwestern & Pacific Railway to build a line west from Denver to Salt Lake City. Construction began almost immediately, and by 1904 rails had reached the summit of Rollins Pass, 65 miles from Denver and 6,400 feet higher. The company was reorganized in 1912 as the Denver & Salt Lake Railroad, and in 1913 its line reached Craig in northwestern Colorado, as far as it would ever extend. Two things saved the road: traffic from the coalfields of northwestern Colorado and a tunnel under the Continental Divide, both of which ultimately proved useful to the Denver & Rio Grande Western, which merged the D&SL in April 1947.

D&SL climbed 6,400 feet in 65 miles — an average grade of 1.86 percent. The westbound climb began right at the South Platte River bridge in Denver, and after a few miles the grade increased to 2 percent and stayed at 2 percent all the way to Ladora, north of Tolland and northeast of what is now the east portal of the Moffat Tunnel. At Ladora the grade increased to 4 percent, and it remained 4 percent for 13 miles to the summit of Rollins Pass at Corona. Eastbound trains faced 16

miles of 4 percent grade from Vasquez, northwest of present-day Winter Park, to Corona. The route over the pass was a temporary line, necessary only until a 3-mile tunnel could be built. The 4 percent grades would have handicapped operation at sea level; more than two miles above sea level they proved the easiest aspect of the Moffat Road's operating conditions: winter weather prevailed much of the year, and practically every winter of its existence the Rollins Pass route was closed for weeks or months at a time.

The Moffat Tunnel opened in 1928, not a 3-mile tunnel at 9,900 feet but a tunnel more than 6 miles long at 9,200 feet, shortening D&SL's route by about 23 miles (and D&SL had recently emerged from another reorganization as the Denver & Salt Lake Railway). When the line over Rollins Pass was abandoned, D&SL's motive power needs were half what they had been: older locomotives were stored, and many were scrapped in the late 1930s.

When D&RGW's Dotsero Cutoff opened in 1934, the Rio Grande obtained trackage rights over more than half the length of the D&SL,

In the 39 years between 1908, when it was built, and 1947, when it was photographed, Mallet 200 acquired a lead truck, disk main drivers, built-up coal bunker sides, and a brakeman's cab on the tender. Photo by Richard H. Kindig.

Lima-built 407, one of the last locomotives to carry Lima's old rectangular builder's plate, was based on a Harriman design, probably as a matter of convenience. The extended smokebox was later emphasized by a Coffin feedwater heater. Lima photo.

from Denver to Orestod, 128 miles, and began acquiring D&SL stock. When the D&RGW merged D&SL in 1947 it added the Mikados, Mallets, and remaining Consolidations to its roster; Ten-Wheelers 302 and 303 were assigned D&RGW numbers, but were scrapped in July 1948.

Freight locomotives

D&SL's first two 2-8-0s came from Schenectady in 1904; a third joined them a year later. They had 57" drivers, 22" × 28" cylinders, piston valves, and Stephenson valve gear. The rest of the Consolidations had 55" drivers, the same size cylinders, and slide valves; Walschaerts valve gear replaced Stephenson on the last ten, built in 1910.

In 1908 the Moffat Road became the fourth railroad in the United States to purchase a Mallet: 0-6-6-0 No. 200. It looked much like Baltimore & Ohio 2400, except for slightly higher domes and stack. The high-pressure cylinders were an inch larger in diameter; the low-pressure cylinders, an inch and a half larger; the 55" drivers, an inch smaller; the total weight, 28,000 pounds greater. Two duplicates came from Schenectady just a year later, and seven more in 1910. In 1912 the road began fitting two improvements to the Mallets: lead trucks to guide them into curves and mechanical stokers to ease the work of their firemen. D&SL ordered two more 0-6-6-0s, 210 and 211, which were delivered in 1913; the final five came in 1916.

Shortly before 212-216 were delivered, the D&SL received ten Mikados, eight from Lima in 1915 and two from Alco's Schenectady Works in 1916. The Lima 2-8-2s bore a strong resemblance to the Harriman-design 2-8-2s that Lima had recently built for Southern Pacific, Illinois Central, and Central of Georgia; the two that Alco built were of the same dimensions (26" × 30" cylinders and 55" drivers) but were nondescript in appearance. The Mikes appear to have carried a cross-compound air pump on each side; it is difficult to say so conclusively without seeing photos of both sides of a locomotive taken on the same day. They

had difficulty with the curves of the line over Rollins Pass and were too powerful for their weight, so until the Moffat Tunnel opened they were assigned to the west end of the railroad. They were eventually fitted with Coffin feedwater heaters; their tenders, like those of the Mallets, were given brakemen's cabs taller than the locomotive stack and cab; and tender side boards to increase coal capacity.

Passenger locomotives

In 1904 the DNW&P bought a pair of 68"-drivered 4-4-0s from the Chesapeake Beach Railway, a 28-mile road connecting Seat Pleasant, Maryland, on the District of Columbia border, with the resort town of Chesapeake Beach (the road's backers included David Moffat and Otto Mears). One day one of the 4-4-0s was assigned to the construction train. It reached the bottom of the 4 percent grade and would go no farther. Both Americans were rebuilt with 60" drivers and thereafter were moderately useful on light trains, usually the local passenger runs between Denver and Tolland.

The first Ten-Wheeler, 300, arrived from Schenectady in 1904. It had 63" drivers and inboard piston valves and weighed 186,000 pounds. The next, 301, arrived a year later. It also had inboard piston valves but the drivers were only 57" in diameter and the locomotive was about 4,000 pounds lighter. The road's third 4-6-0, 302, built in 1907, also had

57" drivers but had slide valves and Stephenson valve gear and weighed 189,000 pounds. The final 4-6-0, 303, was delivered in 1910. It was considerably heavier, 215,000 pounds, and had 63" drivers, slide valves, and Walschaerts valve gear. Both 302 and 303 had extended smokeboxes and had single-stage air pumps on their right sides.

Switchers

D&SL's only switchers were its first two locomotives, which were used in constructing the railroad. They were scrapped in 1939 after several years in storage.

Recommended reading: *The Giant's Ladder*, by Harold A. Boner, published in 1962 by Kalmbach Publishing Co., P. O. Box 1612, 21027 Crossroads Circle, Waukesha, WI 53187

Published rosters:
Railway & Locomotive Historical Society Bulletin, No. 77, page 32
Railroad Magazine, March 1941, page 82

D&SL STEAM LOCOMOTIVES BUILT SINCE 1900

Type	Class	Numbers	Qty	Builder	Built	Retired	D&RGW number Note
0-6-0	51	20, 21	2	Schenectady	1903	1939	
2-8-0	42	100-102	3	Schenectady	1904-1905	1937	
2-8-0	44	103-123	21	Schenectady	1906-1910	1937-1955	1031-103
							(111-113, 118-123 to D&RGW
2-8-2	63	400-407	8	Lima	1915	1948-1956	1220-122
2-8-2	63	408, 409	2	Schenectady	1916	1952, 1956	1228, 122
0-6-6-0	76	200-209	10	Schenectady	1908-1910	1947-1952	3360-336
2-6-6-0	76	210-216	7	Schenectady	1913, 1916	1949-1951	3370-337
							(211-216to D&RGW
4-4-0	19	390, 391	2	Pittsburgh	1899	1937	Ex-Chesapeake Beac
4-6-0	30	300	1	Schenectady	1904	1947	
4-6-0	33	301, 302	2	Schenectady	1905, 1907	1942, 1948	795 (302
4-6-0	34	303	1	Schenectady	1910	1948	79

DETROIT, TOLEDO & IRONTON RAILROAD

The Detroit, Toledo & Ironton was formed in 1905 by the merger of the Detroit Southern and Ohio Southern railroads, both bankrupt. The new company's route made a long arc southwest from Detroit, south through Lima, Ohio, and southeast to the Ohio River at Ironton. In 1920 Henry Ford purchased the railroad, rebuilt the main line, and added a branch to Dearborn and electrified it. A visible aspect of Ford's ownership of the railroad was nickel and chromium plating of many parts of the locomotives. Ford sold the railroad in 1929 to the Pennroad Corporation, a holding company associated with the Pennsylvania Railroad. In 1951 control of the DT&I was transferred from Pennroad to the Pennsylvania Railroad and the Wabash Railway (which was controlled by the Pennsy). The road's locomotive roster underwent major upheavals when Ford purchased the road in 1920 and when Pennroad became owner in 1929. Most of the earlier locomotives were sold for further use instead of being sold for scrap.

The DT&I began dieselization with two switchers in 1941, added seven more in 1948, and completed the job in 1955 — ironically, considering the period of Ford ownership, entirely with locomotives from the Electro-Motive Division of General Motors. The first road diesels, GP7s, were delivered in 1951; more arrived in 1953. GP9s completed the dieselization of the DT&I. The last steam run was made by Mika do 805 on December 24, 1955, from Leipsic, Ohio, to Flat Rock.

Freight locomotives

The DT&I did not get off to a good start. In 1905 it took delivery of 30 57"-drivered 2-8-0s numbered 88-117 from Alco's Brooks Works. In April 1909, after the railroad defaulted on payments, they were repossessed and sold to the Wabash; Chicago, Milwaukee & Gary; New Iberia & Northern; and Duluth, South Shore & Atlantic. Four were repurchased in 1910 — 103, 106, 108, and 109 — and were renumbered second 89, 88, 90, and 91. To further complicate things, second 89 was renumbered second 92 about 1921. All four were sold between 1929 and 1936. In 1909 and 1910 Alco's Schenectady and Richmond works delivered 20 2-8-0s; DT&I was able to keep up the payments on those. They were numbered 100-119, had 57" drivers, and weighed 227,000 pounds, 54,000 more than their predecessors.

The next major group of locomotives was a batch of 15 Russian Decapods acquired in 1918, most likely because they were light, easy on the track, and cheap. Soon after Pennroad took control of the DT&I, former Pennsylvania Railroad locomotives began to replace older power, mostly the Decapods, which were sold, five to the Minneapolis, Northfield & Southern in 1933 and ten to the Seaboard Air Line in 1935. Between 1929 and 1935 DT&I received 18 class H10s 2-8-0s. A more significant change was the shift of the railroad's traffic base from coal and ore at the south end of the line to the automobile industry at the north end. That called for fast freight trains, which meant fast locomotives. DT&I asked Lima for a proposal; Lima's answer was a 2-8-4 that weighed 411,500 pounds, almost twice as much as the Pennsy H10s and, more important, was capable of sustained speed. Lima delivered four in December 1935 and two more in December 1939. With their vestibule cabs and 12-wheel tenders they were decades more modern than anything else on the property. They looked like condensed Nickel Plate Berkshires; the Berks they came closest to in their principal dimensions — 63" drivers and 411,500 pounds total weight — were those of Missouri Pacific.

The road was pleased with its 2-8-4s, but they bordered on being too much engine for the condition of the railroad, even though they were among the lightest of their type. When DT&I went back to Lima for more locomotives it got 2-8-2s, equally modern and among the largest of the Mikados at 369,500 pounds (the USRA heavy Mike weighed 320,000 pounds). The first four Mikes were delivered in 1940; four more arrived in 1941, and the final four in 1944. The last four 2-8-2s had 12-wheel tenders like those of the 2-8-4s, but the first eight Mikados had 8-wheel tenders, some of which were given to 2-8-4s, depending on the runs the locomotives were assigned to. As business increased, the road

Consolidation 200, fresh out of Fordson Shops in 1926, was a Brooks product of 1916. Photo by Clarence J. Root.

DT&I's Mikados are one of the few examples of a road reverting to a smaller locomotive after purchasing large ones. The 800s looked like the Berkshires, but most had short 8-wheel tenders. Lima photo, collection of P. E. Percy.

bought two Pennsylvania L1 2-8-2s in 1948, and leased several 2-8-2s from the Chesapeake & Ohio and three 4-8-2s from the Wabash.

Passenger locomotives

In 1915 DT&I acquired a 4-4-0 which Baldwin had built for the Midland Pennsylvania Railroad but never delivered. DT&I assigned it to the Toledo-Detroit Railroad. It was damaged in a fire in 1924 and retired in 1929. It was displayed for a while at the Henry Ford Museum, then traded in 1980 to the Illinois Railway Museum.

In 1926 DT&I bought two Atlantics from the Michigan Central, 8077 and 8085, and numbered them 44 and 45 (the second use of those numbers). Number 44 was never used on the DT&I and may have been purchased for parts; 45 was assigned to special service, then turned over to the Henry Ford Museum in 1929.

Pennroad control also had its effect on DT&I's passenger service. In 1929 three elderly PRR Atlantics took over passenger traffic from a pair of gas-electric cars. Passenger runs north of Springfield, Ohio, by then a single train each way, were discontinued in 1932. A mixed train replaced the Springfield-Ironton passenger train at the same time, and within a few years it was trimmed to a Springfield-Jackson run (which lasted until 1955). Two of the unemployed Atlantics were scrapped and the third was sold to a quarry.

Switchers

DT&I's only switchers were six 0-8-0s built to USRA design by Lima as an add-on to an order from Ford Motor Company. All six were usually assigned to Flat Rock yard.

Recommended reading: *The Detroit, Toledo & Ironton Railroad*, by Scott D. Trostel, published in 1988 by Cam-Tech Publishing, P. O. Box 341, Fletcher, OH 45326-0341 (LCC 88-071455)

DT&I STEAM LOCOMOTIVES BUILT SINCE 1900

Type	Numbers	Qty	Builder	Built	Retired	Notes
0-8-0	250-255	6	Lima	1924	1955	
2-6-0	65	1	Baldwin	1901		Ex-Detroit Southern
2-6-0	69	1	Dickson	1902		Ex-Detroit Southern
2-8-0	70-74	5	Rogers	1902		Ex-Detroit Southern
2-8-0	75-79	5	Rhode Island	1902		Ex-Detroit Southern
2-8-0	88-91 (1)	4	Brooks	1905		
2-8-0	88-91 (2)	4	Brooks	1905		
2-8-0	92-99	8	Brooks	1905		
2-8-0	94, 95 (2)	2	Brooks	1915		Ex-Toledo-Detroit
2-8-0	100-107 (2)	8	Schenectady	1909		
2-8-0	100-117 (1)	18	Brooks	1905		
2-8-0	108-117 (2)	10	Richmond	1910		
2-8-0	200, 201	2	Brooks	1916		
2-8-0	400-417	18	PRR, BLW, Pitsburgh., Lima, Brooks 1907-1916		1944-1956	Ex-Pennsylvania
2-8-2	315	1	PRR	1916		
2-8-2	317	1	Baldwin	1916		
2-8-2	800-811	12	Lima	1940-1944	1954-1956	
2-8-4	700-705	6	Lima	1935, 1939	1953-1956	
2-10-0	300-314	15	Brooks	1918		Russian Decapods
4-4-0	16	1	Baldwin	1914		Ex-Toledo-Detroit
4-4-2	44, 45	2	Alco	1901		Ex-Michigan Central
4-4-2	600-602	3	PRR, Alco	1901-1904	1938-1939	Ex-Pennsylvania
4-6-0	80-84	5	Baldwin	1903-1904		Ex-Detroit Southern
4-6-0	85-87	3	Baldwin	1905		

DULUTH, MISSABE & IRON RANGE RAILWAY

In 1901 United States Steel Corporation purchased the Duluth & Iron Range Railroad and the Duluth, Missabe & Northern Railway. Both railroads connected the iron mines of northern Minnesota with Lake Superior. The D&IR ran northeast along the shore of the lake to Two Harbors, then inland to Virginia, Tower, Babbitt, and Winton. The DM&N climbed the escarpment immediately west of Duluth to Proctor, then ran northwest to Coleraine, Hibbing, and Virginia. The two railroads remained separate for some years, then gradually moved toward consolidation. At the beginning of 1930 the DM&N leased the D&IR and integrated the operations of the two railroads. In 1937 the DM&N consolidated with the Spirit Lake Transfer Railway to form the Duluth, Missabe & Iron Range Railway, and in 1938 DM&IR acquired the assets and property of the D&IR.

When the rosters of the two roads were consolidated in 1930, Duluth, Missabe & Northern numbers remained unchanged, and Duluth & Iron Range numbers were prefixed by a 1 — 80 became 180, 305 became 1305, and so forth. Most of the Duluth & Iron Range's early locomotives were scrapped in the late 1920s and early 1930s, just before and after the creation of the DM&IR. Duluth, Missabe & Northern sold most of its early locomotives to short lines and industries as it received new ones.

DM&IR stayed with steam longer than most other roads. Its ex-Bessemer & Lake Erie 2-10-4s and ex-Union Railroad 0-10-2s were modern and powerful, and the first visits by diesel demonstrators were not impressive. The ore-shipping season lasted less than eight months a year, and the road was unwilling to spend money on motive power that would be used only part-time. Thawing frozen ore cars at the beginning and end of the shipping season required steam; dieseliza-tion would require the installation of stationary boilers and extensive piping (eventually infrared heaters were installed).

In 1959 15 EMD SW9s arrived to take over switching. EMD suggested an all-SW9 roster would meet Missabe's needs, but the road found single units insufficient for most assignments. For a year the road leased diesels from several other U. S. Steel railroads, then ordered its first six-motor SD9s in 1955. More arrived from EMD in 1957, 1958, and 1959, and a group of SD18s completed dieselization of the DM&IR in 1960.

Freight locomotives

The Duluth & Iron Range switched from 2-8-0s to 4-8-0s in 1893, and its last Twelve-Wheelers were built by Schenectady in 1900. It returned to the Consolidation type in 1905 when Baldwin delivered nine 2-8-0s with 54" drivers and 22" × 28" cylinders. Between 1906 and 1910 Baldwin built another 25 such locomotives. The earliest of the K class weighed 193,400 pounds; the last, 198,850 pounds.

In 1913 D&IR split an order for six 2-8-2s between Baldwin and Lima. Like the K-class 2-8-0s they had 54" drivers, but the cylinders were considerably larger (27" × 30") and total weight was 287,600 pounds. As traffic increased, the D&IR took note of DM&N's 2-10-2s and went shop-

The last locomotives purchased by the Duluth, Missabe & Northern were four 0-10-0s built by Baldwin in 1928. Number 93's twin cross-compound air compressors were a necessity for easing long trains of ore cars down to the Lake Superior docks. Photo from J. C. Seacrest collection.

Mallet 211 was one of five rebuilt from compounds to simple engines. Forward and rear cylinders the same size is the clue. Photo by Frank A. King.

ping for Santa Fes of its own. They would have required strengthening of track and bridges and lengthening of roundhouse stalls, so the D&IR stayed with the Mikado. Baldwin delivered the three locomotives of the N-1 class in 1916. They differed from the N class chiefly in having 58" drivers. D&IR's final 2-8-2s came from Baldwin in 1923, the three locomotives of the N-2 class, heavier than the N-1s but no more powerful.

The Duluth, Missabe & Northern chose a 56"-drivered Ten-Wheeler as its first standard road engine, acquiring 29 of them from Pittsburgh between 1893 and 1900. The road's first Consolidation was delivered by Pittsburgh in 1894 to move ore cars up the 2.2 percent grade between the ore dock and Proctor, and another was delivered in 1895. DM&N turned to the 2-8-0 for its next group of road engines. The 49 Consolidations in the C-1, C-2, and C-3 classes differed only in details. All had 56" drivers and 22" × 28" cylinders and weighed between 180,000 and 185,500 pounds. Rebuilt with superheaters and piston valves, most of the C-3 Consolidations remained on the roster until DM&IR dieselized.

DM&N's ore traffic more than tripled between 1900 and 1909, and the road discovered that the limiting factor in its operation was getting empty ore cars back up the 6 miles of 2.2 percent grade from the Duluth ore docks to Proctor. A 2-8-0 could pull 55 loaded ore cars from the mines to Proctor, and from there to the docks was chiefly a matter of

braking — but coming back up the hill the same Consolidation was good for only 28 empty ore cars. The road briefly considering electrifying that part of the line but concluded that Mallets could do the job at lower cost.

Baldwin delivered eight compound 2-8-8-2s in 1910. They were good for 55 empty ore cars up the hill at 12 mph; after mechanical stokers were applied, they could take 85 empties up the hill but at a lower speed. The Mallets were equipped with a two-section boiler, the front part of which was a feedwater heater, much like those on Santa Fe's articulateds. The devices weren't successful, so the road removed them and filled the resulting void with 6 or 7 tons of steel plates for adhesion. The Mallets were eventually fitted with superheaters, mechanical stokers, and Elesco feedwater heaters. The four additional Mallets delivered in 1916 and 1917 came from Baldwin equipped with superheaters and stokers and were shorter, since their fireboxes were over the last two pairs of drivers — the fireboxes of the earlier Mallets were almost entirely behind the drivers.

DM&N's traffic soon outstripped the capacity of its 2-8-0s, and in 1916 it took delivery of six 2-10-2s, E-class locomotives 500-505. Their 60" drivers and larger fireboxes gave them more speed, and their 28" × 32" cylinders yielded 71,200 pounds of tractive force, 80 percent more than the Consolidations. Three years later the DM&N received ten USRA light 2-10-2s, which were slightly heavier and slightly less powerful than the E class but generally of a better design. DM&N limited its ore trains to 35 mph, so the usual counterbalancing difficulties of the 2-10-2 which restricted speed were not a problem.

Between 1929 and 1937 DM&N and successor DM&IR converted five Mallets to simple articulateds for road service — as compounds they were too slow. The rebuilt locomotives were generally assigned to former Duluth & Iron Range territory.

About 1940 the road anticipated an increase in ore traffic because of

Last of the 1941 group of 2-8-8-4s was No. 227. The Elesco feedwater heater is unusual for a locomotive built in 1941; Worthington heaters were more common by then. The box on the pilot carries sand for traction. Photo by Philip R. Hastings.

the war and recognized that its newest road locomotives were 20 years old. DM&IR decided it needed a locomotive that could haul 25 percent more than the rebuilt Mallets on the Iron Range Division (the former D&IR) and used Western Pacific's simple 2-8-8-2 as the basis for its design. A larger cab required a longer and thus heavier frame and therefore a four-wheel trailing truck; another major difference was in grate area: 125 square feet, where WP's locomotives had 145 square feet — DM&IR burned high quality coal, and WP burned oil. DM&IR also specified one-piece cast engine beds and roller bearings on all axles. Eight M-3 2-8-8-4s arrived from Baldwin in 1941. DM&IR was pleased with them and ordered ten duplicates, class M-4, in 1943 to handle wartime traffic on the Missabe Division. Baldwin completed the Yellowstones late enough in the year that traffic had subsided, so some of the M-4s were delivered to the Denver & Rio Grande Western for use as helpers over Tennessee Pass. D&RGW thought as highly of them as the Missabe Road did. A curiosity of the Yellowstones is that some of each group had Worthington feedwater heaters and the rest had Elescos.

After World War II DM&IR's original Mallets began to show their age. The road was not ready to dieselize and looked around for used locomotives: 0-10-2s from the Union Railroad in Pittsburgh, 2-10-4s from the Bessemer & Lake Erie, and 2-8-2s from the Elgin, Joliet & Eastern — U. S. Steel railroads all.

Passenger locomotives

The Missabe Road and its predecessors were not major passenger carriers. Duluth & Iron Range received six 4-6-0s in 1900 to eliminate doubleheading of 4-4-0s. The Ten-Wheelers had 58" drivers — they were high-wheeled passenger machines only by comparison with a roster dominated by 51"- and 54"-driver freight engines (the 4-4-0s they replaced had 63" drivers). The advent of steel cars in 1913 required heavier power, four 69"-driver 4-6-2s.

Duluth, Missabe & Northern bought a pair of 4-6-0s with 67" drivers in 1906. They had wide fireboxes but were extremely poor steamers. Baldwin, which built the locomotives, suggested reducing the cylinder diameter from 20" to 18¾" to reduce the amount of steam used; DM&N altered one of the pair but without much success. Baldwin's next solution was a pair of 63"-drivered 4-6-0s that were successful enough that the road ordered a third in 1910. The Ten-Wheelers weren't adequate after steel passenger cars replaced wood, so DM&N ordered three Pacifics from Baldwin. They had the same 69" drivers as D&IR's Pacifics but bigger boilers and cylinders 3" greater in diameter (25" × 28"), and at 245,700 pounds were 26,000 pounds heavier. That was the extent of passenger power development on the Missabe Road until 1953, when Budd delivered an RDC-3 that could make a Duluth-Ely and a Duluth-Hibbing round trip in a day.

Switchers

Duluth & Iron Range took delivery of four 0-6-0s from Baldwin in 1906 for switching the ore dock at Two Harbors. By 1927 they had been superseded by 2-8-0s bumped from road service by larger engines. Duluth, Missabe & Northern had a wider variety of switchers. Two 0-6-0s weighing 120,000 pounds, heavy for their time, were delivered by Pittsburgh in 1900 for use in the yard at Proctor. They were the last 0-6-0s the road received, and were replaced with 0-8-0s, beginning with four Baldwins classified S-3 in 1907. Three more of the same dimensions (51" drivers, 21" × 28" cylinders, 164,000 pounds) arrived from Baldwin in 1910 and were classed S-4. Alco's Schenectady Works delivered six S-2s in 1910 with the same size drivers and cylinders but 43,500 pounds heavier. The last four 0-8-0s, class S-5, came from Baldwin in 1917. They were not much heavier than the S2s but had 24" × 28" cylinders — about the same size as the USRA 0-8-0. The S-3 and S-4 classes were sold to Oliver Iron Mining in 1927, and the S-2s were sold to American Steel and Wire in 1948.

In 1928 DM&N received four 0-10-0s from Baldwin. They were the heaviest, most powerful ten-coupled switchers at the time and DM&N's most expensive locomotives at $85,715 each. They had 57" drivers and 28" × 30" cylinders, and weighed 352,250 pounds. Until bridges were strengthened between Duluth and Proctor they were restricted to the yards at Proctor and Two Harbors; later they also worked transfer runs between Duluth and Proctor. They were built with tender boosters, which were removed in the 1930s to reduce maintenance.

In 1949 the Duluth, Missabe & Iron Range bought nine 0-10-2s from the Union Railroad in Pittsburgh, another U. S. Steel road. They were initially assigned to Proctor Yard and the hill between there and Duluth. DM&IR found them somewhat slippery and increased the weight on the drivers by adjusting the equalizing levers to the trailing truck and adding 10,000 pounds of steel plate toward the front of the engine.

Historical and technical society: Missabe Railroad Historical Society, 719 Northland Avenue, Stillwater, MN 55082

Recommended reading: *Locomotives of the Duluth Missabe & Iron Range*, by Frank A. King, published in 1984 by Pacific Fast Mail, P. O. Box 57, Edmonds, WA 98020

Published rosters:
Railroad Magazine: August 1938, page 85; December 1951, page 102; October 1956, page 58; October 1961, page 27
Trains Magazine, February 1955, page 46

DM&IR STEAM LOCOMOTIVES BUILT SINCE 1900

Type	Class	Numbers	Qty	Builder	Built	Retired	Notes
Duluth & Iron Range							
0-6-0	F	28-31	4	Baldwin	1906	1927	
2-8-0	K	90-98	9	Baldwin	1905	1956-1961	
2-8-0	K	200-224	25	Baldwin	1906-1910	1950-1959	
2-8-2	N	300-303	4	Baldwin	1913	1959-1962	
2-8-2	N	304, 305	2	Lima	1913	1961, 1959	
2-8-2	N-1	306-308	3	Baldwin	1916	1958-1959	
2-8-2	N-2	309-311	3	Baldwin	1923	1958-1959	
4-6-0	M	101-106	6	Schenectady	1900	1929-1933	
4-6-2	A	107-110	4	Baldwin	1913	1953-1955	
4-8-0	J	84-89	6	Schenectady	1900	1933	
Duluth, Missabe & Northern							
0-6-0	S-1	56, 57	2	Pittsburgh	1900	Sold 1920	
0-8-0	S-2	80-85	6	Schenectady	1910	Sold 1948	
0-8-0	S-3	58-61	4	Baldwin	1907	Sold 1927	
0-8-0	S-4	62-64	3	Baldwin	1910	Sold 1927	
0-8-0	S-5	86-89	4	Baldwin	1917	1954-1958	
0-10-0	S-6	90-93	4	Baldwin	1928	1955-1958	
2-8-0	C-1	302-312	11	Alco	1899-1903	1933-1948	
2-8-0	C-2	313-318	6	Pittsburgh	1904	Sold 1919	
2-8-0	C-3	319-350	32	Pittsburgh	1905-1907	1919-1955	
2-8-8-2	M	200-207	8	Baldwin	1910	1950-1953	
2-8-8-2	M-1	208, 209	2	Baldwin	1916	1954, 1958	
2-8-8-2	M-2	210, 211	2	Baldwin	1917	1957	
2-10-2	E	500-505	6	Baldwin	1916	1959-1962	
2-10-2	E-1	506-515	10	Brooks	1919	1959-1963	
4-6-0	F	27-33	7	Pittsburgh	1900	1923-1939	
4-6-0	F-1	100, 101	2	Baldwin	1906	Sold 1933	
4-6-0	F-2	102, 103	2	Baldwin	1907	1932, sold 1933	
4-6-0	F-3	104	1	Baldwin	1910	Sold 1933	
4-6-2	P	400-402	3	Baldwin	1913	1955-1958	
Duluth, Missabe & Iron Range							
0-10-2	S-7	601-609	9	Baldwin	1936-1937	1958-1963	Ex-Union Railroad
2-8-2	N-4	1312-1321	10	Alco	1923	1958-1961	Ex-EJ&E 746-755
2-8-2	N-5	1322-1325	4	Lima	1923	1958-1961	Ex-EJ&E 756-759
2-8-2	N-6	1326-1337	12	Baldwin	1929-1930	1958-1962	Ex-EJ&E 761...774
2-10-4	E-4-7	700-717	18	Alco, BLW	1937-1943	1961	Ex-B&LE 621...647
2-8-8-4	M-3	220-237	18	Baldwin	1941, 1943	1958-1963	

ERIE RAILROAD

The Erie entered the 20th century fresh out of bankruptcy. In 1901 Frederick Underwood became the road's president, a post he would hold for 25 years, and E. H. Harriman joined Erie's board of directors. The road undertook a number of construction projects, including freight bypasses with lower grades and double track for the main line.

Erie's main line ran northwest from Jersey City, New Jersey, to Binghamton, New York, turned west through New York's Southern Tier, then made a long arc south through Youngstown and Lima, Ohio, and Huntington, Indiana, before it reached Chicago. A network of branches covered northern New Jersey, and secondary lines reached Rochester, Buffalo, and Dunkirk, N. Y., and Cleveland and Cincinnati, Ohio. The road was built with a track gauge of 6 feet; it converted to standard gauge in 1880. The early choice of wide gauge ultimately proved expensive, but it produced one minor benefit: The standard gauge Erie was a railroad of generous clearances.

Erie's New York-Chicago route was 40 miles longer than New York Central's and 90 miles more than Pennsy's, and it seemed to make a point of avoiding big cities. It had no major grades, except for a couple of hills in western New York, the sawtooth-profile country of eastern Ohio, and the hilly country of northern New Jersey between the Hudson and Delaware rivers. As a result, the Erie developed into a fast carrier of freight, not passengers. Its New York-Chicago passenger trains never numbered more than three each way, and they took 4 to 8 hours longer than the trains of the New York Central and Pennsylvania.

Erie's last steam operation was on March 17, 1954, when K-1 Pacific 2530 (Rogers, 1906) brought a morning commuter train into Jersey City from Spring Valley, N. Y.

Freight locomotives

Erie was using the Consolidation type long before 1900, and continued to purchase 2-8-0s in quantity well into the 20th century. In 1900 it took delivery of three groups of Camelback 2-8-0s, classes H-10, H-11, and H-12, 75 engines in all. The H-10s and H-11s had 56" drivers and 21" × 28" cylinders (as did the H-9s of 1899); the H-12s had 62" drivers and the same size cylinders. Baldwin delivered 15 more Camelback Consolidations in 1901, similar to the H-13s in dimensions but with a piston stroke 2" longer.

The four 2-8-0s of the H-14 class were acquired with the Erie & Wyoming Valley; their 54" drivers and 22" × 30 cylinders gave them more pulling power than any of Erie's own Consolidations.

Erie continued to add 2-8-0s to its roster in 1902. The H-16 class, 1510-1529, came from Baldwin as Vauclain compounds. The H-17 and H-18 classes were delivered by Rogers and Cooke, respectively. They had 56" drivers and 22" × 30" cylinders, and weighed an even 200,000 pounds, about the same as the H-16s. Cooke built the five engines of class H-19, tandem compounds. The Vauclain compounds were converted to simple engines between 1904 and 1911 (the first two conversions were done by Baldwin), and the Cooke tandem compounds were simpled in 1908. All the Camelback 2-8-0s in classes H-9 through H-19 (except H-15, which consisted of five 1884 Dicksons from the Erie & Wyoming Valley) were scrapped in 1927 after being stored for several years for accounting reasons.

The 45 H-20 Consolidations of 1903 and 1904 brought changes: single cab, bituminous-burning firebox above the rear drivers, 62" drivers, 22" × 32" cylinders, slide valves, and Stephenson valve gear. They had a tractive force of 42,500 pounds, slightly less than the biggest of the preceding Camelbacks. The 260 H-21-class 2-8-0s were just like them. Many of the H-20s and H-21s were later superheated, fitted with larger cylinders, and equipped with Baker or Walschaerts valve gear.

The extensive H-22 class, Nos. 1800-1886, was neither particularly successful nor well liked. The first 37 of the group were diverted from an order built for the Harriman railroads, which had found themselves oversupplied with 2-8-0s; Erie ordered 50 more. They had 22" × 30" cylinders and 57" drivers and had only slightly more tractive effort than the H-20s and H-21s. Some were converted to 0-8-0s, but that didn't

prolong their service; all were scrapped between 1927 and 1940 without being rebuilt or superheated. The final 2-8-0 on the roster was 1540, which was built in 1906 for display at an exposition and then sent to the Rock Island, which found it too heavy. Baldwin sold it to the New York, Susquehanna & Western, which also found it too heavy and transferred it to the Erie, which at the time owned the NYS&W.

In 1907 Schenectady built three Camelback 0-8-8-0s for pusher service over Gulf Summit between Deposit, N. Y., and Susquehanna, Pa. When built, they were the largest locomotives in the world. On the job they proved mostly that it took a skilled and strong fireman to produce the power they were designed to deliver. Baldwin rebuilt them in 1921 as 2-8-8-2s with mechanical stokers and other improvements.

Erie's next try at articulation was to convert a 2-8-0 to a 2-6-8-0 by purchasing running gear for the front low-pressure engine and a boiler extension that was mostly feedwater heater — an articulated like the Santa Fe had in great numbers. Meadville Shops converted H-22 No. 1830 in 1910, and in 1916 restored it to its original form (eventually it became a C-2-class 0-8-0). The 2-8-0 boiler didn't have sufficient steaming capacity to propel the Mallet at more than 2 or 3 mph.

Erie kept looking for a good pusher engine. Baldwin delivered Triplex No. 5014 in 1914: a 2-8-8-8-2, essentially a 2-8-8-0 with another eight-drivered engine beneath the tender. All six cylinders were the same size, 36" × 32". The middle set was high-pressure, and exhausted to low-pressure cylinders fore and aft. Unlike other Mallets, it had no provision for working simple — two or three revolutions of the drivers would have exhausted the boiler. It weighed 853,050 pounds, and was said to be capable of pulling 640 cars, subject, of course, to the limitations of couplers and draft gears. It went to work as a pusher, and Erie bought two more. The biggest problem of the Triplexes was boiler capacity: The feedwater pumps couldn't deliver water to the boiler fast enough for the fire to turn it to steam. In addition, when a Triplex was in the shop (and because of size limitations, it had to be Lehigh Valley's shop at Sayre, Pa.), it was like having three Consolidations or Mikados out of service.

Erie had a long-standing custom of honoring superior engineers by painting their names on the cabs of locomotives. Triplex 5014 for some years carried the name of Matt H. Shay.

The seven articulateds turned out to be a digression in the development of Erie freight locomotives. The natural progression from the 2-8-0 was to the 2-8-2. Between 1911 and 1913 Erie purchased 155 Mikados from Baldwin (65), Schenectady (85), and Lima (5). They had 63" drivers and 28" × 32" cylinders, and weighed about 329,000 pounds — just a bit more locomotive than a USRA heavy Mike. Classed N-1 and numbered from 3000 to 3154, they were built with superheaters and were hand-fired; in 1927 they were equipped with mechanical stokers and feedwater heaters.

In 1918 the road received 15 USRA heavy 2-8-2s built by Brooks, classifying them N-2 and numbering them 3200-3214. In 1923 Erie returned to its own design for 40 N-3 class Mikes, 3155-3194, continuing the number series of the N-1s. The principal difference between the

0-8-8-0

The 0-8-8-0 was developed for pusher service. It could pull more than the couplers and freight car frames of its era could stand. The cars could withstand compression better than tension, so much of the power to get heavy trains up a grade was applied at the rear — ahead of the caboose, which was usually a light, wood-frame car. Later 0-8-8-0s were built as extra-heavy switchers for hump yard duty.

An interesting trait of the wheel arrangement was that it was used almost exclusively in the East. Its territory was bounded on the south by the Norfolk & Western, which bought five 0-8-8-0s and five 2-8-8-2s in 1910 to test each type (it chose the 2-8-8-2); on the east by Boston & Maine's yard at Mechanicville, N. Y., and on the

west by various New York Central hump yards. There was one exception. Bingham & Garfield used 0-8-8-0s to move long trains of copper ore down from mines in the mountains south of Salt Lake City. Ownership passed first to Utah Copper Co., then to Kennecott Copper, which built a new electrified line in 1948.

Total built: 85
First: Erie 2600, 1907
Last: Boston & Maine 801, 1922
Longest lived: Delaware & Hudson 1600, 1910-October 1952
Last in service: Delaware & Hudson's last 0-8-8-0s were scrapped in 1952.
Greatest number: Baltimore & Ohio, 30
Heaviest: Bingham & Garfield 106, Alco 1918, 477,000 pounds
Lightest: Pennsylvania 3397, Baldwin 1912, 409,000 pounds

Like most 0-8-8-0s, New York Central's were heavy switchers, ideal for pushing long strings of cars over humps. Alco photo, collection of C. W. Witbeck.

N-1 and N-3 was the booster-equipped cast trailing truck on the N-3.

One final 2-8-2 came from Baldwin in 1926. It was to have had uniflow cylinders, which have steam admission ports at the ends and exhaust ports in the middle. At some point during construction the uniflow design proved impractical and the locomotive was completed with conventional cylinders.

Increases in traffic during the early Teens prompted Erie to seek a

freight locomotive larger than the Mikado. It received a single experimental 2-10-2, No. 4000, class R-1, from Baldwin in 1915. Like the N-1 Mikados it had 63" drivers and 31" × 32" cylinders, and the rods and pistons were of lightweight design to ease the counterbalancing problems common to the 2-10-2 type. It was equipped with superheater, mechanical stoker, and lateral motion devices on the driver axles. Because the boiler was so wide, it had paired sand domes mounted

2-8-8-8-2 AND 2-8-8-8-4 — TRIPLEX

The Triplexes were another in a long succession of attempts by locomotive designers to put as much tractive force as possible under the control of one man — 160,000 pounds. That was more than could be used to pull a train. The couplers, draft gears, and frames of 1914 freight cars could not transmit such forces. (For purposes of comparison, Electro-Motive's four-unit FT demonstrator 103 of 1939 was rated at 228,000 pounds maximum tractive effort.)

As built in 1914, Erie's 5014 didn't have enough grate area. It was sent back to Baldwin to have its grate enlarged to 122 square feet. Engines 5015 and 5016 were built with grates that size. Erie put its three Triplexes to work as pushers, and used them until 1927, when they were retired and stored before scrapping.

Virginian's Triplex was slightly smaller: 34" × 32" cylinders where the Erie locomotives had 36" × 32"; 56" drivers instead of 63"; 108 square feet of grate area. It was slower and ran out of steam faster than the Erie engines. An unanticipated difficulty was that in one tunnel No. 700 had only 4" of clearance, which left no room at all for exhaust steam and smoke. It never made a successful trip. In 1920 Virginian sent it back to Baldwin, which transformed most of it into a 2-8-8-0 and used the running gear of the tender to make a 2-8-2. Both those locomotives lasted until 1953.

Total built: 4
First: Erie 5014, April 1914
Last: Virginian 800, December 1916
Longest lived: Erie 5015, scrapped in 1933
Greatest number: Erie, 3
Heaviest: Erie 5015 and 5016, 857,000 pounds
Lightest: Virginian 700, 844,000 pounds

Virginian 700 had smaller cylinders and drivers than the Erie Triplexes and had a four-wheel truck at the rear for better tracking in reverse, drifting downgrade after pushing a train up a hill. Baldwin photo; collection of H. L. Broadbelt.

side by side. The locomotive was immediately successful, and Erie ordered 40 more from Baldwin, Schenectady, and Lima. Production R-1s weighed 417,200 pounds, about 10,000 pounds more than No. 4000.

Between 1915 and 1917 Schenectady built 30 R-2 Santa Fes. They were shorter and somewhat lighter than the R-1s, 404,000 pounds, with large shallow fireboxes over the rear drivers and small inboard-bearing trailing trucks. They looked like a regression in design, but they were just as powerful as the R-1s and were good steamers. The R-1s and R-2s were delivered with small Vanderbilt tenders so they could fit on existing turntables. Many eventually got larger tenders.

Erie's third group of 2-10-2s were USRA heavy Santa Fes built by Brooks in 1919. Though they were lighter and less powerful than Erie's own design, they lasted longer. Most of the R-1s and about half the R-2s were scrapped before World War II; the USRA 2-10-2s were scrapped

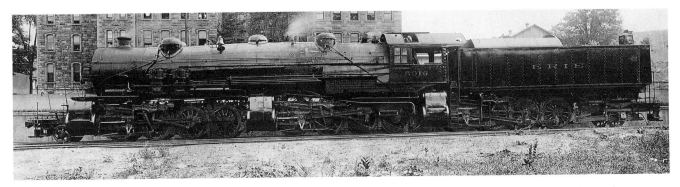

between 1949 and 1952.

Decapods constitute another side trip in Erie's progression of freight locomotives. The road had six Camelback Vauclain compound 2-10-0s that were built in 1891 and 1893 for pusher service on Susquehanna Hill. They were simpled in 1904 and 1905, demoted to yard service, and scrapped between 1924 and 1926. More significant, though, are Erie's Russian Decapods. The Erie was pleased enough with their performance while they were on lease from the USRA that it purchased 75 in 1921. They proved useful in local freight service because of their high tractive effort and low axle loading. Later Erie sold 16 of them to the New York, Susquehanna & Western and 8 to various other roads.

Erie started 1927 with a change in management. Frederick Underwood retired at the end of 1926. The Van Sweringen brothers, who had gained control of the road, appointed as president John J. Bernet, who had recently completed a thorough upgrading of the Nickel Plate. Bernet's job was to turn Erie into a fast freight road like the Nickel Plate. In short order he found that Erie was spending 50 percent more for locomotive maintenance than other roads. He weeded out the oldest locomotives — all those 2-8-0s, for instance — and divided an order for 50 2-8-4s equally between Lima and Brooks. The Brooks engines, 3300-

3324, were class S-1, and the Limas (3325-3349) S-2. The major differences between them were boiler pressure — 225 pounds for the S-1s and 250 for the S-2s — and the trailing trucks. The Brooks engines had cast trailing trucks and full-length frames, and the S-2s had Lima's own built-up trailing truck, through which drawbar forces were transmitted. Both classes differed from Lima's original design of 1924 in having 70" drivers instead of 63". Two more groups of 2-8-4s followed in quick succession: S-3s 3350-3384 from Baldwin in 1928 and S-4s 3385-3404 from Lima in 1929.

Passenger locomotives

In 1901 Baldwin delivered two groups of Ten-Wheelers, G-12s 909-918 and G-13s 919-933. Both classes were Camelbacks and had 62" drivers; the G-12s were single-expansion engines and the G-13s were Vauclain compounds. In 1908 four of the G-13s were converted to simple engines and reclassified G-16; the rest were similarly rebuilt in 1915 and 1916, though the last two rebuilt retained their G-13 classification. The G-15 class, 950-974, was built by Baldwin in 1903 and 1904 for suburban

RUSSIAN DECAPODS

During World War I the Russian government purchased a large number of lightweight 2-10-0s from American locomotive builders. They had a wide coal-burning firebox over the rear drivers, a high boiler, large steam and sand domes, and 52" drivers. They were light locomotives, weighing about 201,000 pounds in working order. Their axle loading was only about 35,000 pounds per axle and they could exert a tractive force of 51,500 pounds. The USRA "light" locomotives were designed with a maximum axle loading of 54,000 pounds; the tractive force of the Russian Decapod was the same as that of the USRA 0-8-0 and almost as much as that of the light 2-8-2.

After 857 locomotives had been shipped, the Russian revolution forced cancellation of the order in 1917, leaving 200 completed Decapods orphaned in the U. S. They were turned over to the United States Railroad Administration, which allocated them to American railroads, mostly in the East and the South. Conversion for use in the U. S. was primarily a matter of new tender and lead-truck wheels, wide tires for the drive wheels to reduce the gauge from 5 feet to 4'8½", and replacement of the European screw couplers and buffers. As modified, weights ranged from 185,000 to 210,000 pounds.

Some railroads received them enthusiastically while others rejected them — the Pennsylvania took delivery of the largest number, 56, but used them little if at all, having its own ideas about Decapods. The Erie eventually rostered 75 Russian Decapods, more than any other road; Seaboard Air Line was second with 37.

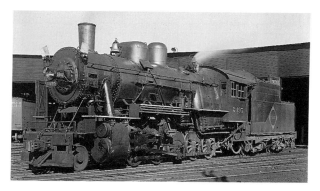

Erie 2495, photographed in 1940, illustrates the characteristics of the Russian Decapod: high-mounted boiler, low drivers, wide firebox above the drivers, and tall domes. Photo by Donald W. Furler.

Number 541, built by Baldwin in 1917, was one of the group shipped to Russia. Characteristic Russian details include the elaborate railings along the running board, dual headlights on the pilot beam, buffers and screw couplings, and the hood over the front of the tender. BLW photo, collection of H. L. Broadbelt.

trains out of Jersey City. They had single cabs, a firebox over the rear drivers that could burn either bituminous or anthracite, and 68" drivers. They were quite successful and eventually were fitted with super-heaters, piston valves, and Baker or Walschaerts valve gear.

Erie purchased three groups of Vauclain compound Atlantics between 1899 and 1903: E-1s 502-507 and 532-534, E-2s 535-544 (later renumbered 935-943 and 934), and E-3s 545-559. The E-1s and E-2s were Camelbacks; the E-3s had single cabs. All three classes had 76" drivers; the E-2s and E-3s had the same cylinders, which were larger than those of the E-1s. All three classes were converted to single-expansion engines between 1904 and 1906.

Erie received three Atlantics in 1905 that could be considered experimental, two Vauclain balanced compounds from Baldwin and one Cole balanced compound from Alco. The Baldwin engines had 72" drivers; the Alco, 78". The Baldwins were simpled in 1917 and the Alco engine in 1919; all three were given 74½" drivers.

When the road realized that its principal passenger trains needed more than an Atlantic or a Ten-Wheeler, it tested a San Pedro, Los Angeles & Salt Lake 4-6-2 built to the standard design used by several railroads in E. H. Harriman's empire. The Harriman Pacific had 77" drivers, 22" × 28" cylinders, 49.5 square feet of grate area, and weighed 225,295 pounds; Erie's K-1 Pacific, based on the design, had 74½" drivers, 22½" × 26" cylinders, 56.5 square feet of grate area, and weighed 243,550 pounds. Alco's Schenectady Works built three, 2510-2512, in 1905; 2510 and 2512 were equipped with Cole superheaters. Rogers built 41 K-1s in 1905 and 1906 and Baldwin built 15 in 1908. All had piston valves, Stephenson valve gear, and outside-journal trailing trucks; the Rogers and Baldwin engines were not superheated. Between 1912 and 1917 the shops at Meadville, Pa., and Hornell, N. Y., rebuilt the K-1s with superheaters, outboard piston valves, and Baker valve gear.

In 1910 Alco built an experimental Pacific, No. 50000, designed by Francis J. Cole, chief consulting engineer at the Schenectady Works. It had a much larger boiler than was common at the time, but the weight of the boiler required that other parts be trimmed down. It had 79" drivers and 27" × 28" cylinders, carried 185 pounds of boiler pressure, exerted a tractive force of 40,630 pounds — 10,000 pounds more than Erie's K-1 — and weighed 269,000 pounds. It demonstrated on several railroads and came to the Erie in November 1911. The road liked the

Mikado 3005, built by Baldwin in 1911, leads a way freight west near Alfred, N. Y., in 1950. Modifications to the 2-8-2 since construction include Elesco feedwater heater, disk main drivers, and a large 12-wheel tender. Photo by R. G. Nugent.

Lima-built S-4 No. 3389 represents the ultimate development of steam freight power on the Erie. Erie's 2-8-4 was the basis of the design of Berkshires for Pere Marquette, Wheeling & Lake Erie, Chesapeake & Ohio, Virginian, and Richmond, Fredericksburg & Potomac. Lima photo.

The K-1 Pacifics were built with inside valves and Stephenson valve gear; No. 2557 shows how they looked after rebuilding with outside valves and Baker gear. Photo by H. W. Pontin.

Only Erie had USRA heavy Pacifics, and the 1923 copies that Baldwin built were an improvement on a good design. The K-5-As were rebuilt in 1941 with cast frames and cylinders and pilot-mounted air pumps. Some received full sets of disk drivers; others, like No. 2941, had only their main drivers replaced. Photo by Vic Neal.

big Pacific well enough to buy it in September 1912; it was renumbered 2509 and classed K-3. It worked until 1950, a longer career than most one-of-a-kind engines.

In June 1912 Erie ordered 5 Pacifics similar to Alco 50000 from Lima, that builder's first large road engines for a Class 1 railroad. The K-2s, numbered 2900-2904, were delivered in 1913. Alco built 10 more, 2905-2914, class K-2-A, in 1917.

Between 1913 and 1916 Alco and Baldwin delivered 44 K-4 Pacifics. They had 69" drivers and were somewhat lighter than the K-2s, but could exert slightly more tractive effort. Baldwin built 10 similar 4-6-2s, class K-4-A, in 1923, for fast freight service. After only six years of service they were rebuilt as passenger engines with 75" drivers.

Among the USRA designs was a heavy Pacific resembling in some of its dimensions Alco 50000 and the Pennsylvania Railroad's K4. USRA allocated 20 heavy Pacifics to Erie, 10 from Baldwin and 10 from Richmond. Erie numbered them 2915-2934 and classed them K-5. No other roads got them (USRA allocated light Pacifics only to Atlantic Coast Line, Baltimore & Ohio, and Louisville & Nashville). Baldwin built 10

copies, class K-5-A, Nos. 2935-2944, in 1923; they differed principally in having Delta trailing trucks. The K-5s and K-5-As were fitted with Elesco feedwater heaters, and the K-5-As were rebuilt in 1941 with cast frames and cylinders, disk drivers, boosters, air pumps mounted on the pilot, and large 12-wheel tenders; some also received roller bearings. There was also one renumbering. K-5 2917 had been in several accidents and came to be considered a jinxed engine — crews refused to take it out. The road renumbered it 2945 in 1930.

Baldwin delivered a single Pacific in 1926, No. 2960, class K-5-B. Its principal difference from the K-5-As was an inch more in cylinder diameter, which gave it a tractive force of 47,200 pounds. Like Mikado 3199, it was ordered with uniflow cylinders, but construction halted partway along and the locomotive was completed with conventional cylinders.

The Erie was all but alone among major eastern railroads in halting passenger locomotive development with the Pacific, lacking even the experimental or tentative ventures of other roads that for all practical purposes stopped with the Pacific. Erie had nothing like the experimental Hudsons of Baltimore & Ohio, the mass-produced but nonethe-

less experimental duplex-drives of the Pennsylvania, and Maine Central's pair of nobody-really-knows-why Hudsons.

Switchers

The first switchers Erie received after 1900 were 30 0-6-0s, class B-5, numbers 50-79, built in early 1904 by Cooke and Schenectady. Later that same year Cooke delivered six B-4 class 0-6-0s — the difference between the two was an inch less in cylinder diameter on the B-4. Erie continued to obtain switchers from various builders, including its own Meadville shops, through 1912. The engines were typical of the period, with slide valves, Stephenson gear, 50" drivers, and main rods connected to the second drivers. Meadville built the 10 locomotives of the B-6 class in 1912. They had main rods connected to the rear drivers and slide valves actuated by Baker valve gear.

B Odd class 0-6-0T No. 2 was built for the Undercliff Terminal Company and purchased by the Erie in 1915 for use as a shop goat.

Switching was upgraded in 1918 when Alco's Pittsburgh Works delivered 16 USRA 0-8-0s. Between 1927 and 1930 Baldwin delivered 55 more 0-8-0s, 200-244, class C-3, and 245-254, class C-3-A. Except for 52" drivers

The C-3 0-8-0s were delivered with huge tenders intended for road engines; a general swap of tenders ensued when they reach Erie rails. Baldwin photo.

they were copies of the USRA design. They were delivered with huge 12-wheel tenders that were intended for road locomotives; upon delivery the switchers were coupled to small Vanderbilt tenders.

Erie converted 33 of its H-22 Consolidations into 0-8-0s by removing the lead trucks. The conversions were most likely done in the late Teens or early 1920s. In 1939 Erie purchased two 0-8-0s from the Buffalo Creek Railroad, numbering them 298 and 299 and classifying them C-4.

Historical and technical society: Erie Lackawanna Historical Society, 116 Ketcham Road, Hackettstown, NJ 07840

Recommended reading: *Erie Power*, by Frederick Westing and Alvin F. Staufer, published in 1970 by Alvin F. Staufer, Route 4, Medina, OH 44256

Published rosters:

Railroad Magazine: October 1935, page 88; May 1949, page 110

Railway & Locomotive Historical Society Bulletin, No. 131 (entire issue)

ERIE STEAM LOCOMOTIVES BUILT SINCE 1900

Type	Class	Numbers	Qty	Builder	Built	Retired	Notes
0-6-0	B-4	44-49	6	Cooke	1904	1929-1945	
							No. 45 rebuilt to 0-6-0T
0-6-0	B-5	50-64	15	Cooke	1904	1928-1950	
0-6-0	B-5	65-79	15	Schenectady	1904	1931-1950	
0-6-0	B-5	80-84	5	Baldwin	1910	1948-1950	
0-6-0	B-5	85-99	15	Meadville Shops	1911-1912	1942-1950	
0-6-0	B-5	110-114	5	Lima	1911	1947-1950	
0-6-0	B-5	115-119	5	Schenectady	1912	1944-1950	
0-6-0	B-6	100-109	10	Meadville Shops	1912	1948-1950	
0-6-0T	B Odd	2	1	Rogers	1912	1947	
0-8-0	C-1	120-135	16	Pittsburgh	1918	1950	USRA
0-8-0	C-2	1804-1886	33	Erie Shops	1927-1940		
							Rebuilt from H-22 2-8-0
0-8-0	C-3	200-244	45	Baldwin	1927, 1929	1950-1953	
0-8-0	C-3-A	245-254	10	Baldwin	1930	1950-1953	
0-8-0	C-4	298, 299	2	Brooks	1914, 1916	1950	
2-8-0	H-9	1400-1409	10	Brooks	1899	1927	
2-8-0	H-10	1450-1469	20	Brooks	1900	1927	
2-8-0	H-11	1470-1499	30	Rogers	1900	1927	
2-8-0	H-12	1425-1449	25	Brooks	1900	1927	
2-8-0	H-13	1410-1424	15	Baldwin	1901	1927	
2-8-0	H-14	1500-1503	4	Schenectady	1900	1927	
2-8-0	H-16	1510-1529	20	Baldwin	1902	1927	
2-8-0	H-17	1530-1544	15	Rogers	1902	1927	
2-8-0	H-18	1545-1564	20	Cooke	1902	1927	
2-8-0	H-19	1565-1569	5	Cooke	1902	1927	
2-8-0	H-20	1570-1615	45	Schenectady	1903-1904	1927-1947	
2-8-0	H-21	1616-1790	175	Rogers, Cooke	1904-1906	1927-1952	
2-8-0	H-21	2000-2034	35	Cooke	1907	1927-1952	
2-8-0	H-21	2035-2084	50	Baldwin	1910	1927-1952	
2-8-0	H-22	1800-1886	87	Baldwin	1905-1906	1927-1936	
							33 rebuilt to C-2 0-8-0
2-8-0	H-27	1540	1	Baldwin	1906	1936	
2-8-2	N-1	3000-3154	155	BLW, Sch., Lima	1911-1913	1947-1951	
2-8-2	N-2	3200-3214	15	Brooks	1918	1950-1952	USRA
2-8-2	N-3	3155-3194	40	Baldwin	1923	1949-1952	
2-8-2	N-3-A	3199	1	Baldwin	1926	1950	
2-8-4	S-1	3300-3324	25	Brooks	1927	1950-1952	
2-8-4	S-2	3325-3349	25	Lima	1927	1950-1952	
2-8-4	S-3	3350-3384	35	Baldwin	1928	1950-1952	
2-8-4	S-4	3385-3404	20	Lima	1929	1950-1952	
2-10-0	J-2	2425-2499	75	BLW, Rich, Sch.	1919	1929-1950	
							Russian Decapod
2-10-2	R-1	4000-4041	42	BLW, Sch., Lima	1915-1917	1939-1949	
2-10-2	R-2	4100-4129	30	Schenectady	1915-1917	1939-1949	
2-10-2	R-3	4200-4224	25	Brooks	1919	1949-1952	USRA heavy
0-8-8-0	L-1	2600-2602	3	Schenectady	1907	1930	
							Rebuilt to 2-8-8-2 by Baldwin
2-6-8-0	M-1	2900	1	Meadville Shops	1910		Rebuilt to 2-8-0 1916
2-8-8-8-2	P-1	5014-5016	3	Baldwin	1914, 1916	1929-1933	
4-4-2	E-1	502-527, 532-534					
			29	Baldwin	1899-1901	1927-1928	
4-4-2	E-2	934-943	10	Baldwin	1902	1930-1933	
4-4-2	E-3	545-559	15	Baldwin	1903	1927-1936	
4-4-2	E-4	535, 536	2	Baldwin	1905	1947, 1942	
4-4-2	E-5	537	1	Schenectady	1905	1942	
4-6-0	G-12	909-918	10	Baldwin	1901	1927	
4-6-0	G-13	919-933	15	Baldwin	1901	1927	13 rebuilt to G-16
4-6-0	G-15	950-974	25	Baldwin	1903-1904	1941-1950	
4-6-2	K-1	2510-2568	59	Schenectady, Rogers, Baldwin	1905-1908		
4-6-2	K-2	2900-2904	5	Lima	1913	1942, 1947	
4-6-2	K-2-A	2905-2914	10	Schenectady	1917	1947-1949	
4-6-2	K-3	2509	1	Schenectady	1910	1950	Alco 50000
4-6-2	K-4	2700-2743	44	Schen, BLW	1913-1916	1947-1954	
4-6-2	K-4-A	2744-2753	10	Baldwin	1923	1949-1950	
4-6-2	K-5	2915-2934	20	BLW, Richmond	1919	1950-1952	USRA heavy
4-6-2	K-5-A	2935-2944	10	Baldwin	1923	1950-1952	
4-6-2	K-5-B	2960	1	Baldwin	1926	1951	

FEEDWATER HEATERS

After the water in the boiler becomes steam and is piped away to do its work in the cylinders, it has to be replenished. How do you add water to a pressurized boiler? Early locomotives used pumps driven by the crosshead or cranks or eccentrics on the axles. By 1900 pumps had been replaced by injectors, which used steam from the boiler to force water into the boiler — a seeming paradox. The device was based on a steam jet: Condensing steam imparted its velocity to the feedwater to create a pressure greater than that in the boiler.

There were two principal types. Lifting injectors were mounted at cab or boiler level and could draw water up several feet, like a suction pump; non-lifting injectors were mounted under the cab (below the bottom of the tender tank) and forced the water up to the boiler. One injector was mounted on each side of the locomotive. They fed through check valves at the front end of the boiler so the addition of cold water would have the least effect on the water boiling over the firebox.

The injector preheats the feedwater and most of the heat in the steam is returned to the boiler, but it uses steam directly from the boiler. The Elesco exhaust steam injector was a simpler way of capturing the energy in exhaust steam. It was an injector that could operate on either live steam in the conventional manner or exhaust steam. Even allowing for the complexities of feedwater heater systems, it was less efficient.

The trouble with injecting cold water into the boiler is that it's like adding a cup of cold water to a boiling pot of soup: the temperature goes down and the boiling stops. When the temperature of the water in the boiler drops, so do steam pressure and speed. How can boiler feedwater water be preheated? Because a great deal of heat goes up the exhaust stack, locomotive designers made numerous attempts to use it to preheat the feedwater. Trevithick patented a feedwater heater in 1804, and the Stourbridge Lion of 1829 had a rudimentary feedwater heater. In the 1850s the Reading applied a heater designed by James Millholland to some of its locomotives. Some early feedwater heaters

used combustion gases as a source of heat; others that were more successful used exhaust steam. The devices were universally complex and difficult to maintain, and fuel was cheaper than maintenance. The first practical feedwater heaters appeared about 1920.

Two types of heaters were developed, closed and open. In closed heaters, exhaust steam is piped through a tank of feedwater but does not come into direct contact with the water. Elesco and Coffin feedwater heaters are of the closed type. A single pump moves water from the tender through the heater tubes and into the boiler. The exhaust steam condenses to water as it passes through the feedwater heater,

The most recognizable feedwater heater is the Elesco bundle-type, a product of the Superheater Company. Inside the cylindrical tank, which is usually mounted atop the smokebox, is a chamber containing exhaust steam and tubes through which the feedwater circulates. Steam travels from the cylinders to the heater through the large vertical pipes alongside the smokebox. The feedwater pump is usually hung on the left side of the locomotive; here on Central Vermont 404 (built by Schenectady in 1905) it is above the running board and ahead of the air pump. The later and less common Elesco coil-type heater worked the same way but had the tubes arranged more compactly at the top of the smokebox see the Central of Georgia 4-8-4 on page 72. Photo by Jim Shaughnessy.

Locomotives built with Coffin feedwater heaters usually had the horseshoe-shaped heater tank hidden in the smokebox. Coffin feedwater heaters added after the locomotive was built were usually hung in front of the smokebox, like that on Denver & Salt Lake Mikado 409. Photo by Ralph Hallock.

The Worthington type S heater was a higher-capacity unit than the BL, with separate pumps and heating chamber; the SA was a refinement of it that incorporated a float valve in the heater chamber. Northern Pacific 2684, built by Baldwin in 1943, illustrates the Worthington SA feedwater heater, with the heater chamber partly countersunk into the top of the smokebox and the pumps on the pilot deck. Baldwin photo; collection of H. L. Broadbelt.

and it is piped back to the tender; an oil skimmer removes the cylinder lubricants.

In an open feedwater heater, exhaust steam is mixed directly with the feedwater. Open heaters require an oil separator to remove cylinder and valve lubricant from the steam, and two pumps are needed, one to bring cold water from the tender and the other to pump hot water into the boiler. Worthington and Wilson feedwater heaters are of the open type. The open type ultimately proved the more popular; most modern steam locomotives had Worthington type SA feedwater heaters.

The effect of the feedwater heater was to raise the temperature of the feedwater anywhere from 135 to 185 degrees Fahrenheit; fuel savings were estimated at 8 to 16 percent. Most locomotives built after the mid-1930s had feedwater heaters, but as for retrofitting, railroads differed. The costs of the device and of its maintenance had to be balanced against the saving in fuel. Canadian National seemed to put feedwater heaters on all its locomotives, and rare was the Southern Pacific locomotive without a Worthington BL hung on the left side. Pennsylvania did not apply feedwater heaters to its old power, and Illinois Central removed the Elesco heaters from its 2-8-4s during rebuilding.

Feedwater heater systems usually replaced the injector on the left side of the locomotive; the right injector was retained.

The Worthington Model BL feedwater heater was a single unit containing hot- and cold-water pumps and the heater chamber. Southern Pacific used them on everything from Moguls to cab-forwards. Photo by F. J. Peterson.

FLORIDA EAST COAST RAILWAY

Henry M. Flagler built the Florida East Coast south from Jacksonville, Florida, to Miami, 366 miles, in 1885 and 1886. In 1905 construction was begun to extend the line another 156 miles southeast across the Florida Keys to Key West. The extension was extremely expensive to build, and hurricanes in 1906, 1909, and 1910 wiped out long portions of the line. The extension opened in 1912.

The Florida land boom of the 1920s brought prosperity to the road, and FEC double-tracked and signaled its main line and built branch lines. Between 1924 and 1926 it bought 125 new locomotives to handle the enormous increase in traffic.

A hurricane in September 1926 triggered the collapse of the land boom, and FEC suddenly had competition as the Seaboard Air Line Railroad opened a line from the center of the state to Miami. Traffic fell off — FEC's revenues for 1927 were only 60 percent of the previous year's. Misfortune followed misfortune: The stock market crashed in 1929; FEC declared bankruptcy in 1931; and when a hurricane on Labor Day 1935 destroyed 42 miles of the Key West Extension, FEC abandoned the line south of Florida City rather than repair it.

FEC was primarily a passenger carrier. Freight consisted of southbound general merchandise and northbound fruit and vegetables. For its entire length along the Florida peninsula FEC's main line was no more than a few miles from the ocean, and its profile was flat — really flat. It started at 8 feet above sea level at Jacksonville, climbed to 9 feet at South Jacksonville, dropped to 7 at St. Augustine, reached a summit of 16 feet at West Palm Beach, dropped to 7 at Fort Lauderdale, and made a final back-breaking climb to Miami at 15 feet. (A branch west from New Smyrna Beach reached the heady altitude of 70 feet at Lake Helen.)

Little information is available on FEC's early-20th-century locomotives. The railroad didn't retain many records, and to early rail enthusiasts the Florida East Coast was as remote as Maine's Bangor & Aroostook or Ontario's Algoma Central.

In 1915 the road began to convert its locomotives from coal to oil. Both fuels had to be brought a considerable distance; oil was easier to handle and had the public-relations advantage of burning cleaner and without cinders.

Atlantic 64 was built by Schenectady in 1905. It is typical of the time, with Stephenson gear and inside piston valves. Alco photo; collection of C. W. Witbeck.

Richmond built Pacific No. 147 in 1920. The high-mounted headlight, paired single compressors and wood pilot all make the engine look older. Alco photo; collection of C. W. Witbeck.

The USRA heavy Mountain was the basis for FEC's last group of 4-8-2s, 801-823, built in 1926. Number 803 carries two cross-compound air pumps on her right side, balancing a feedwater heater pump out of sight on the left side. Photo by James G. LaVake.

Eight-wheel switcher 279 has a long string of refrigerator cars in tow at Jacksonville in 1950. Note that the numerals on the cab are separate pieces of polished metal, not painted. Photo by William J. Husa Jr.

When the Florida boom turned to bust in 1927 FEC found it had far more locomotives than it needed, and in 1936 it defaulted on equipment trust payments for some of them. Indeed, FEC's steam locomotive development is perhaps most significant as a source of second-hand power for other railroads.

Dieselization began with two Electro-Motive E3 passenger units in 1939, but didn't accelerate until the early 1950s. Between 1952 and 1954 the number of steam locomotives dropped from 66 to 9; 6 steamers remained on the roster through 1958.

Road locomotives

Virtually all FEC power was dual purpose. Its first locomotives other than 4-4-0s were five 63" drivered 4-6-0s, 28-32, delivered by Schenectady in 1897 (they are included in the roster below for completeness); seven more, 33-39, with the same dimensions followed in 1900. Baldwin deliv-

ered Ten-Wheelers 40-44 in 1902, FEC's last Baldwin locomotives. Four of the earlier group of 4-6-0s and three of the Baldwins were sold for industrial use between 1925 and 1934; the other Ten-Wheelers were scrapped between 1925 and 1930.

In 1904 and 1905 Alco's Schenectady Works built 20 Atlantics numbered 45-64. The drivers were no more than 70" in diameter. Except for one sold to a construction company and one that blew up in 1923, they were dismantled or sold for scrap in 1925 and 1930.

Between 1907 and 1922 FEC bought 87 4-6-2s. Although details changed over the 15 years, the Pacifics all had the same dimensions: 69' drivers, 22" × 26" cylinders, and 204,000 pounds total weight — light as Pacifics go.

In 1923 FEC turned to the 4-8-2. Its traffic surges — vacationers and perishable fruits and vegetables — required a powerful locomotive ghtly built track and roadbed required that the weight be spread out. EC's first 4-8-2s, 301-315, were among the lightest built, weighing only 87,000 pounds, just 10,000 pounds more than a USRA light Pacific. hey had 68" drivers and a tractive force of 43,100 pounds.

Alco's Schenectady Works built 52 larger and heavier Mountains, umbers 401-452, between 1924 and 1926. They had 26" × 28" cylin- ers, an inch larger than the 301 series, and 73" drivers. They weighed etween 313,000 and 321,500 pounds, slightly less than a USRA light 8-2, and had a tractive effort of 44,100 pounds (the USRA light 4-8-2 was ated at 53,900 pounds).

As the Florida boom continued, FEC bought its first and only pure reight power, 15 copies of the USRA heavy 2-8-2 numbered 701-715, rom Schenectady in 1925.

FEC's third group of 4-8-2s was built by Schenectady in 1926 pri- narily for freight service but with an eye toward the long trains of eavyweight Pullmans that rolled south each winter. They were based n the USRA heavy 4-8-2, with 69" drivers and 28" × 30" cylinders, but veighed about 4,000 pounds more and had a tractive force of 60,800 ounds. They were the last steam locomotives FEC bought.

Switchers

FEC bought most of its switchers as add-ons to orders for road loco- notives. The 0-6-0s built in 1907 and 1917 had construction numbers nmediately above the Pacifics. The five 0-6-0s built by Richmond had onstruction numbers immediately above 4-8-2s 301-315; 0-8-0s 251- 55 and 256-261 followed 4-8-2s 401-420 and 421-432 respectively; and 62-267 followed the 2-8-2s. The 0-8-0s were about the size of USRA witchers.

Recommended reading: *Speedway To Sunshine*, by Seth H. Bramson, ublished in 1984 by Boston Mills Press, 98 Main Street, Erin, ON, Cana- a N0B 1T0 (ISBN 0-919783-12-0)

Published rosters: *Railroad Magazine*, January 1948, page 90

FEC STEAM LOCOMOTIVES BUILT SINCE 1900

Type	Numbers	Qty	Builder	Built	Scrapped	Notes
0-6-0	75, 76	2	Schenectady	1907	1916	Renumbered 201, 202
0-6-0	137-140	4	Schenectady	1917, 1920	1923, 1934	Renumbered 203-206
0-6-0	158-160	3	Schenectady	1922	1934	Renumbered 207-209
0-6-0	210-214	5	Schenectady	1924	1941, 1952	
0-8-0	251-279	29	Richmond	1924-1926	1930-1955	
2-8-2	701-715	15	Schenectady	1925	1954-1955	
4-4-2	45-64	20	Schenectady	1904, 1905	1923-1930	
4-6-0	28-39	12	Schenectady	1897, 1900	1925-1934	
4-6-0	40-44	5	Baldwin	1902	1930	
4-6-2	65-74	10	Schenectady	1907	1929-1930	
4-6-2	77-136	60	Schenectady	1910-1917	1930-1937	
4-6-2	141-150	10	Richmond	1920	1934-1952	
4-6-2	151-157	7	Schenectady	1922	1935-1942	
4-8-2	301-315	15	Richmond	1923	1941-1954	
4-8-2	401-452	52	Schenectady	1924-1926	1936-1955	
4-8-2	801-823	23	Schenectady	1926	1951-1955	

FEC STEAM LOCOMOTIVES SOLD TO OTHER RAILROADS

Type	Numbers	Date sold	Subsequent owner and number
4-6-2	69	1930	Georgia Northern 106
4-6-2	80	1935	Savannah & Atlanta 750
4-6-2	88	1930	Sold for scrap; Georgia Northern 107
4-6-2	96	1941	Georgia & Florida 500
4-6-2	101, 103, 105, 108		
		1930	Atlanta, Birmingham & Coast 71-74; ACL 7071-7074
4-6-2	109	1930	Louisiana & Arkansas 309
4-6-2	110	1930	Atlanta, Birmingham & Coast 75; Atlantic Coast Line 7075
4-6-2	111	1930	Atlanta, Birmingham & Coast 76; Apalachicola Northern 301
4-6-2	112	1930	Atlanta, Birmingham & Coast 77; Atlantic Coast Line 7077
4-6-2	115	1930	Atlanta, Birmingham & Coast 78; Apalachicola Northern 300
4-6-2	117	1930	Atlanta, Birmingham & Coast 79
4-6-2	118-122	1930	Atlanta, Birmingham & Coast 80-84; ACL 7080-7084
4-6-2	123	1930	Atlanta, Birmingham & Coast 85; Apalachicola Northern 302
4-6-2	125	1930	Atlanta, Birmingham & Coast 86; Atlantic Coast Line 7086
4-6-2	127-129	1934	Georgia & Florida 501-503
4-6-2	130	1936	Georgia Northern 130
4-6-2	131	1935	Atlanta & St. Andrews Bay 131
4-6-2	132-135	1934-37	Georgia Northern 504-507

FEC STEAM LOCOMOTIVES SOLD TO OTHER RAILROADS

(continued)

4-6-2	136, 141	1936, 35	Savannah & Atlanta 752, 751
4-6-2	142, 143	1934	Atlanta & St. Andrews Bay 142, 143
4-6-2	144	1934	Georgia & Florida 508
4-6-2	145, 146	1935, 34	Atlanta & St. Andrews Bay 145, 146
4-6-2	149	1941	Georgia & Florida 509
4-6-2	150	1942	Apalachicola Northern 510; Kansas City, Mexico & Orient 152
4-6-2	151, 152	1941	Georgia & Florida 510, 511
4-6-2	154	1935	A&StAB 154; Columbia, Newberry & Laurens 154
4-6-2	155	1942	Apalachicola Northern 515; Kansas City, Mexico & Orient 153
4-6-2	156	1941	Georgia & Florida 512
4-6-2	157	1941	Columbia, Newberry & Laurens 157
0-6-0	203	1923	Georgia & Florida 27
0-6-0	206	1934	Atlanta & St. Andrews Bay 206
0-6-0	207	1934	Georgia & Florida 28
0-6-0	208	1934	Atlanta & St. Andrews Bay 208
0-6-0	211, 212	1941	Georgia & Florida 29, 30
0-8-0	251-253	1936	Louisiana & Arkansas 251-253
0-8-0	254, 255	1936	Illinois Terminal 36, 37
0-8-0	264, 265, 267	1930	Illinois Terminal 34, 33, 35
4-8-2	304, 305	1941	National Railways of Mexico 3200, 3201
4-8-2	307-309	1941	National Railways of Mexico 3206, 3202, 3207
4-8-2	311-315	1941	National Railways of Mexico 3208, 3203, 3204, 3209, 3205
4-8-2	401	1936	St. Louis Southwestern 675
4-8-2	402	1936	Western Railway of Alabama 185
4-8-2	403-408	1936	Western Pacific 171-176
4-8-2	409, 411	1936	St. Louis Southwestern 676, 677
4-8-2	410, 412	1936	Western Pacific 177, 178
4-8-2	413, 416	1936	St. Louis Southwestern 678, 679
4-8-2	414, 415	1936	Western Pacific 179, 180
4-8-2	417, 420	1936	Atlanta, Birmingham & Coast 351, 372; ACL 7351, 7372
4-8-2	418, 419	1936	Western Railway of Alabama 187, 186
4-8-2	421, 422	1948	National Railways of Mexico 3314, 3315
4-8-2	425-427	1948	National Railways of Mexico 3316-3318
4-8-2	429	1948	National Railways of Mexico 3319
4-8-2	433, 434	1945	National Railways of Mexico 3300, 3301
4-8-2	441-452	1945	National Railways of Mexico 3302-3313

4-8-2 — MOUNTAIN

In 1910 the Chesapeake & Ohio confronted the necessity of lifting its passenger trains over the Allegheny Mountains with doubleheaded Pacifics. It conferred with American Locomotive Company to develop a new locomotive type that would combine the eight drivers of the Mikado with the four-wheel lead truck of the Pacific. Alco's Richmond Works built two 4-8-2s for C&O in 1911 and the wheel arrangement was christened the Mountain type.

C&O's new engines shared a number of components with the road's first group of Mikados, and two characteristics were typical of 2-8-2s: The main rods were connected to the third set of drivers and the drivers were only 62" in diameter. Most locomotives with four-wheel lead trucks had their main rods connected to the second set of drivers; most later 4-8-2s had drivers in the 69"-73" range. C&O found the engines too slow for its passenger trains.

In 1913 the St. Louis, Iron Mountain & Southern, a Missouri Pacific subsidiary, bought seven similar but lighter 4-8-2s for passenger trains on its line through through the hilly country between St. Louis and Little Rock. That same year the Rock Island took deliv

New York Central L-3-b 3037, built by Lima in 1940, was built as a freight locomotive, but NYC eventually discovered its modern 4-8-2s were equally good in passenger service. Lima photo; collection of P. E. Percy.

ery of two 69"-drivered 4-8-2s slightly heavier than the C&O engines for heavy passenger trains across the high plains of Kansas and Colorado. The Rock Island engines set the pattern for most subsequent 4-8-2s.

The Mountain type ultimately developed into a fast dual-service locomotive, but in the 1920s and 1930s its role seemed to depend on where it ran. Western railroads such as Southern Pacific, Union Pacific, and Santa Fe used the 4-8-2 as a long-distance heavy passenger locomotive until the advent of the 4-8-4. Eastern roads such as New York Central, Pennsylvania, and Baltimore & Ohio considered it primarily a fast freight engine. In the South a number of railroads progressed from the light Pacific to a lightweight Mountain because their track and bridges couldn't support the concentrated weight of a heavy Pacific.

Surprisingly the Mountain type was not eclipsed by the 4-8-4. In the late 1930s Boston & Maine turned to the type to replace 2-8-4s and 2-10-2s in accelerated freight service and at the same time handle heavy summer passenger trains. New York Central bought 115 4-8-2s (it called them Mohawks) for fast freight service between 1940 and 1943 and discovered that lightweight rods, disk drivers, and improvements in counterbalancing made the 69"- and 72"-drivered machines as speedy as its Hudsons. In 1942 Baltimore & Ohio,

which had previously acquired only four 4-8-2s (and experimental ones at that), began building 4-8-2s in its Mount Clare shops, starting with the boilers of outdated Pacifics and Mikados. B&O was happy enough with the results that it continued the rebuilding program until 1948. Canadian National's last new steam locomotives, 20 semi-streamlined 4-8-2s for fast passenger service, were built after its 203 4-8-4s, the largest fleet of Northerns in North America.

Other names: Mohawk (New York Central)
Total built: 2,201
First: C&O 316 and 317, 1911
Last: Baltimore & Ohio 5592-5594, 1948
Longest lived: Norfolk & Western 104 and 105, built 1916, scrapped 1958
Last in service: National Railways of Mexico still had 13 4-8-2s on its roster in 1961, and they were active for several years afterward.
Greatest number: New York Central, 600
Heaviest: Illinois Central 2600-2619, 423,893 pounds
Lightest: Alaska Railroad 802, 268,000 pounds
Recommended reading: *North American Steam Locomotives: The Mountains*, by Jack W. Farrell, published in 1977 by Pacific Fast Mail, P. O. Box 57, Edmonds, WA 98020 (LCC 76-13756)

Chesapeake & Ohio 316 was the first Mountain type. Its low drivers (62") and main rods connected to the third drivers proved to be nontypical, as was the inboard-bearing trailing truck C&O 316-318 were the only 4-8-2s so equipped. Alco photo.

FUEL

In the beginning most American locomotives burned wood. It was inexpensive and easily obtained in most sections of the country. In the early 1800s trees were considered primarily an impediment to agriculture, and railroads constituted a good market for a by-product of clearing the land. As land was cleared, railroads had to go farther and farther for fuel, and some railroads in the Northeast resorted to buying timberland in the South and bringing in wood by ship. The price of wood rose but it was still cheaper than coal. Railroads turned to coal only after it became readily available.

As late as 1950 woodburners could still be found on a few short lines and lumber-mill and logging railroads in Florida, where wood was plentiful and close at hand. Wood was clean-burning and left little residue, but the great quantities of sparks it produced required complex spark arrestors inside the oversize stacks. Wood had to be loaded into the tender by hand, and a wood fire required constant attention from the fireman. The heat content of wood varied greatly, depending on the kind of wood and how dry it was. Wood was bulky for the amount of heat it contained. It took 5,000 pounds of wood to equal 2,000 pounds

of coal, and even then it was not as good a fuel. An average 4-4-0 of the 1860s would have produced about 400 horsepower as a wood burner and 500 with bituminous coal as the fuel. By 1870 about half the locomotives in the U. S. still burned wood, but coal was rapidly becoming the norm.

Coal

Coal. That's what you think of when you think of steam locomotives. It's not that simple, though. You can't just dig it out of the ground and put it in the tender. Lumps must be between 1 and 4 inches in size, and the coal must be washed to remove rocks, dirt, and other impurities. Moreover, there are several varieties of coal.

Anthracite or hard coal, which is found primarily in eastern Pennsylvania, was the only type of coal mined in any quantity before 1840. Railroads hadn't reached the bituminous-coal areas of the country, and without railroads to transport the coal, mining wasn't an economic proposition. The earliest coal-burning locomotives used anthracite, and not particularly well — it burns slowly. A wide, shallow fire was necessary to produce enough heat to power a locomotive. The narrow, deep firebox of 19th-century locomotives wasn't suitable for anthracite; it required a grate with two to three times the usual area. Since the distance a fireman could fling coal through the firedoor was limited, the firebox had to be wider, not longer. John E. Wootten (1822-1898), general manager of the Philadelphia & Reading, introduced such a firebox in 1877.

Anthracite was considered the best coal for home heating. For that use it was cleaned and graded so the pieces were all the same size. The demand for anthracite soon made it an expensive locomotive fuel. Culm, the material left over from the grading process, eventually found use as a locomotive fuel, but it required the wide Wootten firebox.

Bituminous, or soft coal, is the most common form of the mineral. Bituminous fueled the majority of modern North American steam locomotives because its deposits were widespread. Sometimes railroads

The tender of Live Oak, Perry & Gulf 100, shown at Foley, Florida, in February 1938, illustrates the high volume-to-heat ratio of wood. Photo by M. B. Cooke.

burned a mixture of coal or would use different grades for different services. For instance, the Central Railroad of New Jersey coal dock at Jersey City had separate bins and chutes for bituminous coal for Baltimore & Ohio locomotives and anthracite for Reading and CNJ engines.

Lignite, sometimes called brown coal, is a low-grade coal of relatively recent origin. It contains high proportions of volatile matter and moisture. It is light, and can be lifted off the grate easily by the draft, so special grates are necessary. Because lignite emits sparks, extra netting was needed in the smokebox, and therefore the smokebox had be longer; ashpan openings also had to be screened. Railroads that burned lignite — for example, the Burlington and the Chicago & North Western on their lines west of Omaha — did so because it was near at hand.

The phrase "burned what they hauled" is often used to explain why coal-carrying railroads were late converts to the diesel locomotive. "Burned what was nearby" is a more accurate way of putting it. Part of the cost of fuel is the cost of transportation. Railroads that had to bring in coal from a distance — those in New England, for example — were among the first to dieselize.

Oil

Crude oil came under consideration as a locomotive fuel in the 1880s. It appeared to have several virtues. It left no ashes, it was easy to handle, and it had a higher heat content per pound than coal. The problem was burning it in a firebox. Early experimenters tried unsuccessfully to vaporize it or convert it to a gas. A Scot, Thomas Urquhart, locomotive superintendent of the Grazi-Tsaritzin Railway in Russia, was successful, and by 1886 the railway was using oil in 143 locomotives. Urquhart's success was based on three innovations: He used steam to atomize the oil and spray it into the firebox, he placed the burner so heat would not cause its openings to clog, and he used a wall of firebrick to form a combustion chamber and serve as a reservoir of heat.

In 1894 Baldwin equipped a demonstrator locomotive, a Vauclain compound 4-6-0, to burn oil using the Urquhart system. It had a long, narrow, shallow firebox, less than ideal for the experiment. It made a short test run on the Reading, then pulled a heavy train to Baltimore on the Baltimore & Ohio. On that 92-mile trip it burned 905 gallons (6,637 pounds) of oil to evaporate 8,867 gallons (70,933 pounds) of water. It made several other test runs on the Reading, proving that oil could be used as a locomotive fuel.

Oil was used most often as a locomotive fuel in the Southwest, where the oil fields were. It was occasionally used elsewhere to avoid the danger of sparks from coal (in forested country, for example) or for convenience — Milwaukee Road's *Hiawatha* Atlantics and Chicago & North Western's rebuilt *400* Pacifics both burned oil to avoid the need to stop for coal and for the ease of maintaining the fire at high speed.

GREAT NORTHERN RAILWAY

Completed in 1893, Great Northern was the second railroad through the northern tier of states between the upper Mississippi Valley and the Pacific Northwest. It was largely the creation of one man, James J. Hill. Its main line from St. Paul to Seattle made an easy crossing of the Rockies over Marias Pass in Montana, but it had a far more difficult time crossing the Cascade Mountains in Washington. Secondary lines traversed Minnesota in several directions; the numerous branches that reached north from the main line across North Dakota resembled the skeleton of a fish. GN also had extensive branches in Manitoba and British Columbia; it gradually sold or abandoned most of those. In 1931 GN opened a route south from Spokane, Washington, to a connection with Western Pacific at Bieber, California, that was part new construction, part trackage rights on Southern Pacific, and part traffic agreements and trackage rights on Spokane, Portland & Seattle.

GN and Northern Pacific, which it controlled, jointly constructed and owned the Spokane, Portland & Seattle, and jointly owned nearly all the stock of the Chicago, Burlington & Quincy (the four roads merged in 1970 to form Burlington Northern).

Great Northern's passenger trains had a good reputation. For years the premier train was the Chicago-Seattle *Oriental Limited*. In 1929 GN inaugurated a new train which carried James J. Hill's nickname, *Empire Builder* (a secondary train carried the *Oriental Limited* name until 1931). Other trains served such diverse destinations as Duluth, Minnesota, Winnipeg, Man., Great Falls, Mont., and Vancouver, B. C. GN freight trains carried lumber from the Pacific Northwest, wheat from the northern plains, and iron ore from the Mesabi Range.

The most generous description of Great Northern steam locomotives is homely. Most had Belpaire fireboxes. The older locomotives had low, straight running boards, domes of an archaic shape, and either rectangular tenders that hunkered down over their trucks or Vanderbilt tenders that were taller than the locomotives. Rebuildings and shoppings resulted in more external piping than locomotives of most other roads. Larger locomotives carried paired air pumps on the smokebox front; locomotives without smokebox-mounted pumps had odd-looking headlights carried above the center of the smokebox door. Many loco-

motives were built or retrofitted with slant-front cabs, and a few particularly unfortunate ones were given backward-sloping cab fronts.

Considering only new locomotives, GN steam power development ended in 1930 with the S-2 Northerns and R-2 2-8-8-2s. However, well into the 1940s the road continued to rebuild, modernize, and improve its steam power, with the result that the 2-8-0s, for instance, were thoroughly modern locomotives in spite of their construction dates.

GN began experimenting with diesels early, starting with switchers and light road switchers, and it was an early purchaser of Electro-Motive FT freight diesels. By the mid-1950s it was fully dieselized except during wheat harvest season. The last run of a steam locomotive occurred without ceremony in August 1957.

Freight locomotives

In the 1890s GN like many other railroads bought large numbers of Twelve-Wheelers, one of which was for a brief period the world's largest locomotive. The 4-8-0s had 55" drivers and consequently were slow machines; they were intended for service in the mountains. The usual successor to the 4-8-0 (and its predecessor, too) was the 2-8-0, usually with drivers in the 60"-63" range. GN's Consolidations had the same 55" drivers as the Twelve-Wheelers and generally worked the same mountain territory. Some of the Consolidations were fitted with super-

Great Northern rostered 150 Prairies built in 1906 and 1907. Unstable at speed, they proved useful for branchline service, and 15 were rebuilt into Pacifics. Baldwin photo.

heaters and piston valves in the 1920s; many were converted to 0-8-0s or switching.

GN turned to the 2-6-2 for fast freight trains on the flatter parts of the system, receiving 150 of the type from Baldwin in 1906 and 1907. Their 69" drivers held the potential for good speed, but the basic flaw of the 2-6-2 was that it was unstable at speed. Fifteen of the Prairies were converted to low-drivered dual-service Pacifics; the remaining 2-6-2s were scrapped in the late 1930s and early 1940s.

After the Prairies GN turned its attention to articulateds, discussed below, for several years. The road took delivery of its first 2-8-2s in 1911. These turned out to be what GN was looking for, and over the next seven years Baldwin delivered 145 of the type. The O-1 class Mikados had 63" drivers and 28" × 32" cylinders. They weighed 280,000 pounds and could exert a tractive force of 60,930 pounds — heavier, more powerful, and less complex than the L-2 2-6-6-2s delivered just three years earlier.

The single O-2 class 2-8-2 was a small-drivered engine acquired through merger. The O-3 class consisted of nine heavy USRA Mikados, four diverted from the Spokane, Portland & Seattle and five received in 1920 from the El Paso & Southwestern. A postwar increase in traffic resulted in an order to Baldwin for 45 O-4 class Mikes, delivered in 1920. They had the same size cylinders and drivers as the O-1s but were slightly more powerful. They were the first GN locomotives with Vanderbilt tenders.

By the 1920s GN's 2-6-6-2s had been eclipsed by faster, more powerful locomotives. The 2-6-6-2 boilers, though, were the right size to make 2-8-2s. The 45 members of the L-2 class, the light 2-6-6-2s, went into the shops first, emerging as O-5 class Mikados 3300-3344. They had 63" drivers and 25" × 30" cylinders, and were about the same weight as the original O-1 but less powerful. Next were the L-1s, which became the O-6 class, also with 63" drivers.

Between 1929 and 1931 GN converted 22 of its odd 2-6-8-0s into class O-7 2-8-2s with 69" drivers, and in 1932 the shops built from scratch three enormous O-8 class Mikes with 69" drivers and an axle

The 69" drivers of GN's O-8 class Mikados put them in the same league with the 2-8-4s of Erie and Nickel Plate. Photo by H. W. Pontin.

Great Northern was one of the first users of articulated locomotives. The complex running gear of 2-6-6-2 No. 1800, an L-1 built in 1906, obscures that fact that its boiler is no bigger than that of a medium-size Mikado. Baldwin photo.

loading of more than 80,000 pounds. In the 1940s the O-7s were rebuilt to O-8 specifications. The O-8s generally take honors for North America's heaviest, fastest, and most powerful Mikados.

In 1923 the road was casting about for a replacement for the 2-8-8-0s

2-6-6-2

The 0-6-6-0 appeared on the scene in 1904, about the same time as the 2-10-2. The articulated was more flexible than the Santa Fe type if slightly more complex (the first 2-10-2s were four-cylinder compounds). Great Northern considered its curving line over the Cascades and asked if Baldwin could build a Mallet with lead and trailing trucks. Samuel Vauclain of Baldwin persuaded GN to take five, because a single engine on GN's roster would be treated as an experiment. The 2-6-6-2s arrived in 1906 and GN ordered more. The Mallet had become a road locomotive.

The first 2-6-6-2s were basically 0-6-6-0s with the addition of guiding axles fore and aft. The firebox was over the rear drivers, but there was plenty of room above the 55" or 56" drivers. About 1910 the first 2-6-6-2 appeared with a firebox behind the drivers and supported by a trailing truck, and most subsequent 2-6-6-2s followed that pattern.

The 2-6-6-2 remained a low-speed locomotive, far more likely to be seen bringing hopper cars down from the coal mines than wheeling mainline freight. Baltimore & Ohio's high-speed 2-6-6-2s were handicapped by small fireboxes. By the time the simple articulated became accepted practice, the large firebox supported by a four-wheel trailing truck was also the norm. The high-speed six-coupled articulated came on the scene as the 2-6-6-4 and 4-6-6-4 types.

The 2-6-6-2 also found employment in the logging industry in the western United States, often as a tank engine. Non-common-carrier engines are not included in the statistics below.

Nearly all 2-6-6-2s were built as compounds, and a few were later converted to single-expansion locomotives. Those built as simple locomotives are a heterogeneous group:
- Uintah 50 and 51, 3-foot gauge tank engines; built by Baldwin in 1926 and 1928
- Baltimore & Ohio 7400 and 7450, experimental engines with 70" drivers and one with a watertube firebox; Baldwin, 1930
- National Railways of Mexico 361-370, 3-foot gauge; Alco, 1929-1937
- National Railways of Mexico 2030-2037, standard gauge, equipped with Boxpok drivers and cast trailing trucks; Alco, 1937

Total built: 918
First: Great Northern 1800, 1906
Last: Chesapeake & Ohio 1309, 1949
Last in service: NdeM 2033, retired 1963
Greatest number: Chesapeake & Ohio, 250
Heaviest:
Standard gauge: Baltimore & Ohio 7400, 466,000 pounds
Narrow gauge: Uintah 51, 246,000 pounds
Lightest:
Standard gauge: Great Northern 1805-1829, 263,000 pounds
Narrow gauge: National of Mexico 240-245 (361-366), 204,000 pounds

Norfolk & Western ranked second in the number of 2-6-6-2s with 190 members of the Z1 and Z1a classes like No. 1462 on its roster.

The need for a wide firebox over 63" drivers made the 2-8-8-0s Great Northern's tallest engines. Photo by Russell D. Porter.

Pacific 1383, an H-7, was a product of GN's shops — starting with an E-14 Ten-Wheeler of 1909. Photo by H. W. Pontin.

in heavy freight service. The O-4 Mikado of 1920 was taken as a starting point; adding a fifth driving axle created the Q-1 class 2-10-2 of 1923, numbers 2100-2129. The N-1s weighed 422,340 pounds, about 10 percent more than a USRA heavy 2-10-2, and developed a tractive force about 18 percent greater. They were joined in 1928 by 15 Q-2 Santa Fes rebuilt from P-1 class 4-8-2s originally ordered for passenger service. The Q-2s were a little heavier than the USRA light 2-10-2s and considerably more powerful.

Articulateds

The completion of the first Cascade Tunnel in 1901 reduced the grade of GN's line over the mountains between Wenatchee, Wash., and Seattle from 4 percent to 2.2 percent and eliminated several switchbacks. Train lengths could be increased, but that would require larger locomotives. The road viewed with interest Baltimore & Ohio's pioneer 0-6-6-0 and ordered a version with lead and trailing trucks from Baldwin. Five 2-6-6-2s were delivered in 1906, class L-1, numbers 1800-1804. They weighed 355,000 pounds, about 20,000 pounds more than B&O No. 2400; tractive effort was about 1,500 pounds less. They entered helper service over the Cascades. In 1907 and 1908 GN acquired 45 more 2-6-6-2s for road service. The L-2s, engines 1810-1854, had the

same running gear and 55" drivers and used the same boiler as the H-2 Pacific. The Mallets weighed 250,000 pounds and developed 54,520 pounds of tractive effort. Twenty more L-1s, 1905-1924, were delivered in 1908.

In 1910 Baldwin delivered 35 Mallets classed M-1 and numbered 1950-1984. They were noteworthy for having six drivers in the front, low-pressure engine and eight in the rear. Articulated locomotives in which the two engines had different numbers of drive wheels were rare and in most instances were the result of rebuilding and experimentation.

The reasons for equal numbers of drivers fore and aft were probably based on convenience — initial engineering and spare parts. An argument based on getting the same pulling power from the two engines could just as easily be turned around — the front engine carries less weight, so it should be smaller.

The 2-6-8-0 arrangement was most likely derived from the idea of replacing the trailing wheel of the 2-6-6-2 with a fourth driving axle. The firebox of early 2-6-6-2s was entirely above the drivers, and railroads may have thought the contribution the trailing axle made to smoother riding in reverse was minimal. GN simpled the 2-6-8-0s in the early 1920s and classed them M-2, then in the late 1920s rebuilt 22 of them to O-7 class Mikados.

The M-1s were followed in 1912 by the 2-8-8-0s of the N-1 class, numbers 2000-2024. Where GN's previous Mallets had 55" drivers, the N-1s had 63". The firebox was placed over the rear two pairs of drivers, and for the firebox to have sufficient depth the boiler had to be mounted quite high; the N-1s were the tallest locomotives on the road. In the mid-1920s they were converted to single-expansion engines, class N-2, and in the early 1940s they were again rebuilt with new frames and roller bearings and classed N-3. Tractive effort increased each time: 93,250 pounds as built; 100,000 pounds as simple engines; and 104,236 pounds as modernized.

The Mikados and Santa Fes that replaced the early Mallets on the line over the Rockies were replaced between 1925 and 1930 by simple 2-8-8-2s. Baldwin built the first four R-1s, numbers 2030-2033 in 1925, and GN's shops built ten more, 2034-2043, in 1927 and 1928. An improved version, the R-2 class, numbers 2044-2059, rolled out of the road's shops at Hillyard in Spokane in 1929 and 1930. With a tractive effort of 153,000 pounds the R-2s were considered the most powerful simple articulateds in the world. Both classes of 2-8-8-2s had 63" drivers; the R-1s had inboard-bearing trailing trucks, and the R-2s had cast Delta trailing trucks.

In October 1937 Spokane, Portland & Seattle took delivery of six Northern Pacific-design 4-6-6-4s numbered 900-905. In November of that year, to equalize locomotive mileage on the Spokane-Wishram-Bend-Bieber route, 903 and 904 were sold to Great Northern and numbered 4000 and 4001. Engine 4000 was returned to SP&S in 1946, 4001 in 1950.

Normally steam locomotives stayed on home rails, but occasionally they worked on other roads for convenience or better utilization of equipment. The owner collected a per-mile rental, but where this was a regular occurrence, railroads supplied locomotives to a common pool in proportion to their mileage to avoid having to pay rental to each other.

Passenger locomotives

Among Great Northern's Ten-Wheelers were several groups that had 73" drivers and were obviously passenger engines. Many were rebuilt into Pacifics. GN rostered only 10 Atlantics. The type was well suited to flatland running, and GN had 1,000 miles of that between St. Paul and the Rockies, but the K-1 class 4-4-2s, delivered by Baldwin in 1906, were simply small passenger engines. They were balanced compounds with inside high-pressure cylinders coupled to the first pair of drivers and outside low-pressure cylinders driving the second pair. They had 73" drivers, so they were not especially speedy; their 23,000 pounds of tractive effort was about what other railroads were getting from Atlantics with 79" or 80" drivers. In the mid-1920s GN rebuilt them as superheated single-expansion engines with booster-equipped cast trailing trucks. Tractive effort with the booster cut in was a respectable 36,800 pounds.

GN's first Pacifics came from Rogers in 1905, delicate-looking engines with 21" × 28" cylinders and 73" drivers. In 1906 and 1907 Baldwin delivered 34 H-2 class Pacifics built with drawbar pull, not speed, in mind. They had slide valves, Walschaerts valve gear, 69" drivers, 22" × 30" cylinders, and inside-journal trailing trucks. All but one were upgraded with piston valves, 23½" cylinders, and outside-frame trailing trucks and reclassed H-3. Twenty H-4 Pacifics were delivered by Baldwin in 1909 and 25 more, almost identical to the first group, by Lima in 1914. Their 73" drivers gave them less tractive effort and more speed than the H-2s. They were the last Pacifics GN would buy from a commercial builder. For successive classes GN rebuilt 4-6-0s and 2-6-2s, engines that were short on firebox size and steaming capacity or lacked sufficient boiler length to accommodate a superheater. The H-5 and H-7 classes were rebuilt from E-14 Ten-Wheelers and had 73" drivers; the H-6 Pacifics were rebuilt from Prairies and had 69" drivers.

Along with the H-4 Pacifics of 1914 GN ordered 15 4-8-2s for passenger service over the mountains — P-1s 1750-1764. They were based on the O-1 Mikados of 1911 and had 63" drivers. They proved too slow for passenger trains and GN assigned them to freight service. In 1928

Many consider the P-2 Mountain types, built by Baldwin in 1923, to be GN's best looking and best locomotives. Photo by H. W. Pontin.

they were rebuilt into Q-2 class 2-10-2s (the only 4-8-2s rebuilt to another wheel arrangement; Illinois Central and St. Louis-San Francisco rebuilt 2-10-2s into 4-8-2s) and were much more successful than they had been as 4-8-2s.

In 1923 Baldwin delivered 28 Mountains in the P-2 class, numbers 2500-2527, which were as successful at hauling passenger trains as the P-1s weren't. They had 73" drivers and 29" × 28" cylinders and could exert a tractive force of 54,823 pounds (later 57,580 pounds; 69,780 with booster). Their over-square cylinders (diameter greater than stroke) were unusual; yet more unusual for Great Northern was the conventional radial-stay firebox.

GN purchased its first Northerns in 1929, six fairly conservative Baldwins with Belpaire fireboxes and 73" drivers. They weighed 472,000 pounds and exerted a tractive effort of 68,500 pounds. The S-1s were purchased for passenger service but were soon assigned to freight.

They were followed in 1930 by 14 passenger 4-8-4s, class S-2, also from Baldwin. They were 50,000 pounds lighter and produced 10,000 pounds less tractive effort. They were the first 4-8-4s with 80" drivers, and like GN's second group of 4-8-2s they had radial-stay fireboxes.

Switchers

GN worked its yards with a group of 0-6-0s built from about 1880 to 1917. In 1918 Baldwin delivered 40 eight-wheel switchers that were larger than the USRA 0-8-0. The C-1 class, numbers 810-849, were GN's top-rank switchers, and they outlasted successive classes of 0-8-0s, which were created by removing the lead trucks from 2-8-0s.

Historical and technical society: Great Northern Railway Historical Society, c/o Connie L. Hoffman, 1781 Griffith, Berkley, MI 48072
Recommended reading:
Locomotives of the Empire Builder, by Charles F. Martin, published in 1972 by Normandie House, Chicago

The Great Northern Railway, by Charles and Dorothy Wood, published in 1979 by Pacific Fast Mail, Edmonds, WA (LCC 77-91780)

Published rosters: Railroad Magazine: August 1935, page 88; January 1949, page 82; February 1957, page 34

STEAM LOCOMOTIVES BUILT SINCE 1900

Type	Class	Numbers	Qty	Builder	Built	Notes
0-6-0	A-8	70-72	3	Rogers	1900	
0-6-0	A-9	380-399	20	Baldwin	1912	
0-6-0	A-9	1...94	56	GN, BLW, Rog	1903-1912	
0-6-0	A-10	95-99	5	Brooks	1898-1900	
0-6-0	A-11	30, 31	2	Lima	1917	
0-8-0	C-1	810-849	40	BLW	1918	
0-8-0	C-2	850-869	20	Brooks	1901	Rebuilt from 2-8-0
0-8-0	C-3	875-899	25	Brooks	1903	Rebuilt from 2-8-0
0-8-0	C-4	780-786	7	BLW, Rogers	1902-1907	Rebuilt from 2-8-0
0-8-0	C-5	870-873	4	Rogers	1901	Rebuilt from 2-8-0
2-6-2	J-1	1500-1549	50	Baldwin	1906	
2-6-2	J-2	1550-1649	100	Baldwin	1907	
2-8-0	F-5	1095-1109	15	Rogers	1901	
2-8-0	F-6		20	Brooks	1901	To 0-8-0 850-869
2-8-0	F-7	1134-1139	6	Cooke	1901	
2-8-0	F-8	1140-1253	114	Rogers, Baldwin	1901-1905	
2-8-0	F-9		24	Brooks	1903	To 0-8-0 875-898
2-8-0	F-12	1326, 1327	2	Alco	1907	
2-8-2	O-1	3000-3144	145	Baldwin	1911-1918	
2-8-2	O-2	3149	1	Alco	1915	
2-8-2	O-3	3200-3208	9	Alco	1919-1920	USRA
2-8-2	O-4	3210-3254	45	Baldwin	1920	
2-8-2	O-5	3300-3344	45	GN	1922-1925	Rebuilt from 2-6-6-2
2-8-2	O-6	3350-3371	22	GN	1925-1926	Rebuilt from 2-6-6-2

Type	Class	Numbers	Qty	Builder	Built	Notes
2-8-2	O-7	3375-3396	22	GN	1929-1931	Rebuilt from 2-6-6-0
2-8-2	O-8	3397-3399	3	GN	1932	
2-10-2	Q-1	2100-2129	30	Baldwin	1923	
2-10-2	Q-2	2175-2189	15	GN	1928	Rebuilt from 4-8-2
2-6-6-2	L-1	1800-1804	5	Baldwin	1906	Renumbered 1900-1904
2-6-6-2	L-1	1905-1924	20	Baldwin	1908	
2-6-6-2	L-2	1800-1844	45	Baldwin	1907-1908	
2-6-8-0	M-1	1950-1984	35	Baldwin	1910	
2-8-8-0	N-1	2000-2024	25	Baldwin	1912	
2-8-8-2	R-1	2030-2043	14	Baldwin, GN	1925-1928	
2-8-8-2	R-2	2044-2059	16	GN	1929-1930	
4-6-6-4	Z-6	4000, 4001	2	Alco	1937	SP&S 903, 904
4-4-2	K-1	1700-1709	10	Baldwin	1906	
4-6-0	E-2	910, 911	2	Alco	1915	
4-6-0	E-6	925-939	15	Rogers	1902	
4-6-0	E-8	1053-1072	20	Rogers	1901-1903	
4-6-0	E-14	1010-1054	45	Baldwin	1909	
4-6-0	E-15	1078-1090	13	Baldwin	1910	
4-6-2	H-1	1400-1405	6	Rogers	1905	
4-6-2	H-2	1440	1	Baldwin	1907	
4-6-2	H-3	1406-1439	34	Baldwin	1906-1907	Former H-2 class
4-6-2	H-4	1441-1460	20	Baldwin	1909	
4-6-2	H-4	1461-1485	25	Lima	1914	
4-6-2	H-5	1350-1374	25	GN	1921-1927	Rebuilt from 4-6-0
4-6-2	H-6	1710-1724	15	GN	1923	Rebuilt from 2-6-2
4-6-2	H-7	1375-1384	10	GN	1926-1927	Rebuilt from 4-6-0
4-8-0	G-3	720-769	50	Rogers	1899-1900	
4-8-0	G-4	770-779	10	Brooks	1900	
4-8-2	P-1	1750-1764	15	Lima	1914	Rebuilt to 2-10-2
4-8-2	P-2	2500-2527	28	Baldwin	1923	
4-8-4	S-1	2550-2555	6	Baldwin	1929	
4-8-4	S-2	2575-2588	14	Baldwin	1930	

GREEN BAY & WESTERN RAILROAD

By John Gruber

In 1900 the Green Bay & Western operated 262 miles of road from Green Bay, Wisconsin, west to Winona, Minnesota, on the Mississippi River, and (through subsidiary Kewaunee, Green Bay & Western) from Green Bay east to Kewaunee on Lake Michigan in 1900. It was affiliated with the Lackawanna Coal & Iron Co. and the Delaware, Lackawanna & Western Railroad and was part of the Lackawanna's plan for a western extension to Omaha and Sioux City.

Railroad car ferry service, inaugurated at Kewaunee in 1892, was boosted during World War I to avoid the congestion of Chicago. From 1925 to the 1970s Ford auto parts provided significant traffic. Lake Michigan ferry service declined sharply in 1982 and ended in 1990. Lumber, grain, and coal were the principal commodities for years; paper and paper products are GB&W's livelihood today.

GB&W's traffic level and light rail and bridges combined to keep its motive power about 20 years behind that of larger railroads. The last 2-6-0 was delivered in 1924, a year after GB&W bought its first 2-8-0; Mikados arrived about 35 years after the type first appeared as a wide-firebox road locomotive. Passenger service was unimportant, because GB&W ran crosswise to the principal traffic flow. Even though mixed trains replaced passenger trains in 1935, drawings exist of a proposed streamlined Atlantic resembling Milwaukee Road's *Hiawatha* engines. It would have been ideal for a two-car streamliner connecting Green Bay and Wisconsin Rapids with the *Hiawatha* at Winona, Burlington's *Zephyr* at East Winona, and Chicago & North Western's *400* at Merrilan.

GB&W's roster is complicated by the assignment of locomotives to subsidiaries Ahnapee & Western and Kewaunee, Green Bay & Western; a renumbering in the mid-1930s; and two classification systems established by motive power superintendents in the early 1920s and the mid-1930s (the later one is used here). A GB&W tradition began with the first Mogul in 1907. Thereafter all new locomotives, steam and diesel, came from Alco.

Green Bay & Western's Moguls were light engines, weighing about 140,000 pounds. Number 56 (later 256) was the last, built by Alco's Schenectady Works in 1924. Superheater, piston valves, and Walschaerts valve gear were state of the art, but the narrow firebox between the drivers and the wheel arrangement itself were long since passé. Alco photo.

The Mikados were modern, well-designed locomotives, with Boxpok drivers, cast trailing trucks, and welded tenders. They were delivered with green-and-white striping on the running boards. Photo by Robert A. LeMassena.

GB&W entered the 20th century with a stable of 4-4-0s, which continued to pull its passenger trains until the advent of heavier mixed trains in 1935; the last 4-4-0 was scrapped in 1941.

Seventeen new Moguls, purchased from 1907 to 1924, came with 19" × 26" cylinders and 56" drivers, becoming heavier through the years. Number 27, the first, weighed 128,000 pounds; No. 56, the last, 141,000 pounds. GB&W added technological improvements such as superheaters, piston valves, and Walschaert valve gear to its locomotive orders beginning in late 1914. Its shops applied Nicholson Thermic Siphons to seven 2-6-0s between 1925 and 1927.

Of the seven Consolidations purchased between 1923 and 1929, three were secondhand. The two 1923 locomotives had 22" × 28" cylinders, 51" drivers, and, at 199,000 lbs, were heavy for the road. The ex-Chicago, Peoria & St. Louis locomotives joined the roster in 1927; they had 20" × 26" cylinders, 55" drivers, and weighed 170,000 pounds.

The two Consolidations of 1929, lighter than earlier Consolidations, were well suited to moving freight across Wisconsin on GB&W's 70-pound rail. They had 21" × 28" cylinders, 55" drivers, Baker valve gear, carried 200 pounds boiler pressure, and weighed 174,000 pounds GB&W's first-line road power until 1937, they served on secondary runs after the Mikados arrived and were the last steam locomotives to operate on the GB&W. Number 350 (formerly 49) is preserved at Mid-Continent Railway Historical Society in North Freedom, Wisconsin.

Heavier rail and bridges made possible the Mikados in 1937 and 1939, but even then, their specifications were determined by weight restrictions. They had 22" × 30" cylinders and 64" driving wheels, and carried 245 pounds boiler pressure. At 282,000 pounds and 285,000 pounds, the locomotives were the lightest "important" Mikados built between 1930 and 1943. Statistics kept by the railroad showed that from February 1937 to October 1939, No. 401, for example, ran 134,152 miles, using a ton of coal each 16.55 miles. The railroad was an early diesel user, purchasing its first switcher in 1938 and ending steam service in 1950.

GB&W switchers were 0-6-0s; five were secondhand, purchased from 1923 to 1925 during a post-World War I traffic boom. The two exceptions came from American in 1912 and 1921. Number 92, purchased secondhand from the Chicago & Alton in 1933 as an 0-6-0, was restored to its original 2-6-0 wheel arrangement in 1935 and renumbered 261. Two pre-1900 0-4-0s and an 0-6-0 remained in service until the 1920s.

Recommended reading:

Green Bay & Western, the First 111 Years, by Stan Mailer, published in 1989 by Hundman Publishing, Inc., 5115 Monticello Dr., Edmonds, WA 98020.

The Story of the Green Bay & Western, by Ray and Ellen Specht, published in 1966 as Bulletin 115 of the Railway & Locomotive Historical Society.

Published rosters:

Railroad Magazine, June 1942, page 152

Railway & Locomotive Historical Society Bulletin, No. 115, pages 70-73

GB&W STEAM LOCOMOTIVES BUILT SINCE 1900

Type	Class	Post-1937 Numbers	Pre-1935 Numbers	Qty	Builder	Built	Retired	Notes
0-6-0	A-28	140	40	1	Schenectady	1912	1945	
0-6-0	A-31	141-144	41, 42, 90, 91	4	Brooks	1905	1941	Ex-NYC
0-6-0	A-28	145	60	1	Alco	1921	1948	
0-6-0	A-28	146	80	1	Schenectady	1900	1941	Ex-NYC
0-6-0			92	1	Baldwin	1899	To 2-6-0 261	
			Built as 2-6-0, purchased from Chicago & Alton as 0-6-0					
2-6-0			27-30, 36-37	6	Schenectady	1907-1912	1936	
2-6-0	B-25	250-256	50-56	7	Schen, Pitt	1913-1924	1939-1948	250, 252, 253 were B-27
2-6-0	B-25	257, 258	38, 39	1	Schenectady	1914, 1921	1945	
2-6-0	B-27	259, 260	71, 72	2	Schenectady	1915, 1921	1947	
2-6-0	B-35	261		1	Baldwin	1899	1943	Ex-0-6-0 92
2-8-0	C-31	301-303	44, 64, 74	3	Schenectady	1913	1939	Ex-CP&StL
2-8-0	C-38	350, 351	49, 69	2	Schenectady	1929	1950	
2-8-0	C-43	398, 399	45, 65	2	Brooks	1923	1948, 1949	
2-8-2	D-47	401-406		6	Alco	1937, 1939	1952	

GULF, MOBILE & NORTHERN RAILROAD

The Gulf, Mobile & Northern was formed at the beginning of 1917 by reorganizing the New Orleans, Mobile & Chicago — and that was a 1909 reorganization of the Mobile, Jackson & Kansas City Railroad. The original purpose of the MJ&KC was to tap the pine woods of southern Mississippi, and the GM&N was still relatively lightweight railroading. The new company's first order of business was to extend its main line 40 miles north to Jackson, Tennessee, to connect with northern railroads. By 1920 the road consisted of a 408-mile main line from Mobile, Alabama, to Jackson, and three branches totaling 57 miles.

GM&N's roundhouses contained 4-4-0s and 4-6-0s from the MJ&KC, plus four Pacifics and eight Mikados built in 1912 during the brief period when the Louisville & Nashville and the Frisco jointly controlled the NOM&C. The Pacifics and the Mikes were light engines, weighing 198,000 and 196,000 pounds respectively (the USRA light Pacific weighed 277,000 pounds; the light Mikado, 290,000 pounds).

In 1940 the road was consolidated with the new Gulf, Mobile & Ohio Railroad. GM&O purchased no new steam locomotives during World War Two. In 1947 GM&O merged the Alton Railroad and moved quickly to dieselize all its operations. GM&O's last revenue steam run occurred on October 7, 1949.

Freight locomotives

GM&N's extension to Jackson called for more locomotives and more powerful ones for the increased traffic, but while the USRA controlled the railroads during World War I the road could do little more than plan. Soon after the war Baldwin delivered four 2-8-2s practically identical to those already on the roster, with 57" drivers, 22" × 28" cylinders, and 40,418 pounds tractive effort.

GM&N acquired ten Russian Decapods. They were lighter than the Mikes, but carried more weight on their drivers. They had a tractive effort of 51,500 pounds, 27 percent greater than the 2-8-2s.

In 1922 GM&N made preferential traffic agreements with the Burlington, and to connect with CB&Q it acquired 145 miles of trackage rights over the Nashville, Chattanooga & St. Louis from Jackson to Paducah, Kentucky. More locomotives were necessary, so GM&N bought five 2-10-0s of a standard Baldwin design. They had 57" drivers, which made

Gulf, Mobile & Ohio 261, photographed in 1941, shows off more than a decade of modifications to the original design, among them a Coffin feedwater heater mounted on the front of the smokebox, a second sand dome, and a large single-phase air pump replacing one of the original pair. Photo by Bernard Corbin.

Gulf, Mobile & Northern Decapod 251, built in 1923, illustrates GM&N's standard freight locomotive as built, clean and relatively uncluttered. Baldwin photo; collection of H. L. Broadbelt.

them faster than the Russian Decapods. By 1927 GM&N had 16 such 2-10-0s. GM&N's only switchers were eight 0-6-0s purchased in 1927 and 1928 from Indiana Harbor Belt.

Passenger locomotives

Passenger service wasn't a major consideration, so in 1921 GM&N sold its four Pacifics to Louisville & Nashville — and in 1924 acquired two Atlantics from the Buffalo, Rochester & Pittsburgh. In 1928 GM&N bought two Pacifics similar those it had sold — 69" drivers, 22" × 28" cylinders, 213,000 pounds. One of them, No. 425, still operates on the Blue Mountain & Reading, a tourist railroad at Temple, Pennsylvania.

New Orleans Great Northern locomotives

At the end of 1929 GM&N acquired control of the New Orleans Great Northern, whose line ran from New Orleans to Jackson, Mississippi. NOGN's roundhouses held two 0-6-0s, a 4-4-0, 12 Ten-Wheelers, three Russian Decapods, and three 4-8-2s built by Richmond in 1927.

The area around New Orleans is characterized by swampy, spongy ground and bayous and inlets requiring bridges and trestles, all of which restrict axle loads. NOGN needed something larger and faster than the typical small Mikado, and instead of a large Mikado it chose a small, light Mountain, with a four-wheel lead truck not for speed (the engines had 63" drivers) but for spreading the weight. The 4-8-2s weighed 273,000 pounds and were the second lightest of that type built

for service in North America. (Alaska's 4-8-2s were half a ton lighter, and Tennessee Central's were a ton heavier.) The main rods drove on the third axle instead of the second, a trait common to low-drivered Mountains. Tractive effort was a modest 45,700 pounds. The 4-8-2s were sold in 1947 to the Georgia & Florida by GM&N successor Gulf, Mobile & Ohio.

Historical and technical society: Gulf, Mobile & Ohio Historical Society, P. O. Box 463, Fairfield, IL 62837.

Published rosters:
Railroad Magazine, May 1934, page 136.
Railroad History, No. 158, page 125

GM&N STEAM LOCOMOTIVES BUILT SINCE 1900

Type	Numbers	Qty	Builder	Built	Notes
6-0	10, 11	2	Brooks	1909	Ex-NOGN 13, 11
0-6-0	12-19	8	Brooks, Cooke	1905-1906	Ex-Indiana Harbor Belt
0-6-0	60-63	4	Brooks	1900-1903	Ex-Hocking Valley
2-8-2	101-108	8	Baldwin	1912	Ex-NOM&C; 101-104 to TA&G
2-8-2	109-112	4	Baldwin	1920	
2-10-0	90-92	3	Rich, BLW	1918	Ex-NOGN; 92 to Gainesville Midland
2-10-0	201-210	10	Baldwin	1918	Received 1920-1921; 2 to AT&N
2-10-0	250-265	16	Baldwin	1923-1927	
4-4-0	30-37	8	BLW, Rogers	1900-1907	Ex-NOM&C
4-4-0	102	1	Baldwin	1907	Ex-NOGN 102
4-4-2	40, 41	2		1935	Ex-BR&P, purchased 1921
4-6-0	10, 12	2	Baldwin	1907	Ex-NOM&C
4-6-0	11	1	Baldwin	1907	Ex-Brinson, purchased 1917
4-6-0	52-60	9	BLW, Brooks	1906-1910	Ex-NOGN 52-60
4-6-0	70-72	3	Rich, Schen	1912, 1914	Ex-NOGN 70-72
4-6-0	70-88	19	BLW, Rogers	1903-1908	Ex-NOM&C
4-6-2	40-43	4	Baldwin	1912	Sold to Louisville & Nashville 1921
4-6-2	425, 426	2	Baldwin	1928	
4-8-2	400-402	3	Richmond	1927	Ex-NOGN 200-202; sold to G&F

The peak of New Orleans Great Northern locomotive development was a trio of light 4-8-2s. Gulf, Mobile & Northern 400, originally NOGN 200, is shown at Bogalusa, Louisiana, in 1940, with a temporary stack for the photograph. Photo by John B. Allen.

HIGH-PRESSURE BOILERS AND WATERTUBE FIREBOXES

Until the 1920s the standard boiler pressure was 200 pounds. Saturated steam at that pressure contained about as much water as could be tolerated in the cylinders. As steam locomotives grew even larger, clearances imposed limits on cylinder diameter, and cylinder volume was limited by the amount of steam that could pass through the valves. Increasing boiler pressure offered advantages. For the same force on the piston, the diameter of the cylinder could be less; a smaller volume of steam at higher pressure could pass through the valves more easily. However, increasing the pressure created several problems: more water in the steam; foaming or priming due to minerals dissolved in the water; and rust because more oxygen remained dissolved in the water.

Water treatment, which prevented foaming, permitted an increase in boiler pressure. Lima's 2-8-4 of 1924 carried 240 pounds in combination with limited cutoff — the valves cut off steam supply to the cylinders at some point short of the full piston stroke to take advantage of the expansion of the steam. By the late 1920s most locomotives were designed to work at 250 pounds, and in the late 1930s a number were built to carry 300 pounds.

Another problem of increased pressure was structural. The thickness of the boiler shell depended on the diameter of the boiler and the pressure carried in it; pressures of up to 500 pounds per square inch were feasible without requiring excessively heavy construction. The structural problem was much greater at the firebox. The pressure limit for a staybolted firebox of either conventional shape or Belpaire design was about 300 pounds. Pressures above that called for a water-tube firebox.

The conventional firebox depended for its shape and position on thousands of staybolts that passed through the water space between the firebox wall and the outer shell of the boiler. The staybolts bore the brunt of thermal expansion and contraction and were a source of problems; the watertube firebox was one of several attempts to elimi-

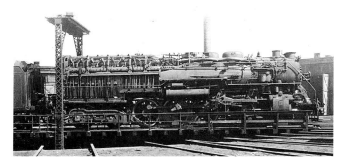

New York Central 800, photographed without its boiler jacket in 1938, illustrates the complexity of its multipressure workings. Photo by Paul T. Roberts.

nate them. It consisted of one or more longitudinal drums at the top of the firebox and longitudinal tubes or headers at the bottom, all connected to the main part of the boiler; and vertical tubes that formed the sidewalls of the firebox connecting the tubes at the bottom with the drums at the top. Watertube fireboxes are common in ships and stationary power plants, where they are in stable environments and work at steady loads. In railroad service they presented problems of maintenance accessibility, insulation, and susceptibility to vibration. The difficulties of the conventional staybolted firebox were easier to solve — or at least easier to fix, and watertube fireboxes were strictly experimental in North America.

A number of experimental locomotives were built with watertube fireboxes and high-pressure boilers. Baltimore & Ohio had the most; below the fireboxes and boilers they were conventional single-expansion engines. B&O's early experimentals worked at ordinary pressures, the later ones at 350 pounds. Delaware & Hudson had four watertube-firebox, high-pressure experimentals: three cross-compound 2-8-0s of 350,

Baldwin's experimental three-cylinder compound 4-10-2 of 1926 had a water-tube firebox that eliminated the maintenance problems of staybolts but brought problems of its own. Baldwin photo.

400, and 500 pounds pressure, and a final triple-expansion 4-8-0 of 500 pounds. They extracted the maximum energy from their fuel and were enormously powerful but spent most of their time in the shops.

In 1929 New York Central ordered and in 1931 Alco delivered a high-pressure, three-cylinder compound 4-8-4, No. 800. Superimposed on a relatively conventional boiler that carried 250 pounds of pressure was a drum that carried 850 pounds; it was heated by a closed-circuit system of water tubes at 1300 pounds. The center cylinder, which measured $13\frac{1}{4}'' \times 30''$, worked at 850 pounds; the two outside cylinders were fed a mixture of exhaust from the center cylinder and 250-pound steam from main part of the boiler. Crews were uneasy about the figures on the pressure gauge and the tendency of the water-level gauge to fluctuate wildly, and the boiler of No. 800 was prone to leak. The engine was scrapped in 1939.

In 1931 Canadian Pacific built a 2-10-4 on the same principles with even higher pressure, 1600 pounds, in the closed system. It was a bi-pressure simple locomotive, not a compound. Its career paralleled that of NYC 800.

ILLINOIS CENTRAL RAILROAD

by John S. Ingles

By 1900 Illinois Central's principal route extended 917 miles from Chicago to New Orleans, much of it double track, and most of it paralleled by one or more secondary lines. Another main line reached west from Chicago to Omaha, Nebraska, Sioux Falls, South Dakota, and Albert Lea, Minnesota. Major branches reached St. Louis, Missouri, Evansville, Indiana, and Shreveport, Louisiana. Expansion right after the turn of the century brought IC rails to Indianapolis, Ind., and Birmingham, Alabama.

By the mid-1880s Edward H. Harriman was on IC's board of directors and vice-president of the road. He began to assemble a system of railroads which soon after the turn of the century included Union Pacif-ic, Southern Pacific, Chicago & Alton, Central of Georgia, and Erie, with Illinois Central connecting them all. Harriman established common standards for locomotives, cars, structures, and signals.

The development of IC steam power was fairly ordinary until the mid-1930s, when the road undertook a massive rebuilding program that yielded locomotives tailored for specific jobs. The products of that program kept Illinois Central in steam longer than most roads — by 1945 most of IC's locomotives had been rebuilt and were essentially less than 10 years old. Other factors favoring steam were the absence of major grades, and a plentiful supply of coal in southern Illinois.

IC experimented early with diesels and dieselized switching early, particularly along Chicago's lakefront, where smoke was a consideration. (It was for the same reason that IC electrified its Chicago suburban service.) In the early 1950s diesels began to arrive from Electro-Motive, several dozen each year. They went to work, replacing steam little by little, as IC worked off its investment in the rebuilding program. By 1956 steam had disappeared from the main lines. At the end of 1960 IC had 219 steam locomotives on its roster; a year later none. However, a steam locomotive was refurbished at IC's shops at Markham Yard in Chicago in 1962 — New York Central 4-4-0 No. 999, for display at Chicago's Museum of Science & Industry.

Freight locomotives

During the early days freight was handled by 4-4-0s with small driving wheels. The 2-6-0 appeared on IC in the 1870s, and IC continued to purchase the type through 1902, when the road turned to 2-8-0s for mainline freight service.

IC's first 2-8-2s were delivered by Baldwin in May 1911. By November 1912 there were 150 in service, numbered 1551-1700. They were standard Harriman-design Mikados, with $63\frac{1}{2}$" drivers and 27" × 30" cylinders; they weighed about 283,000 pounds and had a tractive force of 54,158 pounds. Fifty more 2-8-2s of the same design came from Baldwin in May 1914. Lima built 97 between March 1915 and February 1916, and delivered another 50 in September and October 1918. In 1923 Lima, Baldwin, and Schenectady furnished yet another 125 Mikes, still of the Harriman design, for a grand total of 507 numbered from 1501 to 2017.

IC's first 2-10-2, No. 2901, was delivered by Lima in February 1921, the first of an order of 68. They rolled on drivers an inch bigger than the Mikes — $64\frac{1}{2}$" — and had 30" × 32" cylinders. Weight was 382,000 pounds, just a ton more than the USRA heavy 2-10-2, and tractive effort was slightly less. IC dubbed them the Central type, and in December 1922 and January 1923 57 more arrived from Lima.

IC tested Lima's Super Power 2-8-4 in 1926. It was impressed enough to order 50 duplicates that year, numbers 7000-7049, then buy Lima's original and add it to the series as No. 7050. After a few years of experience with the 2-8-4s IC discovered some drawbacks. The 2-8-4s rode

Illinois Central had 507 Mikados like No. 1996 (Baldwin, 1923). The smokebox front is pure Illinois Central in appearance, but the shape of the cab and tender reveal Harriman influence. Photo by C. W. Witbeck.

poorly above 40 mph, sometimes so roughly that the reverse gear wheel would suddenly spin into full forward gear. When that happened the throttle had to be closed at once and the valve gear returned to the proper position — and several engineers broke an arm doing so. The trailing truck, through which pulling and pushing forces were transmitted, had a tendency to derail when the locomotive was backing a heavy train. Operating costs for the 2-8-4s increased faster than normal as the fleet aged. IC rebuilt one into a singularly unsuccessful 4-6-4, and in 1939 settled for simply modifying the 2-8-4s with cylinders 1" less in diameter and boiler pressure raised from 240 to 265 pounds.

Passenger locomotives

In 1902 IC took delivery of two experimental locomotives for passenger service: No. 1000, a Baldwin 4-4-2 with 21" × 28" cylinders and 79" drivers, weighing 178,600 pounds; and No. 1001, a Rogers 2-6-2 with 20" × 28" cylinders, 75" drivers, weighing 231,070 lbs. After a year of testing the road ordered 25 Atlantics from Rogers, delivered in 1903 and 1904. They had 20" × 28" cylinders and 79" drivers, and weighed 188,000 lbs. Number 1001, the Rogers 2-6-2, was rebuilt to a 4-6-2 and traded numbers with the original Atlantic.

The first attempt at rebuilding the 2-8-4s resulted in the only Hudson designed for freight service in North America. It was too powerful for its weight. Photo by C. W. Witbeck.

Rebuilding altered the appearance of IC's 2-8-4s; removing the Elesco feed-water heater made most of the difference. IC 8049 appears in its original form on page 284 as Lima 1.

With the advent of steel passenger cars train weights increased. Larger, more powerful engines were needed. IC ordered five 4-6-2s in November 1905 from Alco's Schenectady Works, followed by 13 more over the next two years. Numbered 1031-1048, they had 75½" drivers and 25" × 26" cylinders; at 249,000 pounds they were relatively light Pacifics. In September 1907 IC ordered five Harriman Common Standard design 4-6-2s, numbers 1049-1053, from Baldwin. They were about 8,000 pounds lighter than the Schenectady Pacifics, with 24" × 28" cylinders, 77½" drivers, 190 pound boiler pressure, and tractive effort of 42,453 pounds. The next nine years brought another 150 Pacifics from Alco's Brooks, Richmond, and Schenectady plants. Engines 1054-1138 had the same dimension as the first Schenectady 4-6-2s; 1139-1203 had 26" × 28" cylinders and weighed 278,000 pounds, about the same as a USRA light Pacific.

Longer, heavier passenger trains required yet larger engines. Alco's Schenectady Works delivered 14 4-8-2s in October 1923. They were followed in December 1924 and January 1925 by 25 from Lima, and in 1926 by 20 from Schenectady, for a total of 60 Mountains. They weighed

10,000-15,000 pounds more than a USRA heavy Mountain; the combination of "square" 28" × 28" cylinders and 73½" drivers gave them about the same tractive effort as the 69"-drivered USRA 4-8-2. Because of weight limitations on the Ohio River Bridge at Cairo, Ill., they had short tenders carrying 10,000 gallons of water and 18 tons of coal. The Mountains also proved useful for for fast freight trains.

Rebuilt locomotives

Illinois Central purchased its last steam engines from outside builders in 1929 (0-8-0s 3555-3569, from Lima) but motive power development did not stop there. The road's progression through the locomotive types had been ordinary — 2-8-2, 2-10-2, and 2-8-4 for freight; 4-6-2 and 4-8-2 for passenger; 0-6-0 and 0-8-0 for switching. The upgrading and rebuilding program undertaken between 1935 and 1945 changed that, bringing new wheel arrangements to the road and new duties to old ones. The program was sparked in part by a need to speed up IC freight trains. The 2-10-2s and 2-8-4s were comparatively new, but slow. Rebuilding was carried out both at IC's principal shops at Paducah, Kentucky, and at roundhouses all over the system. Moguls became

0-6-0s, Mikados became 0-8-0s and 0-8-2s; and Centrals (2-10-2s) became 2-8-2s, 2-10-0s, 0-10-0s, and 4-8-2s. In total, 434 engines were rebuilt. Many were renumbered, often not in sequence or into a new series that overlapped the old one. Some entire classes of locomotives were rebuilt; other classes were split — some rebuilt, some not.

The program began tentatively. In 1934 and 1935 a few Mikados, Pacifics, and Mountains received one-piece cast cylinders and BK stokers. Then in June 1935 the four newest 4-6-2s, Nos. 1200-1203, were modernized while undergoing Class 3 repairs at Paducah. They received BK stokers and large tenders, and were renumbered 1135-1138 in July 1937. In fall and winter 1935 a few more big 4-6-2s had BK stokers applied. In April 1936 the modernization program began in earnest. Heavy 4-6-2s (the 1139-1203 group) undergoing Class 3 repairs received BK stokers and extended tenders for greater water capacity, and a few had boiler pressure increased.

The first 2-8-2 to be modernized was No. 1919. During Class 3 repairs at Paducah Shops in May 1936 it was fitted with a BK stoker and large tender. A few Mikes were given one-piece cast cylinders between 1934 and 1937; after March 1937 all 2-8-2s in for Class 3 repairs received BK stokers and extended tenders and had boiler pressure raised from 175 to 225 pounds.

IC next pondered its rough-riding 2-8-4s and considered the requirements of its merchandise traffic — short, fast trains that carried less-than-carload-lot freight between major cities on overnight schedules. Between Chicago and Memphis it had tried Mikados (too slow), Pacifics (not powerful enough), and Mountains (too much engine for the trains). The road needed something between a 4-6-2 and a 4-8-2 and decided to build a 4-6-4 for freight service (a 4-7-2 was out of the question). IC started with the boiler of 2-8-4 No. 7038, used $73\frac{1}{2}$" drivers, and kept the Berkshire-size cylinders (27" × 30" or $27\frac{1}{2}$" × 30" — the authorities differ). The resulting homebuilt Hudson had a tractive effort of 68,360 pounds, almost as much as the 2-8-4 and far too much for its weight on drivers, making No. 1 extremely slippery. IC made several unsuccessful attempts to solve the problem by shifting more weight to the

The 2600-class engines were IC's finest 4-8-2s. They were built by the road's shops at Paducah, Kentucky, in 1942 and 1943. The web-spoke drivers were uncommon; the absence of an air tank under the running board is accounted for by a reservoir cast integral with the frame.

drivers. In September 1937 No. 1 was taken to Decatur and tested extensively with the University of Illinois dynamometer car. No report was released, but it's safe to assume that the tests proved the design was a failure. Number 1 was modified for passenger service in 1945 (primarily by reducing cylinder diameter by 3") and renumbered 2499. The rest of the 2-8-4s were rebuilt in kind.

In 1936 a few 2400-class 4-8-2s were equipped with one-piece cast-steel cylinders. During winter 1937 plans were drawn and materials were ordered for a 4-8-2 with a strengthened 2900-class 2-10-2 boiler, built on a one-piece cast engine bed with cylinders and air reservoir cast integral. The 4-8-2, No. 2500, was completed in March 1937 and proved to be a good engine. In June 1937 engines 2501 and 2502 were completed and were followed almost every month by one or more 4-8-2s until September 1942, when a total of 55 were in service. These were followed by the 2600-class 4-8-2s, construction of which started in November 1942. They differed from the 2500s in that they were built from scratch; their boilers were the first made at Paducah. Twenty engines, 2600-2619, were built between November 1942 and August 1943. The new and rebuilt 4-8-2s became IC's top-rank road power and effected a major acceleration of the road's freight service — even coal trains moved faster behind 4-8-2s than they had behind 2-10-2s.

The rebuilding program included locomotives for all classes of service: switching, transfer, local freight. The use of boilers from 2901-class locomotives for 4-8-2s left numerous sets of frames, wheels, and cylinders for 2-10-2s available. Some of the frames were shortened to create 2-8-2s, and others became 2-10-0s, both types using boilers from Mikados. The 2-8-2 cylinders were given to 2-8-0s, which then became 0-8-0s. At times it seemed that every component that went into the rebuilding program was used in one form or another.

Switchers

IC's switchers were nothing unusual — 0-6-0s and 0-8-0s — until the rebuilding program, which provided new wheel arrangements. The roster had included two 0-10-0s, former Alabama & Vicksburg engines (IC subsidiary Yazoo & Mississippi Valley had leased A&V and Vicksburg, Shreveport & Pacific since 1926), and five more were rebuilt from A&V 2-10-2s 470-474. Parts left over from building 4-8-2s were combined to make 0-8-2s and 2-10-0s for transfer and hump service.

Oddities

Probably the oddest locomotives produced by IC's rebuilding program were 11 Atlantics rebuilt for local freight service. They traded their 80" drivers for 63½", and boiler pressure was increased 40 pounds, to 225, for greater tractive effort. Nearly 70 light Pacifics were fitted with 61" drivers, also for light freight duty.

The ten 2-6-6-2s on the roster were acquired in 1926 from then-subsidiary Central of Georgia in exchange for ten 2-10-2s. The Mallets spent most of their lives at IC's hump yard in Memphis.

Historical and technical society: Illinois Central Historical Society, c/o Jim Kubajak, 14818 Clifton Park, Midlothian, IL 60445

Published rosters:

Railroad Magazine: December 1936, page 116, and January 1937, page 82; May 1951, page 118, and June 1951, page 104; February 1958, page 75

Trains Magazine: October 1948, page 23

Paducah Shops was the road's principal rebuilding facility. Locomotives entered the erecting hall at one end and were carried sideways by a crane to the pit track where all the work was done. IC photos.

IC STEAM LOCOMOTIVES BUILT SINCE 1900

Type	Numbers (rebuilt)	Numbers (original)	Qty	Builder	Built	Notes
0-6-0		65-196		Brks, Rog, BLW	1898-1905	
0-6-0		201-209	9	Brooks	1906-1907	
0-6-0		210-341	132	Alco	1912-1918	
0-6-0		350-360		Brooks, Pitt	1900, 1901	Ex-541-598 class, truck removed
0-6-0	380-383	3330-3336	7	Baldwin	1901-1911	Ex-A&V and VS&P
0-6-0		3350	1	Baldwin	1911	Ex-A&V or VS&P
0-8-0		801, 802	4	Baldwin	1926	Chicago & Illinois Western
0-8-0		803, 804	4	Lima	1929	Chicago & Illinois Western
0-8-0	3300-3330		31	IC		From 651-785 series 2-8-0s
0-8-0	3400-3413		14	IC		From 941-993 series 2-8-0
0-8-0	3487-3499		11			From 3960-3972 series 2-8-2
0-8-0	3500-3554	3500-3554	55	Baldwin	1921-1927	
0-8-0	3555-3569	3555-3569	15	Lima	1929	
0-8-0		3570				
0-8-2	3650-3699		50	IC		Ex-1501-1550
0-10-0	3600, 3601	3400, 3401	2	Baldwin	1911	Ex-A&V 430, 431
0-10-0	3602-3606		5	IC		Ex 2-10-2 3100-3104, trucks removed (formerly A&V 470-474)
2-6-0	3701-3756	541-598	57	Rog, Pitt, Brks, BLW	1901-1902	
2-8-0	790-793	641-644	4	Cooke	1903	Ex-CJRR
2-8-0	700-740	651-730	80	Rog., Schen, Brks	1902-1903	
2-8-0	741-769	731-785	55	Rogers	1904	
2-8-0	850-855	794-883		Brooks	1904-1907	
2-8-0	900-911	941-993		Baldwin	1909, 1911	
2-8-2		1501-2017	517	Lima, Schenectady, Baldwin	1911-1923	
2-8-2	2100-2140		41	IC		1501 class boiler, 2901 class cylinders and frame altered for four axles
2-8-2	2199 (2020)		1	IC		1501 class boiler, 7000 class frame
2-8-2		3795-3940		IC	1915-1923	Rebuilt from 2-8-0
2-8-2	3766-3797		32	IC		Ex-3795-3940 class
2-8-2		3960-3972	13	Baldwin	1916-1924	Ex-VS&P 361-368, A&V 460-463
2-8-2	3962, 3969		2	Baldwin		Ex VS&P 362, 367
2-8-4	8000-8048	7000-7049	50	Lima	1926	Rebuilt except 7038
2-8-4	8049	7050	1	Lima	1924	Ex-Lima No. 1
2-10-0	3610-3624		15	IC		1501 class boiler, 2901 class cylinders and frame
2-10-2	2700-2747		48	IC		Ex-2901-3025
2-10-2	2750		1	IC		Ex-2997
2-10-2	2800-2819		20	IC		Ex-2901-3025, new boiler
2-10-2		2901-3025	125	Lima	1920-1923	
2-10-2	3100-3104		5	Baldwin	1919, 1922	Ex-A&V
2-6-6-2	6000-6009		10	Richmond	1919	Ex-Central of Georgia
4-4-2	1001		1	Baldwin	1902	
4-4-2		1002-1026	25	Rogers	1903-1904	
4-4-2	2000-2008		9	IC		63 1/2" drivers
4-6-0		5060-5065	6	Baldwin	1905-1907	
4-6-2	2099	1000	1	Rogers	1902	Rebuilt from 2-6-2, later 61" drivers
4-6-2		1031-1048	18	Schenectady	1905-1907	
4-6-2		1049-1053	5	Baldwin	1909	
4-6-2		1054-1138	85	Brooks, Rich	1910-1913	
4-6-2		1139-1203	75	Brooks, Schen	1916-1920	
4-6-2	1000-1002	1300-1302	3	Baldwin	1919, 1922	Ex-VS&P 380-382
4-6-2	1130-1132	1310-1312	3	Baldwin	1924	Ex-A&V 480-482
4-6-2	2030-2097		59	IC		Ex-1027-1134; 61" drivers
4-6-2	2098		1	IC		Ex-1049, 61" drivers
4-6-2	2099		1	IC		Ex-1000, 61" drivers
4-6-4	2499	1		IC		Rebuilt from 2-8-4 No. 7038
4-8-2		2400-2414	15	Schen.	1923	
4-8-2		2415-2459	45	Lima, Schen.	1925, 1926	
4-8-2		2300-2307	8	IC		Ex-2400 class, 73 1/2" drivers
4-8-2		2350-2352	3	IC		Ex-2400 class, 70" drivers
4-8-2	2500-2555		56	IC	1937-1942	2901 class boilers
4-8-2	2600-2619		20	IC	1942-1943	

KANSAS CITY SOUTHERN RAILWAY AND LOUSIANA & ARKANSAS RAILWAY

Kansas City Southern was built between 1890 and 1897 as the Kansas City, Pittsburg & Gulf Railroad. It was the creation of one man, Arthur Stillwell, and it ran from Kansas City, Missouri, almost straight south along the Missouri-Kansas and Arkansas-Oklahoma state lines to Port Arthur, Texas. Most of the country it traversed was relatively flat, except for encounters with the Ozark Plateau in southwest Missouri and northwest Arkansas and the Ouachita Mountains between Heavener, Okla., and DeQueen, Ark.

Between 1896 and 1907 William Edenborn built a railroad between New Orleans and Shreveport, Louisiana, the Louisiana Railway & Navigation Co. In 1923 it was extended west almost to Dallas, Texas, through the purchase of a Missouri-Kansas-Texas branch. During the same years William Buchanan turned a logging railroad into the Louisiana & Arkansas Railway, with a line from Alexandria, La., north to Hope, Ark., and a branch west from Minden, La., to Shreveport. In 1928 LR&N and L&A merged as the Louisiana & Arkansas Railway, and in 1939 Kansas

City Southern purchased almost all the stock of the L&A. Operation of the railroads was unified, but the L&A maintained a separate corporate existence, as did the branch west into Texas — state laws required that railroads operating in Texas be chartered there.

KCS dieselized its principal passenger trains, starting with the *Southern Belle*, before World War II. After the war it continued dieselization and was noteworthy for purchasing a four-unit set of Fairbanks-Morse "Erie-Built" cab units for freight service — in its way a continuation of the unorthodoxy of the road's Mallets (see below). Dieselization was completed in 1953.

Freight locomotives

The most numerous class of 2-8-0s was the E-3 class, built by Pittsburgh and Baldwin between 1906 and 1908. They were delivered with short rectangular tenders, but some later received longer Vanderbilt tenders. They had 55" drivers and weighed 220,380 pounds.

The larger, more powerful E-4 class Consolidations had wide fire-

![Kansas City Southern 0-6-6-0 locomotive No. 707]

Kansas City Southern was unique in operating the 0-6-6-0 as a road engine. Number 707 trails an auxiliary water tank as it leads freight through Cedar Grove, Louisiana in 1933. Photo by C. W. Witbeck.

Cylinders the same size fore and aft are evidence that 2-8-8-0 No. 757, shown leading a freight north out of Neosho, Missouri, has been converted to a single-expansion engine. Photo by William K. Barham.

0-6-6-0 and 2-6-6-0

North America's first Mallet was Baltimore & Ohio 0-6-6-0 No. 2400. The lack of a lead truck restricted it to low-speed pusher and yard service; most subsequent articulateds had lead trucks. Most of the 32 0-6-6-0s were built for pusher service and later relegated to yard service — or were soon fitted with lead trucks, making them 2-6-6-0s. However, Kansas City Southern operated 0-6-6-0s as road freight engines for a number of years — and with genuine pilots, not footboards. Canadian Pacific's six homebuilt 0-6-6-0s deserve special mention: They were the only Mallets built in Canada; their front engines had the cylinders at the rear; and the last built was the first simple articulated in North America.

The 2-6-6-0 was one of the rarest wheel arrangements, almost a footnote to the 0-6-6-0. Nineteen were built as 2-6-6-0s; twelve others were built as 0-6-6-0s and retrofitted with lead trucks.

Most 0-6-6-0s and 2-6-6-0s were retired in the 1930s. Both types were soon superseded by 2-6-6-2s and by eight-coupled articulateds — if you opted for the complexity of an articulated, you might as well make it a big one. There were so few that all are listed below, not just the first, last, heaviest, and so on.

Type	Road	Numbers	Qty	Builder	Built	Retired	Notes
0-6-6-0	B&O	2400	1	Schenectady	1904		
0-6-6-0	D&SL	200-209	10	Schenectady	1908-1910	1947-1952	To 2-6-6-0
0-6-6-0	WM	951-959	9	Baldwin	1909-1910	-1952	Rebuilt from 2-6-6-2, 1929-1931
0-6-6-0	CP	1950-1955	6	CP	1909-1911		To 2-10-0,1916-1917
0-6-6-0	WSB	1000, 1001	2	Alco	1910	1935	

West Side Belt 1000 and 1001 converted to 2-6-6-0,1912; later became Pittsburgh & West Virginia 20 and 21; sold to Delaware & Hudson, which converted them to 0-6-6-0s and numbered them 1500 and 1501

Type	Road	Numbers	Qty	Builder	Built	Retired	Notes
0-6-6-0	KCS	700-711	12	Alco	1912	1937, 1947	
0-6-6-0	NYC	1300	1	Alco	1913		
2-6-6-0	VGN	500-503	4	Richmond	1909	1933	
2-6-6-0	VGN	510-517	8	Baldwin	1910	1933	
2-6-6-0	D&SL	210-216	7	Schenectady	1913, 1916	1949-1951	

Western Maryland's nine 0-6-6-0s were built as 2-6-6-2s in 1909 and 1910. With the arrival of large 2-10-0s, the articulateds were stripped of their lead and trailing trucks and put to work as heavy switchers. Photo by Leslie R. Ross.

Virginian 500 was the first 2-6-6-0 built. It was one of four, which were followed by eight larger 2-6-6-0s, then Virginian turned to eight- and ten-coupled power and electric locomotives. Richmond Works photo.

Pacifics like No. 808 (built by Schenectady in 1919) were KCS's most modern passenger power. The second sand dome is unusual on a passenger engine. Photo by Charles E. Winters.

The Lima 2-10-4s of 1937 (Lima's last of that wheel arrangement) were massive machines an inch short of 16 feet tall. The 42" wheel of the lead truck makes the 70" drivers look small by comparison; lead truck wheels were usually 33" in diameter. The dome casing on top of the boiler encloses two sand domes fore and aft and a steam dome between them. The external steam line along the top of the boiler was later removed. Lima photo.

boxes over the rear drivers. They were built in 1913 with 57" drivers and 24" × 30" cylinders; they weighed 254,000 pounds. Twelve were rebuilt with cast frames and 63" disk drivers; to compensate for the larger drivers, the engines were given 26" × 30" cylinders and boiler pressure was raised from 175 pounds to 200. The rebuilt 2-8-0s had a tractive effort of 54,948 pounds, an increase of about 2,000 pounds.

KCS was unconventional in the matter of freight locomotives. The 0-6-6-0s of 1912 were unorthodox — road engines without lead trucks. When KCS bought its E-4 Consolidations, most roads had turned to Mikados. When the first 2-8-8-0s were built, the 2-10-2 was current practice, and the second batch of 2-8-8-0s came along in the same year Lima introduced the 2-8-4.

The road made a major leap in 1937 when it purchased ten 2-10-4s, five oil-burners (900-904) and five coal-burners (905-909). They weighed 509,000 pounds, 14,000 more than the 2-8-8-0s. They had a tractive effort of 93,300 pounds, about three-fourths of what the 2-8-8-0s could exert, but their 70" drivers and large fireboxes (107 square feet of grate area) could provide sustained speed, which the articulateds could not.

To handle wartime traffic, KCS purchased six 2-10-2s from Wabash and four USRA light 2-10-2s from Ann Arbor in 1942. Both groups were

slow engines, but changes in side rods and counterbalancing later permitted speeds up to 40 mph.

Articulateds

In 1912 KCS purchased 12 0-6-6-0s, the largest group of that type built and the last built in any quantity. KCS used them as road engines between Pittsburg, Kan., and Westville, Okla., on a stretch of line with grades up to 1.75 percent. They had 56" drivers and burned oil. All but two were retired in 1937 when the 2-10-4s arrived.

A surge in traffic at the beginning of World War I sent KCS looking for larger locomotives. Schenectady delivered seven 2-8-8-0s in 1918. They had 57" drivers, an inch larger than their predecessors; like the 0-6-6-0s, they carried their water and fuel oil in short Vanderbilt tenders. Ten more 2-8-8-0s came from Brooks in 1924, nearly identical except for piston valves on the low-pressure cylinders. For a while in the 1920s No. 753 was equipped with a booster on the rear tender truck — neither tender boosters nor Vanderbilt tenders were common, and the combination was rare. Between 1941 and 1943 KCS rebuilt all its 2-8-8-0s into single-expansion engines.

Passenger locomotives

The D-7 class Ten-Wheelers were generally assigned to passenger trains south of Shreveport, La. They had 67" drivers and a tractive effort of 26,389 pounds. The road had only one class of passenger engines that could be considered modern, 11 Pacifics built by Alco's Schenectady Works in 1912 (800-807) and 1919 (808-810). They had 75" drivers and weighed 258,000 pounds, 19,000 less than the USRA light Pacific. They were interesting in appearance, with high-mounted headlights and blank smokebox doors (not even a number plate) that for a period were painted silver, as were the cylinder heads. Some of the Pacifics were fitted with a second sand dome, and some were given disk drivers, either a complete set or just the main drivers. An unfortunate few were equipped with air horns that sounded like a cawing crow for assignment to the Kansas City-Port Arthur *Flying Crow*.

Switchers

KCS's newest 0-6-0s were built in 1913, and many older 0-6-0s lasted

L&A's M-21 Mikados, built by Baldwin between 1923 and 1927, looked older than they were because of the striping on the drivers and the shape of the domes. Baldwin photo; collection of H. L. Broadbelt.

until dieselization. Most KCS switchers were 0-8-0s rebuilt from E-1 and E3 2-8-0s. Both classes had 55" drivers. The K-class engines, 1000-1012, weighed 189,850 pounds. The K-1s, 1020-1031, weighed 240,000 and had a tractive effort of only 47,124 pounds, somewhat less than might be expected for a switcher of that weight. L&A's three ex-Florida East Coast 0-8-0s worked occasionally on KCS.

Oddities

In Kansas City KCS served customers on spurs that had extremely steep grades — up to 10 percent, according to some reports. Conventional locomotives would have had great difficulty on such track, so KCS purchased two 3-truck Shays. The first, No. 900, built in 1913, had 18" × 20" cylinders and 48" wheels — the largest used on a Shay. Number 901, delivered a year later, was the largest standard-model Shay in Lima's catalog, with 17" × 18" cylinders and 46" wheels.

Louisiana & Arkansas locomotives

L&A was noteworthy for seven Russian Decapods, four former Louisiana Railway & Navigation Ten-Wheelers that were rebuilt for passenger service, and two groups of Mikados. The M-21 class, built by Baldwin between 1923 and 1927 were small (57" drivers, 256,000 pounds) and modern, with trailing truck boosters and (the later ones) feedwater heaters. The M-22 class, built by Lima in 1936, were larger but still comparatively light. They weighed 301,000 pounds and had 63" drivers. Their 23" × 32" cylinders were small, but 240 pounds of boiler pressure made up for that. Tractive effort with booster was a respectable 71,300 pounds; without the booster it was approximately 60,000 pounds, the same as the USRA heavy Mikado.

Historical and technical society: Kansas City Southern Historical Society, c/o Lowell McManus, P. O. Box 282, Leesville, LA 71496-0282

Published rosters: *Railroad Magazine*: April 1939, page 121; June 1952, page 100; April 1957, page 74

KCS and L&A STEAM LOCOMOTIVES BUILT SINCE 1900

Type	Class	Numbers	Qty	Builder	Built	Retired	Notes
Kansas City Southern							
0-6-0	F-2	81-100	20	Bald., Pitts.	1901-1908	1932-1950	
0-6-0	F-3	70-73	4	Schenectady	1913	1948, 1949	
0-8-0	K	1000-1012	13	KCS	1924-1929	1948-1954	
0-8-0	K-1	1020-1031	12	KCS	1925-1927	1950-1955	
2-8-0	E-1	460-474	15	Baldwin	1900, 1903		Converted to 0-8-0s
2-8-0	E-2	450-453	4	Baldwin	1903	sold 1917	Built for PS&N
2-8-0	E-3	475-532	48	Pitts., Bald.	1906-1908	1939-1954	
							Many converted to 0-8-0s
2-8-0	E-4	550-564	15	Richmond	1913	1951-1953	
							559, 560 sold to L&A 1940
2-10-2	L	200-205	6	Brooks	1917	1951-1953	Ex-Wabash
2-10-2	L-1	220-223	4	Baldwin	1919	1951, 1952	Ex-Ann Arbor
2-10-4	J	900-909	10	Lima	1937	1952, 1953	
0-6-6-0	G	700-711	12	Schenectady	1912	1937, 1947	
2-8-8-0	G-1	750-756	7	Schenectady	1918	1939-1951	
2-8-8-0	G-2	757-766	10	Brooks	1924	1947-1953	
4-6-0	D-7	600-606	7	Baldwin	1903	1939-1948	
4-6-2	H	800-807	8	Schenectady	1912	1951-1954	
							800, 806 to L&A 1939
4-6-2	H-1	808-810	3	Schenectady	1919	1951-1953	
Shay	S	900, 901	2	Lima	1913, 1914	1928, 1929	
Louisiana Railway & Navigation Co.							
0-8-0		79, 80	2	Baldwin	1906		
2-6-0		82	1	Baldwin	1909		
2-8-0		90, 91	2	Baldwin	1912		
2-8-0		98, 99	2	Baldwin	1919		
2-10-0		100-105	6	Baldwin	1918		Russian Decapod
2-10-0		106	1	Alco	1918		Russian Decapod
4-4-0		54	1	Baldwin	1900		
4-6-0		92-97	6	Baldwin	1913, 1915		
							To L&A 392-394, 95, 396, 297
4-6-0	D-20	170	1	Baldwin	1903		
Louisiana & Arkansas							
0-8-0	K-21	251-253	3	Alco	1924		Ex-Florida East Coast
0-8-0	K-22	1007	1	Baldwin	1903		Ex-KCS
2-8-0		425	1	Baldwin	1901		Ex-Colorado Midland
2-8-0	E-24	490, 491, 494, 526		Alco			
			4	Alco	1906		Ex-KCS
2-8-0	E-25	559, 560	2	Alco	1913		Ex-KCS
2-8-2	M-20	544	1	Alco	1928		Ex-Denkman Lumber Co.
2-8-2	M-21	551-556	6	Baldwin	1923-1927		
2-8-2	M-22	561-565	5	Lima	1936		
4-4-0		301, 302	2	Baldwin	1911, 1912		
4-6-0		202-207	6	Baldwin	1906		
4-6-0		297	1	Baldwin	1915		Ex-LR&N 97
4-6-0	D-20	172-177	6	Baldwin	1903		
4-6-0	D-22	392-394, 396	4	Baldwin	1913		Ex-LR&N 92-94, 96
4-6-0	D-25	500-511	12	Baldwin	1913-1920		
4-6-0	E-24	526	1	Baldwin	1908		
4-6-2		309	1	Alco	1913		Ex-Florida East Coast
4-6-2	H-20	800, 806	2	Alco	1912		Ex-KCS
Louisiana Railway & Navigation Co. of Texas (later Louisiana, Arkansas & Texas)							
2-6-0		455	1	Baldwin	1901		Ex-Missouri-Kansas-Texas
2-8-0		241-243	3	Alco	1903		
							Ex-Buffalo, Rochester & Pittsburgh
2-8-0		671-675	5	Alco	1901		Ex-Missouri-Kansas-Texas
4-6-0		231, 233	2	Baldwin	1905		Ex-Missouri-Kansas-Texas
4-6-0		239, 240	2	Alco	1907		Ex-Missouri-Kansas-Texas

LEHIGH & HUDSON RIVER RAILWAY

The Lehigh & Hudson River had a single line from Easton, Pennsylvania, to Maybrook, New York. It connected the railroads that clustered at the confluence of the Delaware and Lehigh Rivers with the New York, New Haven & Hartford at Maybrook. Its principal traffic was anthracite moving from the coalfields of eastern Pennsylvania to New England; the road eventually developed into a bridge route for general freight. It was jointly owned by Central Railroad of New Jersey; Delaware, Lackawanna & Western; Erie; Lehigh Valley; Pennsylvania; and Reading.

The road discontinued passenger service in 1939. Through its history it had only one switcher, an 0-6-0 built in 1894. Most of the road's traffic consisted of trains received from one connection and delivered intact to another, and there were almost no industries located along the line. L&HR dieselized quickly in 1950 with 13 Alco RS-3s.

Two mergers and a fire killed the road. The creation of Erie Lackawanna in 1960 and Penn Central in 1968 changed traffic patterns throughout the Northeast, and L&HR's traffic fell off. When the former New Haven bridge over the Hudson at Poughkeepsie burned, L&HR's eastern connection disappeared, turning L&HR into a rural short line. It became part of Conrail in 1976.

Freight locomotives

L&HR's early-20th-century power consisted of Camelback Ten-Wheelers and Consolidations typical of the anthracite railroads. In 1916 Baldwin delivered four 2-8-2s numbered 70-73. They had 56" drivers, 25" × 30" cylinders, and Wootten fireboxes for burning hard coal. Four more Mikados, Nos. 80-83, came from Baldwin in 1918 — USRA light 2-8-2s. They looked considerably larger than the 1916 Mikados, mostly because of their 63" drivers. The other differences weren't as significant: cylinder diameter an inch greater, 7,000 pounds more weight, and 530 pounds more tractive effort.

L&HR's next engines were 2-8-0s 90-95, delivered by Baldwin in 1925 and 1927. Ordinarily a Consolidation would be seen as a step backward

Consolidations 90-95 were large by anyone's standards. The 100 square feet of grate area was the same as Lima's Super-Power Berkshire, and more than Reading's 4-8-4s. Baldwin photo.

from the Mikado — but not these. They weighed 309,700 pounds, almost 18,000 pounds more than the USRA light Mikes. Their drivers were 61" in diameter, not significantly smaller, but their cylinders were 1" larger in diameter and 2" more in stroke: 27" × 32", the same as those of the USRA heavy Mikado. Tractive effort was 71,500 pounds, almost as much as a USRA heavy 2-10-2.

During World War II the road needed additional power. Speed was becoming important, so the road looked for something faster than its heavy 2-8-0s. New locomotive designs were restricted by the war, so L&HR chose duplicates of Boston & Maine's most recent Baldwin 4-8-2s, even to the centipede tenders. Mountain types Nos. 10-12 tipped the scales at 415,200 pounds, heavy as 4-8-2s went. Tractive force was 67,000 pounds, almost as much as the big 2-8-0s, but 73" drivers gave the 4-8-2s speed.

Historical and technical society: Anthracite Railroads Historical Society, P. O. Box 519, Lansdale, PA 19446-0519

Published rosters:

Railroad Magazine: February 1942, page 81; December 1958, page 70
Railway & Locomotive Historical Society Bulletin, No. 47, page 72

L&HR STEAM LOCOMOTIVES BUILT SINCE 1900

Type	Numbers	Qty	Builder	Built	Retired	Notes
2-8-0	50-57	8	Baldwin	1903-1906	1925-1938	Camelback
2-8-0	58-69	12	Baldwin	1908	1930-1938	Camelback
2-8-0	90-95	6	Baldwin	1925, 1927		
2-8-2	70-73	4	Baldwin	1916		
2-8-2	80-83	4	Baldwin	1918		USRA
4-4-0	8	1	Baldwin	1906	1928	
4-6-0	20	1	Baldwin	1906	1936	Camelback
4-6-0	23-34	12	Baldwin	1907	1923-1934	Camelback
4-8-2	10-12	3	Baldwin	1944		

Mountain No. 11, a copy of Boston & Maine's R-1-d 4-8-2s, heads a freight near Warwick, N. Y., in May 1944. Photo by Donald W. Furler.

LEHIGH & NEW ENGLAND RAILROAD

The Lehigh & New England extended from the anthracite-, slate-, and cement-producing region of eastern Pennsylvania to a connection with the New Haven at Campbell Hall, New York. Like the parallel Lehigh & Hudson River, its original purpose was to move anthracite from eastern Pennsylvania to New England. The road later carried considerable cement traffic, but never became a bridge route as L&HR did. It wasn't a passenger carrier of any consequence. As early as 1930 its passenger service consisted of local trains on 10 miles of track at the Pennsylvania end of the line and a single train at the New York end. Its *Official Guide* listing said of most of the line, "Passenger service not established." All passenger service was discontinued in 1938. Dieselization occurred quickly and was complete by the end of 1949.

Low-drivered Camelback 2-8-0s were the mainstay of LNE freight service until Alco's Schenectady Works delivered seven medium-size conventional 2-8-0s in 1922. They had 61" drivers and 27" × 32" cylinders. They weighed 233,000 pounds; their fireboxes were as wide as the Wootten fireboxes used on previous LNE engines.

The Decapods were purchased specifically for a stretch of 2.74 percent grade between Bath and Summit, Pa. They were the largest, most powerful 2-10-0s built. They weighed 400,000 pounds and with tender booster working could exert a tractive force of 106,200 pounds, more than a USRA 2-8-2 working compound. They had 61" drivers and 30" × 32" cylinders. During World War II LNE purchased four Pennsylvania Railroad L1 2-8-2s.

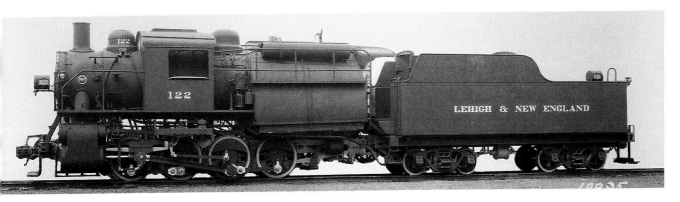

Switchers 120-122, turned out by Baldwin in 1927, were the last Camelbacks built for service in North America. Baldwin photo; collection of H. L. Broadbelt.

Lehigh & New England's latter-day roster included two 0-6-0s and 19 0-8-0s, 13 of which were Camelbacks — and three of those were the last Camelbacks built in the United States (Nos. 120-122, Baldwin, 1927). The conventional-cab 0-8-0s, Nos. 131-136, built by Baldwin between 1927 and 1931, had Wootten fireboxes and enormous rear overhangs that looked long enough to justify trailing trucks.

The two 0-6-0s were latecomers. Though built in 1931, No. 206 had slide valves. Number 207 was enough of a curiosity that it got its picture in the 1938 *Locomotive Cyclopedia*.

Historical and technical society: Anthracite Railroads Historical Society, P. O. Box 519, Lansdale, PA 19446-0519

Published rosters: *Railroad Magazine*: March 1933, page 94; November 1946, page 114

The seven Consolidations built by Schenectady in 1922 — LNE's only Alco steam locomotives — were chunky engines, but not particularly large as 2-8-0s go. Photo by James D. Bennett.

What looks like a tiny cab perched on the back of the boiler of 2-10-0 No. 404 gives an indication of the size of the locomotive. L&NE's Decapods and Alco Consolidations had tender boosters. Photo by Theodore A. Gay.

L&NE STEAM LOCOMOTIVES BUILT SINCE 1900

Type	Class	Numbers	Qty	Builder	Built	Notes
0-6-0	B-4	206	1	Baldwin	1931	
0-6-0	B-5	207	1	Baldwin	1936	
0-8-0	I-1	101	1	Baldwin	1913	Camelback
0-8-0	I-2	111-115	5	Baldwin	1913	Camelback
0-8-0	I-3	116-119	4	Baldwin	1915	Camelback
0-8-0	I-4	120-122	3	Baldwin	1927	Camelback
0-8-0	I-5	131-136	6	Baldwin	1927-1931	
2-8-0	E-8	25, 27	2	Baldwin	1906	
2-8-0	E-9	29	1	Baldwin	1909	Camelback
2-8-0	E-12	151, 152	2	Baldwin	1911	Camelback
2-8-0	E-13	153, 154	2	Baldwin	1915	Camelback
2-8-0	E-14	301-307	7	Schenectady	1922	
2-8-2	G-1	501-504	4	Juniata	1915	
2-10-0	F-1	401-404	4	Baldwin	1927-1931	

2-8-0 — CONSOLIDATION

More Consolidations were built than any other wheel arrangement. The first 2-8-0 was designed by Alexander Mitchell of the Lehigh & Mahanoy Railroad and built by Matthias Baldwin in 1866. The locomotive was named *Consolidation* in honor of the recent consolidation of the Beaver Meadow, Penn Haven & White Haven and Lehigh & Mahanoy railroads into the Lehigh Valley, and the name was soon applied to the wheel arrangement. Its eight drivers offered more adhesion than previous six-coupled engines, and the radial lead truck provided stability lacking in the 0-8-0s that had been used for heavy freight.

The development of the 2-8-0 paralleled locomotive development in general. Until the turn of the century 57" drivers were the largest generally used on the type, and the firebox was either a narrow, deep one for bituminous coal between the rear drivers

The heaviest nonexperimental Consolidations were Reading's I-10sa class, built by Baldwin between 1921 and 1923. They tipped the scales at 322,690 pounds. Reading 2008, photographed at Rutherford, Pennsylvania, in 1948, shows that the Wootten firebox was just about as wide as Reading's clearances allowed. Photo by A. D. Hooks.

or a wide Wootten firebox for anthracite over the drivers. Adopting a shallow firebox about the same width as the boiler for bituminous coal gave the Consolidation greater steaming capacity and also required that the boiler be mounted higher, resulting in a fundamental change in appearance. The use of drivers between 60" and 63" in diameter added another few inches to the height.

Some railroads adopted the Consolidation almost immediately for heavy duty; other railroads were a decade or more into the 20th century before they turned to eight-coupled locomotives. In fairly simple form the 2-8-0 became almost the universal type for freight service between 1900 and 1910. After that the type began to develop in two directions. There was still a demand for light, simple 2-8-0s, and builders continued to produce such locomotives through the 1920s. Consolidations also began to accrue technological improvements like superheaters, mechanical stokers, and feedwater heaters. On several railroads, notably Eastern coal-haulers, the type began to grow in girth and rear overhang — bigger boilers and wider, longer fireboxes. The object was to put as much weight as possible on the drivers and not worry much about speed. Productivity of locomotives and engine crews was measured by the number of cars they moved, not how fast they did the job. Besides, coal didn't spoil on the way from the mine to the consumer. The ultimate development in this direction were the heavy 2-8-0s of Western Maryland and Lehigh & Hudson River; Delaware & Hudson's high-pressure experimentals were side trips outside the mainstream of development.

Those were the two extremes. The majority of 2-8-0s became second-rank locomotives when railroads turned to freight locomotives with trailing trucks. From the Teens to the end of steam, Consolidations did all the jobs that weren't done by Mikes, Berkshires, and Northerns — and sometimes did those too, or pinch-hit for Pacifics, or stood in for switchers.

Total built: About 21,000 for common-carrier railroads
First: Lehigh Valley *Consolidation*, 1866
Last: Mexican Railway 220, 1946
Heaviest: D&H 1402, 356,000 pounds (Alco, 1930)

Green Bay & Western 351, setting out cars at East Winona, Wisconsin, in 1944, typifies the great majority of 2-8-0s, light to medium-size machines that did railroading's unglamorous jobs. Photo by Robert A. LeMassena.

LEHIGH VALLEY RAILROAD

The Lehigh Valley of 1900 extended west from Jersey City and Perth Amboy, New Jersey, to Easton, Bethlehem, and Allentown, Pennsylvania, then northwest through Wilkes-Barre and Sayre, Pa., and Ithaca, New York, to Geneva, then west to Buffalo. Branches reached Niagara Falls and Rochester; several branches and alternate routes served the Finger Lakes area south of Geneva and Auburn, N. Y.; and a network of branches covered the anthracite-producing area around Hazelton and Pottsville, Pa. Some of LV's expansion was relatively late. The line from Geneva to Buffalo was opened in 1892, and the line from Easton to Jersey City in 1899; both extensions avoided cities and even medium-size towns. LV was leased briefly by the Reading in 1892 and 1893, and around the turn of the century several railroads purchased and briefly held interests in the road: New York Central, Reading, Erie, Lackawanna, and Central of New Jersey.

In the mid-1920s Leonor F. Loree, president of the Delaware & Hudson, tried to assemble a New York-Chicago railroad based on D&H, LV, Wabash, and Buffalo, Rochester & Pittsburgh. He got the backing of the Pennsylvania Railroad. In 1928 he lost a battle for control of the BR&P, and suddenly the PRR held 44 percent of LV's stock. Pennsy kept LV out of the hands of other railroads but exercised no influence on the road's policies and operations.

LV was the weakest of the railroads from New York to Buffalo. It had to rely on connecting roads at Buffalo, and most of those were aligned to some extent with one of LV's competitors. Its freight business was also affected negatively by government regulation that forced it to sell its Great Lakes boats and its coal mining subsidiary. Although LV's passenger trains used Pennsylvania Station in New York (LV had no passenger terminal of its own on the New Jersey waterfront), its trains were older and slower than those of the New York Central and the Lackawanna. It was the dominant passenger carrier to Allentown, Bethlehem, and Wilkes-Barre.

Much of LV's main line ran alongside rivers and lakes or through the flat country of New Jersey and western New York, but between Mauch Chunk (now Jim Thorpe) and Wilkes-Barre, Pa., the road had a major struggle to cross the divide between the Lehigh and Susquehanna rivers. There was a long stretch of ascending grade somewhat less than 1 percent along the Lehigh River westbound, followed by 10 miles of 1.2 percent to the summit. Eastbound passenger trains faced about 10 miles of 1.81 percent grade out of Wilkes-Barre; a longer bypass for freight had a grade of 1.16 percent. Many of LV's heavy locomotives were designed for the line over Penobscot and Wilkes-Barre mountains.

In the 19th century LV had a reputation for motive power innovation. It originated the 2-8-0, 4-8-0, and 2-10-0 wheel arrangements (one of the two Decapods was rebuilt as a 2-8-2, then a 2-8-0; the other, a 4-8-0), but shortly after the turn of the century moved away from slow, drag freight engines in favor of faster machines, generally types with fire boxes supported by trailing trucks. It made that move before it switched from Camelbacks to locomotives of conventional configuration, with the result that LV was the only road to operate Camelback Pacifics, Mikados, and (except for one engine) Prairies. About 1910 the road standardized on four wheel arrangements: Mikados for heavy freight, Pacifics for passenger and light freight, Ten-Wheelers for local and branchline service, and 0-8-0s for switching and short-distance coal trains.

LV's locomotives underwent a general renumbering in 1905; the 1905 numbers are used in the text and roster.

In the late 1920s LV acquired several diesel locomotives to work the waterfront in New York and New Jersey, and in 1937 began buying diesel switchers in earnest. In 1945 it bought four two-unit FTs for helper service. LV dieselized quickly between 1948 and 1951. Mikado 432 had the honor of the last steam run on September 14, 1951.

Freight locomotives

Between 1880 and 1900 LV acquired large numbers of Camelback

Lehigh Valley had the only Camelback 2-8-2s; No. 261 was built at Alco's Schenectady Works in May 1907. The handrail below the sand dome that ends abruptly at a cluster of hot injector pipes must have been cursed by engineers. Alco photo, collection of C. W. Witbeck.

2-8-0s of the 20" cylinder, 50" driver size. Between 1899 and 1902 Baldwin delivered 102 M-35-class Consolidations, Vauclain compounds with 52½" drivers and 21" × 30" cylinders, and at the same time 15 M-37-class 2-8-0s, Vauclain compounds with 55½" drivers. The M-36 class 2-8-0s, built by Alco's Schenectady Works in 1907, were single-expansion engines with 21" × 30" cylinders and 62½" drivers. Four were later fitted with 21½" cylinders and were classed M-36½. (LV used "½" instead of a letter to indicate subclasses.)

LV's shops at Sayre built two groups of conventional 2-8-0s, the M-38½ class, Nos. 900-914, in 1909 and 1910; and the M-38 class, Nos. 915-934, in 1912 and 1913. Both had 63" drivers and weighed 215,000 pounds; the M-38½ engines had 22" × 30" cylinders, the M-38s, 23" × 30". Between 1919 and 1929 all 35 were rebuilt to L-5½ class 0-8-0s.

The first Mikados on the road were unique — the only Camelbacks

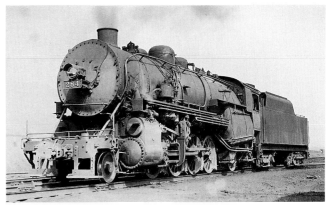

Mikado 284 is an N-6, one of 20 that Sayre Shops rebuilt from 2-10-2s in 1928 and 1929. The inside-journal trailing truck is a holdover from the 2-10-2; the tender booster is a touch of modernity. Photo by W. R. Osborne.

Wyoming type 5103 was built by Baldwin in 1932. The odd rear tender truck originally carried a booster. Photo by Ray Ollis Jr.

2-8-2s ever. Baldwin delivered 37, Nos. 220-256, in 1903 and 1906, and Schenectady built the last ten, 257-266, in 1907. They had 56" drivers and 22½" × 28" slide-valve cylinders; they weighed 234,810 pounds and had a tractive force of 43,031 pounds.

Later Mikados were of conventional configuration. The 42 engines of the N-2 class, Nos. 300-341, built by Baldwin in 1912 and 1913, had 56" drivers, 27" × 30" cylinders, and wide Wootten fireboxes. In weight and tractive force they were about equal to a USRA heavy 2-8-2. The N2½ class of 1913 and 1916, Nos. 350-394, were improved versions of the N-2, with 63" drivers, increased boiler pressure, and mechanical stokers; the N-3s (395-414, 1916; 415-419, 1917; and 420-424, 1922) had the same specifications.

The N-4, N-4B, and N-5 Mikes of 1923 and 1924 were different. They had conventional fireboxes, booster-equipped cast trailing trucks, and 63" drivers. N-4s 425-434 and N-4Bs 460-464 had 27" × 30" cylinders; the N-5s 440-459 and 465-499 had 27" × 32" cylinders and 4,000 pounds more tractive effort.

The last 2-8-2s added to the roster were 20 N-6s, Nos. 275-294, rebuilt from 2-10-2s in 1928 and 1929. They had the same dimensions as the N-5s but kept the Wootten fireboxes and inside-bearing trailing trucks of the 2-10-2s. Their success can be measured by their scrapping dates — more than half were scrapped before World War II, about the same ratio as the 2-8-2s built between 1912 and 1917.

To handle the traffic surge of World War I LV set aside its preference for relatively fast locomotives and bought 40 2-10-2s from Baldwin in 1917 and 36 more in 1919. Numbered 4000-4075 and classed R-1 they had 63" drivers and 29" × 32" cylinders and were slightly lighter and less powerful than USRA heavy 2-10-2s. When traffic dropped after the war the 2-10-2s proved too slow for mainline freight. In 1920 LV sold 4060-4071 to the Hocking Valley, a coal hauler in eastern Ohio; Nos. 4072-4075 followed them to HV in 1922. Twenty more 2-10-2s were rebuilt to class N-6 2-8-2s in 1928 and 1929.

By 1930 Lehigh Valley's traffic had changed. General merchandise had become more important than coal, and it had to move faster. In 1931 the road took delivery of two 4-8-4s, one from Baldwin and one from Alco. The Baldwin engine, No. 5100, class T-1, had 70" drivers and 27" × 30" cylinders; it weighed 413,170 pounds and developed a tractive force of 66,400 pounds. The Alco engine was numbered 5200 and classed T-2. The drivers were the same size, but the cylinders were 26" × 32"; it was almost 11,000 pounds heavier and was rated at 300 pounds more tractive force. LV christened them the Wyoming type.

The Wyomings performed well, and in 1932 each builder delivered 10 more — T-1s 5101-5110 from Baldwin and T-2s 5201-5210 from Alco. In 1934 Baldwin delivered 5 more 4-8-4s, numbered 5125-5129 and classed T-3. With an eye toward passenger service, they had 77" drivers; they weighed 435,000 pounds. They rarely worked passenger trains but occasionally pulled milk trains, where their high drivers were useful — a slow milk train can quickly become a yogurt train.

Passenger locomotives

The Ten-Wheelers built in the 20th century were passenger or dual service locomotives with 69" drivers. The J-55 class was built with 23" cylinders, but 65 of them were rebuilt with 21" cylinders to reduce the demand on the boiler and reclassed J-55½. There was a similar difference between the J-56 and J-57 conventional-cab 4-6-0s; the J-56½ Ten-Wheelers (Nos. 1818-1820) had 73" drivers. The J-25 class, built by Sayre Shops in 1917 and 1918, were intended for freight and mixed-train service. They were light engines (137,000 pounds) with 20" × 24" cylinders and 63" drivers.

LV had a brief fling with the Prairie type, ten Camelbacks with 76½" drivers built by Baldwin in 1902. They proved incompatible with LV's curving main line and were converted to Pacifics in 1906. The road returned to the Atlantic type in 1903. Already on the roster were 17 Baldwin Camelbacks built between 1896 and 1901, some simple and some compound (later simpled), some with 76½" drivers and some with 80½" drivers (later 77"). The 17 members of the F-3 class built by Baldwin and Schenectady between 1903 and 1910 had 77" drivers, as did the F-6 class (LV's only conventional-firebox, conventional-cab Atlantics), built at Sayre Shops in 1910 and 1911. All the Atlantics were scrapped by 1929.

In 1886 LV's Wilkes-Barre Shops built a Camelback 4-6-2 with an experimental double firebox. A collision in 1898 ended its career as a Pacific; its boiler was used to rebuild a 4-6-0 in 1899. The road returned to the 4-6-2 in 1905 and 1906 with eight Camelbacks classed K-1. Large for their time (238,380 pounds), they were joined in 1906 by the 10 members of the K-2 class, rebuilt from 2-6-2s. They had the same size cylinders and drivers as the K-1s, 22" × 28" and 76½", but were much lighter, 201,700 pounds.

The K-2½, K-3, and K-4 classes were all products of Sayre Shops. All had 25" × 28" cylinders, 77" drivers, boiler pressure of 215 pounds, and a tractive force of 41,534 pounds. K-3s 2026-2035 were rebuilt from K-1 and K-2 Camelbacks; the others were built from scratch. The K-4s had conventional fireboxes and burned bituminous coal.

The K-5 and K-5½ Pacifics, Nos. 2100-2149, were built by Baldwin between 1916 and 1919 as dual-service machines. The combination of 27" × 28" cylinders and 73" drivers gave them a tractive force of 48,723 pounds. Engines 2101 and 2102 were streamlined in 1938.

K-6B Pacific 2094 is a 1924 product of Alco's Brooks Works. The inward-sloping cab sides are a Lehigh Valley characteristic. The built-up coal bunker let the engine run from Jersey City to Buffalo with a single stop for coal at Towanda, Pennsylvania. Photo by Donald W. Furler.

The biggest Pacifics were the K-6B class. Alco built Nos. 2090-2099 in 1924. Sayre Shops added two more: No. 2089 in 1925 and No. 2088 (rebuilt from K-3 2025) in 1926. They had 77" drivers and 25" × 28" cylinders, weighed 291,000 pounds, and exerted a tractive force of 41,534 pounds. In 1939 and 1940 LV streamlined three of the K-6Bs, adding about 10,000 pounds; with booster working, the tractive effort of the streamlined Pacifics was 51,934 pounds.

In 1923 and 1924 LV acquired six 4-8-2s, Nos. 5000-5005, that were Alco's first built-from-scratch three-cylinder engines. They were near-duplicates of the two New York Central L-1b 4-8-2s that Alco had converted to three cylinders in 1922, with 69" drivers and 25" × 28" cylinders. They tested in freight service, then went to work pulling passenger trains over the mountains between Mauch Chunk and Wilkes-Barre, eliminating the need for helpers.

LV found, as did most other roads with three-cylinder power, that the cost of maintaining the third cylinder rose sharply when they ran at speeds over 30 mph. In 1939 the road rebuilt all six 4-8-2s as two-cylin-

Number 5128 is one of five 4-8-4s built with 77" drivers for passenger duty but used principally in freight service. Photo by W. R. Osborne.

LV STEAM LOCOMOTIVES BUILT SINCE 1900

Type	Class	Numbers	Qty	Builder	Built	Retired	Notes
0-6-0	G-13	3400-3402	3	Baldwin	1905	1931, 1932	
0-6-0	G-14	3420-3452	33	Baldwin, LV	1907-1914	1930-1951	Camelback
0-8-0	L-1	3030, 3031	2	Baldwin	1901	1926	
0-8-0	L-1½	3000-3003	4	LV	1920, 1921	1923, 1924	
							Rebuilt from 2-8-0s
0-8-0	L-2	3033-3049	17	LV, BLW, Schen	1902-1910	1929-1936	
0-8-0	L-3	3050-3069	20	LV, BLW, Schen	1905-1910	1931-1940	Camelback
0-8-0	L-4	3100-3104	5	LV	1912	1928-1938	
0-8-0	L-5	3125-3174	50	LV, Baldwin	1911-1916	1932-1951	Camelback
0-8-0	L-5½	3176-3210	34	LV	1919-1929	1939-1951	
							Rebuilt from 2-8-0s
0-8-0	L-6	3198, 3199	2	LV	1908	1932, 1926	
							Rebuilt from 2-8-0s
2-6-2	I-1	2230-2239	10	Baldwin	1902		Camelback, rebuilt to K-2
2-8-0	M-35	700-769, 780-812					
			102	Baldwin	1899-1902	1916-1951	Camelback
2-8-0	M-36	813-832	20	Schenectady	1907	1928-1945	Camelback
2-8-0	M-36½	816, 820, 826, 828					
			4	Schenectady	1907	1926-1930	Camelback
2-8-0	M-37	950-954	15	Baldwin	1899, 1900	1923-1932	Camelback
2-8-0	M-38	915-934	20	LV	1912, 1913		
							Rebuilt to 0-8-0 1924-1929
2-8-0	M-38½	900-914	15	LV	1909, 1910		
							Rebuilt to 0-8-0 1919-1929
2-8-2	N-1	220-266	47	BLW, Schen	1903-1907	1924-1932	Camelback
2-8-2	N-2	300-341	42	Baldwin	1912, 1913	1938-1951	
2-8-2	N-2½	350-394	45	Baldwin	1913, 1916	1937-1951	
2-8-2	N-3	395-424	30	Baldwin	1916-1922	1938-1951	
2-8-2	N-4	425-434	10	Baldwin	1923	1940-1951	
2-8-2	N-4B	460-464	5	Baldwin	1923	1948-1951	
2-8-2	N-5B	440-459, 465-499					
			55	Schenectady	1923, 1924	1947-1951	
2-8-2	N-6	275-294	20	LV	1928, 1929	1939-1949	
							Rebuilt from 2-10-2s
2-10-2	R-1	4000-4075	76	Baldwin	1917, 1919	1948-1951	
		4060-4075 sold to Hocking Valley in 1920; 20 rebuilt to N-6 2-8-2s 1928-1929.					

der engines, changed their class from S-1 to S-2, and put them in freight service, where they proved disappointing.

Switchers

Lehigh Valley had only 36 six-wheel switchers built in the 20th century, three end-cab G-13s and 33 Camelback G-14s. The two classes shared cylinder and driver dimensions — 20" × 24" and 51". Development of the 0-8-0 began in 1901 and culminated in the L-5½ class, converted from 2-8-0s by Sayre Shops mostly between 1924 and 1929. They weighed almost as much as a USRA 0-8-0 but smaller cylinders (22" × 30") and larger drivers (55½") made them less powerful.

Historical and technical society: Anthracite Railroads Historical Society, P. O. Box 519, Lansdale, PA 19446-0519

Recommended reading: *Eastern Steam Pictorial*, by Bert Pennypacker, published in 1966 by P & D Carleton, 158 Doretta Street, River Vale, NJ 07675

Published rosters:

Railroad Magazine: August 1935, page 88; July 1949, page 103; August 1949, page 110 (reclassification)

Railway & Locomotive Historical Society Bulletin, No. 126, page 37

ype	Class	Numbers	Qty	Builder	Built	Retired	Notes
-4-2	F-3	2400-2416	17	BLW, Schen	1903-1910	1923-1929	
-4-2	F-4	2460-2467	8	Baldwin	1900, 1901	1923-1928	Later F-5
-4-2	F-6	2475-2479	5	Sayre	1910, 1911	1925-1939	
-6-0	J-25	1131-1165	35	LV	1917, 1918	1940-1951	
-6-0	J-54/A	1550-1556	7	Baldwin	1900	1923-1929	Camelback
-6-0	J-55½	1590-1694	105	BLW,Schen	1904-1908	1912-1948	Camelback
-6-0	J-56/56½/57	1800-1820	21	LV	1911, 1912	1928-1949	
-6-2	K-1	2000-2007	8	Baldwin	1905, 1906	1923	
				Camelback; 2004-2006 rebuilt to K-3			
-6-2	K-2	2230-2239	10		1906	1923-1924	
				Camelback, rebuilt from 2-6-2s; 7 rebuilt to K-3 1919-1920			
-6-2	K-2½	2010-2020	11	LV	1913, 1914	1937-1950	

Type	Class	Numbers	Qty	Builder	Built	Retired	Notes
4-6-2	K-3	2021-2035	15	LV	1917-1921	1938-1950	
							2025 rebuilt to K-6B
4-6-2	K-4	2050-2064	15	LV	1915-1917	1938-1951	
4-6-2	K-5	2100-2129	30	Baldwin	1916, 1917	1941-1951	
							2101, 2102 streamlined 1938
4-6-2	K-5½	2130-2149	20	Baldwin	1918, 1919	1939-1949	
4-6-2	K-6B	2088-2099	12	Brooks, LV	1924-1926	1950-1951	
				2088 rebuilt from K-3 2025 in 1926; 2093, 2097, 2089 streamlined 1939-1940.			
4-8-2	S-2	5000-5005	6	Brooks	1923, 1924	1948	
4-8-4	T-1	5100-5110	11	Baldwin	1931, 1932	1950, 1951	
4-8-4	T-2	5200-5210	11	Schenectady	1931, 1932	1950, 1951	
4-8-4	T-2B	5211-5220	10	Schenectady	1943	1952	
4-8-4	T-3	5125-5129	5	Baldwin	1934, 1935	1951	

LIMA LOCOMOTIVE WORKS

The Lima Machine Works was established in 1869 in Lima, Ohio, to produce agricultural and sawmill equipment. In the 1870s a Michigan logger, Ephraim Shay, developed a geared locomotive for use on wood-railed logging tramways. In 1878 Lima Machine Works built a locomotive to Shay's design for one of Shay's neighbors; then it built several other logging locomotives of conventional design. In the early 1880s, Lima Machine Works began building and marketing Shay locomotives in earnest. In 1891 the company acquired the Lima plant of the Lafayette Car Works, moved its operations there, and reorganized as the Lima Locomotive & Machine Company. A fire set things back temporarily, but the company rebuilt the facilities just in time for a lull in business resulting from the Panic of 1893.

By the turn of the century business had rebounded to the point that plant capacity was restricting production of Shays. The company built a new plant and began building conventional locomotives and undertaking contract repair work for Class 1 railroads. In 1911 Lima built its first locomotives for Class 1 railroads, 23 0-6-0 switchers for Southern and Mobile & Ohio. The firm was reorganized in 1912 as the Lima Locomotive Corporation and began constructing new shop facilities. In 1914, the production of conventional locomotives exceeded that of Shays for the first time. However, the company was earning barely enough to survive. In 1916 it was sold to Joel Coffin, who owned several companies that built locomotive parts. The firm became the Lima Locomotive Works.

During World War I Lima was in a strong position because it had not taken on munitions work as Alco and Baldwin did, but it built only 160 USRA locomotives (of a total of 1830). By then Lima was building large groups of engines for many Class 1 railroads; in particular, New York Central had become Lima's best customer. The early 1920s brought yet another round of new shop buildings.

Super-Power

During the early 1920s, railroads began to recognize that speed was

WILLIAM E. WOODARD (1873-1942) was born in Utica, New York. He attended Utica public schools and graduated from Cornell University in 1896 with a degree in mechanical engineering. He married Phebe Hatfield in 1901. Woodard worked for Baldwin and Dickson before joining Schenectady Locomotive Works in 1900. At Schenectady (which became part of American Locomotive Co. in 1902) Woodard worked as chief draftsman, manager of the electric locomotive and truck department, and assistant mechanical engineer.

In 1916 Woodard moved to Lima Locomotive Works as vice-president in charge of engineering. He is best known for the designs of Michigan Central (New York Central System) H-10 Mikado No. 8000 and Lima 2-8-4 demonstrator No. 1, both of which combined high horsepower and high speed. As a result of the success of those designs, locomotives began to be measured by horsepower instead of tractive effort — force per unit of time instead of simply force. He was granted more than 100 patents for devices such as tandem main rods, articulated trailing trucks, and throttle mechanisms.

At the time of his death at age 68 he was vice-president in charge of design and a director of Lima.

Lima's plant lay in a V between Baltimore & Ohio's Cincinnati-Toledo line and Nickel Plate's main line and shops. Baldwin-Lima-Hamilton photo.

as important as locomotive efficiency in freight service. The railroads and the locomotive builders tried various approaches to the problem, including high-pressure boilers, three-cylinder locomotives, articulation, water-tube fireboxes, and just plain bigger locomotives. Lima's chief engineer, William E. Woodard, who had come to Lima from Alco in 1916, approached the matter from the standpoint of boiler capacity. In 1922 Lima built an experimental 2-8-2 based on New York Central's H-7. Among the differences were a larger grate area, an improved superheater, an Elesco feedwater heater, larger cylinders, lightweight rods, and a booster on the trailing truck. The locomotive, Michigan Central H-10 No. 8000, weighed 334,000 pounds, only 6,000 pounds more than the H-7. The new locomotive could outpull NYC's H-7 and do it while burning less coal.

The H-10 was a prelude, a warm-up. Woodard saw that sustained power output depended not on boiler pressure, weight on drivers, and driver and cylinder dimensions, but on the capacity of the boiler to generate steam. That required grate area. More steam requires more fire, and more fire requires more fuel — but that fuel must burn to produce heat. If it is piled deep in a small firebox, it will not burn completely but instead go out the stack as black smoke.

The H-10's firebox, with 66.4 square feet of grate area, was at the limit of what a 2-wheel trailing truck could carry. Woodard added an axle to the trailing truck to support a 100-square-foot grate, creating the 2-8-4 wheel arrangement. Other specifications: 28" × 30" cylinders, 63" drivers, 65 percent cutoff, 240 pounds boiler pressure. It was numbered 1 and given a class designation of A-1.

The four-wheel trailing truck deserves special mention. It was fabricated rather than cast, it was equipped with a booster on the rear axle, it carried the ashpan, and it transmitted the pulling forces. The frame of the A-1 ended aft of the rear driving wheels. The trailing truck was connected to the rear of the frame with a hinge pin, and the rear end of the trailing truck supported the rear end of the boiler on sliding pads. The chief reason given for this arrangment was to avoid the problem of sharp drawbar angles between the engine and the tender created by the long firebox. Woodard's Super-Power concept became the basis for Lima's locomotive innovations during the next two decades, which included Chesapeake & Ohio's high-drivered 2-10-4s, the modern 2-8-4s of such roads as the Nickel Plate and Pere Marquette, and the 2-6-6-6s of C&O and Virginian.

In 1947 Lima merged with General Machinery Corporation of Hamilton, Ohio, to form the Lima-Hamilton Corporation. In 1951 it was merged with Baldwin Locomotive Works to form the Baldwin-Lima-Hamilton Corporation.

Recommended reading:

Lima: the history, by Eric Hirsimaki, published in 1986 by Hundman Publishing, Inc., 5115 Monticello Drive, Edmonds, WA 98020.
"The Lima story," by David P. Morgan, in *Trains Magazine*, January 1952, pages 12-21, and March 1952, pages 18-23

LOUISVILLE & NASHVILLE RAILROAD

By Charles B. Castner

The Louisville & Nashville of 1900 consisted of 3,200 route miles in 13 states. The main line ran 921 miles from Cincinnati through Louisville, Nashville, and Birmingham to New Orleans. Important secondary lines reached Memphis; St. Louis; Evansville, Indiana; Pensacola, Florida; the Kentucky coal fields; and the coal and ore-producing sections of northern Alabama.

L&N operated through rolling hills and mountainous terrain in much of Kentucky, Tennessee, north Alabama, and Georgia. Grades and curves reduced the tonnages L&N could move over the northern half of its system, but after 1900 the road upgraded much of its main line to reduce grades and curves for more economical train operation.

In 1902 Atlantic Coast Line purchased of a majority of L&N stock, and ACL and L&N began to exchange growing volumes of traffic via direct, or "family," connections at Atlanta and Montgomery. In 1924 the two roads leased the Clinchfield, giving L&N an outlet to the Carolinas for Kentucky coal. Meanwhile, between 1902 and 1907 L&N greatly improved its Cincinnati-Knoxville-Atlanta route, and inaugurated Cincinnati-Atlanta passenger service in 1905. Between 1909 and 1915 the road built lines into the Hazard-Elkhorn and Harlan coalfields of eastern and southeastern Kentucky.

Coal became L&N's top commodity, and the road invested millions in locomotives, cars, facilities, and line improvements. Two-thirds of the coal traffic came from the Kentucky coalfields, and a sizeable share of that volume flowed up the double-tracked Harlan-Corbin-Cincinnati line on its way to northern and midwestern markets. Mines in Alabama, Tennessee, Illinois, and Indiana also generated traffic for the road. Agricultural products long ranked second in L&N's freight traffic mix. Most of that traffic moved northward. Manufactured products ranked

Mikado 1480 was the first of L&N's J-2A class, built by South Louisville Shops in 1921. It was heavier and more powerful than the USRA heavy Mikado. L&N photo.

third, and lumber and forest products, fourth. Passengers accounted for less than 10 percent of L&N's revenues. The road was part of the principal Washington-New Orleans route and two Midwest-to-Florida routes.

Between 1902 and 1905 L&N erected new shops in Louisville. The 35-building, 70-acre plant replaced outmoded Civil War-era shops downtown. The centerpiece was a 40-bay erecting and boiler shop. South Louisville Shops designed and built new locomotives. Believing that it could build more cheaply than buy from outside, L&N produced 400 engines between 1905 and 1923; 282 were designed by Millard F. Cox, superintendent of machinery, in four types: Pacifics, Consolidations, Mikados, and eight-wheel switchers. Several designs utilized interchangeable parts.

South Louisville Shops also upgraded and modernized older engines, as did smaller shops at Corbin, Ky., Decatur, Ala., and Paris and Etowah, Tenn. All large roundhouses had drop pits and traveling cranes to facilitate wheel swaps and running repairs. L&N steam power policy was conservative. While the company introduced new types to meet changing traffic conditions, it stayed with basic wheel arrangements and modestly proportioned power. Until 1900, L&N relied on 4-4-0s and

4-6-0s to pull its passenger trains and 2-6-0s and 2-8-0s to work freight.

Forty-two 2-8-4s built between 1942 and 1949 represented L&N's only venture into large steam power. No ten-coupled or articulated locomotives were ever on the roster. The road preferred to double-head or use helpers on major grades. L&N shied away from experimental power and gadgetry, but it added devices to improve performance — superheaters, feedwater heaters, stokers, mechanical lubricators, power reverses, firebox syphons, and overfire jets. Engines assigned to fast freights and heavy limiteds were fitted with auxiliary or high-capacity tenders to reduce the number of water and fuel stops.

After 1920 the road adopted USRA locomotive designs. It bought more than 330 USRA Pacifics, Mountains, Mikes, and eight-wheel switchers, and those engines handled most mainline passenger, freight and heavy switching duties through the Depression and World War II.

In 1940 L&N needed new power. The road considered 4-8-4s for passenger service north of Mobile (weight restrictions kept the 4-8-2s off the Mobile-New Orleans line, and a 4-8-4 would have been heavier) but instead purchased 16 Electro-Motive E6s — and the diesels could run to New Orleans. At the same time it ordered the first of the M-1 2-8-4s.

In 1948 an M-1 was pitted against a three-unit EMD F3 on the roller-coaster Cincinnati-Louisville line; test results favored the F3s, leading to a decision in 1949 to dieselize everything but freight service in the coalfields. Passenger service was fully dieselized by 1954. By then flue time for the M1s was running out and operating costs for steam were soaring. L&N had little choice but to sideline the M-1s after 1956 and retire all other remaining steam locomotives. Merger with NC&StL in August 1957 brought enough diesels to the system that by 1959, L&N could finally sell its last 2-8-4s for scrap.

Freight locomotives

After 1900 L&N's 2-6-0s and small 2-8-0s were supplanted by larger Consolidations in two major groups. First were a series of some 300 medium-size engines, classes H-23, H-25, and H-27 (Nos. 975-1280), built by Rogers, Baldwin, and South Louisville between 1903 and 1911. All three classes had 57" drivers. The H-23s and H-25s had 21" × 28" cylinders; the H-27s, 21" × 30". Weight ranged from 183,400 to 196,000 pounds. The newer H-25 and H-27s had piston valves, Walschaerts valve gear, and superheaters.

L&N's heaviest 2-8-0s were the 94 members of the H-28 and H-29 classes (Nos. 1281-1374) turned out by South Louisville between 1911 and 1914. With large boilers, wide fireboxes, and bigger cylinders these engines produced 10,000 pounds more tractive effort than the H-25 and H-27s. Many H-29s were fitted with mechanical stokers and auxiliary water tenders and handled freight assignments on some divisions through the 1940s. Until bridges were strengthened along the Gulf coast around 1940, Consolidations powered all fast freights into New Orleans. Some 2-8-0s became yard and heavy transfer power.

The two H-24s were light engines (154,000 pounds) built to an older design; the two H-26s had 51" drivers and were purchased from the builder three years after their construction.

L&N 2-8-2s came in three basic groups: the home-built J-1 and J-2 machines; USRA light Mikados, class J-3; and the heavy USRAs, class J-4. South Louisville produced 50 J-1s between 1914 and 1918. With long boilers, mechanical stokers, and 57" drivers, they wrestled long coal trains from Eastern Kentucky to Cincinnati and Louisville. The 34 J-2s, slightly larger (28" × 30" cylinders instead of 27" × 30"; 326,000 pounds instead of 302,000), followed between 1918 and 1921. Both classes spent their working years in eastern and western Kentucky and in heavy transfer and yard service in Cincinnati and Louisville.

The light USRA Mikes gave L&N fast freight engines that could be used systemwide. Lima delivered 18 in 1919, and Alco followed with 75 between 1920 and 1923. Numbered 1500-1592, the class went to the more level divisions, eventually running all the way to New Orleans. The crews liked them, and they gave less mechanical trouble than any other class of freight power.

The 165 J-4 and J-4A USRA heavy Mikes became L&N's standard mainline heavy freight power. Numbered 1750-1914, all had mechanical stokers and many were later equipped with feedwater heaters, thermic firebox syphons, and bigger tenders. The final 24 (Baldwin, 1929)

The M-1s were the biggest locomotives on L&N. Engines 1957 and 1985 (Baldwin, 1942, and Lima, 1949) roll into Corbin, Kentucky, doing what they were built for. The name "Berkshire" was never used on the L&N; "Big Emma" was the usual nickname ("Cumberland" was suggested but never caught on). Photo by John A. Krave.

also got boosters. They worked Cincinnati-Montgomery and Cincinnati-Corbin, ran as far south as Atlanta, Mobile, and Pensacola, and went to Evansville and East St. Louis. The J-4s ran until the mid-1950s, and it was J-4 1882 (leased to subsidiary Carrollton Railroad in northern Kentucky) that ended L&N steam operation in January 1957.

Brooks delivered a three-cylinder version of the USRA heavy Mike, No. 1999, in 1924. In road service only a few years, it sat out the Depression, then worked the hump at DeCoursey Yard near Cincinnati.

The 42 M-1 2-8-4s, "Big Emmas," were the ultimate development of L&N steam. The first 20, Nos. 1950-69, were built by Baldwin in 1942 and 1944. Lima delivered a second batch of 22, Nos. 1970-91, in 1949. They were a quantum leap beyond the 2-8-2s. They had 69" drivers;

their 25" × 32" cylinders combined with 265 pounds of boiler pressure to give them 65,290 pounds of tractive effort; a booster added 14,100 pounds to that for starting. Vastly higher boiler capacity, larger fireboxes, cast steel frames and cylinders, roller bearings, and 12-wheel tenders gave the M-1s greater horsepower to work heavy trains at higher speeds on 12 percent less fuel than the 2-8-2s.

Kentucky engines, the 2-8-4s stayed mostly on three coalfields divisions, Cincinnati, Cumberland Valley, and Eastern Kentucky — indeed, their size and weight kept them there. On the EK M1s regularly rolled 9,500-ton coal trains (124 cars) from Neon to DeCoursey, with helpers up short grades at Jackson and Ravenna. Similarly, M1s worked 8,300-ton trains off the CV and up the Cincinnati Division to DeCoursey, again with helpers on two grades. During and just after World War II four M1s were assigned to passenger service between Cincinnati and Corbin.

The M-1s were the largest engine L&N could use. Anything larger — articulateds, ten-coupled engines, even 4-8-4s — would have required longer turntables, roundhouse stalls, and shop bays. It would have cost as much to accommodate larger locomotives as the locomotives themselves.

Passenger locomotives

By the 1890s 4-6-0s had replaced 4-4-0s as mainline passenger engines. The type was well represented by a number of small 4-6-0s acquired before 1890 as well as by some 35 bigger Ten-Wheelers built by Cooke, Rogers, and Baldwin between 1890 and 1904. Although replaced by 4-6-2s after 1905, 4-6-0s (and some 4-4-0s) continued in locals and branchline service well into the 1930s, and a few survived into the 1940s.

Heavier and longer trains required engines of greater capacity, so in 1905 L&N purchased its first Pacifics, K-1s 150-154, from Rogers. They were light, 187,800 pounds, and had 69" drivers — but that was 22,000 pounds and 2" more than the newest Ten-Wheelers, and their wider fireboxes and longer boilers gave the Pacifics greater steaming capacity. So successful were the 4-6-2s that between 1906 and 1909 South Louisville built 40 more, K-1s 155-174 and K-2s 175-194. The K-2s came

with superheaters, piston valves, and cylinders a half inch larger; many K-1s were likewise upgraded, including No. 152, which survives in operating condition at Kentucky Railway Museum. The K-1s and K-2s took over on the Cincinnati-Atlanta and Cincinnati-New Orleans main lines. In later years most of them wound up on the flatter Gulf Coast-South Alabama divisions. One K2 was rebuilt with a trailing truck booster and assigned to the heavy *New Orleans Limited* out of Mobile.

Two groups of slightly larger Pacifics, classes K-3 and K-4, were designed and built at South Louisville between 1912 and 1921. They had straight boilers and running boards, piston valves, superheaters and fireboxes with divided or partially sloped grates. The K-3s were numbered 195-211; the K-4s, 2212-2215 (classed K-4A and numbered separately for accounting reasons) and 216-239. The K-3s had 21½" × 28" cylinders, an inch larger than the K-2s, and weighed 211,500 pounds; the K-4s had 22" cylinders and weighed 233,300 pounds, still light for a Pacific, and were L&N's first Pacifics with outside-journal trailing trucks.

In 1919 six USRA 4-6-2s arrived, class K-5, Nos. 240-245. Though the USRA considered them light Pacifics, they were much larger than L&N's design — 25" × 28" cylinders, 73" drivers, 277,000 pounds total weight — and exerted 7,000 pounds more tractive effort. After the war L&N bought 20 more, Nos. 264-271 from Baldwin in 1923 and 272-283 from Brooks in 1924 — but between the last USRA Pacific in 1919 and the first copy in 1923, South Louisville Shop turned out 18 Pacifics, K-4Bs 246-263, almost identical to the prewar K-4s. The K5s took over top passenger assignments on the northerly divisions and later roamed systemwide. They were stoker-equipped and highly regarded by crews and roundhouse forces.

Brooks delivered a lone three-cylinder version of the USRA Pacific in 1925, No. 295, class K-7. It was stored during the 1930s, then in 1940 was rebuilt at Louisville, losing its middle cylinder, and streamlined for the L&N's segment of the Chicago-Miami *South Wind*. Three more heavy Pacifics were streamlined in 1940 and 1941 for the *Dixie Flagler* and *South Wind*.

Two groups of small secondhand 4-6-2s joined the roster in the

L&N's homemade Pacifics were small engines with thin, high-mounted boilers. K-1 No. 166 was built in 1906 and later rebuilt with piston valves and Walschaerts valve gear. Phillip Kotheimer collection.

1920s, four purchased from the Gulf, Mobile & Northern in 1921 and seven acquired with the Louisville, Henderson & St. Louis Railway in 1929.

L&N's biggest passenger engines were the 22 L-1 class 4-8-2s, Nos. 400-421. They were based on the USRA light Mountain, with 70" drivers instead of 69". Baldwin delivered 16 in 1926 and six more that were slightly heavier in 1930. The L-1s replaced K-5 Pacifics on the heaviest mainline limiteds between Cincinnati and Atlanta and down the main line to Birmingham. After 1940 they ranged as far south as Mobile (they weighed too much for the bridges along the Gulf Coast west of Mobile) and west to Evansville and East St. Louis. Some went into freight service in the early 1950s. In 1953 the 14 remaining 4-8-2s were renumbered 470-483 to open a block of numbers for GP7s.

Switchers

Switching was dominated by 0-6-0s and 0-8-0s, though the road also utilized older 2-6-0s and 2-8-0s for yard and transfer work.

First of the two groups of 0-6-0s were nearly 80 small six-wheel switchers rebuilt by Louisville and several other shops in the early 1900s from 1880s-vintage 2-8-0s. Many were reboilered; all retained their original numbers in the 600, 700 and 800 series. They were among the longest-lived of all L&N steam, puttering about yards and industries until the late 1940s.

Baldwin and Alco outshopped 35 bigger 0-6-0s (classes B-4 and B-6, Nos. 2055-2089) between 1903 and 1907. Three 0-6-0s were acquired secondhand in the 1920s, two from American International Shipbuilding Corp. and a third from the Louisville, Henderson & St. Louis.

For heavy switching L&N had 60 eight-wheel switchers, 34 homemade C-1s (Nos. 2100-2117 and 2124-2139) and 26 C-2s of USRA design (2118-2123 and 2140-2159) built between 1919 and 1925. The C-1s engines had similar-sized boilers to the homebuilt heavy 2-8-0s.

Mountain-type 402, almost pure USRA light 4-8-2, leads train 33 across the Ohio River from Cincinnati to Covington, Kentucky, on Memorial Day 1948. Locomotive numbers on the headlight glass were an L&N trait. Photo by Richard J. Cook.

Historical and technical society: Louisville & Nashville Historical Society, P. O. Box 17122, Louisville, KY 40217

Recommended reading:

"Big Emma," by Charles B. Castner, in *Trains Magazine*, December 1972, page 22

Louisville & Nashville Steam Locomotives, by Richard E. Prince, published in 1968 by Richard E. Prince (SBN: 9600088-0-2)

Published rosters:

Railroad Magazine: January 1936, page 88; June 1949, page 112

Trains Magazine: March 1955, page 27

L&N STEAM LOCOMOTIVES BUILT SINCE 1900

Type	Class	Numbers	Qty	Builder	Built	Retired	Notes
0-6-0	B-0	30	1	Baldwin	1911	1948	Ex-LH&StL
0-6-0	B-4	2055-2059	5	Manch	1903	1946-	
0-6-0	B-4	2070-2089	20	Manch, Rog	1905, 1907	1946-	
0-6-0	B-5	2060-2069	10	Baldwin	1903-1904	1934-1951	
0-6-0	B-7	633-648	12	L&N			Ex-H-3 2-8-0
0-6-0	B-8	649-658	9	L&N			Ex-H-4 2-8-0
0-6-0	B-9	2090, 2091	2	Lima	1918		
0-6-0	B-10	701-801	11	L&N			Ex-H-5 2-8-0
0-6-0	B-11	724-812	12	L&N			Ex-H-6 2-8-0
0-6-0	B-12	704-805	6	L&N			Ex-H-5 or H-6 2-8-0
0-8-0	C-1	2100-2117	18	L&N	1915-1918		
0-8-0	C-1	2124-2139	16	L&N	1922-1923		
0-8-0	C-2	2118-2123	6	Alco	1919		
0-8-0	C-2	2140-2159	20	Alco	1922-1925		
2-6-0	F-8	545-549	5	Rogers	1906		
2-6-0	F-9	550-556	7	Baldwin	1889-1907	1927-1930	
							Ex-Louisville & Atlantic
2-8-0	H-18	909-923	15	Cooke	1899-1900	1928-1934	
2-8-0	H-19	924-933	10	Rhode Island	1901	1933-1949	
2-8-0	H-20	934-943	10	Cooke	1902	1928-1949	
2-8-0	H-21	950-974	25	Rogers	1902-1903	1933-1934	
2-8-0	H-23	975-994	20	Baldwin	1903	1933-	

Type	Class	Numbers	Qty	Builder	Built	Retired	Notes
2-8-0	H-23	1000-1179	180	BLW, Rog, L&N	1905-1907	1933-	
2-8-0	H-24	848, 849	2	Rogers	1904	1948, 1947	
2-8-0	H-25	1180-1233	54	Rog, BLW, L&N	1907-1910	1947-	
2-8-0	H-26	996, 997	2	Richmond	1907	1940	
2-8-0	H-27	1234-1280	47	BLW, L&N	1910-1911	1934-1952	
2-8-0	H-28	1281-1305	25	L&N	1911	1950-	
2-8-0	H-29	1306-1350	45	L&N	1912-1913	1949-	
2-8-0	H-29A	1351-1374	24	L&N	1913-1914	1949-	
2-8-0	H-30	61, 62	2	Brooks	1922		
							Ex-Cumberland & Manchester
2-8-2	J-1	1416-1449	35	L&N	1915, 1917	1950-	All to J-1A
2-8-2	J-1	2400-2415	15	L&N	1914	1950-	All to J-1A
2-8-2	J-1A	1450-1461	12	L&N	1918	1950-	
2-8-2	J-2	1462-1479	18	L&N	1918-1919	1950-	
2-8-2	J-2A	1480-1495	16	L&N	1921	1950-	
2-8-2	J-3	1500-1592	93	Lima, Alco	1919-1923	1951-	
2-8-2	J-4	1750-1890	141	Brooks, Rich	1918-1927	1951-	
2-8-2	J-4A	1891-1914	24	Baldwin	1929		
2-8-2	J-5	1999	1	Brooks	1924	1950	Three-cylinder
2-8-4	M-1	1950-1991	42	BLW, Lima	1942-1949	1954-	
4-4-0	D-0	7	1	Baldwin	1916	1947	
							Ex-Cumberland & Manchester
4-6-0	G-11	305-309	5	Rhode Island	1901	-1940	
4-6-0	G-13	314	11	Baldwin	1903-1904	1934-1948	
4-6-0	G-23	31-33	3	Baldwin	1912	1947-1951	Ex-LH&StL
4-6-2	K-1	150-174	25	Rogers, L&N	1905-1907	1940-1947	15 to K-2A
4-6-2	K-2	175-194	20	L&N	1909-1910		All to K-2A
4-6-2	K-3	195-211	17	L&N	1912-1913	1940-1951	
4-6-2	K-4	216-239	24	L&N	1914-1918	1940-	
4-6-2	K-4A	2212-2215	4	L&N	1914	1948-	
4-6-2	K-4B	246-263	18	L&N	1920-1922		
4-6-2	K-5	240-245	6	Richmond	1919	1951-	
4-6-2	K-5	264-283	20	BLW, Brooks	1923, 1924	1951-	
4-6-2	K-6	296-299	4	Baldwin	1912	1950-1951	Ex-GM&N
4-6-2	K-7	295	1	Brooks	1925		Three-cylinder
4-6-2	K-8	81-87	7	Richmond	1923-1927	1948	Ex-LH&StL
4-8-2	L-1	400-421	22	Baldwin	1926, 1930	1951	

MAINE CENTRAL RAILROAD

By 1900 the Maine Central had a near-monopoly on railroading in the state of Maine north of Portland and south of the Canadian Pacific line that cuts across the middle of the state. It reached northeast from Portland through Bangor to the Canadian border at Vanceboro and northwest from Portland to St. Johnsbury, Vermont, and Lime Ridge, Quebec. A dense network of branches covered central Maine, extending north from the Portland-Bangor line and east along the coast. During the first 15 years of the 20th century MEC gained control of the few remaining short lines in central Maine, including two 2-foot-gauge railroads, the Sandy River & Rangeley Lakes and the Bridgton & Saco River.

Maine Central itself had come under control of the Boston & Maine in 1884. B&M control ended in 1914, but from 1933 to 1955 the two roads worked under an agreement for joint employment of officers and unified operation — in effect, merger without getting the Interstate Commerce Commission involved in the matter. Locomotives ran through between Boston & Bangor, 250 miles, and were interchanged freely.

MEC's principal connection for both freight and passenger business was the Boston & Maine at Portland; in turn MEC was the principal connection for the Bangor & Aroostook, which reached north from Bangor. Passenger traffic peaked in the summer as vacationers flocked to the seacoast and mountains in long, heavy Pullman trains — from the Washington-Philadelphia-New York-Ellsworth *Bar Harbor Express* to camper specials, carrying children to and from summer camps.

In 1911 the Portland Terminal Company, a wholly owned MEC subsidiary, was formed to handle all the switching, interchange, and station business of MEC and B&M in Portland. The two railroads immediately assigned several switchers to the company, including two brand-new MEC 0-6-0s, whose numbers were reused the next year.

In 1900 Maine Central adopted a new locomotive numbering and classification scheme, with several classes for each wheel arrangement in use (2-6-0, 4-4-0, and 4-6-0) depending on cylinder diameter. The six-wheel switchers underwent renumbering in 1917 and again in 1920; several switchers were transferred to the Portland Terminal; and recently vacated numbers were quickly reassigned to new 0-6-0s, as if the locomotive superintendent had decided there was no sense throwing away numbers that still had plenty of wear left in them.

There were two systems of indicating subclass, neither used consistently. One appended a number such as 65 or 70 (for the Pacifics) or 110 (the Mikes) that was a key to the tonnage rating; the other, used in the Railway & Locomotive Historical Society roster (and here), was a simple sequential number. The ex-B&M 2-10-2s appear variously as class A, SF, and Sf.

Some roads bought locomotives by the dozen or even the gross (Pennsy, for instance). Maine Central's practice was to buy six to twelve locomotives per year, a few each of several types. In 1912, for example, it bought seven Consolidations and two Pacifics; in 1913, eight Consolidations, two Pacifics, and two 0-6-0s for Portland Terminal, and in 1914 four Conolidations, three Pacifics, and three Mikados. The road's light Pacifics, for example, came from Schenectady over eight years: two in 1907, three in 1909, one in 1910, two each in 1911 and 1912, and three each in 1913 and 1914.

Maine Central and Portland Terminal bought a few diesel switchers before World War II but did not begin dieselizing in earnest until the late 1940s. The official last run of steam took place on June 13, 1954, when Pacific 470 powered an excursion train from Portland to Bangor and back. The engine was placed on display at Waterville, Maine.

Freight locomotives

MEC had only a few 2-6-0s built in the 20th century: eight from Schenectady, Nos. 308-315, and four from Manchester, 316-319, that were the same size as Boston & Maine's B-15 Moguls; and two heavier, 58"-drivered machines acquired with the Portland & Rumford Falls.

Railroads usually favored either Ten-Wheelers or Moguls for light duties, but not both — few railroads rostered great numbers of both

Maine Central's O-3 Ten-Wheelers were chunky locomotives, easily identified by the air reservoir on the pilot. Number 406 is ready to leave Portland on train 59 to Rockland in July 1945. Photo by Peter Ascher.

The O-4 Ten-Wheelers, MEC's only Lima power, were assigned to lines east of Bangor. Photo by Peter Ascher.

types. Maine Central was a Ten-Wheeler road, with 67 of the type built in the 20th century, more than twice as many as any other type of road engine.

The four members of the G class were small, light freight power, with 55" drivers. Numbers 106 and 107 weighed 104,000 pounds; 108 and 109, 115,000. The N class engines were passenger power. Numbers 279-283 had 69" drivers and weighed 142,000 pounds; 284-289, 73" drivers, 156,000 pounds. They were classed together because of their 19" cylinders.

The O class Ten-Wheelers of 1903 and 1905 had 21" × 26" cylinders and 63" drivers — dual-service engines — and weighed 164,000 pounds. They had inside piston valves and Stephenson valve gear. Engines 364-372, class O-1, had the same dimensions and were 3,000 pounds heavier, with outside piston valves and Walschaerts valve gear. The O-2 class, 373-382, were the same but had noticeably larger boilers and weighed 179,300 pounds. The O-4s, which continued the 63" drivers but had 20" × 28" cylinders, are noteworthy on two counts: their 182,000-pound weight was 24,000 pounds less than the O-3s of 1918, they were Maine Central's only Lima locomotives, and they were built quite late for

their type — 1923, just a year before Lima began advocating four-wheel trailing trucks and Super Power.

The 12 members of the O-3 class were considerably larger than the other 4-6-0s on the roster — 67" drivers, 22" × 28" cylinders, and 206,500 pounds total weight. While nowhere near Pennsy's G5 and Southern Pacific's T-40 in weight, they were still large Ten-Wheelers, heavier than many Pacifics and the equivalent in pulling power of MEC's light Pacifics.

Maine Central began buying 2-8-0s in 1910. The first nine, class W, Nos. 501-509, had 63" drivers and 22" × 28" cylinders; the W-1 class of 1912 and 1913 (510-524) and the W-2s of 1914 (525-528) had the same drivers and 23" × 28" cylinders.

In 1910 Boston & Maine bought four oil-burning 2-6-6-2s for operation through the Hoosac Tunnel in northwest Massachusetts. The electrification of the tunnel a year later made them redundant; moreover their combination of 61" drivers and a small firebox wasn't a happy one. B&M sold them to Maine Central, which put them to work on the 2 percent grade through Crawford Notch in the White Mountains of New Hampshire, both as road engines and as helpers. They were converted to coal in 1912. After they were replaced by 2-8-2s they worked occasionally between Portland and Bangor, and one was leased to the New Haven during the winter of 1919-1920. Three were scrapped in 1929; No. 1203, which had been fitted with a superheater during repairs after a head-on collision, remained in service until 1931.

New England wasn't Mikado country. New Haven had 33 of the type, and they were first-rank freight power only briefly; Boston & Albany's Mikes were supplanted in quick succession by 2-10-2s, 2-6-6-2s, and 2-8-4s. Boston & Maine, Central Vermont, and Bangor & Aroostook stuck with 2-8-0s long enough that when they advanced to the next type the Mikado was no longer the latest word.

Maine Central's first 2-8-2s, Nos. 601-603, were delivered by Alco's Schenectady Works in 1914. They had 63" drivers and 26½" × 30" cylinders and weighed 298,000 pounds — about the size of the USRA light Mikado, but with about 3,000 pounds less tractive effort. Seven more were delivered in 1915, six in 1916, and four in 1918. In 1919 the USRA allocated six light 2-8-2s to MEC, which numbered them 621-626 and classed them with its previous 2-8-2s. In 1924 MEC returned to its own design for another six Mikes from Schenectady. Trailing-truck boosters augmented their starting tractive effort.

Between 1936 and 1947 MEC added ten-coupled road freight locomotives to its roster, eight Boston & Maine 2-10-2s that had been replaced by 4-8-2s and diesels.

Passenger locomotives

MEC began buying Pacifics in 1907, three years before neighboring (and controlling) Boston & Maine bought its first 4-6-2. Engines 450 and 451 had 73" drivers and 22" × 28" cylinders and weighed 210,000 pounds, light as Pacifics go. By the time the last of the series, 463-465, arrived from Schenectady in 1914, weight was up to 238,500 pounds, still less than B&M's contemporary P-2, which had the same size drivers and cylinders. Three larger, booster-equipped Pacifics numbered 466-468 were delivered by Schenectady in 1917. They had the same 73" drivers but cylinder diameter was 25" and weight was 260,000 pounds. Two more of the same type, 469 and 470, followed in 1924.

The C-3 Pacifics, built in 1917 and 1924, were up-to-date engines with cast trailing trucks and boosters. Photo by Peter Ascher.

Maine Central's two Hudsons were among the lightest of their type. They had much the same shape as Boston & Maine's P-4 Pacifics but are also identifiable as being descendants of MEC's C-3 Pacifics. Trains collection.

Mikado 629 and Consolidation 509, meeting north of Lewiston, Maine, in 1951, illustrate the "speed" lettering applied to MEC's locomotives in later years. Photo by S. K. Bolton.

Maine Central's two Hudsons have always been something of an enigma. Two-of-a-kind locomotives on a roster usually have as interesting a story behind them as singletons. They were delivered by Baldwin in 1930. Like Pacifics 469 and 470 they had 73" drivers, and their smaller cylinders, 23" × 28", were more than compensated for by 240 pounds of boiler pressure (195 for the Pacifics). They had less grate area, 62.6 square feet, than many locomotives carried with a two-wheel trailing truck. Total weight was 312,590 pounds; tractive force was 41,300 pounds, plus 12,000 pounds for the booster. They were the lightest 4-6-4s built to that time; only Baltimore & Ohio's *Lord Baltimore* and the National of Mexico's Hudsons weighed less. They were Pacific-size Hudsons.

No explanation has come to light of why MEC bought 4-6-4s, and why only two. Consider the factors. Passenger traffic increased through the 1920s, and by the end of the decade the road was probably in the market for a larger passenger engine. The choice was a heavy 4-6-2, a light 4-8-2, or a light 4-6-4. A heavy Pacific would have pressed the limits of MEC's track, roadbed, and bridges, and MEC may have chosen

to keep axle loadings less than the maximum allowed. Both a Mountain and a Hudson would spread the weight over one more axle, but the Mountain would have the complication of a longer rigid wheelbase, eight drivers instead of six. Adding a booster to the 4-6-4 would create the equivalent of an eight-drivered locomotive for starting trains. MEC restricted the Hudsons to the Portland-Bangor main lines; B&M permitted them on both its Boston-Portland routes and considered them good for a somewhat heavier load than its P-4s. (MEC restricted B&M's P-4s, which were among the heaviest of Pacifics, to the same territory.)

But why only two Hudsons? MEC had a history of buying two or three locomotives of a type each year. There were probably plans to buy two more in 1931 and perhaps another two in 1932 or 1933, and the Depression probably canceled those plans.

Switchers

MEC's 0-6-0s ranged in weight from 90,000 to 165,300 pounds. Numbers 167-180, built between 1916 and 1920, were about the size of USRA 0-6-0s, of which MEC had a pair. A number of early 0-6-0s were assigned to Portland Terminal when it was formed in 1911. MEC had a single 0-8-0 on its roster, purchased from Boston & Maine in 1946.

Portland Terminal Company

Between 1912 and 1920 Portland Terminal purchased 12 0-6-0s of its own. In 1935 it bought two 0-8-0s from Boston & Maine, and it returned the favor in 1951 when it sold four 0-6-0s to B&M. If Maine Central's pair of Hudsons were a curiosity, Portland Terminal's single 4-6-4, ex-MEC 702, is an outright oddity, but easily explained — a movable source of steam for melting snow in the yards.

Published rosters:

Railroad Magazine: May 1932, page 212; January 1947, page 106; June 1953, page 104

Railway & Locomotive Historical Society Bulletin: No. 55, page 64 (early locomotives); No. 56, page 87 (later power); No. 152, page 55 (all-time roster)

MEC STEAM LOCOMOTIVES BUILT SINCE 1900

Type	Class	Numbers	Qty	Builder	Built	Retired	Notes
0-6-0	K	154	1	Schenectady	1900	1930	Ex-185, 182
0-6-0	K	155	1	Manchester	1902	1937	Ex-182
0-6-0	K	161-166	6	Schenectady	1909-1910	1946-1947	
							First 165 and 166 to PT 821 and 822 in 1911
0-6-0	K	165, 166	2	Schenectady	1912	1939, 1947	
							Second 165 and 166
0-6-0	K	167-174	8	Schenectady	1909-1918		
0-6-0	K	175, 176	2	Schenectady	1900		
							First 175 to PT 803 in 1911; first 176 renumbered 154 in 1920
0-6-0	K	175, 176	2	Cooke	1919	1948, 1951	USRA
0-6-0	K	177-186	10	Schenectady	1920	1949, 1954	
0-6-0	K	180-182	3	Manchester	1902		
							180 and 181 to PT 801 and 802 in 1911; 182 renumbered 155 in 1920
0-6-0	K	183, 184	2	Brooks	1904		To PT 807, 808 in 1911)
0-6-0	K	185-187	3	Manchester	1906		To PT 809-811 in 1911
0-6-0	K	188	1	Manchester	1905		Ex-P&RF 31
0-6-0	K	189	1	Cooke	1924	Sold 1950	
							Ex-S. D. Warren Co.
0-8-0	J-2	199	1	Schenectady	1922	1951	Ex-B&M 617
2-6-0	P	308-315	8	Schenectady	1900	1925-1928	
2-6-0	P	316-319	4	Manchester	1902	1930-1936	
2-6-0	P	320, 321	2	Manchester	1902	1940	Ex-P&RF 13, 14
2-8-0	W	501-509	9	Schenectady	1910	1927-1953	501 preserved
2-8-0	W-1	510-524	15	Schenectady	1912-1913	1936-1953	519 preserved
2-8-0	W-2	525-528	4	Schenectady	1914	1951-1954	
2-8-2	S	601-620	20	Schenectady	1914-1918	1936-1952	
2-8-2	S	621-626	6	Schenectady	1919	1951-1956	USRA
2-8-2	S	627-632	6	Schenectady	1924	1951-1952	
2-10-2	A	651-658	8	Schenectady	1920, 1923		Ex-B&M
2-6-6-2	X	1201-1204	4	Schenectady	1910	1929, 1935	Ex-B&M
4-4-0	E	84, 85	2	Manchester	1901, 1900	1926, 1924	Ex-Somerset 2, 7
4-4-0	E	86, 87	2	Manchester	1907	1927	Ex-Somerset 10, 12

Type	Class	Numbers	Qty	Builder	Built	Retired	Notes
4-4-0	H	140-149	10	Manchester	1905, 1907	1934-1942	
4-4-0	H	150-152	3	Schenectady	1909	1935-1940	
4-6-0	G	106, 107	2	Baldwin	1905	1930, 1935	
							Ex-Somerset 20, 21
4-6-0	G	108, 109	2	Manchester	1906	1937, 1935	
							Ex-Somerset 22, 23
4-6-0	N	279-283	5	Schenectady	1901, 1903	1928-1935	
4-6-0	N	284-289	6	Schenectady	1904-1906	1935-1938	
4-6-0	O	351-363	13	Schenectady	1903, 1905	1933-1948	
4-6-0	O-1	364-372	9	Rhode Island	1906	1942-1953	
4-6-0	O-2	373-382	10	Baldwin	1907-1908	1939-1953	
4-6-0	O-3	401-412	12	Pitt, Schen	1918, 1920	1948-1953	
4-6-0	O-4	383-390	8	Lima	1923	1949-1952	
4-6-2	C	450-465	21	Schenectady	1907-1914	1936-1956	
							459 was class C-1; 464, C-2
4-6-2	C-3	466-470	5	Schenectady	1917, 1924	1952-1953	470 preserved
4-6-4	D	701, 702	2	Baldwin	1930	1950, 1955	

Portland Terminal Company

Type	Class	Numbers	Qty	Builder	Built	Retired	Notes
0-6-0	K	801, 802	2	Manchester	1902	1923, 1924	Ex-MEC 180, 181
0-6-0	K	803	1	Schenectady	1900	1929	Ex-MEC 175
0-6-0	K	804	1	Manchester	1899	1929	Ex-B&M 161
0-6-0	K	805, 806	2	Baldwin	1903	1928, 1929	Ex-B&M 192, 194
0-6-0	K	807, 808	2	Brooks	1904	1939, 1936	
							Ex-MEC 183, 184; Camelback
0-6-0	K	809-811	3	Manchester	1906	1936-1939	Ex-MEC 185-187
0-6-0	K	820	1	Manchester	1909	1936	Ex-B&M 288
0-6-0	K	821, 822	2	Schenectady	1910	1945, 1943	Ex-MEC 165, 166
0-6-0	K	824-829	5	Manchester	1912-1913	1944-1950	
0-6-0	K	830-835	6	Schen, Pitt	1917-1920	1950-1953	
							830-832, 834 sold to B&M 1951
0-8-0	J	851, 852	2	Schenectady	1916	1951	Ex-B&M 600, 601
4-6-4	D	702	1	Baldwin	1930	1955	Ex-MEC 702

MEXICAN RAILWAY (Ferrocarril Mexicano)

The Mexican Railway was built with British capital and opened in 1872 from the port of Veracruz, on the Gulf of Mexico, to Mexico City, 264 miles. From Veracruz to Paso del Macho in the state of Veracruz, 48 miles, the line climbed from sea level to 1,560 feet, an average grade of 30 feet to the mile and a maximum of 1.7 percent. West of Esperanza, in the state of Puebla, 112 miles from Veracruz at an elevation of 8,045 feet, the line lay across the central plateau of Mexico, with grades of no more than 1.5 percent.

In the 64 miles from Paso del Macho to Esperanza, though, the line climbed 6,485 feet, about 101 feet per mile or an average grade of 1.92 percent. The steepest grades were in the 25 miles from Orizaba, Ver.C., to Boca del Monte, Pue., the Maltrata Incline, where actual grades of nearly 4 percent and 16.5-degree curves created a compensated grade of 4.7 percent. (The figure for compensated grade includes both the slope or inclination and the curve resistance — think of it as "effective grade.") Andrew Talcott, the West Point graduate who engineered the line, believed making the route as short as possible would reduce maintenance expenses. A shorter route had to be steeper, and he calculated that balancing maintenance costs against costs of operating trains called for a grade of 4.6 percent for the mountainous section. The line was built with a calculated maximum compensated (or effective) grade of 4.7 percent, but there were short stretches, a few hundred yards, as steep as 5.24 percent.

Oddities

The railway found the initial answer to the problem of the Maltrata Incline in a locomotive developed by Robert Fairlie, a British engineer. Fairlie's design was an 0-6-6-0: On a single frame it carried a boiler with two barrels, one pointing each way, two smokeboxes and two stacks, and a center firebox. The frame sat on two sets of 0-6-0 running gear, one pointing each way. The whole affair sounds impossible, but the first Fairlies came from Avonside Engine Co. of Bristol, England, in 1871, and there were 24 on the roster from various British builders by the end of 1883. Neilson of Glasgow delivered 12 with 42" drivers and 16" × 22" cylinders between 1888 and 1901. North British built 10 of the same dimensions between 1903 and 1907, and in 1907 built two larger Fairlies (48" drivers, 17" × 25" cylinders, 268,448 pounds weight, 45,900 pounds tractive effort). The final group came from Vulcan Foundry in 1911. They were larger still, with 48" drivers, 19" × 25" cylinders, 306,477 pounds weight, and 57,528 pounds tractive effort — in weight and tractive effort about halfway between the USRA light and heavy Mikados.

Electrification of the line between Paso del Macho and Esperanza between 1923 and 1928 put the Fairlies out of work; one remained on the roster until 1936. FCM's operations were merged with those of National Railways of Mexico in 1959. Dieselization came gradually in the 1960s, first replacing steam, then also replacing the electrics.

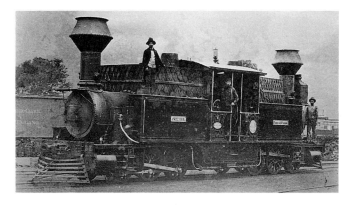

Fairlie 32, *Orizava*, built by Yorkshire Engine Co. of Sheffield, England, illustrates the concept: double boiler, single firebox and cab, swiveling 0-6-0 running gear at each end. G. M. Best collection.

Other standard gauge locomotives

The rest of FCM's steam locomotives were less exotic. Most of the 19th-century locomotives that weren't Fairlies were 2-8-0s and 4-6-0s. Locomotives purchased in the 20th century were of only three types: 2-8-0, 4-6-0, and 4-6-2.

Sixteen 2-8-0s with 50" drivers were delivered by Baldwin between 1899 and 1908. They were classed G-3 but later renumbered and divided into the G-23 and G-24 classes. Eleven ex-Mexican Central 2-8-0s built by Cooke in 1903 and 1904 came to FCM by way of National Railways of Mexico after the Mexican revolution. They had 55" drivers and 22" × 26" cylinders and weighed 211,420 pounds. Along with them came a single ex-Mexican National 2-8-0, somewhat lighter, with 58" drivers.

In 1921 Baldwin delivered 11 Consolidations with 54" drivers, Nos. 200-210 (200 and 201 later swapped numbers). The last locomotives ordered by the road's British management were 10 Baldwin 2-8-0s with 22" × 28" cylinders and 60" drivers and that weighed 192,000 pounds; they looked very much like U. S. Army World War II Consolidations. They were delivered in 1946 and numbered 211-220. After the Mexican government took ownership in 1946 nine old 2-8-0s joined the roster, 1906 Baldwins with 58" drivers, originally built for the National Railroad of Mexico and the Mexican International Railway. Much renumbered by National Railways of Mexico, they were again renumbered (300-308) by FCM.

The Pittsburgh and Dickson 4-6-0s had 60" drivers; the Baldwin 4-6-0s, 54". They underwent some minor renumbering: No. 35 was scrapped; 36 became 35; 38 became 36; 40 became 38.

Three Pacifics numbered 120-122 came from Baldwin in 1910. They were light, low-drivered machines — 216,491 pounds, 63" drivers, 23" × 28" cylinders — but low drivers were what the 4.7 percent grade called for. In 1928 Alco's Schenectady Works delivered four more Pacifics numbered 130-133. They had larger drivers (69") and smaller cylinders (20" × 28") — but three cylinders, not two. They were successful enough that FCM bought three more from Montreal in 1938, and they remained in service into the 1960s.

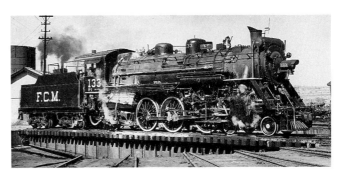

Three-cylinder Pacific 133 was a curiosity when it was built by Alco in 1928; in 1960, when it posed on the turntable at Apizaco, it was an absolute rarity. Photo by Stan Kistler.

Narrow gauge locomotives

The Mexican Railway had three narrow gauge branches, each a different gauge and each constructed only part of the way to its intended destination. In March 1909 FCM bought the Ferrocarril de Atlamaxac, a 2-foot gauge line extending from Muñoz on the Mexicano main line in the state of Tlaxcala to Galera, Pue., 18 miles. The Mexicano changed the gauge to 30" and extended the line another 15 miles to Chignahuapan, Pue., with the intention, never fulfilled, of continuing to Zacatlan. Mexicano sold three of the four 2-foot gauge locomotives (a Baldwin 2-6-0 and two German-built 0-4-4-0Ts), keeping only a two-truck Shay, and ordered four identical 30" gauge 2-8-0s from Baldwin. The branch was abandoned in 1958.

In November 1909 FCM purchased the Ferrocarril de Córdoba a Huatusco, a 2-foot gauge, 20-mile line from Córdoba to Coscomatepec, Ver .C. (The 29-mile extension to Huatusco remained only a proposal.) With the line came three Baldwin 2-6-0s, two built in 1902 and third in 1905, to which FCM added the former Atlamaxac Shay. The branch was abandoned in 1951.

Consolidation 211, the first of 10 built by Baldwin in 1946, was obviously derived from the U. S. Army's 2-8-0 of World War II. Photo by C. W. Witbeck.

FCM purchased a 3-foot gauge railroad extending 74 miles from San Marcos, Pue., to Mucio Martinez, Pue., in 1913. The goal of the line was Huajuapan de León in the state of Oaxaca; because of the Mexican revolution, rails never reached that point and were eventually pulled up between Ixcaquixtla and Mucio Martinez. FCM received three 2-8-0s that had been built for the predecessor company by Baldwin in 1902 plus a fourth engine that was beyond repair. The 2-8-0s were eventually joined by a secondhand 4-6-0 and later replaced by three former National Railways of Mexico 2-8-0s. The branch was abandoned in 1958.

The 5-mile standard gauge branch from Santa Ana to Tlaxcala, the capital of the state of the same name, purchased in 1910, was powered first by mules, then by homemade gasoline cars, both of which are outside the scope of this book.

Recommended reading: *Railroads In Mexico*, Volume I, by Francisco Garma Franco, published in 1985 by Sundance Publications, 250 Broadway, Denver, CO 80203 (ISBN 0-913582-39-5)
Published rosters: *Trains Magazine*, May 1961, page 23

FCM STEAM LOCOMOTIVES BUILT SINCE 1900

Type	Class	Numbers	Qty	Builder	Built	Notes
Standard gauge						
0-6-6-0	R-1	171-180	10	North British	1904, 1907	Fairlie
0-6-6-0	R-2	181, 182	2	North British	1907	Fairlie
0-6-6-0	R-3	183-185	3	Vulcan Foundry	1911	Fairlie
2-8-0	G-23	50-54	5	Baldwin	1904-1908	Built as G-3 class
2-8-0	G-24	59-69	11	Baldwin	1899-1907	Built as G-3 class
2-8-0	GR-26	80-90	11	Cooke	1903-1904	Ex-NdeM
2-9-0	GR-34	91	1	Cooke	1903	Ex-NdeM
2-8-0	GR-27	200-210	11	Baldwin	1921	
2-8-0	GR-28	211-220	10	Baldwin	1946	
2-8-0	GR-42	300-308	9	Baldwin	1906	Ex-NdeM
4-6-0	F-4	69, 70	2	Pittsburgh	1900	To 31, 32
4-6-0	F-4	33-36	4	Dickson	1902	36 renumbered 35
4-6-0	F-5	37-40	4	Baldwin	1904, 1906	38 to 36; 40 to 38
4-6-2	M	120-122	3	Baldwin	1910	
4-6-2	MR-3	130-133	4	Schenectady	1928	Three-cylinder simple
4-6-2	MR-3	134-136	3	Montreal	1938	Three-cylinder simple
24-inch gauge (Huatusco Branch, Córdoba to Coscomatepec)						
2-6-0	E-1	1-3	3	Baldwin	1902, 1905	
Shay	S-H	4	1	Lima	1905	Two-truck
30-inch gauge (Zacatlan Branch, Muñoz to Chignahuapan)						
2-8-0	E-2	11-14	4	Baldwin	1910	
36-inch gauge (Huajuapan Branch, San Marcos to Ixcaquixtla)						
2-8-0	G-028	24-26	3	Baldwin	1899	Ex-NdeM 259, 257, 258
2-8-0	E-3	20-22	3	Baldwin	1902	
4-6-0	EE-4	23	1	Schenectady	1911	

MINNEAPOLIS, ST. PAUL & SAULT STE. MARIE RAILWAY

In 1900 the Minneapolis, St. Paul & Sault Ste. Marie extended from Minneapolis east across Wisconsin and Michigan to a connection with Canadian Pacific at Sault Ste. Marie, Ontario; and northwest from Minneapolis across Minnesota and North Dakota to another connection with CP at Portal, N. D. CP had obtained control of the Soo Line (Sault is pronounced "Soo") in 1888, not so much to form an alternate route to western Canada south of Lake Superior as to prevent Grand Trunk from doing so.

In 1904 the road completed a line from Glenwood, Minn., north to the Canadian border at Emerson, Manitoba. In 1908 it acquired control of the Wisconsin Central Railway and in 1909 leased the property. WC's main line ran from Chicago to St. Paul and Minneapolis via Waukesha, Oshkosh, and Stevens Point, Wis. A long branch reached north to Lake Superior at Ashland, Wis., and another to Superior, Wis., and Duluth, Minn., was nearly complete. It opened a line between the Twin Cities and Superior in 1912, and in 1921 purchased the Wisconsin & Northern, a 134-mile line from Neenah to Crandon.

The Soo Line's principal traffic was wheat. The road was created by the consolidation of two railroads, both established by flour millers in the Twin Cities. One was built as an alternate route to the East that avoided Chicago and Chicago-railroad freight rates; the other reached from the Twin Cities to the wheat-growing areas of Minnesota and North Dakota. Leasing the Wisconsin Central gave the Soo Line access to the lumber and paper industries of Wisconsin, the iron mines of northern Wisconsin and upper Michigan, and to Chicago, the railroad center of the country.

The road entered five years of bankruptcy at the end of 1937, the result of drought in the Midwest and the Depression. A new corporation, the Minneapolis, St. Paul & Sault Ste. Marie Railroad, took over in 1944, and in 1950 it began using the Soo Line name for everything but legal matters. At the beginning of 1961 Soo Line, Wisconsin Central, and Duluth, South Shore & Atlantic (another CP subsidiary) merged to form the Soo Line Railroad. In 1985 it purchased what remained of the Milwaukee Road, and in 1987 it spun off most of the old Wisconsin Central to form a new, independent Wisconsin Central. About that same time Canadian Pacific acquired full ownership of Soo Line. The railroad is now considered a unit of the CP Rail system.

The Soo Line-Wisconsin Central relationship was interesting. The WC was the busiest part of the Soo and carried the most freight. WC retained corporate identity and its own officers. Its rolling stock, even that purchased under Soo Line stewardship, was marked with WC initials and numbered separately. Locomotives numbered 2000 and above and subclasses numbered 20 and higher were WC property (except for 4-8-2s 4000-4003), even in the early diesel era.

The road was not a major passenger carrier. Its Chicago-Minneapolis route was 19 to 52 miles longer than those of its competitors, and Soo never approached its rivals in the matter of speed. After 1933 its summer-only Chicago-Vancouver train (handled by CP west of Portal) ran on the Chicago & North Western between Chicago and St. Paul.

Soo Line didn't need Mallets; it had no mountains to battle. The western part of the road was prairie country, and the line east to the Soo — Sault Ste. Marie — lay through forested country in which the obstacles were rivers, lakes, and swamps. Soo Line had only two grades of consequence, neither severe. Both were on the Wisconsin Central: the Lake Superior escarpment south of Superior, Wis., and Byron Hill in the moraine country of Wisconsin south of Fond du Lac.

The road bought a few diesel switchers before World War II, but didn't begin dieselization in earnest until the end of the 1940s. By early 1955 dieselization was complete, but as late as July 1958 11 steam locomotives — 2-8-0s, 2-8-2s, and 4-6-2s — were still on Soo Line's roster, stored serviceable.

Freight locomotives

Soo Line's freight Ten-Wheelers were all inherited — Nos. 612 and 613 from the Wisconsin & Northern and 2629-2654 from Wisconsin Cen-

Soo's Pacifics were light machines but sufficient for all but the heaviest of the road's passenger trains. Number 2711 is shown at speed with train 2, a Stevens Point-Chicago accommodation train, at Van Dyne, Wisconsin, on September 24, 1949. Photo by Jim Scribbins.

Mikado 1017, built by Brooks in 1920 and part of Soo Line's newest class of 2-8-2, shuffles ore cars at Ashland, Wisconsin, in late 1951.

tral. The E-22 class had 63" drivers; the E-24 and E25 Ten-Wheelers had 57" drivers, which would be considered small on anything but a switcher. The WC Ten-Wheelers were purchased as part of a general upgrading of WC's motive power just before and after 1900.

The Soo began buying 2-8-0s in 1893 — 27 cross-compounds with 51" drivers from Schenectady and Rhode Island. Between 1900 and 1909 Schenectady delivered 51 cross-compound 2-8-0s, Nos. 428-474 and 2425-2428. The early ones had 55" drivers; the later ones, 63". All were later converted to simple engines and superheated.

Between 1910 and 1913 46 more Consolidations arrived from Schenectady, single-expansion engines with 63" drivers, weighing 225,000 pounds — Nos. 475-499 for Soo Line and 2429-2449 for Wisconsin Central. WC's pre-Soo Line 2-8-0s consisted of 25 built by Brooks between 1903 and 1907. They had 63" drivers and 21" × 26" cylinders; at 163,400

pounds they were lighter than any of Soo's own 20th-century 2-8-0s.

The first decade of the 20th century brought Soo's only oddities: a single Vauclain compound Decapod from Baldwin in 1900 (at the time the world's largest locomotive) and ten cross-compound Prairies from Schenectady in 1907. All were later simpled. The 2-10-0 found its niche working the ore dock at Ashland, Wis.

Soo Line acquired its first Mikado in 1904 with the purchase of the Bismarck, Washburn & Great Falls. Number 3 was a 50"-drivered Vauclain compound weighing 166,900 pounds, built by Baldwin in 1901. It was the first Mikado built for service in the U. S. — the first 2-8-2 with a firebox behind the drivers and supported by a trailing truck.

The first 2-8-2s built for Soo Line were delivered by Schenectady in 1913, numbered 1001-1010 and classed L-1. They were about the size of the USRA light Mikado, with 63" drivers. Larger cylinders — 28" × 30" — and 170-pound boiler pressure combined to give them about the

Mountain 4008 is about to hit the Milwaukee Road crossing at Duplainville, Wis., on July 26, 1947, with a northbound fast freight. High-capacity tenders were a later addition to the 4-8-2s. Photo by Jim Scribbins.

same tractive effort as the USRA engine. In 1920 Brooks delivered 25 more Mikes with the same dimensions but slightly heavier, Soo Line 1011-1023 and Wisconsin Central 3000-3011.

In 1941 and 1942 the Soo purchased a dozen secondhand 2-8-2s, four Baldwins from the Rock Island, which it classed L-3 and numbered 1030-1033, and eight Brooks engines from the Chicago, Indianapolis & Louisville (Monon), which it classed L-4 and numbered 1024-1027 and 1034-1037.

Soo Line had several competitive disadvantages between Chicago and the Twin Cities: It was longer, most of the route was single track, and only about half of that was signaled. About all it could do was run faster. In 1926 it turned to the 4-8-2 for freight and heavy passenger service. Alco's Brooks Works delivered 10 class N-20 Mountains in 1926. They were updated versions of the USRA light 4-8-2, weighing 344,500 pounds and equipped with trailing-truck boosters that gave them 64,620 pounds starting tractive effort. The first four, Nos. 4000-4003, were Soo

Line engines; 4004-4009 were Wisconsin Central power. Schenectady delivered eight more in 1928. Engines 4010-4017 weighed 342,000 pounds. In 1930 Soo Line erected the final three, Nos. 4018-4020, in its Shoreham Shops at Minneapolis using boilers built by Alco. Oddly, they weighed 338,700 pounds — successive batches of the same type of locomotive usually weighed more, not less.

Yet more speed for Soo Line freights came with the delivery of four Lima 4-8-4s in 1938, Nos. 5000-5003, class O-20. They were mid-size Northerns, weighing 453,500 pounds, and their 75" drivers would have made them passenger engines only a few years before. They were rated at 66,000 pounds tractive effort; trailing truck boosters added another 13,400 pounds. Assigned to fast Chicago-Twin Cities freight trains, the 4-8-4s acquired a reputation for availability — they were able to turn at the terminals and be on their way quickly.

Passenger locomotives

Wisconsin Central had 15 Atlantics built by Brooks between 1902 and 1905. Their 79" drivers were the largest on the railroad. Most were off the roster by 1940.

Only one group of Ten-Wheelers built after 1900 could be considered passenger engines, by virtue of their 69" drivers — Nos. 605-611, class E-1, built by Baldwin in 1902 and 1903. The roster included two groups of passenger 4-6-0s built in 1898, WC 227-230 (later Soo Line 2625-2628, class E-23) built by Brooks, and Baldwin-built Vauclain compounds 600-604, class E, which had 73" drivers.

There were four groups of Pacifics. Number 700, formerly Bismarck, Washburn & Great Falls 4, was a slide-valve engine with 62" drivers built by Baldwin in 1904. The rest were Schenectady products. The H-1s, Nos. 701-722, and the H-20s, 2700-2703, had 69" drivers and 20" × 26" cylinders and weighed between 202,000 and 206,000 pounds. The H-1s had inside piston valves and Stephenson valve gear. The H-2 class also had 69" drivers. Larger cylinders, 24" in diameter, more than compensated for 170-pound boiler pressure and gave them a tractive effort of 30,760 pounds. The remaining classes — H-3, H-21, H-22, and H-23 — had 75" drivers and 25" × 26" cylinders. The H-3s, Nos. 727-737, and

H-21s, 2704-2713, weighed 258,000 pounds and were built between 1911 and 1913. The H-22 class, Nos. 2714-2717 were 6,000 pounds heavier, and the H-23s, 2718-2723, built in 1923, weighed 271,000 pounds, somewhat lighter than the USRA light Pacific.

Switchers

Soo Line rostered only 0-6-0s. They were 51"-drivered engines, and as the type developed they grew heavier, though not even the B-4s, the only switchers with outside piston valves and outside valve gear, approached the USRA 0-6-0 in weight or tractive effort. Consolidations handled heavier switching chores.

Historical and technical society: Soo Line Historical & Technical Society, 3410 Kasten Court, Middleton, WI 53562

Published rosters:

Railroad Magazine: February 1934, page 130; June 1947, page 124; May 1953, page 106

Trains Magazine: December 1958, page 23

Railway & Locomotive Historical Society Bulletin, No. 54, page 150 (Wisconsin Central)

The four Lima Northerns of 1938 were the final development of steam power on the Soo Line. Number 5001 is heading north with 60 cars in tow on September 25, 1949, at Van Dyne, Wis. Photo by Jim Scribbins.

SOO LINE STEAM LOCOMOTIVES BUILT SINCE 1900

Type	Class	Numbers	Qty	Builder	Built	Notes
0-6-0	B-1	326-333	8	Cooke	1902-1907	
0-6-0	B-2	334-339	6	Schenectady	1909-1910	
0-6-0	B-3	340-343	4	Schenectady	1912	
0-6-0	B-4	344-354	11	Brks, Sch	1915-1920	
0-6-0	B-22	2317-2320	4	Brooks	1900	
0-6-0	B-23	2321-2328	8	Brooks	1899-1908	
2-6-0	D-2	108-172	65	Schenectady	1903-1907	Built as cross-compound
2-6-2	J	800-809	10	Schenectady	1907	Built as cross-compound
2-8-0	F-7	428-430	3	Schenectady	1900	Built as cross-compound
2-8-0	F-8	431-444	14	Schenectady	1902-1903	Built as cross-compound
2-8-0	F-9	445-472	28	Schenectady	1905-1906	Built as cross-compound
2-8-0	F-10	473, 474	2	Schenectady	1909	Built as cross-compound
2-8-0	F-11	475-484	10	Schenectady	1910	
2-8-0	F-12	485-499	15	Schenectady	1912-1913	
2-8-0	F-20	2400-2424	25	Schenectady	1903-1907	Ex-WC 160-184
2-8-0	F-21	2425-2428	4	Schenectady	1909	
2-8-0	F-22	2429-2443	15	Schenectady	1911	
2-8-0	F-23	2444-2449	6	Schenectady	1914	
2-8-2	L	1000	1	Baldwin	1901	Ex-BW&GF 3
2-8-2	L-1	1001-1010	10	Schenectady	1913	
2-8-2	L-2	1011-1023	13	Brooks	1920	
2-8-2	L-3	1030-1033	4	Baldwin	1913	Ex-Rock Island
2-8-2	L-4	1024-1027	4	Brooks	1912	Ex-Monon
2-8-2	L-4	1034-1037	4	Brooks	1912	Ex-Monon
2-8-2	L-20	3000-3011	12	Brooks	1920	
2-10-0	G	950	1	Baldwin	1900	Built as compound
4-4-2	K	2900-2914	15	Brooks	1902-1905	Ex-WC 257-271
4-6-0	E-1	605-611	6	Baldwin	1902-1903	
4-6-0	E-2	612, 613	2	Schenectady	1913, 1915	Ex-Wisconsin & Northern 4, 5
4-6-0	E-22	2629-2639	11	Brooks	1900	Ex-WC 231-241
4-6-0	E-24	2640-2644	5	Brooks	1900	Ex-WC 242-246

Type	Class	Numbers	Qty	Builder	Built	Notes	Type	Class	Numbers	Qty	Builder	Built	Notes
4-6-0	E-25	2645-2654	10	Brooks	1900	Ex-WC 247-256	4-6-2	H-22	2714-2717	4	Schenectady	1914	
4-6-2	H	700	1	Baldwin	1904	Ex-BW&GF 4	4-6-2	H-23	2718-2723	6	Schenectady	1923	
4-6-2	H-1	701-722	21	Schenectady	1904-1907		4-8-2	N-20	4000-4009	10	Brooks	1926	4000-4003 owned by Soo
4-6-2	H-2	723-726	4	Schenectady	1910		4-8-2	N-20	4010-4017	8	Schenectady	1928	
4-6-2	H-3	727-737	11	Schenectady	191911-1913		4-8-2	N-20	4018-4020	3	Soo LIne	1930	
4-6-2	H-20	2700-2703	4	Schenectady	1909		4-8-4	O-20	5000-5003	4	Lima	1938	
4-6-2	H-21	2704-2713	10	Schenectady	1911-1913								

MISSOURI-KANSAS-TEXAS RAILROAD

In 1891 the Missouri, Kansas & Texas Railway had just survived a period of control by Jay Gould and a short receivership. It had lines from Kansas City and Sedalia, Mo., and Junction City, Kan., that converged on Parsons, Kan., whence a single line ran south through Fort Worth and Waco, Texas, to a point between San Antonio and Houston. Branches in Texas reached west to Henrietta and east to Jefferson. The Katy began to expand, and by 1904 its rails reached St. Louis, Houston, San Antonio, Tulsa, Oklahoma City, and Shreveport. By 1915 it had acquired two long lines, one reaching northwest from Waco almost to Lubbock, Texas, and the other running from Fort Worth north along the western border of Oklahoma and into the Oklahoma panhandle.

The company was reorganized as the Missouri-Kansas-Texas Railroad in 1923, and pruned a few routes. It survived the Depression with its finances intact, but just barely. World War II increased the Katy's traffic but wore out its track. It dieselized, but its locomotive maintenance was no better than its track maintenance. In the 1950s the Katy

Katy's line through western Oklahoma was also the place to find the last of its 4-4-0s. Engine 312, built by Baldwin in 1890 and rebuilt in the 1920s, provides ample power for train 54 near Altus, Okla., in May 1946. Glossy black paint and white trim were as much Katy trademarks as the red-and-white herald on the tender. Photo by Preston George.

Missouri-Kansas-Texas found the 2-6-0 ideal for light freight service on light rail. Number 555, photographed at Altus, Oklahoma, in April 1946, is not only a modern-looking Mogul (especially for one built in 1904) but also a well-maintained one. Photo by Preston George.

began to fall apart. Rehabilitation began with a change of management in 1965. Mergers began to swallow up neighboring railroads, and Katy's attitude was first protest, then "count us in." In May 1988 Katy was purchased by Missouri Pacific, a subsidiary of Union Pacific, and its operations were absorbed by UP.

For more than two decades before dieselization Katy's image was one of standard American railroading. Motive power development ceased with the Mikado and the Pacific, which were entirely adequate for Katy's traffic and topography. The road had a reputation for clean, good-looking steam engines, and for that reason attracted more than its share of attention from railroad enthusiasts.

Until 1912 Katy reused engine numbers as they became available. In 1912 a new numbering system was adopted so like engines would have adjacent numbers (the 1912 numbers are used here).

After World War II MKT needed new locomotives. Larger steam locomotives would cost less than diesels, but would require new turntables, bridges, and rail. In early 1946 Electro-Motive's F3 demonstrator No. 291 paid a visit. Even with one of its four units shut down (Katy must have said it was in the market for a 4500-h.p. engine) it was faster and more powerful than the steam locomotives. It could run from one end of the railroad to the other without change, it was kind to Katy's 90-pound rail, and it used one-third the fuel. The road bought its first diesel switchers in 1946 and completed dieselization in 1952.

Freight locomotives

The flat country the MKT traversed and the light construction of most of its lines meant that small freight engines would be sufficient, and the road stayed with the 2-6-0 longer than most other railroads. Ten Moguls delivered by Schenectady in 1902 had wide bituminous-burning fireboxes over the rear 63" drivers, setting a pattern for most of the Katy's subsequent 2-6-0s, built until 1907.

In 1923 the D-8 Moguls were reclassified J-5 and were superheated and fitted with piston valves. They were renumbered, with some engines getting new numbers so other engines could have theirs. In 1938 those still on the roster had their boiler pressure increased from 200 to 210 pounds and were converted to oil burners. There were still 35 2-6-0s in service in 1944, and most of them survived into the 1950s.

Between 1900 and 1902 Katy acquired ten 2-8-0s with 56" drivers, mostly from Baldwin; the K-6 engines had 21" × 26" cylinders, the K-8s 22" × 28". Three engines (plus a fourth built in 1895) were Camelbacks with Wootten fireboxes for low-grade coal from mines near McAlester, Oklahoma. They were rebuilt with conventional fireboxes and cabs.

Alco's Schenectady Works delivered five 2-8-0s in 1901. They had fireboxes over the rear pair of 60" drivers. Fitted with superheaters and piston valves between 1912 and 1916, they were sold to Louisiana Railway & Navigation Co. in 1923.

After a decade of tentativeness about the 2-8-0, Katy ordered 40 of the type from Schenectady. They were delivered in 1910 with 61" drivers and 22" × 30" cylinders. They were road freight engines, successors to the 2-6-0s. The delivery of the first 2-8-2s in 1913 reduced the 2-8-0s to secondary status. Most were scrapped in the early 1930s.

In 1913 and 1914 Schenectady delivered 70 Mikados, classes L-1-a and L-1-b, Nos. 701-770. Like the Consolidations that preceded them they had 61" drivers, but they had much larger 26½" × 30" cylinders. They weighed 287,500 pounds and exerted a tractive force of 57,250 pounds — lighter than a USRA light Mike and a little more powerful.

Alco delivered 35 more 2-8-2s in 1915, the L-2-a class, and 25 L-2-bs in 1918. They had 28" cylinders and weighed 314,000 pounds. The principal difference between the two classes was grate area: 62.8 square feet for the L-2-a and 70.4 for the L-2-b. However, the L-2-as, Nos. 801-835, acquired a reputation for rough riding and slipperiness and were scrapped in 1934. The L-2-bs lasted until diesels took over.

Subsequent Mikados were built by Lima, 20 in 1920 and 40 in 1923. They had the same dimensions as the Alco L-2s but weighed 324,000 pounds, 10,000 pounds more. Four Lima Mikes were equipped with feedwater heaters of various types, but the road decided such devices weren't worth the maintenance expense. A number of Mikes received tender boosters, and the entire L-2-d class had trailing truck boosters (five were built with them, and the others were fitted with them soon

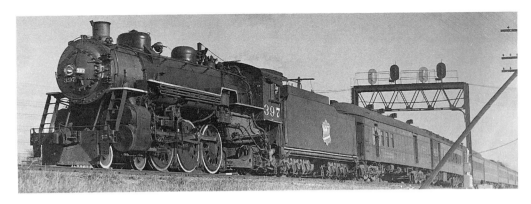

Pacifics for passenger service and Mikados for freight were as far as steam locomotive design progressed on the MKT. Number 397, leading the *Texas Special* east of Dallas in January 1948, has changed considerably since Schenectady delivered it in 1917: sheet-steel pilot, Boxpok drivers, cast trailing truck, and 12-wheel tender. Photo by C. W. Witbeck.

after delivery). The tender boosters were removed in the 1930s, and the trailing truck boosters in the early 1940s.

Passenger locomotives

MKT operated 4-4-0s until 1950 on branch lines in Oklahoma. Between 1923 and 1925 the road rebuilt 12 Baldwin 1890-vintage 4-4-0s. Six were still on the roster in 1948 and were renumbered 1301-1306, reusing numbers that had been assigned to former Wichita Falls & Northwestern 4-4-0s scrapped in 1932. Baldwin delivered seven Atlantics in 1895. They were similar to Atlantic Coast Line's 4-4-2s, except for 70" drivers. They were scrapped in 1923 and 1924.

Katy purchased 73 passenger Ten-Wheelers between 1899 and 1909. They had 68", 69", or 72" drivers and ranged in weight from 136,000 to 181,800 pounds. They were split almost equally between Baldwin and Schenectady. Katy also rostered four Ten-Wheelers with 64" drivers: No. 289, rebuilt in 1908 from a 2-6-0 that had been damaged in a wreck, and Nos. 295-297, former Texas Central engines. As Pacifics took over passenger service, the Ten-Wheelers found themselves unemployed. In 1930 only 15 remained on the roster, and by 1940 all were gone.

Katy's Pacifics were all about the same size: 73" drivers, 24" × 28"

cylinders for the H-1 and H-2 classes and 25" × 28" for the H-3s, weight ranging from 242,000 to 281,000 pounds. The last Pacifics, built by Lima in 1923, were slightly heavier and more powerful than the USRA light Pacific. Nine of the H-3-a class had Baker valve gear instead of Walschaerts, and engines 409 and 410 were built with boosters, which were removed during the 1940s. The Lima Pacifics were built with cast trailing trucks, and most of the earlier Pacifics received them during visits to the shop. Some of the H-3 Pacifics were fitted with Boxpok drivers in later years. In the late 1920s 10 H-3-a engines were fitted with large 12-wheel tenders to eliminate water stops. The tenders introduced the distinctive red-and-white enameled herald that soon became standard on Katy.

Switchers

Until 1919 the core of Katy's switcher fleet was a group of 25 0-6-0s built by Schenectady and Baldwin between 1904 and 1910. They had 57" drivers and 21" × 26" cylinders and weighed 148,000 pounds. Nine smaller 0-6-0s came from Baldwin in 1911: 51" drivers, 19" × 26" cylinders, and 141,000 pounds. Six of those were scrapped in the 1930s, but nearly all the larger 0-6-0s remained in service until dieselization.

In 1919 the USRA assigned ten 0-8-0s to the Katy, which refused them — too big and too expensive. In 1920 Katy changed its mind and ordered 20 such machines from Lima, numbered 39-58; Alco's Richmond Works delivered 10 more in 1923, engines 59-68. The road returned to Lima in 1925 for another ten 0-8-0s, 30,000 pounds heavier than the previous 0-8-0s and with 10,000 pounds more tractive effort. They were the last steam engines Katy bought.

Katy's had five narrow gauge switchers on its roster: two outside-frame 2-foot gauge engines for pushing ties and timbers around the Denison, Texas, tie-treatment plant, and three 3-foot gauge engines that worked at a ballast quarry at Rich, Okla. Many other roads also had such engines but listed them as maintenance equipment.

Historical and technical society: Katy Railroad Historical Society, 2210 S. Main Street, Fort Scott, KS 66701

Recommended reading: *Katy Power*, by Joe G. Collias and Raymond B. George Jr., published in 1986 by M M Books, P. O. Box 29318, Crestwood, MO 63126 (ISBN 0-9612366-1-2)

Published rosters:

Railway & Locomotive Historical Society Bulletin, No. 63, entire issue
Railroad Magazine: October 1934, page 46; February 1948, page 114

MKT STEAM LOCOMOTIVES BUILT SINCE 1900

Type	Class	Numbers	Qty	Builder	Built	Notes	Type	Class	Numbers	Qty	Builder	Built	Notes
0-4-0T	A	90, 91	2	Cooke, Mont.	1917	3-foot gauge	2-8-2	L-1-b	761-770	10	Schen	1914	
0-4-0T	A	92, 93	2	Davenport	1917, 1922	2-foot gauge	2-8-2	L-2-a	801-835	35	Alco	1915	
0-4-0T	A	95	1	Lima	1912	3-foot gauge	2-8-2	L-2-b	836-860	25	Alco	1918	
0-6-0	B-1	5-13	9	BLW	1911		2-8-2	L-2-c	861-880	20	Lima	1920	
0-6-0	B-2	14-38	25	Alco, BLW	1904-1910		2-8-2	L-2-d	881-920	40	Lima	1923	
0-8-0	C-1-a	39-58	20	Lima	1920		4-4-0	C	1301-1304	4	BLW	1910, 1911	Ex-WF&NW
0-8-0	C-1-b	59-68	10	Alco	1923		4-4-0	E-3	306-317	12	MKT	1923-1925	
0-8-0	C-2-a	101-110	10	Lima	1925	Renumbered 70-79	4-6-0	F	216-220	5	BLW	1899	
2-6-0	D-7	410-430	21	BLW	1900-1901		4-6-0	G-7	221-230	10	BLW	1902	
2-6-0	D-7	443-447	5	BLW	1900-1901		4-6-0	G-5-a	221-230	10	Schen	1904	
2-6-0	D-7	452-475	24	BLW	1901		4-6-0	G-5-b	231-238	8	BLW	1905	
2-6-0	D-7	1001-1005	5	BLW	1900		4-6-0	G-5-c	239-245	7	Schen	1907	1926-1931
2-6-0	D-7	1204-1211	8	BLW	1900-1901		4-6-0	G-6	246, 247	2	BLW	1905	Balanced compound
2-6-0	J-5	427-451	25	Schen	1907	Formerly D-8	4-6-0	G-8-a	258-267	10	BLW	1906	
2-6-0	J-5	476-600	125	Schen, BLW	1902-1906	Formerly D-8	4-6-0	F	268-276	9	Schen	1909	
2-6-0	E	93, 94	2	Alco	1908	Ex-WF&S	4-6-0	F	277-288	12	Schen	1909	
2-6-0	E	99-101	3	BLW	1909	Ex-WF&S	4-6-0	G-9	289	1	MKT	1908	Built from 2-6-0
2-8-0	G	676-669	4	BLW	1901	Ex-Texas Central	4-6-0	F	295-297	3	Alco	1989	Ex-Texas Central
2-8-0	G	682-693	12	Schen	1906-1907	Ex-Texas Central	4-6-2	H-1	357-366	10	Alco	1910	
2-8-0	K-6-a	608-612	5	BLW	1901		4-6-2	H-2-a	350-356	7	Alco	1911	
2-8-0	K-6-b	614, 615	2	BLW	1900, 1901	Camelback	4-6-2	H-2-b	367-376	10	Alco	1912	
2-8-0	K-7	671-675	5	Schen	1901	Sold LR&N 1923	4-6-2	H-3-a	377-388	12	Alco	1915	
2-8-0	K-8	668, 669	2	Schen	1902		4-6-2	H-3-b	389-398	10	Alco	1917	
2-8-0	K-8	670	1	BLW	1902	Camelback	4-6-2	H-3-c	399-408	10	Lima	1920	
2-8-0	K-10	616-655	40	Schen	1910		4-6-2	H-3-d	409-413	5	Lima	1923	
2-8-2	L-1-a	701-760	60	Schen	1913,1914								

MISSOURI PACIFIC RAILROAD

In the early 1880s the Missouri Pacific Railway was the nucleus of financier Jay Gould's empire. In the late 1880s that empire fell apart around the edges, but MP and its subsidiaries stayed together. By the turn of the century MP proper extended west from St. Louis to Pueblo, Colorado. The St. Louis, Iron Mountain & Southern reached southwest from St. Louis to Texarkana, on the Arkansas-Texas state line. There it connected with the Texas & Pacific, whose main line extended from New Orleans through Shreveport, Louisiana, and Dallas and Fort Worth, to El Paso, at the western tip of Texas. The International-Great Northern ran southwest from Longview, Texas, on the T&P, to Galveston and Laredo. Secondary main lines reached Omaha, Nebraska, Memphis, Tennessee, and Lake Charles, La., and a long line described an arc northwest from Little Rock, Arkansas, to Kansas City. There were extensive networks of branches in southeast and northeast Kansas and west-central Missouri.

In 1917 MP and the Iron Mountain consolidated to form the Missouri Pacific Railroad. In 1924 MP acquired control of the New Orleans, Texas & Mexico, which with its subsidiary St. Louis, Brownsville & Mexico formed a route from New Orleans through Houston to Brownsville, Texas. At the same time IGN was placed under NOT&M ownership. Of the numerous Texas subsidiaries, major and minor, only the Texas & Pacific had much identity of its own, and its locomotives are described separately in this book.

MoPac's route west from St. Louis encountered heavy going across the divide between the Meramec and Missouri Rivers at Kirkwood, 13 miles west of St. Louis, then more hilly country west of Sedalia, Mo. The St. Louis, Iron Mountain & Southern climbed through the east end of the Ozarks between St. Louis and Poplar Bluff, Mo. Elsewhere on the system grades were no problem. Early in the 20th century MP constructed two major river-level freight routes, from Jefferson City, Mo., to Kansas City, and from East St. Louis down the Mississippi to a connection with the Iron Mountain at Poplar Bluff.

The road adopted a new numbering and classification system in 1905. Numbers below 5000 were assigned to freight engines, 5000-8999 to passenger engines, and 9000-9999 to switchers. In the beginning newer, larger locomotives got lower numbers. The classification system used a letter or two for the wheel arrangement (P for Pacific, MK for Mikado, MT for Mountain, and so on), followed by the driver size.

MP began buying diesels early: switchers in 1937, including two pairs of Electro-Motive units that were the only ones of their kind; a pair of E3s for the *Eagle* in 1939; and FTs in 1943. The last road trip behind steam was made on April 7, 1955, by 2-8-0s 40 and 124, which pulled a train of nine dead 2-8-0s and a 2-8-2 from Bush to Dupo, Ill., for scrapping. The last steam engine in service was 0-6-0 No. 9301, which remained active until November 1955.

Freight locomotives

Missouri Pacific and the Iron Mountain received their last 4-6-0s between 1900 and 1902, 101 engines that were renumbered 2301-2401 in 1905. They had 61" drivers; some had slide valves and some inside piston valves, and a number of the Iron Mountain engines were built with Belpaire fireboxes. Two of the class were still active in the summer of 1955, some time after dieselization was officially complete, on a line between Gurdon and Norman, Ark. Their weight, 158,500 pounds, was all several bridges on that line could support, and MoPac had no diesels that light. By September 1955 the bridges were replaced or strengthened and diesels took over.

The Texas subsidiaries rostered dozens of freight and dual-service Ten-Wheelers with drivers between 57" and 63" — which is about all we know about them. Corporate changes, frequent swapping of power among the roads, frequent renumbering of engines, and destruction of the records of the steam locomotives by the railroads upon dieselization have rendered the picture incomplete.

St. Louis, Iron Mountain & Southern bought 19 Twelve-Wheelers in 1901 and 1903 for freight service on the grades between St. Louis and

The Consolidations numbered 1-172 were the first locomotives delivered after the renumbering of 1905, and their low numbers stood out in a roster of mostly 4-digit engine numbers. They were among MP's longest-lived engines. Number 89 is shown waiting out the weekend between mine-switching jobs at Webb City, Missouri, in July 1949. Photo by Arthur B. Johnson.

Poplar Bluff. They were typical Brooks 4-8-0s, with Belpaire fireboxes, inside valves, Stephenson valve gear, and 55" drivers. In 1905, when the line along the east bank of the Mississippi between East St. Louis and Thebes opened, most freight traffic moved to that route. Too slow for service there, the 4-8-0s were demoted to yard work all across the MP map. By the early 1920s they were rebuilt with longer main rods connected to the third drivers. That meant a heavier main rod, hard to counterbalance, but it was not a problem at switching speeds.

The first group of post-1900 Consolidations comprised 45 engines built by Brooks and Baldwin, Iron Mountain 1851-1890 and 1921-1925 (later MP 501-545). They had 55" drivers, slide valves, and narrow fireboxes between the rear drivers. Twenty-five of them had Belpaire fireboxes, not unusual for Brooks power of the time. They were followed by 401-487, which differed chiefly in having inboard piston valves and a wider firebox above the rear drivers. Many of the class were rebuilt with outside valves and Walschaerts or Baker valve gear.

The best-known MP 2-8-0s were built by Baldwin, Brooks, and Schenectady between 1905 and 1910, Nos. 1-172. They had 22" × 30" cylinders, 63" drivers, and slide valves. The first 76 had Stephenson valve gear; the others, Walschaerts. They were rebuilt considerably over the years, with piston valves, Baker valve gear, mechanical stokers or equipment for burning oil, and, amazingly, new cast frames. In 1942 North Little Rock Shops assembled the remnants of several members of the class plus some spare parts and a new tender to create No. 173.

The other 2-8-0s were acquired with various Texas subsidiaries. Engines 1031-1040 were former Frisco power acquired with the NOT&M. StLB&M 1011-1030 were ordered just before Frisco's bankruptcy took the StLB&M out of its hands.

The first Mikados arrived only a year after the last of the low-numbered Consolidations. Between 1911 and 1914 Schenectady delivered 50, Nos. 1201-1250, in 1911; Baldwin added 30 more (1251-1280) in 1913 and 1914. They had 63" drivers and 27" × 30" cylinders. Typical of the first locomotives built with superheaters, they worked at the relatively low pressure of 170 pounds and developed 50,160 pounds tractive effort. Delivered as hand-fired coal burners, most were later equipped with mechanical stokers or converted to oil. Some of the class were extensively modernized with feedwater heaters, cast trailing trucks, boosters, and large sand domes. The Schenectady engines weighed 275,500 pounds; the Baldwins were about 10,000 pounds heavier.

MoPac was allotted 15 USRA light 2-8-2s and got another 10 that the Pennsylvania Railroad refused. Lima built Nos. 1301-1315, MP's original allocation, and 1318-1325. Baldwin built No. 1316; Schenectady, 1317. After World War I International-Great Northern received ten oil-burning 2-8-2s from Baldwin — four in 1921 and six in 1924 — that were based on the USRA light Mikado but were 17,000 pounds lighter.

The largest group of 2-8-2s, engines 1401-1570, were based on the USRA heavy Mikado, modified with a larger boiler and cast trailing truck. All were built with mechanical stokers, some had trailing-truck boosters, and they were MP's first locomotives with a head brakeman's shelter on the tender deck. They weighed between 320,000 and 338,000

Missouri Pacific's Berkshires of 1930 refined Lima's original 2-8-4 with full-length frames, conventional trailing trucks, and outside journal lead trucks. By 1940 their 63" drivers were a handicap. Lima photo.

pounds. Ten Mikes built for the St. Louis, Brownsville & Mexico by Brooks in 1926 were almost identical, but eight were oil-fired and two were fitted to burn lignite. They carried Worthington BL feedwater heaters on their left flanks in the spot usually occupied by the air pumps. On the oil burners the pumps were mounted crosswise under the cab, a location which proved vulnerable to dirt; they were later moved to the pilot beam (where the lignite-burners carried them).

Engines 1536-1570 and StLB&M 1111-1120 had extra space between the second and third drivers. They were built about the time three-cylinder Mikado No. 1699 was being tested (see below), and the extra space would have provided room for a third main rod, had No. 1699 been successful.

For most roads the next freight locomotive after the Mikado was the Santa Fe. The type usually found employment dragging heavy trains up stiff grades. MoPac, with little in the way of steep grades, had only three small classes of 2-10-2s, all of which eventually gravitated to hump yard and transfer service — the grades up to the Mississippi River bridge in St. Louis and up the humps required just as much pull or push as did the grades out on the main line through the Ozarks. Brooks built 14 of the type, Iron Mountain 1501-1514, in 1916. They were chunky engines with 63" drivers and 30" × 32" cylinders; they weighed about 370,000 pounds. MP renumbered them 1701-1714 in 1924.

Baldwin delivered ten more 2-10-2s in 1926, Nos. 1720-1729. Four of them were fitted with tender boosters, and No. 1729 for a while had

two. During the latter part of World War II all ten were upgraded with roller bearings, lightweight rods, trailing truck boosters, and large tenders for road service. Five more 2-10-2s joined the roster in 1942, former Wabash engines that had been outpaced by 4-8-2s and 4-8-4s. MP assigned them to helper service on Kirkwood Hill.

The only other ten-coupled power on the MP system was a group of eight secondhand Russian Decapods acquired from the Southern Railway, the St. Louis & Hannibal, and the Marion & Eastern. Converted to burn oil, they were assigned to the New Orleans, Texas & Mexico.

MoPac's first 2-8-4s, International-Great Northern 1121-1125, were delivered by Schenectady in 1928. They were similar to Chicago & North Western's J-4s that Alco's Brooks Works had built the year before; they in turn had duplicated the principal dimensions of Lima's A-1.

MP took delivery of 25 Berkshires of its own, numbered 1901-1925, from Lima in 1930. They had the same dimensions as the I-GN engines but at 412,200 pounds were 8,000 pounds heavier. Departures from Lima's design included conventional frames and trailing trucks, two sand domes instead of one, and Worthington BL feedwater heaters. The MP 2-8-4s lacked the boosters of the I-GN engines. They went into service between St. Louis and Kansas City, where they occasioned some bridge strengthening and relocation of coal and water facilities (the 2-8-4s had larger tenders than the 2-8-2s they replaced, and got more mileage out of their fuel and water). Because of the Berkshires, MP established helper service on Kirkwood Hill. In the flatter country west

MoPac's shops at Sedalia, Missouri, took in the 2-8-4s and rebuilt them into 4-8-4s. They had twin sand domes like the 2-8-4s. Photo by Gordon B. Mott.

of there the Mikados had made good time with about the same size train, 40 to 50 cars, they could pull over the hill, but the Berkshires could pull 60 to 70 cars over the hill and 100 or more west of there along the Missouri River. Helpers for the short distance up Kirkwood Hill let MP take advantage of the 2-8-4s' capacity for the whole distance between St. Louis and Kansas City.

As freight trains accelerated in the late 1930s, the Lima Berkshires, Nos. 1901-1925, were handicapped by their 63" drivers. When they were built, 63" was the standard size for 2-8-4s, except for the Erie's fleet of 70"-drivered Berks. Between 1940 and 1942 the shops at Sedalia, Mo., lengthened their boilers, rolled new cast underframes with 75" drivers under them, and created 25 handsome 4-8-4s. The 28" × 30" cylinders were unchanged; with a boiler pressure of 250 pounds, the new Northerns exerted slightly more tractive effort than the Berkshires.

MP needed more 4-8-4s in 1942 during the brief period when the War Production Board required railroads to pool orders for locomotives and use designs already in production. MP chose Denver & Rio Grande Western's 1800-class Northern (Baldwin, 1938) as a prototype; MP 2201-2215 were built simultaneously with Northern Pacific's A-5 4-8-4s, Nos. 2680-2689. The MP engines had the 73" drivers, 26" × 30"

cylinders, and 285-pound boiler pressure of the D&RGW engines, and were about 16,000 pounds heavier; resemblance to the NP engines was more a matter of components and details. Both classes of MP 4-8-4s were intended for freight service, but they worked passenger trains from time to time.

Passenger locomotives

MP received the last of its passenger Ten-Wheelers from Brooks in 1901 and 1902, 69"-drivered engines that were soon renumbered 7501-7529. International-Great Northern received six Baldwin 4-6-0s with 67" drivers in 1911 (ultimately Nos. 379-384). Eight more 67"-drivered Ten-Wheelers, 371-378, joined them between 1921 and 1924, rebuilt from 63"-drivered 4-6-0s 351-358. NOT&M engines 361 and 362 became passenger engines the same way. NOT&M 385-389, 69"-drivered passenger 4-6-0s, were built by Brooks in 1921 — late for Ten-Wheelers and for narrow fireboxes (MP's 4-6-0s were all narrow-firebox engines).

In a reversal of the usual progression, Alco's Brooks Works delivered 15 4-4-2s in 1904, two years after MP's first 4-6-2s. Ten Atlantics were assigned to Missouri Pacific, and five to the Iron Mountain. Their 79" drivers were and would remain the highest on the railroad. The engines were successful; 25 more numbered 5506-5540 arrived on the

Schenectady built 4-6-2 No. 6603 in 1924 as No. 6447. Its original USRA appearance is masked by the heavy cast pilot, Elesco feedwater heater, and 12-wheel tender. Collection of Louis A. Marre.

property in 1907. They were typical of the period, with inside-bearing trailing trucks, inboard valves, and Stephenson valve gear (the last few were built with outboard valves and Walschaerts gear). After 1941 many were rebuilt with cast trailing trucks, some with boosters, and a few with disk drivers. In 1942 two Atlantics, 5513 and 5538, were fitted with 73" drivers and assigned to light, fast freight trains in level territory.

MP's first Pacifics — the first built for service in North America — were delivered by Brooks in 1902 and 1903. Nine, numbered 1115-1123, were assigned to MP and 12, numbered 1616-1627, to the Iron Mountain. Typical of Brooks products of the day, they had inside valves, Stephenson valve gear, and inside-bearing trailing trucks. They weighed 193,000 pounds and exerted a modest 26,835 pounds of tractive effort. In 1905 they were classed P-69 and numbered 6501-6521. In 1920 the entire class was rebuilt with superheaters, outside piston valves, and Baker valve gear (one engine was fitted with Walschaerts gear).

Seven years elapsed until the next 4-6-2s arrived in 1910. Numbers 6401-6439 were built by Brooks and Schenectady in 1910 and 1912. Like the first Pacifics they had 69" drivers, but their 26" × 26" cylinders were 2" larger, engine weight was 259,000 pounds, and tractive effort was 40,930 pounds. Five more, Nos. 6440-6444, were delivered by Schenectady in 1921, with the same dimensions but differing in such details as cast trailing trucks and headlights centered on the smokebox door (earlier 6400s had high-mounted lights). The 6400s were eventually fitted with 73" drivers, and several of the class received roller bearings, cast pilots, and large oil tenders.

Ten heavier Pacifics, 6445-6454 (renumbered 6601-6610 in 1934), were delivered by Schenectady in 1924. They combined the boiler and cylinders of the USRA heavy Pacific with the 73" drivers of the light Pacific — the same formula used for Southern Railway's handsome Ps4s. The only significant difference between the MP and Southern

MP's first 4-8-2s, Iron Mountain 5201-5207, were the second group of that type built. Number 5201 poses half on, half off the turntable at Alco's Schenectady Works in July 1913. Alco photo.

engines was the use of cast trailing trucks by MP. Two more groups of heavy Pacifics arrived from Schenectady in 1924 and 1925. The first, Nos. 6611-6613, looked like their predecessors, 6445-6454, but 6614-6619 were oil burners with 12-wheel tenders intended for MP's premier train, the St. Louis-Texas *Sunshine Special*. (Until the advent of air conditioning, train travel meant open windows, and open windows meant cinders unless the steam locomotive was an oil burner.) The second group, 6620-6629, were coal burners with 12-wheel tenders. Both groups were fitted with Elesco feedwater heaters in the 1930s, and by the 1940s no two engines in the class had the same combination of disk main drivers, roller bearings, pilots, and tender.

Two more groups of heavy Pacifics were delivered in 1926 and 1927 for MP's Texas subsidiaries, International-Great Northern 1151-1155 and St. Louis, Brownsville & Mexico 1156-1161. The I-GN engines had Baker valve gear, front-end throttles, and Worthington SA feedwater heaters; the StLB&M engines had Worthington BL heaters, air pumps on the pilot, and extra-large tenders. The latter group spent most of their lives on the St. Louis-Kansas City-Omaha run before transfering south to their home rails. Missouri Pacific had one more 4-6-2, an experimental three-cylinder engine described below.

St. Louis, Iron Mountain & Southern was the second road to purchase 4-8-2s. In 1913 Alco's Schenectady Works delivered seven Mountains for St. Louis-Little Rock passenger service. Numbered 5201-5207, they were light engines, weighing 296,000 pounds, and their main rods were connected to the third pair of 63" drivers. After they were replaced by faster engines they handled freight duties in Louisiana and Texas.

In 1919 the USRA assigned MoPac seven light 4-8-2s, Richmond-built 5301-5307. MP later ordered nine similar engines from Schenectady. The principal differences were 73" drivers and cast trailing trucks. Numbers 5308-5312 were delivered in 1921, and 5313-5316 in 1923.

Brooks delivered five 4-8-2s, Nos. 5335-5339, in 1927. They had the same 73" drivers and 27" × 30" cylinders as USRA derivatives of 1921 and 1923, but the boiler pressure was 250 pounds instead of 210, and they weighed 386,700 pounds, 23,000 more than Nos. 5308-5316. Sche-

nectady built five more like them, Nos. 5340-5344, in 1930.

In 1939 the shops at Sedalia, Mo., undertook major rebuilding of the USRA Mountains of 1919 to increase their power and speed. The engines received new 75" disk drivers, cast engine beds, roller bearings, lightweight rods, and new tenders; boilers were lengthened and pressure was raised to 250 pounds, and oil replaced coal. They were practically new engines, and they got new numbers, 5321-5327 (though not in sequence). The most significant part to survive rebuilding may have been their value on the company's accounts.

Switchers

MP's switcher fleet consisted of ordinary 0-6-0s, mostly equipped with slide valves. The exceptions were 20 six-wheel switchers built by Alco in 1920 and 1921, Nos. 9301-9320. They had 51" drivers, 21" × 28" cylinders, piston valves, and Walschaerts valve gear. They weighed 160,500 pounds and had a tractive force of 39,100 pounds — about the same all around as a USRA 0-6-0.

Standardization came to MP's yards in the form of 85 eight-wheel switchers, all copies of the USRA design as modified by MP: heavier by 12,000 to 18,000 pounds and possessed of 7,750 pounds more tractive effort. The later engines had cast frames and front-end throttles mounted in front of the stacks.

MP had a single Mallet, a 2-8-8-2 built by Baldwin in 1912 for hump yard work at Dupo, Ill., on the Iron Mountain. In the 1920s hump duties were taken over by 0-8-0s, and the Mallet was stored. It was revived in 1927 and given a 12-wheel tender with Bethlehem Auxiliary Locomotives (tender boosters) on both trucks. It then went back to work on the hump at Dupo, along with a similarly equipped 2-10-2, until 1947 when the boosters were removed. The Mallet was put into transfer service across the Mississippi River bridge and occasionally worked as a helper on Kirkwood Hill.

Experimental locomotives

In 1925 Alco's Schenectady Works delivered two three-cylinder locomotives to MoPac, a 2-8-2 and a 4-6-2. They virtually replicated two engines that Brooks had built for Louisville & Nashville a year before

Mountain 5323, shown at St. Louis in November 1939, a month after emerging from Sedalia Shops, shows almost no trace of it USRA light 4-8-2 origins. The 75" drivers were the largest used on any 4-8-2 in North America. Collection of Louis A. Marre.

(MP's engines were heavier). Before delivery the 2-8-2 went through its paces at Pennsylvania Railroad's Altoona test plant, setting records for tractive effort and low coal consumption; the 4-6-2 meanwhile outperformed MP's other Pacifics. MoPac soon discovered the difficulties of maintaining locomotives that had one-third of their moving parts tucked between the frames. Once their novelty had worn off, the three-cylinder engines became power of last resort instead of first choice. In 1937 the Mikado was converted to a two-cylinder engine and renumbered 1571, distinguishable from the 170 USRA-copy Mikes only by a smokebox front with the door a little above center. The Pacific remained in storage longer, then became a test bed for Franklin poppet valves. Rebuilding in 1942 included conversion to two cylinders and oil fuel, roller bearings, Elesco exhaust steam injector, and a new number: 6001. The rebuilding was successful. Number 6001 proved the equal of 4-8-2 for many assignments, but the poppet valves, like the three-cylinder running gear, didn't warrant duplication.

Historical and technical society: Missouri Pacific Historical Society, c/o Bill Herbert, P. O. Box 187, Addis, LA 70710

Recommended reading:
Mopac Power, by Joe G. Collias, published in 1980 by Howell-North Books, 11175 Flintkote Avenue, Suite C, San Diego, CA 92121 (ISBN 0-8310-7117-6)

"Those Sedalia 4-8-4's," by Lloyd E. Stagner, in *Trains Magazine*, May 1984, pages 20-28

Published rosters: *Railroad Magazine*: April 1938, page 60, and March 1938, page 67; September 1951, page 98; March 1966, page 34 (1906 roster)

MP STEAM LOCOMOTIVES BUILT SINCE 1900

Type	Class	Numbers	Qty	Builder	Built	Retired	Notes
0-6-0	SW-51	9301-9320	20	Alco	1920-1921	-1955	
0-6-0	SW-51	9401-9475	75	Brooks, Richmond, Baldwin	1902-1910	1949-1950	
0-6-0	SW-51	9501-9543	43	Cooke, Manchester, Schenectady	1903-1904	1932-1948	
0-6-0	SW-52	9580, 9581	2	Baldwin	1905		
0-6-0	SW-53	9583	1	Baldwin	1910		
0-6-0	SW-52	9584-9587	4	Baldwin	1906		
0-6-0	SW-52	9588-9591	4	Baldwin	1921		
0-8-0	SW8-51	9601-9605	5	Alco	1927	-1955	
0-8-0	SW8-51	9606-9610	5	Alco	1927	-1955	
0-8-0	SW8-51	9701-9720	20	Baldwin	1924-1925	-1955	
0-8-0	SW8-51	9721-9750	30	Lima	1926, 1929	-1955	
0-8-0	SW8-51	9761-9785	25	Alco	1927	-1956	
2-8-0	C-63	1-172	172	Baldwin, Brooks, Schenectady	1905-1910	1937-	
2-8-0	C-63	173	1	MP	1942	1956	
2-8-0	C-55	401-487	84	Brooks	1903-1904	1949-1955	
2-8-0	C-55	501-545	45	Brooks, BLW	1901-1903	1925-1945	
2-8-0	C-54	1001-1003	3	Alco	1913-1914	-1935	
2-8-0	C-50	1004, 1005	2	Baldwin	1907	-1935	San Antonio, Uvalde & Gulf, SAU&G

MP STEAM LOCOMOTIVES BUILT SINCE 1900

Type	Class	Numbers	Qty	Builder	Built	Retired	Notes
2-8-0	C-55	1006-1008	3	Brooks	1906	1935-1948	SAU&G
2-8-0	C-51	1009	1	Baldwin	1920	1948	
						San Antonio Southern	
2-8-0	C-57	1011-1030	20	Baldwin	1914	-1949	StLB&M
2-8-0	C-55	1031-1040	10	Baldwin	1907		NOT&M
2-8-0	C-57	1051-1073	23	BLW, Schen	1912, 1913		I-GN
2-8-2	MK-63	1201-1280	80	Alco, BLW	1911-1914	-1954	
2-8-2	MK-63	1301-1325	25	Lima, BLW, Alco	1919	1949-1955	USRA
2-8-2	MK-63	1401-1570	170	Alco	1921-1925	1949-1955	
2-8-2	MK-	1699	1	Schenectady	1925	1953	Three cylinders
2-8-2	MK-63	1101-1110	10	Baldwin	1921, 1924	1949-1955	I-GN
2-8-2	MK-63	1111-1120	10	Brooks	1926	1949-1955	StLB&M
2-8-4	BK-63	1121-1125	5	Alco	1928	1953-1954	
2-8-4	BK-63	1901-1925	25	Lima	1930		Rebuilt to 4-8-4
2-10-0	D-52	941-948	8	Alco	1918		Russian Decapod
2-10-2	SF-63	1701-1714	14	Brooks	1916	1953	
2-10-2		1715-1719	5	Brooks	1917	1953	Ex-Wabash
2-10-2	SF-63	1720-1729	10	Baldwin	1926	1955	
2-8-8-2	ML-55	4000	1	Baldwin	1912	1946	
4-4-0	E-63	914	1	Baldwin	1905		StLB&M
4-4-0	E-67	927	1	Baldwin	1904		StLB&M
4-4-0	E-63	953	1	Baldwin	1905		
						San Benito & Rio Grande Valley	
4-4-2	A-79	5501-5540	40	Brooks	1904, 1907	1937-1948	
4-6-0	TN-56½	236	1	Baldwin	1920		Sugar Land
4-6-0	TN-57	212	1	Baldwin	1910		Rio Grande City
4-6-0	TN-57	213, 214	2	Baldwin	1916		Sugar Land
4-6-0	TN-57	233	1	Cooke	1905		NOT&M
4-6-0	TN-57	235	1	Baldwin	1912		SAU&G
4-6-0	TN-57	285	1	Cooke	1901		I-GN
4-6-0	TN-57	299	1	Alco	1913		SAU&G
4-6-0	TN-60	310	1	Alco	1907		
						Houston & Brazos Valley	
4-6-0	TN-61	2301-2401	101	Brooks	1900-1902		
4-6-0	TN-61	2402, 2403	2	Baldwin	1901		
4-6-0	TN-63	252-261	10	Baldwin	1905		StLB&M
4-6-0	TN-63	291	1	Rhode Island	1902		I-GN
4-6-0	TN-63	297	1	Alco	1913		SAU&G
4-6-0	TN-63	301-306	6	Dickson	1903		NOT&M
4-6-0	TN-63	315-360	46	Cooke, Baldwin, Brooks	1901-1908		I-GN
4-6-0	TN-67	320, 333, 339	3	Cooke	1901-1903		I-GN
4-6-0	TN-67	361, 362	2	Baldwin	1903		NOT&M
4-6-0	TN-67	371-378	8	IGN	1921-1925		I-GN
4-6-0	TN-67	379-384	6	Baldwin	1911		I-GN
4-6-0	TN-69	385-389	5	Alco	1921		NOT&M
4-6-0	TN-69	7501-7529	29	Brooks	1901-1902	-1935	
4-6-2	P-73	6000	1	Schenectady	1925	1952	Three cylinders
4-6-2	P-73	6401-6439	39	Schen, Brooks	1910, 1912	1948-1954	
4-6-2	P-73	6440-6444	5	Schenectady	1921		
4-6-2	P-69	6501-6521	21	Brooks	1902-1903	-1953	
4-6-2	P-73	6601-6629	29	Schenectady	1924, 1925	1949-1954	
4-6-2	P-73	1151-1155	5	Alco	1926	1954	I-GN
4-6-2	P-73	1156-1161	6	Alco	1927	1954	StLB&M
4-8-0	TW-55	1801-1819	19	Brooks	1901, 1903		
4-8-2	MT-63	5201-5207	7	Schenectady	1913	1948	
4-8-2	MT-69	5301-5307	7	Richmond	1919	To 5321-5327	USRA
4-8-2	MT-73	5308-5316	9	Schenectady	1921, 1923	-1955	
4-8-2	MT-73	5335-5344	10	Brooks, Schen	1927, 1930	-1956	
4-8-2	MT-75	5321-5327	7	MP	1939	1954	Ex-5301-5307
4-8-4		2101-2125	25	MP	1940-1942	1949-1953	
4-8-4		2201-2215	15	Baldwin	1943	1956	

MOBILE & OHIO RAIL ROAD

The Mobile & Ohio extended from Mobile, Alabama, north to St. Louis, with a branch from Artesia, Mississippi, to Montgomery, Ala., and trackage rights on Southern Railway and Illinois Central between Memphis, Tenn., Corinth, Miss., and Birmingham, Ala. It was controlled by the Southern Railway from 1901 to 1938.

In 1940 the M&O was purchased by the new Gulf, Mobile & Ohio Railroad, which then consolidated with the Gulf, Mobile & Northern. M&O purchased no new steam locomotives. In 1947 GM&O merged the Alton Railroad and moved quickly to dieselize all its operations. M&O's last steam operation occurred on October 7, 1949.

M&O's locomotives were renumbered in 1910. It was a renumbering calculated to confuse engine crews (historians, too). This group of 0-6-0s, for instance, gave their numbers to that group of 0-6-0s; other 0-6-0s kept their old numbers. One can imagine an engineer saying, "Looks like we got

No. 12 today, Horace," and the fireman replying, "She's a good steamer, Ralph," and then their surprise on discovering their engine wasn't the No. 12 it used to be. The 1910 numbers are used here.

Freight locomotives

M&O used 57"- and 63"-drivered 4-6-0s for freight service until the advent of eight-coupled power. The type grew from 129,000 pounds (Nos. 178-187) to 167,495 pounds (310-321 and 325-384 — and later in life they weighed in at 179,500 pounds). The largest group of Ten-Wheelers comprised 60 built by Baldwin between 1905 and 1907. They had 63" drivers, 21" × 28" cylinders, and 33,320 pounds tractive effort.

Between 1911 and 1916 M&O purchased 21 Mikados from Baldwin. The last three, Nos. 418-420, had Southern valve gear; the others had Walschaerts valve gear. They had outboard-bearing trailing trucks (unlike the 1912 Pacifics), 63" drivers, and 27" x 30" cylinders, and weighed 273,000 pounds.

In 1914 M&O bought 15 Consolidations, eight from Alco and seven from Baldwin. Like M&O's early Mikados, they had 63" drivers; the cylinders were 3" smaller. Intended to replace some of M&O's older small locomotives, the 2-8-0s were not popular with crews. The fire-

Ten-Wheeler 377, one of 60 such engines on Mobile & Ohio's roster, leads a mixed train at Starkville, Mississippi, in February 1942. Photo by C. W. Witbeck.

For mainline freight service M&O relied on 2-8-2s. Number 459, built by Richmond in 1922, was a copy of the USRA light 2-8-2. Photo by R. J. Foster.

In the 1920's Mobile & Ohio bought ten 4-6-2s that were copies of the USRA light Pacific. The principal point of difference between the USRA locomotive and M&O's Pacifics was the cab roof: the USRA cab roof had a deeper curve. Photo by John B. Allen.

box, about the same size as that of the 2-8-2, required that the boiler be mounted higher to clear the rear drivers, and the rear pair of drivers tended to derail. M&O returned to the 2-8-2 wheel arrangement for subsequent orders, and ten of the 2-8-0s were scrapped before 1940.

M&O's second group of Mikados were copies of the light USRA design. Alco's Richmond Works built 10 in 1922; Lima, 17 in 1923 and 1924; Baldwin, 5 in 1926; and Alco's Schenectady Works delivered the final 5 in 1928.

Passenger locomotives

Only one group of Ten-Wheelers could be considered passenger engines because of their 69" drivers: Nos. 230-239, built by Baldwin in 1906. Three were later fitted with 63" drivers. Mobile & Ohio's first Pacifics, 250-253, were Baldwin products of 1912, identical to a group of Southern Railway Ps-2s and built with them. They were relatively light machines (232,000 pounds) with 72" drivers and inboard-bearing trail-

ing trucks. Between 1923 and 1926 Baldwin delivered ten copies of the USRA light Pacific.

Switchers

M&O was well endowed with switchers. The most numerous were USRA switchers, ten allocated by the USRA, Nos. 40-49, built by Cooke in 1918, and 13 copies built by Richmond and Schenectady in 1927 and 1928. The road had several groups of earlier 0-6-0s; eight built by Lima in 1911 survived to receive GM&O numbers.

Historical and technical society: Gulf, Mobile & Ohio Historical Society P. O. Box 463, Fairfield, IL 62837.

Published rosters:

Railroad Magazine, September 1934, page 88.

Railroad History, No. 157, page 85

M&O STEAM LOCOMOTIVES BUILT SINCE 1900

Type	Numbers	Qty	Builder	Built	Retired	Notes
0-6-0	11-14	4	Rogers	1900	1931-1934	built as 6-9
0-6-0	15-17	3	Baldwin	1905	1934-1940	
0-6-0	18-22	5	Baldwin	1904-1905	1934-1943	built as 10-14
0-6-0	23-27	5	Baldwin	1906-1907	1934-1945	built as 72-76
0-6-0	30-37	8	Lima	1911	1940-1948	
0-6-0	40-49	10	Cooke	1918	1948-1950	USRA
0-6-0	50-62	13	Rich, Schen	1927, 1928	1948-1950	USRA design
2-8-0	540-554	15	BLW, Rich	1914	1935-1948	
2-8-2	400-420	21	Baldwin	1911-1916	1946-1949	
2-8-2	450-486	37	Richmond, Lima, Baldwin, Schenectady	1922-1928	1946-1950	
4-6-0	178-187	10	Rogers	1900	1918-1934	
4-6-0	220-227	8	Baldwin	1903	1918-1940	
4-6-0	230-239	10	Baldwin	1906	1931-1949	
4-6-0	300-306	7	Baldwin	1904	1918-1940	
4-6-0	310-321	12	Baldwin	1904	1930-1940	
4-6-0	325-384	60	Baldwin	1905-1907	1918-1949	
4-6-2	250-253	4	Baldwin	1912	1939-1940	
4-6-2	260-269	10	Baldwin	1923-1926	1946-1949	

NASHVILLE, CHATTANOOGA & ST. LOUIS RAILWAY

By Charles B. Castner

The Dixie Line's principal antecedent was the Nashville & Chattanooga. Chartered in 1845, N&C linked the Tennessee cities of its name by 1854, creating a land route from west of the Appalachians to the Southeast. By 1900 the road had added St. Louis to its corporate name; its efforts to reach that city were thwarted by the Louisville & Nashville, which in 1880 bought control of the NC&StL (hereafter "NC"). By the turn of the century NC extended southeast to Atlanta (it leased the Western & Atlantic from the state of Georgia), southwest to Memphis, and northwest to Paducah, Kentucky. In Nashville it built new shops and jointly with L&N built a new union station there, which opened in 1900. NC's last major extension was an Ohio River bridge at Paducah, built jointly with Chicago, Burlington & Quincy in 1917. After 75 years of control L&N merged the NC in 1957.

NC's Nashville-Atlanta main line encountered the Cumberland range of the Appalachians just north of Chattanooga, and trains tackled grades up to 2.5 percent on Cumberland Mountain. Pusher engines based at Cowan, Tenn., assisted trains up both the north and south slopes. Undulating profiles and curves also characterized the W&A Division through North Georgia and the Nashville Division west to Bruceton; somewhat flatter terrain was found in west Tennessee and Kentucky.

About half of NC's freight traffic moved to and from other railroads at Paducah, Memphis, Martin, and Nashville on the north and Atlanta on the south. Manufactured goods moved south and perishables north; coal from mines in southeast Tennessee also contributed to the traffic mix. NC's principal passenger route was the Nashville-Atlanta portion of the Chicago-Florida "Dixie Route," operated in conjunction with Chicago & Eastern Illinois and Louisville & Nashville north of Nashville, and Central of Georgia, Atlantic Coast Line, and Florida East Coast south of Atlanta.

The 25 4-8-4s constituted NC's only modern steam. By 1947 well over half of NC's locomotives were over 30 years old. Pressed by increasing competition and the need to reduce operating costs, NC in 1948 and 1949 bought its first road diesels, 30 F3s and F7s. Already in service were 20 yard switchers, and L&Ns E7s were running through on the St. Louis-Atlanta *Georgian*. The new power, assigned to Nashville-Atlanta runs, virtually doubled the steam tonnage ratings and allowed NC to dieselize most mainline runs by 1951. By 1953 NC had completely dieselized. A lowly H7 Consolidation, No. 406, ended all steam on the NC when it brought the Union City, Tenn., branch freight into Bruceton for the last time on January 4, 1953. A sample of NC super-steam survives: J3 4-8-4 No. 576 was donated to the city of Nashville in 1953 and stands on display in Centennial Park.

Freight and pusher locomotives

After 1900, 2-8-0s and 2-8-2s became NC's preferred freight power, later augmented by dual-service 4-8-2s and 4-8-4s. Several 2-8-0s had pushed trains up Cumberland Mountain well before 1900, but the type was not bought in large numbers until 1899, when Baldwin began delivering 24 engines (NC's class H5) with 56" drivers, long straight boilers,

NC&StL's first 2-8-2s looked lighter and older than they were. They weighed 272,000 pounds, only 20,000 pounds less than a USRA light Mikado. The high mounted headlight, capped stack, and sharply tapered boiler all contributed to an appearance of antiquity. Baldwin photo.

The Mikes put in time in Cumberland Mountain helper service. Passenger train helpers were coupled ahead of the road engine, in this case a J3 4-8-4, and were as likely to run backward as forward. Photo by Hugh M. Cromer.

NC's J2-class 4-8-4s were among the lightest of the type, weighing 381,000 pounds as built. Only the J2s, the "Gliders," had outside lead truck journals. Alco photo.

and fireboxes between the drivers. One engine was a Camelback with a modified Wootten firebox to burn slack coal (the leftovers from the cleaning and grading process, also called culm); it was later rebuilt with a conventional firebox.

Between 1903 and 1907 Baldwin delivered 51 heavier 2-8-0s (the H6, H7, and H8 classes) with wider fireboxes over the rear drivers and larger boilers. The H6s and H7s had 56" drivers; the five H8s had 50" drivers for pusher service on Cumberland Mountain. NC's most powerful Consolidations, ten H9s with 56" drivers and 46,000 pounds tractive effort, came from Baldwin in 1911. Many H6s and H7s were upgraded at Nashville with superheaters, piston valves, power reverse, and Walschaerts valve gear in the 1920s. The 2-8-0s wound up on branch lines or in yard and transfer duty. Some remained in service right up to dieselization.

After 1915 a fleet of 50 2-8-2s gradually replaced 2-8-0s on mainline freight. First to come were 29 L1s, Nos. 600-628, built by Baldwin between 1915 and 1918. They had superheaters, 58" drivers, and Vanderbilt tenders; they were later fitted with mechanical stokers. The L1 "Jitneys" (as crews called them) ranged over the entire NC; after World War II, they were concentrated west of Nashville.

NC's second group of 2-8-2s comprised 10 USRA light Mikados, Nos. 650-659, delivered by Alco's Schenectady Works in 1918, and 12 Baldwin

copies, Nos. 660-671, delivered in 1922 and 1923. The Baldwin engines had cast trailing trucks, boosters, and Vanderbilt tenders. Four of the original USRA engines were later fitted with booster-equipped cast trailing trucks. With 63" drivers and more boiler capacity than the L1s, the L2s handled mainline freights systemwide through World War II, ending up as Cumberland Mountain pushers in the late 1940s.

During World War I NC acquired five Russian Decapods, which had an extensive tour of duty on the Huntsville and Paducah branches. For years, NC assigned low-wheeled 4-6-0s and 2-8-0s to shove trains up Cumberland Mountain, but in 1915 it took delivery of three 2-8-8-2 compound Mallets from Baldwin. They took over all pusher duties, each replacing two Consolidations. They were replaced by pairs of Mikes in 1945, which in turn gave way to 4-8-4s.

Passenger and dual-service locomotives

NC's most successful 4-6-0s were 16 Baldwin and Rogers machines built between 1902 and 1908, classes G6, G7, and G8. Similar in size, with 66" drivers, they handled most passenger service in the early 1900s. The seven G8s were compounds, with all four cylinders driving the first axle. They were later rebuilt as two-cylinder simple engines and were shifted to Nashville-Memphis service about the time of World War I.

In 1909 Baldwin delivered a final batch of four Ten-Wheelers.

Because the engines steamed poorly, they went back to Philadelphia in 1912 and were rebuilt as 4-6-2s, to become NC's first of that type (class K1, Nos. 500-503).

Meanwhile the Dixie Line's first new Pacifics, eight class K2 engines numbered 530-537, arrived from Baldwin in 1912 and 1913 with larger boilers and 72" drivers. The K2s took over the Chattanooga Division; No. 535 was christened *Marie* after the daughter of a former engineer. The K2s were later improved with mechanical stokers and feedwater heaters, and two, Nos. 535 and 536, were streamlined for the *City of Memphis* (in 1947) and the *Dixie Flagler* (in 1940). In addition No. 535 was extensively rebuilt with cast cylinders, roller bearings, and a 12-wheel tender. For several years, it averaged 14,000 miles a month on daily round trips with the streamliner between Memphis and Nashville. Baldwin delivered eight lighter Pacifics, class K1A, in 1915, for Atlanta Division trains. They had 69" drivers and weighed 237,000 pounds.

Meanwhile, growing bridge traffic called for larger mainline power, and in 1919 NC received its first 4-8-2s, five USRA light Mountains from Alco's Richmond Works. NC classed them J1 and numbered them 550-554. The J1s were successful on Chattanooga Division runs, and were followed in 1922 and 1925 by eight copies from Baldwin, Nos. 555-561. They were built with with feedwater heaters and Delta trailing trucks; boosters were added soon after delivery.

By 1929 the 4-8-2s weren't meeting all NC's traffic needs. The road designed a dual-service 4-8-4, using the USRA light 4-8-2 as a starting point, and Alco delivered five in 1930. NC classed them J2, numbered them 565-569, and called them Dixies. They were the first 4-8-4s in the South, and were notable for having one-piece cast frames with brackets to support piping and auxiliary appliances normally hung on the boiler, feedwater heaters, large fireboxes, and free-steaming boilers. Lateral-motion driving wheel boxes on the first and second driving axles enabled the J2s to literally glide in and out of curves, and crews soon dubbed them "Gliders." Turntable lengths dictated short tenders. First assigned to the difficult Chattanooga Division, the J2s went into Atlanta after 1940, and later to Memphis.

J3s of both groups doublehead the northbound *Dixie Flyer* through Bass, Alabama, on March 30, 1946. The principal difference between the "Yellow Jackets" and the "Stripes" was the running board skirt. Photo by Hugh M. Comer.

C. M. Darden, NC's motive power chief from 1930 to 1959, designed many of the J2s' features. In 1941, when NC urgently needed more power, Darden called on Alco for an improved version, the 20 great J3s, Nos. 570-589. Streamstyled, with clean boilers, conical smokebox noses, and retractable-coupler pilots, the J3s had roller bearings throughout, Boxpok drivers, and large semi-Vanderbilt tenders with six-wheel trucks (thanks to new 110' turntables at Nashville, Chattanooga, and Atlanta). The first 10 boasted yellow panels along the running boards and were quickly nicknamed "Yellow Jackets." Later J3s without the panels but with brightly painted running board edges were called "Stripes."

Switchers

NC purchased few new switchers, preferring to rebuild older power or use engines already in service, such as its 2-8-0s. Between 1891 and 1904 NC bought 17 0-6-0s from Rogers and Baldwin, and during the Teens it converted seven 2-8-0s to eight-wheel switchers by removing the lead trucks. They were all off the roster by the late 1930s.

Oddities

In 1918 Mikado 616 was given a tender fitted with a tractor engine, the running gear of 2-8-0 No. 304 in place of the customary pair of trucks. The tractor had 51" drivers, 20" × 24" cylinders, and slide valves, and was supplied with steam at boiler pressure. NC soon discovered drawbacks to the arrangement. The boiler wasn't able to supply steam for both sets of running gear; coal and water capacity were limited; and as coal and water were used, the weight available for adhesion of the tender engine diminished. Number 616 soon had a conventional tender again.

Recommended reading:
Nashville, Chattanooga & St. Louis Railway History and Steam Locomotives, by Richard E. Prince, published in 1967 by Richard E. Prince, Green River, Wyoming
"Gliders, Yellow Jackets & Stripes," by David P. Morgan, in *Trains Magazine*, December 1963, pages 22-35
Historical and technical society: Louisville & Nashville Historical Society, Box 17122, Louisville, KY 40217
Published rosters: *Railroad Magazine*: October 1939, page 90; January 1952, page 109

NC&STL STEAM LOCOMOTIVES BUILT SINCE 1900

Type	Class	Numbers	Qty	Builder	Built	Retired	Notes
0-6-0	B2-29	60, 61	2	Baldwin	1904	1936	
0-8-0	C1-28	770-773	4	Rogers	1902	1936	
							Rebuilt from 2-8-0 1916 and 1922
0-8-0	C2-40	775, 776	2	Brooks	1900	1936	
							Rebuilt from 2-8-0 1920 and 1919
2-8-0	H5-29	350-373	24	Baldwin	1899-1901	1934-1950	
2-8-0	H6A-39	374-383	10	Baldwin	1902-1903	1946-1952	
2-8-0	H7B37	410-419	10	Baldwin	1907	1947-1952	
							Some rebuilt to H7C-40
2-8-0	H7C-40	400-409	10	Baldwin	1904-1907	1948-1951	
2-8-0	H7C-40	384-399	16	Baldwin	1903-1904	19486-1951	
2-8-0	H8C-44	420-424	5	Baldwin	1904-1906	1948-1951	
2-8-0	H8G-40	430, 431	2	Brooks	1900		Rebuilt to 0-8-0 775, 776
2-8-0	H9-46	450-459	10	Baldwin	1911	1950-1953	
2-8-2	L1-55	600-628	29	Baldwin	1915-1918	1942-1950	
2-8-2	L2-55	650-659	10	Schenectady	1918	1951	USRA
2-8-2	L2A-55	660-671	12	Baldwin	1922-1923	1951	
2-10-0	P1-51	950-954	5	Rich, BLW	1918	1950	Russian Decapod
2-8-8-2	M-1-99	900-902	3	Baldwin	1915	1945	
4-4-0	D0-20	50	1	Baldwin	1902	1934	Ex-Georgia RR 35
4-6-0	G6-24	250-254	5	Baldwin	1902	1945-1949	
4-6-0	G7-25	270-273	4	Rogers	1904	1936	
4-6-0	G8-29	280-286	7	Baldwin	1906, 1908	1947-1949	
4-6-2	K1-34	500-503	4	Baldwin	1909	1942-1948	
							Rebuilt from 4-6-2 191?
4-6-2	K1A-37	504-511	8	Baldwin	1915	1948	
4-6-2	K2	530-537	8	Baldwin	1912-1913	1949-1951	
4-8-2	J1-54	550-562	13	Rich, BLW	1919-1925	1949-1950	
4-8-4	J2-57	565-569	5	Schenectady	1930	1951	
4-8-4	J3-57	570-589	20	Schenectady	1942-1943	1951-1952	

NATIONAL RAILWAYS OF MEXICO (Ferrocarriles Nacionales de Mexico)

The standard gauge Mexican Central Railway was completed in 1884 from El Paso, Texas, to Mexico City via Chihuahua, Zacatecas, Aguascalientes, and Querétaro (each the capital city of the state of the same name). The 3-foot gauge Mexican National Railroad (FCNM) opened in 1888 from Laredo, Texas, to Mexico City via Monterrey, Nuevo Leon; Saltillo, Coahuila; and San Luis Potosí, capital of the state of the same name. It was standard-gauged in 1903. National Railways of Mexico was formed in 1908 as successor to FCNM, and in 1909 it acquired the Central. It gradually took over most of the other railroads in Mexico.

The Mexican Revolution of 1911 destroyed the country's railroads, and not until the United States was clear of World War I could they resume construction and buy new rolling stock. National Railways of Mexico ordered large numbers of locomotives, primarily from Baldwin, in 1921 and 1924. In 1921 NdeM bought a number of secondhand engines, including 57 Ten-Wheelers from Illinois Central.

In the late 1920s and mid-1930s NdeM bought an interesting assortment of new locomotives: two three-cylinder 4-6-2s; five 4-8-0s; ten 4-6-4s; and 18 simple 2-6-6-2s, eight standard gauge and ten narrow. New steam and diesel locomotives north of the border in the 1940s created a surplus of older locomotives, which found a ready purchaser in NdeM. The road bought its last new steam locomotives in 1946, 32 light 4-8-4s.

NdeM began dieselizing right after World War II, but went at it slowly. By the end of 1965 dieselization was almost complete. On the standard gauge part of the system only a few 4-8-4s remained in helper service, and only 14 narrow-gauge steam engines were active.

NdeM adopted a new numbering system in 1908 when it acquired the Central, but standard and narrow gauge locomotives were treated as if they were completely separate, so there were hundreds of duplicate numbers. In the years after the revolution many secondhand engines carried their previous numbers, some locomotives were assigned low numbers followed by "A," and several major industries acquired locomotives that NdeM used. A complete renumbering and reclassification in 1930 cleared up the duplicate numbers. NdeM assigned numbers below 500 to narrow gauge engines, with blocks of numbers for subsidiary railroads. The 1930 numbers are used in the text and table below. Locomotives that did not survive until the 1930 renumbering are omitted in the table. An "R" as the second letter of the locomotive class indicates a superheater (*recalentador*).

Information on Mexican locomotives is sketchy at best. Most of what follows was constructed from *Railroad History*, issue 160. Secondhand locomotives are listed in the roster but are not discussed below.

Freight locomotives

NdeM began existence with a large number of Moguls and Consolidations inherited from the Central and the National. In 1921 and 1924 NdeM took delivery of several groups of freight locomotives, most of them from Baldwin: 55 Consolidations (class GR-20, Nos. 1137-1191); five light Mikados (KR-1, 2101-2105); 40 medium-weight Mikados (KR-2, 2106-2145); and 28 narrow gauge Consolidations (G-030, 262-289). They were a varied lot:

Numbers	Drivers	Cylinders	Weight	Tractive force
1137-1191	55"	21" × 28"	166,000	34,350
2101-2105	48"	20" × 28"	180,000	35,700
2106-2145	57"	25" × 30"	270,000	53,125
262-289	41"	18" × 22"	110,265	26,600

The KR-2 Mikados had the same boiler as the MR-6 Pacific, delivered at the same time. The KR-1 Mikados were curiously anachronistic, with inside-bearing trailing trucks, old-looking domes, and capped stacks. In addition, two groups of five 2-8-0s were purchased by industries and acquired by NdeM later on: the GR-23 class, Nos. 1232-1236, and G-24, 1237-1241.

The road had 22 compound 2-6-6-2s on its roster built between 1908

The NdeM locomotives that Baldwin built in 1921 and 1924 included two types of Mikados, KR-1 800 (later 2101) and KR-2 941 (later 2136), MR-6 Pacific 159 (later 2531), and PR-7 Twelve-Wheeler 5-A (later 2856). The larger 2-8-2, the 4-6-2, and the 4-8-0 all had the same boiler. Baldwin photos; collection of H. L. Broadbelt.

and 1911. In 1928 Schenectady delivered six 3-foot gauge simple 2-6-6-2s, with 43" drivers and 15" × 22" cylinders; two more came in 1934, and a final two in 1936. Then in 1937 Schenectady delivered eight standard gauge simple 2-6-6-2s, with 57" drivers and 18" × 30" cylinders. They worked at 250 pounds pressure, weighed 394,000 pounds, developed 72,474 pounds tractive effort. They two classes were the largest groups of simple 2-6-6-2s in North America. The only other simple 2-6-6-2s were two high-drivered experimentals on the Baltimore & Ohio and Uintah's two narrow-gauge tank engines.

NdeM purchased its last new steam locomotives in 1946, 32 4-8-4s, half of them built by Alco and half by Baldwin. They had 70" drivers and were intended primarily for freight service. At 387,000 pounds they were among the lightest of their type. They were called Niagras on NdeM.

Passenger locomotives

NdeM had little in the way of fast passenger power. FCNM had 20 Ten-Wheelers with 69" drivers built between 1902 and 1904 (NdeM's F-34 and F-35 classes, Nos. 821-840), and six Pacifics with 68" drivers. The first of the 4-6-2s was built by Baldwin in 1906 as a four-cylinder balanced compound. NdeM classed it M-3 and numbered it 2506. The other five Pacifics came from Schenectady in 1907. The three M-1s (Nos. 2502-2504) and the M-2 (No. 2505) had the same dimensions, except aft of the trailing truck: No. 2505 was 36" shorter. The single M-4, No. 2507, was also a four-cylinder compound. Both compounds were later converted to two-cylinder simple engines. In 1921 Baldwin delivered 20 medium-size Pacifics with 67" drivers (Nos. 2511-2530); four more identical 4-6-2s followed in 1924 (Nos. 2531-2534), accompanied by 10 narrow gauge 4-6-0s (181-190) and a standard gauge 4-8-0.

At first glance the Twelve-Wheeler was a curiosity. The type flourished from 1890 to 1900, and Norfolk & Western, which had more of them than anyone else, was a decade behind the times when it received its last 4-8-0s in 1912. More than that, NdeM's locomotive (delivered as No. 5-A, later 2856) bore little resemblance to the typical Twelve-Wheeler. Instead of 55" drivers and a narrow firebox between the rear drivers, it had 67" drivers and a wide firebox over the rear drivers. Comparison of the Twelve-Wheeler with the Pacifics and Mikados delivered the same year offers a clue. All three types had the same boiler — same grate area, same firebox dimensions, same number of tubes. The only difference was the working pressure — 180 pounds for the Pacifics, 190 for the Mikados, and 200 for the Twelve-Wheeler. The Pacifics and the Twelve-Wheeler had the same drivers and lead truck wheels. The Pacifics had 25" × 28" cylinders; the Twelve-Wheeler, 28" × 28". Fittings were identical, except for an Elesco feedwater heater and Baker valve gear on the 4-8-0; the Pacifics and Mikes had Young valve gear. The Pacifics weighed 253,950 pounds; the Mikados, 262,260; and the Twelve-Wheeler, 276,950. Tractive forces were 40,000, 53,000, and 55,700 pounds, respectively.

Perhaps, while the Pacifics and Mikes were under construction, the railroad thought about replacing the trailing truck of the Pacific with a fourth pair of drivers to use the weight of the firebox of the Pacific for tractive effort, and asked Baldwin to add such a locomotive to the group. To provide room for the drivers under the firebox, Baldwin raised the boiler; the 4-8-0 was 6" taller than the Pacifics and 9" taller than the Mikados. The resulting locomotive apparently was successful, and in 1935 Baldwin delivered five more with the same running gear and a slightly larger boiler.

In 1928, just after the three-cylinder craze died out north of the border, Schenectady delivered a pair of three-cylinder 4-6-2s, virtually identical to four it had just built for the Mexican Railway. The last purely passenger locomotives NdeM bought new were ten Hudsons, the lightest of their type in North America (292,000 pounds, 4,000 pounds more than the 1935 4-8-0s). They had 73" drivers, highest on the railroad, and their basic specifications were those of the USRA light Pacific.

Niagra 3031, built by Alco in 1946 (despite the round plate on the side of the smokebox) stands awaiting duty on a helper assignment at Tula, Hidalgo, on January 28, 1966. Photo by William J. Husa, Jr.

In March 1963 two 4-6-4s were running in North America: No. 2703, shown at Encarnacion with a freight train, and No. 2708. Photo by B. L. Bulgrin.

Switchers

The Central brought with it a group of 25 0-6-0s built by Baldwin and Brooks between 1902 and 1907. NdeM built one 0-6-0 and rebuilt two narrow gauge 2-8-0s into standard gauge 0-8-0s, and that was it for

National Railways of Mexico was the only North American railroad to buy single-expansion 2-6 6-2s in quantity. Standard gauge 2034, built by Alco in 1937, is a thoroughly modern locomotive, and gives the impression of being a slightly under-scale Challenger. Photo by A. M. Payne.

NdeM 367, an Alco product of 1934, looks like what Chesapeake & Ohio would have had for a narrow gauge division. Photo by Everett L. DeGolyer Jr.

genuine, no-lead-truck switchers. The narrow gauge roster included four 2-8-0s that were briefly converted to 0-8-0s.

Published rosters:

Railroad History, No. 160, page 60 (all-time roster)

Railroad Magazine: June 1961, page 16

NdeM STEAM LOCOMOTIVES BUILT SINCE 1900

Type	Class	Numbers	Qty	Builder	Built	Retired	Notes
Standard gauge							
0-6-0T	B-3	504	1	Kitson	1904	1959	NdeT
0-6-0T	B-4	505	1	Kitson	1904	1955	NdeT
0-6-0	B-7	508, 509	2	Kitson	1905	1955, 1953	NdeT
0-6-0	B-9	604, 605	5	Schenectady	1899-1900	1922-1958	Ex-IM
0-6-0	B-10	606, 607	2	Cooke	1900	1957, 1960	Ex-CyP
0-6-0	B-12	600	1	Brks	1902		
0-6-0	B-12	611-634	24	Brks, BLW	1902-1907	1945-1962	
0-6-0	B-13	635-637	3	Baldwin	1906	1951-1960	
0-6-0	B-13	638	1	NdeM	1913	1957	
0-8-0	C-1	639, 640	2	NdeM		1960, 1946	
						Rebuilt from narrow gauge 2-8-0s	
2-4-2T	L-1	2501	1	Dickson	1907		Ex-Hines Consol.Mining

Type	Class	Numbers	Qty	Builder	Built	Retired	Notes
2-6-0	E-2	652	1	Baldwin	1904	1933	Ex-CyM
2-6-0	E-3	653	1	Cooke	1906	1933	Ex-Central 119
2-6-0	E-4	654-667	14	Cooke	1903-1904	1946-1962	
							Ex-Central 130-143
2-6-0	ER-7	670-674	9	Cooke	1906	1924-1963	
						Ex-Central 110-118; four retired before 1930	
2-8-0	G-5	523-533	11	Baldwin	1901, 1903	1955-1959	
						Ex-Nacional de Tehuantepec	
2-8-0	G-6	534-550	17	Baldwin	1903-1908	1944-1962	Ex-NdeT
2-8-0	G-7	1033-1036	4	Baldwin	1905	1946-1957	
						Ex-Vera Cruz y Isthmus	
2-8-0	G-10	1043-1046	4	Baldwin	1899-1900	1930-1959	
						Ex-Hocking Valley	
2-8-0	G-11	1047-1050	4	Baldwin	1902	1930-1955	Ex-HV
2-8-0	G-12	1051	1	Baldwin	1907	1957	
2-8-0	G-14	1061-1110	56	BLW, Rog, RI	1899-1900	1922-1962	
						Ex-Central 716-771 (second numbers); six retired before 1930	
2-8-0	G-15	1111-1121	15	Brooks	1902	1930-1960	
						Ex-Central 252-266; four retired before 1930	
2-8-0	G-16	1123-1132	10	Baldwin	1901-1902	1954-1963	
						Ex-El Paso & Southwestern	
2-8-0	G-17	1133, 1134	2	Rogers	1903	1958, 1933	

NdeM STEAM LOCOMOTIVES BUILT SINCE 1900 (continued)

Type	Class	Numbers	Qty	Builder	Built	Retired	Notes
						Ex-Illinois Central, 1921	
2-8-0	G-18	1135, 1136	2	Schenectady	1903	1960, 1957	Ex-IC, 1921
2-8-0	GR-20	1137-1191	55	Brks, BLW	1921, 1924	1953-1963	
2-8-0	G-21	1220	1	Baldwin	1920		
						Ex-Mississippi Export, 1942	
2-8-0	G-22	1230	1	Baldwin	1907	1957	
2-8-0	GR-23	1232-1236	5	BLW, Cooke	1921	1962	
2-8-0	G-24	1237-1241	5	Baldwin	1921	1948-1962	
2-8-0	G-25	1242	1	Baldwin	1902	1931	
2-8-0	G-26	1243-1306	68	Cooke	1903-1904	1930-1963	
		Originally Central 800-867; 852, 819, 835, and 851 retired before 1930; parts used for 1362					
2-8-0	G-27	1307-1329	25	Cooke	1906	1930-1963	
		Originally Central 870-894; 873 and 886 retired before 1930; parts used for 1363					
2-8-0	G-28, GR-32	1330-1361	32	Cooke	1907	1955-1963	
2-8-0	G-29	1364	1	Baldwin	1900		Ex-KCS, 1929
2-8-0	G-30	1365, 1366	2	Baldwin	1906	1958, 1953	
						Ex-Bullfrog Goldfield, 1927	
2-8-0	G-31	1365, 1366	4	Baldwin	1902	1931, 1957	
		Ex-Central 935-938; first two retired 1930; 1366 later renumbered 1367					
2-8-0	GR-32	1362, 1363	2	NdeM	1938	1946	
						Built from retired locomotives	
2-8-0	G-33	1368-1380	15	Baldwin	1904	1930-1958	
		Originally FCNM 555-569; Nos. 559 and 560 retired before 1930					
2-8-0	GR-34	1381-1433	55	Cooke	1902-1903	1930-1963	
		Originally FCNM 500, 501, 503, 505-554; Nos. 502 and 504 retired before 1930					
2-8-0	G-35	1434-1439	6	Baldwin	1907	1953-1957	
						Ex-Colorado Midland, 1921	
2-8-0	G-36	1440-1444	5	Baldwin	1904	1946, 1953	
2-8-0	G-37	1445-1447	3	Baldwin	1903	1957-1958	Ex-KCS, 1921
2-8-0	GR-38	1448	1	Brooks	1921	1962	
						Ex-Chihuahua y Oriente, 1934	
2-8-0	GR-39	1450-1454	5	Baldwin	1906	1950, 1962	
						Ex-Rock Island, 1942	
2-8-0	GR-40	1455-1459	5	Brooks	1909-1910	1946-1962	
						Ex-Rock Island, 1942	
2-8-0	G-40	1481	1	Baldwin	1903		Ex-KCS, 1921
2-8-0	G-41	1482-1485	4	Pittsburgh	1910	1953-1954	Ex-NOdeM
2-8-0	GR-42	1501-1531	31	Baldwin	1906	1946-1962	
		Ex-FCNM, IM; previously NdeM 1449-1479, class G-39					
2-8-0	GR-43	1550-1586	37	Schen, BLW	1909-1913	1953-1963	
						Ex-Chicago & North Western, 1942-1943	
2-8-0	GR-44	1590, 1591	2	Pittsburgh	1911	1949, 1953	
						Ex-Bessemer & Lake Erie, 1943	
2-8-0	GR-48	1650-1656	7	Baldwin	1922-1926	1957, 1962	
						Ex-Norfolk Southern, 1948	
2-8-0	GR-52	1781, 1784	2	Baldwin	1920, 1921	1960, 1961	Ex-FdelP
2-8-0	GR-53	1803	1	Baldwin	1906	1960	
2-8-2	KR-1	2101-2105	5	Baldwin	1921	-1963	
2-8-2	KR-2	2106-2145	40	BLW, Brks	1921, 1924	1953-1963	
2-8-2	KR-3	2200-2214	15	BLW, Schen	1918	1957-1963	
						Ex-Nickel Plate, 1945-1946	
2-8-2	KR-3	2215-2224	10	Lima	1923-1924	1953-1963	
						Ex-Nickel Plate, 1945-1946	
2-8-2	KR-4, -5	4100-4116	17	Brooks	1916-1918	1949-1958	
						Ex-Pittsburgh & Lake Erie, 1945-1946	
2-8-2	KR-7, -8	2250, 2251	2		1949	1962, 1961	
						Rebuilt from narrow gauge 400, 401	
2-8-4	UR-1	3350-3354	4	Baldwin	1939	1957, 1962	Ex-NS, 1950
2-10-2	SR-1	3100-3105	6	Brooks	1919	1953-1959	
						Ex-Texas & Pacific, 1941	
2-6-6-2	H-1	2001, 2002	2	Schen	1911	1946	Ex-NOdeM, 1925
2-6-6-2	HR-2	2003	1	Baldwin	1908	1961	
2-6-6-2	HR-3	2004-2022	20	Baldwin	1910-1911	1958-1961	
		previously 1101-1114, 1116-1120; No. 1115 retired 1923					
2-6-6-2	HR-4	2030-2037	8	Schenectady	1937	1961-1963	
4-4-0	D-3	644	1	Baldwin	1910	1941	
						Ex-Atlanta, Birmingham & Atlantic	
4-4-0	D-4	510, 511	2	Pittsburgh	1895, 1900	1939	NdeT
4-6-0	F-13	513-516	4	Pittsburgh	1904	1952-1953	NdeT
4-6-0	F-16	751, 752	2	Baldwin	1900	1946, 1953	Ex-VCyl
4-6-0	F-21	757, 758	3	Schenectady	1900	1930-1946	
						Ex-IM; one retired before 1930 renumbering	
4-6-0	F-22	759-766	8	Baldwin	1900-1903	1949-1960	Ex-VCyl
4-6-0	F-26	369-372	4	Cooke	1900	1927-1955	Ex-IM
4-6-0	F-28	NdeT 519	1	Pittsburgh	1901	1939	
4-6-0	F-34	821-835	15	Brooks	1902-1903	1948-1962	Ex-FCNM
4-6-0	F-35	836-840	5	Baldwin	1904	1953-1958	Ex-FCNM
4-6-0	F-36	841-897	57	Rogers, Brooks, Baldwin	1898-1901	1931-1962	Ex-IC, 1921

NdeM STEAM LOCOMOTIVES BUILT SINCE 1900 (continued)

Type	Class	Numbers	Qty	Builder	Built	Retired	Notes
4-6-2	M-1	2502-2504	3	Schenectady	1907	1953, 1956	
4-6-2	M-2	2505	1	Schenectady	1907	1956	
4-6-2	M-3	2506	1	Baldwin	1906	1956	
4-6-2	M-4	2507	1	Schenectady	1907	1957	
4-6-2	MR-5	2508-2510	3	Baldwin	1903-1904	1953-1957	
						Ex-El Paso & Southwestern, 1921	
4-6-2	MR-6	2511-2534	24	Baldwin	1921, 1924	1962	
4-6-2	MR-7	2686, 2687	2	Schenectady	1928	1962	Three cylinders
4-6-4	NR-1	2700-2709	10	Schenectady	1937	1957-1962	
4-8-0	PR-6	2013, 2855	2	Schenectady	1905, 1903	1930, 1946	
				Ex-Butte, Anaconda & Pacific; No. 2013 retired before 1930 renumbering			
4-8-0	PR-7	2856	1	Baldwin	1924	1962	
4-8-0	PR-8	3000-3004	5	Baldwin	1935	1962-1963	
4-8-2	TR-1	3200-3205	6	Richmond	1923	1956-1961	Ex-FEC
4-8-2	TR-2	3206-3209	4	Richmond	1923	1956-1957	Ex-FEC
4-8-2	TR-3	3300-3319	20	Schenectady	1925-1926	1948-1964	Ex-FEC
4-8-4	QR-1	3025-3056	32	BLW, Sch	1946	-1965	
Narrow gauge							
2-6-0	E-02	167	1	Cooke	1920	1948	
4-6-0	F-05	103, 104	2	Cooke	1902	1954	MdeIS

Type	Class	Numbers	Qty	Builder	Built	Retired	Notes
4-6-0	F-031	181-190	10	Baldwin	1924	1954-1965	
2-8-0	G-014	226-230	5	Baldwin	1900, 1905	1930-1953	
2-8-0	G-019	115, 116	2	Baldwin	1909	1954	MdeIS
2-8-0	G-020	117-119	3	Baldwin	1909	1954, 1956	MdeIS
2-8-0	G-021	120, 121	3	Baldwin	1906, 1908	1930-1954	MdeIS
2-8-0	G-024	FCI 73-75	3	Kerr, Stuart	1904	1965, 1968	
2-8-0	G-024	OM 142, 143	2	Kerr, Stuart	1904	1968	
2-8-0	G-024	OM 144, 145	2	Baldwin	1902	1968, 1965	
2-8-0	G-027	249-252	4	Baldwin	1900	1951-1965	
2-8-0	G-029	260, 261	2	Baldwin	1900	1965, 1960	Ex-FCNM
2-8-0	G-030	262-289	28	Baldwin	1921, 1924	1952-1969	
2-8-0	G-031	290-294	5	Schenectady	1936	SG 900-906, 1948-1952	
2-8-0	G-031	295, 296	2	NdeM	1944	SG 901, 1949; 907, 1952	
2-8-0	G-031	297	1	Baldwin	1910	SG 903, 1950	
2-8-2	KR-03	400	1	Baldwin	1903	SG 2250, 1949	
						Ex-D&RGW 458	
2-8-2	KR-04	401	1	Baldwin	1903	SG 2251, 1949	
						Ex-D&RGW 459	
2-6-6-2	HR-01	361-370	10	Schenectady	1928-1936	1951, 1954	

NEW YORK CENTRAL SYSTEM

The New York Central System was the longest eastern trunk railroad and was second only to the Pennsylvania Railroad in revenue. NYC served most of the industrial part of the country, and its freight tonnage was exceeded only by the coal-carrying railroads. In addition it was a major passenger carrier — it carried perhaps two-thirds the number of passengers as the PRR, but NYC's average passenger traveled one-third again as far as Pennsy's.

The system was assembled in the 1860s and 1870s by Cornelius Vanderbilt (nicknamed "Commodore") and his son William Henry Vanderbilt. In 1900 its nucleus was the New York Central & Hudson River Railroad, which ran from New York up the east bank of the Hudson to Albany, then west to Buffalo. Its principal western connection and affiliate was the Lake Shore & Michigan Southern, which reached from Buffalo through Cleveland and Toledo to Chicago. The other western connection and affiliate at Buffalo was the Michigan Central, whose main line ran west across southern Ontario to Detroit, then to Chicago.

The New York Central Railroad (the second company of that name) was formed in 1914 by merger of NYC&HR and LS&MS. Considered part of the New York Central Railroad were Ohio Central Lines (Toledo & Ohio Central, Kanawha & Michigan, and Kanawha & West Virginia), the

West Shore Railroad (Weehawken, N. J. to Buffalo, parallel to NYC's own line), and Boston & Albany Railroad (neatly defined by its name).

The NYC system included several railroads that retained their identities until relatively late. Michigan Central consisted of a Buffalo-Detroit-Chicago main line (Canada Southern from Buffalo to Detroit, MC proper beyond), secondary lines to Grand Rapids and Mackinaw City, and a number of branches south of the Detroit-Chicago main. The Big Four (Cleveland, Cincinnati, Chicago & St. Louis) had main lines from Cleveland through Columbus to Cincinnati, from Cleveland southwest through Indianapolis to St. Louis, and from Cincinnati northwest through Indianapolis to Chicago; branches covered much of Ohio and Indiana and reached west to Peoria (Peoria & Eastern) and north to Jackson, Mich. (Cincinnati Northern). Pittsburgh & Lake Erie (Youngstown, Ohio-Pittsburgh-Connellsville, Pa.) was 80 percent owned by NYC. Several terminal roads around Chicago were semi-autonomous components of the system: Indiana Harbor Belt, Chicago Junction, Chicago & Indiana Southern, and Chicago River & Indiana.

The Toronto, Hamilton & Buffalo was owned jointly by NYC, MC, and CS (73 percent total), and Canadian Pacific (27 percent); it was not considered part of the New York Central System. However, the most significant steam locomotives on its roster were ex-NYC Hudsons 5311 and 5313 and a pair of Berkshires that looked more like NYC power than any of NYC's own 2-8-4s.

NYC's most famous early locomotive was 4-4-0 No. 999, built by West Albany Shops in 1893 primarily for publicity purposes. It earned its fame on May 10, 1893, when it turned its 86" drivers fast enough to move the four-car *Empire State Express* at 112.5 mph between Batavia and Buffalo, N. Y.

NYC experimented early with diesels and three-power locomotives (diesel, third-rail electric, and battery) and before World War II bought a number of switchers but no road engines. During the war NYC designed a high-horsepower 4-8-4 for passenger service. The first one was delivered concurrently with four Electro-Motive diesels: two 5400-h.p. FTs and two pairs of E7s. The new 4-8-4s and the diesels were tested intensively. NYC studied the costs of dieselizing, of staying with steam, both short-term and long-term, and of electrifying its main line from Harmon, N. Y., to Buffalo. Dieselization won out. The last New York Central steam-powered train was a transfer run in Cincinnati on May 2, 1957, pulled by H-7 Mikado No. 1977.

NYC's locomotive roster is complex. In earlier years the subsidiaries had their own locomotive numbering systems. Around 1905 most were brought into a unified NYC numbering scheme, with blocks of numbers and classes allotted to each subsidiary: for instance, MC was assigned 7500-8999 and classes beginning at 80; P&LE, 9000-9499 and classes from 100. Boston & Albany and Peoria & Eastern had separate systems. When locomotives were transferred between subsidiaries they were often renumbered.

In the early 1920s there was a start at renumbering (the next group of locomotives purchased was numbered 1-200), and a general renumbering in 1936 compressed blocks of numbers that had developed holes. There was a minor renumbering after World War II, and another in 1951. In the roster below, the first number is usually the number as built and the second is a later number. (The roster was compiled from several sources, none of which had the entire story, and is admittedly incomplete. Additions and corrections are welcomed.)

Freight locomotives

By 1900 the Consolidation was rapidly becoming NYC's standard freight locomotive. Each subsidiary had its own design, and there was considerable experimentation with compounding. In 1903 NYC&HR got the first of the G-5 class, which had 63" drivers, 23" × 32" cylinders, a wide firebox over the rear drivers, inside valves, and Stephenson valve gear. By 1907 (after nearly 600 had joined the roster) the type had evolved into the G-6, with outside valves and Walschaerts valve gear. Many of the G-5s were rebuilt into Mikados of the H-5 class.

NYC moved a lot of perishable freight, largely foodstuffs, that required more speed than the Consolidations could provide. In 1910 NYC designed a freight Pacific with 69" drivers and tractive effort of 36,900 pounds. Brooks delivered 50 (class K-10a, Nos. 3000-3049) that

went into freight service on the Hudson Division. The road immediately split an order among Schenectady, Brooks, and Baldwin for 50 more with 26" × 26" cylinders, 2" larger than the K-10s. They were classed K-11 and numbered 3050-3099. In 1912 the K-10s were given larger cylinders and reclassed K-11, and Schenectady began delivery of 100 more, 3100-3199. In 1916 fast freights were taken over by the L-1 4-8-2s (also with 69" drivers and square cylinders), and the Pacifics moved into secondary passenger service. Some were fitted with oil burners for service in the Adirondacks, some became passenger terminal switchers, and 28 were given 72" drivers and reclassed K-14.

The 595 class G-5 2-8-0s were built between 1903 and 1907 as saturated engines with inside valves and Stephenson valve gear, and by 1911 they needed upgrading. NYC considered rebuilding them with superheaters, new cylinders, and Walschaerts valve gear, realized that new boilers and fireboxes would be necessary too, and sent five of them to Baldwin to be converted to 2-8-2s, NYC's first. Eventually 462 G-5s were converted to H-5s. Baldwin got no further orders, but Lima built 10, NYC's West Albany Shops, 20, and Alco's Brooks Works, 427. In addition, Schenectady and Lima built 179 new H-5s, for a total of 641. The remaining G-5s were upgraded with superheaters and Walschaerts valve gear and reclassed G-6. The H-5s had 63" drivers, 25" × 32" cylinders (2" larger than the G-5s), and 51,000 pounds starting tractive force (4,000 pounds better than the G-5s).

In 1912 and 1913 Brooks delivered 70 H-7 2-8-2s, 35 each for Lake Shore & Michigan Southern and Michigan Central. They had 63" drivers and 27" × 30" cylinders, and were relatively heavy at 322,000 pounds. Schenectady delivered 60 more in 1920, 10 for MC and 50 for CCC&StL. All but the first ten LS&MS Mikes were transferred to MC in 1917, when 4-8-2s took over fast freight on the Lake Shore. The original ten H7s were retired early, but the others received a variety of modifications: mechanical stokers, feedwater heaters, cast trailing trucks, boosters, and large tenders.

The H-6 class, which comprised 194 USRA light Mikados, followed the H-7s. Soon after delivery 11 NYC engines and all 24 IHB engines were reassigned. The 15 Lake Erie & Western engines went with the road when it became part of the Nickel Plate in 1923. The New York Central System also received 30 USRA heavy Mikes, all assigned to Pittsburgh & Lake Erie or Pittsburgh, McKeesport & Youghiogheny.

In 1922 Lima built an experimental 2-8-2, Michigan Central 8000. William E. Woodard, Lima's chief engineer, started with the H-7e and created a locomotive that was only slightly heavier, 334,000 pounds, but could exert 4,470 more pounds tractive effort plus another 11,000 pounds for the booster. In the interest of squeezing more energy out of the fuel the engine had a feedwater heater and an improved superheater; a mechanical stoker and front-end throttle were original equipment. The engine was enough better than the H-7 that NYC ordered 200 more for assignment to NYC, MC, CCC&StL, B&A, and P&LE — 75 from Lima and 125 from Schenectady. They were classed H-10a and, inaugurating a new system-wide numbering scheme, were numbered 1-200. They were followed in 1924 by 91 in the H-10b class, Nos. 201-251 and 320-369. The major differences in appearance were air pumps on the pilot, 12-wheel tenders, and the lack of an outside dry pipe. Like the H-7s they received a variety of modifications during their service. All but the P&LE engines were renumbered in 1936; MC 8000 became 370 in

1932, 2090 in 1936, and 2100 in 1948.

USRA assigned ten light 2-10-2s to Boston & Albany. When B&A freight trains were speeded up in the early 1920s the 2-10-2s couldn't keep up. In 1926 they were sold to CCC&StL, then to NYC proper the next year, and almost immediately afterward to Canadian National.

Good as the H-10 Mikado was, Lima set new efficiency goals: a locomotive that could equal the H-10 in drag freight service on 20 percent less coal and in fast freight service on 12 percent less — or get 10 percent more drawbar pull out of the same amount of coal. The result was Lima's 2-8-4 demonstrator of 1924. Lima sent the A-1 east to Selkirk Yard, south of Albany, N. Y., with "Boston & Albany" on its tender, and the locomotive entered regular service over the Berkshire Hills between Selkirk and Springfield, Massachusetts. B&A ordered 25 that year, 20 more in 1926, and 10 in 1930. The three groups were classed A-1a (the A class had been used previously for 0-4-0s) and numbered 1400-1424; A-1b, 1425-1444; and A-1c, 1445-1454. All had 63" drivers and 28" × 30" cylinders. The first two groups had Elesco feedwater heaters and Lima's articulated trailing truck; the A-1c class had Coffin feedwater heaters concealed in their smokeboxes, conventional cast trailing trucks, and full-length frames. By the end of World War II B&A's 2-8-4s were worn out. They were retired in 1949 when B&A began to dieselize. Two were sold to the Tennessee, Alabama & Georgia but were scrapped not long after they moved south.

Even though NYC had begun dieselization, in 1947 subsidiary Pittsburgh & Lake Erie ordered seven 2-8-4s: class A-2a, Nos. 9400-9406. They were NYC's last steam purchase, and the last steam locomotives Alco built. By the time they were delivered in 1948, diesel production had taken over Alco's tender shop, so the tenders carried Lima's diamond-shaped builder's plate. The A-2as had anachronistic spoked 63" drivers and 26" × 32" cylinders. They looked much like the 4-8-4s but

had vestibule cabs. They were scrapped in early 1957.

In 1916 the Central ordered and tested a single 69"-drivered 4-8-2 for freight service. It proved fast and economical. Schenectady delivered 29 more within the year, and by the end of 1918 the road had 185 4-8-2s in freight service. The Central classed them L-1 and numbered them 2500-2684; as to name, though, Mountain wouldn't do. NYC advertised itself as "the Water Level Route," implying you could sleep comfortably as your train rolled along the banks of the Hudson and the Mohawk and the shore of Lake Erie — you wouldn't spend the whole night being tossed up and down mountains and flung around curves. On the New York Central 4-8-2s were Mohawks.

Between 1925 and 1930 Alco's Schenectady Works added another 300 Mohawks to the roster, the L-2 class: NYC 2700-2899, CCC&StL 6200-6274 (later 2900-2974), and NYC 2474-2499 (later 2975-2999). They had 69" drivers, but instead of the L-1s' 28" × 28" cylinders, the L-2s had 27" × 30" cylinders, the same as the USRA light Mountain. They weighed between 363,000 and 370,000 pounds, about 15 tons more than the L-1s.

In the late 1930s Mohawks occasionally substituted for Hudsons in passenger service. L-1s and L2s were limited to 60 mph, but NYC rebuilt two of the last L-2s with lightweight rods, cast engine beds, and

improved counterbalancing and found they were good for 80 mph. Orders quickly went to Alco and Lima for 65 L-3 Mohawks, Nos. 3000-3064, delivered between 1940 and 1942. They had the same 69" drivers but smaller cylinders, $25\frac{1}{2}" \times 30"$, and higher boiler pressure, and Nos. 3000-3024 were fitted with roller bearings specifically for passenger service. They proved equal to the Hudsons on passenger trains and could work freight as well.

The final group of 4-8-2s, the 50 L-4s, delivered by Lima in 1942 and 1943, were just a bit larger than the L-3s: 72" drivers and $26" \times 30"$ cylinders. A quirk of NYC's 600 4-8-2s was that though obviously road engines, most had footboards instead of a pilot. Number 2500 was built with a pilot, as were the passenger L-3s and the L-4s.

Passenger locomotives

The New York Central System accumulated 313 Atlantics, two-thirds of them assigned to the NYC&HR, between 1901 and 1907. They came into favor quickly as the logical successor to the 4-4-0 on NYC's fast, level track; they went out of favor almost as quickly because of the requirement that all trains into Grand Central Terminal in New York carry only steel passenger cars, which were much heavier than wood

cars. Few of Central's Atlantics lasted to be renumbered in 1936.

The Ten-Wheelers didn't fare so badly. The best known of the early 4-6-0s were Lake Shore & Michigan Southern's 80"-drivered Brooks engines, but the 4-6-0s that were most numerous and lasted longest were the F-2s, built between 1905 and 1908 for freight service, with 69" drivers and $22" \times 26"$ cylinders. In 1912 NYC began to fit them with superheaters and reclass them F-12, and they proved to be excellent branchline and suburban engines. Of the more than 140 built, nearly half were still on the roster for the 1936 renumbering and remained in service another 12 to 15 years, outlasting many newer locomotives.

The Lake Shore & Michigan Southern had a brief fling with the 2-6-2 while the NYC&HR was in its Atlantic phase. The Prairies were definitely passenger engines, with 81" or 79" drivers. The first group, the J-40 class, carried too much weight on their drivers. A few were transferred to the Toledo & Ohio Central and lasted until the mid-1920s; the rest were retired early. The J-41 Prairies were larger and more successful, at least to the point of all being converted to K-41 Pacifics.

The Central's first Pacifics were five class K engines for NYC&HR and ten for B&A, all delivered by Schenectady in 1903. Both had 75" drivers, inside valves, and Stephenson valve gear (later members of all classes had outside valves and Walschaerts valve gear). The Ks had $22" \times 26"$ cylinders and weighed 218,000 pounds; the K-1s, $21" \times 28"$ and 207,000 pounds. Over the next 12 years Schenectady and Brooks turned out 56 more Ks in subclasses Ka through Km for the B&A, and 50 for the Big Four. At the same time, Michigan Central and Canada Southern received a total of 70 almost identical K-80-class engines.

Between 1907 and 1910 NYC&HR and LS&MS received 192 K-2 Pacifics. They were about 40,000 pounds heavier than the K class and had 79" drivers and $22" \times 28"$ cylinders. They were followed between 1910 and 1924 by 281 superheated K-3s. They were not much heavier

NYC's F-12 Ten-Wheelers survived remarkably long. Number 1234 stands at Yorktown Heights, New York, awaiting suburban passenger work in 1950. The Baker valve gear actuates the inside valves through rocker arms. Photo by John P. Ahrens.

The K-3 Pacifics were standard mainline passenger power until the advent of the Hudsons. Number 4888, built by Brooks in 1923, stands ready for work at Livernois Yard in Detroit in 1939. Photo by Robert A. Hadley.

than the K-2s but had 23½" × 26" cylinders and the same 79" drivers. Successive groups of K-3s were heavier, and the last had boosters.

Three classes of passenger Pacifics followed the K-3s: ten K-4s with 72" drivers for Pittsburgh & Lake Erie, built by Brooks in 1917 and 1918; 35 heavy K-5s built between 1924 and 1927 for MC, CCC&StL, and P&LE; and ten K-6s for B&A in 1925 and 1926. The K-5s were a preliminary step toward the Hudsons — they had the same 79" drivers and 25" × 28" cylinders — and the K-6s had the usual B&A modification, 75" drivers. The first five K-6s carried a cross-compound air pump on the left side of the smokebox front; the smokebox door was circular but offset to the right, and the headlight was carried slightly above center. The resulting face was lopsided — and fortunately not repeated on the Central, a road generally characterized by good-looking engines.

During the 1920s NYC's passenger traffic increased greatly. The Pacifics were good for about nine cars at mainline speeds, but the road wanted an engine that could pull 12 to 14 — an engine with greater tractive effort for starting trains and greater boiler capacity for prolonged high-speed running. Clearances, track, and bridges precluded

a super Pacific, but a four-wheel trailing truck could support a larger firebox and spread the weight. NYC ordered a single 4-6-4 from Alco's Schenectady Works in 1926. NYC 5200, built in February 1927, was the first of the type. (The Chicago, Milwaukee & St. Paul had already designed such an engine but couldn't afford to build it.) The new engine had 79" drivers and 25" × 28" cylinders and worked at a boiler pressure of 225 pounds. It was equipped with a booster, which added 11,000 pounds for starting to the rated 42,300 pounds of tractive effort, and an Elesco feedwater heater countersunk into the top of the smokebox. NYC dubbed the new locomotive the Hudson type and classed it J-1.

It was obviously a success. Between 1927 and 1931 Schenectady built 204 more J-1s: NYC 5201-5344, MC 8200-8229, and CCC&StL 6600-6629. Schenectady and Lima each built ten J-2 Hudsons for Boston & Albany, essentially the same except for 75" drivers, which gave them 2,500 pounds more tractive effort, in deference to B&A's non-water-level profile. In 1934 West Albany Shops streamlined No. 5344 and named it *Commodore Vanderbilt*. It was America's first streamlined steam locomotive and one of the two that were streamlined twice* — in

---

* Baltimore & Ohio 5304 was the other, streamlined for the *Royal Blue* and the *Cincinnatian*.

4-6-4 — HUDSON

Soon after Lima's Super-Power 2-8-4 hit the rails in 1925, it became clear that a four-wheel trailing truck would be as beneficial to a passenger engine. The standard passenger locomotive of the time was the Pacific; substituting a four-wheel trailing truck created the 4-6-4.

Credit for designing the first 4-6-4 is usually given to the Chicago, Milwaukee & St. Paul, which drew up plans for such a locomotive in 1925. It used the name "Milwaukee type" on some documents, and the name "Baltic," used in Europe for 4-6-4 tank locomotives, was also used in connection with the design. However, the Milwaukee Road soon thereafter entered bankruptcy and set aside its plans for new passenger locomotives until 1929.

New York Central Hudsons

By the mid-1920s the New York Central's 4-6-2s had reach the limits of its track and clearances, but passenger train weights continued to increase. In November 1926 NYC experimentally applied a four-wheel trailing truck to a K-3 Pacific and at the same time ordered a single 4-6-4 from American Locomotive Company.

Number 5200 emerged from Alco on February 14, 1927. The new locomotive carried a bit less weight on its 79" drivers than NYC's K-3 Pacific, but carried more on the trailing truck, which supported a much larger firebox. After extensive testing, NYC ordered 59 more Hudsons — named for the river NYC followed from New York to Albany. Within four years the New York Central system had 225 4-6-4s

— 145 J-1s like 5200 and 20 75"-drivered J-2s on subsidiary Boston & Albany. In 1937 the Central received 40 J-3s, which had the same basic specifications except for smaller cylinders and higher boiler pressure; 10 streamlined J-3s came in 1938, making 275 in all — well over half the 4-6-4s built for service in North America.

Other Hudsons

Canadian Pacific had the second largest group of Hudsons, 65 built between 1929 and 1940, all to the same specifications, which were based on CP's G3 Pacific. They were slightly heavier than NYC's Hudsons and could exert a little more tractive effort.

The other Hudsons can be grouped by size. Most were 79"- or 80"-drivered machines, larger and heavier than NYC's — of the "standard size" Hudsons, only Santa Fe's 3450-class were lighter. The group is diverse, including Canadian National, Burlington, Milwaukee Road (the F6 class), Lackawanna, and New Haven.

In 1937 and 1938, 84"-drivered Hudsons were delivered to three railroads: Milwaukee Road, Chicago & North Western, and Atchison, Topeka & Santa Fe. The Milwaukee and C&NW engines were streamlined as was one of Santa Fe's. Milwaukee's were for fast Chicago-Twin Cities service on lightweight *Hiawatha* trains; the North Western engines were used on conventional heavyweight passenger trains between Chicago and Omaha. Santa Fe's engines were assigned to conventional trains between Chicago and La Junta, Colorado.

New York Central J-1a 5200 was North America's first Hudson. The design was used virtually unchanged for 274 more 4-6-4s for NYC and its subsidiaries — the most visible change was a larger tender. Alco photo.

Three railroads had lightweight Hudsons, which probably would have been Pacifics but for restrictions on weight per axle. The New York, Chicago & St. Louis (Nickel Plate) ordered four light 4-6-4s in November 1926. Alco's Brooks Works delivered them less than a month after NYC 5200 emerged from Schenectady. Maine Central received two slightly smaller 4-6-4s from Baldwin in 1930, and National Railways of Mexico got ten even lighter 4-6-4s from Alco in 1938.

A number of Hudsons were rebuilt or experimental locomotives. Baltimore & Ohio used the wheel arrangement as a vehicle for testing the watertube firebox: one 4-6-4 was rebuilt from a Pacific and three were built from scratch. One of those, *Lord Baltimore*, could also be classified with either the lightweights or the 84"-driver locomotives but truly belongs in the experimental group. Wabash used boilers from three-cylinder 2-8-2s to create semistreamlined 4-6-4s; Chesapeake & Ohio and Frisco rebuilt Pacifics into Hudsons; and Illinois Central rebuilt a Lima 2-8-4 into a 4-6-4 for freight service. The rebuilds were generally successful except for *Lord Baltimore* and IC's locomotive.

Hudsons were early candidates for scrapping. They were intended for fast mainline passenger trains, which were often the first to be dieselized, and the type wasn't well suited to heavy freight, local, or branchline work. A number of Hudsons were preserved, though none from the New York Central. Canadian Pacific 2860 remains active in excursion service between North Vancouver and Squamish, British Columbia.

Total built: 487
First: New York Central 5200, Alco, 1927
Last and heaviest: Chesapeake & Ohio 310-314, Baldwin, 1948, 443,000 pounds.
Longest-lived: Nickel Plate 173.
Last in service: National Railways of Mexico 2703 and 2708, 1963.
Greatest number: New York Central, 275
Lightest: National Railways of Mexico 2700-2709, Alco 1938, 292,000 pounds.
Recommended reading: *North American Hudsons*, by Lloyd E. Stagner, published in 1987 by South Platte Press, Box 163, David City, NE 68632.

J-3a Hudson 5411 rolls through Trenton, Michigan, with the *Cleveland Mercury* in June 1953. A Worthington type SA feedwater heater has replaced the original Elesco unit. Photo by John Krave.

1939 the plain-looking shroud was removed and the engine was reshrouded to match the Dreyfuss-styled streamlined Hudsons of 1938.

NYC ordered 50 more Hudsons in late 1936. The principal differences in the J-3a class were 22½" × 29" cylinders, 275 pounds pressure, and Boxpok or Scullin disk drivers. The first 40, Nos. 5405-5444, looked like the J-1s; Nos. 5445-5454 were streamlined by Henry Dreyfuss for the *20th Century Limited*. They were also classed J-3a, odd for a road on which subclasses proliferated freely. Two more J-3as, 5426 and 5429, were streamlined in 1941 for the *Empire State Express*.

NYC's Hudsons were America's best-known steam engines. They were many in number and ran through populous territory, NYC had an active public-relations department, model manufacturers (including Lionel and American Flyer) copied them in practically every scale — and they were fast, powerful, and good-looking.

In the early 1940s NYC was pleased with the job its dual-service Mohawks were doing in passenger service but wanted more boiler capacity, which meant a larger firebox supported by a four-wheel trailing truck — a 4-8-4. Alco delivered a single 4-8-4, No. 6000, in March

Niagara 6001, first of the production 4-8-4s, wheels the *Iroquois* west through Berea, Ohio, during its first winter of service. With their high headlights and smoke lifters the Niagaras brought a new look to the New York Central. Photo by Richard J. Cook.

1945. It had 75" drivers which were soon replaced by 79" drivers — the frame had been designed for that possibility. Central immediately ordered 26 more, the last one equipped with poppet valves. Central looked at the map for a river to go with its Hudsons and Mohawks and chose Niagara as the name for the 4-8-4s.

The Niagaras were the largest locomotives NYC's clearances would allow. There was no space at all for a steam dome, the sand dome was shaped like a saddlebag, and the stack was only 7" high. To conserve weight the cab, running boards, and smoke lifters were aluminum. The 4-8-4s had roller bearings on all axles, lightweight rods, and nickel-steel boilers. The smokebox front was a radical departure from NYC's standard centered-headlight look: a small circular door below center on a large irregularly shaped large door, and a headlight up toward the top. A cast number plate and oval NYC emblem and a drop-coupler pilot were reminders of previous NYC engines.

The road tested the Niagaras extensively. Several were assigned to Harmon-Chicago service and ran up more than 25,000 miles a month (at least 27 trips in 30 days). Their power output was about 6000 h.p.,

and with extra attention and priority treatment by the roundhouses they were the equal of a three-unit E7. The catch was that the diesels didn't need priority treatment. The last Niagara was retired in 1956.

Even before the Niagaras were delivered NYC considered a duplex-drive 4-4-4-4 with 20" × 26" cylinders and 79" drivers. It would have looked like an extended Niagara with an outside journal lead truck. The preliminary sketch even assigned a class, C-1a (the previous occupants of the C class, 4-4-0s, were either gone or soon would be).

Articulateds

New York Central, the Water Level Route, is not the first road that springs to mind when articulateds are mentioned, but it rostered 91 Mallets in three wheel arrangements. The most numerous were 74 2-6-6-2s. The first, the sole member of class NE-1a, was built in 1910 for Boston & Albany. It tested successfully there — B&A got 13 NE-2s soon afterward — then moved to NYC&HR's coal-hauling Pennsylvania Division, where it proved successful. Schenectady delivered 60 more NE-2s between 1911 and 1921. A few were active until the early 1950s.

The next most numerous group were the NU-1-class 0-8-8-0s for hump yard service — 16 of them, built between 1913 and 1921 for LS&MS, P&LE, MC, CS, and NYC. There was also a single 0-6-6-0, class NB-1a, built by Schenectady in 1913 for work as a passenger train pusher west out of Albany.

Switchers

NYC rostered almost 300 six-wheel switchers in the B-10 and B-11 classes, plus large numbers of earlier 0-6-0s (and a few later ones). NYC's 0-10-0s came before the 0-8-0s. The ten-wheel switchers were hump engines, designed to replace two 0-6-0s and to handle any train the largest road engine could bring into a yard. Most had 52" drivers and weighed 274,000 pounds. They proved cumbersome. Only three of the 20 built were still on the roster at the end of World War II.

USRA allocated 75 0-8-0s to the New York Central System, and subsequent 0-8-0s built as late as 1944 were copies of the USRA design. In 1927 Brooks built three heavy switchers for Indiana Harbor Belt. They were three-cylinder simple engines, the most powerful 0-8-0s built, with a tractive force of 75,700 pounds — plus 13,800 pounds from the boosters on the front trucks of their tenders.

Oddities and experimental locomotives

NYC exploited the double-ended flexibility of tank engines for suburban service in New York and Boston. The J-class 2-6-6Ts of 1901 and 1902, Nos. 1407-1422, were built for local trains on the Hudson and Harlem divisions. The electrification of Grand Central displaced them to B&A, where they worked in suburban service briefly before being rebuilt to conventional 2-6-0s. B&A received 18 almost identical engines of its own, Nos. 300-317, in 1906 and 1907. They were rebuilt and modernized in the late 1920s and remained in service until dieselization. Both groups had 63" drivers and 20" × 24" cylinders, and fireboxes that were short but almost as wide as a Wootten firebox.

In 1910 and 1912 NYC&HR received ten 2-4-4Ts for the 8-mile Yonkers Branch of the Putnam Division. With 57" drivers, 16" × 22" cylinders, and a total weight of 140,000 or 142,000 pounds, they are among the smallest road engines described in this book. Electrification of the line in 1926 put them out of work.

Boston & Albany planned for years to electrify its suburban operations but in 1928 took delivery of five 4-6-6-Ts from Schenectady. They were big-boilered 63"-drivered engines that looked like condensed, telescoped versions of parent NYC's Hudsons.

The Niagaras weren't the first 4-8-4s on New York Central rails. Timken demonstrator No. 1111 put in considerable mileage on the road in 1930, and looked very much like a New York Central engine. In 1931 Alco delivered an experimental multipressure, three-cylinder, compound 4-8-4, No. 800. The middle cylinder worked at 850 pounds, and two outside cylinders used a mixture of exhaust from the middle cylinder and steam direct from the boiler at 250 pounds. Inside the boiler and firebox was a closed-loop steam system that carried pressures up to 1300 pounds. It was not a success.

Historical and technical society: New York Central System Historical Society, P. O. Box 745, Mentor, OH 44060

PAUL W. KIEFER (1888-1968) was born in Delaware, Ohio. He attended public schools in Delaware and Glenville, Ohio, then studied in the night school of the Cleveland YMCA and at the Central Institute in Cleveland. He married Minnie Battles in 1912. Before 1916 he completed a four-year machinist apprenticeship at the Collinwood Shops of the Lake Shore & Michigan Southern in Cleveland, also serving as an instructor in the apprentice program. He then became successively locomotive machinist, mechanical inspector, and locomotive construction inspector. He continued to rise through NYC's ranks, and from 1926 to 1949 he was chief engineer, motive power and rolling stock, New York Central System. He retired as chief engineer, equipment, in 1953.

Simply put, Kiefer's best-known contributions to locomotive design are NYC's Hudson and Niagara. In 1947 he received a gold medal from the American Society of Mechanical Engineers for his work. He wrote numerous articles on freight car design and a book, *A Practical Evaluation of Railroad Motive Power*, published in 1947 by the Steam Locomotive Research Institute. Kiefer died September 2, 1968.

Recommended reading: "The Hudson," by Frederick Westing, in *Trains Magazine*, November 1957, pages 44-59

Published rosters: *Railroad Magazine*, May-August 1940 (May, page 81; June, page 113; July, page 85; August, page 128); December 1955, page 68; February 1956, page 67 (postwar renumbering)

NYC STEAM LOCOMOTIVES BUILT SINCE 1900

This roster is based on one compiled and published by William D. Edson and Edward L May in 1966. Long out of print, it is the definitive NYC roster, starting with Mohawk & Hudson's *DeWitt Clinton* and finishing with Pittsburgh & Lake Erie 9406. In the condensation here NYC's penchant for reassigning and renumbering can only be hinted at. The earlier number is generally as built; the later one is usually the 1936 number. I have ignored the postwar renumberings that served to clear number blocks for diesels.

Type	Class	Earlier Nos.	Later Nos.	Qty	Builder	Built	Subsidiary
0-6-0	B-2	311-376		66	Sch, Cke	1900-1903	NYC&HR
0-6-0	B-10	100-199		200	Schen	1903-1906	N&YC&HR
0-6-0	B-10	450-609	6600-6709	210	Alco	1907-1912	N&YC&HR
0-6-0	B-10	117-119	40-42	3	Brooks	1910	IHB
0-6-0	B-10	115-143		29	Alco	1907-1913	B&A
0-6-0	B-10	4518-4552		35	RI	1907-1908	LS&MS
0-6-0	B-10	4600-4614	IHB 15-29	15	Cooke	1906	LS&MS
0-6-0	B-10	7307-7372		66	Alco	1905-1912	CCC&StL
0-6-0	B-10	8590-8596	6991-6995	7	MLW	1909-1910	CS
0-6-0	B-10	8750-8799	6861-6897	50	Alco	19051912	MC
0-6-0	B-10	8790-8799	IHB 30-39	10	Brooks	1905	MC
0-6-0	B-11	610-629	6711-6729	20	Schen	1913	NYC
0-6-0	B-11	1-8		8	Pitt, Brks	1913, 1914	Detr. Term.
0-6-0	B-11	20-27	43-50	8	Baldwin	1913	IHB
0-6-0	B-11	144-152	6745-6754	9	Schen	1913, 1916	B&A
0-6-0	B-11	7373-7425		53	Alco,Li,Ba	1913-1918	CCC&StL
0-6-0	B-11	8597-8599	6997-6999	3	MLW	1913	CS
0-6-0	B-11	8798-8844	6898-6944	47	Pitt,Li,Ba	1912-1913	MC
0-6-0	B-54	4365-4374	NKP 32-41	10	Pittsburgh	1902	LE&W
0-6-0	B-55, 56	4375-4517	7000-7012	43	Alco	1902-1907	LS&MS
0-6-0	B-56f, g	4553-4587	7053-7087	35	Sch, Pitt	1910, 1911	LS&MS
0-6-0	B-58	9, 10, 111...119, 130-135		15	NYC, Sch	1905-1915	IHB, CJ
0-6-0	B-59-60d	136-167		32	Sch, Brks	1905-1912	CJ
0-6-0	B-60, 61	103...110		7	Alco	1907-1916	CR&I
0-6-0	B-61-61c	180-202		23	Schen	1913-1916	CJI
0-6-0	B-62	221-234		14	Cooke	1918	USRA, CJ
0-6-0	B-72	514, 515	7277, 7278	2	P&E	1900, 1901	P&E
0-6-0	B-73-74a	8-31	7279-7302	24	Sch, Dick	1901-1903	CCC&StL
0-6-0	B-82c, e	8663-8693		31	Sch, MC	1899-1905	MC
0-6-0	B-82d	8540-8543		4	CS	1899-1900	CS
0-6-0	B-82e	8506-8510		5	MC	1899-1904	MC
0-6-0	B-84b, d	8572-8581		10	CS	1901-1905	CS
0-6-0	B-84a, c	8720-8747		28	MC, Schen	1903-1906	MC
0-6-0	B-95b	29-31	9505-9507	3	Brooks	1901	T&OC
0-6-0	B-96a	415-417	9508-9510	3	Baldwin	1902	T&OC
0-6-0	B-97a, b	418-425	9511-9518	8	Brooks	1903, 1905	T&OC
0-6-0	B-97a, b	560-563		4	Brooks	1903, 1905	K&M
0-6-0	B-98a,b,c	426-434	9519-9527	9	Brooks	1905-1907	T&OC
0-6-0	B-98b, e	564-567	9528-9531	4	Brks, Rich	1906, 1911	K&M
0-6-0	B-104	9011-9070		60	Pitt., P&LE	1902-1913	P&LE
0-6-0	B-104	9122...9160		36	P&LE	1906-1912	PMcK&Y
0-6-0	B-105	253-255	9147-9149	3	Pittsburgh	1906	PMcK&Y
0-8-0	U-1a	9540-9542	7270-7272	3	Schen	1913	T&OC
0-8-0	U-1a, b	4280-4289	7280-7299	20	Schen	1913	LS&MS
0-8-0	U-1a, e	150-166		17	Schen	1913, 1916	IHB
0-8-0	U-2a-h	636-774	7336-7474	139	Alco, Lima	1916-1918	NYC
0-8-0	U-2c-g	8904-8939	7504-7539	36	Lima	1917-1918	MC
0-8-0	U-2c	8900-8903	7550-7553	4	Lima	1917	MC
0-8-0	U-2f	200-239	7560-7599	40	Lima	1918	NYC
0-8-0	U-2i	167-171		5	Lima	1918	IHB-CR&I
0-8-0	U-2j	42-47	7475-7480	6	Lima	1918	B&A
0-8-0	U-2k, l	54-65	7481-7492	12	Lima, Sch	1923, 1924	B&A
0-8-0	U-3a	4250-5252	NKP 205-207	3	Lima	1920	USRA, LE&W
0-8-0	U-3c, c	7200-7234	7600-7634	35	Lima	1922, 1924	CCC&StL
0-8-0	U-3b, c	240-319	7640-7719	80	Lima	1920-1922	NYC
0-8-0	U-3a	300-319		20	Baldwin	1919	USRA, IHB
0-8-0	U-3a	7440-7449	7740-7749	10	Bks,Li,Ba	1919, 1920	USRA, CCC&StL
0-8-0	U-3a	9543-9547	7753-7757	5	Pittsburgh	1918	USRA, T&OC
0-8-0	U-3a	9548-9550	7758-7760	3	Lima	1920	USRA, K&M
0-8-0	U-3b	48-53	7220-7225	6	Lima	1920-1921	B&A
0-8-0	U-3b, e, g	320-339		20	Lima	1921-1925	IHB
0-8-0	U-3d, e	350-360		11	Lima	1923-1924	CR&I
0-8-0	U-3c	386-405	7786-7805	20	Schen	1922	NYC
0-8-0	U-3a	406-414	7806-7814	9	Baldwin	1919	NYC
0-8-0	U-3a	415-439	7815-7839	25	Brooks	1918	USRA, NYC
0-8-0	U-3a	8940-8949	7840-7849	10	Lima	1920	USRA, MC
0-8-0	U-3b	8950-8985	7850-7885	36	Lima, Alco	1920-1926	P&E
0-8-0	U-3h	7495, 7496	73, 74	2	Brooks	1926	P&E
0-8-0	U-3e, f	4300-4349	7900-7949	50	Sch, Lima	1924-1925	NYC

NYC STEAM LOCOMOTIVES BUILT SINCE 1900 (continued)

Type	Class	Earlier Nos.	Later Nos.	Qty	Builder	Built	Subsidiary
0-8-0	U-3b	7485-7494	7985-7994	10	Lima	1920-1921	CCC&StL
0-8-0	U-3j	9000-9024	7950-7974	25	Lima	1929	P&LE
0-8-0	U-3k		8000-8049	50	Lima	1937	P&LE
0-8-0	U-3l		8050-8074	25	Schen	1944	P&LE
0-8-0	U-4a	100-102		3	Brooks	1927	3-cyl., IHB
0-8-0	U-33	30-41		12		1917-1918	Ex-2-8-0, B&A
0-8-0	U-60, 61	7450-7484	7200-7234	35	CCC&StL	1917-1922	CCC&StL
0-10-0	M	3650-3652	4601-4603	3	Brooks	1905	NYC&HR
0-10-0	M-1, 1a	4592-4599		8	Brooks	1905, 1907	LS&MS
0-10-0	M-1a	8799	7192	1	Brooks	1906	MC
0-10-0	M-1b	4590, 4591		2	Brooks	1907	`CI&S
0-10-0	M-1c	7498, 7499		2	Brooks	1907	CCC&StL
0-10-0	M-1d, e	8790, 8791	7190, 7191	2	Montreal	1909, 1910	MC
0-10-0	M-1f	95, 96	4600, 8998	2	Brooks	1910	NYC&HR
0-4-4-0	Shay	1896-1900	7186-7189	5	Lima	1923	NYC
0-6-6-0	NB-1	1300		1	Schen	1913	NYC&HR
0-8-8-0	NU-1a	5897-5899	7097-7099	3	Brooks	1913	NYC
0-8-8-0	NU-1b	9090, 9091		2	Brooks	1916	P&LE
0-8-8-0	NU-1c	5900-5905	7100-7105	6	Brooks	1916	NYC
0-8-8-0	NU-1d	8700, 8701	7109, –	2	Brooks	1916	MC
0-8-8-0	NU-1e	5906-5908	7106-7108	3	Schen	1921	NYC
2-4-4T	D-1, 2	37-49	1911-1920	10	Brooks	1910-1912	NYC&HR
2-6-0	E1a,b,d	1691-1761	1907...1922	71	Sch, NYC	1899-1900	NYC&HR
2-6-0	E-1c	1768-1790	1914-1917	23	Baldwin	1900	NYC&HR
2-6-0	E-1b,d,e	1859-1878	1923-1926	4	Sch, NYC	1900-1903	NYC&HR
2-6-0	E-2	1762		1	Schen	1900	Comp., NYC&HR
2-6-0	E-3, 3a	1763-1767	1927-1929	5	Sch, BLW	1900	NYC&HR
2-6-0	E-11	1407-1422		16	NYC	1904	Rebuilt from 2-6-6T
2-6-0	E-48	105...132		16	Schen	1900-1907	To B-58, CJ
2-6-0	E-48	120-127		8		1901-1906	CJ
2-6-0	E-82-82c	283-292	8364-8373	10	Schen	1901-1902	MC
2-6-2	J-40	650-695	4650-4695	46	Brooks	1901-1903	LS&MS
2-6-2	J-41	4700-4734		35	Brooks	1904-1905	To 4-6-2, LS&MS
2-6-6T	D-2a, b	1250-1267	300-317	18	Schen	1906-1907	B&A
2-6-6T	J	1407-1422		16	Schen	1901-1902	Rebuilt to 2-6-0
2-8-0	G-1	2332		1	Schen	1901	Compound, NYC&HR
2-8-0	G-2	2333-2414		82	Schen	1901-1903	Comp., NYC&HR
2-8-0	G-3	2302-2331		30	Schen	1901-1902	NYC&HR
2-8-0	G-4	2415-2429	2685-2699	15	Schen	1903	Compound, NYC&HR
2-8-0	G-5,a,b	2427-2499		23	Sch, Brks	1903-1904	NYC&HR
2-8-0	G-5, 6	2590-2649	990-1049	60	Schen	1905-1908	B&A
2-8-0	G-5c-6l	2700-2986		287	Sch, Brks	1905-1910	NYC&HR
2-8-0	G-5, 6	5449-5499		51	Brooks	1905-1910	IHB, CI&S
2-8-0	G-5r-6v	5600-5699		100	Brks, Sch	1907-1911	LS&MS
2-8-0	G-5a-z	5900-5999		100	Brks, Sch	1904-1906	LS&MS
2-8-0	G-5, 6	6618-6842		125	Brks, Sch	1905-1911	CCC&StL
2-8-0	G-6p, u	7610-7627	1130...1142	18	Montreal	1910	CS
2-8-0	G-5s-6t	7800-7867	1112...1141	68	Brks, Sch	1907-1910	
2-8-0	G-16q	1050-1053		4	Schen	1912	B&A
2-8-0	G-6v	5605-5614	NKP475-484	10	Brooks	1911	LE&W
2-8-0	G-16v, w	5385-5399	NKP 485-499	15	Brks, Sch	1911-1912	LE&W
2-8-0	G-33	2564-2575	964-975	12	Schen	1901	Rblt to 0-8-0, B&A
2-8-0	G-34a	2576-2589	976-989	14	Schen	1903	B&A
2-8-0	G-40	5596-5599		4	Brooks	1902	LEA&W
2-8-0	G-42a, b	5700-5749		50	Brooks	1899-1900	LS&MS
2-8-0	G-43a-e	750-869	1100-1111	120	Brooks	1901-1903	LS&MS
2-8-0	G-44	5515-5539		25	Brooks	1904	LE&W, LEA&W
2-8-0	G-46a, b	1000-1006	5870-5876	7	Brooks	1903-1904	LS&MS
2-8-0	G-46c	5877-5891		15	Brooks	1907	LEA&W
2-8-0	G-46d	5576-5595	9662-9681	20	Brooks	1909	LS&MS
2-8-0	G-46e	9652-9661	1112-1121	10	Schen	1912	T&OC
2-8-0	G-46f	5401-5424	1122-1125	24	Brooks	1910	CI&S
2-8-0	G-46g	5561-5575	1130, 1131	15	Brooks	1911	LS&MS
2-8-0	G-46h	6843-6872	1143-1172	30	Brooks	1912	CCC&StL
2-8-0	G-46i	6873-6882	1173-1182	10	Brooks	1912	P&E
2-8-0	G-46j, k, l	528-552	1183-1199	25	Rich, Brks	1911-1914	K&M
2-8-0	G-47	200, 201	CJ 1, CR&I 2	2	Schen	1913	CR&I
2-8-0	G-66	704-713	6531-6540	10	RI	1899-1900	CCC&StL
2-8-0	G-67-71	714-775	6541-6617	77	Brks, Sch	1901-1903	CCC&StL
2-8-0	G-80-80d	573-619	7700-7746	47	Schen	1901-1904	MC
2-8-0	G-80b	499	7530	1	Schen	1902	MC
2-8-0	G-80d, e	466-479	7540-7553	14	Sch, CS	1904	CS
2-8-0	G-80f	7554-7567		14	MLW	1905	CS
2-8-0		500-509		10	BLW	1901-1902	K&M
2-8-0	G-95a	510-512	9601, 9602	3	Rogers	1903	K&M
2-8-0	G-95a	300-324	9660-9624	25	Rogers	1902-1903	T&OC
2-8-0	G-95c	3	9600	1	Richmond	1907	K&WV
2-8-0	G-96a,b,c	325-351	9625-9651	27	Brooks	1905-1907	T&OC

NYC STEAM LOCOMOTIVES BUILT SINCE 1900 (continued)

Type	Class	Earlier Nos.	Later Nos.	Qty	Builder	Built	Subsidiary
2-8-0	G-96a,b,c	513-527		15	Brooks	1905-1907	K&M
2-8-0	G-97a	608-612	9725-9729	5	Brooks	1904	Z&W
2-8-0	G-100,101	139-165	9318-9335	27	Pittsburgh	1900, 1902	P&LE
2-8-0	G-102, a	166-199	9336-9369	34	Pittsburgh	1903	P&LE
2-8-0	G-102, a	150-153,200	9370-9374	5	Pittsburgh	1905	P&LE
2-8-0	G-102, a	282-292	9411-9421	11	Pittsburgh	1903, 1906	PMcK&Y
2-8-0	G-102b	9422-9424		3	Pittsburgh	1907	PMcK&Y
2-8-0	G-102b	9375-9377		3	Pittsburgh	1907	P&LE
2-8-0	G-103	9378-9392		15	Pittsburgh	1910	P&LE
2-8-0	G-104	9393-9397		5	P&LE	1913	P&LE
2-8-2	H-5a-e	3600-3721	1202-1247	122	Brks, BLW	reblt 1912	NYC
2-8-2	H-5p, q	3722, 3723	1248, 1249	2	Brks, NYC	reblt 1915	NYC
2-8-2	H-5h	3725-3774	1253-1275	50	Schen	new 1913	NYC
2-8-2	H-5f, k	3775-3830	1276-1297	56	Brooks	reblt 1913-1914	NYC
2-8-2	H-5m, n	3831-3852	1302-1314	22	Brooks	reblt 1914	NYC
2-8-2	H-5p	3853-3934	1315-1376	82	Brks, NYC	reblt 1915-1918	NYC
2-8-2	H-5t	3935-3984	1435-1484	50	Lima	new 1916	NYC
2-8-2	H-5p	4071-4115	1377-1530	45	Brooks	reblt 1915-1916	NYC
2-8-2	H-5l	4116-4124	1428-1432	9	Brooks	reblt 1913	NYC
2-8-2	H-5l	6000-6063	1502-1563	64	Brooks	reblt 1913-1915	CCC&StL
2-8-2	H-5s, t	6064-6088	1564-1588	25	Lima	new 1916	CCC&StL
2-8-2	H-5l	6125-6149	1485-1531	25	Brooks	reblt 1913	CCC&StL
2-8-2	H-5l	6698-6722	1625-1649	25	Brooks	reblt 1913-1915	CCC&StL
2-8-2	H-5j	1200-1213		14	Schen	1913-1914	B&A
2-8-2	H-5g	1214-1223		12	Brooks	reblt 1915	B&A
2-8-2	H-5t	1224-1229		6	Lima	new 1916	B&A
2-8-2	H-5r	250-264		15	Schen	new 1916	IHB
2-8-2	H-5u	400-419		20	Sch, Lima	new 1923	IHB
2-8-2	H-5v	420-424		5	Lima	new 1924	IHB
2-8-2	H-6a	6089-6113	1700-1724	25	Baldwin	1918	USRA, CCC&StL
2-8-2	H-6a	9732-9746	1732-1746	15	Schen	1918	USRA, T&OC
2-8-2	H-6a	400-423		24	Lima	1919	USRA, IHB, to SLSF, PM
2-8-2	H-6a	7970-7989	1770-1789	20	Schen	1918	USRA, MC
2-8-2	H-6a	5100-5149	1800…1849	50	Schen	1918	USRA, NYC, 11 to PM
2-8-2	H-6a	5150-5194	1850-1894	45	Lima	1918-1919	USRA, NYC
2-8-2	H-6a	5540-5554	NKP 586-600	15	Baldwin	1918	USRA, LE&W
2-8-2	H-7a	4000-4009		10	Brooks	1912	LS&MS
2-8-2	H-7b	4010-4034	2035-2059	25	Brooks	1912-1913	LS&MS
2-8-2	H-7c, d	7900-7934	2000-2034	35	Brooks	1913	MC
2-8-2	H-7e	6150-6199	1950-1999	50	Schen	1920	CCC&StL
2-8-2	H-7e	7960-7969	2060-2069	10	Schen	1920	MC
2-8-2	H-8a	9500-9504		5	Brooks	1916	P&LE
2-8-2	H-8a,b,c	9550-9579		30	Brooks	1916-1918	PMcK&Y
2-8-2	H-8d	9520-9524		5	Brooks	1920	P&LE
2-8-2	H-9a	9580-9589		10	Brooks	1918	USRA, PMcK&Y
2-8-2	H-9b	9505-9509		5	Schen	1919	USRA, P&LE
2-8-2	H-9c	9590-9594		5	Schen	1919	USRA, PMcK&Y
2-8-2	H-9d	9510-9519		10	Baldwin	1919	USRA, P&LE
2-8-2	H-10a	8000	2090	1	Lima	1922	MC
2-8-2	H-10a	1-190	2101-2290	190	Lima, Sch	1922-1923	NYC, MC, CCC&StL, B&A
2-8-2	H-10a, b	191-211		21	Schen	1923, 1924	P&LE
2-8-2	H-10b	212-251	2312-2351	40	Lima	1924	CCC&StL, MC
2-8-2	H-10b	320-359	2360-2399	40	Schen	1924	NYC
2-8-2	H-10b	360-369	2080-2089	10	Schen	1924	NYC
2-8-2T	HXa, b	555-559	9500-9504	5	Brooks	1902-1912	K&M
2-8-4	A-1a	1400-1424		25	Lima	1926	B&A
2-8-4	A-1b	1425-1444		20	Lima	1926-1927	B&A
2-8-4	A-1c	1445-1454		10	Lima	1930	B&A
2-8-4	A-2a		9400-9406	7	P&LE	1948	P&LE
2-10-2	Z-1	1100-1109		10	Brooks	1919	B&A, to CN
2-6-6-2	NE-1a	1249	1374	1	Schen	1910	B&A
2-6-6-2	NE-2a	1375-1399		25	Schen	1911	NYC&HR
2-6-6-2	NE-2b,c,e	1300-1312		13	Schen	1913-1917	B&A
2-6-6-2	NE-2d, f	1349-1373	1933-1938	25	Schen	1917	NYC
2-6-6-2	NE-2g	1339-1348	1939-1948	10	Schen	1920-1921	NYC
4-4-0	C-3	947, 948	1079, 1080	2	NCYC	1900, 1901	NYC&HR
4-4-0	C-38	1139-1144	249-254	6	Schen	1900	B&A
4-4-0	C-39	1134-1138	244-248	5	Schen	1900	B&A
4-4-0	C-96a	455-457	9556-9558	3	Brooks	1901	T&OC
4-4-0	C-96c	2	9555	1	RI	1906	K&WV
4-4-0	C-97a-d	570-579	9570-9579	10	Schen	1902-1905	K&M
4-4-0	C-97a,b,c	458-466	9559-9567	9	Brooks	1904-1906	T&OC
4-4-0	C-100	23		1	P&LE	1906	Inspection eng., P&LE
4-4-0	C-103-105	9253-9267		15	Pittsburgh	1901-1906	P&LE
4-4-0	C-106	9290-9294		5	Pittsburgh	1907	PMcK&Y
4-4-2	1-40a	4321, 4322		2	Schen	1907	NYC

278

NYC STEAM LOCOMOTIVES BUILT SINCE 1900 (continued)

Type	Class	Earlier Nos.	Later Nos.	Qty	Builder	Built	Subsidiary
4-4-2	I, I-10	3775…3999	775…999	212	Schen	1901-1907	NYC&HR
4-4-2	Ib	3948-3953	400-405	6	Schen	1902	B&A
4-4-2	Ij	6940-6959		20	Schen	1906-1907	CCC&StL
4-4-2	I-1	3000	803	1	Schen	1904	Cole comp., NYC&HR
4-4-2	I-2	10-12	800-802	3	Schen	1901	StL&A
4-4-2	I-3	3804	804	1	BLW	1905	Bal. comp., NYC&HR
4-4-2	I-40	4750-4759	4320-4324	10	Schen	1907	LS&MS
4-4-2	I-60-63	360-369	6900-6939	40	Sch, Brks	1901-1904	CCC&StL
4-4-2	I-80	251-266	8082-8097	16	Schen	1901-1902	MC
4-4-2	I-80	480-489	8072-8081	10	Schen	1901-1902	CS
4-4-2	I-80	319, 323	8070-8071	2	Schen	1903	Toledo, CS & Detroit
4-4-2	I-100a	301-305	9200-9204	5	Schen	1903	P&LE
4-6-0	Fx	U&D 19-41	800-818	22	Schen	1899-1907	NYC
4-6-0	F-2-2g	2065-2166	819-876	102	Schen	1905-08	to F-12, NYC&HR
4-6-0	F2c, f	1900-1919	704-723	20	Schen	1907	To F-12c, B&A
4-6-0	F-2d	1965-1999		35	Schen	1907	to F-12, NYC&HR
4-6-0	F-3	2036-2050	2010-2024	15	BLW	1900	NYC&HR
4-6-0	F-40	5280-5289		10	Baldwin	1902	CI&S
4-6-0	F-41	5290-5299		10	Pittsburgh	1900	CI&S
4-6-0	F-52	611-615	5011-5015	5	Brooks	1900	LS&MS
4-6-0	F-69, 69a	400-405	6234-6239	4	Baldwin	1900	CCC&StL
4-6-0	F-82, a	8150-8159	880, 881	10	CS, Schen	1899-1901	MC, CS
4-6-0	F-82	8106, 8107		2	Schen	1900	MC
4-6-0	F-82	8260-8293	882-889	24	Schen	1900-1906	MC
4-6-0	F-84	8190-8195		6	Schen	1900	MC
4-6-0	F-103-105	9205-9219		3	Pittsburgh	1909-1912	PMcK&Y
4-6-0	F-105a	9220-9224		5	P&LE	1915	PMcK&Y
4-6-2	Kg	2795-2799	510-514	5	Schen	1903	NYC&HR, then B&A
4-6-2	Ka…Km	515-565		51	Schen	1905-1914	B&A
4-6-2	Kb…Kn	6400-6449		50	Brks, Sch	1905-1915	CCC&StL
4-6-2	Ko	6450-6454		5	CCC&StL	1915	CCC&StL
4-6-2	K-1	2700-2709	500-509	10	Schen	1903	B&A
4-6-2	K-2f-k	3438-3494		57	Schen	1907-1910	NYC&HR
4-6-2	K-2a-d			95	Schen	1907-1910	LS&MS
4-6-2	K-2e	3555-3594			Schen	1908	NYC&HR
4-6-2	K-3a-g	3358-3437	4806…4854	80	Sch, BLW	1911-1913	NYC&HR
4-6-2	K-3b, e	4895-4909	4814…4841	15	Schen	1911,1913	LS&MS
4-6-2	K-3f-q	8300-8339	4603-4639	40	Sch, Brks	1913-1923	MC
4-6-2	K-3h	8400-8404	4640-4644	5	Schen	1916	MC
4-6-2	K-3n,p,q	3267-3357	4667-4757	91	Sch, Brks	1918-1923	NYC
7 K-3ns renumbered B&A 500-506, 1937-1938							
4-6-2	K-3j-p	6455-6499	4855-4899	45	Sch, Brks	1917-1923	CCC&StL
4-6-2	K-3r	6500-6504	4800-4804	5	Brooks	1925	CCC&StL
4-6-2	K-4a, b	9224-9234		10	Brooks	1917-1918	P&LE
4-6-2	K-5	5000 (6525)	4925	1	Schen	1924	MC, then CCC&StL
4-6-2	K-5a	8350-8354	4926-4930	5	Brooks	1925	MC, then CCC&StL
4-6-2	K-5b	6505-6514	4905-4914	10	Schen	1926	CCC&StL
4-6-2	K-5b	8355-8364	4915-4924	10	Schen	1926	MC, then CCC&StL
4-6-2	K-5b	9235-9244	4931-4940	10	Schen	1927	P&LE
4-6-2	K-6a, b	590-599	9245-9254	10	Brks, Sch	1925, 1926	B&A, then P&LE
4-6-2	K-10a	3000-3049	4400-4449	50	Brooks	1910-1911	To K-11a
4-6-2	K-11a-f	3050-3199	4450-4599	200	Alco, BLW	1911-1913	NYC&HR
4-6-2	K-14a-f		4390-4399	10	NYC	1924-1925	Rblt from K-11
4-6-2	K-14b		17-19	3	NYC	1929-1930	Ex-K-11, P&E
4-6-2	K-14g, h	575-589		15	Sch, BLW	1911-1913	B&A
4-6-2	K-41a, b	4700-4734		35	NYC	1916-1919	Rblt from 2-6-2
4-6-2	K-80	8410-8437		28	Sch, MLW	1904-1910	CS
4-6-2	K-80	8450-8491		42	Schen	1904-1912	MC
4-6-4	J-1a-e		5200-5344	145	Schen	1927-1931	NYC
4-6-4	J-1b, c, d	8200-8229	5345-5374	30	Schen	1927-1930	NYC
4-6-4	J-1d, e	6600-6629	5375-5404	30	Schen	1929, 1931	CCC&StL
4-6-4	J-2a, b	600-609	5455-5464	10	Schen	1928, 1930	B&A
4-6-4	J-2c	610-619	5465-5474	10	Lima	1931	B&A
4-6-4	J-3a		5405-5454	50	Schen	1937-1938	NYC
4-6-6T	D-1a	400-404	1295-1299	5	Schen	1928	B&A
4-8-0	H-30, a	800-810		11	Schen	1899-1900	B&A
4-8-2	L-1a-d		2500-2684	185	Sch, Lima	1916-1918	NYC
4-8-2	L-2a, c		2700-2899	200	Schen	1925-1929	NYC
4-8-2	L-2b, d	6200-6249	2900-2949	50	Schen	1929	CCC&StL
4-8-2	L-2d	2450-2499	2950-2999	50	Schen	1929-1930	NYC
4-8-2	L-3a, b, c		3000-3064	65	Sch, Lima	1940-1942	NYC
4-8-2	L-4a, b		3100-3149	50	Lima	1942-1944	NYC
4-8-4	HS-1a		800	1	Schen	1931	NYC
4-8-4	S-1a, b		6000-6025	26	Schen	1945-1946	NYC
4-8-4	S-2a		5500	1	Schen	1946	NYC

NEW YORK, CHICAGO & ST. LOUIS RAILROAD

In 1900 much of the Nickel Plate Road of later years was part of the New York Central System. The New York, Chicago & St. Louis Railway (it acquired the Nickel Plate nickname early in life) consisted of a single line from Buffalo, New York, west to Chicago via Cleveland, Bellevue, and Fostoria, Ohio, and Fort Wayne, Indiana. Its origins were with the Lake Erie & Western, but it had been purchased by the Vanderbilts in 1883. Between Buffalo and Cleveland it paralleled the Lake Shore & Michigan Southern — indeed, was within sight of it most of the way. West of Cleveland NKP's line swung to the south, avoiding most of the population centers except Fort Wayne.

The Lake Erie & Western made a long southward-reaching arc from Sandusky, Ohio, to Bloomington, Illinois. It was intended to be a shortcut for traffic moving to and from Chicago & Alton's Bloomington-Kansas City line. Because of disputes with the Vanderbilts' Lake Shore & Michigan Southern over traffic, LE&W's management organized the Nickel Plate in 1881. NKP became part of the Vanderbilt system in 1883. In the late 1880s LE&W extended its main line west to Peoria, Ill., acquired two lines crosswise to its main stem, and was purchased by the LS&MS in 1899.

The Toledo, St. Louis & Western — the Clover Leaf — was a former narrow-gauge railroad from Toledo, Ohio, to St. Louis. Its route passed through almost nowhere of consequence, its narrow-gauge antecedents meant light construction and a sawtooth profile, and its finances were as poorly constructed as its line. Despite all that, it somehow developed a reputation for moving freight fast.

In 1916 the Nickel Plate was purchased by the Van Sweringen brothers of Cleveland, real estate developers who suddenly found themselves in the railroad business. They put John J. Bernet of the NYC in charge. He led a thorough upgrading of the road, turning it into a fast freight carrier. In 1923 the Nickel Plate, the Lake Erie & Western, and the Clover Leaf were consolidated as the New York, Chicago & St. Louis Railroad — but still the Nickel Plate Road.

In 1927 Bernet moved to the Erie, by then also in the Van Sweringen group of railroads, and worked the same transformation — and the motive power of that transformation was 105 Berkshires. Bernet returned to NKP in 1933 to pull the Nickel Plate out of the Depression the same way.

For the first decade and a half of the 20th century NKP's motive power policy was a conservative version of parent New York Central's conservative motive power policy. During its first years of independence it copied NYC engines. The first Berkshires of 1934 were a major leap for the road.

Even though it was part of the New York Central System, Nickel Plate had its own locomotive classification and numbering scheme. About the time it became independent it adopted NYC's class letters, though NKP's Hudsons were class L, not J. For the last 0-8-0s and the 2-8-4s the road followed the class letters of the Van Sweringens' Advisory Mechanical Committee, C for 0-8-0 and S for 2-8-4. Nickel Plate renumbered frequently, and some numbers were applied to as many as five locomotives in the space of 40 years. Lake Erie & Western's engines carried 4-digit NYC numbers and were renumbered into NKP series; Clover Leaf engines simply had 700 added to their numbers. Most of the engines in the 700-class were retired before the 2-8-4s arrived, but two long-lived 0-6-0s, 716 and 717, had to be renumbered out of their way — first to fifth 16 and 17, then to second 316 and 317.

Wheeling & Lake Erie's locomotive history is complex. It includes predecessor railroads of several gauges and numerous renumberings. In the roster below only those W&LE engines that became part of the Nickel Plate roster are shown.

Freight locomotives

Between 1902 and 1913 Nickel Plate acquired 59 Consolidations in the N classes, modest-size engines with 19" × 28" cylinders and 63" drivers. Successive batches grew in weight from 157,000 to 185,000 pounds. Just before the Van Sweringens bought the Nickel Plate, parent New

Nickel Plate Mikado 633 was an upgraded USRA light 2-8-2. NKP characteristics are the cylinder bracing and the large tender, obviously newer than the locomotive. The Elesco feedwater heater was unusual on the road. Photo by R. J. Foster, collection of John A. Rehor.

Berkshire 746, built by Lima in 1944, stands on the ready track at Bellevue, Ohio, on August 21, 1956. Almost two years later, on July 2, 1958, it would head NKP's last mainline steam run from Bellevue to Conneaut. Photo by John A. Rehor.

York Central sweetened the deal with 15 larger 2-8-0s, which NKP classed T and number 460-474. They were former Lake Shore & Michigan Southern G-43 engines built by Brooks in 1903; NYC modernized them with superheaters and Baker valve gear. They weighed slightly less than the newest N-class 2-8-0s, but they had larger cylinders, higher boiler pressure, and almost 7,000 pounds more tractive effort. It was not a major sacrifice on NYC's part — Central by then had nearly 800 2-8-2s, many of them rebuilt from 2-8-0s newer than those bestowed on the Nickel Plate.

Nickel Plate had noticed those Mikados, too, and sent an order to Lima for ten copies of NYC's H-5. Engines 500-509 were delivered in 1917, and soon afterward 25 more, Nos. 510-534, came from Brooks. A year later the USRA assigned ten light Mikados to Nickel Plate: H-6, Nos. 601-610. Because of their price, $56,600 apiece, NKP wasn't enthusiastic about having to take the engines, but after delivery the road changed its mind. The USRA engines weighed only 5,000 pounds more than the H-5s but were good for 6,000 pounds more tractive effort. They were equipped with mechanical stokers that eased the job of the fireman, and large tenders that let trains pass up water stops.

When USRA control ended after World War I, some railroads revert-ed to the locomotive designs they had used before 1918, in many cases to designs inferior to USRA locomotives. Other roads eagerly adopted the USRA designs. Nickel Plate was among the latter. Between 1920 and 1924 it bought 61 copies of the USRA light Mikado. The first five, Nos. 611-615, class H-6b, carried minor improvements in the boiler and firebox, plus cast trailing trucks. Engine 616 had one more: It was Lima's first engine built with a booster on the trailing truck. All subsequent Mikados had boosters.

Merger of the Clover Leaf and the Lake Erie & Western in 1923 added locomotives to NKP's roster. Both roads brought Consolidations to the union. Lake Erie & Western had an assortment of NYC castoffs, most of them newer than NKP's own 2-8-0s, and Clover Leaf's 2-8-0s culminated in 10 built by Lima in 1921 and 1922: high-mounted 57" drivered engines numbered 206-212 and 214-216 (the number of rosters with gaps between 12 and 14 indicates that railroad men were more superstitious than you would suspect). Lake Erie & Western also had 15 USRA light Mikados, which NKP numbered just below the H-6a class. Most NKP and LE&W engines were too heavy for the Clover Leaf, so Clover Leaf locomotives stayed on their own rails for several years, augmented by some of the lightest NKP engines.

Berkshire 766, fresh from Lima in 1944, displays a wealth of detail: safety-tread running boards, four sand hatches, six sanders (and six more on the other side), front-end throttle — all part of a superb machine for moving freight. NKP photo.

By 1930 the Van Sweringens' empire had extended to include Erie and Chesapeake & Ohio. A central Advisory Mechanical Committee was charged with designing new locomotives. C&O needed a heavy freight engine, so the AMC designed a 2-10-4 based on Erie's 2-8-4s. The result was C&O's T-1 of 1930.

Nickel Plate, however, had a surplus of power. It pulled through the Depression primarily with its H-6 Mikados, and scrapped many of its oldest locomotives. In 1933 NKP needed new freight engines and turned to the AMC. Erie's Berkshires were no longer the newest technology around, so the committee started with the C&O 2-10-4, considered NKP's bridges and track, and drew up a 2-8-4 with 69" drivers, 25" × 34" cylinders, 90 square feet of grate area, 245 pounds boiler pressure, and 64,100 pounds tractive force.

Alco built 15 of them, Nos. 700-714, class S, in 1934, and suddenly Nickel Plate had big-league locomotives. The design proved better than anticipated, one of the occasional examples of the whole being greater than the sum of its parts. It was copied for Wheeling & Lake Erie, Pere Marquette, Chesapeake & Ohio, and Richmond, Fredericksburg & Potomac. As World War II gathered momentum NKP suddenly found itself short of power and leased locomotives from other roads until Lima could deliver 25 S-1s, Nos. 715-739, in 1942 and 1943, quickly followed by 30 S-2s, 740-769, in 1944. The S-2s were somewhat heavier and had roller bearings on the driver axles. By the time they were delivered NKP had strengthened its bridges east of Bellevue, Ohio, so the Berkshires could be used over the entire length of the railroad.

NKP tested a four-unit set of F3s in 1948 and opted for 10 more 2-8-4s. It was getting good use out of its steam locomotives, and Berkshires were $226,000 apiece, compared to $568,000 for four-unit F3s. Lima delivered Nos. 770-779 in 1949 — by then the company was Lima-Hamilton, and No. 779 was its last steam locomotive. NKP had been doing more bridge and track work, and the former Clover Leaf route to St. Louis finally hosted Berkshires.

About that same time NKP added a large number of steam locomotives to its roster by leasing the Wheeling & Lake Erie. W&LE's most significant engines were 32 Berkshires like NKP's; also on the roster were large numbers of 0-8-0s and 0-6-0s (some of the latter built in 1944), pre-USRA 2-6-6-2s, and ex-Norfolk & Western 4-8-2s that had come thirdhand from Denver & Rio Grande Western and Richmond, Fredericksburg & Potomac.

EMD returned later with a pair of F7s painted blue and silver — the same colors that had been on NKP passenger diesels since 1947. The F7s worked well on the former LE&W line to Peoria, but engineers reported difficulty with backup moves. NKP began to buy diesel switchers, then GP7s to dieselize the Indianapolis-Michigan City line. Gradually more branches were dieselized, then the line to St. Louis. The Berkshires continued in fast freight service on the Buffalo-Chicago main line, sometimes pulling 175- to 200-car trains.

Finally in 1958 diesels arrived for mainline service. The last mainline steam run was on July 2, 1958, from Bellevue to Conneaut, Ohio, behind No. 746. In spring 1959 a few 0-8-0s were put to work switching the ore docks at Conneaut, but an anticipated return of 2-8-4s to the main line didn't occur.

Passenger locomotives

The 4-4-0s in the O class were passenger engines with 68" drivers. Built in 1904, they were the first 4-4-0s Nickel Plate purchased since 1882. They were superheated between 1911 and 1913; the last one left the roster in 1924.

The Ten-Wheelers in classes P to P-3 were purchased for fast freight service but later served on passenger trains. They had 19" × 24" cylinders, 62" or 63" drivers, and narrow fireboxes between the rear drivers. Weight grew from 136,500 for the Ps to 150,000 for the P-3s. Many of the P class were sold to Akron, Canton & Youngstown in 1920. Some members of other classes were superheated and fitted with piston valves.

The six R-class Ten-Wheelers built by Baldwin in 1907 were slightly larger all around. They had 72" or 73" drivers and were equipped with superheaters, piston valves, and Walschaerts valve gear in 1921 and 1922. Numbers 184, 186, and 187 remained in service until 1948.

Nickel Plate acquired ten Pacifics in 1922, four from Lima and six from Brooks. As built they had 22½" × 26" cylinders and 73" drivers and weighed 245,000 (Lima) and 252,000 pounds (Brooks). They had a USRA look about them but were much lighter and less powerful.

NKP got a new president in 1927, Walter L. Ross, who had been president of the Clover Leaf since 1912 and its general passenger agent before that. He decided NKP would go after the long-haul passenger business in competition with New York Central. That meant new locomotives, and early in March 1927, less than three weeks after New York Central's first Hudson emerged from Schenectady, Nickel Plate took delivery of four 4-6-4s, Nos. 170-173, from Alco's Brooks Works. For the moment NKP had four times as many Hudsons as NYC. They would prove to be among the lightest Hudsons, 314,000 to 318,000 pounds.

Nickel Plate's Hudsons looked bigger than they were after the smoke lifters were added. In actuality they were little more than a USRA light Pacific with a four-wheel trailing truck. Photo by Robert Hally.

They had 73" drivers, like the Pacifics, and 25" × 26" cylinders. The four-wheel trailing truck was necessary for spreading weight, not for carrying an enormous firebox — grate area was 66.7 feet, the same as the USRA light Pacific, and the tractive effort was the same. They shared several features with the H-6 Mikados — which were USRA light 2-8-2s. Lima built four more 4-6-4s in 1929, class L-1b, Nos. 174-177.

In later years both the Pacifics and the Hudsons had their driver diameter increased to 74" by application of thicker tires, and the boiler pressure of the Hudsons was increased from 215 to 225 pounds.

Only two Lake Erie & Western passenger engines, a pair of Baldwin 4-4-0s built in 1902, joined the Nickel Plate roster in 1923. The Clover Leaf contributed several groups of Ten-Wheelers, only two of which could be considered passenger engines because of their 69" drivers, and two Atlantics, typical turn-of-the-century Brooks engines with 73" drivers.

2-8-4 — BERKSHIRE

In 1920, when American railroads emerged from 26 months of government control, the prevailing philosophy of freight-train operation was to hang as many cars as possible behind a locomotive and send it out to drag its way along the line. Three locomotive types were ideal for drag freight: 2-10-2, 2-6-6-2, and 2-8-8-2. The 2-10-2 and the 2-6-6-2 were roughly equivalent in pulling power; the 2-8-8-2 was more powerful. The 2-10-2 had reached the limits of piston thrust and frame strength; the Mallets had the complexity of a second set of moving parts. All three had large cylinders that could use steam faster than the firebox and boiler could make it.

Competition brought the need to accelerate freight trains, but with the locomotives available, speed required sacrificing train length. In 1922 Lima built an experimental 2-8-2 for New York Central, H-10 No. 8000. Lima's William E. Woodard based the design on NYC's H-7 Mikado but added a substantially larger firebox grate, a feedwater heater, larger cylinders, lightweight rods, and a booster — what we would now call "state of the art." The H-10 could both outpull and outrun the H-7, confirming Woodard's views on the importance of increased steaming ability.

Woodard then designed a locomotive to answer the hypothetical question, "What if we make the grate even larger?" One answer was, "You'll need a four-wheel trailing truck to support the firebox," and another was that the resulting locomotive would be able to generate enough steam for sustained speed. The tangible result was Lima

demonstrator No. 1, class A-1, the first 2-8-4. Its 100-square-foot grate was half again as large as the grate of the NYC H-10. It had 28" × 30" cylinders and 63" drivers and carried a boiler pressure of 240 pounds. The frame of the A-1 ended behind the rear drivers, and the trailing truck transmitted the pulling forces and supported the rear of the firebox directly. It also had a booster on the rear axle and carried the ashpan.

In early 1925 the A-1 demonstrated on New York Central's subsidary Boston & Albany across the Berkshire Hills of western Massachusetts. The B&A quickly signed up for 45 copies and the wheel arrangement had a name. Both the wheel arrangement and Lima's Super-Power concept (in simplest terms, a much greater capacity for making steam) were an immediate success. Railroads bought Berkshires by tens and dozens at a minimum (Toronto, Hamilton & Buffalo's two are a special case — a 50-mile run, a fourth of which was on New York Central System tracks).

The 2-8-4s built over the ensuing 24 years fall into four groups: copies of the A-1, with 28" × 30" cylinders and 63" drivers; the Erie's enlarged version of the A-1, with 28½" × 32" cylinders and 70" drivers; the Nickel Plate Berkshires (25" × 34" cylinders and 69" drivers) and the others of that design; and the rest, which don't fit into the first three groups.

The copies of the A-1 were built between 1926 and 1929 for Boston & Albany, Illinois Central, Chicago & North Western, Boston & Maine, Missouri Pacific, and Toronto, Hamilton & Buffalo. B&A 1400-1444 and the IC and B&M engines, all built by Lima, had the

Lima Locomotive Works 1 — the A-1 — was the first Berkshire and the first locomotive with a firebox large enough to require a four-wheel trailing truck. The piping for the booster engine on the trailing truck, the piping for the Elesco feedwater heater, and the outside dry pipe leading from the steam dome to the front-end throttle all contributed to the appearance of power. Lima photo.

Two Boston & Albany Berkshires, both copies of Lima's A-1, begin the eastward climb into their namesake mountains as they pass the tower at Chatham, New York. Photo by Harold Hegeman.

short frame and articulated trailing truck of the original. The others had full-length frames and conventional trailing trucks.

Between 1927 and 1929 John J. Bernet brought Erie out of the drag freight era with the purchase of 105 Berkshires, and the 2-8-4 became a much faster freight engine. The two major differences between the Lima A-1 and the Erie Berkshires were a larger boiler and 70" drivers; the cylinders were a half inch larger, and the locomotives had full-length frames.

In 1933 Bernet became president of the Nickel Plate to pull it out of the Depression the same way he had upgraded the Erie. The Nickel Plate was under the control of the Van Sweringen brothers, as were the Erie, Chesapeake & Ohio, Pere Marquette, and Wheeling & Lake Erie. The unified Advisory Mechanical Committee of the Van Sweringen railroads developed a 2-8-4 that combined design elements from the Erie's Berkshires and C&O's T-1 2-10-4. The Nickel Plate bought 80 2-8-4s between 1934 and 1949, and the same design was used for the Berkshires of the Pere Marquette, Wheeling & Lake Erie, Chesapeake & Ohio, Virginian, and Richmond, Fredericksburg & Potomac. The PM engines had cylinders an inch larger in diameter, the W&LE engines were lighter, the C&O engines were heavier (C&O engines were often heavier than the same type on other roads), and RF&P's had different domes and cabs. The Virginian copied the C&O design for its five Berkshires of 1946.

The rest of the 2-8-4s include 15 Santa Fe engines that shared driver size with the original Lima design but little else; 6 Detroit, Toledo & Ironton locomotives that looked like Nickel Plate engines with 63" drivers; 42 Louisville & Nashville engines that shared some characteristics with the Van Sweringen 2-8-4s; five lightweight Norfolk Southern machines that eventually went to Mexico; and seven 63"-drivered, boosterless Pittsburgh & Lake Erie engines that were Alco's last steam locomotives (1948).

Other names: Lima (Boston & Maine, Illinois Central), Kanawha (Chesapeake & Ohio)

Total built: 611

First: Lima Locomotive Works 1, 1924

Last: Nickel Plate 779, Lima, 1949

Longest lived: Boston & Maine 4003/Santa Fe 4197, 1928-1954

Last in service: National Railways of Mexico 3351 and 3354 (ex-Norfolk Southern 601 and 604), 1963

Greatest number purchased: Erie, 105

Greatest number on roster: Chesapeake & Ohio, 130 (40 acquired with merger of Pere Marquette in 1947)

Heaviest: Chesapeake & Ohio 2760-2784, 469,680 pounds

Lightest: Norfolk Southern 600-604, 335,400 pounds

Recommended reading: *North American Steam Locomotives: The Berkshire and Texas Types*, by Jack W. Farrell, published in 1988 by Pacific Fast Mail, P. O. Box 57, Edmonds, WA 98020 (ISBN 915713-15-12)

Switchers

Nickel Plate's 0-6-0s fall into three groups: the M class, delivered by Brooks, Manchester, and Schenectady between 1900 and 1909; the New York Central-influenced B-10s and B-11s; and 30 engines the road rebuilt from Consolidations 119-148 in the early 1920s.

Nickel Plate received five 0-8-0s from Lima in 1918, numbered 200-204. They were copies of New York Central's contemporary 0-8-0 and had 57" drivers. Influenced by the Lake Erie & Western USRA 0-8-0s, NKP returned to Lima in 1924 and 1925 for 20 copies of the USRA 0-8-0. Lima delivered five more eight-wheel switchers in 1934. They had the same cylinder and driver sizes as the USRA engines but were 18,000 pounds heavier, worked at 200 pounds instead of 175, and had a Type E superheater and front-end throttle. They were classed C-17, using the Advisory Mechanical Committee letter for the type instead of New York Central's U.

Lake Erie & Western had a similar assortment of old 0-6-0s, three ex-NYC B-11s, and three USRA 0-8-0s. Clover Leaf had ten 0-6-0s, a few of which served Nickel Plate until dieselization.

Historical and technical society: Nickel Plate Road Historical & Technical Society, P. O. Box 54027, Cincinnati, OH 45254-0027

Recommended reading:

The Nickel Plate Story, by John A. Rehor, published in 1965 by Kalmbach Publishing Co., 21027 Crossroads Circle, P. O. Box 1612, Waukesha, WI 53187

The Nickel Plate Years, by Eric Hirsimaki, published in 1989 by Mileposts Publishing Co., 3963 Dryden Drive, North Olmsted, OH 44070 (ISBN 0-929886-03-8)

"The engines that saved a railroad," by John A. Rehor, in *Trains Magazine*, October 1962, pages 18-32

Published rosters:

Nickel Plate: *Railroad Magazine*: August 1934, page 88, October 1947, page 119; August 1953, page 100

Wheeling & Lake Erie: *Railroad Magazine*, September 1939, page 116; May 1950, page 122; March 1974, page 30

NKP STEAM LOCOMOTIVES BUILT SINCE 1900

Nickel Plate

Type	Class	Numbers	Qty	Builder	Built	Retired
0-6-0	B-9	100-129	30	NKP	1920-1925	1930-1948
0-6-0	B-10	94-99	6	Brooks	1913	1948, 1949
0-6-0	B-11a	50-59	10	Brooks	1910	1948-1951
0-6-0	B-11b	60-69	10	Lima	1917	1948-1953
0-6-0	B-11c	70-79	10	Lima	1918	1948-1953
0-6-0	M	45-49, 200, 208-213, 217-249				
			40	Alco	1900-1909	1920-1933
0-8-0	C-17	300-304	5	Lima	1934	1962, 1963
0-8-0	U-2	200-204	5	Lima	1918	1953, 1955
0-8-0	U-3b	210-219	10	Lima	1924	1951-1962
0-8-0	U-3c	220-229	10	Lima	1925	1952-1962
2-6-0	F-7	826, 827	2	Baldwin	1907	
2-8-0	G-10s	718	1	NKP	1923	1934
2-8-0	N	119-128	10	Brooks	1902	to 0-6-0
2-8-0	N-1	129-148	20	Brooks	1903, 1904	to 0-6-0
2-8-0	N-2	149-158	10	Brooks	1906	1929-1945
2-8-0	N-3	159-161	3	Baldwin	1907	1933-1945
2-8-0	N-4	162-166	4	Brooks	1908	1933-1945
2-8-0	N-5	448-453	6	Brooks	1911	1933-1948
2-8-0	N-6	454-459	6	Brooks	1913	1934-1949
2-8-0	T	460-474	15	Brooks	1903	1931-1934
2-8-2	H-5a	500-509	10	Lima	1917	1955-1963
2-8-2	H-5b	510-534	25	Brooks	1917	1953-1963
2-8-2	H-6a	601-610	10	Schen	1918	1944-1956
2-8-2	H-6b–f	611-671	61	Lima	1920-1924	1945-1962
2-8-4	S	700-714	15	Schen	1934	1957-1963
2-8-4	S-1	715-739	25	Lima	1942, 1943	1957-1964
2-8-4	S-2	740-769	30	Lima	1944	1960-1964
2-8-4	S-3	770-779	10	Lima	1949	1961-1963
4-4-0	O	176-181	6	Brooks	1904	1920-1924
4-6-0	P	40-54	15	Brooks	1905, 1906	1920-1922
4-6-0	P-1	30-39, 55-64	20	Brooks	1908, 1909	1923-1936
4-6-0	P-2	335-358	24	Brooks	1910, 1911	1923-1933
4-6-0	P-3	359-366	8	Brooks	1913	1933, 1936
4-6-0	R	182-187	6	BLW	1907	1933, 1948
4-6-2	K-1a	160-163	4	Lima	1922	1952, 1953
4-6-2	K-1b	164-169	6	Brooks	1923	1952-1954
4-6-4	L-1a	170-173	4	Brooks	1927	1956-1962
4-6-4	L-1b	174-177	4	Lima	1929	1953-1956

NKP STEAM LOCOMOTIVES BUILT SINCE 1900 (continued)

Lake Erie & Western (to NKP 1923)

Type	Class	NKP Nos.	Numbers	Qty	Builder	Built	Retired
0-6-0	B-11d	80-82	4275-4277	3	Schen	1913	1949-1951
0-6-0	B-55	42-46	4377…4393	5	Brooks	1902	1933-1934
0-6-0	B-54	32-41	4365-4374	10	Pittsburgh	1902	1929-1934
0-8-0	U-3a	205-207	4250-4252	3	Lima 1920		1953-1955
2-8-0	G-41	400-409	5501…5514	10	Brooks	1904	1921-1953
2-8-0	G-6v	475-484	5605-5614	10	Brooks	1911	1933-1955
2-8-0	G-16v	485-494	5385-5394	10	Brooks	1911	1934-1951
2-8-0	G-16w	495-499	5395-5399	5	Schen	1912	1934-1950
2-8-0	G-44	375-398	5515-5538	25	Brooks	1904	1924-1954
2-8-2	H-6a	586-600	5540-5554	5	Baldwin	1918	1944-1958
4-4-0	C-49	300, 301	4246, 4248	2	Baldwin	1902	1922, 1929

Toledo, St. Louis & Western (Clover Leaf) (to NKP 1923)

Type	NKP Class	NKP Nos.	Numbers	Qty	Builder	Built	Retired
0-6-0	B-6	705, 706	5, 6	2	Dickson	1902	1933, 1934
0-6-0	B-7	707-712	7-12	6	Brooks	1907	1933-1946
0-6-0	B-8	714, 715	14, 15	2	Baldwin	1904	1928
0-6-0	B-12	716, 717	16, 17	2	Baldwin	1921	1947
2-6-0	F-6	820-825	120-125	6	Baldwin	1901	1929
2-8-0	G-1	830, 831	130, 131	2	Baldwin	1902	1929
2-8-0	G-2	832, 833	132, 133	2	Schen	1904	1930-1931
2-8-0	G-3	834, 835	134, 135	2	Pittsburgh	1900	1931

Type	NKP Class	NKP Nos.	Numbers	Qty	Builder	Built	Retired
2-8-0	G-4	836	136	1	Rogers	1908	1933
2-8-0	G-7	890-894	190-194	5	Baldwin	1913	1952, 1953
2-8-0	G-8	901-905	201-205	5	Lima	1916	1955, 1956
2-8-0	G-9	906-916	206-216	10	Lima	1921, 1922	1953-1963
2-8-0	G-10	860-889	160-189	20	Brooks	1905	1933-1955
4-4-2	E-3	744, 745	44, 45	2	Brooks	1904	1933
4-6-0	P-4	740-743	40-43	4	Baldwin	1901	1927-1929
4-6-0	P-5	809-811	109-111	3	Richmond	1900	1927, 1929
4-6-0	P-6	850-859	150-159	10	Brooks	1904	1930-1933

Wheeling & Lake Erie (to NKP 1949)

Type	W&LE Class	NKP Nos.	Numbers	Qty	Builder	Built	Retired
0-6-0	B-5	351-386	3951-3986	36	W&LE	1929-1944	1952-1957
0-8-0	C-1	271-275	5101-5105	5	Pittsburgh	1918	1952-1962
0-8-0	C-1a	276-295	5106-5125	20	W&LE	1928-1930	1952-1964
2-8-0	G-1	920	4156	1	Brooks	1905	
2-8-0	G-2	921-927	4301…4320	7	Brooks	1905	
2-8-0	G-3	928	6053	1	Schen	1913	
2-8-0	H-10	6053…6067	2401-2420	20	Schen	1913	1941-1952
2-8-2	M-1	671-690	6001-6020	20	Brooks	1918	1954-1958
2-8-4	K-1 (S-4)	801-832	6401-6432	32	Schen	1913-1942	1959-1964
2-6-6-2	I-3	940-943	8001-8010	10	Baldwin	1919	1941-1955
4-8-2	K-3 (J-1)	844-849	6801-6810	10	N&W	1926	1952-1964

NEW YORK, NEW HAVEN & HARTFORD RAILROAD

The New Haven system reached all but full growth shortly before 1900, and in 1904 it acquired the Central New England. Full growth meant almost all the railroading — indeed, almost all the transportation in southern New England south of the Boston & Albany main line, and several lines reached north of the B&A almost to the Massachusetts-New Hampshire state line. The main line, the "Shore Line," reached from Woodlawn, New York, on New York Central's Harlem Division about 14 miles out of Grand Central, to Boston. A secondary main line reached north from New Haven through Hartford to Springfield, Mass. Other secondary lines ran from Norwalk, Conn., to Pittsfield, Mass.; from Devon, Conn., through Waterbury to Hartford, then northeast to Boston; from Groton, Conn., north to Worcester, Mass.; from Providence, R. I., to Worcester, Mass.; and from Mansfield, Mass., to Fitchburg and Lowell. Branches covered the area.

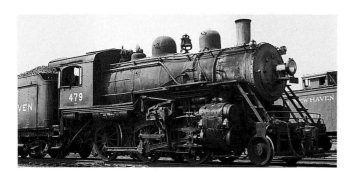

New Haven chose the Mogul as its standard freight locomotive at the turn of the century and had 226 of the type built after 1900. Number 479 was the highest-numbered but not the last built. Southern valve gear and piston valves were added after No. 479 had been in service several years. Photo by Kent W. Cochrane.

The Shore Line was almost gradeless except for five miles of 0.7 percent against southbound trains through Sharon, Mass. Numerous curves with speed restrictions along the shore in Connecticut hampered fast running and required engines that could accelerate quickly. Secondary lines that branched off the Shore Line generally followed rivers. Helper grades were found on the routes that ran crosswise to the watercourses, notably the line from New Haven to Maybrook and the CNE — away from Long Island Sound, Connecticut is hilly country.

The Central New England ran from Hartford, Connecticut, to the northwest corner of the state, then southwest to Poughkeepsie, New York, where it crossed the Hudson on a high bridge, and on to Maybrook and Campbell Hall, where it connected with Erie, Lehigh & Hudson River, Lehigh & New England, and New York, Ontario & Western. NH's chief reason for acquiring CNE was the Poughkeepsie bridge and the western connections. Though under NH control, CNE remained a separate operation until 1927.

New Haven electrified the main line from Woodlawn to Stamford in 1907 and on to New Haven in 1914. Its experience with electric power made it an early experimenter with diesels; by 1940 it had 31 diesel switchers on its roster. By then NH was experiencing the beginnings of a wartime traffic surge. Its newest steam locomotives were 12 years old, and its choices were to extend electrification (expensive, and the road was in bankruptcy), order new steam locomotives (they would take time), or adapt stock diesel locomotives for freight service. The only diesels available were 2000 h.p. passenger engines from Alco and Electro-Motive. Alco had long been NH's prime locomotive builder, and in December 1941 NH took delivery of the first of ten DL-109s geared for freight and equipped with heavy-duty draft gear and couplers. They also had steam generators, because the freights ran at night and the road planned to use them on passenger trains during the day. By 1945 NH had amassed a fleet of 60 such units and effectively dieselized mainline freight and passenger service east of New Haven.

Dieselization gathered speed after the war. The official last run of steam was an excursion behind Pacifics 1372 and 1388 in April 1952, but J-1 Mikado No. 3016 operated on a fan trip on July 19, 1953. Mikados 3006, 3016, and 3020 were used as snow melters until 1956. The three Mikes remained on the property awaiting scrapping. In spring 1958 No. 3016 made another appearance in steam on New Haven rails. It became Eastern & Portland 97 for the filming of *It Happened to Jane*, in which lobster-seller Doris Day kidnaps No. 97, ties up the freight and passenger service of the E&P, gets her lobsters to market alive and well (behind steam, giving them a preview of their eventual fate), and makes a monkey out of the president of the E&P, played by Ernie Kovacs.

NH adopted a new numbering scheme in 1904, right after devising a new classification system in which the newest and largest locomotives got the lowest numbers (B-1, for example) and the oldest of the type got the highest (B-5, for instance). The road soon had to grapple with the problem of another group of B-class engines (B-0? and beyond that, what?). It decided to follow the more usual practice of assigning higher class numbers to successive groups of locomotives.

Freight locomotives

New Haven's post-1900 freight locomotives were atypical. After 226 Moguls built between 1900 and 1910 came 18 Consolidations acquired with the Central New England, then 33 Mikados. For a railroad with NH's traffic density and a wheel arrangement that was the standard freight locomotive for decades, 33 engines hardly justified the time it took the motive power superintendent to find the classification book and decide what the next available class letter was. Fifty 2-10-2s seemed a lot for a New England railroad, but the region is hilly, even mountainous. Seventy 4-8-2s complete the list, and they were appropriate for a fast, water-level railroad. (Actually, the 4-8-2s didn't complete the list. NH's roster of freight engines included 48 other 2-8-2s, most with 63" drivers, and ten 4-6-6-4s with 57" drivers, but they were restricted to electrified territory west of New Haven, and their wheel arrangements were usually given as 1-B+B-1 and 2-C+C-2.)

New Haven inherited a large number of 2-6-0s from predecessors such as the Old Colony and the New York & New England. In 1896 and 1898 Schenectady delivered two groups of ten heavy 2-6-0s (145,000 pounds) with 63" drivers and 20" × 28" cylinders for freight service. They were classed K-1-a and (after 1905) numbered 480-499. Between 1900 and 1907 Baldwin, Cooke, Rhode Island, and Schenectady delivered 195 more with the same size cylinders and drivers but another 6,000 to 9,000 pounds weight. They were classed K-1-b, and like the K-1-a classs had fireboxes atop the frames between the drivers, but the frames were notched aft of the main drivers to allow the grate to slope downward toward the front. The 25 members of the K-1-c class, delivered in 1902 by Rhode Island, had wider fireboxes above the rear drivers. Number 325 in the group delivered by Schenectady in 1900 was a tandem compound classed K-1-d; it was rebuilt to a simple K-1-b in 1905.

The 2-6-0s initially were mainline freight locomotives, and while they could not pull as much as the 51"-drivered 2-8-0s, they were faster, important on a line with heavy passenger traffic. In 1913 NH began to superheat the K-1-bs, fit them with outside valve gear and larger cylin-

The J-1 Mikados had an extremely low profile, with cabs set much lower than customary. Alco photo.

ders, and (later) reclass them K-1-d. Some received new boilers and power reverses. With the arrival of larger locomotivs the 2-6-0s were demoted to local freight, work train, and commuter service.

The Central New England K-6 Moguls differed from the K-1-b class only in having Walschaerts valve gear, and although they were the newest 2-6-0s on the system, they were never superheated. The wide-firebox K-1-c Moguls turned out to be coal gluttons, and six were converted to oil burners in 1931 for work in the electrified zone.

New Haven ordered 25 2-8-0s from Rhode Island in 1895. They were impressive looking, but much of their apparent bulk was an illusion caused by their 51" drivers. They weighed 156,000 pounds, only a ton more than the K-1-b Moguls of a decade later, and were too slow for mainline service. They were relegated to switching and pusher work and were retired in the mid-1920s.

By the time NH absorbed the Central New England in 1927 only three older 50"-drivered 2-8-0s were left on its roster, but there were 15 medium-weight, superheated 2-8-0s built by Schenectady in 1912 for Maybrook-New Haven freight service. New Haven thought well enough of them to fit them with firebox syphons and power reverses and keep them in service through World War II.

New Haven took delivery of two groups of 2-8-2s in 1916. The first, the J-1 class, Nos. 3000-3024, had 63" drivers and 25" × 30" cylinders and weighed 251,750 pounds, a little smaller than a USRA light Mikado. They were notable for an overall height of 13'9", more than a foot

The last steam freight engines NH purchased were the R-3-a class, three-cylinder 4-8-2s. Number 3558, built by Alco in 1928, was still in service in 1950, awaiting helper duties at Hopewell Junction, New York. Photo by John V. Weber.

lower than contemporary New Haven Pacifics, which enabled them to fit under bridges on the Dorchester Branch, the freight route from Readville, Mass., to Boston. Their cabs were noticeably lower but the tenders were of conventional configuration. (A freshly coaled J-1 was likely to have a coal pile towering over the cab, at least as far as the first bridge on the Dorchester Branch.) The last two of the group were built with McClellon boilers and water-tube fireboxes; both received new McClellon boilers in 1928 and conventional boilers in 1942.

Eight heavy 2-8-2s also came from Schenectady in 1916, NH 3100-3104 and CNE 3105-3107, class J-2. They had the same 63" drivers but 26" × 32" cylinders and weighed 309,600 pounds; tractive effort was 58,372 pounds. They were slightly less locomotive than a USRA heavy Mike, but they lacked the mechanical stoker of the USRA engine. It was impossible for a fireman to fling enough coal into the firebox for mainline speeds, and they were relegated to yard and pusher service.

As World War I began, New Haven's only mainline freight power was the group of 25 J-1 Mikados. E. J. Pearson, who had come to the presidency of the road after stints on Milwaukee Road, Northern Pacific, and Missouri Pacific, got NH what it needed in the form of 50 2-10-2s, which Alco's Schenectady Works delivered in 1918. They had 63" drivers and 30" × 32" cylinders and were about halfway between the USRA light and heavy Santa Fes in weight and tractive force. They had shallow fireboxes over the rear two pairs of drivers and roller-skate-wheel inboard-journal trailing trucks. Counterbalancing problems restricted their speed to 25 mph, incompatible with the fast, frequent passenger trains on the New Haven-Boston main line. The USRA 4-8-2s that arrived the next year solved that problem, and most of the 2-10-2s were moved to the New Haven-Maybrook line. However, NH had more 2-10-2s than it needed, so any that needed repairs were simply set aside. During the late 1920s nearly all received Elesco feedwater heaters and thermic syphons, and in the late 1930s a few were fitted with Boxpok drivers. By the beginning of World War II five of the class were being cannibalized. When war traffic surged New Haven needed all 50, and the five hulks were restored to service.

The USRA assigned its first 10 light 4-8-2s to the road for New Haven-Boston freight service. NH classed them R-1 and numbered them 3300-3309, and liked them well enough to order 39 copies, 3310-3348, for delivery in 1920 and 1924. They were assigned to fast freight service on all the main lines except the Maybrook route. They were equipped with steam and signal lines for passenger service, but their long rigid wheelbase was incompatible with the slip switches in Boston's South Station, so what little passenger work they did was on the lines to Springfield and Worcester. Many R-1s received minor improvements in the form of feedwater heaters, syphons or circulators, and large tenders, but by 1940 were beginning to show their age. Readville Shops replaced their Southern valve gear with Baker and equipped them with mechanical lubricators, and they worked hard through the war. Nine original USRA engines were retired in 1946, and the last R-1s in 1951.

In 1924 Schenectady delivered a single 4-8-2, class R-2, No. 3500 (it was to have been No. 3349, simply another R-1-b). It weighed 360,000 pounds, 16,000 more than the R-1-b engines, and its 230-pound boiler pressure gave it a tractive effort of 63,390 pounds. It had an experimental McClellon boiler with a water-tube firebox. At the top instead of a conventional crown sheet were three connected longitudinal drums. Vertical tubes 4" in diameter connected the outside drums to similar longitudinal drums along the outside of the bottom of the firebox, forming the side walls of the firebox. The spaces between the vertical tubes were filled with insulation. The McClellon boiler had no staybolts — they were a constant problem — and the tubes promoted better water circulation. The entire structure was riveted together and lacked structural strength; the twisting forces that resulted as the engine entered and left a superelevated curve tended to work the drums and tubes loose and let the insulation fall out from between the tubes.

In 1926 ten more McClellon-boilered 4-8-2s came from Schenectady. Seven were two-cylinder engines classed R-2-a, Nos. 3501-3507. They were 3,000 pounds heavier than No. 3500 and carried pressure of 265 pounds. They were equipped with duPont-Simplex stokers, which proved troublesome; they were refitted with HT-2 stokers in the 1930s. They later had their Southern valve gear replaced with Baker or Walschaerts gear. The other three engines had three cylinders and were classed R-3. NH had received ten three-cylinder 0-8-0s in 1924 and was pleased enough with their performance to order six more 0-8-0s and test the three-cylinder concept in a road engine. The new 4-8-2s had three 22" × 30" cylinders instead of the 27" × 30" cylinders of the previous Mountain types, and they worked at 265 pounds.

The McClellon boilers were not successful: The water tubes tended to leak, and gaps in the firebox insulation let in cold air. Even so, W. L. Bean, NH's mechanical manager, specified McClellon boilers on ten more three-cylinder 4-8-2s delivered by Schenectady in 1928; they also had one-piece cast steel smokeboxes designed by Bean. The next year all 21 McClellon-boilered engines went back to Schenectady for conventional boilers, and Bean left the New Haven.

The middle cylinders proved to be maintenance problems. The road considered converting the 4-8-2s to two cylinders, but money wasn't available during the Depression. They continued to work through World War II as three-cylinder machines.

Passenger locomotives

In 1896 New Haven received 20 4-4-0s of a more-or-less-standard Schenectady design for its top-rank passenger trains. Schenectady delivered five more, with 78" drivers instead of 73" (the A-3 class), in 1900, and Rhode Island added more to each class in 1902 and 1903, giving the road 50 modern, fast 4-4-0s. During the 1920s many of the A-1s and A-3s were rebuilt with new frames, superheaters, piston valves, Southern valve gear, and steel cabs. A-1 No. 1275 outlasted the rest by several years working in wire-train service.

Between 1897 and 1904 NH rebuilt more than 50 older 4-4-0s for secondary trains with new boilers, cylinders, frames, and 69" drivers. Included were 15 class A-2 4-4-0s built in 1893 with anthracite-burning fireboxes and 78" drivers. In 1903 Rhode Island built 25 4-4-0s of the same size, the last of the type the New Haven purchased.

Rhode Island delivered 20 Ten-Wheelers in 1903 and 1904 for branch-line freight service, the G-3 class, Nos. 950-969. They found work wherever there was light rail and frail bridges. Between 1904 and 1907 52 passenger Ten-Wheelers arrived from Baldwin. They had evenly spaced 73" drivers, and narrow fireboxes between the drivers and above the frames. Two were Baldwin balanced compounds, but their combination of low tractive effort and high maintenance costs prompted the road to convert them to two-cylinder simple engines in 1912 and 1924. Atlantics and Pacifics with larger fireboxes took over mainline passenger duties in 1907, and the 4-6-0s moved into commuter service. Between 1912 and 1924 they were superheated and fitted with outside valve gear, and later all were fitted with new frames.

New Haven bought just one group of 12 Atlantics. Schenectady built them in 1907 after the first group of Pacifics. With their 79" drivers (the Pacifics had 73") they were intended for fast, extra-fare trains between New York and Boston. Soon after they were delivered steel cars replaced wood, and the Atlantics were assigned to light passenger

The Pacifics most characteristic of the New Haven were the I-4s. They were built in 1916 and were top passenger power for 20 years. Elesco feedwater heater, air reservoirs atop the boiler, and 12-wheel tenders were later modifications. Photo by E. R. Meakes.

trains elsewhere. Superheated and equipped with piston valves between 1912 and 1922, they were reclassed H-1 in 1928 to avoid conflict with CNE's 2-8-0s. After 1935 one or two of them found a niche as protection (along with a pair of lightweight coaches) for the *Comet*, a three-unit diesel streamliner that shuttled between Boston and Providence.

The first Pacifics, Nos. 1000-1008, arrived from Schenectady in 1907. They were built with slide valves and Walschaerts valve gear, and their 73" drivers were intended for heavy mainline trains. Baldwin delivered 21 more I-1s, Nos. 1009-1029, later in 1907, and Schenectady added 1030 and 1031 to the class in 1910. By later standards they were relatively light Pacifics, 229,500 to 232,000 pounds. They were superheated between 1912 and 1923 and given cylinders an inch larger, 23" × 28", but were never equipped with feedwater heaters or mechanical stokers.

Brooks built the I-2 class in 1913: Nos. 1300-1349, 73" drivers, 24" × 28" cylinders, superheated, 251,500 pounds. They replaced the I-1s on mainline passenger trains and were also assigned to fast freight service. Six other Pacifics were delivered in 1913, the I-3 class, Nos. 1090-1095, built by Baldwin. They were slightly lighter than the I-2s had the

same cylinders but 79" drivers. They were intended to replace the Atlantics on the Shore Line's prestige trains. The I-2s and I-3s were both replaced in fast mainline passenger service by the I-4s in 1916 and were demoted to secondary passenger trains.

The I-4s were delivered by Schenectady in 1916. Numbers 1350-1399 had 79" drivers and 26" × 28" cylinders but were relatively light, 266,000 pounds, because of the Thames River bridge at New London, Conn. They had large boilers with combustion chambers and were good steamers. A new bridge at New London in 1918 allowed the road to beef up the frames and drivers, and between 1922 and 1930 the entire class was fitted with Elesco feedwater heaters. Air reservoirs atop the boiler replaced the original equipment between the frames, and some I-4s had their stubby tenders replaced by 12-wheel affairs.

The I-4s were New Haven's top mainline passenger locomotives for more than 20 years, but by the mid-1930s they were wearing out, and heavier, longer passenger trains were taxing their abilities. During 1936 the road tested four I-4s to determine specifications for new power, and two of those engines failed during the tests. A 4-6-4 was required, and Baldwin submitted the low bid. The first I-5, No. 1400, was delivered in early 1937. It had 80" drivers, 22" × 30" cylinders, carried 285 pounds boiler pressure, weighed 365,300 pounds, and was streamlined and painted conservative black and silver. After some initial counterbalancing problems were corrected, the I-5s settled down to fast passenger service between Boston and New Haven, 157 miles. Assignments were arranged so eight engines covered 12 trips each way every day, and the remaining two as spares, though not idle. Unlike many streamlined steam engines, the I-5s retained all their shrouding till the end.

Switchers

New Haven began the 20th century by receiving ten T-1-class 0-6-0s from Schenectady. They were cross-compounds, as were ten more built by Rhode Island in 1902 (they were converted to simple engines and reclassed T-1-a between 1907 and 1917). NH returned to simple engines for the next switchers, 116 T-2 class 0-6-0s, built between 1904 and 1913 by Rhode Island, Cooke, and Richmond. The first 19 had their main rods connected to the second drivers and were reclassed T-2-a after the delivery of the next group, on which the third drivers were the main drivers. All were saturated engines with slide valves and Stephenson valve gear.

As trains increased in length and weight, the road turned to 0-8-0s for switching. Between 1920 and 1923 Schenectady delivered 35 copies of the USRA 0-8-0, 15 for New Haven and 20 lettered for Central New England but used all over the New Haven system. In 1927 three Central New England 0-8-0s joined the New Haven roster. They were somewhat lighter than the USRA copies, and although saturated were built with piston valves and Walschaerts valve gear. With their arch-windowed cabs they looked like New Haven power (and were in a way, since NH had owned CNE since 1904). They had been built for service at Maybrook, but after they became NH engines were moved to Boston.

NH's first three-cylinder engines were ten 0-8-0s delivered by Schenectady in 1924. They had 57" drivers and 22" × 28" cylinders, all of which drove on the third axle. Weight was 247,000 pounds, about 15 tons more than the USRA copies. Six more joined the roster in 1927. They worked well, and in low-speed switching and hump service suffered none of the problems of three-cylinder road engines. Builder photos of both groups show huge 12-wheel tenders; soon after delivery the large tenders were swapped with 4-8-2s. NH wasn't the only road to do this, and the most likely explanation for ordering mismatched locomotives and tenders is convenience in delivery — it's much easier to move something with a coupler at each end (engines and tenders are connected by drawbars, not couplers).

Oddities

In 1897 the New England (successor to the NY&NE) sent a wood passenger car to Schenectady, where a vertical-boiler 0-4-0 with 42" drivers was fitted into one end, creating a self-propelled car. It remained in service until 1904. It required the same crew as a locomotive, but it was able to work only as a single-car passenger train. It was sold in 1907 after several years of storage. In 1934 the Besler Systems proposed building a two-car steam-powered lightweight train. NH, in bank-

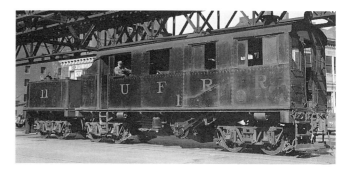

Climax geared locomotives, like Shays and Heislers, were usually found in forests, miles from the nearest city. There were exceptions: New York Central's and Kansas City Southern's Shays, and Union Freight Railroad's Climaxes, which were wrapped in box cabs. Photo by Robert C. Baker.

ruptcy at the time, couldn't afford a new train, so the project began with two existing coaches, which were streamlined and fitted with engineer's compartments at one end of each. The power plant, which was tucked into one end of one of the cars, consisted of a vertical flash boiler and a power truck with four cylinders, two high-pressure cylinders driving one axle and two low-pressure cylinders driving the other.

The Besler train entered service in 1936 on the Bridgeport-Waterbury-Hartford run and proved troublesome. The weight of the two cars and the schedule, which called for much stopping and starting, meant that the power unit had to operate at full capacity most of the time. The train was withdrawn in 1943, and the cars became ordinary passenger equipment again.

A New Haven subsidiary, the Union Freight Railroad, operated along city streets in Boston between South and North Stations, affording a connection for freight between NH and Boston & Maine as well as serving industries along the way. Four box-cab Climax geared locomotives built between 1923 and 1928 worked the line until 1946, when GE 44-

ton diesels took over. Before the Climaxes, the line used geared four-wheel locomotives.

Historical and technical society: New Haven Railroad Historical & Technical Association, P. O. Box 122, Wallingford, CT 06492

Recommended reading: *New Haven Power*, by J. W. Swanberg, published in 1988 by Alvin F. Staufer, 2244 Remsen Road, Medina, OH 44356

Published rosters:

Railway & Locomotive Historical Society Bulletin:

No. 40, page 62 (New York & New Haven, Hartford & New Haven)
No. 41, page 29 (New York, New Haven & Hartford)
No. 43, page 60 (New York, Providence & Boston; Providence & Worcester)
No. 44, page 64 (Housatonic)
No. 46, page 37 (Old Colony)
No. 47, page 79 (Boston & Providence)
No. 49, page 69 (New York & New England)
No. 50, page 7 (Central New England)

Railroad Magazine: January 1939, page 124, and February 1939, page 113; February 1952, page 95

Trains Magazine: February 1950, page 26

NYNH&H STEAM LOCOMOTIVES BUILT SINCE 1900

Type	Class	Numbers	Qty	Builder	Built	Retired	Notes
0-6-0	U-1-c	2520	1	Pittsburgh	1902		
0-6-0	T-1	2300-2319	20	RI, Schen	1900, 1902	1935-1946	Cross-compound
0-6-0	T-2-a	2325-2343	19	Rhode Island	1904	1935-1946	
0-6-0	T-2-b	2373-2469	97	Cke, RI, Rich	1905-1913	1935-1950	
0-6-0	T-3	2350-2355	6	Schenectady	1904-1910	1935	Ex-CNE 1-6
0-8-0	Y-2	10-12	3	Schenectady	1913	1948	Ex-CNE 10-12
0-8-0	Y-3	3400-3414	15	Schenectady	1920, 1923	1949-1952	
0-8-0	Y-3	3415-3434	20	Schenectady	1922	1949-1952	
							Ex-CNE 28-32, 13-27
0-8-0	Y-4	3600-3609	10	Schenectady	1924	1949-1952	Three cylinders
0-8-0	Y-4-a	3610-3615	6	Schenectady	1927	1950-1951	Three cylinders
2-6-0	K-1-b	260-299	40	BLW, Cooke	1907		
2-6-0	K-1-b	325-479	155	Baldwin, Schenectady, Rhode Island			
					1900-1905	1927-1951	
2-6-0	K-1-c	300-324	25	Rhode Island	1902	1927-1949	
2-6-0	K-6	550-555	6	Brooks	1910	1935	Ex- CNE 125-130
2-8-0	F-3	110, 117, 118					
			3	Rogers	1905, 1907	1928	Ex-CNE 110, 117, 118
2-8-0	F-5	150-164	15	Schenectady	1912	1946-1950	Ex-CNE 150-164
2-8-2	J-1	3000-3024	25	Schenectady	1916	1947-1956	
2-8-2	J-2	3100-3107	8	Schenectady	1916	1946	
						3105-3107 were ex-CNE 180-182	
2-10-2	L-1	3200-3249	50	Schenectady	1918	1946-1950	
4-4-0	A-1	1250-1284	35	RI, Schen	1896, 1903	1935-1949	
4-4-0	A-3	1200-1214	15	RI, Schen	1900, 1902	1935-1940	
4-4-0	C-3-c	1525-1549	25	Rhode Island	1903	1925-1935	
4-4-0	C-15	1500-1514	15	NYNH&H	1901-1904	1925-1935	
4-4-2	F-1 (H-1)	1100-1111	12	Schenectady	1907	1900-1947	
4-6-0	G-3	950-969	20	Rhode Island	1903-1904	1926-1944	
4-6-0	G-4-a	800-849	50	Baldwin	1904-1907	1935-1948	
4-6-0	G-4-b	858-859	2	Baldwin	1904	1935	Balanced compound
4-6-0	P-1	50-52	3	Schenectady	1909	Ex-CNE 50-52	
4-6-2	I-1	1000-1031	32	Schen, BLW	1907, 1910	1944-1951	
4-6-2	I-2	1300-1349	50	Brooks	1913	1948-1952	
4-6-2	I-3	1090-1095	6	Baldwin	1913	1947-1948	
4-6-2	I-4	1350-1399	50	Schenectady	1916	1939-1952	
4-6-4	I-5	1400-1409	10	Baldwin	1937	1951	
4-8-2	R-1	3300-3309	10	Rich	1919	1946, 1948	USRA
4-8-2	R-1-a	3310-3339	30	Schenectady	1920	1947-1951	USRA copies
4-8-2	R-1-b	3340-3348	9	Schenectady	1924	1947-1951	USRA copies
4-8-2	R-2	3500	1	Schenectady	1924	1949	
4-8-2	R-2-a	3501-3507	7	Schenectady	1926	1949, 1951	
4-8-2	R-3	3550-3552	3	Schenectady	1926	1949	Three cylinders
4-8-2	R-3-a	3553-3562	10	Schenectady	1928	1949-1951	Three cylinders
Union Freight Railroad							
0-4-0T	5		1	Rhode Island	1907		
0-4-0T	6		1	Cooke	1914		
3-truck	8-11		4	Climax	1923-1928		

NORFOLK & WESTERN RAILWAY

by E. W. King, Jr.

By 1900 the Norfolk & Western extended from Norfolk, Virginia, to Portsmouth, Ohio, where the line divided, going north to Columbus and west to Cincinnati. Important branches reached Durham and Winston-Salem, North Carolina; Hagerstown, Maryland; and Bristol and Norton, Va. Many short branches served the coalfields of Virginia and West Virginia; by far the largest part of N&W's traffic was bituminous coal. Though the road was not a major passenger carrier, it was well known for its Norfolk-Cincinnati trains, and it was the middle portion of a Washington-Chattanooga route operated in conjunction with the Southern Railway. Much of N&W's well-maintained main line was double track.

Of the three Pocahontas Region coal railroads (Chesapeake & Ohio and Virginian were the others) the N&W had the worst grades. Eastbound coal had to be lifted up the 2 percent grade of Elkhorn Mountain into Bluefield, W. Va., up Alleghany Mountain (1 percent) between Bluefield and Roanoke, Va., and up the Blue Ridge (1.2 percent) just east of Roanoke. All three grades required helpers; the line up Elkhorn Mountain was operated with electric locomotives between 1915 and 1950, when a line relocation reduced the grade to 1.4 percent.

N&W established its headquarters and a large shop at Roanoke, and began building its own locomotives and cars there in 1883. Financial difficulties ended such activity 10 years later. Locomotive production resumed in January 1900 with engine 830, the first W1-class 2-8-0, and the road continued to build locomotives until 1953. N&W's engineering staff used a dynamometer car to monitor locomotive performance and conducted research in fuels, drafting, and grates. (N&W's USRA 4-8-2s were able to operate over two and three divisions on passenger trains without having their fires cleaned or ash pans dumped.) The department also developed an annular-ported exhaust nozzle (known as the "waffle-iron" nozzle because of its appearance) that created a good draft while minimizing exhaust back-pressure. The size of the nozzle was the reason for the large-diameter smokestacks characteristic of N&W locomotives.

In the first decade of the 20th century the road was a good customer of Baldwin Locomotive Works, which displayed four N&W engines at the Louisiana Purchase Exposition at St. Louis, Missouri, in 1904. These were cross-compound 2-8-0 No. 61, 4-6-0 No. 90, 4-4-2 No. 606, and 2-8-0 No. 729. Of these, all but 729 were built new for the Exposition. (Alco stole the show, however, displaying America's first Mallet — Baltimore & Ohio 0-6-6-0 No. 2400.)

By the 1940s and 50s most N&W trains moved behind one of three locomotive types, 4-8-4, 2-6-6-4, and 2-8-8-2, all tailored for N&W's requirements by the Roanoke Shops. With their high-pressure boilers (300 pounds), large combustion chambers and grates, roller bearings on all axles (and in the case of the 4-8-4s and the last five 2-6-6-4s, on the side and main rods), huge tenders, and extensive pressure lubrication systems, these locomotives achieved performance levels rarely seen before the diesel era. Except for the 4-8-4s, N&W locomotives were not heavyweights for their types. The A weighed less than all 4-6-6-4s except Union Pacific's original Challengers; the Y-class compound 2-8-8-2s were lighter than most simple 2-8-8-2s.

N&W was the last major railroad to dieselize. During the 1940s the road had been able to obtain horsepower more cheaply from steam locomotives than it could have from diesels. Good coal was inexpensive, and labor costs did not begin to increase sharply until the 1950s. When these factors changed, so did the railroad.

Freight Locomotives

In 1900 the Consolidation was the backbone of N&W's freight locomotive fleet. Except for a handful of class T Vauclain compound and class B cross compounds (all later converted to simple engines), most were 60-ton engines with 50" drivers and 20" × 24" cylinders, little different from 2-8-0s used on other roads.

Twelve-Wheeler 1119, shown at Hagerstown, Maryland, in 1927, was one of 50 M2s built by Baldwin in 1910. Photo by R. P. Morris.

The 2-8-0s that foretold the future were 30 class W engines that came from Baldwin in 1898 and 1899. Numbered 800-829, they had 56" drivers and 21" x 30" cylinders, and weighed 167,830 pounds. In 1900 the first W1s (830-842, 844-865) started rolling out of Roanoke, essentially class W engines with piston valves instead of slide valves. The Ws and W1s had narrow fireboxes which were unable to keep up with the demands of the relatively large drivers and the long piston stroke, so the design was modified with a wide firebox over the drivers. A total of 212 class W2 2-8-0s were built by Roanoke, Baldwin, Richmond, and Cooke between 1902 and 1905.

In 1900 N&W tried the 4-6-0 as a fast freighter. Baldwin built 12 class V engines with 56" drivers, numbers 950-961. Within a year they were rebuilt with 62" drivers for mountain passenger service and reclassed V1; Richmond supplied five more, 962-966, in 1902. Later they were used in light passenger and mixed train service, and four soldiered on through World War II as switchers at Norfolk.

N&W bought its first locomotives with trailing trucks in 1903, 4-4-2s for passenger service, but the road's mechanical engineers preferred to have the weight of the firebox carried by drive wheels on freight locomotives; there was ample room for a firebox above the smaller drivers. N&W never owned a 2-8-2, but instead amassed the nation's biggest fleet of 4-8-0s — 286 engines, between 1906 and 1911.

N&W's first 4-8-0s, class M, 375-399, duplicated the cylinder and driver dimensions of the W2 2-8-0s; they were faster and better steamers than their predecessors. M1s 1000-1099, which differed principally in having Walschaerts valve gear, joined the roster in 1907. The Ms and M1s were deckless; their many-windowed cabs straddled the end of the firebox and the fireman bailed coal from the tender deck.

In 1910 N&W and Baldwin created America's largest production-run Twelve-Wheelers, class M2, numbers 1100-1149. Roanoke built 11 similar 4-8-0s, 1150-1160, in classes M-2a, M-2b, and M-2c during the next two years. The M2s had the same 56" drivers as the earlier Twelve-Wheelers but cylinders 3" larger, 24" x 30"; they weighed 262,000 pounds, as much as contemporary 2-8-2s. The M2s had the same size firebox as the earlier 4-8-0s, and their larger cylinders pushed the limits of boiler capacity. Equipping the M2s with superheaters and stokers helped, but the 4-8-0 design had gone as far as it could.

In the 1920s the road needed a fast freight locomotive — something more powerful than the 4-8-0s and more agile than the Mallets. Since 1916 N&W had used 4-8-2s for passenger service and occasional freight service; the Mountain type was a logical choice for freight. Roanoke built 10 class K3 4-8-2s in 1926. They had 63" drivers and 28" x 30" cylinders. Their main rods were connected to the third drivers, which meant long main rods — long meant heavy, and heavy meant hard to counterbalance. The K2s rode hard, and they raised havoc with the track at speeds over 35 mph. In 1944 six were sold to Richmond, Fredericksburg & Potomac; the following year the remaining four went to the Denver & Rio Grande Western. Wheeling & Lake Erie bought all ten, thirdhand, in 1948.

Articulateds

Traffic began to increased markedly about 1910, and N&W realized that no 4-8-0 — nor any other non-articulated locomotive of the day —

4-8-0 — TWELVE-WHEELER

The 4-8-0 made a brief appearance in the late 1860s as a development of the 2-8-0, itself a new wheel arrangement. Few 4-8-0s were built until the late 1880s, when the type achieved popularity as a road freight engine. Its four-wheel lead truck offered more stability than the two-wheel truck of the Consolidation, but it wasn't necessary for speed, given the 57" drivers that were usually the maximum size used. Twelve-Wheelers offered more boiler capacity than contemporary 2-8-0s; in addition to extra length the boilers were usually greater in diameter. Most Twelve-Wheelers were built with narrow fireboxes, often of the square-cornered Belpaire type.

The 4-8-0 was eclipsed about the turn of the century by larger 2-8-0s with 63" drivers and by the 2-8-2, which had a much larger firebox. Never plentiful (Bruce estimates 600 were built in the United States), after the early 1930s Twelve-Wheelers were rare. Norfolk & Western kept elderly 4-8-0s in service until 1958 because they were N&W's only freight locomotives smaller than articulateds. Rarer than rare were Twelve-Wheelers built after World War I: Delaware & Hudson 1403, *L. F. Loree*, a four-cylinder triple-expansion drag freight engine built by Alco in 1933; and six passenger engines built by Baldwin for National Railways of Mexico, one with 67" drivers in 1924 and five with 69" drivers in 1935.

Other names: Mastodon (also applied to the 4-10-0, of which there

National Railways of Mexico 3000 and her four sisters, built in 1935, were anything but typical Twelve-Wheelers, with their wide fireboxes and 69" web-spoke drivers. They weighed 288,000 pounds, almost as much as a USRA light 2-8-2. Photo by Stan Kistler.

was only one, Central Pacific's *El Gobernador*)
Last: National Railways of Mexico 3000-3004, 1935
Longest lived: Several Norfolk & Western 4-8-0s built in 1906 were retired in 1958
Last in service: National of Mexico 3000-3004 and 2856 (Baldwin, 1924) were still in service in 1963
Greatest number: Norfolk & Western, 286
Heaviest: Delaware & Hudson 1403, 382,000 pounds

would be sufficiently powerful. In May 1910 the road received ten Mallets, five straightforward 0-8-8-0s from Alco (class X1, numbers 990-994) and five Baldwin 2-8-8-2s (class Y1, numbers 995-999) that embodied Baldwin's pet separable boiler concept. There were two sets of flues: The rear set made up the main boiler, and the front set acted as a feedwater heater. The X1s and Y1s had the same weight on drivers, driver diameter, cylinder dimensions, grate area, and boiler pressure. Tests showed the X1 was the better performer, but the leading and trailing trucks of the Y1 gave it better riding stability. The 0-8-8-0s out-

lived the expensive-to-maintain Y1s by ten years; equipped with superheaters and with boiler pressure raised to 230 pounds, they lasted as hump switchers until 1934.

In 1911 N&W borrowed a superheated compound 2-6-6-2 from C&O for testing. The 2-6-6-2 was about equal to N&W's Y1 in weight and rated power, and handily outperformed it. Impressed, N&W obtained a fleet of 190 similar 2-6-6-2s (1300-1489, classes Z1 and Z1a) from Richmond and Baldwin between 1912 and 1918. They replaced double-headed 2-8-0s and 4-8-0s in drag service.

2-8-8-2

by E. W. King, Jr.

The first 2-8-8-2s in North America were two experimental Mallets built by Baldwin in 1909 for Southern Pacific. They embodied a Baldwin concept known as the separable boiler: The front portion was kept full of water and functioned as a feedwater heater; besides the obvious benefit, this would ensure adequate adhesive weight on the front engine at all times. Intended to replace pairs of 2-8-0s on the grueling climb over the Sierra Nevada, these new monsters accomplished that most impressively, using 10 percent less fuel and, amazingly, 50 percent less water. After a redesign to run cab-forward and thus avoid gassing crews in Espee's many tunnels and snowsheds (a change made possible by the use of oil for fuel — it could be piped under pressure from the tender to the burner in the firebox, which was now on the leading end) these big Mallets became one of the greatest success stories in steam locomotive history , fathering ever-more-powerful and efficient cab-forward 2-8-8-2s and, later, 4-8-8-2s.

Norfolk and Western entered the Mallet market in 1910, buying five compound 2-8-8-2s from Baldwin — similar to SP's pioneers, even to separable boilers — and five more straightforward 0-8-8-0s, likewise compound, from Alco's Schenectady Works in May of that year. Except for one single-expansion locomotive obtained by the Pennsylvania in 1911, 2-8-8-2 development followed typical patterns, with engines being made larger and heavier. These were lumbering beasts with immense pulling power, but little capability for speeds over 20 mph.

In 1918 Norfolk & Western went down a different design path and produced a Class Y2 compound 2-8-8-2. Clearances limited the size of the low-pressure cylinders, so to obtain the desired power N&W used smaller cylinders and boiler pressure of 230 pounds — 200 pounds had been considered a maximum. This produced more efficiency and speed than was possible in contemporary designs, and in 1919 the USRA 2-8-8-2s furthered this concept and used an even higher boiler pressure — 240 pounds.

The first fleet of simple 2-8-8-2s was begun in 1924 when Chesapeake & Ohio received the first of its H-7 class. These locomotives looked ferocious but had only modest capacity, with 57" drivers and tractive effort of 108,550 pounds.

By 1931 several roads were operating simple 2-8-8-2s. Western Pacific (137,000 pounds starting tractive effort), Denver & Rio Grande Western (132,000 pounds), and Great Northern (146,000 pounds) had extended the capacity of the wheel arrangement far beyond that of the C&O H-7s and had accomplished it on 63" drivers, thus

Norfolk & Western Y6b 2197, built in 1952 and scrapped in 1959, represents the ultimate development of the compound articulated with efficiency features like a feedwater heater and roller bearings all around. N&W photo.

raising the speed as well. These huge 2-8-8-2s made superb reputations battling the Rockies and Sierras until diesels came.

Many railroads felt their old 2-8-8-2s could be speeded up by converting them to simple locomotives. Southern Railway, Great Northern, Baltimore and Ohio (converting theirs to 2-8-8-0s in the process), Southern Pacific (the early cab forwards), and Union Pacific replaced the low-pressure cylinders and repiped the locomotives for simple operation. These rebuilds were hailed as great successes, though they sacrificed economy for speed.

The speed potential of the USRA 2-8-8-2 and its deriviatives with higher pressure and smaller cylinders was adequate for all its users — N&W, Clinchfield, Northern Pacific, Rio Grande, Interstate, and Virginian. It is a tribute to the USRA designers that no USRA or USRA-derived Mallet was ever converted to simple operation.

Alone among America's railroads, N&W felt that the compound 2-8-8-2 based on the USRA design could be modified to minimize back-pressure problems and "souped up" to be an ideal mountain heavy freight hauler. In tinkering with the design over a period of 33 years the road wound up with a locomotive capable of producing 5600 drawbar horsepower at 25 mph with a top speed of 50 mph — perfect matches for N&W's tonnage, grades, and curves — and all this was achieved while retaining the economies of compound operation and in a locomotive that weighed 100,000 pounds less than either Chesapeake & Ohio's 2-6-6-6 or Union Pacific's 4-8-8-4.

Names: Chesapeake (Chesapeake & Ohio)
First: Southern Pacific 4000, 1909
Last: Norfolk & Western 2200, April 1952
Longest lived: N&W Y3 2001, 1919-March 1958
Greatest number: Norfolk & Western, 227
Heaviest: Western Pacific 251-256, 663,000 pounds
Lightest: (excluding those built for logging roads) Norfolk & Western 995-999 (Class Y1), 400,000 pounds

In 1928 engine 1399 was rebuilt as a simple engine, class Z2, but was not a success. The boiler could not supply four cylinders instead of two. Seventy-four Z1as were rebuilt with piston valves for the low-pressure cylinders and Worthington feedwater heaters, and reclassed Z1b. Most lived to be replaced by diesels in the late 1950s.

In 1918 Y2-class 2-8-8-2s began to roll out of Roanoke. These engines had modest cylinder dimensions offset by higher-than-normal boiler pressure — 230 pounds. In 1918 and 1919 Roanoke and Baldwin built 25 Y2s; in 1924 Roanoke built six more with low-pressure cylinders a half-inch larger — class Y2a (All Y2s were eventually reclassed Y2a).

One of N&W's mechanical engineers, John A. Pilcher, was assigned to the USRA design team. Pilcher showed up with blueprints for the Y2a under his arm, and both USRA Mallets were derived from them. The 2-8-8-2 used an even higher boiler pressure (240 pounds) with the 25" and 39" × 32" cylinders of the Y2a, and the USRA 2-6-6-2 was essentially a scaled-down Y2a. N&W went for the USRA 2-8-8-2 in a big way, obtaining 45 from Alco and 5 from Baldwin in 1919: numbers 2000-2049, class Y3. When more power was needed in 1923 the road obtained 30 more with larger tenders (2050-2079, class Y3a). Ten more 2-8-8-2s came from Richmond in 1927, classed Y3b (later Y4) and numbered 2080-2089. They were N&W's first Ys to sport Worthington BL feedwater heaters and the slant-front cab that would be seen on all the road's subsequent 2-8-8-2s. They were also the last steam locomotives N&W bought from commercial builders.

About 1927 N&W began to raise the boiler pressure of the Y2s and Y3s to 270 pounds, increasing both efficiency and power. In 1928 it applied a new exhaust system to the low-pressure engine of Y3 2049. The "bridge pipe" consisted of a large-diameter connection between the exhaust cavities of the two cylinders, from which a larger pipe extended to the exhaust stand and waffle-iron exhaust nozzle. This reduced back pressure and helped speed up the engines without sacrificing efficiency.

Between 1930 and 1932 came the first modern 2-8-8-2s, the 20 engines of class Y4a (numbers 2090-2109; later classed Y5). They incorporat-

2-6-6-4

by E. W. King, Jr.

As the demands for higher train speeds in the 1920s pressured locomotive designers to produce machines with greater horsepower, several new wheel arrangements were devised to provide for the weight of the larger fireboxes necessary to produce this power — 4-6-4, 2-8-4, 4-8-4, and 2-10-4.

It was the mid-1930s before a locomotive designer took the final step to produce what would turn out to be the ultimate fast, powerful locomotive — a high-drivered simple articulated with a big firebox. Baldwin had built two experimental 70"-drivered 2-6-6-2s for Baltimore and Ohio in 1930, but these were not high-horsepower machines, nor were they satisfactory at high speeds. Their boilers could not produce the steam necessary to make good the performance promised by those twelve high drivers, and the front engine units were slippery and tended to "hunt," or oscillate laterally in an alarming fashion.

In 1934 Baldwin produced three simple articulated locomotives of a new wheel arrangement, 2-6-6-4, for the Pittsburgh & West Virginia. Intended to raise train speeds over a sawtooth profile railroad with sharp curves (otherwise a 2-10-4 similar to those Baldwin built for Bessemer & Lake Erie might have sufficed) the new engines (P&WV class J-1) were equipped with 63" drivers and a rare

Drivers 69" in diameter make Seaboard 2501 a racy-looking engine. It has an Elesco coil-type feedwater heater and a semi-Vanderbilt tender. Baldwin photo, collection of H. L. Broadbelt.

three-axle tender truck booster. These locomotives were designed back-to-front. First consideration was given to providing a firebox-boiler combination capable of the required horsepower output — a deep Belpaire firebox of liberal grate area located entirely behind the driving wheels. Since P&WV's requirements did not include sustained high speed running, the 63" drivers were satisfactory, and the locomotives could develop starting tractive effort comparable to

ed bridge-pipe front engines, waffle-iron nozzles, and slant-front cabs. Boiler pressure was 300 pounds, which would become N&W's standard. The new engines did not, however, incorporate two new developments — roller bearings and one-piece cast steel frame and cylinders — and they spent a lot of time in the shop because their traditional fabricated frames could not handle their increased power and speed. All was put right in 1940 and 1941, when the 19 remaining Y5s (2092 was wrecked in 1937) were equipped with these improvements and 2090-2100 were renumbered 2110-2119.

By the mid-1930s N&W needed a locomotive that could eliminate doubleheading of passenger trains, roll time freights on the mountainous divisions in the middle of the railroad, handle heavy tonnage on the east and west ends where grades were favorable, and run 60 mph or better. Two experimental 70"-drivered 2-6-6-4s, numbers 1200 and 1201, were constructed at Roanoke in May and June of 1936; they were the third group of N&W locomotives to bear the class letter A (the others were a pair of 0-6-2Ts off the roster by 1900 and five passenger 4-6-0s built by Baldwin in 1902 and dismantled in 1928). They were an imme-

many 16-drivered articulateds and much more horsepower at the speeds that P&WV did require. The three J-1s were joined in 1937 by four J-2s, which lacked the troublesome tender booster.

A year later, Seaboard Air Line asked Baldwin for a locomotive that could do the work of two light 2-8-2s, and do it faster. SAL's problem was a congested single-track railroad. Baldwin recommended the same wheel arrangement that had worked so well for P&WV. To meet Seaboard's stringent axle-loading limitations the five locomotives were extremely light, but had 69" drivers for speed. These class R-1 locomotives met Seaboard's requirements, and the road went back to Baldwin for five class R-2 sisters two years later. The builder had evidently learned how to deal with the front-engine instability of the B&O 2-6-6-2s; the SAL engines routinely operated at speeds over 60 mph, and often handled second sections of Seaboard's seasonal Florida passenger trains. Dieselization resulted in all 10 of these fine locomotives being sold to the Baltimore and Ohio in 1947, where they operated until 1953.

Norfolk and Western developed the most powerful 2-6-6-4s and acquired the largest fleet, obtaining 43 locomotives between 1936 and 1950. All were equipped with cast frames and roller-bearing axles, and the last five were the continent's only articulated locomotives equipped with lightweight, roller-bearing side and main rods. The class A 2-6-6-4s set many performance records until they were replaced by diesels in 1959.

The development of the high-speed simple articulated followed two paths, of which the 2-6-6-4 was the less popular. American Locomotive Company was also developing a high-speed simple articulated in the mid-1930s, and Alco's designers were aware of the stability problems suffered by the B&O 2-6-6-2s. Accordingly they designed their high-speed articulated from front to back, starting with a four-wheel lead truck and creating the 4-6-6-4 wheel arrangement, the Challenger. To meet the length limitations of most roads, there was no room for the firebox to be located behind the driving wheels; it was squeezed in above the drivers. Many 4-6-6-4s had grate areas larger than that of C&O's prodigious 2-6-6-6, but the shallow fireboxes with restricted throats resulted in much poorer combustion efficiency. Many roads that owned 4-6-6-4s never operated them at speeds necessitating that four-wheel lead truck.

Total built: 60
First: Pittsburgh & West Virginia 1100, 1934
Last: Norfolk & Western 1242, April 1950
Longest lived: N&W 1200, 1936-1959 (No. 1218 was removed from display in 1985, restored to operating condition, and placed in excursion service in 1987)
Greatest number: Norfolk & Western, 43, 1200-1242
Heaviest: Norfolk & Western 1210-1242, 573,000 pounds
Lightest: Seaboard Air Line 2500-2509, 480,000 pounds

---

diate success, and the road built eight more (1202-1209) in late 1936 and 1937. The As set new records for steam locomotive horsepower. No steam locomotive was their equal until 1941, when the first Lima 2-6-6-6s and Alco 4-8-8-4s hit the road, and both these types outweighed the As by about a hundred tons.

Twenty-five more As were built at Roanoke in two groups during the war. Numbered 1210-1234, they differed only in details from their predecessors. The major visible difference was the use of Alligator crossheads and guides instead of the multiple bearing type; boiler pressure was increased to 300 pounds. The last eight As came from Roanoke in 1949 and 1950, and the final five, 1238-1242, had lightweight Timken roller-bearing side and main rods, a feature found on no other articulated locomotives. Engine 1242 was the last simple articulated locomotive built for service in North America.

While the first two A's were showing their stuff on the road, Roanoke was building the first five of what would prove to be the ultimate Mallet compound, the Y6 2-8-8-2. Incorporating all the improvements of the Y4a class, the Y6s also had one-piece cast steel frames and roller

Class A 2-6-6-4 No. 1238 was one of only five articulated locomotives built in the U. S. with roller bearing rods. Though designed for bituminous coal, the wide firebox would do credit to a Reading locomotive. N&W photo.

bearings on all axles. Their use of American Multiple front-end throttles resulted in an interesting peculiarity: In order that the smokebox not be lengthened — overhang was a consideration — the exhaust stand and nozzle were slanted forward to make room for the superheater header and the throttle mechanism.

The go-ahead was given for thirty more Y6s; these hit the road at about monthly intervals. By October 1940 the class, engines 2120-2154, was complete. Sixteen additional 2-8-8-2s (2155-2170, class Y6a) were built at Roanoke early in World War II, differing only in details. Experiments in the late 1930s and early 1940s had proven the worth of limited cutoff for the compounds, and the new engines incorporated 80 percent limited cutoff in the high-pressure engines and 75 percent in the low-pressure; earlier 2100s were modified to these values.

In 1948 Roanoke began building the the Y6b class. Engines 2171-2187 incorporated all the earlier developments, plus Worthington SA feedwater heaters in place of the earlier BL units. A line relocation west of Bluefield resulted in a need for steam locomotives to replace the side-rod electrics that had battled Elkhorn Mountain for 35 years. Roanoke turned out Y6bs 2188-2200 between August 1950 and April 1952; No. 2200 was the last steam locomotive built for road freight service in the United States. The last five Y6bs had an improved intercepting and reducing valve which increased the power of the low-pres-

sure engines and required the addition of 29,000 pounds of lead to them (the engines still weighed 110,000 pounds less than a Union Pacific 4-8-8-4). Also incorporated was a booster valve which increased the power of the low-pressure engine in compound operation by admitting a small amount of steam at boiler pressure into the receiver. As older 2100-series engines were shopped they received these improvements. These Mallets now could develop 170,000 pounds tractive effort simple, 132,000 pounds compound, and produce 5600 drawbar horsepower at 25 mph — a fine match for the demands of N&W's mountain freight service. That they held the line against diesels as long as they did — the last Y6b ran in revenue service in May 1960 — is a tribute to the continuing intelligent modification of a basically sound design.

N&W put 91 auxiliary water tenders into service between May 1952 and April 1954 to reduce the number of water stops. At least one of those stops was at the foot of a short grade, and eliminating the stop meant trains could hit the grade at speed and rely on momentum. Doing away with the need to coax a standing train into motion on a grade in effect increased the tonnage ratings of the locomotives.

Passenger locomotives

In 1900 the N&W handled its passenger trains with 4-4-0s and 4-6-0s. Shortly after the turn of the century, the road embarked on a two-pronged effort at modernizing its passenger power, ordering four class

A 4-6-0s (numbered 86-90) and six class J 4-4-2s (600-605) from Baldwin. The Exposition locomotives mentioned earlier filled out these classes to five and seven locomotives, respectively. Intended for the relatively flat east and west ends of the railroad, the Js had 79" drivers, the highest N&W ever specified for a new locomotive, and 45 square feet of grate area. The 4-6-0s were not so successful, having a narrow firebox, 20" × 28" cylinders, and 68" drivers. The narrow firebox made them hard to fire and poor steamers.

In 1905 Baldwin combined the running gear of the class A 4-6-0, a larger boiler, and a large firebox carried by a trailing truck behind the drivers. The result was the class E 4-6-2. The five Es, 595-599, were joined in 1907 by 15 class E1 Pacifics numbered 580-594. The E1s had Walschaerts valve gear, the first N&W engines with valve gear outside the frames.

In 1910 N&W received the first of what would eventually be 37 larger 4-6-2s in classes E2, E2a, and E2b (543-579). Those that came from Alco's Richmond Works were the first N&W engines with Baker valve gear, which would become the road's standard, and an outside-bearing trailing truck, which provided more stability than the earlier inside-journal designs.

The E-2s were not heavy Pacifics, though, and the combination of steel passenger cars and longer trains quickly made doubleheading necessary. In 1916 Roanoke created the road's first 4-8-2s, K1s 100-115. These heavy Mountains could handle N&W's heaviest passenger trains. Their cylinder dimensions were "over-square," combining a 29" bore with a short 28" stroke. It was an effort to reduce piston speed, but resulted in the K1s being hard starters. Alco's Brooks Works delivered 10 USRA heavy 4-8-2s (class K2, 116-125) in 1919. They were extremely successful, and the road went to Baldwin for 12 more in 1923 (class K2a, 126-137). Their 28" × 30" cylinders made them superior to the K1s.

Train weights increased throughout the 1920s, and the class J 4-4-2s proved too dainty. Needing more power but not wanting to design and build a special locomotive, N&W bought five 80"-drivered K3s Pacifics from the Pennsylvania Railroad in 1930. These 4-6-2s (N&W class E-3,

N&W's top passenger trains rated J-class 4-8-4s, though the seven cars of the *Powhatan Arrow* hardly tax No. 607 as it whistles into Glen Lyn, Virginia. The train's total weight is about the same as the weight of the engine and tender. Photo by Ben F. Cutler.

500-504) had the highest drivers ever to carry the N&W name and the characteristic Pennsy left-hand lead, which caused considerable consternation the first time one of them was in the shop for wheel work. All N&W engines had right-hand lead.

In the late 1930s N&W needed an entirely new passenger engine. Doubleheading the 4-8-2s was expensive and using 2-6-6-4s on passenger trains — A's 1200 and 1201 were virtual regulars on trains 41 and 42 between Bristol and Monroe — was wasteful. The new passenger engine had to be brawny enough to make track speed up the mountains with the heaviest trains, fast enough to make up time on the level ends of the road, durable enough to run from one end of the railroad to the other without change, and stylish enough to hold its own in a world enamored of flashy diesel-powered streamliners.

N&W's mechanical engineers were up to the challenge, and the

result was five 494,000-pound 4-8-4s numbered 600-604 that rolled out of Roanoke between October 1941 and January 1942. These class J engines — the third group to bear the letter — had roller bearings on all axles, rods, wrist pins, and valve gear, and extensive pressure lubrication. The drivers were the same 70" of the E2 4-6-2s, the K1 4-8-2, and the class A 2-6-6-4, but careful attention to counterbalancing and the use of Timken lightweight tandem rods allowed speeds in excess of 110 mph without damage to either locomotive or track. The huge boilers were designed for 300 pounds pressure, but the safety valves were set at 275; grate area was 107.7 square feet. Tractive effort was 73,300 pounds; No. 602 was fitted with a Franklin high-speed trailing truck booster that added 12,500 pounds. The booster was removed after several engineers unsuccessfully tried to cut it in at too high a speed. It wasn't needed anyway — the relatively small drivers, totally opposite the thinking of the commercial builders, meant this locomotive could handle N&W's grades with a fifteen-car *Pelican* or *Pocahontas* without breathing hard. On top of it all, the Js wore a tasteful bullet-nosed shroud painted glossy black and trimmed with a gold-edged tuscan red stripe.

Wartime restrictions on materials meant that 4-8-4s 605-610 were built without streamlining and with enormous side rods which accentuate the relatively small size of the drivers. N&W photo.

With World War II came the demand for more passenger power, but the War Production Board was unsympathetic. To satisfy bureaucratic requirements Nos. 605-610 had to be classified as freight engines. They were built without shrouds, and certain alloys and the roller bearings were not available for the rods, so they were classed J1. After the war they were streamlined, fitted with roller bearing rods, and reclassed J. Their boiler pressures were raised to 300 pounds, as were those of the earlier Js, giving them a starting tractive effort of 80,000 pounds, highest ever for a 4-8-4.

The Js began to rack up an average of 15,000 miles per month, an astounding figure considering that the longest possible run was 676 miles from Norfolk to Cincinnati. Many railroads didn't approach that mileage figure with diesels. Designed not only for high power and speed capabilities but also for easy servicing and quick turnarounds, Js 600 and 601 both exceeded 2 million miles in their 17-year careers.

Two E-2a Pacifics, 563 and 578, survived to be replaced by diesels.

They were the regular and backup engines on trains 5 and 6 between Bluefield and Norton; curvature west of Richlands, Va., precluded the use of 4-8-2s or 4-8-4s. Bluefield Shop made some minor improvements on the little 4-6-2s — Standard stokers, Hennessey driving box lubricators, and 15,000 gallon tenders, for instance — to insure efficient operation.

In the late 1940s N&W upgraded its 4-8-2s. The K1s got strengthened frames, new cylinders and cabs, lagged firebox sides, and extended pressure lubrication. They were used mainly on local freights until dieselization. The K2s and K2as came in for more dramatic renovation. New cylinders, fireboxes, stokers, roller bearings for all except the driver journals, which were equipped with oil lubrication, and extensive mechanical pressure lubrication were the invisible changes. Intended to handle all passenger trains not assigned to Js, they were streamlined just like them. At a distance it was difficult to tell the difference.

In 1950 N&W built Js 611-613. They were the last steam passenger locomotives built for an American common carrier, and were nearly identical to Nos. 605-610. After dieselization, 611 was put on display in a Roanoke park. It was removed in 1982, overhauled, and placed in excursion service.

Switchers

In 1900 the N&W's switcher fleet consisted of class P, R, and S 0-6-0s and a handful of class I 2-8-0s (the lead trucks were removed about 1904). The road relied upon the cascade effect of new road power releasing older engines for yard service, and as the years passed, switchers were created by applying footboards to older 2-8-0s, 4-8-0s, 2-6-6-2s, and 2-8-8-2s.

Humps in the coal classification yards at Portsmouth and Roanoke required lots of tractive effort. By the late 1920s 2-8-8-2s were used on these jobs, and still weren't powerful enough. N&W tried adding tender truck boosters; Y2a-class 2-8-8-2s 1700, 1711, 1717, and 1720 and Y3 2006 received Bethlehem boosters; No. 1702 got two Franklin boosters, and 1706 and 1714 each got one. Some of these booster-equipped 1700s also spent time as pushers on Alleghany Mountain between Wal-

N&W experimented with a pair of 4-8-0s to create semistreamlined switchers with automatic stokers and injectors. Even with modern controls, they were old locomotives; the simplicity of modern 0-8-0s won out. Photo by H. Reid.

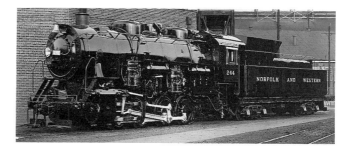

After years of using outmoded road engines for switching, N&W went for the 0-8-0 whole hog with 30 purchased from Chesapeake & Ohio in 1950 and 45 of its own manufacture between 1951 and 1953. Engine 244 was the last reciprocating steam engine built for service on an American common carrier railroad. N&W photo.

ton and Christiansburg, Va. But boosters were expensive to maintain; it proved less expensive to raise boiler pressure to 270 pounds to increase main cylinder tractive effort.

In 1950 Chesapeake & Ohio put 45 almost-new 0-8-0 s up for sale. Virginian bought 15, and N&W obtained 30 that had come from Baldwin only two years before. These were modified USRA 0-8-0s whose design dated from 1918, but with 30 years of improvements they were formidable machines. They had 200 pounds of boiler pressure, 52" drivers, and an engine weight of 244,000 pounds; tractive effort was rated at 57,200 pounds. Not so obvious were the one-piece cast steel frames and front-end throttles. N&W added a second air pump, increased tender water capacity, and raised the boiler pressure to 220 pounds, resulting in a tractive effort of 62,932 pounds. They kept their C&O numbers on N&W — 255-284.

The C&O switchers were so good that Roanoke built 45 more 0-8-0s (200-244) from the same blueprints between March 1951 and December 1953. New 13,000-gallon welded clear-vision tenders were built on the frames and trucks of the USRA 12,000-gallon tenders delivered with the Y3 2-8-8-2s in 1919. Engine 244 was the last reciprocating steam engine built for common carrier service for an American railroad.

Oddities and experimental locomotives

N&W's only Lima locomotive was a 150-ton, 4-truck Shay delivered in August 1907 for service on steep mine branches near Bluestone, W. Va. After about eight years of service, it was sold and eventually wound up on the El Paso & Southwestern.

Two M2 4-8-0s, 1100 and 1112, were shopped at Roanoke in 1947 and 1948 and emerged as "automatic switchers." Automatic controls were added to stoker, draft, and a standby feedwater pump; the smokebox was extended so a fan could be used for draft, and 1112's boiler pressure was raised to 225 pounds. Tender capacities were increased

to 20 tons, and pressure lubrication was added so the locomotives could stay out in the yard for 24 hours without shop attention. Both engines received homely shrouding and skyline casings for the domes. They were moderately successful, but no steam locomotive engineer worth his salt would ever completely trust an automatic water supply.

In May 1954 N&W took delivery of a steam-turbine-electric locomotive from Baldwin-Westinghouse. Numbered 2300, classed TE-1, and named *Jawn Henry** after that legendary steel-drivin' man, it had a Babcock & Wilcox water-tube boiler working at 600 pounds pressure, weighed 818,000 pounds (all on drivers), and was rated at 4500 horsepower. The stoker and injector were controlled automatically with devices like those on the experimental 4-8-0s.

On test, it developed a tractive effort of 199,000 pounds — at 1 mph. *Jawn* could handle more tonnage on less fuel than conventional steam engines, but at lower speeds. Electrical troubles and problems with fly ash cutting the turbine blades were curable and not seen as deterrents to obtaining a fleet of *Jawns*; cost was. The unit cost of additional TE-1's was too high; no other railroads were interested in such machines — they were content with diesels, and many had already dismantled their coal and water facilities. Being a one-of-a-kind was never a happy condition, and so it was for big *Jawn Henry*; like his namesake he died an untimely death, going to the torch in December 1957.

Modern Servicing Facilities

By 1941 Norfolk & Western was aware of the availability record of the diesel and sought a system of servicing its locomotives between runs that would complement their superb road performance. Analysis showed that the combination of roundhouse and turntable was inherently inefficient. While it was obviously necessary to turn locomotives between runs — any new facility would have to include a turntable or wye — much could be done to improve the efficiency of replenishing coal and water, lubrication, inspection, and minor repairs.

The road had spent years researching fuels and grate and draft configurations for efficient combustion, so cleaning the fire and dumping the ashpan were not the time-consuming chores they were elsewhere. New coal and water facilities were designed so even the largest tenders could be filled quickly.

N&W designed a new facility known as a "Lubritorium," a long, brightly lit building with spacious pits for inspecting and lubricating driver bearings and brake rigging, and drops with long hoses for quickly lubricating rods and filling lubricators. Inspections and light repairs could be accomplished easily while the locomotive was being lubricated. Lubritoriums were built at Shaffers Crossing (Roanoke), Bluefield, Williamson, W. Va., and Portsmouth; a modified version was installed at Pulaski, Va. Locomotives stayed out of roundhouse unless heavy repairs were necessary.

The new facilities made it possible to service and turn locomotives in 90 minutes or less, and gave N&W's steam locomotives an availability record that compared favorably with diesels of the day.

Historical and technical society: Norfolk & Western Historical Society, P. O. Box 201, Forest, VA 24551-0201

Recommended reading:
Norfolk & Western Railway, by Richard E. Prince, published in 1980 by Richard E. Prince (SBN 9600088-9-6)
"Faith in Steam," by David P. Morgan, in *Trains Magazine*, November 1954, pages 18-30

Published rosters:
Railroad Magazine: March 1936, page 91; September 1944, page 121; February 1953, page 84; August 1956, page 58
Trains Magazine: November 1954, page 24

---

* Jawn (or John) Henry was, according to legend, a black construction worker who pitted his hammer and drill against a steam drill and died in the attempt. Some accounts place the incident on the Central of Georgia at Leeds, Alabama, in 1888; others say it occurred during the construction of Chesapeake & Ohio's Big Bend Tunnel at Hilldale, West Virginia.

N&W STEAM LOCOMOTIVES BUILT SINCE 1898

Type	Class	Numbers	Qty	Builder	Built	Retired	Notes
0-8-0	S1	255-284	30	Baldwin	1948	1958-60	Ex-C&O 255-284
0-8-0	S1a	200-244	45	N&W	1951-53	1958-1960	
0-8-8-0	X1	990-994	5	Schenectady	1910	1934	
2-8-0	W	800-829	30	Baldwin	1898-99	1926-1934	Rebuilt to W-1
2-8-0	W1	830-842, 844-865					
			34	N&W, BLW, Richmond			
				1900-1901	1926-1934		5 rebuilt to 0-8-0T
2-8-0	W2	673-799,	212	N&W, BLW	1901-1905	1926-1952	
				776 equipped with Walschaerts Valve Gear, reclassed			
2-8-0	B	61-70	10	Baldwin	1898-1904	1933-1934	
				Cross-Compound, simpled 1909-1912; No. 61 built 1904,- Exposition engine			
2-6-6-2	Z1	1300-1314	15	Richmond	1912	1934	
2-6-6-2	Z1a	1315-1489	175	Rich, BLW	1912-1918	1934-1958	
						1331-1489 rebuilt to Z1b	
2-6-6-2	Z2	1399	1			1934	Rebuilt 1928 from Z-1a
2-6-6-4	A	1200-1209	10	N&W	1936-1937	1958-1959	
2-6-6-4	A	1210-1224	15	N&W	1943	1959-1961	
2-6-6-4	A	1225-1234	10	N&W	1944	1958-1959	
2-6-6-4	A	1235-1242	8	N&W	1949-1950	1958-1959	
2-8-8-2	Y1	995-999	5	Baldwin	1910	1924	
2-8-8-2	Y2	1700-1704	5	N&W	1918-1921	1946-1951	All rebuilt to Y2a
2-8-8-2	Y2a	1705-1710	6	N&W	1924	1948-49	
2-8-8-2	Y2	1711-1730	20	Baldwin	1919	1948-1951	All rebuilt to Y2a
2-8-8-2	Y3	2000-2044	45	Schenectady	1919	1957-1958	
2-8-8-2	Y3	2045-2049	5	Baldwin	1919	1957-1958	
2-8-8-2	Y3a	2050-2079	30	Richmond	1923	1958-1959	
2-8-8-2	Y3b	2080-2089	10	Richmond	1927	1958	Changed to Y4
2-8-8-2	Y4a	2090-2109	20	N&W	1930-32	1958-1960	Changed to Y5
2-8-8-2	Y6	2120-2154	35	N&W	1936-1940	1958-1960	
2-8-8-2	Y6a	2155-2170	16	N&W	1942	1958-1960	
2-8-8-2	Y6b	2171-2187	17	N&W	1948-1949	1959-1960	
2-8-8-2	Y6b	2188-2194	7	N&W	1950-1951	1959-1960	
2-8-8-2	Y6b	2195-2200	6	N&W	1951-1952	1959-1960	
4-4-2	J	600-606	7	Baldwin	1903-04	1931-35	
4-6-0	V	950-961	12	Baldwin	1900	1929-1948	
4-6-0	V-1	962-966	5	Richmond	1902	1929-1933	
4-6-0	A	86-90	5	Baldwin	1902-04	1928	
4-6-2	E	595-599	5	Richmond	1905	1934-39	
4-6-2	E1	580-594	15	Baldwin	1907	1931-1938	
4-6-2	E2	564-579	16	Richmond	1910	1938-1958	
4-6-2	E2a	553-563	10	Baldwin	1912	1940-1958	
4-6-2	E2b	543-552	10	N&W	1913-14	1938-1955	
4-6-2	E3	500-504	5	Baldwin	1913	1946-1947	ex-PRR class K3s
4-8-0	M	375-499	125	Rich, BLW	1906-07	1926-1958	
4-8-0	M1	1000-1099	100	Rich, BLW	1907	1926-1947	
4-8-0	M2	1100-1149	50	Baldwin	1910	1950-1957	
4-8-0	M2a	1150-1152	3	N&W	1911	1950-56	
4-8-0	M2b	1153, 1154	2	N&W	1911	1950-56	
4-8-0	M2c	1155-1160	6	N&W	1911-12	1952-57	
4-8-2	K1	100-115	16	N&W	1916-17	1957-58	
4-8-2	K2	116-125	10	Brooks	1919	1957-59	
4-8-2	K2a	126-137	12	Baldwin	1923	1958-1959	
4-8-2	K3	200-209	10	N&W	1926	sold 1944-45	
4-8-4	J	600-604	5	N&W	1941-1942	1958-59	
4-8-4	J-1	605-610	6	N&W	1943	1959	
						Streamlined 1945-47, reclassed J	
4-8-4	J	611-613	3	N&W	1950	1959	

NORTHERN PACIFIC RAILWAY

Northern Pacific was the first of America's three northern transcontinentals, opened in 1883 from Carlton Junction, Minnesota, near Duluth, to a connection with the Oregon Railway & Navigation Company at Wallula Junction, Washington. NP soon fell into financial difficulties, entered receivership in 1893, and was reorganized in 1896. In 1900 it acquired the St. Paul & Duluth, and in 1901, the Seattle & International, a line from Seattle north to the Canadian border at Sumas, Washington. Also in 1901 NP leased its lines in Manitoba (from Emerson through Winnipeg to Portage la Prairie and from Morris to Brandon) to the provincial government. About the turn of the century control of NP was acquired by James J. Hill, builder of the Great Northern. In 1901 NP and GN jointly purchased almost all the stock of the Chicago, Burlington & Quincy, and between 1905 and 1908 NP and GN built the Spokane, Portland & Seattle Railway from Spokane, Wash., down the Columbia River to Portland, Ore.

NP's main line had easy grades northwest across Minnesota. As it headed straight west across North Dakota from Fargo through Jamestown, Bismarck, and Dickinson, it crossed the drainage pattern, resulting in a sawtooth profile with a succession of 1 percent ascending and descending grades. From Glendive to Livingston, Montana, the line climbed steadily, following the Yellowstone River. At Livingston the mountains began, with two major summits over the Belts and the Rockies and a minor summit between them — grades up to 2.2 percent. An alternate route took passenger trains over a much higher pass east of Butte, with long stretches of 2.2 percent. West of the Rockies there was a long descent to the Columbia River at Pasco, Wash., a relatively easy climb along the Yakima River, short stretches of 2.2 percent over the Cascades, then a 1 percent descent to Auburn, Tacoma, and Seattle.

NP's motive power policy was essentially conservative. NP's routes had few long straight stretches where the engineer could really open it up, so speed wasn't a major consideration in the design of its locomotives. Among the important considerations were an on-line source of low-grade coal which required large fireboxes, and areas where the only available water was bad.

In 1940 NP tested Electro-Motive FT demonstrator 103. With a 5,000-ton train it was able to make 36 mph at a spot where previously a well-maintained Z-6 4-6-6-4 with the same train made 16 mph. FTs went into service first on Stampede Pass, where a tight tunnel restricted steam locomotives, and they soon found their way to other divisions. NP stayed with steam longer than most other roads because of its relatively modern fleet of 4-8-4s and 4-6-6-4s and its source of cheap coal. The last steam-powered run was on January 17, 1958, when W-3 Mikado No. 1713 brought a train into Duluth.

Freight locomotives

At the turn of the century NP had a case of compound fever and bought several groups of compound 2-8-0s (some cross-compound, some tandem) in classes Y through Y-3. Two small groups of simple 2-8-0s were delivered in 1903, the Y-4 class with 63" drivers and the Y-5s with 55". The 81 post-1900 Consolidations were in a minority compared with 150 Prairies and 380 Mikados. They were rebuilt to simple engines and were eventually assigned to switching service.

NP wasn't the first road to order Mikados — Bismarck, Washburn & Great Falls bought one in 1902, and Santa Fe took delivery of 15 in 1902 and 1903 — but NP was the first to order them in quantity, 160 class W 2-8-2s built by Brooks between 1904 and 1907. They had 63" drivers, 24" × 30" cylinders, inside valves, Stephenson valve gear, and inside journal trailing trucks. Engine weight was 263,500 pounds. Some were built as tandem compounds, and some were equipped with diamond stacks against the sparking tendencies of NP's low-grade sub-bituminous coal. The W-1 class, Nos. 1660-1699, built by Schenectady in 1910, had 25" × 30" cylinders and Walschaerts valve gear but otherwise resembled the W class.

Twenty tandem compound 2-8-2s were converted to simple engines in 1912, reclassed W-2, and numbered 1900-1919. It is uncertain whether

W-class Mikado 1504, shown out of service (the piston rod is missing), was part of the first large group of Mikados. Photo by Maurice L. Kunde.

NP's Mikados had grown substantially by the time the W-3 class was built. Number 1760 exhibits such NP traits as pressed-steel pilot and the odd headlight displaying the number to both sides and forward. Photo by R. V. Nixon.

or not these were originally W-class engines in the 1500-1659 series.

While the early Mikes were arriving from Brooks and Schenectady, Brooks also delivered 150 2-6-2s for light freight service, class T, Nos. 2300-2449. Six Ts were rebuilt to 2-8-2s in 1918 and 1919 — the W-4 class. Later 18 Prairies were modified, reclassed T-1, and renumbered 2450-2567.

Brooks delivered 135 W-3 Mikados, Nos. 1700-1834, between 1913 and 1920. They had the same 63" drivers as the earlier Mikes, but 28" × 30" cylinders. They had outside-frame trailing trucks and piston-rod extensions (which helped support the pistons and reduce wear on the bottoms of the pistons and cylinders, but at the expense of more piston rod packing). The W-3s weighed 335,800 pounds, about 16,000 pounds more than a USRA heavy Mikado.

The W-5s of 1923 were heavier still, 342,800 pounds, but had the same basic dimensions. They had cast trailing trucks with boosters, air pumps mounted on the smokebox front, and piston rod extensions, and most had either Elesco or Worthington feedwater heaters. In March 1926 W-5 No. 1844 pulled a freight train from Seattle to Minneapolis without change, consuming 353 tons of coal and 442,000 gallons of water (and producing 38 tons of ash) on the 1,898-mile trip.

Articulateds

Like the parallel Milwaukee Road, NP's nonarticulated freight locomotive progression was directly from the 2-8-2 to the 4-8-4, skipping 10-coupled locomotives, except for a pair of prehistoric Decapods. Unlike Milwaukee, NP went in for articulateds. The first were the Z class 2-6-6-2s, Nos. 3000-3015, turned out by Baldwin in 1907. They were identical to Great Northern's and Burlington's first Mallets, with 55" drivers and slide valves fore and aft. They were followed in 1910 by the Z-1 class, Nos. 3100-3105. They had the same size drivers but smaller cylinders and weighed 305,150 pounds, about 50,000 less than the Zs.

Baldwin also sent 2-8-8-2s west to NP in 1910, the Z-2 class, Nos. 4000-4004. They had 57" drivers and 26" × 30" and 40" × 30" cylinders and weighed 443,500 pounds. Between 1913 and 1920 Schenectady and Brooks built the next group of 2-8-8-2s, Z-3s 4005-4025, which had the same size drivers and cylinders as the Z-2s but weighed about 20 tons more. The last 2-8-8-2s, Z-4s 4500-4503, copies of the USRA design, were delivered by Richmond in 1923.

NP's largest articulateds were built not for the Rockies and the

2-8-2 — MIKADO

In 1890 Baldwin built ten 2-8-2 locomotives for the narrow gauge Interoceanic Railway in Mexico, and in 1893 Brooks built four for the Chicago & Calumet Terminal Railway. The Mexican locomotives had a firebox behind the drivers — the locomotives had outside frames and there was no other place for it. The trailing wheel was a tiny one underneath the cab. The engines were converted to 2-8-0s. The Chicago & Calumet locomotives had fireboxes above the frames; the rear axle was a guiding axle for reverse running. Robert Grimshaw's *Locomotive Catechism* of 1893 referred to these locomotives as the Calumet type. The 1899 Brooks catalog called similar engines built for Mexican Central in 1897 as "Consolidation Freight, Double Enders," and made reference to two pairs of leading wheels.

The wheel arrangement was named Mikado in 1897 when Baldwin built a group of 2-8-2s for the Nippon Railway of Japan. The word means "emperor of Japan," and it had come into currency in 1885 with the opening of Gilbert and Sullivan's opera *The Mikado*.

The first Mikado built for service in the U. S. — and the first with a firebox behind the drivers and supported by a trailing truck — was a 50"-drivered Vauclain compound built by Baldwin in 1901 for the Bismarck, Washburn & Great Falls. It later became Soo Line No. 1000. In 1902 and 1903 Baldwin delivered 15 2-8-2s to the Santa Fe, also Vauclain compounds, but AT&SF bought no more for a decade.

Northern Pacific purchased 160 Mikados between 1904 and 1907, but railroads were generally slow to adopt the type in preference to the 2-8-0. The reason was that even 63" drivers, the largest used on 2-8-0s, were low enough to permit a wide firebox over the rear drivers. The switch to 2-8-2s was usually the result of a desire to increase freight train speed, which required not just a wide firebox but also a larger boiler. Like Pacifics, Mikados embodied a good balance between boiler size, grate area, and running gear.

In the Teens Mikados became the standard freight locomotives. USRA's 625 light 2-8-2s outnumbered all other USRA road engines combined — and there were also 233 heavy Mikes. Mikado construction tapered off as railroads turned to larger power for freight

Southern Railway's Ps-4 Pacifics are often considered the ultimate, typical Pacific. SR Ms-4 No. 4913, shown at Alexandria, Virginia, in 1933, fills that role for the Mikado. Photo by W. H. Thrall, Jr.

trains, but Canadian Pacific bought its last four from Montreal Locomotive Works in 1948, and the 3'6" gauge Newfoundland Railway received six, also from Montreal, in 1949.

During World War II several railroads tried to redesignate their 2-8-2s MacArthurs. Wake Hoagland commented on the folly of such a move in the January 1957 issue of *Trains*: "Imagine: Big Mac, Super Mac, a low-slung Mac, an Alco-built Mac!" Nowadays we have Big Macs, but they're not 2-8-2s.

Other names: MacArthur

First: Bismarck, Washburn & Great Falls 3, Baldwin 1901

Last:

Narrow gauge: Newfoundland Railway 324-329, Montreal, 1949

Standard gauge: Canadian Pacific 5470-5473, Montreal, 1948

Last in service: Denver & Rio Grande Western's narrow gauge 2-8-2s

Greatest number: New York Central, 1,387

Heaviest: Great Northern O-8, Nos. 3375-3399, 425,540 pounds

Cascades but for the main line between Mandan, N. D., and Glendive, Mont. East and west of that part of the line Mikados could handle 3,000- to 4,000-ton trains, but the succession of 1 percent ascending and descending grades across western North Dakota restricted the Mikes to 2,000 tons, which meant trains had to be doubleheaded or cut in half. NP needed two Mikes in one locomotive. Chesapeake & Ohio had pioneered the simple 2-8-8-2 and Denver & Rio Grande Western had refined

Northern Pacific's Yellowstones were built not for the grades of the Rockies but for hill-and-dale running across North Dakota. Their cavernous fireboxes were required by the low-grade coal NP obtained from mines along the line. Baldwin photo; collection of H. L. Broadbelt.

it. NP set out to design a simple 2-8-8-2 with 63" drivers and four 26" × 32" cylinders.

The hook was that NP wanted to burn low-grade Rosebud coal in the engines, which meant a large firebox with a grate area of 182 square feet, the largest ever used on a steam locomotive. The front half of the firebox was over the two rear pairs of drivers, and a four-wheel, booster-equipped trailing truck supported the rear half, creating a new wheel arrangement, 2-8-8-4, christened Yellowstone (Z-5, Nos. 5000-5011). NP ordered one locomotive, and Alco delivered it in 1928. It weighed 717,000 pounds, and its auxiliary appliances included a trailing truck booster and two Coffin feedwater heaters. It was the largest steam locomotive in the world, and Alco celebrated by serving dinner to 12 people seated in the firebox. NP asked for bids for 11 more like it, and Baldwin got the job.

Impressive as they were, the Yellowstones steamed poorly and produced less than 5,000 horsepower — it should have been 6,000. After nearly a decade of testing and experimenting, NP found that the grates were too large to maintain a high temperature and complete combustion

of the coal. Blocking off 2 feet at the front did the trick. In 1941 the entire class received new one-piece cast front frames with integral cylinders, and the drivers were fitted with roller bearings.

NP's next need was for a large, fast freight locomotive for the mountains. A 4-8-4 wouldn't have been much more powerful than the W-5 Mikes, a 2-10-4 would have had difficulties with some of the curves, and an updated 2-8-8-4 wasn't considered — possibly because the Z-5s weren't all they could have been. NP and Alco worked together to design a 4-6-6-4 based on Union Pacific's first Challengers. Not long after UP's 4-6-6-4s were delivered, Alco sent 12 west to NP, the Z-6 class, 5100-5111. They had the 69" drivers of the UP engines, cylinders an inch larger (23" × 32"), and about 40 percent more grate area — again for that low-grade coal. Timken provided roller bearings for the axles of Nos. 5104-5111 to furnish a comparison between friction and roller bearings in freight service. Despite the success of Timken 1111, NP wasn't sure roller bearings could stand up to freight service. The friction bearings on Nos. 5100-5103 proved to be a constant source of trouble until they were replaced by roller bearings; by then roller bearings had

come to be standard for modern locomotives. Nine more 4-6-6-4s, Nos. 5112-5120, were delivered in 1937 along with six oil-burning duplicates for Spokane, Portland & Seattle.

Six Z-7 Challengers, Nos. 5121-5126, arrived from Alco in 1941 for wartime traffic. They had thicker driver tires that resulted in 70" diamter, vestibule cabs, and Centipede tenders. The 20 Z-8s of 1943 and 1944, Nos. 5130-5149, were virtually identical. They were the last steam locomotives Northern Pacific bought.

Passenger locomotives

NP inherited three 1899 Baldwin Atlantics with 78" drivers when it acquired the St. Paul & Duluth in 1900. It numbered them 600-602 and classed them N. Three more class N-1 Atlantics joined the roster in 1909: No. 603 from Baldwin and 604 and 605 from Alco.

The 4-6-0s in the P classes were passenger engines with 69" or 73" drivers. Some of the P-1s and all the P-2s were built as cross-compounds and later converted to simple engines. The P-3s were built as compounds but were never simpled; only two remained on the roster in 1925.

Most of the S-4 Ten-Wheelers, built by Baldwin in 1902 as Vauclain compounds, served NP for a half century. Only one of the class had been retired by 1945. Photo by R. V. Nixon.

Compared with Q-class No. 2080, shown on page 35, Q-1 Pacific No. 2119 illustrates the early development of the type, with a larger boiler and outside-frame trailing truck. By 1945 more than half the class, built between 1904 and 1907, had been retired. Photo by R. V. Nixon.

4-8-4 — NORTHERN

In 1926 and 1927 the Northern Pacific took delivery of 12 locomotives from Alco that were designed to meet two requirements: eliminate doubleheading of passenger trains, and burn low-grade coal from company-owned mines at Rosebud, Montana. Meeting the first requirement meant eight drivers, not six, and meeting the second meant a large firebox, which in turn called for a four-wheel trailing truck. A new wheel arrangement was created, the 4-8-4, or "Northern Pacific" type.

The name was quickly shortened to Northern, but no other wheel arrangement had more alternate names. Canadian National christened its first 4-8-4 the Confederation type but soon settled for Northern; the Lackawanna referred to its 4-8-4s as Poconos, for the mountains they traversed. Roads south of the Mason-Dixon Line considered Northern pejorative — and substituted Dixie (Nashville, Chattanooga & St. Louis), Potomac (Western Maryland), and Greenbrier (Chesapeake & Ohio). New York Central, the water-level route, looked at its map for another river, already having used Hudson and Mohawk, and chose Niagara; curiously, National Railways of Mexico seconded the motion.

North America's 4-8-4s eventually ranged in weight from 361,000 to 510,150 pounds and had drivers between 69" and 80" in diameter. NP's first 4-8-4s were just about in the middle of those ranges: 426,000 pounds and 73" drivers. The next 4-8-4s were five passenger engines with 77" drivers for Delaware, Lackawanna & Western, also built by Alco in 1927. Baldwin built a single passenger 4-8-4 for the Santa Fe in 1927, following up with nine more the next year after a period of testing. The Lackawanna and Santa Fe engines weighed about as much as the NP locomotives but were more powerful because of boiler pressure and cylinder size.

North of the border, in 1928 Canadian National split an order for 40 4-8-4s between Montreal Locomotive Works and Canadian Locomotive Company, and ordered 12 from Alco for subsidiary Grand Trunk Western. CN considered the type a dual-service locomotive, and that is what it quickly became all across North America. Northerns had enough pulling power for fast freight trains and enough speed for passenger work. The four-wheel lead truck provided stability, and the four-wheel trailing truck allowed a large firebox for sustained steam production.

The 4-8-4 was the ultimate development of non-articulated steam power, and it became the standard modern American steam loco-

Northern Pacific 2600 was the first 4-8-4. The outside-cradle frame — the heavy frame members below the firebox and outboard of the trailing truck — was also used on Canadian National and Chicago & North Western 4-8-4s. Photo by R. V. Nixon.

motive. The only major western road that didn't buy the 4-8-4 was the Texas & Pacific; the major eastern trunk lines that didn't own 4-8-4s were freight carriers with fleets of high-drivered 2-8-4s; the Baltimore & Ohio, which was preoccupied with watertube fireboxes; and the Pennsylvania, which put its trust first in electrification and then in duplex-drive locomotives. Some railroads discovered the dual-service abilities of the 4-8-4 as dieselization progressed: Northerns that were out of a job in passenger service were assigned to freight trains and vice versa.

Many of the steam locomotives that have recently been active in excursion service are 4-8-4s: Southern Pacific 4449, Cotton Belt 819, Norfolk & Western 611, Santa Fe 3751, Spokane, Portland & Seattle 700, Chesapeake & Ohio 614, several Reading engines, and Union Pacific 844, which UP points out was never retired from service.

Other names:
Confederation (Canadian National)
Dixie (Nashville, Chattanooga & St. Louis)
Golden State, General Service (Southern Pacific)
Greenbrier (Chesapeake & Ohio)
Niagara (New York Central, National Railways of Mexico)
Pocono (Delaware, Lackawanna & Western)
Potomac (Western Maryland)
Wyoming (Lehigh Valley)
Total built: 1,115
First: Northern Pacific 2600, December 1926
Last: Norfolk & Western 613, 1950
Longest lived: Union Pacific 844, 1944 to the present
Last in regular service: National Railways of Mexico
Greatest number: Canadian National, 203 (including Grand Trunk Western)
Heaviest: Atchison, Topeka & Santa Fe 2900-2929, 510,150 pounds
Lightest: Toledo, Peoria & Western 80-85, 361,000 pounds
Recommended reading: *North American Steam Locomotives: The Northerns*, by Jack W. Farrell, published in 1975 by Pacific Fast Mail, P. O. Box 57, Edmonds, WA 98020 (LCC 74-33883)

The S-4s, Nos. 1350-1389, were NP's best-known Ten-Wheelers. They were built by Baldwin in 1902 as Vauclain compounds, and were simpled and superheated between 1918 and 1920. Like the other S classes they had 63" drivers. Initially assigned to passenger service in the Rockies, they later were all-purpose engines: branchline, pusher, local freight, local passenger.

The S-10s, Nos. 320-329, were quite light, 153,000 pounds, and had 57" drivers. Some sources say they were built for Russia but never shipped. Number 328 is in active service at the Minnesota Transportation Museum.

Just as NP was one of the first roads to adopt the Mikado, it turned to the Pacific for passenger trains in 1903 with the delivery of 20 Q-class Pacifics by Alco, Nos. 2080-2099. Their 69" drivers and 22" × 26" cylinders set the pattern for the next four classes of 4-6-2s; they weighed 205,000 pounds. Typical of the period, they had inboard-journal trailing trucks and inside valves; in contrast to the W-class Mikados they had long, thin straight boilers. They were followed by the Q-1 class, 48 engines numbered 2100-2147, delivered between 1904 and 1907. They had outside-frame trailing trucks and larger boilers with a noticeable taper, and weighed about 20,000 pounds more.

In 1906, partway through the construction of the Q-1s, NP bought two Cole compound Pacifics that it classed Q-2 and numbered 2175 and 2176. They had four cylinders, two inside and two outside. In 1909 they were converted to simple engines with 22" × 26" cylinders.

Baldwin delivered 23 Q-3 Pacifics in 1909. They had the same size cylinders and drivers as the Qs and Q-1s, but were built with Walschaerts valve gear and outside valves; weight was up to 237,000 pounds. Baldwin continued delivering Pacifics with 31 Q-4s, Nos. 2177-2207, differing only in cylinder size, 23" × 26". Schenectady delivered 17 Q-4s in 1910.

In 1920 NP was ready for heavier passenger power. In 1915 it had begun buying steel passenger cars, which weighed on average 10 tons more than wood cars. During World War I traffic increased, and train lengths grew to where the Q-4s couldn't keep up with schedules. NP began to draw up specifications: tractive effort, 42,000 pounds; drivers, 73"; cylinders, 26" × 28"; maximum axle load, 62,500 pounds. NP considered the USRA designs. The light Pacific was well within the axle load limit and considerably more powerful than the Q-4; the heavy Pacific had an axle load of 65,666 pounds. Both the USRA 4-8-2 designs were within the axle load limit, but they had 69" drivers and put out more tractive force than NP wanted. NP wanted a fast engine and didn't consider its grades particularly severe. Besides (and this was probably the crucial factor) a 4-8-2 would cost more than a 4-6-2. NP designed two Pacifics that met its specifications and weighed 296,000 and 314,000 pounds. It ordered 20 of the lighter design, then specified efficiency devices like feedwater heaters and stokers. The Q-5s arrived from Brooks with an axle load of 65,433 pounds and a total weight of 323,700 pounds — and, worse, a price tag of $70,916. Each. The Q-5s were more complicated than NP's previous Pacifics, with several previously untried appliances, and the combination of variable-lead valve gear and shop forces that knew only constant-lead valve gear caused NP to limit the locomotives to 55 mph. Eventually most of the bugs were worked out, and in 1923 the Q-6 Pacifics, Nos. 2246-2265, were delivered, nearly identical except for cast trailing trucks.

Within a few years passenger train length and weight had again increased to the point that the Q-5s and Q-6s were inadequate. Aggravating the problem was NP's switch to inexpensive strip-mined sub-bituminous coal. The price was one-fourth that of good eastern coal but the coal had only half the heat value. NP's Pacifics and Mikados didn't perform well on it. NP's mechanical department calculated that a 4-8-2 with 73" drivers would haul the trains, but Rosebud coal would require 115 square feet of grate area. (The USRA light 4-8-2 had 70.3 square feet.) A firebox that size called for a four-wheel trailing truck and created a new wheel arrangement, 4-8-4. It was called the Northern Pacific type, soon shortened to Northern.

Alco's Schenectady Works turned out 12 Northerns (class A, Nos. 2600-2611) in late 1926. They weighed 426,000 pounds, and the axle loading was 65,000, NP's limit, but NP was already rebuilding its bridges and trestles. At 225 pounds boiler pressure tractive effort was 61,600 pounds, and a booster on the rear axle of the trailing truck added 12,000 pounds for starting. Boiler pressure was later increased to 240 pounds, with a resulting 4,000-pound increase in tractive effort. Visually the most interesting feature of the engines was the outside frame cradle at the rear to permit a large ashpan (Chicago & North Western 4-8-4s and Central Vermont 2-10-4s had the same construction).

NP tested the new 4-8-4s on the road with a dynamometer car and came to two conclusions: The engines produced more horsepower when they were worked hard, and they were slightly under-boilered. They replaced double-headed Pacifics between Jamestown, N. D., and Glendive, Mont.; they reduced the need for helpers between Livingston and Missoula, Mont.; and they were able to run farther without change. After some initial difficulties with driver bearings that resulted in broken axles, the 4-8-4s worked well. Most were converted to oil burners, and all had their boosters removed in the late 1940s.

The A-1 class contained a single locomotive, formerly Timken demonstrator No. 1111, the first steam locomotive built with roller bearings on all axles. NP was not especially impressed with the 4-8-4's performance on test runs (it wasn't set up to burn low-grade coal), but its owners had planned to use it for only two years, and that period expired while the engine was on NP rails. Additionally, it suffered crown sheet damage while working on NP. Timken didn't want to take back an unserviceable locomotive, and NP didn't want to repair Timken's locomotive. NP bought it in 1933 (probably less than enthusiastically) and found it durable and inexpensive to operate. It remained in service until 1955, then made a ceremonial last run in 1957 before being scrapped. More significant than its service on NP was the role it played in persuading railroads that roller bearings were practical.

In 1933 NP realized it needed more 4-8-4s. It specified 77" drivers and, because of its experience with the Timken engine, roller bearings on all axles. Baldwin won the bid and delivered ten A-2s, Nos. 2650-2659, in late 1934 and early 1935. They had the same size fireboxes as the A class and 28" × 31" cylinders instead of the A's 28" × 30". They were NP's first locomotives with semi-Vanderbilt tenders — the lower part of the tank was cylindrical and the upper part rectangular. The A-2s were initially assigned to passenger service and later worked on freight trains. Three groups of nearly identical 4-8-4s followed, all from Baldwin: A-3s 2660-2667 in 1938, A-4s 2670-2677 in 1941, and A-5s 2680-1689 in 1943. The A-4s and A-5s had vestibule cabs and pedestal tenders, and the A-4s had solid pilots. Because of wartime restrictions on the production of passenger engines, the A-5s were built for and assigned to freight service.

In 1943 the Baldwin 4-8-4s (and also the Alco 4-6-6-4s) began to develop boiler leaks owing to three factors: high boiler pressure (260 pounds), riveted construction, and alloy steels that became brittle over time. The road reboilered six 4-8-4s before deciding that impending dieselization would solve the problem and as a stopgap reduced the boiler pressure of the 4-8-4s.

Switchers

Northern Pacific's most numerous switchers were the 96 0-6-0s of the L-9 class, built between 1906 and 1910 by Manchester, Baldwin, Dickson, and Pittsburgh. The ten L-10s built by Schenectady in 1912 had the same 51" drivers, 20" × 26" cylinders, and Stephenson valve gear, but outside piston valves instead of slide valves. In addition to a group of 0-8-0s rebuilt from Consolidations — all but one retired before 1934 — NP had four USRA 0-8-0s built in 1919 and 20 copies built in 1920, all from Brooks.

Historical and technical society: Northern Pacific Railway Historical Association, c/o Richard Loops, 550 Amy Lane, Idaho Falls, ID 83406

Recommended reading: *Northern Pacific Supersteam Era 1925-1945*, by Robert L. Frey and Lorenz Schrenk, published in 1985 by Golden West Books, P. O. Box 80250, San Marino, CA 91108 (ISBN 0-97095-092-4)

Published rosters:
Railroad Magazine: May 1939, page 114, and June 1939, page 78; May 1947, page 118; December 1956, page 6
Trains Magazine, February 1946, page 26

NP STEAM LOCOMOTIVES BUILT SINCE 1900

Type	Class	Numbers	Qty	Builder	Built	Notes
0-6-0	L-6	900-919	20	Schenectady	1901	
0-6-0	L-7	1020-1035	15	BLW, Schen	1902-1903	
0-6-0	L-9	1040-1135	96		1906-1910	
				Built by Manchester, Baldwin, Dickson, and Pittsburgh		
0-6-0	L-10	1160-1169	10	Schenectady	1912	
0-8-0	G	1151-1159	9	Richmond	1905	Rebuilt from 2-8-0s
0-8-0	G-1	1170-1173	4	Brooks	1919	USRA
0-8-0	G-2	1174-1193	20	Brooks	1920	
2-6-2	T	2300-2449	150	Brooks	1906-1907	
2-8-0	F-5	45, 46	2	Schenectady	1900	Ex-SLS&E
2-8-0	Y-1	17-29	13	Schenectady	1900	
2-8-0	Y-2	1250-1279	30	Schenectady	1901-1902	
2-8-0	Y-3	1200-1213	14	Schenectady	1901	
2-8-0	Y-4	1280-1293	14	Schenectady	1903	
2-8-0	Y-5	1214-1223	10	Schenectady	1903	
2-8-2	W	1500-1659	160	Brooks	1904-1907	
2-8-2	W-1	1660-1699	40	Schenectady	1910	
2-8-2	W-2	1900-1919	20	Brooks	1905	Rebuilt from compounds
2-8-2	W-3	1700-1834	135	Brooks	1913-1920	
2-8-2	W-4	2500-2505	6	Brooks	1918, 1919	
				Rebuilt from class T at Brainerd in 1909		
2-8-2	W-5	1835-1859	25	Schenectady	1923	
2-6-6-2	Z	3000-3015	16	Baldwin	1907	
2-6-6-2	Z-1	3100-3105	6	Baldwin	1910	
2-8-8-2	Z-2	4000-4004	5	Baldwin	1910	
2-8-8-2	Z-3	4005-4025	21	Schen, Brks	1913-1920	
2-8-8-2	Z-4	4500-4503	4	Richmond	1923	
2-8-8-4	Z-5	5000	1	Schenectady	1928	
2-8-8-4	Z-5	5001-5011	11	Baldwin	1930	
4-4-2	N-1	603-605	3	Baldwin	1909	
4-6-0	P-1	207-218, 220, 226-236	24	Alco	1898-1901	
4-6-0	P-2	240-249	10	Alco	1900-1902	
4-6-0	P-3	1400-1419	20	Alco	1901-1902	
4-6-0	S-2	104-133	30	Schenectady	1900	
4-6-0	S-3	1300-1323	24	Alco	1901-1902	
4-6-0	S-4	1350-1389	40	Baldwin	1902	
4-6-0	S-10	320-329	10	Rogers	1907	

Type	Class	Numbers	Qty	Builder	Built	Notes	Type	Class	Numbers	Qty	Builder	Built	Notes
4-6-2	Q	2080-2099	20	Schenectady	1903		4-8-4	A-1	2626	1	Schenectady	1930	Ex-Timken 1111
4-6-2	Q-1	2100-2147	48	Schenectady	1904-1907		4-8-4	A-2	2650-2659	10	Baldwin	1934-1935	
4-6-2	Q-2	2175, 2176	2	Alco	1906		4-8-4	A-3	2660-2667	8	Baldwin	1938	
4-6-2	Q-3	2148-2170	23	Baldwin	1909		4-8-4	A-4	2670-2677	8	Baldwin	1941	
4-6-2	Q-4	2177-2224	48	BLW, Schen	1909-1910		4-8-4	A-5	2680-2689	10	Baldwin	1943	
4-6-2	Q-5	2226-2245	20	Brooks	1920		4-6-6-4	Z-6	5100-5120	21	Schenectady	1936-1937	
4-6-2	Q-6	2246-2265	20	Schenectady	1923		4-6-6-4	Z-7	5121-5126	6	Schenectady	1941	
4-8-4	A	2600-2611	12	Schenectady	1926		4-6-6-4	Z-8	5130-5149	20	Schenectady	1943-1944	

PENNSYLVANIA RAILROAD

In the first four decades of the 20th century the Pennsylvania Railroad was the country's top railroad in revenue, track miles, and passenger counts. It was an enormous transportation factory, and its plant covered the Middle Atlantic states from New York City to Washington, D. C. Pennsy's lines went practically everywhere in its home state except the anthracite-mining region in the northeast corner; west of Pennsylvania its lines reached to Cincinnati, Louisville, St. Louis, Peoria, Chicago, Mackinaw City, Detroit, and Cleveland. The map was essentially an hourglass with two waists — Pittsburgh and Harrisburg — and a bulge between. Pennsy was all but fully grown by 1900, and its major construction projects after the turn of the century were a terminal in New York City — from which steam locomotives were excluded — and electrification of the routes from New York to Washington and from Philadelphia to Harrisburg.

In 1869 the lines west of Pittsburgh were brought under a new organization, the Pennsylvania Company, and were operated more or less independently until the 1920s. The independence of Lines West extended to locomotives, with types, classes, and detail variations (such as centered headlights, vertical-bar pilots, and even radial-stay fireboxes) not found east of Pittsburgh.

PRR advertised itself as The Standard Railroad of the World. Its standardization was intramural — it deviated from common North American practice in items like Belpaire fireboxes, red paint on its passenger cars, and position-light signals. In the first decade of the 20th century it spurned the compounds and the Mallets that other roads were buying; later it adopted only slowly — if at all — efficiency devices such as feedwater heaters, boosters, and mechanical stokers.

Standardization was manifest in PRR's locomotive roster. Once it found locomotives it liked, it bought and built them by the hundreds and used them systemwide. In contrast to Chesapeake & Ohio, which pulled passenger trains with a multiplicity of wheel arrangements, and New York Central, which used several classes of Pacifics, Hudsons, 4-8-2s, and 4-8-4s on mainline passenger trains, Pennsy had 425 K4-class Pacifics, which it doubleheaded as necessary. About the time the Decapod experienced a minor renaissance as a lightfooted freight engine, Pennsy turned the other way and created an absolute hippopotamus that would have crushed most other railroads' rail to powder.

Between 1910 and 1923 PRR developed a stable of five locomotive types: the E6 Atlantic, K4 Pacific, L1 Mikado, I1 Decapod, and M1 Mountain. It bought great quantities of Mikes and Decapods just before World War I; K4s were added to the roster steadily from 1917 to 1928. The M1 was designed and one was built in 1923; they were built in quantity in 1926 and 1930. That was as far as any of those types went. There was no M2, no I2. The L2 class was a group of USRA light Mikes that

Pennsy's first modern Consolidations were the H6 class. Number 1 is an H6sb, built by Baldwin in 1906.

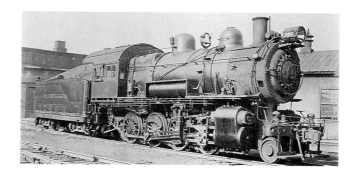

PRR all but spurned, and the two K5s were experimental. The three-cylinder running gears and four-wheel trailing trucks that were adopted by other roads were ignored at PRR's Philadelphia headquarters.

One reason for this was that PRR had turned its attention from steam to electricity. In the late 1920s and early 1930s it developed several standard electric locomotives (which ranged from mediocre to scrapped-when-half-built) before copying a New Haven engine to create the GG1. During the Depression PRR electrified its New York-Washington main line, then extended wires to Harrisburg, Pa., creating a surplus of steam locomotives. PRR's intention to continue the electrification over the Alleghenies to Pittsburgh put its steam locomotive development on hold.

In the late 1930s and early 40s a sudden burst of creativity spawned several duplex-drive designs and a turbine locomotive; when traffic surged during World War II, Pennsy's quickest route to new freight locomotives was to copy Chesapeake & Ohio's 2-10-4. After the war it bought quantities of duplex-drive freight engines (good) and passenger engines (terrible).

Pennsy built more of its own locomotives than any other railroad. Between 1866 and 1904 Altoona Machine Shop built 2,289 locomotives, and from 1891 to 1946 the road's Juniata Works, also at Altoona, Pa., built 4,584 — 6,873 in all. (Lima, smallest of the Big Three, built about 7,500 locomotives.) The shop complex at Altoona included a stationary test plant, one of two or three in the U. S., where locomotive performance could be evaluated under controlled conditions. When Pennsy bought locomotives it usually bought them from Baldwin, which was located in the road's home town, Philadelphia.

Pennsy's classification system was logical, and it applied to electrics as well as steam — the B1 was a six-wheel boxcab switcher, and the L6 was a boxcab freighter with a 1-D-1 wheel arrangement. It would have worked the other way, too: Had Pennsy bought 4-8-4s, the letter R

L1 Mikado No. 1372 (Baldwin, 1918) was the standard road freight engine on the Pennsylvania. PRR was among the first roads to use a cast trailing truck, and for years it favored blind drivers (without flanges) on the inner axles. Photo by W. R. Osborne.

had already been broken in and warmed up by 2-D-2 electric No. 4999. The few subclasses were indicated with lowercase letters; a lowercase s indicating superheating was dropped when superheating became standard.

Locomotive numbers were another matter. In the late 19th century the road assigned blocks of numbers to subsidiary railroads, with high-

4-4-2 — ATLANTIC

It is uncertain just what the first Atlantic was. In 1887 the New York, Providence & Boston added a trailing axle to spread the weight of a 4-4-0 that had proved too heavy for bridges, and Hinkley built an experimental locomotive, the *A. G. Darwin*, with a center cab and a double firebox. The NYP&B engine wasn't an Atlantic; *Darwin* was. Santa Fe bought a similar engine soon afterward.

In 1893 Baldwin Locomotive Works introduced the 2-4-2, the Columbia type. It had high drivers and a wide firebox supported by a rigid trailing axle; it was intended for fast passenger service despite its two-wheel lead truck. The Atlantic Coast Line was in the market for a locomotive with more steaming capacity than its 4-4-0s, and thought the large firebox of the Columbia was the answer. In 1894 Baldwin designed a conventional-cab 4-4-2 for ACL and named it for the railroad. The four-wheel lead truck gave stability at speed and allowed a longer, better-steaming boiler than the 2-4-2; the 72" drivers were a compromise between the 84¼" drivers of the Baldwin exhibition engine and the 57" to 66" drivers of ACL's 4-4-0s. ACL bought 10 Atlantics between 1894 and 1900 (plus a pair of 2-4-2s, just to test the type) but soon decided they were too light. ACL left its name on the type but turned to Ten-Wheelers for mainline duties.

Several other railroads bought Atlantics, either conventional-cab machines with narrow fireboxes or anthracite-burning Camelbacks. The conventional engines were seen as a modest expansion of the 4-4-0, and the Camelbacks were a way to combine high drivers, generally 80" or more, and a wide Wootten firebox. In 1900 Schenectady built the first of 91 Chicago & North Western Atlantics with a bituminous-burning firebox supported by a nonswiveling trailing axle behind the drivers. The type quickly achieved widespread popularity for fast passenger trains.

Another advance in technology ended the development of the Atlantic type — the all-steel passenger car, which typically weighed

Chicago & North Western 1314 was a member of the first group of Atlantics built with a wide bituminous-burning firebox behind the drivers. Collection of John S. Kamacher.

10 to 20 tons more than a wood car (but was longer and had a greater capacity). Trains soon outgrew the Atlantic, and the type was relegated to short, light trains.

The Pennsylvania Railroad, however, developed the Atlantic further about the time most railroads were building up fleets of Pacifics. The E6 turned out to be the equivalent of many roads' light Pacifics, but its success in the steel-car era perhaps can be measured by comparing the counts — 83 E6 Atlantics against 425 K4 Pacifics.

The type experienced a renaissance in the late 1930s when Milwaukee Road bought four enormous streamlined Atlantics for its new *Hiawatha* trains. A few other railroads modernized Atlantics for short, fast trains.

Southern Pacific 3000 was rebuilt in 1927 by the road's Sacramento shops from an earlier A-3 class Atlantic. Improvements included a Worthington BL feedwater heater and a booster-equipped cast trailing truck. In 1946 No. 3000 was dolled up with red and orange paint on its cab and tender to pull the *Sacramento Daylight*, a Sacramento-Lathrop, California, connection to the *San Joaquin Daylight*. Photo by Fred Matthews.

Other names: Chautauqua (applied to Brooks-built locomotives of which *Railroad Gazette* said, "having the general characteristics of the Atlantic type"), Milwaukee (the streamlined *Hiawatha* engines)
Last and heaviest: Milwaukee Road No. 4, 1937, 290,000 pounds
Longest lived: Santa Fe 1550 was built in 1905 and scrapped in December 1953
Last in service: Santa Fe 1473, 1487, 1488, and 1550 were scrapped in 1953
Greatest number: Santa Fe, 178

er numbers assigned to the western parts of the system. That system continued until 1920, but as the locomotive fleet grew — in the mid-1920s PRR had nearly 7,500 locomotives — it began to push against the limits of 4-digit numbers. PRR had to reassign numbers of retired engines to new engines almost immediately. After 1924 blocks of numbers were assigned to new groups of engines.

From a purely logical standpoint, blocks of numbers are redundant if there is a letter classification system; conversely, a number of railroads relied on blocks of numbers to classify their locomotives. The presence of both satisfies a human desire for order. In the roster here there isn't space to give individual numbers of each engine. For a complete listing of all Pennsy locomotives built after 1906, see *Keystone Steam & Electric*, cited below.

In the late 1940s PRR had a lot of old, worn-out locomotives and some undependable new ones. It was reluctant to dieselize, then did so in a rush, acquiring more than a few diesels that were about as reliable as its T1s. By 1956 steam was concentrated in a few areas; the last major passenger assignment for steam was commuter service on the New York & Long Branch Railroad in New Jersey. The elimination of steam was officially complete on November 30, 1957, but the year-end report to the Interstate Commerce Commission included 319 steam locomotives — and at the end of 1958 there were still 21 steam locomotives on the roster.

Freight locomotives

By the turn of the century PRR had progressed beyond the 2-6-0 to the 2-8-0. The first modern Consolidation was the H6, 22" × 28" cylinders and 56" drivers, first built in 1899. In 1901 the design was changed to include a wide firebox over the rear drivers, and in 1905 there was another change to piston valves and Walschaerts valve gear. Mass production of the type ended in 1908, but ten more were built between 1909 and 1913. Most of the nearly 2,000 built were scrapped by the mid-1930s, but more than 100 superheated engines in the H6sa and H6sb classes stayed in service through the 1940s on branches where their 200,000 pounds was all the light rail could handle.

The I1 Decapods were the equivalent of two H8 Consolidations on coal and ore trains. Large as they were, they were outweighed by the 2-10-0s of Lehigh & New England. Photo by Richard J. Cook.

The first H8 2-8-0s were built in 1907. They were larger than their predecessors, with 24" × 28" cylinders and 62" drivers, and about 42,000 pounds heavier. Construction of the class continued until 1913; later members were built with superheaters. Most of the early H-8s received superheaters later, and at the same time many were fitted with larger cylinders and reclassed H9 or H10. Cylinder size was the principal difference among the H8, H9, and H10 classes: 25" × 28" for the H9, built for Lines East, and 26" × 28" for the H10, built for Lines West. The three classes totaled 1,233 engines.

Pennsy built and tested a Mikado in 1914. It had 62" drivers, 27" × 30" cylinders, and weighed 320,700 pounds, about the size of the later USRA heavy Mike. It had the same boiler as the K4s Pacific, introduced that same year, and a number of smaller parts were interchangeable between the two classes. Between 1914 and 1919 Altoona and Baldwin built a total of 574 L1s. They went to work in the Central Region, roughly western Pennsylvania and eastern Ohio, but were soon displaced to the Eastern Region (everything east of Altoona and Renovo, Pa.) by I1 Decapods.

Meanwhile, coal and ore trains were still moving behind double-headed 2-8-0s. PRR designed an enormous 2-10-0, with 30½" × 32" cylinders, 62" drivers, 90,000 pounds tractive force (just about twice that of the H8), and total weight of 386,100 pounds. Juniata built one I1 in 1916, and the road tested it thoroughly. Juniata outshopped 122 of the type in 1918 and 1919, and Baldwin built 475 in 1922 and 1923. The Baldwin engines had Worthington BL feedwater heaters, unusual for Pennsy — not the BL in particular but feedwater heaters in general. Most of the I1s were assigned to the Central Region, displacing L1 Mikes.

Lines West had its own idea about heavy freight power: the N1-class 2-10-2. It had an enormous firebox (79.9 square feet of grate) supported by a trailing truck that appeared not only inadequate but set too close to the drivers. Drivers were the same size as the I1, cylinders a half inch smaller, and weight 435,000 pounds. In 1918 and 1919 Brooks built 35 and Baldwin 25. At the same time the USRA assigned 130 heavy 2-10-2s, class N2, to Lines West. They had the same size cylinders as the N1s, drivers an inch larger, and weighed 55,000 pounds less. After four years of service PRR replaced their conventional radial-stay fireboxes with Belpaires.

The USRA also assigned 38 light 2-8-2s to PRR in 1919. All but five were soon transferred to Missouri Pacific and St. Louis-San Francisco; those remaining were classed L2s and put to work on Pennsy's Grand Rapids & Indiana subsidiary.

Pennsy's last conventional freight locomotive was the M1 4-8-2 of 1923. It was based on the I1 — the same boiler — and many parts were interchangeable. It had 27" × 30" cylinders and 72" drivers, and weighed 385,000 pounds. Following the road's usual practice, Juniata built one which was tested thoroughly. Early modifications were a larger tender — the first one had a low-side tender appropriate for an E6 Atlantic — and mechanical stoker. Baldwin and Lima delivered a total of 200 M1s in 1926, and Baldwin, Juniata, and Lima built 100 M1as in 1930. Designed as a dual-service engine, some M1s were striped and painted for passenger service, but the New York-Washington electrification

Standard mainline fast freight power in the 1930s was the M1 4-8-2. Many of the class were fitted with 16-wheel long-distance tenders. Photo by John P. Ahrens.

freed great numbers of Pacifics, which couldn't be used on freight but could be doubleheaded on passenger trains to release the Mountain types for freight.

World War II hit Pennsy with an enormous traffic surge and no modern freight power. In May 1942 Juniata outshopped a single duplex-drive 4-6-4-4, class Q1. It wasn't a success, and the designers went back to the drawing board. The need for freight locomotives was still there, and the War Production Board had placed a moratorium on new designs. PRR borrowed a Chesapeake & Ohio 2-10-4, made a few minor changes (70" drivers instead of 69", solid drop-coupler pilot, and keystone-shaped number plate), and built 125 J1s at Altoona between 1942 and 1944.

A new duplex-drive design, the Q2 4-4-6-4, was ready in 1944. Tests of the prototype were promising, and PRR quickly canceled an order to Lima for 25 more 2-10-4s and built 25 Q2s at Altoona. Like the Q1, the two sets of cylinders had different diameters and strokes, but both were normally oriented. The Q2s were the most powerful ten-drivered locomotives ever built. They weighed about 40,000 pounds more than the J1s and developed about 5,000 pounds more tractive force, but they were complex. All the Q2s were retired before any of the J1s were.

Passenger locomotives

Pennsy continued to build 4-4-0s until 1910; it created the best of the conventional Atlantics (Milwaukee's *Hiawatha* Atlantics were unconventional); and it was slow to adopt the Pacific. In 1907 Alco's Pittsburgh Works delivered an experimental 4-6-2, class K28, with 24" × 26" cylinders and 80" drivers, and weighing 273,600 pounds. Pennsy used the design as the basis for the Lines East K1 Pacific (none built) and the Lines West K2. Between 1910 and 1913 PRR acquired 227 K2s. Most were built superheated; those that weren't were soon retrofitted with superheaters. In 1913 Baldwin delivered to Lines West 30 K3 Pacifics, somewhat larger and heavier and equipped with mechanical stokers (which Pennsy would adopt only reluctantly years later).

The K2 wasn't quite what Pennsy had in mind. To take advantage of its heavy rail and good roadbed it returned to the Atlantic type in 1910, creating the E6, an engine with 22" × 26" cylinders, 80" drivers, and a weight of 231,500 pounds — in effect, a middle-weight Pacific with only two sets of drivers. The boiler was almost identical to the H8 Consolidation, and superheating allowed an increase in cylinder diameter to 23½", bringing tractive effort up to 31,275 pounds. Juniata built two in 1912 and 80 in 1914, most of them for New York-Philadelphia-Washington service.

In 1911 Alco delivered another experimental Pacific, class K29, with 27" × 28" cylinders and 80" drivers, weighing 317,000 pounds. (At some point Alco must have realized that even if it built an engine PRR would buy a thousand of, Baldwin and Juniata would split the order.) Pennsy combined cylinders, drivers, and overall size of the K29, various features of the E6, and the boiler of the L1s Mikado to create a Pacific it classed K4s. It tested the new engine for three years, then between 1917 and 1924 built 324 of them at Altoona. Passenger traffic increased during the 1920s, and trains grew longer. Doubleheaded K4s became standard practice. While other railroads turned to 4-8-2s, 4-6-4s, and 4-8-2s, in 1927 and 1928 PRR ordered 100 more K4s, 25 from Juniata

DUPLEX-DRIVE LOCOMOTIVES

In the mid-1920s the steam locomotive builders began to bang up against the boundaries of what could be achieved with current materials and technology. Alco pushed three-cylinder locomotives, and Lima developed the Super-Power concept, the most visible aspect of which was the four-wheel trailing truck. Baldwin didn't develop such a specialty until the early 1930s, when it began

advocating duplex, or divided, drive. Ten-coupled locomotives had already reached the practical limits of cylinder and valve sizes, piston thrust, and machinery weight, and Ralph Johnson, Baldwin's chief engineer, foresaw that 4-8-4s soon would. He proposed splitting the 4-8-4 into a nonarticulated 4-4-4-4.

The idea wasn't entirely new. In 1932 the Paris-Lyon-Mediterranée Railway in France received 10 divided-drive compound 2-10-2s. High-pressure cylinders between the second and third axles drove the rear three axles, and low-pressure cylinders in the usual location drove the front two, creating essentially a nonarticulated Mallet — except for a pair of rods inside the frames that connected the second and third driving axles. The locomotives remained in service into the early 1950s.

The duplex layout represented an engineering compromise. Main and side rods could be lighter, since they had to transmit only half the power, and easier to counterbalance; cylinders could be smaller and less subject to the limits imposed by valve size. The disadvantage of a second complete set of moving parts was offset to some extent by the reduced stress on those parts. The other disadvantage was a longer wheelbase: Inserting a set of cylinders between two pairs of drivers added more than four feet to the driving wheelbase, and 4-8-4s already relied on lateral motion devices on least one axle to reduce the rigid wheelbase.

But the worst problem was the independence of the two sets of running gear. When they were in phase (running in unison), they created a surging, fore-and-aft motion in the train. Minor variations in adhesion, caused by something as trivial as the locomotive entering a curve, caused one unit to slip, throwing the load on the

Pennsylvania 6130 was the first of its duplex-drive freight locomotives. Streamlining, 77" drivers, and cylinders alongside the ashpan were among the factors that led to its downfall. The Q2, exemplified by the prototype, No. 6131, can be considered the most successful — or least unsuccessful — of the duplex-drive locomotives. Mechanical difficulties aside, they were intriguing machines. PRR photos.

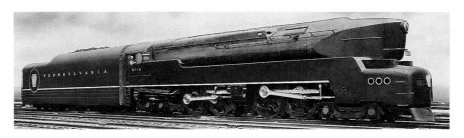

Pennsylvania Railroad's Baldwin-built T1 prototypes of 1942 had a long prow, deep skirting, and portholes — might this be where Buick got the idea? PRR photo.

other, then regain adhesion — among the results were rough handling of the train and radical changes in draft that lifted the fire off the grates. Coupling the two units would have alleviated the problem, but at a cost of even more machinery.

Baldwin got nowhere with its proposals in the early 1930s. Baltimore & Ohio turned down such a proposal, then reconsidered and built its own duplex drive locomotive, No. 5600, in 1937. Both sets of cylinders were the same size, 18" × 26", and the rear cylinders were mounted backwards, under the outer edge of the firebox and ahead of the trailing truck. During testing B&O found that the two sets of drivers gradually got in step with each other — ideally they should be 45 degrees out of phase — so the road turned the tires of one set down from 76" to 75", which, assuming no slipping, made the two sets of drivers go in and out of phase with each other three or four times a mile. The complexities of No. 5600's watertube firebox and duplex drive ensured that the shop forces would become much better acquainted with the locomotive than B&O's engineers and firemen. It was taken out of service in 1943 and scrapped in 1950.

The next duplex drive was Pennsylvania Railroad 6100, a 6-4-4-6 built in the road's shop at Altoona. It spent its first two years on display at the New York World's Fair of 1939 and 1940 looking powerful and fast — and indeed it was, but 6100 proved too long for most of Pennsy's turntables and curves. PRR assigned the loco-

motive to the straight, flat racetrack between Chicago and Crestline, Ohio (just west of Mansfield). It was taken out of service in 1944 and scrapped in 1949.

Baldwin was on the verge of building a demonstrator when Pennsy ordered two 4-4-4-4s, class T1. They were delivered in the spring of 1942, futuristically streamlined and impressive in everything but boiler capacity and grate area.

Also in 1942 Altoona built a duplex-drive freight locomotive, a 77"-drivered 4-6-4-4, class Q1. Like the B&O duplex-drive engine, it had its rear cylinders tucked under the outside edges of the firebox. The two sets of cylinders were of different diameters (to be expected, since one set drove six wheels and the other, four) and of different strokes, 28" in the front and 26" in the rear. It was not a success. Altoona decided to try again and produced a single Q2, a 4-4-6-4, with 69" drivers and cylinders arranged conventionally, though still of different diameter and stroke. The Q2 was successful enough that Pennsy got War Production Board approval to build 25 more in 1944 and 1945. Although the Q2s were the most successful duplex-drive locomotives, diesels sent most of them to storage by 1949 — the task of filling in during peak traffic periods fell to the simpler, easier-to-maintain J1 2-10-4s and M1 4-8-2s.

Encouraged by the success of the Q2, Pennsy continued to pursue the duplex drive concept and in 1945 and 1946 received 25 more 4-4-4-4s from Baldwin and 25 from its own Altoona shops.

The Pennsy re-equipped. T1 5547 with Walschaerts valve gear, making it almost the duplex-drive machine Baldwin proposed in 1939 — but it was a futile gesture. PRR photo.

In service the T1s were less than satisfactory. They were slippery engines, and their poppet valves were troublesome (Baldwin's original proposal included Walschaerts gear and piston valves). Paradoxically streamlining made them dirty engines — smoke tended to swirl around the cab and the train, and their long rigid wheelbase proved incompatible with the sharp curve at the west end of Pennsy's station in Pittsburgh. Most of the T1s were stored by the end of 1949; all were scrapped by the end of 1953.

Eighty-one duplex-drive locomotives were built for North American service, and 80 of them wore the Pennsylvania Railroad keystone. They were an expensive blunder, and they may well have sparked PRR's decision to dieselize. Ultimately what made North American duplex-drive locomotives simply an experiment was that the anticipated difficulties with the 4-8-4 didn't occur.

Other names: None of the duplex-drive wheel arrangements had names.

First, lightest, and longest-lived: Baltimore & Ohio 4-4-4-4 No. 5600, built in 1937, 391,500 pounds, retired in 1943, scrapped in 1950

Last, heaviest, and last in service: Pennsylvania Q2, 619,100 pounds (No. 6199 was built in June 1945; 6186-6195 were retired in January 1956)

Greatest number: Pennsylvania Railroad T1 (52)

Recommended reading: "Duplex-drives," by David P. Morgan, in *Trains Magazine*, November 1959, pages 16-25

and 75 from Baldwin — still hand-fired and still doubleheaded.

In the 1920s PRR needed all the mainline passenger power it had, so it was unable to demote older power to suburban service. It developed a Ten-Wheeler for such service, combining the E6 boiler and 68" drivers. The G5s were quite successful. Pennsy built 90 of its own, and 31 for subsidiary Long Island Rail Road.

Pennsy pushed the Pacific a little further. In 1929 Juniata and Baldwin each built a heavy Pacific with M1-size cylinders. The Baldwin engine had Caprotti poppet valves (removed in 1937), and both had Worthington feedwater heaters and PRR standard-issue coal shovels. They had about 10,000 pounds more tractive effort and 6,000 pounds more weight on the drivers than the K4s, making them slippery engines. They weren't enough better than the K4 to justify duplication, and soon the Depression made new power unnecessary.

Over the years the K4s received almost every imaginable modification: disk drivers, smoke lifters, streamlining, and solid drop-coupler pilots. In later years the headlight and the generator (just ahead of the stack) traded places, and for a minor change it made a major difference (negative) in appearance.

PRR experienced a belated resurgence of interest in large passenger locomotives in the early 1940s — the duplex-drive S1 and T1, described in the sidebar here and the S2 turbine, described on page 000.

Switchers

There were two major classes of 0-6-0s, the B6, which weighed 170,000 to 180,000 pounds; the B8, which weighed about 140,000; and the Lines West B29, lighter still at 135,000 pounds. In addition, the USRA allotted 30 0-6-0s to PRR.

Those were the ordinary switchers. There were two classes of 0-4-0s designed for the street trackage and sharp curves of eastern cities, the A4, built between 1906 and 1913, and the A5, built from 1916 to 1924. The A5 was a thoroughly modern engine, with piston valves and power reverse, and at 131,750 pounds it was among the heaviest 0-4-0s.

In the mid-1920s PRR developed an 0-8-0 and built 90 of them. The C1s had 27" × 30" cylinders and 56" drivers, weighed 278,000 pounds,

Pennsy didn't have a light Pacific — its powerful E6 Atlantic did the same jobs. Photo by Walter Krawiec.

K4 5495 was built at Altoona in 1928, among the last of the class built. For its builder photos PRR painted windows and lamp lenses white. PRR photo.

and developed a tractive effort of 78,107 pounds. By comparison, the USRA 0-8-0 had 25" × 28" cylinders and 51" drivers, weighed 214,000 pounds, and had a tractive effort of 51,000 pounds. Pennsy's C1s switchers were large and not well liked by those who ran and maintained them.

Articulateds

Pennsy made only a few excursions into the articulated locomotive field; most were experimental, one-of-a-kind engines. In 1911 Schenectady built a single 2-8-8-2, class HH1s, that went into pusher service near Pittsburgh. In 1912 Baldwin delivered a single 0-8-8-0, classed CC1, designed to replace pairs of 2-8-0s in pusher service. It wasn't successful enough to warrant repeating. In 1919 Juniata built a single-expansion 2-8-8-0, class HC1s. It too was relegated to pusher service and was never duplicated.

The most successful of Pennsy's own articulateds were ten 0-8-8-0s, class CC2, built by Baldwin in 1919 for Lines West pusher and hump service. All ten eventually were stationed at Columbus, Ohio.

In 1943 PRR bought six USRA 2-8-8-2s from Norfolk & Western to use between Hagerstown, Md., and Harrisburg, Pa. N&W classed them Y3; PRR, HH1, reusing the classification of its first articulated. After the war they went to Columbus to join the CC2s.

Historical and technical society: Pennsylvania Railroad Technical & Historical Society, P. O. Box 389, Upper Darby, PA 19082

Recommended reading:

Keystone Steam & Electric, by William D. Edson, published in 1974 by Wayner Publications, Box 871, Ansonia Station, New York, New York 10023

Apex of the Atlantics, by Frederick Westing, published in 1963 by Kalmbach Publishing Co., P. O. Box 1612, Waukesha, WI 53187

Published rosters: Railroad Magazine: July 1941, page 50, August 1941, page 50, September 1941, page 89, October 1941, page 60, and November 1941, page 77; December 1954, page 22; August 1957, page 36

PRR STEAM LOCOMOTIVES BUILT SINCE 1906

Type	Class	Numbers	Qty	Builder	Built	Retired	Notes
0-4-0	A4	50…6601	64	PRR	1906-1913	1927-1936	
0-4-0	A5s	76…4039	47	PRR	1916-1924	1930-1956	
0-6-0	—	3687, 3688	2	Baldwin	1907, 1913	1925, 1926	
							Ex-Cornwall & Lebanon
0-6-0	—	5411	1	Baldwin	1912	1928	
							Ex-Baltimore & Sparrows Point
0-6-0	B6	7045…9354	49	PRR, BLW, Lima	1910-1913	1948-1952	
0-6-0	B6sa	3…6227	55	PRR	1913-1914	1949-1953	
0-6-0	B6sb	31…6400	238	PRR	1916-1926	1949-1959	
0-6-0	B8	15…9569	247	PRR, Lima	-1913	1929-1956	
0-6-0	B23	8777-8782	6	Schenectady		1926-1934	
0-6-0	B28s	7007-9405	30	Pitt, Cke, Schen	1918-1919	1948-1953	USRA
0-6-0	B29	7028…9786	135	Pitt, Rich, Lima	-1913	1926-1930	
0-8-0	C1	6550-6639	90	PRR	1925, 1927	1948-1953	
0-8-8-0	CC1s	3397	1	Baldwin	1912	1931	
0-8-8-0	CC2s	7250…9359	10	Baldwin	1919	1947-1949	
2-6-0	F27s	8833-8843	11	Schen	1907	1926-1928	
2-8-0	H6b	1…9988	148	Pitt, PRR, BLW	1907-1913	1928-1953	
2-8-0	H8	3193-3217	25	PRR	1907	1933-1956	
2-8-0	H8a	7193…9886	117	PRR, Pitt, BLW	1907-1911	1937-1956	
2-8-0	H8b	21…3577	352	PRR, Baldwin	1908-1913	1934-1957	
2-8-0	H8c	7021-9989	192	Pitt, Brks, PRR	1910-1913	1938-1957	
2-8-0	H9s	24…5174	274	Baldwin, PRR	1913-1914	1947-1958	
2-8-0	H9s	7…9999	312			Converted from H8	
2-8-0	H10s	7001…9895	273	Pittsburgh, Brooks, Baldwin, Lima	1913-1916	-1960	
2-8-0	H10s	6073…9999	200			Converted from H8	
2-8-0	H34a	9602-9605	4	Pittsburgh	1908	1925-1926	
2-8-0	H34b	9616-9619	4	Pittsburgh	1910	1925-1926	
2-8-2	L1s	2…9866	574	PRR, Baldwin	1914-1919	1941-1959	
2-8-2	L2s	9627-9631	5	Schenectady	1919	1948	USRA light
2-10-0	I1	790	1	PRR	1916	1956	
2-10-0	I1	30…6340	122	PRR	1918-1919	1949-1959	
2-10-0	I1	4225-4699	475	Baldwin	1922-1923	1949-1960	
2-10-2	N1s	7008…9866	60	Brooks, Baldwin	1919	1947-1950	
2-10-2	N2s	7036…9859	130	Brooks, Baldwin	1919	1948-1953	
							USRA heavy
2-10-4	J1	6150-6174	25	PRR	1943-1944	1957-1959	
2-10-4	J1, J1a	6401-6500	100	PRR	1942-1943	1957-1959	
2-8-8-0	HC1s	3700	1	PRR	1919	1929	

Type	Class	Numbers	Qty	Builder	Built	Retired	Notes
2-8-8-2	HH1s	3396	1	Schenectady	1911	1928	
2-8-8-2	HH1	373-378	6	Schenectady	1919	1947-1949	
							Ex-Norfolk & Western
4-4-0	D16	340-6460	40	PRR	1907-1908	1928-1935	
4-4-0	D16d	9821-9825	5	PRR	1907-1910	1925-1931	
4-4-2	—	6504, 6532	2	Baldwin	1907		
4-4-2	E2b	7496-8634	70	PRR	-1909	1924-1937	
4-4-2	E2d	6001…6083	32	PRR	-1908	1931-1938	
4-4-2	E3d	10…6441	43	PRR	-1908	1932-1946	
4-4-2	E5	1002…9832	12	PRR	1910-1913	1937-1949	
4-4-2	E6	5075 (1067)	1	PRR	1910	1950	
4-4-2	E6s	13…6085	82	PRR	1912, 1914	1948-1953	
4-4-2	E23s	8735-8738	4	Schenectady	1907, 1910	1928-1929	
4-6-0	G5s	459…3832	40	PRR	1923	1948-1953	
4-6-0	G5s	5700-5749	50	PRR	1924-1925	1949-1955	
4-6-0	G34b	9530…9539	8	Pittsburgh	1907, 1909	1927-1928	
4-6-2	K2	23…9999	153	PRR	1910-1911	1931-1949	
4-6-2	K2a	86…8543	72	PRR, Schen	1911-1913	1931-1949	
4-6-2	K2sb	3371, 3375	2	PRR	1911	1934, 1931	
4-6-2	K3s	7004…8663	30	Baldwin	1913	1947-1949	
4-6-2	K4s	8…8378	425	PRR, Baldwin	1914-1928	1947-1959	
4-6-2	K5	5698, 5699	2	PRR, Baldwin	1929		
4-6-2	K21s	8701-8712	12	Schenectady	1910-1913	1929-1930	
4-6-2	K28	7067	1	Pittsburgh	1907	1933	
4-6-2	K29	3395	1	Schenectady	1911	1929	
4-8-2	M1	4700 (6699)	1	PRR	1923	1950	
4-8-2	M1	6800-6999	200	Baldwin, Lima	1926	1949-1959	
4-8-2	M1a	6700-6799	100	BLW, PRR, Lima	1930	1951-1959	
4-4-4-4	T1	6110, 6111	2	Baldwin	1942	1953	
4-4-4-4	T1	5500-5549	50	PRR, Baldwin	1945-1946	1952-1959	
4-6-4-4	Q1	6130	1	PRR	1942	1952	
4-4-6-4	Q2	6131	1	PRR	1944	1952	
4-4-6-4	Q2	6175-6199	25	PRR	1945	1953-1956	
6-4-4-6	S1	6100	1	PRR	1939	1949	
6-8-6	S2	6200	1	Baldwin	1944	1952	Turbine

Narrow gauge

Type	Numbers	Qty	Builder	Built	Retired	Notes
2-6-0	9663	1	Griffith & Wedge	1909	1928	Ex-Ohio River & Western
2-6-0	9684	1	Cooke	1916	1934	Ex-Waynesburg & Washington
2-6-0	9687	1	Cooke	1920	1934	Ex-Waynesburg & Washington
4-6-0	9661	1	Baldwin	1910	1929	Ex-Ohio River & Western

READING COMPANY

Measured by geographic extent — from the middle of Pennsylvania to tidewater between Perth Amboy and Elizabeth, New Jersey — the Reading was not a major railroad. In traffic it was a giant: It was one of the principal carriers of anthracite coal, and it was a link in several freight routes to Philadelphia and New York. Reading operated an intense commuter and medium-distance passenger service that funneled passengers in and out of its terminal in Philadelphia, and was part of Baltimore & Ohio's Washington-Jersey City route.

Around the turn of the century the Philadelphia & Reading Railroad and its affiliated coal company became properties of the Reading Company, the Reading acquired control of the Central Railroad of New Jersey, and Baltimore & Ohio acquired control of the Reading. In 1923 the Reading Company merged the Philadelphia & Reading Railroad (and several other subsidiaries) and became an operating company. In this entry "Reading" means the Philadelphia & Reading Railroad up to 1923 and the Reading Company thereafter. (The Reading Railroad existed only on the Monopoly game board.)

The Reading owned nearly a third of the anthracite land in eastern Pennsylvania, and its steam locomotives burned anthracite — more specifically culm, the leftovers of the cleaning and grading process. The only way anthracite and culm could produce enough heat for a locomotive was to have a wide, shallow fire. John E. Wootten (1822-1898), general manager of the Philadelphia & Reading, introduced a wide firebox for anthracite in 1877, and it soon became standard on Reading locomotives. Eventually the road turned to a mix of anthracite and bituminous coal, the proportions depending on the route, service, and even the season, but the locomotives kept their Wootten fireboxes.

Reading built well over 600 locomotives at its shops in Reading, Pa., between 1845 and 1948. The last were the G-3 Pacifics of 1948. The road adopted a new classification and numbering system in 1900. It used small letters to separate minor variations in cylinder and driver size; superheating was indicated by an s between the number and the subclass letter.

Reading bought gas-electric cars and diesel switchers early, and

The I-8 Camelbacks were Reading's most numerous class of Consolidations. No. 1591 is shown on a work train in the early 1940s. Photo by W. Frank Clodfelter.

This is a USRA 2-8-0. Reading I-9sb Consolidations 1670-1699 were ordered by the USRA and built to Reading specifications in 1919. Photo by A. D. Hooks.

The I-10 class were Reading's largest 2-8-0s — large enough that their boilers became the basis for 4-8-4s. Baldwin photo; collection of H. L. Broadbelt.

between 1929 and 1933 it electrified most of its Philadelphia suburban service. It proclaimed that diesels were good for switching but not for road service — and at the same time bought Electro-Motive FTs to eliminate the need for helpers on a mountainous route. The last scheduled passenger run with steam power was on May 6, 1952, from Newtown to Philadelphia with Pacific 134. (G-3 Pacifics continued to work on Pennsylvania-Reading Seashore Lines until 1955.) By then freight was dieselized except for traffic peaks. Reading stored its 4-8-4s in serviceable condition, and used them on freight for the last time in spring 1956. Several were leased to the Pennsylvania Railroad that fall, again for a surge of traffic. Between 1957 and 1960 Reading gradually scrapped 25 4-8-4s, leaving just five available for standby freight duties — and for Reading's Iron Horse Ramble excursions, which ran until 1963.

Freight locomotives

Reading had about three times as many Consolidations as all other types of freight engines. The I-7 class 2-8-0s, built between 1898 and 1903, were built to burn bituminous coal because of an increased demand for anthracite for other uses. The I-7s were rear-cab engines with 56" drivers and either narrow fireboxes between the drivers or shallow fireboxes above the rear drivers. A few were converted to Camelbacks with wide fireboxes and classified I-6, reusing a vacated class. Baldwin subsequently built Camelback I-6s.

The I-8 class was the most numerous group of Consolidations, 177 built by Baldwin and Reading Shops between 1905 and 1914. They were Camelbacks with 61½" drivers. Weighing about 226,000 pounds, they were 25 to 30 tons heavier than the I-6s and I-7s. At the same time Reading built the lightweight (154,000 pounds) 50"-drivered I-2 Consolidations to replace I-1s built in the early 1880s. As I-1s went to scrap they gave their numbers to I-2s under construction.

The I-9 Consolidations of the late Teens and the early 1920s were another leap in size and weight, to about 285,000 pounds; driver size went back down to 55½". They had 25" × 32" cylinders and a tractive force of 64,300 pounds — heavier than a USRA light Mikado and able to pull more than a USRA heavy Mike. Engines 1670-1699 were ordered by the USRA but built to Reading specifications. Reading's ultimate

Reading 2100, the first of the T-1-class Northerns, appears to carry a year's worth of grime as it waits to couple to its freight train in April 1946. Photo by Bruce D. Fales.

2-8-0s were the I-10 class, which had 27" × 32" cylinders and 61½" drivers. Their weight of 322,690 pounds put them in the same league as the USRA heavy Mike; their 71,000-pound tractive force was about halfway between the USRA light and heavy 2-10-2s.

For fast freight service Reading had 57 heavy Mikados built by Baldwin and Reading Shops between 1912 and 1917. They had 61½" drivers and 24" × 32" cylinders and weighed 334,425 pounds.

Acquired about the same time were 31 2-8-8-2s that were used mostly in pusher service in the mountains northwest of Reading. They were too slow for mainline freight service, but between 1927 and 1944 11 were converted to enormous 2-10-2s and the remainder were converted to simple articulateds and subsequently had their trailing trucks removed. In 1931 Baldwin built ten 2-10-2s that were slightly bigger than the 2-8-8-2 conversions: 61½" drivers, 30½" × 32" cylinders, 451,000 pounds total weight, 92,570 pounds tractive effort — the largest Santa Fes built. At the opposite end of the scale were Reading's other ten-coupled engines, four Russian Decapods that had short lives and went to scrap in 1935.

The traffic levels of World War II called for fast freight locomotives. Reading had plenty of engines that could pull almost anything they were coupled to, but they were generally deficient in driver size or boiler capacity for sustained speed. Between 1945 and 1947 Reading used the boilers of 30 I-10sa Consolidations as the basis for as many 4-8-4s. The rear ends of the Consolidation boilers remained the same — the Northerns had the same 94.5 square feet of grate that the Consolidations did. The boilers were lengthened at the front and placed on new running gear with 70" drivers. The T-1s were freight engines until they were replaced by diesels, then three found new careers as excursion locomotives, first on the Reading, then under private ownership. Three survive today: Nos. 2100, 2102, and 2124.

Passenger locomotives

Reading's Camelback 4-4-0s were succeeded in passenger service by Camelback 4-4-2s. Driver size ranged from 74" (those were the low-drivered Atlantics) to 86". The latter were used primarily on the Atlantic City Railroad between Camden and Atlantic City, N. J. The last Atlantics, the 1916 rebuilds of the 4-4-4s, were Reading's only non-Camelback examples of their type; the last 4-4-0s, D-11s 410-419, built by Baldwin in 1914, were 110 pounds short of being the heaviest of their type and also were rear-cab engines.

Most of Reading's Ten-Wheelers were built for fast freight service. As they were replaced by larger locomotives they were moved to local passenger service, replacing older 4-4-0s. Several classes had 68½" drivers, and two engines, the experimental L-10s, were built with 74" drivers for passenger service.

The road's first Pacifics, Nos. 105-109, were built by Reading Shops in 1916. In each succeeding year through 1926, except for 1920 and 1922, Reading took delivery of five more 4-6-2s. They had 80" drivers and 25" × 28" cylinders, except for the 74"-drivered G-2sa class of 1926. Engine weight ranged from 273,600 to 305,360 pounds. Reading's last Pacifics were the G-3 class of 1948, essentially built to the 1916 design but modernized with cast trailing trucks, disk main drivers, and feedwater heaters; weight was 329,450 pounds. G-1s 117 and 118 were streamlined in 1937 to pull the Budd-built *Crusader* streamliner between

Philadelphia and Jersey City, and Nos. 108 and 178 received British-looking styling about the same time.

Switchers

Reading had 57 Camelback 0-4-0s built in the 20th century. They were useful for the sharp curves in the industrial and waterfront districts. The newest, the A-5a class, weighed 110,450 pounds, not much compared with even a Mikado or a Pacific, but 11 tons more than General Electric's 44-ton diesel. One 0-4-0, No. 1187, survives as Strasburg Railroad No. 4.

The most numerous Camelback 0-6-0s were the B-7a class, 36 hefty slide-valve, 55"-drivered machines weighing 162,000 pounds, as much as a USRA 0-6-0. The B-8s had 50" drivers on a 108" wheelbase, enabling them to negotiate sharp curves like the 0-4-0s. The five members of the B-6a class were oddities in comparison to the rest of Reading's roster — rear cab, narrow firebox, only 124,900 pounds — but wouldn't have looked out of place among the old 0-6-0s of practically any other road. The 20 B-9a-class 0-6-0s had rear cabs, Wootten fireboxes, and piston valves.

The E-3 eight-wheel switchers were rebuilt from Vauclain compound 2-8-0s built between 1892 and 1896; their 180,000-pound weight let them work on spurs and branches with light rail. The other 0-8-0s, the E-5sa class, were Reading's only superheated switchers. They were rear-cab, Wootten-firebox engines weighing 280,000 pounds.

Experimental locomotives

Most of Reading's experimental locomotives were designed for fast passenger service. Before settling on the Atlantic type in the 1890s the road experimented with high-drivered 2-4-2s and 4-2-2s. Reading decided it didn't trust the two-wheel lead truck at high speeds, and the 4-2-2s had too little weight on their drivers.

In 1915 Reading built four 4-4-4s. They were the first American locomotives with four-wheel trailing trucks, and the trucks themselves were identical with the lead trucks — 36" spoked wheels straddling outside ashpan hoppers. The engines were designed with four-point suspension that proved unsuccessful. In 1916 the 4-4-4s were rebuilt to Atlantics.

Between 1909 and 1911 Reading built six experimental locomotives, 80"-drivered Atlantics 300-303 and 74"-drivered Ten-Wheelers 675 and 676. Engines 300, 303 and 675 had three cylinders; the others had two cylinders and served as a control group. Within a few years the three-cylinder engines were rebuilt with just two cylinders.

Historical and technical societies:
Anthracite Railroads Historical Society, P. O. Box 519, Lansdale, PA 19446-0519
Reading Company Technical & Historical Society, P. O. Box 15143, Reading, PA 19612-5143
Recommended reading: *Reading Power Pictorial*, by Bert Pennypacker, published in 1973 by D. Carleton, 158 Doretta Street, River Vale, NJ 07675
Published rosters:
Railroad Magazine: January 1938, page 72, and February 1938, page 118; May 1944, page 43, and June 1944, page 115; May 1953, page 110
Railway & Locomotive Historical Society Bulletin, No. 167, entire issue

READING STEAM LOCOMOTIVES BUILT SINCE 1900

Type	Class	Numbers	Qty	Builder	Built	Retired	Notes
0-4-0	A-4a	1187-1200	14	Baldwin	1902-1903	1935-	
0-4-0	A-4a	1246-1250	5	Baldwin	1902	1935-	
0-4-0	A-5a	1147-1184	38	BLW, Reading	1906-1913	1929-	
0-6-0T	B-4a	1251	1	Reading	1918		
0-6-0	B-6a	1311-1315	5	Baldwin	1903	1929-	
0-6-0	B-7a	1321-1356	36	BLW, Reading	1906-1913		
0-6-0	B-8a	1316-1318	3	Baldwin	1907		
0-6-0	B-8b	1393-1399	7	Reading	1913, 1921		
0-6-0	B-9a	1451-1470	20	Reading	1917-1918		
0-8-0	E-3a	1400-1409	10	Baldwin	1905	1937-	
0-8-0	E-5sa	1490-1499	10	Baldwin	1924-1925		
2-6-4T	Q-1	376-385	10	Baldwin	1903-1904	1930-1936	
2-8-0	I-2e, f	701...802	53	Reading	1906-1910	1923-1940	
2-8-0	I-7a, b, c	961-1020	60	Baldwin	1898-1900	1923-	
2-8-0	I-7c, d,	1023-1097	75	Baldwin	1901-1903	1926-	
2-8-0	I-6a, b, c	1101-1125	25	Baldwin	1905, 1907	1935-1941	
2-8-0	I-8a	1501-1617	117	BLW, Reading	1905-1914	1937-1945	
2-8-0	I-9s, b	1625-1699	75	Baldwin	1918-1921		
2-8-0	I-9sb	1900-1924	25	Baldwin	1922		
2-8-0	I-10sa	2000-2049	50	Baldwin	1923, 1925	2020-2049 to 4-8-4	
2-8-2	M-1sa	1700-1756	57	Reading, BLW	1912-1917		
2-10-0	J-1sa	1126-1129	4	Baldwin	1917-1918	1935	
2-10-2	K-1sa	3000-3010	11	Reading	1927-1939		
2-10-2	K-1sb	3011-3020	10	Baldwin	1931		
2-8-8-2	N-1sa, c	1800-1810	11	Baldwin	1917-1918	Rebuilt to 2-10-2	
2-8-8-2	N-1sb, c	1811-1830	20	Baldwin	1918-1919	Rebuilt to 2-8-8-0	
4-4-0	D-5f	260-279	20	Baldwin	1901-1902	1928-1936	
4-4-0	D-5h	280-294	15	Baldwin	1906	1925-1940	
4-4-0	D-8b	242-246, 250	6	Reading	1903, 1907	1922-1934	
4-4-0	D-8c	400-409	10	Reading	1911	1932-1940	
4-4-0	D-10a	378	1	Reading	1904	1930 Rebuilt from 4-2-2	
4-4-0	D-10b	385	1	Reading	1905	1933 Rebuilt from 4-2-2	
4-4-0	D-11s	410-419	10	Baldwin	1914	1941-1945	
4-4-0	–	100	1	Baldwin	1902	1925 Renumbered 102 in 1912	
4-4-0	–	103	1	Reading	1903	1912	
4-4-2	P-1c	318-321	4	Baldwin	1900	1930, 1933	
4-4-2	P-2a	304-310	7	Reading	1907-1911	1934-1936	
4-4-2	P-2a	315-317	3	Reading	1907-1911	1923-1934	
4-4-2	P-3a	322-327	6	Baldwin	1900	1930, 1933	
4-4-2	P-3b	329	1	Baldwin	1902	1933	
4-4-2	P-4a	328	1	Baldwin	1902	1933	
4-4-2	P-4b, c	330-339	10	Baldwin	1903-1904	1933-1935	
4-4-2	P-5	340-349	10	Reading	1906	1944-	
4-4-2	P-6a	300, 303	2	Reading	1911, 1909		Three cylinders
4-4-2	P-6b	301, 302	2	Reading	1911		
4-4-2	P-7sa	350-353	4	Reading	1916		Rebuilt from 4-4-4
4-4-2	–	100	1	Reading	1913	1929	
4-4-4	C-1a	110-113	4	Reading	1915		Rebuilt to 4-4-2s 350-353 in 1916
4-6-0	F-2d	29/1025	1	Reading	1903	1916	
4-6-0	L-4b	571-580	10	Baldwin	1900	1928-	
4-6-0	L-5a	587-601	15	Baldwin	1902-1903	593-597 to CNJ	
4-6-0	L-6b	299	1	Reading	1905	1927	
4-6-0	L-7a	602-615	14	BLW, Reading	1905, 1910	1936-	
4-6-0	L-8a	691-700	10	Baldwin	1906		
4-6-0	L-8b	650-654	5	Reading	1911	1944-	
4-6-0	L-10a	675	1	Reading	1911		Three cylinders
4-6-0	L-10b	676	1	Reading	1911		
4-6-2	G-1sa	105-129	30	Reading	1916-1923		
4-6-2	G-1sa	130-134	5	Baldwin	1924		
4-6-2	G-1sb	200-204	5	Baldwin	1925		
4-6-2	G-2sa	175-179	5	Baldwin	1926		
4-6-2	G-3	210-219	10	Reading	1948		
4-8-4	T-1	2100-2129	30	Reading	1945-1947	1957-	

RICHMOND, FREDERICKSBURG & POTOMAC RAILROAD

The rail route between Washington, D. C., and Richmond, Virginia, opened in 1872. The northern portion, from Washington to Quantico, Va., consisted of two Pennsylvania Railroad subsidiaries, which were consolidated in 1890 as the Washington Southern; the southern portion was the RF&P. In 1901 the Richmond-Washington Company was formed to operate the WS and the RF&P as a single railroad; in 1920 the RF&P absorbed the Washington Southern. In the steam era Richmond-Washington was owned equally by Pennsylvania, Baltimore & Ohio, Atlantic Coast Line, Seaboard Air Line, Southern, and Chesapeake & Ohio.

In 1903 Washington Southern and RF&P agreed to furnish road power in proportion to mileage owned. Washington Southern provided the switchers for Potomac Yard in Alexandria, and RF&P the switchers for Richmond. After 1904 locomotives were lettered Richmond-Washington Line in place of the name of the owner. In 1926 the RF&P renumbered its locomotives and classed the roster for the first time, using numbers as class designations.

Atlantic Coast Line and Seaboard diesels worked through to Washington before World War II, and RF&P purchased several diesel switchers before and during the war, but it bought no road diesels until 1949. Freight trains were dieselized first, and by 1952 the RF&P was completely dieselized.

Road locomotives

RF&P's 114-mile double-track main line (there were no branches) was a bridge route, the principal southern connection of Pennsy and B&O and the principal northern connection of ACL and SAL. The road had no major grades, and it carried enough traffic that freight had to move at passenger-train speeds. Accordingly, the road first chose 4-6-0s as dual-purpose road engines, then switched to the 4-6-2. The first Pacifics, built by Baldwin in 1904 for Washington Southern and by Richmond in 1905 for RF&P, had 68" drivers and 20" × 26" or 21" × 26" cylinders and were intended for freight service. Eventually 69" drivers

became standard. Three of the 151 class were superheated and fitted with outside-bearing trailing trucks and remained in service until 1946; the rest were scrapped before World War II.

The 1907 Pacifics, Nos. 201-206 (RF&P 80-85), had 73" drivers for passenger service. They were saturated engines with slide valves (but Walschaerts valve gear) and inside-bearing trailing trucks. Pacific 256-263 (WS 56-59 and RF&P 86-89) were similar but weighed 252,000 pounds instead of 238,000. They were all superheated and given piston valves; Nos. 256-263 also were fitted with new trailing trucks.

More Pacifics were delivered in 1913, Nos. 251-255 (WS 51-55) from Baldwin and 264-268 (RF&P 90-94) from Richmond, superheated but still with inside-bearing trailing trucks. The Baldwin engines weighed 240,000 pounds and were found somewhat slippery; the Richmond engines weighed 258,340 pounds. Eventually all the 200s had 23" × 28" cylinders and a tractive force of 34,500 pounds; most were ultimately assigned to freight.

Baldwin delivered six freight Pacifics in 1914 and 1915. They had 68" drivers (later 69"), 26" × 28" cylinders, and 47,320 pounds tractive effort. They were rebuilt in the late 1920s with Elesco feedwater heaters and cast trailing trucks with boosters (they were delivered with inside-bearing trailers).

Driver size increased again to 75" for Pacifics 301-312 (RF&P 10-21), built by Richmond in 1918 and 1920 and Baldwin in 1924 and 1925. In cylinder size and performance they were between the USRA light and heavy Pacifics, and outweighed the USRA heavy by about 14,000 pounds.

Four final passenger Pacifics, Nos. 325-328, were delivered by Baldwin in 1927, with 75" drivers and 27" × 28" cylinders; they weighed 342,600 pounds and had a tractive force of 48,580 pounds — heavy Pacifics by anyone's standards. Chesapeake & Ohio bought them in 1947.

After World War I Atlantic Coast Line's USRA Pacifics began inter-

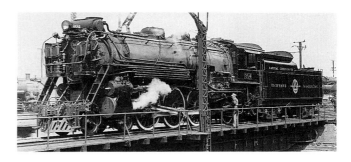

Pacific 304, shown on the Potomac Yard turntable in 1948, is typical of RF&P's large 4-6-2s. Photo by William P. Price.

changing heavier freight trains with RF&P at Richmond. RF&P needed something heavier than a Pacific, and ordered two 4-8-2s from Richmond in 1924; two more were delivered the next year. They were heavier than USRA heavy Mountains but their smaller cylinders and 73" drivers made them slightly less powerful.

In 1937 the road received five 4-8-4s from Baldwin. Although billed as dual-service locomotives (they had 77" drivers), they were too wide to operate through the Capitol Hill tunnel in Washington and too heavy for the Long Bridge across the Potomac between Washington and Arlington, Va., so they worked in freight service. They were named for generals of the Confederacy and numbered 551-555.

In 1938 Baldwin delivered six lighter 4-8-4s for passenger service. They had the same size drivers and cylinders (27" × 30") as the Generals but weighed 406,810 pounds, about 60,000 less. They had long Vanderbilt tenders; the heavy rectangular tenders of the Generals had also been too heavy for the Potomac River bridge. The passenger 4-8-4s were numbered 601-606 and named for governors of Virginia. Like the Generals, the Governors had one-piece cast steel frames; they had friction bearings on all axles (the Generals had roller bearings only on the lead trucks). Another six, Nos. 607-612, arrived from Baldwin in 1942, and ten more, Nos. 613-622, in 1945. These last ten had rectangular tenders and roller bearings on all axles and were named for prominent Virginians, such as George Washington and James Madison.

Freight locomotives

Early in World War II RF&P ran short of freight power. The quickest way to obtain it was to purchase ten 2-8-4s from Lima that were virtual duplicates of Nickel Plate 730-739 and built at the same time. Nickel Plate was a fast freight railroad, and its engines were equally suitable to RF&P's single-speed main line.

Still short of power, in 1944 the road purchased six Norfolk & Western class K3 4-8-2s, definitely freight power with their 63" drivers. They

RF&P 4-8-4 No. 605, *Governor James Madison* (who later rose to higher office), awaits a passenger assignment at Washington in 1940. Photo by Donald A. Somerville.

were stored soon after the war and sold through a dealer to the Wheeling & Lake Erie, where they met up with the other four of the K3 class, which had spent the war years on the Denver & Rio Grande Western.

Switchers

Richmond-Washington's early 0-6-0s were ordinary-looking slide valve engines ranging in weight from 110,000 to 150,000 pounds. The later six-wheel switchers were built with piston valves but were not superheated. and weighed about 170,000 pounds. The 0-8-0s were intended for hump work at Potomac Yard. Engines 71-74 had 24" × 28" cylinders and 51" drivers and weighed 229,000 pounds. The last two 0-8-0s, Nos. 91 and 92, had 26" cylinders and 53" drivers and weighed 259,000 pounds. Wartime traffic through Potomac Yard outstripped even the heavy 0-8-0s, and in 1943 RF&P bought three simple 2-8-8-2s from Chesapeake & Ohio for hump work.

Recommended reading: *The Richmond-Washington Line and Related Railroads*, by Richard E. Prince, published in 1973 by Richard E. Prince (SBN 7600088-76-X)
Published rosters: *Railroad Magazine*: November 1932, page 554; March 1952, page 102

RF&P STEAM LOCOMOTIVES BUILT SINCE 1900

Type	Post-1926 Numbers	Pre-1926 Numbers	Qty	Builder	Built	Retired	Notes
0-6-0	1, 3	RF&P 100, 101	2	Baldwin	1903, 1905	1940, 1941	
0-6-0	2, 4, 5	WS 110-112	3	Baldwin	1903, 1905	1939-1945	
0-6-0	11-13	RF&P 102-104	3	Baldwin	1906	1936	
0-6-0	14, 15	WS 113, 114	2	Baldwin	1906	1936, 1945	
0-6-0	21, 22	RF&P 105, 106	2	Baldwin	1912	1945, 1938	
0-6-0	25-27	WS 115-117	3	Richmond	1908	1936-1945	
0-6-0	31, 32	RF&P 107, 108	2	Baldwin	1919	1949	
0-6-0	35, 36	WS 121, 122	2	Baldwin	1918	1947, 1948	
0-6-0	41	WS 109	1	Richmond	1918	1949	
0-6-0	42-44	RF&P 123-125	3	Richmond	1921, 1923	1949	
0-6-0	45, 46	RF&P 127, 128	2	Richmond	1925	1949, 1953	
0-6-0	47, 48		2	Rich, BLW	1918-1927	Sold 1951	
0-8-0	71-73	WS 118-120	3	Richmond	1914, 1918	1948-1953	
0-8-0	74	RF&P 126	1	Richmond	1923	1953	
0-8-0	91, 92	RF&P 130, 131	2	Richmond	1923	1953	
2-8-4	571-580		10	Lima	1943	1952	
2-8-8-2	1-3		3	Schenectady	1925	1949	Ex-C&O
4-6-0	101-105	RF&P 25-29	4	Richmond	1903	1930-1946	

Type	Class	Numbers	Qty	Builder	Built	Retired	Notes
4-6-0		RF&P 30-35	6	Richmond	1900	Sold 1916-1923	
4-6-0		RF&P 36, 37	2	Baldwin	1901	Sold 1916	
4-6-0	106-113	RF&P 38-46	9	Richmond	1901, 1903	1927-1935	
						No. 39 retired before renumbering	
4-6-2	151-160	WS 60-69	10	Baldwin	1904	1929-1946	
4-6-2	161-165	RF&P 70-74	5	Richmond	1905	1929, 1946	
4-6-2	201-206	RF&P 80-85	6	Baldwin	1907	1937-1950	
4-6-2	251-255	WS 51-55	5	Baldwin	1913	1937-1950	
4-6-2	256-259	WS 56-59	4	Richmond	1911	1950	
4-6-2	260-263	RF&P 86-89	4	Richmond	1912	1937-1950	
4-6-2	264-268	RF&P 90-94	5	Richmond	1913	1937-1950	
4-6-2	301-312	RF&P 10-21	12	BLW, Rich	1918-1925	1950	
4-6-2	325-328		4	Baldwin	1927	Sold to C&O, 1947	
4-6-2	401-406	RF&P 1-6	6	Baldwin	1915, 1916	1950	
4-8-2	501-504	RF&P 200-203	4	Richmond	1924, 1925	1950	
4-8-2	515-520		6	N&W	1926	Sold to W&LE, 1948	
4-8-4	551-555		5	Baldwin	1937	1952	
4-8-4	601-622		22	Baldwin	1938-1945	1953-1954	

Locomotives 613-622 were leased to C&O about 1955 and scrapped in 1959.

RUTLAND RAILROAD

The Rutland had an idyllic New England setting, and its steam locomotives were generally good-looking — it was in far better condition aesthetically than financially. It was built as part of a Boston-to-Great Lakes route. Eventually it became a segment of one of three competing Boston-Montreal routes and one of four competing New York-Montreal routes. It served the major population centers of Vermont, Burlington and Rutland, but it didn't have a monopoly at either — and in Vermont population center is a relative term. Its main line extended from White Creek, New York, where it connected with the Boston & Maine, east to Bennington, Vt., then north through Rutland to Burling-

In the late 1940s Consolidation No. 23 (Schenectady, 1907) was equipped with a stoker and had its air pump moved to the pilot; Stephenson valve gear remained. Photo by H. N. Proctor.

The 1912 Ten-Wheelers were relatively modern, with superheaters, piston valves, and Walschaerts gear, and remained in service until dieselization. Photo by L. B. Herrin.

ton, then northwest across a chain of islands in Lake Champlain to connections with Canadian National and Canadian Pacific at the Canadian border. A second main route reached southeast from Rutland to a connection with B&M at Bellows Falls, Vt., on the Connecticut River. A branch nicknamed "The Corkscrew" extended south from Bennington to Chatham, N. Y., and a long branch reached west across the top of New York to Ogdensburg.

The road came under control of the New York Central shortly after 1900, and it enjoyed prosperity for about a decade. Then NYC and New Haven got to quarreling about the Rutland and the New York, Ontario & Western (another perennial hard-luck case), and the Interstate Commerce Commission ruled that Rutland's boats on the Great Lakes competed with parent NYC's trains and therefore had to be sold.

From 1905 to 1913 Rutland's locomotives carried NYC numbers and were built to New York Central designs, but they were second-rank designs. Even the last of the Consolidations, built after NYC had begun acquiring Mikados in quantity, had Stephenson valve gear and inside valves, and Rutland's Ten-Wheelers, if comparatively modern ones, arrived after NYC had added several classes of Pacifics to its own ros-

ter. However, after NYC control ceased, Rutland didn't turn around and acquire large batches of locomotives built to its own designs. Its next locomotives came while the USRA was in control; and after that Rutland would buy only ten more steam locomotives, six Pacifics and four Mountains. The Pacifics looked like New York Central engines, but the Mountains appeared to derive in equal parts from the 1929 Pacifics and contemporary Alco practice.

The purchase of the four Mountains instead of diesels in 1946 is at least explainable. In 1946 only one of Rutland's neighbors, Boston & Maine, had even begun dieselization; the others — NYC, Delaware & Hudson, Central Vermont, Canadian National, and Canadian Pacific — were still solidly in the steam camp. Diesels would have required new servicing facilities, and Rutland had all it could do to afford the new locomotives.

Four years later the situation reversed. Except for the Mountains, Rutland's locomotives were old, tired, and expensive to operate. The road tested Alco's RS-3 demonstrator and a Bangor & Aroostook GP7. It used the scrap value of the unused Addison branch, the oldest and worst freight cars, and the steam locomotives as a down payment on

nine RS-3s (including the demonstrator), six RS-1s, and a GE 70-tonner. It would have made no economic sense to keep the 4-8-2s in service, because they would require all the steam locomotive facilities be kept in place. The Mountains were retired in 1955 and scrapped.

Freight locomotives

The eight F-11 Ten-Wheelers, numbers 50-57, built by Schenectady in 1902, were freight engines with 63" drivers. Between 1907 and 1913 the road received 18 2-8-0s with 63" drivers. They had wide fireboxes over the rear drivers, but even the last of them had inside valves and Stephenson valve gear. They were classed G-34; their eventual Rutland numbers were 14-31. In 1939, as part of a campaign to save the Rutland, which had fallen into bankruptcy, No. 28 was fitted briefly with running board skirting for a named freight train, the *Whippet*. (The locomotive pictured in the advertising for the train was a Southern Pacific *Daylight* 4-8-4.)

When the traffic surge of World War I hit, the Consolidations were the biggest freight locomotives on the property — and they weighed about 210,000 pounds. The USRA allotted six USRA light 2-8-2s to the Rutland, which classified them H-6a, the same classification used on New York Central.

At the end of World War II Rutland's power was worn out. In 1946 the road was able to round up enough money for four 4-8-2s from Sche-

nectady. They had 73" Boxpok drivers and 26" × 30" cylinders; their weight of 348,000 pounds, slightly less than the USRA heavy Mountain, put them in the middle range of weights for North American 4-8-2s. They were light enough to go anywhere on the road, and they often worked on passenger trains. They were delivered in dark green paint, which soon gave way to black. The arrangement of the smokebox front and air pump shields on the pilot echoed the appearance of Toledo, Peoria & Western and Union Pacific 4-8-4s. In size and power Nos. 90-93 were about the equal of Canadian National's last group of 4-8-2s.

Passenger locomotives

Rutland received two groups of Ten-Wheelers in 1902, passenger engines 40-49, class F-12, and dual-service engines 50-57, class F-11. The F-12s had 69" drivers and weighed about 156,000 pounds; the F-11s had 63" drivers and weighed about 10,000 pounds more.

Four 4-6-0s arrived in 1910, passenger engines with 69" drivers, inside piston valves, and Stephenson valve gear: class F-2h, numbers 2036-2039 (later 70-73). They were relatively modern Ten-Wheelers, with fireboxes over the rear drivers, and they weighed 198,000-211,000 pounds. Six more were delivered by Schenectady in 1912, class F-2j, numbers 2074-2079. They were superheated and had outside valves and Walschaerts gear. In 1913 they were renumbered 70-79. Ten-Wheelers 70 and 71 were fitted with superheaters in 1913 and 1914, respectively, and Walschaerts valve gear in 1917; Nos. 72 and 73 received both betterments in 1920.

Mid-1920s prosperity brought with it three Pacifics, 80-82, built by Schenectady in 1925. They were about the size of USRA light Pacifics but had 69" drivers. Three more with 73" drivers and weighing 292,500 pounds were delivered by Schenectady in 1929. The Pacifics were close in most dimensions to New York Central's K-14 class but had a longer piston stroke, 28" instead of the 26" used by NYC.

Switchers

Most of the 0-6-0s had 51" drivers, slide valves, and Stephenson valve gear, differing primarily in weight. Number 106, purchased after New York Central control ended, had piston valves and Walschaerts valve gear. Number 107 had 57" drivers and weighed 168,000 pounds; Rutland acquired it secondhand from a neighboring short line, the Clarendon & Pittsford, in 1946, for $500.

During World War I the USRA allotted two 0-8-0s to the Rutland, but they were diverted to NYC and came to the Rutland after the war.

Historical and technical society: Rutland Railroad Historical Society, P. O. Box 6262, Rutland, VT 05701

Recommended reading: *The Rutland Road*, by Jim Shaughnessy, published in 1981 (second edition) by Howell-North Books, P. O. Box 3051, La Jolla, CA 92038 (ISBN 0-8310-7128-1)

Published rosters:
Railroad Magazine: November 1922, page 130; August 1946, page 33; April 1970, page 26
Railway & Locomotive Historical Society Bulletin, No. 101, page 82
Trains Magazine: March 1946, page 34

Rutland 93 was the last of the four Mountains. They were built by Alco in 1946, the last 4-8-2s built by a commercial builder in North America. Photo by S. K. Bolton Jr.

RUTLAND STEAM LOCOMOTIVES BUILT SINCE 1900

Type	Class	Numbers	Qty	Builder	Built	Retired	Notes	Type	Class	Numbers	Qty	Builder	Built	Retired	Notes
0-6-0	B-2-a	100, 101	2	Cooke	1907	1951, 1952		2-8-0	G-34d	26-31	6	Schenectady	1913	1951, 1952	
0-6-0	B-9	102-104	3	Manchester	1902	1945, 1946		2-8-2	H-6a	32-37	6	Schenectady	1918	1951, 1952	
0-6-0	B-2-b	105	1	Manchester	1913	1951		4-6-0	F-11	50-57	8	Schenectady	1902	1946-1951	
0-6-0	B-2-c	106	1	Schenectady	1914	1953		4-6-0	F-12	40-49	10	Sch., Man.	1902	1932-1951	
0-6-0	B-3	107	1	Schenectady	1914	1953		4-6-0	F-2-h	70-73	4	Schenectady	1910	1951, 1952	
0-8-0	U-3	109, 110	2	Pittsburgh	1918	1951		4-6-0	F-2-j	74-79	6	Schenectady	1912	1951-1953	
2-6-0	E-1-d	144, 145	2	Schenectady	1900	1946		4-6-2	K-1	80-82	3	Schenectady	1925	1952	
2-8-0	G-34a	18-23	6	Schenectady	1907	1939-1951		4-6-2	K-2	83-85	3	Schenectady	1929	1951-1953	
2-8-0	G-34b	14-17	4	Schenectady	1910	1948, 1951		4-8-2	L-1	90-93	4	Schenectady	1946	1955	
2-8-0	G-34c	24, 25	2	Schenectady	1911	1950, 1951									

ST. LOUIS-SAN FRANCISCO RAILWAY

The St. Louis & San Francisco Railroad (the "Frisco") approached 1900 with a fresh grip on its finances, the result of a reorganization in 1896. Its main line reached from St. Louis to Oklahoma City; major branches extended from Monett, Missouri, south through Fort Smith, Arkansas, to Paris, Texas, and northwest through Wichita to Ellsworth, Kansas. In 1901 Frisco leased the Kansas City, Fort Scott & Memphis, a line from Kansas City through Springfield, Mo., and Memphis, Tennessee, to Birmingham, Alabama; and the following year, 1902, the road completed a line from Sapulpa, Okla., near Tulsa, to Carrolton, Texas, on the outskirts of Dallas, creating an X-shaped map, with St. Louis-Texas and Kansas City-Birmingham routes crossing at Springfield, Mo. In 1903 the Oklahoma City line was extended southwest to Quanah, Texas. In 1907 Frisco purchased the St. Louis, Memphis & Southeastern, a line from St. Louis south paralleling the Mississippi River to a junction with the Kansas City-Memphis line.

Frisco controlled the Chicago & Eastern Illinois and Gulf Coast Lines (New Orleans to Brownsville, Texas) and was itself part of the empire of Benjamin F. Yoakum, which collapsed in 1913. The St. Louis-San Francisco Railway emerged from the rubble in 1916 without C&EI and

GCL. Its only major expansion thereafter was acquisition of two routes to the Gulf of Mexico at Pensacola, Florida, and Mobile, Ala.

Frisco's main line southwest from St. Louis started climbing right at the yard limits, crossing a watershed into the valley of the Meramec River. Down through the Ozarks it followed the top of a ridge much of the way, but it was hill-and-dale running. The Kansas City-Memphis route similarly sliced through the mountains. The outer reaches of the system across the plains of Oklahoma and Texas were easier going.

Frisco's roster included a number of locomotives inherited from predecessors, subsidiaries, and short lines, among them St. Louis, Memphis & Southeastern; Jonesboro, Lake City & Eastern; Gulf, Texas & Western; and Muscle Shoals, Birmingham & Pensacola.

Frisco's reputation for maintenance included cleanliness, even polished rods. Its shops seemed at times to overdo modernization of older power — for example, Scullin disk drivers on a 1900 Consolidation used as a switcher, or front-end throttles on turn-of-the-century 4-4-0s.

Frisco's 4200-series Mikados, built by Baldwin in 1930, were among the heaviest of the type. Baldwin photo; collection of H. L. Broadbelt.

Frisco's homebuilt Mountains in the 4400 series were the heaviest built. SLSF photo.

Frisco bought a few diesel switchers for use in St. Louis during World War II, and its first road diesels were E7s for the *Texas Special* and the *Meteor*, but it believed that fast freight schedules meant high-horsepower steam locomotives (the homebuilt 4-8-2s and the Baldwin 4-8-4s, for example) and moderate-length trains. A change of management in 1947 changed motive power policy as well, and dieselization began in earnest in 1948. The last steam-powered revenue train was a local freight between Birmingham and Bessemer, Alabama, in February 1952, pulled by USRA 2-8-2 No. 4018.

Freight locomotives

Frisco's first 2-8-0s were delivered in 1881 and its last 2-6-0s in 1892. Between 1900 and 1902 Dickson, Pittsburgh, and Richmond delivered a total of 33 Consolidations, Nos. 801-833, with 21" × 28" cylinders and 57" drivers. The next major group of 2-8-0s, Nos. 970-989, was delivered by Baldwin in 1906. They had the same size cylinders, drivers 2" smaller, and 12 tons more weight; more important, the firebox was above the rear drivers instead of between them, increasing the grate area (and thus the steaming capacity) by 55 percent.

In 1907 Baldwin delivered 51 Consolidations numbered 1200-1250 that were the next size larger: 22" × 30" cylinders, 57" drivers, 198,000 pounds, 43,300 pounds tractive effort. At the same time Schenectady delivered Nos. 1251-1295, about the same size but slightly heavier. Within a year all 45 were transferred to the Rock Island, also part of the

Yoakum empire. Replacements came from Baldwin and Brooks in 1909 and 1910. The first 15, Nos. 1251-1265, were duplicates of 1200-1250 but were superheated. Engines 1266-1305 were larger and heavier still — 26" × 30" cylinders, 63" drivers, 241,900 pounds. The last group of 2-8-0s, Nos. 1306-1345, built by Schenectady in 1912, had the same dimensions.

Schenectady delivered seven 2-8-8-2s in 1910. Intended to be the equivalent of two 2-8-0s, they were handicapped by small boilers and fireboxes. After holding down various jobs in the Ozarks, none of them for long, the Mallets were banished to coal mine duty in Alabama in the mid-1920s.

Frisco's next attempt to go beyond the 2-8-0 was a batch of 2-10-2s built by Baldwin between 1916 and 1918. They were numbered 1-60, had 29" × 30" cylinders and 60" drivers, and weighed 380,000 pounds. They proved to be good pullers, but they had two drawbacks. Their Jacobs-Shupert fireboxes leaked and had to be replaced immediately. (The Jacobs-Shupert firebox was constructed from plates and channels riveted together to form an extremely rigid structure. It had no staybolts, which were a perennial source of problems, but the flexing that resulted from the motion of the locomotive played hob with the joints between the plates and channels.) The other problem was counterbalancing: At speeds over 35 mph the 2-10-2s kinked the rails. When competitive pressures meant higher speeds for freight trains, the 2-10-2s were out of a job. Frisco used boilers from 33 of them to build 4-8-2s

between 1936 and 1942; all but two of the rest were scrapped by 1940. Engines 19 and 40 were renovated to work a branch to Fort Leonard Wood that opened in 1941.

During World War I the Frisco received 20 Russian Decapods. They were particularly useful on Oklahoma branches with light rail. Frisco treated them well, converting some to oil and fitting others with mechanical stokers, and with one exception they remained in service until the end of steam. Engine 1621 was destroyed in a dynamite explosion in the 1920s, and SLSF traded a Ten-Wheeler to the Fort Smith, Subiaco & Rock Island for the short line's sole Russian Decapod, which became second No. 1621. Five were sold to Eagle-Picher Mining in 1951, and one of those five engines, No. 1630, is active at Illinois Railway Museum in Union, Ill.

Frisco's progress from 2-8-0 to 2-8-2 via 2-8-8-2 and 2-10-2 is attributable to the USRA, which assigned 33 light Mikados, Nos. 4000-4032. They came to SLSF slightly secondhand from the Pennsylvania, which rejected them, and Indiana Harbor Belt, and at first Frisco told the USRA it didn't want them either. The road soon discovered they were good steamers, and eventually fitted them all with cast trailing trucks and boosters. Most of the USRA Mikes also had their cab roofs raised to

increase headroom, an alteration no other railroad found necessary.

Between 1923 and 1926 Baldwin delivered 65 heavy 2-8-2s based on the USRA heavy Mike. Engines 4100-4164 had the same size cylinders and grate, but drivers were an inch larger, 64", and were 10 to 12 tons heavier. Boiler pressure of 210 pounds instead of 190 gave them 5,000 pounds more tractive effort, and trailing-truck boosters added another 8,750 pounds.

In 1928 the road ordered 20 even heavier Mikados. Traffic fell off in 1929, eliminating the need for new power, but construction was too far along for the order to be canceled. The engines, Nos. 4200-4219, were delivered in 1930. They had the same drivers and cylinders as their predecessors but 10 square feet more grate area and 235 pounds boiler pressure. Tractive effort was 68,500 pounds, plus 9,600 more with the booster working. They had outside-journal lead trucks, two air pumps behind shields on the pilot, concealed Coffin feedwater heaters, Baker valve gear, and welded tenders.

The final Mikados were Nos. 1350-1356, rebuilt from 2-8-0s in the 1305 series between 1943 and 1946. Most of the changes took place at the rear: The frame was extended, a booster-equipped trailing truck was added, and a combustion chamber was spliced into the boiler just ahead of the firebox. Up front, a Coffin feedwater heater was countersunk into the smokebox.

As traffic and train speeds increased in the mid-1930s Frisco needed new locomotives. The shops at Springfield were given the task of building them — the road was in receivership, and money would go further at home than at Baldwin's plant in Philadelphia. The starting point for the new engines was the collection of displaced 2-10-2s. The first group of 4-8-2s used only a few components: trailing trucks, boosters, small appliances, and just enough of the boilers to qualify the

Frisco's 1910 Baldwin Pacifics were small engines. Streamlining made them look larger; there was plenty of empty space inside the shell. Streamlined or no, the bell and the whistle were out front where they could be heard. SLSF photo.

engines as rebuilt, not new. The first Mountain type, No. 4300, emerged from the shop on July 15, 1936. It had 27" × 30" cylinders and 70" Scullin disk drivers; weight was 431,110 pounds and tractive force was 66,400, plus 8,450 for the booster. The new engine was soon joined by ten more, 4301-4310, in St. Louis-Monett fast freight service.

The road wanted more 4-8-2s, but money was still tight. The second group of rebuilds used the entire 2-10-2 boiler, from smokebox to cab. New running gear included the same Scullin 70" wheels and 29" × 32" cylinders, the largest used on any 4-8-2 (a few engines had web-spoke drivers). The engines were the heaviest Mountains built, 449,760 pounds. Engines 4400-4412 were oil burners and considered dual-service engines; 4413-4422 were coal-burning freight locomotives.

As World War II continued, Frisco needed yet more locomotives and turned to the 4-8-4 type. Wartime restrictions precluded a completely new design, so Frisco's designers began with Chicago, Burlington & Quincy's O-5A. They kept the 74" drivers and 28" cylinder diameter but lengthened the stroke by an inch to 31", reduced the grate area and total heating surface, and increased the boiler pressure from 250 to 255 pounds — weight was almost the same and tractive force was 3,700 pounds better at 71,200 pounds. The first 12, Nos. 4503-4514, coal burners for freight service, were delivered by Baldwin in 1942. In November of that year three oil-burning passenger 4-8-4s arrived, Nos. 4500-4502, painted blue and white and lettered in red for the *Meteor*. The tenders of the freight engines carried red-and-white Frisco Faster Freight emblems until 1946, when the new president of the railroad asked how much tonnage the emblems could pull and ordered them painted over. As traffic increased — Frisco served Fort Leonard Wood and Fort Sill — the road needed ten more 4-8-4s, delivered by Baldwin in 1943. They had trailing truck boosters, which worked so well that Springfield Shops applied them to the earlier Northerns.

Passenger locomotives

In 1927 Frisco considered the purchase of gas-electric cars for local service, but reduced the order and modernized six 4-4-0s with oil burning apparatus, superheaters, piston valves, Walschaerts valve gear, and front-end throttles. The six survived into the late 1940s — at least one into the 1950s. The 1100 and 1400 classes of 4-6-0s had 69" drivers for passenger service. Most of the 1100s were converted to oil and remained in service until the late 1940s; the 1400s remained coal burners, were downgraded to freight work, stored during the Depression, and then returned to service (still in freight) during World War II.

The first Pacifics came from Brooks (Nos. 1000-1009) and Baldwin (1010-1014) in 1904. Both groups had 69" drivers. The Brooks engines had piston valves and weighed 204,000 pounds; the Baldwins, slide valves and 191,000 pounds. Frisco purchased several more groups of Ten-Wheelers, then returned to the 4-6-2 in 1910 with 25 somewhat larger superheated engines from Baldwin, Nos. 1015-1039. They also had 69" drivers; later rebuildings gave 73" drivers to some of the class, changed the original 26" × 28" cylinders to 24" × 28", and converted them from coal to oil.

In 1912 Schenectady delivered 20 heavier Pacifics (262,600 pounds) with 69" drivers. They were built alongside the 1306-series 2-8-0s and had many parts interchangeable with them. Numbered 1040-1059, they underwent the same cylinder and fuel changes as Nos. 1015-1039.

To compete with Santa Fe's diesel-powered streamliners from Kansas City to Tulsa and Oklahoma City, Frisco created a pair of three-car streamlined trains to run as the *Firefly* between Kansas City and Oklahoma City via Tulsa — and shrouded three Pacifics like nothing before or since. The trains entered service December 10, 1939, apparently with unrebuilt equipment; the complete streamliners made their debut on March 29, 1940.

Frisco's final Pacifics came from Baldwin in 1917. They shared a number of features with the 2-10-2s, including Jacobs-Shupert fireboxes that leaked; in addition they were short of boiler capacity. They were assigned to undemanding duties. Between 1937 and 1941 Springfield rebuilt them as Hudsons. Changes included a larger firebox, booster-equipped four-wheel trailing truck, 74" drivers in place of 73", concealed Coffin feedwater heater, and skirting. The rebuilding redeemed them, and they released 1500-series 4-8-2s for freight service.

The poor performance of the 1060-series Pacifics resulted in an order for 15 medium-size 4-8-2s, Nos. 1500-1514, delivered by Baldwin in 1923. Their 26" × 28" cylinders and 69" drivers made them a little smaller than the USRA light Mountain; their 342,200 pounds put them between the two USRA designs in weight. They took over all St. Louis-Springfield service, and five more delivered in 1925 resulted in their territory being extended to Oklahoma City. In 1926 Baldwin delivered ten more, 1520-1529. They were primarily passenger engines, but worked occasionally in freight service. Six 1500s were placed on display after dieselization; No. 1522 was removed from the National Museum of Transport in 1988 and restored for excursion service.

Switchers

Of Frisco's 0-6-0s, the most interesting looking were Nos. 3713-3752, built by Baldwin between 1907 and 1911. They were short and chunky, with high-mounted boilers. They had piston valves and Stephenson valve gear and weighed 154,500 pounds. The USRA assigned seven 0-6-0s to the road in 1919. Unlike its neighbors (Katy, MoPac, Rock Island) Frisco had no 0-8-0s; many 2-8-0s worked in yard service.

Historical and technical society: Frisco Railroad Museum, P. O. Box 276, Ash Grove, MO 65604

Recommended reading: *Frisco Power*, by Joe G. Collias, published in 1984 by M M Books, P. O. Box 29318, Crestwood, MO 63126 (ISBN 0-9612366-0-4)

Published rosters: *Railroad Magazine*: November 1934, page 41; July 1948, page 98

SLSF STEAM LOCOMOTIVES BUILT SINCE 1900

Type	Numbers	Qty	Builder	Built	Notes	Type	Numbers	Qty	Builder	Built	Notes
0-6-0	3539-3548	10	Baldwin	1923		2-8-0	819-828	10	Pittsburgh	1902	
0-6-0	3648-3657	10	Baldwin	1906		2-8-0	829-833	5	Richmond	1902	
0-6-0	3670	1	Pittsburgh	1902	Ex-StLM&SE 12	2-8-0	834, 835	2	Brooks	1903	
0-6-0	3671-3695	25	Baldwin	1904-1906		2-8-0	850, 851	2	Brooks	1905	Ex-New Iberia & Northern 1, 2
0-6-0	3700-3712	13	Dickson	1906		2-8-0	860, 861	2	Brooks	1900	Ex-MSB&F
0-6-0	3713-3752	40	Baldwin	1907-1911		2-8-0	870, 871	2	Pittsburgh	1900	Ex-MSB&F
0-6-0	3800-3806	7	Schenectady	1919	USRA	2-8-0	956-965	10	Dickson		Ex-StLM&SE 270-279
2-6-0	72, 73	2	Baldwin	1913	Ex-JLC&E	2-8-0	970-989	20	Baldwin	1906	10 to NOT&M 1911
2-6-0	365, 366	2	Schenectady	1909	Ex-GT&W 3, 4	2-8-0	1200-1265	66	Baldwin	1907, 1909	
2-6-0	367, 368	2	Brooks	1910	Ex-GT&W 5, 6	2-8-0	1251-1295	45	Schenectady	1907	Sold to CRI&P 1908
2-8-0	76, 77	2	Baldwin	1920	Ex-JLC&E	2-8-0	1266-1280	15	Baldwin	1909-1910	
2-8-0	801-818	18	Dickson	1900	Built as 501-518	2-8-0	1281-1292	12	Brooks	1910	

SLSF STEAM LOCOMOTIVES BUILT SINCE 1900 (continued)

Type	Numbers	Qty	Builder	Built	Notes
2-8-0	1293-1305	13	Baldwin	1910	
2-8-0	1306-1345	40	Schenectady	1912	7 rebuilt to 2-8-2s 1350-1356
2-8-2	1350-1356	7	SLSF	1943-1946	
2-8-2	4000-4032	33	Lima, Schen	1919	USRA
2-8-2	4100-4164	65	Baldwin	1923-1926	
2-8-2	4200-4219	10	Baldwin	1930	
2-10-0	1613-1632	20		1918	
	Russian Decapods built by Richmond, Baldwin, Brooks, and Schenectady				
2-10-0	1621	1	Baldwin	1918	
					Ex-FtSS&RI 101 to replace first 1621
2-10-2	1-60	60	Baldwin	1916-1918	
					33 rebuilt to 4-8-2 1936-1942
2-8-8-2	2001-2007	7	Schenectady	1910	
4-4-0	182, 183	2	Pittsburgh	1902	Ex-StLM&SE 23, 24
4-4-0	200-204	5	Pittsburgh	1902	
4-4-0	205-219	15	Dickson	1903	
4-4-0	220-229	10	Rhode Island	1903	
4-6-0	74, 75	2	Baldwin	1916	Ex-JLC&E
4-6-0	467	1	Baldwin	1913	Ex-GT&W 8
4-6-0	479-484	6	Baldwin	1910	Ex-StLB&M 38-43
4-6-0	516-530	15	Baldwin	1903	
4-6-0	558-567	10	Cooke		
4-6-0	573, 574	2	Pittsburgh	1902	Ex-StLM&SE 21, 22
4-6-0	575-584	10	Pittsburgh	1902	Ex-KCFS&M 575-584
4-6-0	585-599	15	Dickson	1903	
4-6-0	600-609	10	Richmond	1902	
4-6-0	610-616	7	Baldwin	1903	
4-6-0	617-623	7	Baldwin	1903	
4-6-0	624-628	5	Baldwin	1903	
4-6-0	629-633	5	Schenectady	1905	
4-6-0	634-668	35	Baldwin	1904	
4-6-0	669-693	25	Dickson	1903	
4-6-0	695-699	5	Brooks	1906	
4-6-0	700-704	5	Dickson	1903	
4-6-0	705-724	20	Brooks	1906	Cross-compound
4-6-0	727-741	15	Schenectady	1905	
4-6-0	742-759	18	Baldwin	1902	Vauclain compound
4-6-0	760-774	15	Baldwin	1903	
4-6-0	775-778	4	Baldwin	1903	Ex-StLM&SE 620-623
4-6-0	779-784	6	Baldwin	1903	Ex-BE&SW 624-629
4-6-0	785-799	15	Baldwin	1903	
4-6-0	1100-1111	12	Schenectady	1907	
4-6-0	1400-1409	10	Baldwin	1907	
4-6-2	1000-1009	10	Brooks	1904	
4-6-2	1010-1014	5	Baldwin	1904	
4-6-2	1015-1039	25	Baldwin	1910	
4-6-2	1040-1059	20	Schenectady	1912	
4-6-2	1060-1069	10	Baldwin	1917	Rebuilt to 4-6-4 1937
4-8-2	1500-1529	30	Baldwin	1923-1926	
4-8-2	4300-4310	11	SLSF	1936-1937	
4-8-2	4400-4422	23	SLSF	1939-1942	
4-8-4	4500-4524	25	Baldwin	1942-1943	

ST. LOUIS SOUTHWESTERN RAILWAY

The St. Louis Southwestern, early nicknamed the Cotton Belt, began life as a narrow gauge feeder line to start Texas cotton on its way to St. Louis. Jay Gould tried to hem it in, but it built northeast, then fell into Gould's hands. Shortly after 1900 it reached St. Louis by trading trackage rights with Missouri Pacific in southeast Missouri and southwest Illinois and teaming up with MoPac to build a bridge across the Mississippi at Thebes, Ill. By then Cotton Belt was at its full extent: St. Louis to Fort Worth, with branches to Sherman, Hillsboro, Waco, and Lufkin, Texas, Shreveport, Louisiana, Memphis, Tennessee (by trackage rights on Rock Island), and Cairo, Illinois.

Rock Island purchased control of Cotton Belt in 1925 and sold it almost immediately to Kansas City Southern. In 1932 Southern Pacific

The K1-class Consolidations were Cotton Belt's big freight locomotives until the 4-8-4s arrived in 1930. Photo by R. J. Foster.

Cotton Belt's finest freight engines were its home-built 4-8-4s. Number 814 was the last of the 1937 group. Photo by R. J. Foster.

acquired control of Cotton Belt to establish a St. Louis connection for its Texas lines. The road continued to be more or less independent until about 1950, when it began to look more and more like a piece of SP.

Cotton Belt began dieselizing in earnest with FTs in 1944 and 1945. Between 1951 and 1953 it cut its passenger-train miles by more than half, with the result that by the end of 1952 the road's passenger trains were dieselized. By mid-1953 diesels had replaced the last steam engines in freight service. The official last run was a work train on October 28, 1953, behind 2-8-0 No. 502 (Baldwin, 1906).

Freight locomotives

At the beginning of the 20th century Cotton Belt freight rolled behind 2-6-0s and 4-6-0s. The road bought Moguls through the first decade of the century, and the last four, G1s Nos. 425-428, had a number of features in common with the G1 Consolidations (including cylinder size and thus the same classification). They were intended for heavy switching and transfer service around St. Louis.

Cotton Belt bought its first 2-8-0s in 1906, ten small 55"-drivered engines with slide valves, Stephenson valve gear, and narrow fireboxes — class G1, Nos. 500-509. In the 1920s five were superheated and given new cylinders and valve gear, and three were converted to 0-8-0s. The

G1s were followed in 1909 and 1901 by the G2s, Nos. 510-529, which differed principally in having a 30" piston stroke and Walschaerts valve gear. Later all were superheated and fitted with piston valves, and two of the class were converted to 0-8-0s.

Between 1912 and 1923 Baldwin delivered 76 K1-class engines, Nos. 550-589 with 57" drivers and 750-785 with 61". Both groups had 25" × 30" cylinders; weight ranged from 228,000 pounds for the first ones as built to 243,775 pounds for the last. All were eventually converted to oil fuel, and 15 received tender boosters in 1927. Many K1s displaced by diesels were not scrapped but sold to the Southern Pacific of Mexico and its successor, the Ferrocarril del Pacifico.

During World War II StLSW bought several groups of 2-8-0s from Erie, Chicago & North Western, and Detroit, Toledo & Ironton, and seven 4-8-2s from Rock Island.

Until the late 1920s Cotton Belt was an also-ran, secondary railroad. In 1929 the investors that had acquired the road began to upgrade it, and new locomotives were at the top of the list. In the late 1920s all sorts of high-capacity freight locomotive designs were available, but Cotton Belt needed an engine that was compatible with 85-pound rail, 90-foot turntables, and wood bridges. Baldwin proposed a high-drivered 2-8-4, then a 4-8-4, then built ten 4-8-4s — and Cotton Belt's leap from 2-8-0 to 4-8-4 is one of the longest in North American railroading. The new engines, Nos. 800-809, had 70" drivers and 26" × 30" cylinders, and weighed 422,500 pounds, about the same weight as Rio Grande's 1700s, Great Northern's S-2s, and Timken demonstrator No. 1111.

The L1s went into service moving 30 percent more tonnage than the K1s and doing it faster. The road's new fast freight, the *Blue Streak*, was good publicity; better for the finances was an ever-increasing amount of freight moving to and from Southern Pacific at Corsicana, Texas. In 1937 Cotton Belt built five more 4-8-4s in its own shops at Pine Bluff, Ark. Engines 810-814 incorporated two refinements, Boxpok drivers and roller bearings on all axles; the Baldwin 4-8-4s received them in the early 1940s. Wartime traffic required more power, so Pine Bluff built another five, Nos. 815-819, in 1942.

By 1952 Cotton Belt was almost totally dieselized. Eleven 4-8-4s moved west to parent Southern Pacific for freight service out of El Paso, Texas. When those routes were dieselized, the 4-8-4s were moved again and found a new career in passenger service, first in San Francisco-San Jose commute service, then on SP's main lines out of Oakland. Number 819, the last of the 1942 4-8-4s, was put on display at Pine Bluff. It was restored for excursion service in 1985.

Passenger locomotives

Cotton Belt's passenger business was primarily local (Missouri Pacific served all of Cotton Belt's important cities and towns faster and more frequently). The road bought 4-4-0s with 69" drivers until 1906. Most were scrapped in the early 1930s, but three lasted into the 1940s. In 1909 Baldwin delivered six small Atlantics numbered 600-605. They had 70" drivers, a narrow firebox between the trailing wheels, slide valves, and Stephenson valve gear — they were not so much Atlantics as they were Americans with trailing axles. In the mid-1920s they were modernized with piston valves, Walschaerts valve gear, and super-heaters, and were converted to oil burners. Until 1930 they were Cotton Belt's only locomotives with trailing trucks. Two 4-4-2s were scrapped in the early 1930s; the other four lasted most of the way through the

Eighteen Ten-Wheelers were the mainstay of passenger and fast freight service until the arrival of 4-8-4s and ex-Florida East Coast 4-8-2s. The Scullin disk drivers under No. 665 would have been more at home on a New York Central Hudson. Photo by R. J. Foster.

1940s — and one was sold in 1952 to the Cotton Plant-Fargo Railway, probably for use as a stationary boiler.

Six E2 Ten-Wheelers were adapted for passenger service by the expedient of thicker driver tires, increasing their 61" drivers to 70".

In 1913 Baldwin delivered ten G0-class 4-6-0s with 69" drivers. Other than being Ten-Wheelers long after Pacifics had become the standard passenger engine, they were as modern as the Atlantics were archaic, with wide fireboxes, superheaters, piston valves, and Walschaerts valve gear, and at 209,200 pounds they were 13 tons heavier than the Atlantics. Eight more with Baker valve gear came from Baldwin in 1916. In the 1920s they were converted to oil burners, and later several were fitted with disk drivers.

In the early 1920s the road considered ordering copies of the light USRA Pacific, but nothing came of it nor of a proposal for a heavy 73"-drivered 4-8-2. By the mid-1930s the road needed something larger than the G0 Ten-Wheelers. The new 4-8-4s were far too expensive (and too valuable in freight service) to use on short passenger trains. In 1936 Florida East Coast defaulted on an equipment trust. and StLSW entered a bid for five 12-year-old light 4-8-2s. They were a bargain at $12,500 each — the Baldwin 4-8-4s of 1930 had cost $110,849 each. Cotton Belt classed them L0 and numbered them 675-679.

Historical and technical society: Cotton Belt Rail Historical Society, P. O. Box 2044, Pine Bluff, AR 71613

Recommended reading: *Cotton Belt Locomotives*, by Joseph A. Stra-

pac, published in 1977 by Shade Tree Books, P. O. Box 2268, Huntington Beach, CA 92647 (LCC 77-78935)

Published rosters: *Railroad Magazine*: September 1932, page 196; February 1947, page 110; July 1953, page 96

SLSW STEAM LOCOMOTIVES BUILT SINCE 1900

Type	Class	Numbers	Qty	Builder	Built	Retired	Notes
0-6-0	C3	95-97	3	SLSW	1895-1900	1916, 1917	
							Built at Pine Bluff
0-6-0	C4	86-94	9	Rogers, Bald.	1901, 1903	1925-1933	
							87, 87 Ex-Dallas Terminal
0-8-0	G2	500, 504, 509, 524, 528					
			5	SLSW	1927-1929	1945-1953	
2-6-0	D2	300-330	31	Rogers	1901-1904	1929-1944	
2-6-0	D3	331-340	10	Baldwin	1906, 1909	1945-1955	
2-6-0	E3	400-404	5	Rogers	1905	1934-1956	
2-6-0	E4	450-459	10	Baldwin	1909	1947-1950	
2-6-0	G1	425-428	4	Baldwin	1912	1946	
2-8-0	G1	500-509	10	Baldwin	1906	1935-1953	
						500, 504, 509 to 0-8-0	
2-8-0	G1	530-532	3	Alco	1904-1905	1945	Ex-Erie
2-8-0	G2	510-529	20	Baldwin	1909-1910	1945-1953	
						524, 528 to 0-8-0; 6 to SPdeM 1947	
2-8-0	G2	545-548	4	Schen, Rich	1909,1911	1946-1949	Ex-DT&I
2-8-0	J1	533-536	4	Schenectady	1903, 1904	1945-1949	Ex-Erie
2-8-0	K1	540, 541	2	Schenectady	1909, 1910	1945	Ex-C&NW
2-8-0	K1	550-589	40	Baldwin	1912-1917	1934-1952	
							15 to FdelP 1950
2-8-0	K1	750-785	36	Baldwin	1920-1923	1934-1956	
							25 to FdelP 1950
4-4-0	C2	40-57	18	Rogers, Pitt	1900-1903	1927-1944	
4-4-0	D1	58-62	5	Baldwin	1906	1933	
4-4-2	E1	600-605	6	Baldwin	1909	1933-1952	
						601 sold to Cotton Plant-Fargo	
4-6-0	E2	209-224	16	Rogers, Pitt	1900, 1901	1925-1944	
4-6-0	F1	250-255	6	Baldwin	1910	1945-1953	
4-6-0	G0	650-667	18	Baldwin	1913, 1916	1945-1952	
4-8-2	L0	675-679	5	Schenectady	1924	1952, 1953	Ex-FEC
4-8-2	M1	680-686	7	Brooks	1920, 1923	1953	Ex-CRI&P
4-8-4	L1	800-819	20	BLW, SLSW	1930-1943	1953-1959	

SEABOARD AIR LINE RAILROAD

By Albert M. Langley, Jr., and W. Forrest Beckum, Jr.

Most major railroad systems in the United States were formed by the turn of the century, but the Seaboard did not emerge until 1900. Financier John Skelton Williams of Richmond, Virginia, merged existing companies and constructed connecting segments to form a railroad which stretched from Portsmouth and Richmond, Va., to both coasts of Florida, and from the ports of Wilmington, North Carolina, Savannah, Georgia, and Jacksonville, Fla., to Birmingham and Mont-

gomery, Alabama, and Chattahoochee, Fla. SAL had several subsidiaries that it eventually absorbed — Macon, Dublin & Savannah; Georgia, Florida & Alabama; and Charlotte Harbor & Northern — plus another that remained independent, Gainesville Midland.

SAL's line south through the Carolinas was inland and crossed numerous rivers, resulting in a sawtooth profile (the easy route along the coastal plain was already taken by Atlantic Coast Line). The short

Seaboard's Q-3 class was based on the USRA light Mikado, modernized and lengthened slightly — note the space between the cylinders and the first drivers. Baldwin photo; collection of H. L. Broadbelt.

lines it acquired were lightly constructed, as were many of the branches in Florida. SAL competed in the Northeast-to-Florida passenger market with Atlantic Coast Line (ultimately its merger partner); its line to Atlanta and Birmingham competed with the Southern Railway. It carried manufactured goods south and perishables north just like ACL, but had to work harder doing it. Other major commodities were forest products and phosphate.

Seaboard began dieselizing its Florida passenger trains in 1938, the same year Atlantic Coast Line turned to 4-8-4s. After World War II SAL amassed a diverse fleet of diesels in an effort to dieselize quickly. The road reported dieselization complete in 1953, but one 0-4-0T continued to work on the street trackage at Columbus, Ga., until 1959.

Freight locomotives

Seaboard turned to the 2-8-0 relatively early. In 1902 and 1903 Richmond delivered 20 L-3 class Consolidations, 57"-drivered engines weighing 145,200 pounds. They were notable for having wide fireboxes over the rear drivers. Baldwin delivered the ten members of the H class in 1904, also with 57" drivers and wide fireboxes but weighing almost 34,000 pounds more. With 21" × 30" cylinders and 200 pounds pressure they were rated at 39,500 pounds tractive effort. The last 2-8-0s built for the Seaboard were the H-1 class, 20 engines delivered by Baldwin in 1911. They had 56" drivers and 23" × 30" cylinders and weighed about 214,000 pounds as built. The last engine of the class, No. 919, was built with a superheater, and the combination of 25" × 30" cylin-

ders and 170 pounds pressure gave it a tractive effort of 48,450 pounds.

SAL acquired a number of 2-8-0s with short lines, and during World War II it purchased five from Chicago & North Western which proved to be its most powerful Consolidations.

Consolidations were SAL's standard drag freight power and Pacifics and Ten-Wheelers pulled fast freights until 1914, when Richmond delivered 19 Mikados numbered 300-318 and classed Q. They had 63" drivers and weighed 282,000 pounds. The combination of 185 pound pressure and 27" × 30" cylinders proved less than optimal, and later the cylinders were reduced to 26" and pressure raised to 200 pounds; the Mikes were also eventually fitted with mechanical stokers.

The USRA assigned ten light 2-8-2s to Seaboard in 1918. The Q-1s had almost the same specifications as the Q class but were equipped with mechanical stokers. SAL returned to its own design for the Q-2 class, 15 of which were delivered by Schenectady in 1922. They later received the same modifications as the Q class. The next year, 1923, saw the first of the Q-3 Mikados, based on the USRA light Mike but with differences: cast trailing truck with booster, air pumps mounted on the smokebox front, and 17" extra space between the cylinders and the first drivers. SAL purchased a total of 117 Q-3s from Schenectady, Richmond, and Baldwin, and in 1931 used the remains of No. 441, which had suffered a boiler explosion, to build a new engine numbered 451.

World War I brought three groups of ten-coupled freight locomotives. Baldwin delivered ten 2-10-2s in 1918. They had 63" drivers and 29"

Mountain 263, at Richmond in 1938 on the northbound *Orange Blossom Special*, typifies the modernized M-2, with Elesco coil-type feedwater heater and 12-wheel tender. Photo by Bruce D. Fales.

× 32" cylinders and weighed 336,000 pounds. Seaboard classed them B and numbered them 400-409; in 1925 they were renumbered 2400-2409 to make room for 2-8-2s. In 1919 the USRA assigned 15 light 2-10-2s to Seaboard; they became class B-1, Nos. 485-499 (later 2485-2499). They had 57" drivers and weighed 352,000 pounds. The B-class engines were considered mainline power and worked out of Hamlet, primarily westward to Charlotte and Rutherfordton; the USRA engines were found to be slow and hard on the track and were banished to the Atlanta-Birmingham line. Both classes later benefited from recounterbalancing and disk main drivers. The USRA engines, surprisingly, outlasted the B class by several years.

The other ten-coupled engines were Russian Decapods. USRA allocated 20 to Seaboard, which found them ideal for logging and phosphate service on light-rail branches in Florida. Eventually 14 more came to the Seaboard from other railroads.

In 1924 the Georgia, Florida & Alabama, which had a line from Richland, Ga., south through Bainbridge, Ga., and Tallahassee, Fla., to the Gulf of Mexico, asked Baldwin for a 2-10-0 that was faster than its two Russian Decapods. Baldwin's response was a light, fast 2-10-0 which

quickly became a standard item in Baldwin's catalog. GF&A bought six and liked them. SAL acquired the GF&A in 1928 and was impressed enough with the Baldwin Decapods to order eight more in 1930. They were assigned primarily to Montgomery-Savannah and Montgomery-Bainbridge fast freight service.

Articulateds

In 1917 and 1918 Richmond delivered 16 Mallets, Nos. 500-515, to work between Hamlet, N. C., and Richmond, Va. They were 2-8-8-2s intended for fast freight service, with 63" drivers, larger than normal for the type. They were quickly found to be too large for the Seaboard not only in pulling capacity but in size and weight. They also proved that compound Mallets were intended for low-speed work. In 1920 they were sold to Baltimore & Ohio and converted to simple 2-8-8-0s.

Seaboard tried articulateds again in 1935, Baldwin simple 2-6-6-4s that were considered the first successful high-speed articulateds. They had 69" drivers and four 22" × 30" cylinders, and at 230 pounds boiler pressure could exert a tractive force of 82,300 pounds; they weighed 480,000 pounds and were numbered 2500-2504. Baldwin delivered five more, Nos. 2505-2509, in 1937, with just minor differences: Walschaerts valve gear instead of Baker, Worthington feedwater heaters instead of Elesco coil type, and single crosshead guides instead of the alligator type. The articulateds' territory was extended beyond Hamlet to Atlanta and Birmingham, and northeast from Norlina to Portsmouth, Va. Displaced by diesels in 1947, they were sold to B&O just as the 2-8-8-2s had been.

Passenger locomotives

The last Ten-Wheelers SAL purchased were the K class, built in 1910 with 72" drivers for passenger service. They were narrow-firebox engines, and over the years were the subject of considerable tinkering with cylinders, valves, and driver size. Most were fitted with smaller drivers and reclassed L-2-S or L-4-S.

The first Pacifics arrived in 1911. They were superheated engines with 72" drivers, but they were light, only 214,400 pounds. Baldwin built five more in 1912, and Richmond seven in 1913, including replace

2-10-0 — BALDWIN STANDARD DECAPODS

by E. W. King, Jr.

Seaboard Air Line 533, built in 1930, illustrates Baldwin's standard light Decapod design. Baldwin photo, collection of H. L. Broadbelt.

In the early 1920s Baldwin decided to pursue the light-axle-loading market that existed in the short lines and even some of the Class 1 railroads. It developed two sizes of light superheated 2-10-0s available with a choice of fuel (oil or coal, with another choice of mechanical stoker or hand firing).

The heavier of the two designs developed 60,000 pounds starting tractive effort with an axle loading of just 46,000 pounds. It had 25" × 30" cylinders, 57" drivers, 64.7 square feet of grate area, and boiler pressure of 215 pounds. The engine weighed about 250,000 pounds. By comparison, the USRA heavy Mikado developed about the same tractive effort, but had an axle loading of 60,000 pounds and total engine weight of 326,000 pounds. Gulf, Mobile & Northern bought 16 of the type between 1923 and 1927 (Nos. 250-265), and Kansas City, Mexico & Orient, five in 1925 (Nos. 801-805, later Santa Fe 2565-2569).

The lighter model found wider acceptance: Between 1924 and 1933 Baldwin built 22 for six railroads. They had 24" × 28" cylinders, 56" drivers, 54.3 square feet of grate area, and 190 pounds boiler pressure; starting tractive effort was 46,510 pounds. Total weight was just 212,000 pounds, with 38,000 pounds on each driver axle and 22,000 pounds on the lead truck. For comparison, the Russian Decapods of 1918 weighed 185,000 to 210,000 pounds, had an axle loading of 35,000 pounds, and exerted 51,500 pounds tractive effort.

Free-steaming and fast, Baldwin's light 2-10-0s were the antithesis of Pennsylvania Railroad's I1 Decapods. They found homes on Alabama, Tennessee & Northern (Nos. 401-403); Durham & South-

ern (Nos. 200-202; No. 202 was the only locomotive built in the U. S. in 1933); Georgia, Florida & Alabama (Nos. 400-405, later Seaboard Air Line 523-528); Great Western (No. 90); Osage Railway (No. 10, later Midland Valley 110); and Seaboard Air Line (Nos. 529-536). Canadian Locomotive Company built 10 virtual duplicates between 1926 and 1930 for Edmonton, Dunvegan & British Columbia (Nos. 51-58) and its successor, Northern Alberta Railways (Nos. 101 and 102).

In the 1950s Gainesville Midland, a short line in Georgia, bought four of the locomotives secondhand (AT&N 402 to GM 203, and SAL 524, 530, and 533 to GM 207, 208, and 209). They remained active until 1959, and three survive today. Great Western 90, its smokebox extended to enable it to burn lignite, hauled sugar beets for its owner until the early 1960s; it now operates on the Strasburg Railroad in Pennsylvania. Alabama, Tennessee & Northern 401 was sold to Woodward Iron Company in Alabama and soldiered on into the early 1960s, then was donated to Mid-Continent Railway Museum in North Freedom, Wisconsin.

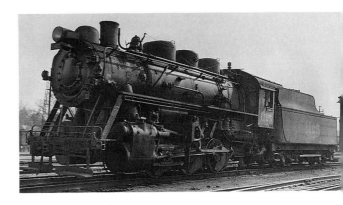

Seaboard's F-7 0-6-0s, built by Baldwin in 1927 and 1928, represent the ultimate development of the six-wheel switcher. Photo by Ernest Sevde.

ments for two that had collided head-on. They were delivered as Nos. 1-20 and renumbered 851-870. In 1940 P-class engines 865 and 868 were streamlined for the Wildwood-Tampa-St. Petersburg section of the *Silver Meteor*.

The P-1 Pacifics, Nos. 800-849, delivered by Baldwin and Richmond in 1912 and 1913, were freight Pacifics with 63" drivers and 22" × 28" cylinders. They weighed 220,000 pounds and developed 33,826 pounds tractive effort. After the Mikados arrived SAL rebuilt 41 P-1s with 69" drivers to better fit them for passenger service and reclassed them P-2 and P-3. During World War II SAL bought ten light Pacifics from Western Maryland for freight and passenger service. They had 68" drivers and weighed 201,700 pounds; SAL classed them P-4 and numbered them 871-880.

In quick succession after the Pacifics came the M-class Mountains for Richmond-Hamlet-Atlanta passenger service, Nos. 200-209 from Richmond in 1914 and 210-214 from Schenectady in 1917. They had 69" drivers and 27" × 28" cylinders and weighed 316,000 pounds. Ten more 4-8-2s almost identical to the Ms came from Schenectady in 1922. They were classed M-1 and numbered 215-224.

In search of more speed, SAL modified the design with 72" drivers for the M2 class, built by Baldwin between 1924 and 1926. They had cast trailing trucks (no boosters, though), and like the previous 4-8-2s they had small Vanderbilt tenders and were hand-fired. They were later fitted with stokers or converted to oil, and received 12-wheel tenders or had their small tenders enlarged. Initially their territory was Richmond-Hamlet-Savannah; later they worked to Atlanta, Tampa, and Miami.

Switchers

SAL had a small group of 0-4-0 tank engines for street trackage in Columbus, Ga., the last of which was delivered by Baldwin in 1936. The L-5-class 0-6-0s, built between 1907 and 1913, were considered standard switchers until the mid-1920s. USRA assigned ten 0-6-0s to

Seaboard in 1918. Mainstays of the switching fleet in later years were 5(F-7 class 0-6-0s built by Baldwin in 1927 and 1928. They were quite mod ern and were fitted with front-end throttles. With 51" drivers, 23" × 28 cylinders, and a weight of 180,000 pounds, they looked like USRA 0-6-0 at first glance, but they were larger.

The road had only five 0-8-0s, former 2-8-0s purchased from Elgin Joliet & Eastern during World War II.

Historical and technical society: Atlantic Coast Line and Seaboard Ai Line Railroads Historical Society, p. O. Box 325, Valrico, FL 33594-032

Recommended reading:

Seaboard Air Line Railway Steam Boats, Locomotives, and History, b Richard E. Prince, published in 1969 by Richard E. Prince (LCC 69 19844)

Seaboard Air Line Railway Album, by Albert M. Langley Jr., W. Forres Beckum Jr., and C. Ronnie Tidwell, published in 1988 by Union Statio Publishing, 785 Murrah Road, North Augusta, SC 29841 (ISBN 0-9615257 2-X)

Published rosters: *Railroad Magazine*: May 1935, page 88; Septembe 1948, page 114

SAL STEAM LOCOMOTIVES BUILT SINCE 1900

Type	Class	Numbers	Qty	Builder	Built	Retired	Notes
0-4-0	Odd	468	1	Baldwin	1901	1917	Ex-Georgetown &Western
0-4-0T	Odd	1002	2	Baldwin	1912	1936	
0-4-0T	Odd	1003	1	Baldwin	1913	1949	
0-4-0T	Odd	1001	1	Baldwin	1936	1959	
0-4-2T		1000	1	Porter	1900	1914	Ex-Columbia Belt Line
0-6-0		123	1	Richmond	1900	Sold 1917	Ex-Georgetown & Western
0-6-0		125	1	PRR	1903	1930	Ex-Jefferson Construction Co.
0-6-0		1000, 1001	2	Baldwin	1907	1930	Ex-GF&A, ex-TN
0-6-0		1026	1	Baldwin	1915	1937	Ex-CA&W
0-6-0	F-2	1016-1020	5	Rhode Island	1900	-1935	
0-6-0	F-3	1006-1009	4	Pittsburgh	1900	-1930	
0-6-0	F-4	1010-1015	6	Pittsburgh	1901	-1930	
0-6-0	F-5	1090-1099	10	Cooke	1918	-1952	
0-6-0	F-7	1101-1150	50	Baldwin	1927-1928	-1953	
0-6-0	L-5	1030-1059	30	Baldwin	1907-1913	-1952	
0-8-0	F-9	1175-1179	5	Pittsburgh	1904-1905	-1949	Ex-EJ&E, built as 2-8-0
2-8-0		920-924	5	Baldwin	1906-1913	1946, 1949	Ex-GF&A 200-204
2-8-0		925, 926	2	Baldwin	1910, 1911	1933, 1936	Ex-CH&N 17, 18
2-8-0		927, 928	2	Richmond	1913	1949, 1941	Ex-CH&N 50, 51
2-8-0		929-932	4	Baldwin	1920	1950-1951	Ex-CH&N 71-74
2-8-0		954, 955	2	Baldwin	1900	1916	Ex-Georgetown & Western
2-8-0	H	990-999	10	Baldwin	1904	-1938	
2-8-0	H-1	900-919	20	Baldwin	1911	-1950	
2-8-0	H-2	933-937	5	Schenectady	1910-1912	1948-1949	Ex-CNW
2-8-0	L-3	970-989	20	Richmond	1902-1903	-1935	
2-8-2	Q	300-318	19	Richmond	1914	-1952	
2-8-2	Q-1	490-499	10	Schenectady	1918	1950	USRA
2-8-2	Q-2	319-333	15	Schenectady	1922	-1952	
2-8-2	Q-3	334-451	118	Schen, BLW, Rich, SAL	1923-1931	-1955	
2-8-2	Q-4	480-487	8	Rich, BLW	1912	1946-1950	Ex-Wabash
2-10-0	D	500-520	21	Richmond	1918	-1951	Russian Decapod
2-10-0	D-1	521, 522	2	Baldwin	1918	1949, 1950	Russian
2-10-0	D-2	523-528	6	Baldwin	1924, 1926	1951-1953	Ex-GF&A
2-10-0	D-3	529-536	8	Baldwin	1930	1952-1953	
2-10-0	D-4	540-546	7	Brooks	1918	1949-1950	Russian
2-10-0	D-5	547-550	4	Baldwin, Richmond, Brooks	1918	1949-1951	Russian
2-10-2	B	2400-2409	10	Baldwin	1918	1948-1950	
2-10-2	B-1	2485-2499	15	Baldwin	1919	1950-1953	
2-6-6-4	R-1	2500-2504	5	Baldwin	1935	Sold 1947	
2-6-6-4	R-2	2505-2509	5	Baldwin	1937	Sold 1947	
2-8-8-2	A	500-515	16	Richmond	1917-1918	Sold 1920	
4-4-0		101	1	Baldwin	1905	1936	Ex-GF&A
4-4-0		103	1	Baldwin	1913	1933	Ex-CH&N
4-4-0		122	1	Baldwin	1901	1924	Ex-Georgetown & Western
4-4-0		166	1	Baldwin	1914	1936	Ex-CA&W
4-4-0	G-1	180-184	5	Rhode Island	1900	1903	
4-4-0	G-2	185-199	15	Baldwin	1900	-1933	
4-6-0		684-688	5	Baldwin	1901-1906	1930, 1936	Ex-GF&A
4-6-0		689	1	Baldwin	1910	1934	Ex CH&N
4-6-0		690, 692	2	Baldwin	1907	1930	Ex-Tampa Northern
4-6-0		693-695	3	Baldwin	1914	-1936	Ex-Tampa & Gulf Coast
4-6-0	I-5	581	1	Richmond	1900	1916	
4-6-0	I-5	1575-1599	24	Richmond	1900-1901	1928-1933	
4-6-0	I-12	671-680	10	Baldwin	1909-1913	1936-1948	Ex-CA&W
4-6-0	I-13	681-683	3	Baldwin	1915	-1946	Ex-CA&W
4-6-0	K	658	1	Baldwin	1910	1940	
4-6-0	L-2	600-649	49	Rich, BLW	1902-1907	1936-1950	
4-6-0	L-2-S	652-654, 659	4	Baldwin	1910	-1950	Rebuilt from K, 1933
4-6-0	L-4	700-796	97	BLW, Rich	1903-1907	1922-1952	
4-6-0	L-4-S	650, 651, 655-657, 660-664	10	Baldwin	1910	-1952	Rebuilt from K, 1933
4-6-2	P	851-870	20	Rich, BLW	1911-1913	-1951	
4-6-2	P-1	800-849	50	BLW, Rich	1912-1913	-1952	
4-6-2	P-4	871-880	10	Baldwin	1909, 1911	-1952	
4-8-2	M	200-214	15	Rich, Schen.	1914, 1917	-1950	
4-8-2	M-1	215-224	10	Schenectady	1922	-1952	
4-8-2	M2	235-270	36	Baldwin	1924-1926	-1954	

SHAYS AND OTHER GEARED LOCOMOTIVES

Until the mid-1920s special-purpose railroads did the industrial jobs that are now handled by trucks, tractors, fork-lifts, and earth-movers. Conventional steam locomotives weren't the best motive power for some of those special jobs — snaking logs out of the woods, for example. Logging railroads were lightly built, with grades that followed the course of the land and curves that would challenge an 0-4-0. In the 1870s a Michigan lumberman, Ephraim Shay, had a local foundry build a small locomotive that would be cheaper to operate than teams of mules or oxen. The locomotive destroyed Shay's track, even though it weighed less than a car of logs. Shay reasoned that a locomotive with trucks instead of big drive wheels would ride better on his track. He designed such a locomotive and asked Lima (Ohio) Machine Works to build one. It was a flat car with two four-wheel trucks, an upright boiler, and a pair of vertical cylinders. The cylinders drove a longitudinal shaft that drove the axles through bevel gears to reduce speed and increase torque.

The Shay was a success, and it became Lima's specialty — and put Lima into the locomotive business. It evolved into a machine with a longitudinal boiler offset to the left to balance the weight of the cylinders (usually three) on the right. It was available in a variety of sizes, with two, three, even four trucks, and a number of Class 1 railroads bought Shays for special service. The last Shay was built in 1944 for Western Maryland, for use on a branch with 9 percent grades.

The Shay was the most common type of geared locomotive — Lima built about 2,770 between 1880 and 1944. The other two common types were the Climax and the Heisler. The Climax Manufacturing Company of Corry, Pa., built approximately 1,100 geared locomotives between 1888 and 1928. There were several types. The most common had a pair

![Shay No. 15]

Shay No. 15 of the West Side & Cherry Valley, a tourist-carrying successor to the West Side Lumber Company, displays the basic elements of a Shay: three slide-valve cylinders, longitudinal driveshaft, bevel gears driving each axle, and boiler off-center to balance the cylinders. Photo by Robert L. Hogan.

The workings of the Climax are easy to see in this tiny 1910 Climax that is part of the collection of the British Columbia Provincial Museum. Photo by Jay Lentzner.

Meadow River Lumber Company three-truck Heisler No. 6 was still active at Rainelle, West Virginia, in 1955. Photo by John B. Allen.

of inclined cylinders just aft of the smokebox driving a transverse shaft which was geared to a central longitudinal driveshaft that in turn drove all the axles through skew bevel gears.

Heisler Locomotive Works of Erie, Pennsylvania, built more than 600 geared locomotives between 1891 and 1941. They had two cylinders arranged in a V under the boiler driving a central longitudinal shaft gear to the outer axle of each truck; side rods connected the outer and inner axles.

SOUTHERN PACIFIC LINES

In 1900 Southern Pacific consisted of several long routes and clusters of branches. From Oakland, California, the main lines radiated east over the Sierra Nevada and across the desert to Ogden, Utah (the original Central Pacific); north through the Sacramento Valley and over the Cascades and Siskiyous to Portland, Oregon; and southeast through the San Joaquin Valley and over the Tehachapis to Los Angeles, then east through Tucson, Arizona, and El Paso, San Antonio, and Houston, Texas, to New Orleans. Secondary lines covered central California, and Houston was the hub of a group of lines covering much of Texas east of San Antonio. In 1900 SP purchased the narrow gauge Carson & Colorado, which extended from a connection with the Virginia & Truckee at Mound House, Nevada, 300 miles south across desert and mountains to the Owens Valley of California, where it connected with nothing for another decade. SP's route along the coast from San Francisco to Los Angeles was nearly complete in 1900; it opened in 1901.

In 1900 Edward H. Harriman bought control of the SP from the estate of Collis P. Huntington, the last of its founders. He immediately began a campaign of line relocations and improvements that included double

track over the Sierra, a trestle across the Great Salt Lake, and a new water-level line south of San Francisco. SP soon benefited from Harriman's program of locomotive and car standardization, and for more than a decade SP, Union Pacific, Illinois Central, and Chicago & Alton all had locomotives built to the same designs.

The 1920s saw several new lines drawn on SP's map. In 1924 SP purchased the El Paso & Southwestern, which had a line from Tucson, Ariz., to El Paso parallel to SP's own line, then northeast to a connection with the Rock Island at Tucumcari, New Mexico. The Natron Cutoff from Black Butte, Calif., to Eugene, Ore., via Klamath Falls was completed in 1926, bypassing the curves and grades of the route through Grants Pass. About the same time SP opened a line from Klamath Falls to the Oakland-Ogden route at Fernley, Nevada. The Southern Pacific of Mexico was completed from Nogales, Ariz., to a connection with National Railways of Mexico a few miles north of Guadalajara, capital of the state of Jalisco.

Every SP route out of California eventually came up against mountains, and the worst combination of grades and operating conditions

Mogul 1623, shown at Tracy, California, in 1942, was built by Cooke in 1899. It was typical of SP's fleet of more than 300 2-6-0s. Photo by Richard W. Biermann.

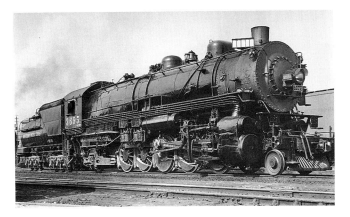

Southern Pacific's standard road freight engine was the 2-10-2. The two cross-compound air pumps on the right side of No. 3695 balance a Worthington BL feedwater heater on the left. Photo by Gerald M. Best.

was on the route east to Ogden (though crews working over the Siskiyous or the Tehachapis might debate that). The line climbed 7,000 feet in the 105 miles from Sacramento to the summit of Donner Pass — which was in a heavy snow area. Much of the route was protected by snowsheds, so crews had to battle smoke instead of snow. Beyond the Sierra and beyond the mountains east of Los Angeles lay hundreds of miles of desert.

SP's principal commodities included perishable fruit and vegetables moving east from California, lumber south and east from Oregon, and general merchandise moving west. SP was the principal passenger carrier on the West Coast and operated suburban services south from San Francisco to San Jose and in Oakland, Berkeley, and Alameda.

For years the state of Texas required that railroads doing business in the state have their principal offices there. SP had a long list of Texas subsidiaries that were consolidated in 1934 as the Texas & New Orleans Railroad. The point of demarcation was El Paso. West lay the Pacific Lines; east, the Texas & Louisiana Lines. The T&L Lines were practically a separate railroad. At least after the 1901 renumbering, Pacific Lines engines had four-digit numbers and T&L engines, three-digit. Locomotives transferred between Pacific Lines and T&L were renumbered, and when they returned there was no guarantee they'd get their old numbers back. Pacific Lines' four-digit locomotive numbering had plenty of growing room, and there was little renumbering or reuse of old numbers. The T&L roster was cramped by its three-digit numbers, and there were several renumberings.

The acquisition of the El Paso & Southwestern in 1924 and the San Antonio & Aransas Pass in 1925 added non-standard locomotives to the roster. Many were were eventually assigned to SP's lines in Mexico.

SP's motive power policy was conservative. It was still acquiring Ten-Wheelers in 1920 and Moguls in 1930, both products of the road's shops and both the heaviest of their type (242,500 and 215,230 pounds, respectively). Of the two major innovations of the 1920s, SP went whole hog for the less successful — three cylinders. Fireboxes supported by four-wheel trucks appeared on only two types, 4-8-4s and 4-8-8-2s. The

HARRIMAN STANDARDIZATION

Harriman's takeover of SP in 1900 amounted to an all-but-merger of SP and Union Pacific. One manifestation of this situation (and of Harriman's quest for efficiency) was unified purchasing of standard locomotives and cars. At the time Union Pacific's mechanical department was in tatters after a period of control by the Goulds followed by bankruptcy, so SP's mechanical department drew up plans for Common Standard locomotives of ten wheel arrangements. Parts were interchangeable among as many classes as possible, and everything was specified in detail, even the shape and size of the builder's plate and the placement of gauges in the cabs.

The equipment purchases for the Associated Lines, as the Harriman roads were known, were made by the Union Pacific Equipment Association, and they were massive purchases. For five months at the end of 1907 and beginning of 1908 the entire production of Alco's Brooks Works was an order of 125 engines of five types for SP, UP, and subsidiaries from the Oregon & Washington to the Cananea, Rio Yaqui y Pacífico. The Associated Lines assigned new locomotives where they were needed, which wasn't necessarily the road lettered on their cabs, and sometimes purchased more engines than were necessary, accounting for a group of Common Standard 2-8-0s on the Erie, of which Harriman was a director.

Harriman died in 1909, and Union Pacific control of Southern Pacific ended in 1913, but Harriman's policies influenced locomotive design for several more years — and his Common Standard locomotives remained in service until the end of steam.

Depression halted locomotive development for several years; in the late 1930s and early 1940s SP purchased large numbers of 4-8-4s and 4-8-8-2s.

During World War I SP was one of the few major roads that acquired no USRA locomotives. They would have had to be converted to oil in any event, and SP had its own ideas about locomotive design. The road was desperate enough for locomotives, though, that it built 2-6-0s, 2-8-0s, 4-6-0s, and 4-6-2s from spare parts, in effect getting brand-new locomotives of decade-old designs. The traffic surge of World War II was so intense that SP bought whatever used locomotives it could find and searched through its dead lines for everything that could be restored to service.

Diesel switchers appeared in the late 1930s, but road diesels not until 1947. SP dieselized from the ends toward the middle. As diesels took over the outer districts, steam locomotives were moved to California, even the best 2-8-0s and 4-8-4s of subsidiary St. Louis Southwestern. By 1956 steam was in service only to cover traffic surges. Delivery of a large number of diesels in 1956 and a recession in 1957 gave SP enough diesel power even for peak season. The last steam freight run was November 30, 1956, and diesels replaced the last steam in regular passenger service (Peninsula commute service) on January 22, 1957. A final Oakland-Reno excursion was operated with 4-8-4 No. 4460 on October 19, 1958, and the last operation of steam in regular service was between Laws and Keeler, Calif., on August 25, 1959, with 50-year-old narrow gauge 4-6-0 No. 9.

SP used several classification systems, starting in the late 1880s with one based on cylinder size, then a rudimentary alphabetic scheme about 1895. In 1904 the Harriman roads adopted a new scheme that consisted of a letter for type followed by a series of numbers and fractions for driver size, cylinder bore and stroke, and weight on drivers. The system was informative but cumbersome — the first Atlantics, for example, were class A-79$\frac{1}{2}$ $^{15\&25}/_{28}$ 200. Later, suffix letters were added to indicate superheater and feedwater heater. About 1912 SP adopted a simpler class system, which is used here.

Freight locomotives

In the 1890s SP's standard freight engine was the 4-8-0. At the turn of

SP's cab-forwards gave the engineer a forward view unequaled by any other steam engine. Number 4133, built by Baldwin in 1930, was an AC-6, the last class with flat-front cabs. Baldwin photo; collection of H. L. Broadbelt.

The Lima-built AC-9s were SP's only coal-burning articulateds of conventional layout. The skyline casing over the domes wasn't quite enough to qualify them as streamlined. Photo by R. H. Kindig.

the century it returned to the 2-8-0 for heavy trains and the 2-6-0 for light duties, at the same time adopting such new technology as piston valves, oil fuel, and compounding. The M-4 Moguls had 63" drivers and 20" × 28" cylinders, and weighed 146,000 pounds. Many were built as Vauclain compounds, but by the mid-Teens were converted to simple engines with 21" × 28" cylinders. The type evolved only slightly; the classes differ primarily in weight. The three M-6s built by Sacramento Shops in 1917 and 1918 from spare parts weighed 179,000 pounds and were essentially 1902 engines, even to Stephenson valve gear. The M-21s, built by Houston Shops between 1928 and 1930, were the largest of the type built, weighing 215,230 pounds, but they followed the same basic design, with 63" drivers and 22" × 28" cylinders — 250 pounds of boiler pressure gave them 45,710 pounds of tractive effort.

In the ten years between 1901 and 1911 SP amassed a fleet of more than 350 Harriman Common Standard 2-8-0s with 57" drivers and 22" × 30" cylinders. They were the road's standard freight engine. The shops at Sacramento and Los Angeles assembled 19 more from spare parts, condemned engines, and new components between 1917 and 1919 to help alleviate a power shortage.

The first 2-8-2s, the Mk-2 class, Nos. 3200-3215, appeared in 1911, with 57" drivers and 23¾" × 30" cylinders and a weight of 264,800 pounds. The Mk-4s, 3216-3240, only slightly heavier but superheated, were delivered in 1913, along with the first of the Mk-5 class, which had 63" drivers, 26" × 28" cylinders, and a weight of 280,300 pounds. The Mk-6s, which had the same dimensions, were delivered in the middle of a run of Mk-5s. The Mikado seems to have been an interim type on SP. Pacific Lines had only 83 in four classes, and the Texas & Louisiana Lines had just a single group of 57 Mk-5s.

Brooks delivered an initial batch of ten 63"-drivered 2-10-2s in 1917, F-1s 3601-3610, and three months later a single 57"-drivered F-2 which was rebuilt to F-1 specifications in 1920. SP's class letters stood for the common name of the type in most cases. The 2-10-2s were F for Freight; crews called them "Decks" — for Decapod. The F-3 class, delivered in 1921, set the pattern for subsequent 2-10-2s: 63" drivers, 29½"

T-32-class Ten-Wheeler 2381 was one of fourteen built mostly from spare parts by SP's shops between 1917 and 1920. SP photo.

$\times$ 32" cylinders, weight of 385,000 pounds. F-4s 3668-3687 were shipped from Baldwin in a single train called the "Prosperity Special" to symbolize the end of the post-World War I slump. A number of 2-10-2s were converted to coal in the 1920s for use out of El Paso; later they were restored to oil. Many of the 2-10-2s were leased or sold to the T&NO in the 1940s and 1950s. The last 2-10-2, No. 3769, was built with Uniflow valves and Walschaerts valve gear, and in 1929 was fitted with Caprotti poppet valves, which proved too delicate. In 1937 it was rebuilt to F-5 specifications.

Shortly after the last 2-10-2s were delivered SP decided to try Alco's three-cylinder concept in the form of a 4-10-2. Schenectady delivered 16 in 1925, 23 in 1926, and 10 in 1927. They were dubbed the Southern Pacific type on SP (Union Pacific's were the Overland type) and they were put into service over the Sierra. They proved not to be a replacement for 2-8-8-2s; most eventually worked out of Los Angeles.

Articulateds

In 1909 Baldwin delivered two 57"-drivered 2-8-8-2 Mallets, the first of that wheel arrangement, to replace double-headed Consolidations over the Sierra. They pulled well, but their length and exhaust were incompatible with the snowsheds — the crews couldn't see forward at all, and that problem was secondary to just breathing. One trip made in reverse was more successful, except for difficulties with the tender, but it led to a suggestion: Put the cab over and around the smokebox. The heat and noise would have been terrific, and the overhang on curves left little room for a cab anyway, but the proposal led to another solution: separate the engine from the tender, attach the tender at the smokebox end, add plumbing to bring the fuel oil to the firebox, enclose the cab, and add headlight and pilot. The idea was outrageous, outlandish, and outstandingly successful. Later in 1909 Baldwin delivered 15 cab-forward 2-8-8-2s, class MC-2 (Mallet Consolidation), Nos. 4002-4016. Between 1911 and 1913 Baldwin shipped 32 more of the type

west. Between 1928 and 1931 most were rebuilt to simple articulateds and reclassified AC. They remained in service until the late 1940s.

SP tried the same concept for a passenger engine in 1911: a dozen MM-2-class cab-forward 2-6-6-2s. (The MM-1 class consisted of a dozen light T&NO 2-6-6-2s built in 1910 and displaced in the early 1920s by 2-10-2s.) They proved unstable and by 1914 all had been fitted with four-wheel lead trucks. They were simpled in the late 1920s and 1930s and the entire class wound up in freight service in Oregon.

The second generation of cab-forwards consisted of 4-8-8-2s with 63" drivers and four 24" $\times$ 32" cylinders. The first ten arrived from Baldwin in 1928: Nos. 4100-4109, class AC-4. Northern Pacific's first 2-8-8-4 was introduced that same year. SP's AC-4 wasn't quite a Yellowstone backing up: It had the same size drivers, but the cylinders were 2 inches less in diameter, the firebox was much smaller (SP didn't have to contend with NP's low-grade coal), total weight was about 50 tons less, and tractive force was 116,900 pounds, compared to 140,000 pounds for NP's Yellowstone. Which was the better engine? NP bought 12 Yellowstones; Baldwin kept building cab-forwards until SP had 195 of the type in classes AC-4 through AC-12, except for AC-9. They were SP's trademark, even more than the *Daylight* 4-8-4s.

In 1939 Lima delivered 12 coal-burning 2-8-8-4s for service between El Paso and Tucumcari. They were SP's only modern articulateds of

Pacific 2416 was a member of the first group of Harriman standard 4-6-2s. Some of the class were extensively rebuilt; others like No. 2416 changed but little during their service lives. Photo by F. J. Peterson.

conventional layout. They had the same driver and cylinder dimensions as the cab-forward 4-8-8-2s and, like the Lima-built 4-8-4s, they had skyline casings over the domes and silver striping on the pilots. They were converted to oil burners in 1950.

Passenger locomotives

By 1900 SP had adopted the 4-6-0 for passenger service, but purchased two groups of 4-4-0s, E-23s 1445-1458 in 1900 and E-27s 1526-1540 in 1911. Both classes had 73" drivers and were intended for light passenger service. Most were scrapped in the mid-1930s. Number 1455 was sold to the T&L Lines and survived until 1948; No. 1445 was scrapped in 1951 after serving several years as a stationary boiler at Indio, Calif. Most of T&L's own E-23s had long lives, as did three groups of 4-4-0s inherited from the San Antonio & Aransas Pass and Dayton & Goose Creek. All survived thanks to frail branch lines that could support nothing larger.

From Oakland east to Sacramento, north to Redding, and south to Bakersfield was level country, ideal for high-drivered Atlantics. Sixteen 4-4-2s numbered 3000-3015 were delivered by Baldwin in 1902, Vauclain compounds with 84" drivers. They were followed in 1903 by 13 A-2 Atlantics with 79" drivers, also Vauclain compounds. Engines 3016-3024 had Vanderbilt boilers, which had cylindrical fireboxes set into

the rear of the boiler; T&L engines 285-288 had conventional boilers. Of the A-1s and A-2s only No. 288 was converted to a simple engine, and it was scrapped with the rest of the class.

The largest group of Atlantics was the A-3 class, Nos. 3025-3071 and 289-292. They were built between 1904 and 1908 by Baldwin, Schenectady, and Brooks as simple engines with 81" drivers. All were superheated by the mid-1920s, and many were fitted with feedwater heaters or booster-equipped cast trailing trucks (they were delivered with inside-journal trailing trucks), but they retained their Stephenson valve gear. The A-5s were built for the Mexican Lines, served on the Arizona Eastern, and were assigned to Pacific Lines in 1924. They had the same dimensions as the A-3 class.

In 1927 and 1928 Sacramento and Los Angeles Shops each rebuilt two A-3s with new cylinders, outside valve gear, and booster-equipped trailing trucks. At least one was later painted red and orange and assigned to the *Sacramento Daylight*, a Sacramento-Lathrop section of the *San Joaquin Daylight*.

T-25-class Ten-Wheelers 2274-2281 and T-26s 2283-2300 were built in 1901 by Cooke and Baldwin, respectively. Both classes had 69" drivers; the Baldwins were Vauclain compounds. Ten T-23 Ten-Wheelers were delivered by Baldwin in 1903. They were numbered 2301-2310 and had 63" drivers and 21" × 28" cylinders. The T-28 and T-31 classes followed the same design with cylinders an inch larger and a little more weight (176,330 pounds for the T-23 as built; 196,200 with superheater; 203,300 and 208,000 for the T-28 as built and with superheater; 208,000 for the T31, built superheated). Twelve T-28s were built for the T&L Lines in 1908 and 1911 — Ten-Wheelers weren't nearly as popular east of El Paso as they were on Pacific Lines.

Brooks built T-32s 2363-2370 in 1913. They were large engines with 69" drivers and 23" × 28" cylinders and a weight of 218,500 pounds, but

SP's heavy Pacifics were like Texas & New Orleans P-13 No. 631, shown at San Antonio in 1937 at the head of train 5 — train number indicators were another Harriman standard. Photo by Guy L. Dunscomb.

like the previous 4-6-0s had narrow fireboxes between the rear drivers. Between 1917 and 1920 Sacramento and Los Angeles Shops copied the design for 14 more of the class. In 1927 No. 2371 was reclassed T-40 when it was fitted with a feedwater heater, which increased its weight to 242,500 pounds — the heaviest of all 4-6-0s.

Baldwin delivered 28 Pacifics, Nos. 2400-2427, between 1904 and 1907. They had 77" drivers, 22" × 28" cylinders, outside piston valves, Stephenson valve gear, and inside-journal trailing trucks; they weighed 222,000 pounds. They were superheated in the late Teens. Between 1927 and 1929 eight of the class (and one P-2) were modernized with Walschaerts valve gear, booster-equipped cast trailing trucks, and feedwater heaters; they were reclassed P-4 but retained their original numbers. The P-3s (2428-2437) were almost identical; the P-5s (2438-2452 and 600-609) were built with Walschaerts valve gear. In 1917 and 1918 Sacramento Shops scraped up enough spare parts to build two more P-3s — brand-new 1904 engines (without those P-3s SP would have had to accept USRA engines).

The P-6s (2453-2458 and 610-621), built by Brooks in 1913, marked the first real development of the Harriman Common Standard Pacific on SP: They weighed 277,300 pounds, and while they had the same 77" drivers, they had 25" × 28" cylinders and a large tapered boiler instead of the thin straight boiler of the early Pacifics.

The P-8 and P-10 Pacifics (2461-2475 and 2478-2491) were heavy Pacifics with 73" drivers and 25" × 30" cylinders; the P-9s (622-630) and P-13s (631-633) were near-duplicates of the P-10s. The P-10s were built with feedwater heaters — the P-8s had them added — and the last eight P-10s were built with boosters. The P-14 class (650-652) were former Pacific Lines P-6s rebuilt and streamlined in 1937 for the *Sunbeam* and the *Hustler*.

Contemporaneous with the heavy Pacifics were the 4-8-2s. Sche-

nectady delivered 28 in 1923 and 1924, and Sacramento Shops built 49 copies between 1925 and 1930. All had 73" drivers (like the heavy Pacifics), 28" × 30" cylinders, trailing-truck boosters, and Worthington BL feedwater heaters. The El Paso & Southwestern 4-8-2s, the Mt-2 class, had cylinders an inch larger and Baker valve gear, but were rebuilt with 28" cylinders and Walschaerts gear in the early 1940s. They were ordered by EP&SW but delivered to SP and renumbered almost immediately well above any 4-8-2s SP had planned.

The 4-8-4s are straightforward except for the renumbering of the GS-1s as they crossed the dividing line at El Paso. Baldwin delivered 14 Northerns in 1930, 4400-4409 for Pacific Lines and 700-703 for T&L Lines. They were classed GS-1 — some say for General Service and others say for Golden State. They were modest-size Northerns weighing 442,300 pounds; they had 73" drivers and 27" × 30" cylinders. Even with inch-smaller cylinders, their higher boiler pressure (250 pounds) gave them about 5,000 pounds more tractive effort than the Mountains. In the early 1940s seven Pacific Lines GS-1s were transferred to the T&L and were renumbered 704-710; in the 1950s Nos. 700-703 and 705-709 moved west and were renumbered into the 4400s, some with an interim 4470-series number.

4-10-2 — SOUTHERN PACIFIC

The 4-10-2 was a logical combination of Alco's advocacy of three-cylinder locomotives and the successful 2-10-2. The weight of the third cylinder and its machinery required a four-wheel lead truck, creating a new wheel arrangement. In 1925 Alco built two 4-10-2s — Southern Pacific 5000 in April and Union Pacific 8800 in May — and asked the railroads to name the type. SP suggested Southern Pacific; Union Pacific, Overland (UP was the Overland Route). SP ordered 15 more almost immediately, but UP tested its 4-10-2 extensively before ordering nine more.

By 1927 SP had amassed 49 of the type. They went to work in freight and passenger service over Donner Pass, but proved too rigid for the curves there. They were moved south and spent most of their lives on the Sunset Route east from Los Angeles before retirement between 1953 and 1955. Number 5021 was donated to the Southern California Chapter of the Railway & Locomotive Historical Society and is displayed at the Los Angeles County Fairgrounds in Pomona.

Union Pacific's 10 Overlands were assigned to Salt Lake City-Los Angeles service. UP was pleased with its three-cylinder 4-12-2s, but rebuilt the 4-10-2s as two-cylinder engines in 1942. Two were scrapped in 1948 and two in 1949. The other six lasted until 1953 (one engine) and 1954 (five).

In 1926 Baldwin built a three-cylinder compound 4-10-2 with a watertube firebox and sent it around the country on a demonstration tour. The railroads found it overly heavy and complex and were wary of most of its features: a cylinder between the frames, compounding, and watertube firebox. By then it was evident the two-cylinder 4-8-4 was the ideal high-speed, heavy freight and passenger engine. Baldwin No. 60000 returned to Philadel-

Southern Pacific was the principal user of the 4-10-2, with 49 locomotives like No. 5024 on its roster. Photo by Gerald M. Best.

phia in 1928 and was stored until 1932, when it was placed on displayed at the Franklin Institute. It remains there today.

Other names: Overland (Union Pacific)
Total built: 60
First: Southern Pacific 5000, April 1925
Last: SP 5048, July 1927
Longest lived: SP 5021, built 1926, retired for preservation March 1956
Greatest number: Southern Pacific, 49
Heaviest: Baldwin 60000, 457,500 pounds
Lightest: Union Pacific 5090-5099, 360,100 pounds
Recommended reading: *Three Barrels of Steam*, by James Boynton, published in 1973 by Glenwood Publishers, P. O. Box 194, Felton, CA 95018 (ISBN 0-911760-13-X)

The 4-8-2s were built for heavy passenger service and were eventually bumped to secondary and commuter trains and freight service. Number 4334, a product of SP's Sacramento Shops, has been equipped with a skyline casing. Collection of R. W. Brown.

After a seven-year hiatus SP took delivery of six more 4-8-4s, Nos. 4410-4415, built by Lima, as were all subsequent 4-8-4s. Dimensionally they were the same as the GS-1s, but in appearance they were wonderfully different: broad running board skirting, skyline casing over the domes, conical smokebox front, and red, orange, and black paint to match the new San Francisco-Los Angeles *Daylight* streamliner (see page 379). Later in 1937 Lima delivered another 14 with 80" drivers, 26" × 32" cylinders, and 280 pounds pressure: GS-3s 4416-4429. They were followed by the 28 GS-4s and two GS-5s in 1941 and 1942: half an inch less cylinder diameter and 20 pounds higher pressure. The two GS-5s were identical to the GS-4s except that they had roller bearings, Timken on No. 4458 and SKF on 4459. The 4-8-4s went to work on all the principal passenger trains and also the San Francisco-Los Angeles *Overnight* merchandise freight trains. The GS-6 class was built under wartime restrictions. They had to be dual-service engines, not passenger power, so they reverted to the 73"-drivered GS-2 design; they lacked skirting and were painted black. (Western Pacific received six identical engines, and Central of Georgia used the same design for its "Big Apple" 4-8-4s.) GS-4 No. 4449 was placed on display in Portland, Oregon, in 1958. It was restored to operating condition in 1975 for the *American Freedom Train*, then regained its *Daylight* colors and has since operated over much of the SP system.

In 1952 SP leased 11 Cotton Belt 4-8-4s that had been displaced by diesels, classified them GS-7 and GS-8, and got another three to five years' service out of them, first on the Rio Grande Division out of El Paso, then in San Francisco commute service.

Switchers

The entire SP system had only 39 0-8-0s. They fell into three groups: engines built by Sacramento Shops using boilers of retired A-3 Atlantics,

engines built by Houston starting with boilers of 2-6-6-2s, and former El Paso & Southwestern engines built as 0-8-0s. The Depression cut off the Atlantic-to-0-8-0 program, and by the time it resumed diesel switchers were available. The rest of the switcher fleet comprised 0-6-0s, mostly with 51" drivers and 19" × 26" cylinders. Those built after World War I had 57" drivers and 20" × 26" cylinders.

Oddities

The cab-forwards can be considered oddities only in comparison to other locomotives. They were SP's solution to an operating problem, they worked well, and SP was obviously pleased enough with them to keep buying them.

Southern Pacific had one Camelback, Ten-Wheeler No. 2282, built for the Sonora Railway to use anthracite coal from mines in northern Mexico. After only a few months in Mexico it was transferred to Pacific Lines and was soon converted to conventional configuration.

SP's narrow gauge line from Laws to Keeler in California's Owens Valley, a remnant of the Carson & Colorado, remained in steam until

1954, when a custom-built diesel took over.

Historical and technical society: Southern Pacific Historical & Technical Society, 9510 West 122nd Street, Overland Park, KS 66213

Recommended reading:

Steam Locomotive Compendium, by Timothy S. Diebert and Joseph A. Strapac, published in 1987 by Shade Tree Books, P. O. Box 2268,

Huntington Beach, CA 92647 (ISBN 0-930742-12-5)

Cab-Forward, by Robert J. Church, published in 1982 by Central Valley Railroad Publications, P. O. Box 116, Wilton, CA 95693

Published rosters: *Railway & Locomotive Historical Society Bulletin*, No. 94, entire issue

SP STEAM LOCOMOTIVES BUILT SINCE 1900

Type	Class	Numbers	Qty	Builder	Built	Retired	Notes
Pacific Lines							
0-6-0	S-8	1295-1297	3	Brks, BLW	1908-1909	1940-1950	
							Ex-Arizona Eastern
0-6-0	S-10	1210-1221	12	Baldwin	1913	1954-1958	
0-6-0	S-10	1232-1246	15	Baldwin	1918	1953-1957	
0-6-0	S-10	1298, 1299	2	Baldwin	1917, 1918	1957, 1958	
							Ex-Arizona Eastern
0-6-0	S-11	1222-1231	10	Lima	1914	1953-1958	
0-6-0	S-12	1247-1284	38	SP	1919-1923	1949-1958	
0-6-0	S-14	1285-1294	10	Lima	1924	1953-1958	
0-6-0	S-16	1002	1	Baldwin	1903	1935	Ex-EP&SW
0-6-0	S-17	1003-1014	12	Schen	1907	1932-1936	Ex-EP&SW
0-6-0	S-22	1100	1	Brooks	1922	1951	
							Ex-South San Francisco Belt
0-6-0	S-51	1122-1194	73	BLW, Brks	1906-1911	1939-1951	
0-6-0	S-51	1195-1209	15	Baldwin	1912	1946-1951	
0-6-0	S-57	1077-1101	25	Baldwin	1901-1902	1932-1940	
0-6-0	S-57	1102-1106	5	Baldwin	1903	1934-1938	Vanderbilt boilers
0-6-0	S-57	1107-1111	5	Baldwin	1903	1932-1945	
0-6-0	S-57	1112-1121	12	Schen	1904	1935-1952	
0-8-0	SE-2	1301-1306	6	Baldwin	1901, 1903	1935-1950	Ex-EP&SW
0-8-0	SE-2	4500	1	Baldwin	1901	1950	Ex-EP&SW
0-8-0	SE-3	4509-4512	4	T&NO	1930, 1936	1956-1958	
0-8-0	SE-4	1307-1314	8	SP	1930-1937	1956-1958	
0-8-0	SE-4	4501-4508	8	SP	1930-1937	1956-1958	
2-6-0	M-4	1615-1719	103	Schen, Cooke	1899-1901	1932-1957	
2-6-0	M-6	1725-1769	45	Baldwin	1901	1934-1958	
							Vauclain compound
2-6-0	M-6	1780-1802	23	Baldwin	1902-1903	1939-1958	
							Vauclain compound
2-6-0	M-6	1803	1	Baldwin	1902	1953	Ex-CRYyP
2-6-0	M-6	1823-1825	3	SP	1917, 1918	1946-1957	
2-6-0	M-7	1720-1724	5	Baldwin	1901	1934-1954	
							Vanderbilt boiler, Vauclain compound
2-6-0	M-7	1770-1779	10	Baldwin	1902	1954-1958	
							Vanderbilt boiler, Vauclain compound
2-6-0	M-9	1804-1818	15	Brooks	1908	1934-1958	
2-6-0	M-9	1819-1822	4	Baldwin	1909	1950-1953	
2-6-0	M-9	1826, 1827	2	SP	1918	1952, 1953	
2-6-0	M-9	1828-1830	3	Brooks	1908	1950-1954	
							Ex-Arizona Eastern
2-6-0	M-11	1831-1836	6	Baldwin	1909	1949-1956	
							Ex-Arizona Eastern
2-6-2	Pr-1	1900-1903	4	Baldwin	1902	1932-1935	Ex-EP&SW
2-6-2	Pr-2	1904, 1905	2	Baldwin	1904	1935, 1932	
2-8-0	C-3	2606-2611	6	Schen	1900	1935-1951	Cross-compound
2-8-0	C-4	2612-2623	12	Schen	1901	1935-1957	Cross-compound
2-8-0	C-5	2624-2677	54	Baldwin	1901-1903	1934-1953	
							Vauclain compound
2-8-0	C-5	2678-2693	16	Baldwin	1903-1904	1935-1952	
2-8-0	C-8	2694-2751	58	Baldwin	1904	1952-1958	
2-8-0	C-9	2513-2599	87	Baldwin	1906-1907	1949-1958	
2-8-0	C-9	2752-2830	79	Baldwin	1905-1908	1951-1958	
2-8-0	C-9	2858-2860	3	Brooks	1908	1953-1954	
							Ex-Arizona Eastern
2-8-0	C-10	2831-2838	8	Baldwin	1911	1952-1958	
2-8-0	C-10	2839-2857	19	SP	1917-1919	1949-1958	
2-8-0	C-11	2502	1	Schen	1904	1934	Ex-Butte County
2-8-0	C-11	2861-2864	4	Baldwin	1920-1921	1958	Ex-Cotton Belt
2-8-0	C-12	2503	1	Baldwin	1902	1936	Ex-Butte County

Type	Class	Numbers	Qty	Builder	Built	Retired	Notes
2-8-0	C-12	2865-2868	4	Baldwin	1923	1958	Ex-Cotton Belt
2-8-0	C-13	2501	1	Lima	1905	1925	
							Ex-Salem, Falls City & Western
2-8-0	C-15	2505-2508	4	Baldwin	1900	1939-1950	Ex-EP&SW
2-8-0	C-16	2509	1	Baldwin	1901	1923	Ex-EP&SW
2-8-0	C-17	2510, 2511	2	Baldwin	1902, 1905	1949	Ex-EP&SW
2-8-0	C-18	3400-3409	10	Baldwin	1902, 1903	1932-1959	Ex-EP&SW
2-8-0	C-19	3410-3426	17	Baldwin	1904	1934-1959	Ex-EP&SW
2-8-0	C-20	3440-3444	5	Baldwin	1906	Sold 1951	Ex-EP&SW
2-8-0	C-21	3445-3449	5	Baldwin	1906-1907	Sold 1951	Ex-EP&SW
2-8-0	C-22	3452-3469	18	Schen	1907	Sold 1951	Ex-EP&SW
2-8-0	C-23	3450, 3451	2	Schen	1907	Sold 1951	Ex-EP&SW
2-8-0	C-32	2500	1	Baldwin	1906	1948	Ex-Nacozari
2-8-2	Mk-2	3200-3215	16	Baldwin	1911	1934-1956	
2-8-2	Mk-4	3216-3240	25	Baldwin	1913	1934-1956	
2-8-2	Mk-5	3236-3249	14	Baldwin	1913	1951-1956	
2-8-2	Mk-5	3270-3277	8	BLW, Lima	1913-1917	1952-1956	
2-8-2	Mk-6	3250-3269	20	Lima	1914	1951-1957	
2-8-2	Mk-7	3300-3309	10	Schen	1913, 1916	1950-1954	Ex-EP&SW
2-8-2	Mk-8	3310-3314	5	Schen	1918	1951-1954	Ex-EP&SW
2-8-2	Mk-9	3315-3324	10	Schen	1920	1950-1955	Ex-EP&SW
2-8-2	Mk-10	3295, 3296	2	Brooks	1923	1953	Ex-Minarets & Western
2-8-2	Mk-11	3297, 3298	2	Brooks	1914	1953, 1954	Ex-C&IM
2-8-4	B-1	3500-3509	10	Lima	1928	1950-1951	Ex-B&M
2-10-2	F-1	3601-3652	52	Brooks, BLW		1917, 1919	1952-1958
2-10-2	F-2	3600	1	Brooks	1918	To T&NO 1946	
2-10-2	F-3	3653-3667	15	Baldwin	1921	1952-1958	
2-10-2	F-4	3668-3717	50	Baldwin	1922	1951-1958	
2-10-2	F-5	3718-3768	51	Baldwin	1923-1924	1949-1956	Most to T&NO
2-10-2	F-6	3769	1	Baldwin	1924	1955	Uniflow valves
2-6-6-2	MM-3	3930, 3931	2	Schen	1920	1954, 1951	
							Ex-Verde Tunnel & Smelter
2-8-8-2	MC-1	4000, 4001	2	Baldwin	1909	1948, 1949	Rebuilt to AC-1
2-8-8-2	MC-2	4002-4016	15	Baldwin	1909	1935-1949	Rebuilt to AC-1
2-8-8-2	MC-4	4017-4028	12	Baldwin	1911	1935-1948	Rebuilt to AC-2
2-8-8-2	MC-6	4029-4048	20	Baldwin	1912-1913	1936-1949	Rebuilt to AC-3
2-8-8-4	AC-9	3800-3811	12	Lima	1939	1953-1956	
4-4-0	E-23	1445-1458	14	Cooke	1900	1932-1945	
4-4-0	E-27	1526-1540	15	Baldwin	1911	1934	

Type	Class	Numbers	Qty	Builder	Built	Retired	Notes
4-4-2	A-1	3000-3015	16	Baldwin	1902	1922-1925	
							Vauclain compound
4-4-2	A-2	3016-3024	9	Baldwin	1903	1915-1918	
							Vanderbilt boiler, Vauclain compound
4-4-2	A-3	3025-3071	47	Sch, BLW, Brks		1904-1908	1932-1952
4-4-2	A-5	3072-3074	3	Baldwin	1911	1935	
4-4-2	A-6	3000-3003	4	SP	1927-1928	1948-1952	Rebuilt from A-3
4-6-0	T-23	2301-2310	10	Baldwin	1903	1949-1954	
4-6-0	T-25	2274-2281	8	Cooke	1901	1926-1934	
4-6-0	T-26	2283-2300	18	Baldwin	1901	1934-1951	
							Vauclain compound
4-6-0	T-27	2282	1	Baldwin	1900	1928	Camelback
4-6-0	T-28	2311-2352	42	Baldwin	1907-1911	1949-1957	
4-6-0	T-31	2353-2362	10	Baldwin	1912	1953-1957	
4-6-0	T-32	2363-2370	8	Brooks	1913	1953-1956	
4-6-0	T-32	2371-2384	14	SP	1917-1920	1952-1957	
4-6-0	T-35	2101	1	Schen	1900	1926	Ex-EP&SW
4-6-0	T-36	2102-2104	3	Manch	1902	1934-1947	Ex-EP&SW
4-6-0	T-37	2105, 2106	2	RI	1903	1952, 1951	Ex-EP&SW
4-6-0	T-57	2385	1	Baldwin	1906		Ex-Bullfrog-Goldfield
4-6-0	T-58	2386	1	Baldwin	1907		Ex-Las Vegas & Tonopah
4-6-2	P-1	2400-2427	28	Baldwin	1904-1907	1934-1954	9 rebuilt to P-4
4-6-2	P-3	2428-2437	10	Baldwin	1911	1947-1954	
4-6-2	P-3	2459, 2460	2	SP	1917, 1918	1952, 1948	
4-6-2	P-5	2438-2452	15	Baldwin	1912	1947-1953	
4-6-2	P-6	2453-2458	6	Baldwin	1913	1955-1957	
4-6-2	P-7	2476, 2477	2	Lima	1917	1958	Ex-Arizona Eastern
4-6-2	P-8	2461-2475	15	Baldwin	1921	1953-1958	
4-6-2	P-10	2478-2491	14	Baldwin	1923-1924	1954-1958	
4-6-2	P-11	3100-3109	10	Baldwin	1907	1939-1950	Ex-EP&SW
4-6-2	P-12	3120-3129	10	Brooks	1917	1947-1958	
4-8-2	Mt-1	4300-4327	28	Schen	1923-1924	1952-1957	
4-8-2	Mt-2	4385-4390	6	Brooks	1924	1951, 1953	
4-8-2	Mt-3	4328-4345	18	SP	1925-1926	1953-1958	
4-8-2	Mt-4	4346-4366	21	SP	1926-1929	1953-1958	
4-8-2	Mt-5	4367-4376	10	SP	1929-1930	1953-1958	
4-8-4	GS-1	4400-4409	10	Baldwin	1930	1954-1957	
4-8-4	GS-2	4410-4415	6	Lima	1936	1954-1958	
4-8-4	GS-3	4416-4429	14	Lima	1937	1954-1958	

SP STEAM LOCOMOTIVES BUILT SINCE 1900 (CONTINUED)

Type	Class	Numbers	Qty	Builder	Built	Retired	Notes
4-8-4	GS-4	4430-4457	28	Lima	1941-1942	1956-1958	
4-8-4	GS-5	4458, 4459	2	Lima	1942	1958, 1956	Roller bearings
4-8-4	GS-6	4460-4469	10	Lima	1943	1954-1958	
4-8-4	GS-7	4475-4481	7	Baldwin	1930	1955-1957	Ex-Cotton Belt
4-8-4	GS-8	4485-4488	4	StLSW	1937, 1942	1956, 1958	Ex-Cotton Belt
4-10-2	SP-1	5000-5015	16	Schenectady	1925	1951-1954	
4-10-2	SP-2	5016-5038	23	Schenectady	1926	1953-1955	
4-10-2	SP-3	5039-5048	10	Schenectady	1927	1953-1954	
4-6-6-2	MM-2	3900-3911	12	Baldwin	1911	1946-1948	Built as 2-6-6-2
4-8-8-2	AC-4	4100-4109	10	Baldwin	1928	1953-1955	
4-8-8-2	AC-5	4110-4125	16	Baldwin	1929	1952-1955	
4-8-8-2	AC-6	4126-4150	25	Baldwin	1930	1953-1955	
4-8-8-2	AC-7	4151-4176	26	Baldwin	1937	1954-1958	
4-8-8-2	AC-8	4177-4204	28	Baldwin	1939	1954-1958	
4-8-8-2	AC-10	4205-4244	40	Baldwin	1942	1955-1958	
4-8-8-2	AC-11	4245-4274	30	Baldwin	1942-1943	1954-1958	
4-8-8-2	AC-12	4275-4294	20	Baldwin	1943-1944	1955-1958	

Narrow gauge

Type	Class	Numbers	Qty	Builder	Built	Retired	Notes
4-6-0		8, 9, 18	3	Baldwin	1907-1911	1954, 1960, 1955	Ex-NCO
4-6-0		6, 7	2	Baldwin	1903	1934, 1935	Ex-NCO

Texas & Louisiana Lines

Type	Class	Numbers	Qty	Builder	Built	Retired	Notes
0-6-0	S-3	45-52	8	Schen	1899-1900	1930-1947	
0-6-0	S-5	53-77	25	Baldwin	1902-1903	1939-1941	
0-6-0	S-7	78-81	4	Schen	1904	1947-1950	
0-6-0	S-8	82-102	21	Baldwin	1906-1911	1941-1949	
0-6-0	S-8	111-116	6	Baldwin	1906-1907	1946-1949	Ex-H&TC
0-6-0	S-9	103-110	8	Baldwin	1912	1947-1950	
0-6-0	S-9	117-128	12	Baldwin	1913	1947-1954	
0-6-0	S-10	129-136	8	Baldwin	1917-1918	1950-1953	
0-6-0	S-13	137-146	10	Baldwin	1920-1921	1952-1956	
0-6-0	S-14	147-166	20	Lima, T&NO	1924-1926	1952-1957	
0-6-0	S-19	26-29	4	Schen	1901, 1903	1936-1937	
							Ex-SA&AP, EP&SW
0-8-0	SE-3	175-186	12	T&NO	1930-1936	1952-1957	
2-6-0	M-4	410-459	50	Schen, Cke	1899-1901	1934-1955	
2-6-0	M-6	482-485	4	Baldwin	1903	1947-1953	
2-6-0	M-6	515-517	3	Baldwin	1903	1947-1953	
2-6-0	M-7	460-469	10	Baldwin	1902	1928-1929	

Vanderbilt boiler, Vauclain compound

Type	Class	Numbers	Qty	Builder	Built	Retired	Notes
2-6-0	M-9	550-556	7	Brooks	1908	1948-1955	Ex-H&TC
2-6-0	M-10	560-565	6	Baldwin	1909	1947-1953	Ex-H&TC
2-6-0	M-11	500-514	15	Baldwin	1912	1952-1957	
2-6-0	M-17	495	1	Baldwin	1905	1946	Ex-SA&AP
2-6-0	M-18	496	1	Lima	1911	1932	Ex-SA&AP
2-6-0	M-19	497-499	3	Baldwin	1911	1932, 1946	
2-6-0	M-20	481	1	Baldwin	1919	1953	
							Ex-Dayton & Goose Creek
2-6-0	M-21	520-529	10	T&NO	1928-1930	1950-1954	Ex-H&TC
2-8-0	C-8	800-807	8	Baldwin	1904	1950-1955	
2-8-0	C-9	808-857	50	BLW, Brks	1905-1908	1946-1958	
2-8-0	C-20	867-869	3	Cooke	1921	1953-1955	Ex-SA&AP
2-8-0	C-21	870	1	Lima	1909	1950	Ex-SA&AP
2-8-0	C-22	871-876	6	Pittsburgh	1900	1936-1947	Ex-SA&AP
2-8-0	C-23	877-884	8	Baldwin	1913	1939-1954	Ex-SA&AP
2-8-0	C-24	885-894	10	Lima	1913	1935-1955	Ex-SA&AP
2-8-0	C-25	895, 896	2	Schen	1913	1957, 1956	Ex-Texas Midland
2-8-2	Mk-5	738-794	57	T&NO,BLW,Brks		1913-1921	1953-1957
2-10-0	D-1	897-899	3	Baldwin	1918	1934, 1937	Ex-SA&AP
2-10-2	F-1, F-4, F-5						
-		900...999	83	BLW, Brks	1917-1924	1953-1957	Ex-Pacific Lines
2-10-2	F-1	970-981	12	Brooks	1918	1954-1956	
2-6-6-2	MM-1	900-911	12	Baldwin	1910	1929-1930	Ex-950-961
4-4-0	E-23	261-265	5	Cooke	1900	1941-1951	
4-4-0	E-39	205-209	5	Baldwin	1924	1946	Ex-SA&AP
4-4-0	E-40	220-223	4	Baldwin	1922	1947, 1954	Ex-SA&AP
4-4-0	E-41	224	1	Baldwin	1921	1946	
							Ex-Dayton &Goose Creek
4-4-2	A-2	285-288	4	Baldwin	1903	1921	Vauclain compound
4-4-2	A-3	289-292	4	Schen, BLW	1904	1932	
4-6-0	T-28	700-711	12	Brooks, BLW		1908, 1911	1954-1955
4-6-0	T-38	369-376	8	Baldwin	1907-1908	1930-1937	Ex-SA&AP
4-6-2	P-5	600-609	10	Baldwin	1912	1952-1957	ex-900-909
4-6-2	P-6	610-621	12	Brooks	1913	1952-1954	ex-920-931
4-6-2	P-9	622-630	9	Baldwin	1923	1953-1955	
4-6-2	P-13	631-633	3	Baldwin	1928	1954-1955	
4-6-2	P-14	650-652	3	Brooks	1913	1953-1954	Ex-2455-2457
4-8-4	GS-1	700-703	4	Baldwin	1930	1954-1956	

SOUTHERN RAILWAY

by Dale Roberts and Bill Schafer

The banking house of J. P. Morgan coerced two financially hyper-extended railroads to combine on July 1, 1894, to form the Southern Railway. Although the Southern system ultimately comprised dozens of subsidiaries and affiliates, its two fundamental components were the Richmond & Danville and the East Tennessee, Virginia & Georgia. By 1918 the Southern either owned or controlled over 8,000 miles of railroad spanning the Southeast, from Cincinnati and St. Louis to Jacksonville, and from Washington to Memphis and New Orleans.

Southern's heart and soul lay in the Piedmont Plateau and the Appalachians. This meant grades — lots of them — nearly everywhere. The Washington-Atlanta main line, for example, followed the Appalachian foothills nearly its entire distance, slicing across dozens of watersheds. Other main lines zig-zagged through the mountains to reach operating and traffic centers such as Asheville, Knoxville, and Chattanooga. The financial frailty of Southern's predecessors meant that most lines were cheaply constructed. This meant curves.

Until well after World War II, the Southeast lagged behind the rest of the country in economic and population growth. About the only good thing the Southern had going for it during the steam era was the availability of inexpensive labor. This, combined with the railway's conservative, paternalistic management, meant that its operation favored relatively simple motive power. Besides, except on the main trunks, delicate bridges and light rail imposed weight restrictions.

The steam locomotives of the Southern family were a mix of antiques inherited from predecessors and basic workaday engines of conservative design, the newest of which was built in 1928. Except for a modest fleet of 2-8-8-2s, the largest locomotives were World War I-era 2-10-2s.

By the time the economy improved, Southern had a new management which decided that superannuated motive power and difficult operating characteristics were great reasons to give diesel-electric locomotives a try. The first diesels — six Fairbanks-Morse power cars

Southern had more than 300 K- and Ks-class Consolidations like No. 753. The engine has been fitted with Universal valves, piston valve replacements for its original slide valves. Photo by Frank E. Ardrey, Jr.

for local passenger schedules — were placed in operation in 1939. Fourteen years later the Southern was all-diesel, the largest railroad up to that time to completely dieselize.

Although the Southern possessed extensive repair shops at strategic points on its system, it never got into the business of building its own motive power. In the twentieth century, Southern favored Baldwin and American Locomotive's Richmond Works.

Many Southern locomotives came equipped with Baker, Stephenson, and the home-grown Southern valve gear. As locomotives were modernized, many received Walschaerts gear.

Southern steam locomotives possessed dignity and style, and for years Southern let its engineers and roundhouse foremen customize or personalize the engines. In his monograph on elegant engines of the Deep South, *The Georgian Locomotive*, H. Stafford Bryant, Jr., described Southern's motive power as "really not quite of this prosaic world; they were high Chippendale with brass eagles, stars on the cylinders, Mason-

Southern's heaviest 2-8-0s were the ten members of the Ks-3 class, built by Alco's Richmond Works in 1926 for service in the coal-mining area north of Knoxville, Tennessee. Photo by Walter H. Thrall, Jr.

Southern's 4-6-2s weren't all Ps-4s. P-1 No. 1292, built by Baldwin in 1906, was built with 63" drivers for service in the mountains. Its slide valves are driven by Southern valve gear. Collection of Bruce R. Meyer

ic wheels, polished candlesticks about the headlight." No two Southern steam locomotives matched precisely, particularly modernization in the programs carried out just before and during World War II.

Southern planned a major upgrading program for its locomotives, but the Depression intervened. In the years just before and after World War II it applied a number of improvements such as mechanical stokers, feedwater heaters, single-guide multiple-bearing crossheads, mechanical lubricators, rebuilt cabs, Walschaerts valve gear in place of Baker, and enlarged tenders. Each roundhouse performed these tasks with individuality; you could tell where an engine was assigned and maintained by the arrangement of its handrails, the style of its headlight, or the striping on its running boards.

In general, Southern numbered its steam locomotives according to the owning company:

Nos.	Owning Company
1-5249	Southern Railway proper
6000-6499	Cincinnati, New Orleans & Texas Pacific Railway
6500-6696	Alabama Great Southern Railroad

6800-6979	New Orleans & Northeastern Railroad
7000-7084	Miscellaneous subsidiaries
8000-8051	Russian Decapods and USA 2-8-0s assigned during WWI
8200-8375	Georgia Southern & Florida Railway
8550-8556	St. John's River Terminal (Jacksonville)

If a locomotive was superheated, a small "s" followed the class letter, such as "Ps-4." No "s" meant slide valves and saturated steam. The numbers in the roster below are 1903 numbers.

Freight Locomotives

Among the earliest locomotives ordered by the new Southern Railway were light Consolidations in the G and H series, constructed between 1895 and 1901. In size and weight, they matched power inherited from Southern's predecessors. The next group of 2-8-0s was the slightly larger J-class, constructed between 1902 and 1904. The class I Consolidations, with 63" driving wheels, anticipated the legions of 63"-drivered Mikados that followed in the subsequent two decades. The I-class was built in 1907 and 1909 for fast freight and mixed train service; it was scrapped in the early 1930s.

Next came the class K 2-8-0s, standard road freight engines that could go nearly anywhere on the system. Over 400 K-class locomotives were delivered to the Southern and its subsidiaries between 1903-1910. When the Ms-class Mikados began appearing in 1911 (there were 183 of them; the first was No. 4501, now owned and operated for excursion service by the Tennessee Valley Railroad), the 2-8-0s were gradually bumped to branch lines and local and yard work.

Many of the K-class were superheated (and reclassed Ks) in the 1920s and 1930s and received Economy or Universal valve chests. These were piston-valve kits which bolted onto the original slide valve cylinders and were common on the Southern but seldom seen elsewhere. Other K-class engines received new cylinder and valve assemblies and were reclassed Ks-1 or Ks-2.

Southern found two niches for 2-8-0s that resulted in two final orders in 1926. Like a number of Northeastern anthracite haulers that preferred heavy 2-8-0s for work in the coalfields, Southern ordered ten Ks-3s for mine run service on the branches north of Knoxville. Stoker- and feedwater heater-equipped, these were Southern's heaviest Consolidations, each packing more punch than an Ms-class Mike. Five lighter Ks-4s were ordered in the same year and assigned to the New Orleans & Northeastern, a line known for small engines and restrictive axle loadings. Light as it was, the Ks-4 was the heaviest steam locomotive ever assigned to the NO&NE.

During World War I USRA consigned 25 light Mikados to the Southern. These Ms-1 locomotives performed so well that Southern ordered 45 virtual copies in 1922 and 1923.

The seven Ms-2 locomotives were stock Ms Mikados with the running gear of surplus 2-8-0s or 2-6-0s installed under the tender. Drawing steam from the locomotive's boiler, these "auxiliary tender tractors" were a modest success on the heavy grades of the Asheville Division. The experiment lasted from 1915 until about 1924.

Five Ms-3 Mikes were constructed for subsidiary New Orleans & Northeastern 1914. Their overall weight of 209,000 pounds was eclipsed by nearly all of the Ks-series 2-8-0s.

The 166 Ms-4s delivered between 1923 and 1928 represent the high-water mark of Southern 2-8-2s. Based on the USRA heavy Mike, the Ms-4 quickly became the standard mainline freight locomotive between Alexandria and Atlanta, Chattanooga and Macon, and several other arteries on the Southern proper. Ms-4s also served as the standard freighters on subsidiaries Alabama Great Southern and Cincinnati, New Orleans & Texas Pacific. Their preeminence on the hottest freight assignments lasted until after World War II, and they were considered suitable for occasional passenger duty.

Five Ms-5 and Ms-6 Mikados were fashioned from surplus Ss-class 2-10-2s between 1929 and 1931. The conversion program was halted by the Depression.

The only Southern locomotives known to have been equipped with Vanderbilt tenders were the Ms-7s, seven ancient Mikados bought secondhand from the Erie in 1942 when new diesels were not available. They operated mostly on the AGS to relieve wartime congestion, and remained in service until bumped by diesels.

Southern's investment in articulated locomotives was modest. Two four-truck Shays were delivered by Lima in 1907 for service on steep branch lines around Knoxville; eight years later they were sold to the Chesapeake & Ohio. Subsidiary Alabama Great Southern received a single 2-6-8-0 compound in 1909. It later served on the CNO&TP, eventually winding up on Southern's Asheville Division, where it joined two others built for the Southern in 1911. All three were scrapped in 1935.

Initially ordered for service in the Appalachian coalfields, Southern's twelve Ls-1 2-8-8-2 Mallets were received in 1918-1919. Eleven more were delivered between 1924 and 1926. Southern forsook compound power with the delivery of eight simple 2-8-8-2 Ls-2 engines between 1926 and 1928. Their success as mountain haulers resulted in their prompt assignment to service over the 4.7 percent Saluda grade in North Carolina. Southern planned to convert all of the Ls-1s to Ls-2 specifications, and succeeded in simpling three of the compounds before the Depression intervened.

The first ten-coupled engines arrived in 1917-1918 in the form of 80 Ss-class 2-10-2s. The Santa Fes were heavy and rough on the railway's

The green-and-gold Ps-4 was the epitome of Southern steam power. Number 6482, shown at Cincinnati in 1947, exhibits two CNO&TP traits: the odd number plate under the headlight and the Wimble smoke duct that slides forward over the stack to protect tunnel roofs from the exhaust blast. Photo by Robert A. Hadley.

unsteady roadbed. Some were assigned to the CNO&TP and equipped with Southern's unique smoke deflectors — an extension of the smokestack designed to channel smoke over the top of the boiler and to exhaust it behind the cab. But the tunnels were too much for the leviathans, and as soon as the Ms-4s showed up in the 1920s, many of the Santa Fes found themselves on the curvy Asheville Division. These were equipped with "floating" front drivers (Franklin lateral motion driving boxes and spherical bearings forward on the connecting rods) to cope with the bends found on the Blue Ridge and Saluda grades.

Southern received 50 USRA light Santa Fes, the Ss-1 class. Until the late 1920s, many Ss-1s could be found pounding down the Alexandria-Atlanta main line until they too were bumped by the classy Ms-4 Mikes. Their rigid wheelbase, longer than that of the Ss, ruled out service on the Asheville Division, so the USRA 2-10-2s served the remainder of their careers operating in all directions out of Knoxville.

By the time the Ms-4s were delivered, it became apparent that Southern owned too many 2-10-2s. Five of the USRA Santa Fes were cut down to make class Ms-5 and Ms-6 Mikados, but again the Depression halted the conversion program. Nobody needed surplus 2-10-2s, so many of the

Ss-class succumbed to the scrapper's torch prior to World War II. As with the Ms-2 Mikados, a single Ss operated with a 2-6-2 auxiliary tractor under its tender from 1918 to 1926.

Passenger locomotives

Southern inherited numerous 4-6-0s from its predecessors. Passenger versions of this wheel arrangement were classified in the F-series, and many were built new for Southern passenger service until 1907. By that time, though, the Pacific had so thoroughly shown its superiority that the Ten-Wheeler was relegated to branch line and secondary schedules. A few F-class locomotives survived until after World War II on lines requiring light axle loadings, but most of Southern's Ten-Wheelers were scrapped by the end of the Depression.

Ten graceful Atlantics joined the roster in 1906. Fleet but feeble, the class C 4-4-2s originally ran out of Atlanta but were restricted to the Georgia lowlands, Macon-Brunswick mostly, after steel cars arrived. All but one were scrapped during the Depression; they had the largest driving wheels (79") of any Southern steam locomotive.

The first P-class Pacifics appeared in 1903. They were not superheated and had slide valves, like the first K-class Consolidations. The class eventually counted 100 members, the last delivered in 1910. Virtually all were later superheated. Those engines whose cylinders received the Universal or Economy steam chest treatment were classed Ps; others received entirely new valve and cylinder assemblies and were reclassified Ps-2.

For service in the mountains, Southern ordered 25 P-1 class 4-6-2s with 63" drivers in 1906. Four of these later were rebuilt with 67" drivers and reclassed P-5. It does not appear that any P-1 or P-5 engines were superheated; most were retired during the Depression.

Out of deference to frail trestles, five ultra-light Ps-3 4-6-2s were

Southern's largest passenger locomotives were 4-8-2s that predated the famous Ps-4s. Number 1472 was a Baldwin product of 1917. Green-and-gold livery was pioneered by the Ps-4s and later applied to passenger engines in other classes. Photo by Richard E. Prince.

built for the New Orleans & Northeastern in 1914. They lasted until the diesels showed up after World War II.

The Ps-4 Pacific was Southern's trademark locomotive. Deliveries began in 1923, equipped with USRA 10,000-gallon tenders. Indeed, the locomotive itself was a modified USRA heavy Pacific with smaller (73") drivers and a slightly shorter boiler and frame. So successful was the design that additional batches arrived in 1926 and 1928, most with twelve-wheel 14,000-gallon tenders. A total of 64 Ps-4s were built for the Southern proper and subsidiaries CNO&TP and AGS.

Until 1926, the Ps-4, as all Southern locomotives, were black. But on a visit to London in 1925, President Fairfax Harrison was smitten by the green locomotives he saw on the London & North Eastern Railway there, "relieved by gilded lettering and numbering. [He] must immediately have envisioned such gaily colored steam locomotives as rocketing through his own northern Virginia meadows," to quote Bryant again. Upon his return, Harrison saw to it that the 1926 group of Ps-4s arrived in a rich Virginia green, with gold leaf striping and lettering. The colors were an instant hit and the scheme was applied to all Southern passenger power, from 4-8-2s to 4-4-0s, within a few years. The tradition continued when Southern began operating steam locomotives in excursion service in 1966, with the debut of Ms-class Mikado 4501 in green-and-gold passenger garb. She was joined by Ks-1 Consolidation 722, similarly attired, in 1970. One magnificent example of the glory years survives: Ps-4 1401 has formed the centerpiece of the Smithsonian's railroad collection at its Museum of American History in Washington since 1962.

In 1917 Baldwin and Southern designed the railway's first 4-8-2 passenger locomotives. The thirty Ts-class engines went to work pulling trains of steel cars on the principal main lines of the Southern, CNO&TP,

and AGS. Ironically, they were bumped to hillier territory by the Ps-4 Pacifics. In 1919 the USRA assigned 25 light Mountains to the Southern, the Ts-1 class. True to the name of their wheel arrangement, Southern's Mountains could be found on passenger trains in the toughest terrain: between Bristol and Memphis, Atlanta-Birmingham, Macon-Chattanooga, and on the Asheville Division. Most 4-8-2s were incrementally modernized through the end of World War II, and with few exceptions wore their green livery to the end.

Switchers

Southern's switchers featured more individualistic customization than any other group. Records of Southern switchers are incomplete, but we can make some generalizations.

Most unusual were the shop engines assigned to various engine terminals. These included 0-4-2Ts, 0-4-4Ts and 0-6-0Ts as well as more conventional engines, most of which were not formally assigned a class.

The A-1s and A-2s were generally light 0-6-0 switchers inherited from Southern predecessors. A-3 and A-4 classes were lighter 0-6-0s built after 1894 for the Southern. A-5s belonged to the NO&NE.

The standard switcher prior to World War I was the A-7 class 0-6-0, the heaviest of its type. About 150 A-7s worked throughout the system. Built between 1904 and 1914, many lasted until the end of steam, particularly where industrial clearances were tight.

Another class produced prior to World War I was the As-10 0-8-0.

Twelve were built between 1914 and 1917 by Baldwin and Lima. The USRA 0-8-0 became Southern's standard heavy-duty yard goat. Twenty were assigned to the Southern during World War I and given the As-11 class. So successful was their performance that nearly fifty more were ordered between 1918 and 1926. CNO&TP, AGS, and NO&NE also rostered As-11s. The USRA 0-8-0s were among the last steam locomotives retired. All remained in service until the end of steam operation.

Historical and technical societies:

Southern Railway Historical Association, P. O. Box 33, Spencer, NC 28159

Southern Railway Historical Society, P. O. Box 4094, Augusta, GA 30917-4094

Recommended reading: *Southern Railway System Steam Locomotives and Boats*, by Richard E. Prince, published in 1970 by Richard E. Prince (SBN 9600088-4-5)

Published rosters:

Railroad Magazine: June 1937, page 80, and July 1938, page 134; March 1950, page 114

Trains Magazine: December 1949, page 18

SOUTHERN STEAM LOCOMOTIVES BUILT SINCE 1900

Type	Class	Numbers	Qty	Builder	Built	Retired	Notes
Southern Railway							
0-6-0		1562-1565	4	Baldwin	1903		
0-6-0	A-3	1562-1565	4	Baldwin	1903	1929	
0-6-0	A-4	1566-1575	10	Pittsburgh	1906	1925-1949	
0-6-0	A-4	1576-1600	25	Baldwin	1906	1927-1951	
0-6-0	A-7	1615-1751	137	Baldwin, Pittsburgh, Lima 1904-1914		1934-1953	
0-6-0	A-8	1601-1607	7	Baldwin	1904	1933-1948	
0-8-0	As-10	1898, 1899	2	Baldwin	1914	1953	
0-8-0	As-11	1839-1897	59	Brooks, Richmond, Lima 1918-1926		1952-1954 5 to CNO&TP, 1 to NO&NE	
2-10-2	Ss	5000-5079	80	BLW, Rich	1917-1918	1938-1952	
2-10-2	Ss-1	5200-5249	50	BLW, Brooks	1917-1918	1938-1952	
2-6-8-0	Ls	4002, 4003	2	Baldwin	1911	1935	
2-8-0		205-219	15	Schenectady	1903-1907		
2-8-0		505-509	5	Pittsburgh	1903		
2-8-0		510-548	39	Baldwin	1903		
2-8-0	H-1	251, 252	2	Richmond	1900	1934, 1938	
2-8-0	H-1	290-312	23	Richmond	1900	1935-1952	
2-8-0	H-1	313-322	10	Richmond	1901	1935-1952	
2-8-0	H-1	353-377	25	Baldwin	1901	1933-1949	
2-8-0	H-3	323-352	30	Pittsburgh	1900	1933-1952	
2-8-0	H-4	378-402	25	Baldwin	1907	1933-1954	
2-8-0	I	549-552	4	Pittsburgh	1907	1935-1938	
2-8-0	I	553-556	4	Baldwin	1909	1934-1935	
2-8-0	J	440-454	15	Pittsburgh	1903	1933-1952	
2-8-0	J	455-469	15	Richmond	1902	1935-1950	
2-8-0	J	480-489	J	Baldwin	1903-1904	1934-1950	
2-8-0	J	505-548	44	Pitt, BLW	1903	1934-1951	
2-8-0	J-1	403-408	6	Baldwin	1900	1933-1939	
2-8-0	J-2	470-479	10	Baldwin	1902	1936-1950	
2-8-0	Ks	566-883	318	Richmond, Baldwin, Pittsburgh 1903-1910		1935-1953	
2-8-0	Ks-3	2500-2509	10	Richmond	1926	1952-1953	
2-8-2	Ms	4501-4635	135	BLW, Rich	1911-1914	1939-1953	
2-8-2	Ms-1	4750-4774	25	Schen, Rich	1918, 1923	1951-1953	
2-8-2	Ms-4	4800-4914	115	Richmond, Schenectady, Baldwin 1923-1928		1952-1954	
2-8-2	Ms-6	4995-4999	5	Brooks	1918	1952 Ex-2-10-2, 4998 is Ms-5	
2-10-0		8000-8019	20	Richmond	1918		
2-10-0		8025-8034	10	Baldwin	1918		
2-6-8-0	Ls	4002, 4003	2	Baldwin	1911	1935	
2-8-8-2	Ls-1	4004-4026	23	Baldwin	1918-1926	1937-1950	
2-8-8-2	Ls-2	4050-4058	9	Baldwin	1926, 1928	1951-1952	
4-4-2	C	1905-1914	10	Richmond	1906	1934-1942	
4-6-0		915-917	3	Baldwin	1903		
4-6-0		1005-1008	4	Richmond	1900		

SOUTHERN STEAM LOCOMOTIVES BUILT SINCE 1900 (continued)

Type	Class	Numbers	Qty	Builder	Built	Retired	Notes
4-6-0		1009-1018	10	Baldwin	1901-1902		
4-6-0		1061-1074	14	Richmond	1900-1901		
4-6-0		1075	1	Baldwin	1902		
4-6-0	Es-20	3458	1	Schenectady	1900		Ex-GS&F 137
4-6-0	F-11	1001-1040	40	Schenectady, Richmond, Baldwin	1899-1906	1929-1939	
4-6-0	F-12	1051-1084	34	BLW, RIch	1897-1903	1928-1948	
4-6-0	F-14	1085-1112	28	Baldwin	1903-1904	1933-1947	
4-6-0	F-16	1113	1	Baldwin	1914	1934	
4-6-0	F-7	915-918	4	Baldwin	1903	1933-1937	
4-6-0	F-8	919-928	10	Baldwin	1907	1933-1946	
4-6-0	Fs-17	1114	1	Baldwin	1914	1947	
4-6-2	P-1	1275-1299	25	Baldwin	1906	1935-1947	
4-6-2	Ps	1200-1250	51	BLW, Rich	1903-1910	1938-1951	Many to Ps-2
4-6-2	Ps	1300-1324	25	Baldwin	1910-1911	1937-1953	
4-6-2	Ps	1360-1365	6	Baldwin	1910	1940-1952	Ex-GS&F 500-505
4-6-2	Ps-2	1251-1270	20	Rich, BLW	1911-1912	1947-1952	
4-6-2	Ps-2	1325-1359	35	Rich, BLW	1912-1914	1946-1951	
4-6-2	Ps-4	1366-1409	44	Schenectady, Richmond, Baldwin	1923-1928	1949-1953	
4-8-2	Ts	1450-1472	23	Baldwin	1917	1949-1953	
4-8-2	Ts-1	1475-1499	25	BLW, Rich	1919	1952-1953	5 to CNO&TP, 3 to AGS
	Shay	4000, 4001	2	Lima	1907	1916	

Cincinnati, New Orleans & Texas Pacific

Type	Class	Numbers	Qty	Builder	Built	Retired	Notes
0-6-0		6000-6012	11	BLW,Pitt,Dick	1900-1904	1922-1939	
0-6-0	A-7	6015-6020	6	Pitt, Rich	1906-1907	1935-1948	
0-8-0	As-10	6025-6028	4	Lima	1917	1952	
0-8-0	As-11	6029-6033	5	Brooks	1918	1952-1954	Ex-SR 1878-80, 91, 92
0-8-0	As-11	6034-6045	10	BLW, Lima	1922, 1926	1952-1954	
2-8-0	G-4	6101-6179	79		1899-1903	1923-1934	Built by Rhode Island, Schenectady, Pittsburgh, and Baldwin
2-8-0	Ks	6180-6229	50	Rich, BLW	1905-1911	1939-1950	13 to NO&NE
2-8-2	Ms	6250-6284	35	Baldwin	1911, 1913	1949-1950	
2-8-2	Ms-1	6285-6319	35	Schen, Rich	1918, 1922	1952-1953	
2-8-2	Ms-4	6320-6337	18	Richmond	1926	1953-1954	

Type	Class	Numbers	Qty	Builder	Built	Retired	Notes
2-8-2	Ms-4	6350-6374	25	Baldwin	1928	1952-1954	
4-6-0		6420-6423	4	Baldwin	1903, 1906	1924,1927	
4-6-2	Ps	6450-6470	21	Rich, BLW	1907-1913	1938-1951	
4-6-2	Ps-4	6471-6482	12	Schen, Rich	1924,.1926	1952-1953	
4-8-2	Ts	6490-6494	5	Baldwin	1917	1951-1953	
4-8-2	Ts-1	6495-6499	5	Rich, BLW	1919	1951-1953	Ex-SR 1495-1498 and 1475

Alabama Great Southern

Type	Class	Numbers	Qty	Builder	Built	Retired	Notes
0-6-0	A-9	6501, 6502	2	Baldwin	1903	1932, 1929	
0-6-0	A-7	6510-6518	9	Pitt, Rich	1905-1907	1936-1949	
0-8-0	As-10	6530-6533	4	Lima	1917	1952-1953	
0-8-0	As-11	6534-6537	4	Lima	1926	1953-1954	
2-8-0	H-7	6550-6558	9	Rich, BLW	1902-1903	1924-1938	
2-8-0	K	6565-6595	31	Rich, BLW	1905-1909	1939-1953	
2-8-0	Ks-1	6599	1	Baldwin	1909	1947	
2-8-2	Ms	6600-6611	12	BLW, RIch, Lima	1913-1917		1949-1950
2-8-2	Ms-1	6612-6621	10	Richmond	1922	1952-1953	
2-8-2	Ms-4	6622-6629	8	Richmond	1926	1952-1954	
2-8-2	Ms-7	6630-6636	7	Baldwin, Schenectady, Lima	1911-1913	1949-1952	Ex-Erie
2-6-8-0	Ls	6399	1	Baldwin	1909	1935	
4-6-0		6654-6657	4	Richmond	1900, 1902	1923-1928	
4-6-0		6660	1	Schenectady	1905	1932	
4-6-0		6661	1	Baldwin	1906	1931	
4-6-2	Ps	6675-6683	9	BLW, Rich	1907, 1909	1939-1949	
4-6-2	Ps-4	6684-6691	8	Schen, Rich	1923, 1926	1949-1953	
4-8-2	Ts-1	6692-6694	3	Baldwin	1919	1952	
4-8-2	Ts	6695, 6696	2	Baldwin	1917	1954, 1948	

New Orleans & Northeastern

Type	Class	Numbers	Qty	Builder	Built	Retired	Notes
0-6-0	A-8	6815-6826	12	BLW, Rich	1901-1907	1928, 1934	
0-8-0	As-11	6849	1	Brooks	1918	1952	
4-6-0	E-21	6875-6885	11	Baldwin	1904-1907	1928-1940	
4-6-0	Es-22	6886-6888	3	Baldwin	1911-1912	1946-1948	
4-6-0	Es-23	6889-6891	3	Baldwin	1912	1940, 1948	
4-6-0	Es-22	6892, 6893	2	Baldwin	1912	1947	
4-6-0	Fs-21	6894, 6895	2	Baldwin	1912	1939	
2-8-0	Hs-6	6898, 6899	2	Baldwin	1910	1949	
2-8-0	Ks	6900-6911	12	BLW, Rich	1906-1911	1939-1951	Ex-CNO&TP

Type	Class	Numbers	Qty	Builder	Built	Retired	Notes
2-8-0	Ks	6915	1	Baldwin	1907	1950	Ex-CNO&TP
2-8-0	Ks	6920, 6921	2	Rich, BLW	1905, 1907	1951, 1950	Ex-CNO&TP
2-8-0	Ks-4	6922-6926	5	Baldwin	1914	1949-1952	
2-8-2	Ms-3	6940-6944	5	Baldwin	1914, 1916	1946	
New Orleans Terminal Company							
0-6-0		7071-7077	7	Baldwin	1905	1923-1936	
2-6-0		7080-7084	5	Baldwin	1905	1933-1937	
Georgia Southern & Florida							
4-4-0	B-14	8200-8202	3	Baldwin	1900	1928, 1932	
4-4-0	B-16	8210-8213	4	Schenectady	1900-1901	1929-1934	

Type	Class	Numbers	Qty	Builder	Built	Retired	Notes
4-6-0	Fs-11	8230-8233	4	Baldwin	1906-1907	1929-1938	
4-6-0	Fs-17	8250-8257	8	Baldwin	1914-1915	1947-1949	
4-6-0	Es-20	8300-8305	6	Schen, BLW	1900-1904	1928-1939	
2-8-0	Ks	8330-8338	9	Baldwin	1910	1951-1952	
2-8-0	Ks-1	8339-8344	6	Richmond	1912	1949-1953	
0-6-0	A-7	8370-8375	6	BLW, Rich	1910, 1912	1948-1953	
St. Johns River Terminal							
0-6-0	A-4	8550, 8551	2	Baldwin	1908, 1909	1941, 1947	
0-6-0	A-7	8555, 8556	2	Baldwin, Lima	1909, 1912	1953	

SPOKANE, PORTLAND & SEATTLE RAILWAY

The Spokane, Portland & Seattle is significant for never having a steam locomotive of its own design — indeed, much of its life it had to make do with castoffs from its owners. In the diesel era it was independent in motive power matters, ordering from Alco when Great Northern and Northern Pacific were buying only Electro-Motive products.

The road was built between 1905 and 1908, to give its two owners, Great Northern and Northern Pacific, access to Portland, Oregon. (GN and NP were both controlled by James J. Hill.) The main line ran from Spokane, Washington, southwest to Portland. About half the distance was along the north bank of the Columbia River, with no significant grades. A subsidiary, the Oregon Trunk Railway, ran south from the Columbia at Wishram, Washington, climbing through the canyon of the Deschutes River to the plateau country of central Oregon at Bend. It became a strategic part of the Great Northern line that reached south to a connection with Western Pacific at Bieber, California.

Number 1 on the SP&S roster was a six-wheel switcher, one of five built by Manchester in 1907. Photo by Donald M. Gunn.

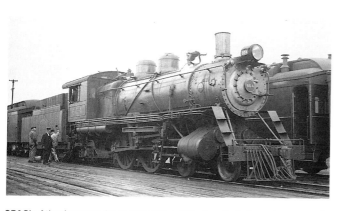

SP&S's Atlantics were duplicates of Great Northern's, balanced compounds with inside high-pressure cylinders driving the first axle and outside low-pressure cylinders driving the second axle. Their rebuilding to simple locomotives and the addition of booster-equipped cast trailing trucks duplicated GN's modifications. SP&S removed the boosters in 1931, a year before this photo was taken. Photo by R. V. Nixon.

Modern passenger power came to SP&S in the form of three 4-8-4s built alongside NP's A-3 Northerns. The only differences were in the firebox and tender — SP&S's locomotives were oil burners. Photo by H. W. Pontin.

The two parent roads tended to wrangle over their child, and they vied with each other to see which could be stingier. Most SP&S steam locomotives were acquired secondhand from GN or NP. The thirty that were built new — seven 0-6-0s, ten Atlantics, two Ten-Wheelers, three Northerns, and eight Challengers — were GN or NP designs. When the USRA allocated four heavy 2-8-2s and eight 0-8-0s to SP&S, Great Northern and Northern Pacific conferred with the USRA and agreed to provide the necessary locomotives instead. GN took the Mikes and NP took the switchers.

In its early years SP&S used 2-6-2s, 2-8-0s, 4-6-0s, and 4-4-2s. It received its first Mikados in 1925, three from GN (500-502) and one from NP (525). The ten Atlantics were the mainstay of passenger service. They were converted from compounds to simple engines in 1923 and

1924, and because passenger trains were becoming longer, they were fitted with trailing truck boosters in 1927. They were still inadequate, and the road converted six of its ex-GN 4-6-0s to Pacifics between 1927 and 1930.

In 1933 GN and NP took over management of SP&S on an alternate-year basis and closed most of its offices and shops. In 1937 GN and NP recognized that the road needed new locomotives and added three 4-8-4s and six 4-6-6-4s to NP orders, the only difference being oil fuel instead of coal. The 4-6-6-4s arrived first, SP&S's first new locomotives since 1914, when 0-6-0s 7 and 8 were delivered. Because of a business recession, two of the Challengers were placed in storage; two others were sold or leased to Great Northern to equalize locomotive mileage on trains between Spokane and Bieber.

In 1940 GN and NP began dieselization of the SP&S with four switchers. That same year SP&S resumed management of its own affairs. During World War II traffic increased significantly and the road had a rash of accidents. It had to beg for more power from its parents — Mikados plus two new 4-6-6-4s. Dieselization resumed after the war and continued slowly. A last-of-steam excursion ran behind 4-8-4 No. 700 on May 20, 1956 (No. 700 was restored to operating condition in 1990), and the last run of a steam locomotive was made by 4-6-6-4 No. 910 on June 23 of that year.

Historical and technical society: Spokane, Portland & Seattle Railway Historical Society, c/o Gerald Howard, 6207 N. Concord, Portland, OR 97217

Recommended reading:
North Bank Road, by John T. Gaertner, published in 1990 by Washington State University Press, Pullman, WA 99164-5910 (ISBN 0-87422-070-X)
The Northwest's Own Railway, by Walter R. Grande, published in 1992 by Grande Press, 4243 S.W. Admiral Street, Portland, OR 97221-3669 (ISBN 0-9634128-0-9)

Published rosters: *Railroad Magazine*: March 1939, page 118; November 1952, page 38

SP&S STEAM LOCOMOTIVES BUILT SINCE 1900

Type	Class	Numbers	Qty	Builder	Built	To SP&S	Retired	Notes
0-6-0	A-1	1-5	5	Manch.	1907	New	1946-1952	
0-6-0	A-3	7, 8	2	Schenectady	1914	New	1952	
2-6-2	F-1	450-466	17	Baldwin	1906-1907	1908, 1925	1937-1949	
								Ex-GN 1549…1638
2-8-0	N-6	325-328	4	Schenectady	1901	1925, 1936	1945-1949	
								Ex-NP 1255, 1260, 1251, 1261
2-8-0	N-6	329	1	Richmond	1902	1936	1948	Ex-NP 1273
2-8-0	N-7	335-339	5	Schenectady	1903	1925	1945-1946	
								Ex-NP 1283…1291
2-8-0	N-2	355-364	10	Baldwin	1907	1909	1952-1954	
								Ex-GN 1255-1264 (not in order)
2-8-0	N-2	365	1	Rogers	1905	1925	1952-	Ex-GN 1208
2-8-0	N-2	366-368	3	Baldwin	1907	1936	1953-1954	
								Ex-GN 1228, 1240, 1253
2-8-0	N-2	369	1	Rogers	1903	1945	1950	Ex-GN 1182
2-8-0	N-3	370	1	Pittsburgh	1904	1911	1940	
								Ex-Astoria & Columbia River 19
2-8-2	O-1	500-512	13	Baldwin	1913-1918	1925-1944	1945-1951	
								Ex-GN 3026…3134
2-8-2	O-2	525	1	Schenectady	1910	1925	1947	Ex-NP 1698
2-8-2	O-3	530-539	10	Brooks	1913-1917	1926-1944	1953-1957	
								Ex-NP 1701…1765
2-8-2	O-4	550, 551	2	Baldwin	1920	1950	1953	
								Ex GN-3211, 3214
4-4-2	C-1	600-609	10	Baldwin	1909	New	1937-1949	
								Same as GN K-1
4-6-0	D-1	100-109	10	Baldwin	1910	1910	1937-1930	
								Ex-GN 1043-1052, 6 rebuilt to 4-6-2
4-6-0	D-2	150, 151	2	Baldwin	1911	New	1950, 1948	
4-6-0	D-5	156	1	Baldwin	1904	1911	1937	
								Ex-Spokane & Inland Empire 2
4-6-0	D-6	159	1	Rogers	1902	1912	1941	
								Ex-Pacific & Eastern 3
4-6-0	D-7	160-162	3	Baldwin	1910	1925	1944	
								Ex-GN 1074-1076
4-6-2	H-1	620-625	6	Baldwin	1910		1952-1953	
								Rebuilt from 102-105, 107, 109
4-6-2	H-1	626	1	Baldwin	1910	1945	1953	Ex-GN 1378
4-8-4	E-1	700-702	3	Baldwin	1938	New	1960	
								Same as NP A-3
4-6-6-4	Z-6	900-905	6	Alco	1937	New	1960	
								Same as NP Z-6
4-6-6-4	Z-8	910, 911	2	Alco	1944	New	1960	
								Same as NP Z-8

STOKERS

By 1900 large steam locomotives had reached the limit of hand firing, about 5,000 pounds of coal per hour, roughly equivalent to a continuous output of 1,500 horsepower. A mechanical substitute for the fireman was necessary — or a conversion to oil fuel, which remained experimental in 1900.

Development of a mechanical stoker was a challenge. Consider what it had to do — transport coal from tender to engine, put it inside the firebox, and spread it evenly on the grate. The coal bunker of the tender was open to the elements, lumps of coal varied widely in size, and the machinery inside the firebox was subject to high temperatures

Stokers began to appear shortly after 1900. The components varied widely — almost everything was tried. The conveyors that moved the coal from tender to locomotive included open troughs with pistons or hinged flaps pushing the coal, and screw conveyors operating in tubes; often the mechanism included a crusher to break up larger lumps of coal. Some conveyors delivered coal directly to the underside of the grate; others transferred it to elevators that raised it above the grate. The elevators included endless chains with buckets in a tube on the backhead inside the cab, and vertical screws. Inside the firebox the coal was spread over the grate by oscillating paddles or steam jets. After the early experiments, most stokers had screw conveyors, screw elevators, and steam jets to distribute the coal.

Some railroads resisted mechanical stokers on the grounds they were expensive to purchase, install, and operate, and they tended to waste coal, putting more into the firebox than a skilled fireman. In an effort to get around the human limit, railroads used two, sometimes three firemen to increase the output of their locomotives, but even that quickly reached a limit — there's only so much room in a cab. Ultimately the Interstate Commerce Commission required mechanical stokers on all coal-burning passenger engines with 160,000 pounds or more on the drivers; for freight engines, the break point was 175,000 pounds.

The horizontal stoker tube lay beneath the cab floor and above the drawbar. At the far end of the tube a screw elevator lifted the coal to just beneath the level of the firedoor.

STREAMLINING

Streamlining was a phenomenon of the 1930s. A new profession, industrial design, arose during the Depression, and its practitioners said, in effect, "Look how smoothly and efficiently fish swim through water and birds fly through air. If we design objects that have smooth curved lines like fish and birds, those objects will be efficient."

And it was so. Curves replaced square corners, and horizontal lines replaced verticals. Objects were designed to be unified in appearance instead of collections of parts — "eye appeal" was the watchword. Ribbon spools that used to live in the open air on top of typewriters were concealed by hinged lids. Cooling coils on top of refrigerators were tucked down behind, to gather dust and cat hair out of sight and at the same time free a place to store bananas. Automobile windshields were tilted back and headlights were faired into the fenders.

The passenger train of the 1920s was not streamlined. The cars were sheathed with steel plates held together by thousands of rivets, or with narrow vertical boards with V-grooves at every joint. Roofs had protruding ventilators; underbodies were cluttered with generators, battery boxes, and other mechanical equipment. Each car was separate, and between cars there were spaces. The cars were usually painted dark olive, a color whose virtues were that it held up well and didn't show dirt. Pulling the train was a collection of wheels of various sizes, flailing levers, and what appeared to be the contents of a plumbing supply warehouse, all painted black.

Two streamlined trains burst into this nonstreamlined world in 1934, Union Pacific's M-10000 and Burlington's *Zephyr*. The UP train was golden yellow and medium brown, and although it was riveted, the rivets were comparatively small; the exterior of the *Zephyr* was unpainted fluted stainless steel. The new trains were attention-getters, and other railroads looked on enviously.

In December 1934 the New York Central unveiled a streamlined steam locomotive, *Commodore Vanderbilt* — a three-year-old J-1 Hudson, No. 5344, wearing an aerodynamically designed shroud but painted a

New York Central Hudson No. 5344 was streamlined in 1934 and given the name *Commodore Vanderbilt*. In 1939 it was reshrouded to match the 10 J-3a Hudsons delivered the previous year. Photo by Glenn Grabill Jr.

Milwaukee Road 1, shown at speed on a nine-car *Hiawatha* near West Lake Forest, Illinois, was the first steam locomotive built streamlined. Photo by Lucius Beebe.

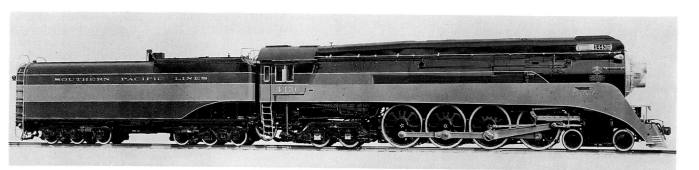

Among the best looking streamlined locomotives were Southern Pacific's *Daylight* 4-8-4s. The actual streamlining is almost minimal: running-board skirting and a "skyline" casing along the top of the boiler — and a vivid red, orange, and black paint scheme. Lima Locomotive Works photo.

conservative dark gray. In April 1935 the first steam locomotive to be built streamlined emerged from Alco's plant at Schenectady: Milwaukee Road No. 1, a huge Atlantic (first of that wheel arrangement since 1914) dressed in light gray, orange, and maroon for the road's new *Hiawatha*. Steam locomotives proved amenable to streamlining, and Alco, Baldwin, Lima, Montreal, and Roanoke built them: Atlantics and Hudsons for the Milwaukee Road, Hudsons for Chicago & North Western, Santa Fe, New York Central, and New Haven, Jubilees and Hudsons for Canadian Pacific, and 4-8-4s for Canadian National, Grand Trunk Western, Norfolk & Western, and Southern Pacific.

Railroads also streamlined existing locomotives, sometimes with the help of industrial designers, the likes of Raymond Loewy, Henry Dreyfuss, and Otto Kuhler, and sometimes on their own. The degree of streamlining varied. New York Central's *Mercury* Pacifics were completely shrouded and almost unrecognizable; New York, Ontario & Western got considerable mileage out of a simple running-board skirt and maroon paint on a 4-8-2. The esthetics of the home-streamlined

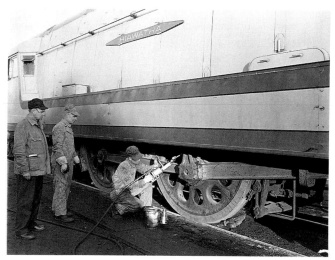

A Milwaukee Road *Hiawatha* Atlantic illustrates the difficulty of servicing streamlined locomotives. *Trains* collection.

locomotives varied, too. The "inverted bathtub" styling of NYC's *Mercury* Pacifics soon became outdated; Chicago & North Western's home-styled Pacifics were better looking than the road's Alco-built Hudsons; Lackawanna's winged locomotives were almost laughable.

Steam locomotive streamlining was of two types: the shovel-nose, flat-sided styling of the *Commodore Vanderbilt* and Milwaukee's Atlantics, which more or less copied the profile of the *Zephyr*, and the bullet or torpedo shape that resulted from simply smoothing the basic shape. The streamlining had little effect on the aerodynamics of the locomotive except at the highest speeds; the real purpose was appearance.

Streamlining also created a problem. Any part that was covered with sheet metal for the sake of appearance was inaccessible for maintenance. Doors and hatches helped, but chances were good that a streamlined locomotive would come out of the shop with a bit less shrouding than it had when it entered.

Three preserved locomotives active in the 1990s are streamlined: Canadian Pacific Royal Hudson 2860, Southern Pacific Daylight 4-8-4 No. 4449, and Norfolk & Western class J 4-8-4 No. 611.

SUPERHEATING

At normal atmospheric pressure at sea level, water boils at 212 degrees Fahrenheit (100 degrees Centigrade). If the water is heated in a pressurized vessel, the boiling point is higher. At 200 pounds pressure, for example, water boils — turns to steam — at 387 degrees Fahrenheit. Steam which is at the boiling temperature for a given pressure is said to be saturated. If the temperature of the steam is reduced, it will begin to condense back to water; if the temperature is raised, still at that pressure, the steam is said to be superheated.

When saturated steam is piped through the throttle, the dry pipe, and the valves to the cylinders, where it expands and the pressure drops, some of the heat in it (not a great proportion of it, in actuality) is converted to work. Some of the steam condenses into water.

Water in the cylinders creates problems. Water is incompressible, and if too much is in the space between the piston and the cylinder head as the piston moves toward the cylinder head, something has to give — either relief valves or the cylinder head. The higher the steam pressure, the more water condenses as the steam expands in the cylinder. Locomotive designers found that boiler pressure much over 200 pounds resulted in more water condensation than relief valves could handle; 200 pounds boiler pressure became the accepted maximum for saturated steam locomotives.

However, if the steam is heated above the boiling point after it is no longer in contact with the water from which it has been formed, the situation changes. The primary benefit is that the same weight of steam takes up a greater volume — less water has to be heated and converted to steam to do the same amount of work. In addition, the problem of condensation in the cylinders is greatly reduced.

In 1898 Wilhelm Schmidt equipped two locomotives of the Royal Prussian Railway with superheaters. He noted a 25 percent increase in efficiency and applied the device to a number of other locomotives. The Canadian Pacific noted Schmidt's experiments and sent one of its mechanical engineers, A. W. Horsey, to Europe to observe the locomotives firsthand. In 1901 CP equipped 4-6-0 No. 548 with a Schmidt smokebox superheater, the first application of the device outside Europe. In 1903 CP installed superheaters of a newer Schmidt design in two more 4-6-0s, both compounds. The railroad soon found that superheating was far more effective than compounding. In 1904 it bought its first group of locomotives built with superheaters, and by the

An Illinois Central locomotive in the Paducah roundhouse offers a good view of a Type A superheater header and the tubes running back into the flues. Photo by Bruce Meyer.

end of 1906 had 197 superheated locomotives in service and 175 more on order. At the time there were approximately 15 superheated locomotives in the United States.

How does the superheater work?

The customary route of steam to the cylinders is from the steam dome, where it is collected, through the throttle, into the dry pipe, which runs forward through the boiler into the smokebox, then through steam pipes which lead down each side of the smokebox to the valves. The superheater consists of a two-chambered manifold or header at the top of the smokebox. From the intake or saturated side of the header hairpin-shaped tubes run into the flues, reaching almost as far as the rear tube sheet. Saturated steam goes through the tube, absorbing more heat from the exhaust gases, then returns to the superheated side of the header, from which it is piped to the cylinders.

Type E superheaters consist of single U-shaped tubes in all or nearly all flues; the steam makes two passes through the flue (one back, one forward). Type A superheaters consist of double-U-shape tubes in a few rows of oversize flues. The steam makes four passes through the flue.

Advantages and disadvantages

For a given amount of fuel, a superheated locomotive was 25 to 30 percent more powerful than the same engine without a superheater. Railroads quickly saw that superheating could provide the fuel economy of the compound without its mechanical complexity. After 1912 nearly all new road locomotives were built with superheaters, and most railroads retrofitted them to existing locomotives. Railroads took longer to see that superheating would help switchers; some railroads continued to buy non-superheated switchers into the 1920s.

The superheater was a simple device with no moving parts, but it brought a few problems with it. The high temperatures of superheated steam required cylinder and valve lubricants with higher flash points, and the large flat surfaces of slide valves wore quickly with superheated steam, so piston valves became necessary. Placing superheater tubes inside the flues provided places where cinders could accumulate, and the tubes themselves eventually wore through from the cutting action of the cinders. Larger flues were required so the superheater tubes could fit inside them; that in turn meant fewer flues and a resulting decrease in the total heating surface. Those difficulties were minor, though, compared with the advantages.

When superheaters were introduced, locomotive designers experimented with lower boiler pressures, larger cylinders, and sometimes smaller boilers. The resulting locomotives were no better and sometimes worse than previous saturated locomotives. Locomotive designers soon recognized that a well-balanced saturated engine design also made for a well-balanced superheated engine.

On many modern locomotives the throttle was located not in the steam dome but ahead of superheater header in the smokebox — the front-end throttle. Later designs placed the throttle in the superheater header.

TANK ENGINES

A tank engine has no tender — it carries its fuel and water in tanks and bunkers alongside the boiler, over it like a saddle, or on a frame extension behind the cab. Common in Europe, tank engines were rare in North America. They were used in special situations.

Suburban service

Suburban passenger service has a unique set of operating conditions: frequent stops and starts and short runs — 10 or 12 miles, sometimes less. Turning the locomotive at the end of the run took time and required either a turntable, which was expensive to build and maintain, or a wye, which required real estate. One easy solution was to run the engine around the train and make the return trip in reverse, but this swapped the problems of turning the engine for new disadvantages: no guiding axle at the rear of the locomotive, the crew exposed to the weather (the rear of the cab was usually open), and a tender blocking the view of the track.

Suburban tank engines replaced the tender with a coal bunker and water tank carried on an extension of the locomotive frame. The extension was supported by a truck that also guided the locomotive into curves when running in reverse. The price of such convenience was limited fuel and water capacity and thus limited range.

The principal users of suburban tank engines in North America were Boston & Albany, Canadian National, Canadian Pacific, Central of New Jersey, Illinois Central, New York Central, and Reading. Elsewhere,

Central Railroad of New Jersey 227, a 4-6-4T, leaves Elizabethport, N. J., with the shuttle train for Newark, 7 miles away. The narrow coal bunker allows the crew to look out directly to the rear; the headlight and pilot duplicate equipment at the front of the locomotive. Photo by C. A. Brown.

short-distance suburban runs were taken over by streetcars and rapid transit, or major suburban operations were electrified. Many railroads begrudged the purchase of specialized locomotives for service that was usually not a money-maker.

Other uses for tank engines

Tank engines could be used for switching in assignments where they weren't far from fuel and water supplies. Railroads often used

The ultimate development of the suburban tank engine in North America was Boston & Albany's 4-6-6T, which looked like a condensed or concentrated New York Central Hudson. Alco built five of them in 1928. Note that the water tank extends under the rear of the cab. Photo from Alco Historic Photos.

Quincy Railroad 2, an Alco product of 1924, carried enough water in the side tanks and fuel oil in the rear tank for the 6-mile run between Quincy, California, and the connection with the Western Pacific at Quincy Junction. Photo by Guy L. Dunscomb.

them to move cars and locomotives around the shops; the lack of a tender made that much more space available on a turntable or a transfer table. The weight of the water in saddle and side tanks assisted adhesion and allowed the engine to pull a little more (and in addition it wasn't pulling the weight of a tender).

A few short lines took advantage of the virtues of the tank engine: It could operate equally well in either direction, and the complication of a tender was absent.

TENDERS

By the 1850s the tender had developed into a U-shaped water tank surrounding the fuel space and resting on what was essentially a flat car. Water was put into the tank through a covered hatch or manhole in the top, the tender deck; a gate at the front of the fuel space helped contain the wood or coal. For the most part, tenders retained that form through the steam era. The rear wall of the coal bunker acquired a slope to move coal forward so the fireman could reach it easily, and

the floor of the bunker was raised to be level with the cab floor, creating additional space underneath for water or the stoker mechanism. Locomotives that burned oil had a tank in place of a coal bunker; for locomotives converted from coal to oil, the oil tank was often a separate part designed to drop into the coal bunker.

Tender size depended on locomotive size: the larger the engine, the more fuel and water it used. There was a tradeoff: the cost of tow-

ing large amounts of fuel and water versus the cost of more frequent water and fuel stops. The ratio between the fuel and water capacities was usually based on two water stops per fuel stop — water is easier to obtain and store than coal or oil. A pound of coal, on the average, could turn 6 pounds (0.7 gallons) of water to steam, yielding an approximate ratio of 10,000 gallons of water to 14 tons of coal. In practice the proportion might be different. A railroad with track pans (New York Central for instance) could take on water without stopping and emphasize coal capacity.

Tender size also depended on turntable length. Many roads bought large locomotives with small tenders, then replaced the tenders with larger ones when longer turntables were installed.

In the Teens one-piece cast steel tender underframes became available, but the body of the tender continued to be a separate piece supported by a floor on top of the underframe. In 1927 the first water-bottom tender appeared. The underframe was a solid steel casting to which the sides were fastened, creating a single structure and increasing capacity by 1,500 to 2,000 gallons.

The riding quality of a tender depended on its load. A locomotive fresh out of the engine terminal had a heavy tender; at the end of the run, a light one — and a water stop near the end of the run resulted in a rear-heavy tender, with little coal up front and lots of water at the rear. A few railroads had dissimilar trucks under their tenders to compensate; most didn't.

In the late 1930s the cast bed frame or pedestal or centipede tender appeared. The water-bottom frame was a single casting with pedestals for five axles supporting the middle and rear and a swiveling four-wheel truck supporting the front. The five rigid axles (which could move laterally) provided extra stability.

Vanderbilt tenders

A round tank holds more than a rectangular tank with the same sur

The tender deck had a manhole for filling the water tank plus such items as drain holes for spilled water, a box housing train control apparatus, and, ahead of the manhole on this NYC tender, a housing for the top of the water chute. Most tenders had their capacities marked on the rear. NYC photo.

The pedestal tender, with a four-wheel lead truck and a ten-wheel rigid frame, was introduced in the late 1930s. The all-welded tender of DM&IR 225 carries a bell for backup moves. Photo by Bruce R. Meyer.

face area, and a cylinder is stronger than a box. On May 31, 1901, a patent was issued to Cornelius Vanderbilt (grandson of the Commodore) for a tender with a cylindrical water tank. It was lighter than a rectangular tender of the same capacity because of the inherent strength of its construction; rectangular tanks required a great deal of internal bracing. Some railroads went for Vanderbilt tenders in a big way. The Harriman roads liked them; the New York Central never had one, curious given the ancestry of the inventor.

Doghouses

Freight-train operation often called for a brakeman on the head end. There wasn't much room for him in the cab — he could squeeze onto a corner of the fireman's seat, but the fireman didn't like that, or he could stand in the gangway between the engine and the tender, which was uncomfortable, unsafe, and in the way of the fireman. In 1937 the Brotherhood of Railroad Trainmen and the members of the Association of American Railroads agreed that new locomotives constructed for road freight service would need a seat for the head brakeman, as would

Some railroads equipped their tenders with scoops for taking on water at speed from track pans. NYC photo.

385

any locomotives receiving Class 1 or Class 2 repairs. Railroads could either provide a third seat in the cab or provide a shelter on the tender.

It was easier to provide a third seat in the cab on new locomotives, but not for older locomotives (Baltimore & Ohio, for example, did so by extending the left side of the cab and cutting back the left side of the tender). A shelter on the tender deck was more customary for older locomotives if the tender deck was low enough or bridge clearances sufficiently generous. The agreement stipulated that the cabin be equipped with a seat equivalent to that provided for the engine crew, including sufficient leg and foot room, and a heater. The design and construction of the cab were left to the railroad — more likely, to the shop foreman.

TEXAS & PACIFIC RAILWAY

Texas & Pacific's main routes were completed by 1882. They ran from New Orleans northwest to Shreveport, Louisiana, then west through Dallas and Fort Worth to El Paso (the last 92 miles by trackage rights on Southern Pacific). A line from Texarkana southwest to Marshall, Texas, formed a natural extension of Missouri Pacific's Iron Mountain subsidiary; other routes from Texarkana ran south to Shreveport and west through Paris and Sherman to Fort Worth. A few branch lines built around the turn of the century completed the map. T&P set aside its goal of California (the Civil War had taken it out of the running for first transcontinental railroad; when it resumed construction SP had already built east from California to El Paso) and settled down as a regional carrier. The discovery of oil in 1918 at Ranger, about 95 miles west of Fort Worth, changed the fortunes of Texas and the T&P. Over the next several years the road undertook an extensive rebuilding.

Texas & Pacific No. 600 was the first 2-10-4. It was a development of Lima's A-1, and had the same short frame and articulated trailing truck. The empty space above the trailing truck would be occupied by an ashpan on a coal-burning engine. Lima photo.

Pacific 715 illustrates trademarks of T&P power after the 1920s: shielded air pumps on the pilot and Elesco feedwater heater with a diamond-shaped T&P herald on its front. Photo by Charles M. Mizell, Jr.; collection of Harold K. Vollrath.

Like many western railroads T&P used the 4-8-2 for long-distance heavy passenger service. In the late 1940s a few Mountains and Pacifics were trimmed in blue and gray to match T&P's streamlined passenger cars. Photo by Elliott B. Kahn.

T&P became part of Jay Gould's empire in 1881, and was in and out of financial difficulty over the next four decades, all the while remaining part of the Missouri Pacific system. MP had no influence on T&P motive power until after World War II — and then it was evidenced in the colors of T&P's road diesels.

Missouri Pacific freight diesels started operating between Texarkana and Longview — between MP proper and International-Great Northern — in 1947, and T&P's own freight diesels began to arrive in 1949. The last steam passenger train operated from Shreveport to New Orleans on November 9, 1951, behind USRA Mikado No. 800. The last steam-powered freight was a banana train from New Orleans to Shreveport pulled by Pacific No. 719 in April 1952.

Freight locomotives

Ten-Wheelers were the backbone of T&P's freight power until ten 2-8-0s were delivered by Baldwin in 1912, medium-size engines with 57" drivers. The road passed over the 2-8-2 and acquired 44 2-10-2s between 1916 and 1919. They all had 63" drivers and 28" × 32" cylin-

ders and weighed from 323,500 to 339,300 pounds — somewhat lighter and faster than the USRA light 2-10-2.

In 1918 the USRA allotted 11 light Mikados to T&P, which numbered them 550-560 and classed them H-1. They were orginally intended for the Chicago & Alton and the Long Island Rail Road, and in 1919 they were transferred to the Chicago, Rock Island & Pacific. Meanwhile 11 more light Mikes, 800-810, originally ordered for the Rock Island, were delivered by Baldwin in 1919.

The oil boom increased T&P's traffic beyond the capacity of the 2-10-2s and USRA Mikes, and the reconstruction of the railroad allowed heavier power. Lima stretched its Super-Power 2-8-4 with a fifth pair of 63" drivers, increased the cylinder size to 29" × 32", and created a new wheel arrangement, the 2-10-4 — the Texas type. Total weight was 448,000 pounds, 300,000 of that on the drivers — 60,000 pounds per axle, compared to 53,500 for the road's heaviest 2-10-2s and 55,000 pounds for the USRA light Mikados. The first ten 2-10-4s shouldered aside 2-10-2s in 1925, hauling 44 percent more tonnage on 42 percent

2-10-4 — TEXAS

In 1919 Santa Fe purchased a group of 2-10-2s. One of them, No. 3829, was built with an experimental four-wheel trailing truck, but was otherwise identical to the rest of the group. The experiment was inconclusive: No. 3829 was not converted to a 2-10-2, nor were other 2-10-2s fitted with four-wheel trailing trucks.

In 1925 Lima stretched its Super-Power 2-8-4 design with a fifth set of drivers to increase tractive effort while keeping the axle loading low. The new wheel arrangment, 2-10-4, was named Texas in honor of the first road to buy the type, Texas & Pacific. Between 1925 and 1929 the type was built with drivers in the 60"-64" range, and suffered to some extent from the counterbalancing problems that plagued low-drivered 2-10-2s. In 1930 Chesapeake & Ohio stretched Erie's 70"-drivered Berkshire into a Texas with 69" drivers, creating a 2-10-4 that was both powerful and fast. It set a pattern for 2-10-4s designed thereafter. The only 2-10-4s built with low drivers after 1930 were for railroads that already had such locomotives. The largest drivers used on the type were 74", on Santa Fe 5001-5035 (No. 5000 had 69" drivers).

With one exception the 2-10-4 was a freight locomotive — Canadian Pacific used semistreamlined 2-10-4s in passenger service through the Rockies. While Texas types remained in service quite late on a few railroads to protect traffic peaks, the job they did — hauling heavy freight trains long distances at high speeds — was the one for which railroads were most willing to spend money to dieselize. They were generally outlived by smaller locomotives.

Other names: Colorado (Chicago, Burlington & Quincy), Selkirk (Canadian Pacific)
Total built: 429
First: Texas & Pacific 600, 1925
Last: Canadian Pacific 5935, March 1949
Longest lived: Central Vermont 707, 1928-1959; Chicago, Burlington & Quincy 6310-6321 may be runners-up

In 1942 the Pennsylvania Railroad was caught between an immediate need for heavy freight locomotives and a ten-drivered duplex that needed more drawing-board work. PRR copied Chesapeake & Ohio's 12-year-old T-1 for the 125 members of the J1 class, which many consider Pennsy's best modern engines. Photo by Don Wood.

Last in service: Duluth, Missabe & Iron Range's ex-Bessemer & Lake Erie 2-10-4s were scrapped in 1961, but it is doubtful they were used in the two years before that; 1959 scrap dates are listed for 2-10-4s of Canadian Pacific (Nos. 5930-5935); Santa Fe, and Central Vermont (No. 707)
Greatest number: Pennsylvania Railroad, 125
Heaviest: Pennsylvania Railroad J1, 575,800 pounds
Lightest: Central Vermont 700-709, 419,000
Recommended reading: *North American Steam Locomotives: The Berkshire and Texas Types*, by Jack W. Farrell, published in 1988 by Pacific Fast Mail, P. O. Box 57, Edmonds, WA 98020 (ISBN 915713-15-12)

less fuel and doing it in 33 percent less time. During the next four years T&P purchased 60 more of the type. Engine 610, first of the I-1a class, was put on display in 1951 at the Southwestern Exposition & Fat Stock Show; it was restored to service in 1975 to pull the American Freedom Train and later worked in Southern Railway's excursion program.

Passenger locomotives

Texas & Pacific had 137 4-6-0s built after the turn of the century. The D-9 and D-10 classes had 63" drivers for dual service; the D-7s and D-11s had 67" drivers for passenger service, as did the D-9½ class, which were rebuilt from D-9s.

T&P built a pair of Atlantics in 1907, slide-valve 75"-drivered machines. They turned out to be rear-heavy and unstable, and their 28,000 pounds of tractive effort was no more than that of the considerably lighter D-9 Ten-Wheelers that preceded them — and not enough once steel passenger cars arrived. The two Atlantics were good enough to superheat but not duplicate.

In 1919 Baldwin and Brooks each delivered seven Pacifics. They had 73" drivers and 26" × 28" cylinders, and they had light-looking cast trailing trucks. The P-1 class Baldwins, built as 600-606 and renumbered 700-706, weighed 275,000 pounds; the Brooks engines, numbered 707-713 and classed P-1a, weighed 281,000 pounds. Alco's Richmond Works delivered eight more 4-6-2s in 1923, virtual duplicates of the Brooks engines except for heftier-looking trailing trucks.

Schenectady delivered five 73"-drivered 4-8-2s in 1925. Classed M-1 and numbered 900-904, they had 27" × 30" cylinders and carried 210 pounds pressure, giving them a tractive force of 52,500 pounds, plus 10,200 pounds from the trailing-truck booster. Baldwin delivered five more in 1928, the M-2 class, Nos. 905-909. They had the same dimensions and at 365,000 pounds were 4,500 pounds heavier than the M-1s.

Switchers

The USRA allocated 14 0-6-0s to T&P, and the design was copied for the B-8a class, Nos. 471-478, built by Cooke in 1923. The road had a good-size fleet of 0-8-0s, all with 51" drivers and 21" × 28" cylinders — 3" smaller than those of a USRA 0-8-0, but T&P's engines worked at 250

The C-2a class was the ultimate development of T&P's switcher fleet, with tender booster, front-end throttle (under the dome in front of the stack), and an outside pipe carrying superheated steam to the turret for the auxiliaries. Baldwin photo; collection of H. L. Broadbelt.

pounds, compared to 175 for the USRA. Baldwin built them all. Eight C-2s, Nos. 482-489, were delivered in 1925, followed by two C-2a class engines, Nos. 480 and 481, with tender boosters in 1926. Five more came in 1927, booster-equipped 490 and 491 and plain C-2s 492-494.

Experimental locomotives

T&P was an all-oil-burner railroad by 1920 — and soon afterward oil prices began to rise. In 1923 it converted 2-10-2 No. 524 to burn lignite, a low-grade brown coal. The conversion involved sealing the firebox and adding a turbine-driven fan to furnish air. The color and texture of the lignite quickly gained No. 524 the nickname "Snuff Dipper," and the forced-draft pressurized firebox worked just about as well as you'd expect. Fortunately for T&P, further oil discoveries in 1927 dropped the price of oil, and No. 524 was restored to burning oil.

Historical and technical society: Missouri Pacific Historical Society, c/o Bill Herbert, P. O. Box 187, Addis, LA 70710

Recommended reading: *Texas & Pacific*, by Don Watson and Steve Brown, published in 1978 by Boston Mills Press, 132 Main Street, Erin, ON N0B 1T0, Canada (ISBN 0-919822-83-5)

Published rosters:

Railroad Magazine: July 1933, page 130; October 1948, page 126

Trains Magazine: March 1950, page 25

Type	Class	Numbers	Qty	Builder	Built
0-6-0	B-5	3-5, 8, 10, 15, 22-25, 27, 41, 46, 52, 102, 113-115, 127-134, 140, 169	28	T&P	1902-1907
0-6-0	B-6	317-323	7	Cooke	1902
0-6-0	B-7	450-456	7	Baldwin	1916
0-6-0	B-8	457-470	14	Pittsburgh	1919
0-6-0	B-8a	471-478	8	Cooke	1923
0-8-0	C-2	482-489	8	Baldwin	1925
0-8-0	C-2	492-494	3	Baldwin	1927
0-8-0	C-2a	480, 481	2	Baldwin	1926
0-8-0	C-2a	490, 491	2	Baldwin	1927
2-8-0	F-1	401-410	10	Baldwin	1912
2-8-2	H-1	550-560	11	Schenectady	1918
2-8-2	H-2	800-810	11	Baldwin	1919
2-10-2	G-1	500-505	6	Baldwin	1916
2-10-2	G-1a	506-513	8	Baldwin	1917
2-10-2	G-1b	514-525	12	Baldwin	1919
2-10-2	G-1c	526-543	18	Brooks	1919
2-10-4	I-1	600-609	10	Lima	1925
2-10-4	I-1a	610-624	15	Lima	1927
2-10-4	I-1b	625-639	15	Lima	1928
2-10-4	I-1c	640-654	15	Lima	1928
2-10-4	I-1d	655-669	15	Lima	1929
4-4-0	A-1	2	1	Cooke	1900
4-4-0	A-3	11, 16-21, 31-34	10	T&P	1900
4-4-2	E-1	339, 340	2	T&P	1906
4-6-0	D-7	264-266	3	Rogers	1900
4-6-0	D-7	267-274	8	Cooke	1901
4-6-0	D-9	257-263	7	Rog.	1900
4-6-0	D-9	275-316	42	Cooke	1901-1902
4-6-0	D-9	324-338	15	Cooke, Rog.	1903
4-6-0	D-9	349-358	10	Rogers	1906
4-6-0	D-9½	359, 360	2	T&P	
4-6-0	D-10	361-400	40	Baldwin	1907
4-6-0	D-11	411-420	10	Baldwin	1912
4-6-2	P-1	600-606	7	Baldwin	1919
4-6-2	P-1a	707-713	7	Brooks	1919
4-6-2	P-1b	714-721	8	Richmond	1923
4-8-2	M-1	900-904	5	Schenectady	1925
4-8-2	M-2	905-909	5	Baldwin	1928

THREE-CYLINDER LOCOMOTIVES

Most North American steam locomotives of conventional layout had two cylinders, one on each side of the engine. The cylinders applied thrust to the driving wheels at 90 degree intervals in the rotation, with the right side leading the left on most railroads. This was called "quartering," and ensured the engine would not stall on dead center. The idea of a three-cylinder locomotive appeared fairly early. In 1846 George Stephenson built two engines in which the outside cylinders worked in unison and the inside cylinder, which produced as much power as the sum of the outside cylinders, applied thrust 90 degrees from it — think of a three-legged race, and you'll understand the concept.

In 1881 F. W. Webb of the London & North Western Railway patented a three-cylinder compound in which the outside high-pressure cylinders drove the rear drivers on cranks 90 degrees apart, and the inside low-pressure cylinder drove a crank on the front axle. The two sets of drivers were not coupled, and the arrangement of the reversing gear was such that the two sets of drivers could turn in opposite directions (and sometimes did). If a locomotive stopped with two of the three cylinders on dead center, it had to be pushed off dead center before it would start. Despite their quirks LNWR acquired more than 100 of them. They were scrapped soon after Webb's retirement in 1903.

Baldwin built three balanced three-cylinder simple 2-6-0s for the Erie & Wyoming Valley in 1894. All three cylinders drove the same axle, on which the crank and crankpins were 120 degrees apart. The Stephenson valve gear eccentrics for all three cylinders were on that axle, too, probably leaving barely enough room to stick in an oil can.

Between 1909 and 1912 the Reading rebuilt one 4-4-2 and built two more and a 4-6-0 with three cylinders. All were soon restored to two-cylinder configuration because of metallurgical problems with the crank axles. Ten years elapsed before another three-cylinder engine was built.

In 1922 Alco rebuilt a New York Central 4-8-2 with three 25" × 28" cylinders replacing the original pair of 28" × 28" cylinders. It proved successful in service, and in 1923 Alco's Brooks Works built another three-cylinder Mountain from scratch, Lehigh Valley 5000. It too was successful, and LV ordered five more.

Alco began advocating three-cylinder locomotives. Among the advantages cited were that the power of the locomotive was divided among three pistons and main rods instead of two, and six power impulses per revolution of the drivers produced more even torque than four. The main drawback was that a third of the machinery was hidden between the frames, accessible only from below.

A number of railroads sampled three-cylinder power, and several went for it in a big way, notably Union Pacific, with 10 4-10-2s and 88 4-12-2s. The latter were quite successful, perhaps because they weren't in a minority. One-of-a-kind locomotives tended to be shoved to the back of the roundhouse when they needed even minor repairs. Non-standard locomotives that became standard by weight of numbers got better treatment.

Alco built 246 three-cylinder locomotives at its Brooks, Schenectady, and Montreal works between 1922 and 1938, almost 40 percent of them for UP. But the three-cylinder era was over in 1930 — why? Lima's Super-Power concept offered high horsepower without mechanical complexity; the railroads were leery of the maintenance problems of the third cylinder, main rod, and valve gear; and the Depression cut the need for new locomotives.

Oddities

Baldwin built a compound watertube-firebox three-cylinder 4-10-2, No. 60000, in 1926. Any one of its three nonstandard features would have been too much for most railroads; all three in an extremely heavy locomotive were more than any railroad wanted. One of the few demonstrator steam locomotives ever built, No. 60000 remained Baldwin property and was eventually placed on display at the Franklin Institute in Philadelphia. The 1938 Pacifics that Alco's Montreal Works built for Ferrocarril Mexicano were essentially duplicates of FCM's 1928 engines. They remained in service quite late.

The head of the third cylinder and the Gresley valve gear levers are plainly visible on the front of Louisville & Nashville Mikado 1999. L&N photo.

The enormous cylinder casting for Baldwin 60000, fresh from the foundry, shows the inclination of the middle cylinder, as does the side view with the crosshead guides and crossheads in place. The main driver axle had a counterbalanced crank for the main rod from the middle cylinder. Baldwin photos.

Valve gear

The three-cylinder locomotives of the 1920s generally used Walschaerts valve gear for the outside cylinders and Gresley conjugating valve gear for the inside cylinder. Gresley gear consisted of a large lever with a fixed fulcrum connected at one end to the valve rod of the left cylinder and at the other to the center of a smaller floating lever, the ends of which were connected to the valve rods of the right and center cylinders. That arrangement and the inclination of the center cylinder (so the rod could clear the first axle) combined to require that the left and right cranks be 120 degrees apart; the right and center cranks, 110 degrees; and the center and left cranks, 130 degrees. The exhaust of a three-cylinder machine was uneven and distinctive — not an even three-beat rhythm but more like a slightly lopsided waltz.

THREE-CYLINDER STEAM LOCOMOTIVES BUILT SINCE 1900

Road	Type	Numbers	Qty	Builder	Built	Retired	Notes
Baldwin	4-10-2	60000	1	Baldwin	1926		Compound, water-tube firebox
BRC	0-8-0	150	1	Baldwin	1925		
CRI&P	4-6-2	999	1	Brooks	1924	1939	
DL&W	4-8-2	1450-1454	5	Brooks	1925	1946	
							Rebuilt to two-cylinder engines 1930-1931
DL&W	4-8-2	2201-2235	35	Schen	1926-1927	1946-1950	
D&RGW	4-8-2	1600	10	Baldwin			
FCM	4-6-2	130-133	4	Alco	1928		
FCM	4-6-2	134-136	3	Montreal	1938		
IHB	0-8-0	100-102	3	Alco	1927		Rebuilt to two-cylinder engines
L&N	2-8-2	1999	1	Brooks	1924	1950	
L&N	4-6-2	295	1	Brooks	1925		
							Rebuilt to two-cylinder engine 1940
LV	4-8-2	5000-5005	6	Brooks	1923-1924		
							Rebuilt to two-cylinder engines 1939
MP	2-8-2	1699	1	Alco	1924		
							Rebuilt to two-cylinder engine 1937, renumbered 1571
MP	4-6-2	6000	1	Alco	1925		
							Rebuilt to two-cylinder engine 1942, renumbered 6001
NdeM	4-6-2	178, 179	2	Alco	1928		Renumbered 2686, 2687
NYC	4-8-2	2568, 2569	2	Schen	1922, 1924	1936	
							Rebuilt from and to two-cylinder engines
NYNH&H	0-8-0	3600-3615	16	Schen	1924, 1927	1949-1952	
NYNH&H	4-8-2	3550-3562	13	Schen	1926, 1928	1950-1951	
Reading	4-4-2	300	1	Reading	1911	1948	
							Rebuilt to two-cylinder engine 1917
Reading	4-4-2	303	1	Reading	1909	1948	
							Rebuilt to two-cylinder engine 1916
Reading	4-4-2	344	1	Reading	1912	1948	
							Rebuilt to two-cylinder engine 1917
Reading	4-6-0	675	1	Reading	1911	1948	
							Rebuilt to two-cylinder engine 1916
SP	4-10-2	5000-5048	49	Schen	1925-1927	1953-1955*	
UP	4-10-2	8800-8809	10	Brooks	1925-1926	1948-1954	
							Rebuilt to two-cylinder engines 1942, renumbered 5090-5099
UP	4-12-2	9000-9087	88	Brks, Sch	1926-1930	1953-1956*	
Wabash	2-8-2	2600-2604	5	Schen	1925		Boilers used for 4-6-4s

* Southern Pacific 5021 and Union Pacific 9000 are on display in the collection of the Southern California Chapter, Railway & Locomotive Historical Society, Los Angeles County Fairgrounds, Pomona, California.

TURBINE LOCOMOTIVES

The traditional steam engine produces reciprocating motion which must immediately be converted into rotary motion. The machinery is difficult to balance, and the torque it produces is not constant. Locomotive designers long envied the designers of steamships and stationary power plants — they could use turbines instead of reciprocating engines — and experimented with steam turbines in locomotives. During the 1920s and 1930s the German State Railway and the London, Midland & Scottish Railway introduced steam turbine locomotives that ran relatively well for a decade or so. Both designs were of conventional appearance and used mechanical transmissions between the turbines and the wheels.

In 1938 General Electric built a pair of 2500 h.p. steam-turbine-electric locomotives in an attempt to equal Electro-Motive Corporation's passenger diesels. The units were painted and lettered for Union Pacific and looked like a cross between UP's *City of Denver* diesels and the streamlined electric locomotives GE built that same year for the New Haven. Each unit had a 2-C+C-2 wheel arrangement; internal workings

Union Pacific 1 and 2 await departure from Omaha on their first run in March 1938. Photo by John P. McGlynn.

Chesapeake & Ohio orange-and-silver steam turbine-electric No. 500 was an enormous piece of equipment, 20 feet longer than today's auto-racks and piggyback flats, and its tender was about the size of today's covered hopper cars. Baldwin photo.

The forward turbine of Pennsylvania 6200 was on the right side of the locomotive between the second and third drivers. Photo by Paul Eilenberger.

included a 1,500-pound pressure boiler, generator, and condensing system — components that needed plenty of care and maintenance. UP ran the locomotives on a few test trips, sent them around the country on a publicity tour, and, after a few trips in revenue service, returned them to GE. In 1943 Great Northern used them briefly to handle a surge in freight traffic between Wenatchee and Spokane, Washington, then sent them back to GE, where they were scrapped.

The Pennsylvania Railroad noted the success of LMS's turbine locomotive. In 1944 Baldwin delivered a steam-turbine locomotive to the Pennsy, No. 6200, class S2. It had a new wheel arrangement, 6-8-6 (it was to have been a 4-8-4, but wartime restrictions on the use of lightweight materials required extra axles) and weighed 589,970 pounds, a little more than Pennsy's J1 2-10-4. Its power unit was an adaptation of a Westinghouse marine power plant. The two turbines, a large one for forward movement and a small one for reverse, were clutched and geared to the second and third driver axles; all four axles were connected with conventional side rods. The Pennsy found it could outpull

conventional locomotives of the same size and above 40 mph was the equivalent of a 6,000 h.p. diesel, but below that speed it used inordinate amounts of steam and coal. It worked in passenger service between Chicago and Crestline, Ohio, for a short period, then was placed in storage and eventually scrapped.

The most spectacular steam turbines were Chesapeake & Ohio's trio, discussed on page 87. In 1954, four years after the C&O turbines had been scrapped, Baldwin-Lima-Hamilton and Babcock & Wilcox teamed up to build a similar locomotive for the Norfolk & Western. Number 2300, named *Jawn Henry*, rode on two pairs of six-wheel trucks, all axles powered, but the basic configuration — coal bunker up front, boiler behind the cab with firebox forward, turbines and electrical equipment at the rear — duplicated the C&O engines. It weighed 818,000 pounds, somewhat less than the C&O engines but still a lot more than an equivalent amount of diesel horsepower. It was scrapped in 1957.

A steam turbine in a stationary power plant or a ship runs at a near-constant speed in a clean, stable environment — and it isn't likely to

encounter either condition in a locomotive. Turbines are delicate where reciprocating engines are robust, and the experimental, one-of-a-kind status of turbine locomotives put them at a disadvantage when it came to maintenance. The diesel engine was a much sturdier machine than the steam turbine and proved adaptable to railroad service. However, like the cross-compound engine, the steam turbine had long since found a niche in the auxiliary department, driving a generator that furnished electricity for the headlight and the lights in the cab.

First: Union Pacific 1 and 2

Last: Norfolk & Western 2300, *Jawn Henry*

Greatest number: Chesapeake & Ohio, 3, Nos. 500-502

The coal bunker of Norfolk & Western 2300 is clearly visible ahead of the cab. The white flags on the front and the dynamometer car behind the tender indicate this is a test run. Photos of 2300 — indeed of any turbine — without a dynamometer car are rare. Photo by Parker Hayden.

UNION PACIFIC RAILROAD

For approximately three decades after Union Pacific completed its main line from Council Bluffs, Iowa, to Promontory, Utah, it was in financial difficulty — and control by Jay Gould for part of that time didn't help matters. In 1897 Edward H. Harriman gained control of the road and began to improve it. At the turn of the century UP's main lines reached from Council Bluffs, Iowa, west to Ogden, Utah, and from Kansas City, Missouri, west to Denver, Colorado, then north to Cheyenne, Wyoming. The Oregon Short Line, a UP subsidiary, extended from Granger, Wyoming, west of Green River, northwest to Huntington, Oregon, on the Snake River; other OSL main lines reached north from Pocatello, Idaho, to Silver Bow, Montana, near Butte; and from McCammon, Idaho, near Pocatello, through Ogden and Salt Lake City to Uvada, Utah, in the southwest corner of the state. The Oregon Railroad & Navigation Co., another UP subsidiary, extended from Huntington to Portland and from Umatilla, Ore., northeast to Spokane. (In 1910 it became the Oregon-Washington Railroad & Navigation Co.) In 1907 the Los Angeles & Salt Lake was completed between its namesake cities, and the southern portion of the OSL was transferred to it.

UP's main line followed the Platte and South Platte rivers and Lodgepole Creek west across Nebraska and southeast Wyoming, climbing gently all the while. The line west from Kansas City similarly followed rivers until it reached the high plains of eastern Colorado and the val-

Mikado 2274, an MK-7 built by Baldwin in 1917, is typical of UP's Harriman Mikes. The trailing truck is an early version of Commonwealth Steel Company's Delta truck. Photo by Arthur Stensvad.

UP's standard road freight power for a decade was the 2-8-8-0. In the late 1930s and early 1940s UP converted them to single-expansion engines and renumbered them in the 3500 series. Photo by J. F. Orem.

ley of the South Platte at Denver. From mile-high Denver it followed the South Platte downstream about half the distance north to Cheyenne, then ascended along other watercourses and over a minor divide to Cheyenne at 6,062 feet. Those were the easy parts.

West out of Cheyenne was Sherman Hill, the thorn in UP's flesh. It was a stiff climb (Harriman's reconstruction program reduced the grade to 1.5 percent) up a natural ramp over a spur of the Laramie Mountains, then a descent to Laramie, elevation 7,165 feet. (Later surveys uncovered routes with easier grades north of Cheyenne, but by then Cheyenne was an established city with major railroad facilities.) West of Laramie was relatively level open country, marked by the North Platte River, the Great Divide Basin, and the Green River, and eventually the Wasatch Mountains and a descent through Weber Canyon to Ogden.

The route northwest to Portland followed the Snake River across southern Idaho and the Columbia River along the top of Oregon — but between the water-level grades were the Blue Mountains of eastern Oregon. The Los Angeles & Salt Lake traversed long stretches of desert

southwest across Utah, followed Meadow Valley Wash for more than 100 miles down to Las Vegas, then encountered steep grades in the mountains southwest of Las Vegas and over Cajon Pass into the Los Angeles basin.

All across the UP system were alternating stretches of easy going and stiff grades, and the road's operating philosophy seemed to be "don't break up trains" — if a Mikado, for example, could bring a train west to Cheyenne, UP wanted an engine that could take that same train over Sherman Hill. The road avoided doubleheading, but helpers were unavoidable.

Locomotives were often transferred from one part of the UP system to another, and part of the transfer was new numbers. The number system was not a simple matter like 5000s for OSL and 6000s for LA&SL, or even a different second digit for each company (essentially that's what the system was, but it was a different set of digits for each type of locomotive). UP sometimes changed engine numbers to indicate a change in fuel from coal to oil or vice versa. The 4-6-6-4s were particularly

OTTO JABELMANN (1891-1943) was born in Cheyenne, Wyoming. He attended grade school there and high school in Seattle, Washington, and Ann Arbor, Michigan, then studied engineering at Stanford and University of Michigan. He began work with UP as a crew caller in 1906, then became machinist apprentice, machinist, and eventually district foreman and superintendent of shops at Cheyenne. At the beginning of 1929 he became system superintendent of shops at Omaha, and in 1933, general superintendent of motive power and machinery at Omaha. In 1936 he was appointed head of the new motive power and machinery department, and in 1939 became vice-president in charge of research and mechanical standards.

Jabelmann was responsible for much of the design of UP's 4-8-4s, 4-6-6-4s, and 4-8-8-4s, particularly the later classes. At the time of his death, January 6, 1943, he was in England with W. Averill Harriman on a special mission connected with lend-lease distribution.

confusing in that regard and in reuse of numbers recently vacated by other engines of the same type.

UP was an early purchaser of diesels for its streamliners but didn't begin dieselizing freight trains until 1947. The road's last 4-8-4, No. 844, was never stricken from the roster but remained active for excursion trains and company specials. In 1962 it was renumbered 8444 to make room for GP30s, and regained its original number in 1989. In 1981 4-6-6-4 No. 3985 was restored to operation.

Freight locomotives

The Union Pacific system bought 472 Consolidations between 1900 and 1909. Nearly all were standard Harriman 2-8-0s, with 57" drivers and 21" × 30" or 22" × 30" cylinders. All were built with Stephenson valve gear; a few were rebuilt with Walschaerts gear. The 2-8-2 fleet numbered 427. The MK-1 and MK-2 classes had 57" drivers, 23¾" × 30" cylinders, and 47,945 pounds tractive force. Later classes had 63" drivers, 26" × 28" cylinders, and 53,628 pounds tractive effort, slightly smaller and less powerful than the USRA light Mikado.

The USRA allotted 20 light Mikes to UP. Upon delivery in 1918 they were classed MK-Special, since they weren't part of the Associated Lines Common Standard hierarchy, and numbered 2295-2314. In 1920 they were renumbered 2480-2499 to allow the number sequence of UP's Harriman 2-8-2s to continue. There was a great deal of shuffling of Mikados among UP proper, Oregon Short Line, and Los Angeles & Salt Lake.

After the 2-8-2s UP freight power developed in two directions: articulateds, discussed below, and 2-10-2s, which Union Pacific, just as reluctant as Southern Pacific to call them Santa Fes, classed TTT (two-ten-two). Between 1917 and 1924 UP added 174 2-10-2s to its roster, all 63"-drivered engines with 29½" × 30" cylinders. There was considerable trading of the 2-10-2s among the subsidiaries.

The 2-8-8-0s that became standard road power across Wyoming were powerful but slow. As a start toward developing a faster freight engine, a year after the delivery of the last 2-10-2 the road received a single experimental three-cylinder 4-10-2 numbered 8000 and classed FTT-1. UP tested it thoroughly and ordered nine more for the Los Angeles & Salt Lake, but the type wasn't quite what the road wanted. It designed and Brooks built a single 4-12-2, No. 9000, class UP-1. The 4-10-2s had 63" drivers like the 2-10-2s that preceded them; the 4-12-2 had 67" drivers. In spite of its long rigid wheelbase and three-cylinder mechanism, the 4-12-2 was remarkably successful. Between 1926 and 1930 UP bought 89 more, and they had long service lives as three-cylinder engines. Most were assigned to UP proper. The engines that were to have been Nos. 9063-9077 were built as Oregon Short Line 9500-9514, and eight that were built for Oregon-Washington were soon transferred to UP. The 4-10-2s didn't fare as well. They were rebuilt as two-cylinder locomo-

4-12-2 — UNION PACIFIC

In the mid-1920s Union Pacific used 2-10-2s and 2-8-8-0s on mainline freight trains. Both types were slow; the 2-8-8-0 had a maximum speed of 20 mph. UP tested a three-cylinder 4-10-2 in 1925 and found it could handle 20 percent more tonnage than a 2-10-2 on 16 percent less fuel — and do it faster. The road ordered nine more, and asked Alco about an engine that could match the pulling power of the 2-8-8-0s at speeds up to 40 mph.

At the time the articulated was still a low-speed machine, suffering from the instability of the front engine and encumbered with the problems of compounding. Great Northern was just then receiving the first nonexperimental simple 2-8-8-2s; true high-speed articulateds were still in the future. A rigid-frame locomotive was indicated, and weight restrictions combined with the power UP needed meant six driving axles. Alco's Brooks Works built a 4-12-2 for UP in 1926; it was delivered before the nine 4-10-2s.

Number 9000 had two outside 27" × 32" cylinders driving the third set of drive wheels and a third 27" × 31" cylinder in the center driving the second axle. The first axle also had a crank in the center to provide clearance for the center main rod. Drivers were 67" in diameter, and the fourth pair was blind (flangeless), a concession to curves that was later found unnecessary due to the lateral-motion devices on the first and last pairs of drivers.

The 4-12-2 was the largest locomotive built with a rigid wheelbase. It was powerful, and it rode well at speed. UP liked No. 9000 and bought 87 more like it. They initially worked UP's main line across Wyoming; after they were displaced by Challengers and Big Boys they moved to Kansas and Nebraska. Number 9000 was donated to the Southern California Chapter of the Railway & Locomotive Historical Society and is displayed at the Los Angeles County Fairgrounds in Pomona.

The type remained unique to UP. Twelve-coupled engines were uncommon elsewhere in the world. Bulgaria had two groups of

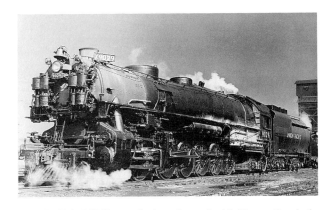

Union Pacific's 4-12-2's were the largest nonarticulated locomotives in the world. No. 9029, standing at Council Bluffs, Iowa, in August 1952, offers a view of the Gresley valve gear that controls the middle cylinder. Photo by R. H. Kindig.

2-12-4 tank engines, and Indonesia had a few 2-12-2Ts. In 1934 Russia built a 4-14-4 that is all but apocryphal. It had 63" drivers and weighed 416,000 pounds, the same as a Boston & Maine 4-8-2. Out of deference to light rail and roadbed it had an axle loading of 20 tons, about the same as a B&M 2-6-0. It made one demonstration run during which it tore the track apart; it was stored and later scrapped.

Total built: 88
First: Union Pacific 9000, April 1926
Last: UP 9087, 1930
Heaviest: UP 9063-9087, 515,000 pounds
Lightest: UP 9000, 495,000 pounds

The 25 Big Boys were about as large as locomotives could be, and they were the heaviest reciprocating-piston steam locomotives ever built. Note that the radius rods of the Walschaerts valve gear are at the bottom of the links for maximum valve travel — the locomotive is ready to start. Photo by R. H. Kindig.

tives in 1942 and renumbered 5090-5099, and were scrapped several years before the 4-12-2s.

Articulateds

In 1909 UP and OWR&N each received three 2-8-8-2s from Baldwin, UP 2000-2002 and OWR&N 700-702. In 1915 they were renumbered 3600-3602 and 3800-3802, and in 1917 the UP engines were transferred to OSL as 3700-3702. All six were scrapped in 1928.

In 1918 Schenectady delivered 15 2-8-8-0s numbered 3600-3614 (the first three numbers were barely cool). World War I interrupted the flow, but it resumed in 1920. By 1924 UP had 64 2-8-8-0s, and OSL and OWR&N each had 3. They became the standard mainline freight power across Wyoming until the 4-12-2s arrived. Between 1937 and 1944 UP converted all 70 to simple articulateds and numbered them 3500-3569 (numbers 3500-3514 had been used for Atlantics until 1933).

In the mid-1930s UP turned its attention from sheer pulling power to horsepower. It needed a locomotive to replace the combination of 2-8-8-0 and 2-10-2 on eastbound freights from Ogden. A 4-12-2 with larger drivers wasn't possible — the long rigid wheelbase of the 67"-drivered 4-12-2s was already a limitation. Arthur H. Fetters, general mechnical engineer, suggested a simple articulated, which would have much shorter rigid wheelbase and lighter rods. Fetters and designers from Alco started with the 4-12-2, split the six sets of drivers into two groups of three, added 2" to their diameter, replaced the ouside 27" and middle 31" cylinders with four 22" × 32" cylinders, and raised the boiler pressure from 220 to 255 pounds — all of it easy on paper — to get the equivalent pulling power, then enlarged the firebox enough to require a four-wheel trailing truck. A new wheel arrangement was created, 4-6-6-4. Shortly after engines 3900-3914 were delivered in 1936, the type was named

Challenger. According to one source the name was chosen because the proposed assignment, Ogden to Green River, would be a challenge to any locomotive. However, in 1935 UP had inaugurated a low-fare Chicago-Los Angeles coach train of the same name and within a year or two applied the name to fast merchandise trains and a railroad-owned hotel at Sun Valley, Idaho. The second group, Nos. 3915-3939, was delivered in 1937 and included minor evolutionary changes. The last six of the group were fitted for passenger service.

Within five years UP wanted more power. Under the direction of Otto Jabelmann the Challenger was expanded to a 4-8-8-4 with 68" drivers and 23¾" × 32" cylinders and a total weight of 772,000 pounds. The type got its name when someone at Alco chalked "Big Boy" on the smokebox of one under construction. (There's no record of other names UP and Alco might have contemplated. They wouldn't have been as good.)

Shortly after the first 20 Big Boys were delivered UP returned to Alco for more Challengers. Jabelmann revised the design with cylinders an inch smaller and firebox 26" shorter but 280 pounds boiler pressure. There were numerous internal improvements, and many components were common to the Big Boys and the last 4-8-4s. The new Challengers incorporated a major difference in their running gear: The front engine was free to move sideways but not at all vertically, resulting in better

4-6-6-4 — CHALLENGER

Union Pacific introduced the 4-6-6-4 in 1936 when it took delivery of Nos. 3900-3914, and Northern Pacific and Spokane, Portland & Seattle were next in line for the type, buying 21 and 6 respectively. The design of those initial 4-6-6-4s was sound — all the Challengers built had practically the same dimensions: 69" or 70" drivers, cylinders ranging from $20\frac{1}{2}$" × 32 to 23" × 32", and total weight of 566,000 to 644,000 pounds. Most had grate areas of 108 square feet, but the NP and SP&S engines had larger grates, 152 square feet, because of NP's low-grade coal. The articulation of the later 4-6-6-4s allowed only horizontal movement of the front engine. Vertical curves in the track were taken up entirely by the spring rigging, resulting in better weight distribution between the front and rear engines and greater stability than other articulateds. As a group, the 4-6-6-4s were the best of the high-speed simple articulateds. Though intended as freight engines, UP used them regularly in passenger service. One Challenger is active today, UP 3985.

Total built: 252
First: Union Pacific 3900, 1936
Last: Clinchfield 663, 1947
Greatest number: Union Pacific, 105
Heaviest: Northern Pacific 5121-5126, 644,000 pounds
Lightest: Union Pacific 3900-3914, 566,000 pounds

Fresh from Alco in 1938, Union Pacific 3939 poses in Los Angeles with the streamlined coaches of the *Challenger*, the road's Chicago-Los Angeles economy coach train. UP photo.

Last of the 1942 group of 4-6-6-4s, UP 3969 is eastbound at Sherman, Wyoming, with a freight bound for Denver in July 1948. Caption. Photo by Jim Ady.

Representatives of the first two classes of UP 4-8-4s lead train 5, the *California Fast Mail*, out of Cheyenne on August 11, 1940. Photo by R. H. Kindig.

weight distribution and stability. During World War II UP was desperate for power and purchased 30 simple 2-8-8-2s from Chesapeake & Ohio and five USRA compound 2-8-8-2s from Norfolk & Western. Both groups were scrapped in 1947.

Passenger locomotives

Most of UP's 4-4-2s were standard Harriman Atlantics with 81" drivers. One class of those, the A-3s, were Vauclain compounds built in 1906 and retired in 1921 and 1923 without being simpled. The non-Harriman Atlantics consisted of four 70"-drivered A-1s built in 1903 for the San Pedro, Los Angeles & Salt Lake. They were scrapped in 1921.

A few groups of 4-6-0s had passenger-size drivers (68", 69", 73", and 79") but UP was not the Ten-Wheeler enthusiast that Southern Pacific was. It progressed to the Pacific early and in quantity. There was little difference among the first six classes, P-1 through P-6. All had 77" drivers, 22" × 28" cylinders, and Stephenson valve gear. The later classes kept the 77" drivers but had 25" × 28" cylinders. The largest, the P-13s (UP 2900-2909, built by Baldwin in 1920) approached the USRA heavy Pacific in weight on drivers and tractive force.

The P-13s were UP's last Pacifics. In 1922 the road turned to the 4-8-2 for heavy passenger service. The 70 Mountains had 73" drivers, 29" × 28" cylinders, and a tractive force of 54,838 pounds. In the 1930s the Mountains were upgraded with one-piece cast frames with integral cylinders, and Walschaerts valve gear replaced Young.

The final step in UP's passenger locomotive progression was to the 4-8-4: 20 in 1937, 15 in 1939, and 10 in 1944. The first group, Nos. 800-819, had 77" drivers and 24½" × 32" cylinders; trailing were 12-wheel semi-Vanderbilt tenders. The second and third groups, 820-834 and 835-844, had 80" drivers, 25" × 32" cylinders, and pedestal tenders. All were converted to oil fuel in 1946.

Switchers

Most of UP's switchers were 0-6-0s with 51" or 57" drivers and Stephenson valve gear. The S-5 and S-6 classes were built with Walschaerts gear and a few early switchers were later fitted with it. Fifteen USRA 0-6-0s, UP 4600-4609 and OSL 4753-4757, were the only exceptions to the Harriman standard switchers. UP had one 0-8-0, rebuilt from a 2-8-0 as an experiment. Unaltered 2-8-0s did much of the heavy yard work.

Historical and technical society: Union Pacific Historical Society, P. O. Box 903, Laramie, WY 82070-0903

Published rosters:

Steam Roster for the Union Pacific System, 1915-1990, by Gordon McCulloh, published in 1990 by Smokerise Publications, P. O. Box 823, Tucker, GA 30084-0823

Railroad Magazine: May 1933, page 83; July 1947, page 114; December 1957, page 72

UP STEAM LOCOMOTIVES BUILT SINCE 1900

Type	Class	Numbers	Road	Qty	Builder	Built	Retired	Notes
0-6-0	S-56	4226	LA&SL	1	Lima	1913	1945	
0-6-0	S-55	4227, 4228	LA&SL	2	Schen	1902	1925	
0-6-0	S-1	4229-4234	LA&SL	6	Baldwin	1904	1929-1947	
0-6-0	S-2	4235-4239	LA&SL	5	Baldwin	1907	1929-1947	
0-6-0	S-3	4240-4242	LA&SL	3	Baldwin	1913	1946-1947	
0-6-0	S-6	4243-4246	LA&SL	4	Baldwin	1921	1946-1956	
0-6-0	S-51	4338-4347	UP	10	Baldwin	1901	1925-1928	
0-6-0	S-1	4350-4359	UP	10	Baldwin	1905	1929-1936	
0-6-0	S-2	4360-4379	UP	20	Baldwin	1906-1907	1927-1936	
0-6-0	S-2	4380	UP	1	Brooks	1908	1929	
0-6-0	S-2	4381-4400	UP	20	Baldwin	1909, 1911	1927-1936	
0-6-0	S-4	4401-4415	UP	15	Baldwin	1913	1933-1956	
0-6-0	S-4	4416-4420	UP	5	Lima	1914	1934-1958	
0-6-0	S-5	4421-4450	UP	30	Baldwin	1916	1947-1960	
0-6-0	S-6	4451-4480	UP	30	Lima	1920	1947-1956	
0-6-0	S-Spl	4600-4609	UP	10	Baldwin	1918	1947-1956	USRA
0-6-0	S-51	4701, 4702	OSL	2	Baldwin	1901	1926	
0-6-0	S-2	4703-4709	OSL	7	Brooks	1908	1928-1947	
0-6-0	S-2	4710-4721	OSL	12	Baldwin	1906	1928-1933	
0-6-0	S-51	4722-4724	OSL	3	Baldwin	1901	1928, 1930	
0-6-0	S-51	4725-4729	OSL	5	Cooke	1901	1927-1930	
0-6-0	S-1	4730-4734	OSL	5	Baldwin	1904	1929-1946	
0-6-0	S-3	4735-4739	OSL	5	Baldwin	1912	1933-1947	
0-6-0	S-4	4740-4744	OSL	5	Lima	1914	1946-1947	
0-6-0	S-5	4748-4752	OSL	5	Baldwin	1918	1946-1954	
0-6-0	S-Spl	4753-4757	OSL	5	Pittsburgh	1919	1937-1955	USRA
0-6-0	S-1, -2	4758-4764	OSL	7	Baldwin	1905-1907	1929	Ex-UP
0-6-0	S-51	4901	OWR&N	1	Pittsburgh	1902	1927	
							Ex-Pittsburgh & Lake Erie	
0-6-0	S-2	4902-4922	OWR&N	21	Baldwin	1907-1913	1933-1955	
0-6-0	S-4	4923-4926	OWR&N	4	Lima	1914	1953, 1955	
0-6-0	S-1	4927-4930	OWR&N	4	Baldwin	1905	1931-1955	
0-6-0	S-51	4931-4933	OWR&N	3	Baldwin	1901-1903	1930, 1940	
0-8-0	S-57	4500	UP	1	UP	1924	1946	
							Rebuilt from 2-8-0	
2-6-0	M-62	4100-4107	OSL	8	Baldwin	1901	1925-1928	
2-8-0	C-57	150-158	UP	9	Baldwin	1902	1928-1946	
2-8-0	C-2	201-310	UP	110	Baldwin	1902	1933-1953	
							Compound	
2-8-0	C-2	311-331	UP	21	Brooks	1908	1930-1957	
2-8-0	C-2	332, 333	UP	2	Baldwin	1905	1957, 1937	
2-8-0	C-2	350-358	UP	9	Baldwin	1904	1933-1957	Ex-SP
2-8-0	C-57	400-479	UP	80	Baldwin	1900-1901	1929-1958	
							Vauclain compound	
2-8-0	C-57	480-499	UP	20	Baldwin	1903	1929-1958	
2-8-0	C-55	510-524	OSL	15	Baldwin	1901	1930-1956	
							Vauclain compound	
2-8-0	C-57	525-539	OSL	15	Baldwin	1901-1903	1946-1958	
2-8-0	C-2	560-618	OSL	59	Baldwin	1904-1907	1933-1958	
2-8-0	C-2	619-622	OSL	4	Brooks	1908	1947-1956	
2-8-0	C-51	705, 706	OWR&N	2	Schen	1909	1947, 1940	
							Ex-North Coast 1, 2	
2-8-0	C-57	710-724	OWR&N	15	Baldwin	1901, 1903	1927-1947	
2-8-0	C-57	725-729	OWR&N	5	Baldwin	1902	1930-1940	
							Compound	
2-8-0	C-2	730-768	OWR&N	39	Baldwin	1906-1908	1930-1957	
2-8-0	C-1	6000-6008	LA&SL	9	Baldwin	1904	1933-1955	
2-8-0	C-2	6009-6060	LA&SL	52	Baldwin	1905, 1907	1928-1957	
2-8-0	C-2	6061-6086	LA&SL	16	Sch, Brks	1907	1928-1957	
2-8-2	MK-1	1900-1929	UP	30	Baldwin	1911	1947-1955	
2-8-2	MK-2	1930-1949	UP	20	Baldwin	1912	1947-1956	
2-8-2	MK-1	2000-2014	OSL	15	Baldwin	1911	1947-1955	
2-8-2	MK-2	2015-2034	OSL	20	Baldwin	1912	1947-1954	
2-8-2	MK-1	2100	OWR&N	1	Baldwin	1910	1955	
							Original Harriman 2-8-2	
2-8-2	MK-1	2101-2140	OWR&N	40	Baldwin	1911	1946-1957	
2-8-2	MK-2	2141-2165	OWR&N	25	Baldwin	1912-1913	1947-1957	
2-8-2	MK-8	2166-2171	OWR&N	6	Baldwin	1918	1947-1957	
2-8-2	MK-3	2200-2290	UP	10	Baldwin	1911	1947-1956	
2-8-2	MK-4	2210-2219	UP	10	Baldwin	1912	1948-1955	
2-8-2	MK-5	2220-2244	UP	25	Baldwin	1913	1947-1957	
2-8-2	MK-6	2245-2259	UP	15	Lima	1914	1947-1957	
2-8-2	MK-7	2260-2279	UP	20	Baldwin	1917	1947-1958	
2-8-2	MK-8	2280-2294	UP	15	Baldwin	1918	1947-1956	
2-8-2	MK-9	2295-2310	UP	16	Brooks	1918	1947-1959	
2-8-2	MK-8	2311-2320	UP	10	Baldwin	1918	1947-1956	
							Ex-OSL 2525-2534	
2-8-2	MK-Spl	2480-2499	UP	20	Schen	1918	1953-1958	USRA

UP STEAM LOCOMOTIVES BUILT SINCE 1900 (continued)

Type	Class	Numbers	Road	Qty	Builder	Built	Retired	Notes
2-8-2	MK-5	2500-2514	OSL	15	Baldwin	1913	1947-1956	
2-8-2	MK-7	2515-2524	OSL	10	Lima	1917		To LA&SL
2-8-2	MK-4	2515-2518	OSL	4	Brooks	1912	1947-1956	Ex-UP 2214…2218
2-8-2	MK-5	2519-2524	OSL	6	BLW	1913	1946-1958	Ex-UP 2220…2241
2-8-2	MK-8	2525-2527	OSL	3	Lima	1914	1949-1954	Ex-UP 2246,54,58
2-8-2	MK-7	2528-2532	OSL	5	BLW	1917	1948-1956	Ex-UP 2266…2278
2-8-2	MK-8	2525-2534	OSL	10	Baldwin	1918	1947-1956	To UP 2311-2320
2-8-2	MK-10	2555-2564	OSL	10	Brooks	1921	1947-1959	Ex-LA&SL 2716-2725
2-8-2	MK-6	2700-2707	LA&SL	8	Schen	1914	1947-1956	
2-8-2	MK-6	2708	LA&SL	1	Baldwin	1914	1947	
2-8-2	MK-7	2709-2715	LA&SL	7	Lima	1917	1947-1957	
2-8-2	MK-10	2716-2725	LA&SL	10	Brooks	1921	1947-1959	To OSL 2555-2564
2-8-2	MK-5	2726-2732	LA&SL	7	Baldwin	1913	1947-1957	Ex-OSL 2515…2524
2-8-2	MK-7	2733-2735	LA&SL	3	Lima	1917	1948-1958	Ex-OSL 2500…2521
2-10-2	TTT-2	3800-3805	LA&SL	6	Baldwin	1918	1952-1958	Ex-OSL 2500…2521 / To OSL 5300-5305
2-10-2	TTT-1	5000-5009	UP	10	Baldwin	1917	1948-1955	5007 to LA&SL 1958
2-10-2	TTT-3	5010-5014	UP	5	Baldwin	1919	1952-1957	5010-5013 to LA&SL
2-10-2	TTT-4	5015-5039	UP	25	Baldwin	1920	1952-1958	
2-10-2	TTT-6	5040-5049	UP	10	Brooks	1923	1952-1958	
2-10-2	TTT-6	5050-5052	UP	3	Baldwin	1923	1955	
2-10-2	TTT-6	5053-5089	UP	37	Lima	1923	1950-1958	
2-10-2	TTT-2	5300-5305	OSL	6	Baldwin	1918	1952-1958	Ex-LA&SL 3800-3805
2-10-2	TTT-6	5306-5313	OSL	8	Brooks	1923	1950-1958	
2-10-2	TTT-5	5314-5318	OSL	5	Baldwin	1923	1952-1958	Ex-OWR&N 5408,9,11-13
2-10-2	TTT-5	5400-5414	OWR&N	15	Baldwin	1922-1923	1954-1956	5408,9,11-13 to OSL
2-10-2	TTT-6	5500-5514	LA&SL	25	Baldwin	1923	1949-1956	Leased from UP
2-10-2	TTT-7	5515-5524	LA&SL	25	Baldwin	1924	1949-1956	Leased from UP
2-10-2	TTT-1	5525-5529	LA&SL	5	Baldwin	1917, 1919	1954-1956	Ex-UP 5007,10-13
2-8-8-0	MC-2	3600-3614	UP	15	Schen	1918	1947-1956	To 3500-3514
2-8-8-0	MC-3	3615-3633	UP	19	Brooks	1920	1947-1954	To 3515-3533
2-8-8-0	MC-4	3634-3638	UP	5	Brooks	1923	1949-1954	To 3534-3538
2-8-8-0	MC-5	3639-3643	UP	5	Brooks	1923	1952, 1954	To 3539-3543
2-8-8-0	MC-6	3645-3664	UP	20	Brooks	1924	1947-1954	To 3545-3564
2-8-8-0	MC-2	3703	OSL	1	Schen	1918	1942	To UP3644, then 3544
2-8-8-0	MC-4	3704, 3705	OSL	2	Brooks	1923	1944	To UP 3565, 3566
2-8-8-0	MC-4	3803-3805	OWR&N	3	Brooks	1923	1944	To 3567-3569
2-8-8-2	SA-57	3570-3599	UP	30	Sch, BLW	1924, 1926	1947	Ex-Chesapeake & Ohio
2-8-8-2	MC-1	3600-3602	UP	3	Baldwin	1909	1928	To OSL 3700-3702
2-8-8-2	MC-57	3670-3674	UP	5	Schen	1919	1947	Ex Norfolk & Western
2-8-8-2	MC-1	3700-3702	OSL	3	Baldwin	1909	1928	Ex-UP 2000-2002
2-8-8-2	MC-1	3800-3802	OWR&N	3	Baldwin	1910	1928	
4-4-0	E-62	1008	OSL	1	Baldwin	1909		Ex-Idaho Northern 200
4-4-0	E-70	1050	LA&SL	1	Schen	1901	1925	Ex-Los Angeles Terminal 8
4-4-2	A-2	3300-3319	UP	20	Baldwin	1904, 1906	1923, 1925	
4-4-2	A-3	3320-3334	UP	15	Baldwin	1906	1921, 1923	Compound

UP STEAM LOCOMOTIVES BUILT SINCE 1900 (continued)

Type	Class	Numbers	Road	Qty	Builder	Built	Retired	Notes
4-4-2	A-1	3376-3379	LA&SL	4	Schen	1903	1921	Ex-3100-3103
4-4-2	A-2	3400-3407	OSL	8	Baldwin	1904	1925-1930	
4-4-2	A-2	3408-3411	OSL	4	Brooks	1908	1928-1929	
4-4-2	A-4	3500-3514	OWR&N	15	Baldwin	1911	1928-1933	
4-6-0	T-69	1320-1329	UP	10	Baldwin	1900	1921-1936	
4-6-0	T-73	1330-1347	UP	18	Baldwin	1900-1901	1921-1932	
4-6-0	T-79	1348-1359	UP	12	Baldwin	1901	1921-1924	
4-6-0	T-63	1360-1369	UP	10	Baldwin	1902-1903	1927-1934	
4-6-0	T-54	1502	OSL	1	Baldwin	1907	1925	Ex-Idaho Northern 101
4-6-0	T-73	1562-1571	OSL	10	Baldwin	1902	1926, 1928	
4-6-0	T-2, -3	1572-1583	OSL	12	Baldwin	1909, 1911	1933-1951	
4-6-0	T-57,61	1584-1587	OSL	4	Baldwin	1907, 1910	1946-1947	Ex-Pacific & Idaho Northern
4-6-0	T-68	1591-1596	LA&SL	6	Brks, Sch	1901	1925	
4-6-0	T-64	1727-1732	OWR&N	6	Baldwin	1901	1927-1948	
4-6-0	T-2, -3	1742-1754	OWR&N	13	Baldwin	1909, 1911	1933-1949	
4-6-0	T-1	1755-1760	OWR&N	6	Brooks	1909	19401-947	
4-6-2	P-1–P-6	2800-2859	UP	60	Baldwin	1904-1911	1927-1947	
4-6-2	P-8, -9	2860-2879	UP	20	Brooks	1912-1913	1947-1954	
4-6-2	P-10	2880-2899	UP	20	Lima	1914	1947-1955	
4-6-2	P-13	2900-2909	UP	10	Baldwin	1920	1947-1954	
4-6-2	P-9, -10	2910, 2911	UP	2	Brks, Lima	1913, 1914	1953	Ex-OSL 3124, 3130
4-6-2	P-3	3100-3113	OSL	14	Baldwin	1906, 1911	1933-1947	
4-6-2	P-8	3114-3123	OSL	10	Schen	1912	1947-1953	
4-6-2	P-9	3124-3128	OSL	5	Brooks	1913	1947	
4-6-2	P-10	3129-3133	OSL	5	Lima	1914	1947, 1952	
4-6-2	P-11	3134-3138	OSL	5	Baldwin	1919	1954-1955	
4-6-2	P-1	3150-3170	LA&SL	21	Baldwin	1904	1926-1954	
4-6-2	P-4	3171-3175	LA&SL	5	Baldwin	1907	1928-1933	
4-6-2	P-8	3176-3181	LA&SL	6	Schen	1912	1947-1949	
4-6-2	P-2	3200-3203	OWR&N	4	Baldwin	1905	1936-1958	
4-6-2	P-1	3204-3207	OWR&N	4	Schen	1904	1933-1955	
4-6-2	P-3	3208-3210	OWR&N	3	Baldwin	1906	1936-1948	
4-6-2	P-6	3211-3217	OWR&N	7	Baldwin	1911	1933-1954	
4-6-2	P-7	3218, 3219	OWR&N	2	Baldwin	1911	1947, 1955	
4-6-2	P-9	3220-3225	OWR&N	6	Brooks	1913	1947-1955	
4-6-2	P-12	3226, 3227	OWR&N	2	Baldwin	1919	1954	
4-8-2	MT-1	7000-7039	UP	40	Brooks	1922	1949-1956	
4-8-2	MT-1	7850-7864	LA&SL	15	Brooks	1923	1950-1956	
4-8-2	MT-2	7865-7869	UP	5	Brooks	1924	1953-1956	Leased to LA&SL
4-8-4	FEF-1	800-819	UP	20	Alco	1937	1954-1961	
4-8-4	FEF-2	820-834	UP	15	Alco	1939	1956-1962	
4-8-4	FEF-3	835-844	UP	10	Alco	1944	1957-1962	
4-10-2	FTT-1	8000	UP	1	Brooks	1925		To LA&SL 8809
4-10-2	FTT-2	8800-8808	LA&SL	9	Brooks	1926	1948-1954	To 5091-5099
4-10-2	FTT-1	8809	LA&SL	1	Brooks	1925		Renumbered 5090
4-12-2	UP-1	9000	UP	1	Brooks	1926	1956	
4-12-2	UP-2	9001-9014	UP	14	Brooks	1926	1953-1956	
4-12-2	UP-3	9015-9029	UP	15	Brooks	1928	1954-1956	
4-12-2	UP-4	9030-9054	UP	25	Schen	1929	1953-1956	
4-12-2	UP-5	9078-9087	UP	10	Schen	1930	1953-1955	
4-12-2	UP-5	9500-9514	OSL	15	Schen	1930	1954-1956	Ex-UP 9063-9077
4-12-2	UP-3	9700-9707	OWR&N	8	Brooks	1928	1953-1956	To UP 9055-9062
4-12-2	UP-2	9708	OWR&N	1	Brooks	1928		Ex-/to UP 9004
4-6-6-4	CSA-1	3900-3914	UP	15	Schen	1936	1956-1962	To-3800-3814
4-6-6-4	CSA-2	3915-3939	UP	25	Schen	1937	1956-1961	To 3815-3839
4-6-6-4	4664-5	3930-3949	UP	20	Schen	1944	1952-1960	
4-6-6-4	4664-3	3950-3969	UP	20	Schen	1942	1958-1961	
4-6-6-4	4664-4	3975-3999	UP	25	Schen	1943	1959-1961	3975-3984 to 3708-3717
4-8-8-4	4884-1	4000-4019	UP	20	Schen	1941	1961-1962	
4-8-8-4	4884-2	4020-4024	UP	5	Schen	1944	1962	
Shay	65-3	59	LA&SL	1	Lima	1902	1949	Ex-New East Tintic 11
Shay	32-2	60	LA&SL	1	Lima	1896	1918	Ex-New East Tintic 10
Shay	80-3	61	LA&SL	1	Lima	1907	1948	

UNITED STATES RAILROAD ADMINISTRATION

World War I began in Europe in July 1914. Long before the United States officially entered the war, it was involved as a supplier of materials to the Allied Powers. The movement of those materials to East Coast ports constituted a major traffic increase for the railroads after several slack years at the beginning of the Teens.

The United States entered the war on April 6, 1917. Five days later a group of railroad executives pledged their cooperation in the war effort and created the Railroad War Board. Among the problems the board had to deal with were labor difficulties, a patriotic rush of employees to join the Army, and a glut of supplies for the war effort choking East Coast yards and ports.

The efforts of the board were not enough for the government. On December 26, 1917, President Woodrow Wilson placed U. S. railroads under the jurisdiction of the United States Railroad Administration for the duration of the war. The director of the USRA was William G. McAdoo, Secretary of the Treasury and Wilson's son-in-law. The government guaranteed the railroads a rental based on their net operating income for the previous three years. Essentially the government was renting the railroads as one would rent a furnished house, with responsibility for anything lost or damaged.

Two years of heavy traffic moving to Atlantic ports had left the Eastern railroads with roundhouses full of locomotives awaiting repairs. To alleviate the motive power shortage, the USRA proposed to design and purchase a fleet of standard locomotives.

The trade magazine *Railway Age* was initially cautious about the concept. Any design would be a compromise, too heavy for some railroads and too light for others. *Railway Age* suggested a 2-8-2 and an

0-6-0: Chicago Junction 221. Alco photo, Collection of C. W. Witbeck.

0-8-0: New York Central 415. Alco photo.

Light 2-8-2: B&O 4500 was the first USRA locomotive built. The cab has a flatter roof than the cab used on subsequent USRA locomotives. BLW photo, collection of H. L. Broadbelt.

Heavy 2-8-2: CM&StP 8600. Alco photo; collection of C. W. Witbeck.

Light 4-6-2: Atlantic Coast Line 494. Alco photo.

Heavy 4-6-2: Erie 2924. BLW photo, collection of H. L. Broadbelt.

0-8-0 that could work nearly full time at full capacity. Such locomotives would have modern features such as superheaters, stokers, and combustion chambers. Boilers, running gear, and tenders could easily be standardized; fittings should not, since railroads had preferences in matters like brake systems, firedoors, and lubricators. The magazine stated that railroads needing large numbers of new locomotives should be permitted to purchase locomotives designed specifically for their needs.

As 1918 progressed, the tone of the editorials in *Railway Age* changed from cautious to hostile. The need for locomotives was immediate — did it make sense to design new ones rather than build to existing designs? Would standardization make any sense? The average locomotive run was about 150 miles, and there were approximately 2000 engine districts and divisions in the U. S., each with unique requirements. The 835 2-8-2s built in the U. S. during 1917 ranged in weight from 160,000 pounds to 340,000 pounds — could any standard locomotive fill all those slots? What would be the effect on mechanical officers, who took such pride in their locomotive designs? One letter printed in the magazine advocated a heavy 2-8-0 and a light 2-10-0 instead of the proposed 2-8-2.

The USRA answered some of the arguments. Standardization would permit a tremendous increase in locomotive production and would provide a fluid reserve of power that could be moved from railroad to railroad. The few railroads with extreme grades or other conditions requiring heavy locomotives would still be able to get the power they needed. Roads needing lighter power could use locomotives that were replaced by the standard ones.

An engineering committee made up of representatives from the three principal locomotive builders (American, Baldwin, and Lima) and the railroads developed twelve standard locomotives in eight wheel arrange-

Light 4-8-2: New York, New Haven & Hartford 3300. Alco photo.

Heavy 4-8-2: Chesapeake & Ohio 133. Alco photo.

2-6-6-2: Wheeling & Lake Erie 8009. BLW photo, collection of H. L. Broadbelt.

2-8-8-2: Virginian 900. Alco photo.

ments: 0-6-0, 0-8-0, 2-8-2, 2-10-2, 2-6-6-2, 2-8-8-2, 4-6-2, and 4-8-2, with light and heavy versions of the Mikado, Santa Fe, Pacific, and Mountain. Specifications were published in April 1918. They were all designed as coal-burning, superheated locomotives. All had Baker valve gear except the 2-8-2s, which had Walschaerts valve gear, and the 2-10-2s, which had Southern valve gear.

The USRA placed orders for 555 locomotives with Alco and 470 with Baldwin (Lima was already working at capacity). Originally the order was split by type, with only the light Mikado to be constructed by both builders, but the USRA soon changed the order so that both builders would construct all twelve types. Even the order for five heavy 4-8-2s was split.

The reason for splitting the orders was to provide a foundation for future construction of the standardized locomotives. The initial duplication of work in creating patterns and jigs would be repaid in flexibility when orders could be placed with either builder for any of the types.

The initial allocations were published in June 1918. Among the roads receiving large batches were Baltimore & Ohio, 100 light Mikados; New York Central, 95 light Mikados; Milwaukee Road, 50 light Mikados (later changed to heavy Mikados); Erie, 50 heavy Mikados (only 15 were delivered), 20 heavy Pacifics, and 25 heavy Santa Fes; Southern, 50 light Santa Fes. All five heavy Mountains, three from Alco and two from Baldwin, were for Chesapeake & Ohio.

The first order was placed on April 30, 1918, and on July 1, 1918,

Baldwin outshopped Baltimore & Ohio light Mikado 4500. *Railway Age* reported the design was "straightforward throughout, with nothing of an unusual nature."

The first heavy 2-8-2, Wheeling & Lake Erie 6001, appeared in August from Alco's Brooks Works, and the first 0-8-0, for the Toledo & Ohio Central (part of the New York Central System), emerged from Alco's Pittsburgh Works in September.

The first USRA 0-6-0, for the Chicago Junction Railway, came in October. *Railway Age* for October 11, 1918, reported that it was very close to Chicago & North Western's very satisfactory new M-3 switcher, and that the USRA locomotive should prove to be efficient.

The war ended in November 1918, perhaps sooner than the USRA anticipated. USRA control of the railroads continued until 1920, and the builders continued to produce USRA locomotives. In January 1919 *Railway Age* reported that the Mikados and switchers were generally giv-

As the years passed, railroads modified their USRA locomotives. Pennsylvania Railroad 7961 has been rebuilt with a Belpaire boiler, and the smokebox front reflects standard Pennsy practice: small door, high headlight, and round number plate. Otherwise the locomotive is still recognizable as a USRA heavy 2-10-2. Duluth, Missabe & Iron Range 506, on the other hand, conceals its ancestry, a USRA light 2-10-2 built for DM&IR predecessor Duluth, Missabe & Northern. The smokebox front and the Southern valve gear remain relatively unaltered, but almost everything else was added or changed by the railroad — Elesco feedwater heater, the steps from the pilot to the running board, air reservoirs atop the boiler, paired air compressors, slant-front cab with all-weather window, cast trailing truck, and built-up coal bunker. Photo by Robert C. Anderson.

ing good service, and in February characterized the heavy 2-10-2 as not the heaviest or most powerful Santa Fe type, but well balanced.

The USRA designs were good. The switchers were heavier and more powerful than contemporary 0-6-0s and 0-8-0s, and the 0-8-0 was the basis for nearly all switchers built after 1920. The Mikados and Pacifics were well balanced — the firebox, boiler, and running gear were the right size for each other. The light Pacific was heavier than most contemporary 4-6-2s and had a larger boiler, so it constituted a step forward in passenger power for many railroads. It also found a niche in freight service: Its 40,000-pound tractive effort was the match of many 2-8-0s with 61" to 63" drivers, and the Pacific could easily outrun the Consolidation. The heavy Pacific was several years ahead of its time, but it was the basis of such late 4-6-2s as the Southern Ps-4 and Baltimore & Ohio P-7. The 2-10-2s and the 2-6-6-2 were considered the least successful of the USRA designs, partly because of the shortcomings of the 2-10-2 type as a whole and partly because railroads soon were looking for horsepower — pulling power combined with speed — instead of pure pulling power.

Far more copies of USRA locomotives were built than originals — vindicating, perhaps, the arguments for standardization. Three decades later, after another war, both the railroads and the locomotive builders suddenly embraced standardization — but the designs weren't Pacifics and Mikados but rather F7s, RS3s, and GP9s.

Recommended reading:

"Uncle Sam's locomotives," by Eugene L. Huddleston, in *Trains Magazine*, March 1991, pages 30-38

"The U. S. R. A. Locomotives," by William D. Edson, in *Railway & Locomotive Historical Society Bulletin*, No. 93, page 73

Published roster: *Railway & Locomotive Historical Society Bulletin*, No. 93, page 80

USRA LOCOMOTIVE TYPES AND THEIR DIMENSIONS

Type	Driver diameter (inches)	Cylinders (inches)	Total weight (pounds)	Weight on drivers (pounds)	Tractive effort (pounds)	Quantity built
0-6-0	51	21 × 28	163,000	163,000	39,100	255
0-8-0	51	25 × 28	214,000	214,000	51,000	175
2-8-2 (light)	63	26 × 30	292,000	220,000	54,700	625
2-8-2 (heavy)	63	27 × 32	320,000	239,000	60,000	233
2-10-2 (light)	57	27 × 32	352,000	276,000	69,600	94
2-10-2 (heavy)	63	30 × 32	380,000	293,000	73,800	175
2-6-6-2	57	23, 35 × 32	448,000	358,000	80,000	30
2-8-8-2	57	25, 39 × 32	531,000	474,000	101,300	106
4-6-2 (light)	73	25 × 28	277,000	162,000	40,700	81
4-6-2 (heavy)	79	27 × 28	306,000	197,000	43,900	20
4-8-2 (light)	69	27 × 30	327,000	224,000	53,900	47
4-8-2 (heavy)	69	28 × 30	352,000	243,000	58,200	15

VALVES AND VALVE GEAR

By E. W. King, Jr.

Between the boiler which produces steam and cylinders which use it are the valves. Steam locomotive cylinders are double-acting, so there are valves at each end of the cylinder. Unlike the internal combustion engine, the valves have a double job, admission and exhaust. Each valve works in a steam chamber connected to the cylinder by ports at each end; similar ports lead to the steam and exhaust pipes. The valve opens and closes ports by sliding across them; its motion is controlled by the valve gear, which is driven by the pistons. Two types of valves were commonly used on steam locomotives, slide and piston.

Slide valves

The slide valve, also known as the D, flat, or hat valve because of its shape, was the first type to see widespread use. It was easily identified by its rectangular steam chest atop the cylinders. It was an outside-admission valve — steam was admitted to the cylinder ports over the outside edge of the valve. The valve moved back and forth over rec-

tangular ports in the valve seat. As boiler pressures increased and super-heated steam came into use, the slide valve began to show limitations. The ports were limited in size, and pressure on the valve increased friction. The slide valve was seldom used on new locomotives after 1910.

Piston valves

The piston valve, introduced in the 1890s, solved these problems. It was round — spool-shaped — and the ports, which were larger, were located around the circumference of the valve, so steam pressure caused no friction. Most piston valves were inside-admission: Steam was admitted to the cylinder ports over the inside edge of the valve and exhaust was outside.

Universal Valves and Economy Steam Chests were bolt-on outside admission piston valves designed to replace slide valves.

Cutoff, lap, and lead

Three terms used in reference to valves and valve gear are cutoff,

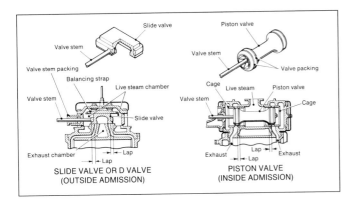

**SLIDE VALVE OR D VALVE
(OUTSIDE ADMISSION)**

**PISTON VALVE
(INSIDE ADMISSION)**

lap, and lead. Cutoff is the point in the piston stroke at which the supply of steam is cut off by closing the valve. It is usually expressed as a percentage of the piston stroke. After the valve closes, the steam in the cylinder continues to expand and push on the piston. The sooner in the stroke the supply is cut off, the less steam is used.

Lap, expressed in inches, is the distance by which the intake edges of the valve overlap the cylinder ports when the valve is in the center of its travel. Lap provides a constant means of cutting off steam admission before the end of the piston stroke. Customary values of lap result in steam being cut off at 82 to 92 percent of the piston stroke; values of 75 percent or less are considered limited cutoff. Cutoffs of less than 60 percent make engines hard to start; without a booster, engines with short cutoff required jockeying of the throttle and reverse lever to start heavy trains.

Lead is the admission of steam to the cylinder just before the piston reaches the end of its stroke, cushioning the piston during its change of direction and starting it on its return stroke with increased snap.

Valve gear

Valve gear had three jobs: moving the valve, reversing the engine,

and allowing the engineer to shorten the cutoff as speed increased. Because the valves covered and uncovered the cylinder ports in the middle of their travel when the pistons were at the ends of their strokes, the motion of the valve could not coincide with the motion of the piston. The movement of the valves had to be 90 degrees out of phase with the movement of the pistons. Outside-admission valves had to be 90 degrees ahead of the piston; inside-admission, 90 degrees behind, regardless of the direction of the engine. The motion of the valves was taken from eccentrics on the axle or the crankpin.

There were two general types of valve gears — direct, in which the movement of the valve was in the same direction as the eccentric, and indirect, in which the valve moved in the oppposite direction. The five most common conventional valve gears in North America were Stephenson, Walschaerts, Baker, Southern, and Young.

Stephenson

Stephenson valve gear was an inside variety, mounted between the frames. For each cylinder two eccentrics were keyed to a driving axle. They gave a rocking motion to links that could be moved vertically by the engineer's reverse lever. The links passed the motion to link blocks which could not move vertically; movement of the reverse lever caused the motion of the link block to range from full forward to full backward motion. The link blocks were connected to rocker arms which actuated the valve rods. Lead was provided by the setting of the eccentrics; it was seen as a valuable characteristic of Stephenson gear that lead increased as the reverse lever was moved toward the center position.

As the steam locomotive grew, frames became larger and heavier and had more bracing, which left little room to apply and maintain Stephenson gear. It was seldom applied to new locomotives after 1910. While it was possible to mount Stephenson gear outside the wheels, it was difficult and done in only a few instances.

Walschaerts

Egide Walschaerts, a Belgian enginehouse foreman, invented the valve gear which bears his name in 1844. It was introduced to North America on Mason bogie locomotives about 1876 and reintroduced on

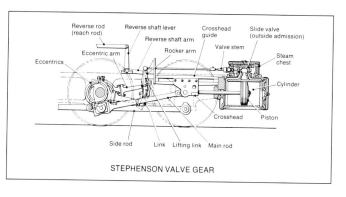

STEPHENSON VALVE GEAR

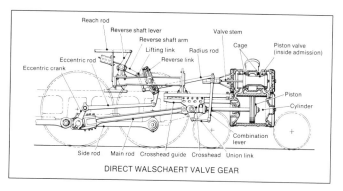

DIRECT WALSCHAERT VALVE GEAR

Baltimore & Ohio 2400, the first Mallet, in 1904. It was the most common outside valve gear in North America.

Walschaerts gear derived its motion from an eccentric crank mounted on the main driver crankpin. The motion was transmitted by an eccentric rod to a link, pivoted at its center on the valve gear hanger. The motion of the link was, in turn, passed by means of a link block to a radius rod which could be moved up and down in the link by the reverse lever. Lead motion was derived from a crosshead connection through a union link and a combination lever, to which the radius rod and valve rods were attached. For outside-admission valves the radius rod was connected to the combination lever below the valve rod; for inside admission, it was connected above the valve rod.

Positioning the radius rod at the extreme top or bottom of the link provided maximum valve travel and power; positioning it near the center resulted in shorter valve travel. Locomotives with direct Walschaerts valve gear moved forward when the radius rod was below the center of the link; those with indirect Walschaerts gear moved forward when the radius rod was above the center.

Baker

Baker valve gear was invented in 1903 by Abner D. Baker, and mar-

keted through the Pilliod Company. The original Baker valve gear was simplified in 1912 and became second in popularity among the outside valve gears. Baker gear replaced the link and sliding link block of the Walschaerts gear with a system of rods and bell cranks. It used the same eccentric crank, eccentric rod, combination lever, and union link as the Walschaerts gear. Its heart was a reversing yoke which was moved back and forth by the reversing linkage. Like the Walschaerts and Stephenson gears, the valve was at its maximum travel at the extreme front and rear positions of the yoke.

Southern

The third most popular outside gear was the Southern, patented in 1912 by William Sherman Brown, a Southern Railway locomotive engineer. Similar in principle to the Baker, it took all its motion from the eccentric crank, eliminating the connection to the crosshead. Southern gear used a radius hanger that performed the function of the reverse yoke of the Baker; it was attached to the eccentric rod some distance from the end. The motion for the valve was taken from the end of the eccentric rod and transmitted to the valve rod through a bell crank. Lead was derived from the difference in the points of connection of the radius hanger and the transmission yoke to the eccentric rod.

411

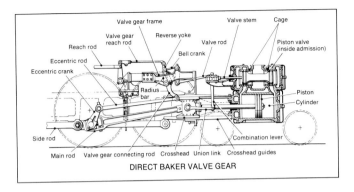

DIRECT BAKER VALVE GEAR

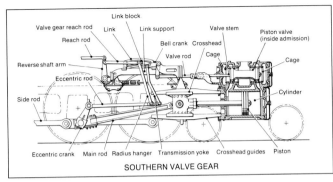

SOUTHERN VALVE GEAR

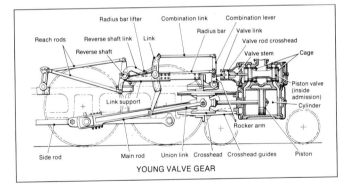

YOUNG VALVE GEAR

Young

Young valve gear, invented by Otis W. Young, was first used in 1915. It took advantage of the quartering of the drivers — 90 degrees apart — to use the motion from one side of the engine to drive the valves on the other, eliminating the eccentric crank and rod. It used links similar to the Walschaerts link that derived their motion from a long union link attached to the crosshead. The radius rods, which were controlled by the engineer as in Walschaerts gear, transmitted their motion to rockers and shafts which took the motion to the opposite side of the engine.

Three-cylinder engines

Valve gear for the middle cylinder of three-cylinder locomotives was a problem. There was little room for it between the frames, and it would receive little maintenance there. Sir Nigel Gresley, a British engine designer, developed an ingenious conjugated valve gear that used a system of levers in front of the cylinders to combine the motion of the valve rods of the outside cylinders to move the valve of the middle cylinder. It could be used with any of the outside gears except the Young, which couldn't be used on three-cylinder engines anyway because the crankpins were 120 degrees apart.

Some three-cylinder locomotives used a double Walschaerts gear on the right side driving two links, one for the inside valve.

Poppet valves

The piston valve had limitations. Because it controlled intake and exhaust simultaneously, any move toward limited cutoff on the intake side created back pressure on the exhaust side. Poppet valves, the kind found in the common gasoline engine, promised to solve the problems.

They were much lighter than piston valves and required less power to operate, and intake and exhaust could be timed separately. The valve mechanism was usually mounted above the frame and behind the cylinders; it was driven either by a crosshead connection or an arrangement that took power from a shaft geared to a crank on the main driver.

Poppet valves worked better than piston valves at high speeds, but they proved expensive and difficult to maintain. Relieving back pressure, while salutary in itself, often created a slippery locomotive. They arrived on the scene too late for designers to master their use.

Recommended reading: "Concerning Stephenson, Walschaert, Baker, Southern, and Young," by E. W. King, Jr., in *Trains Magazine*, May 1984, pages 34-41

Drawings by Allen J. Brewster, from *Trains Magazine*

VIRGINIAN RAILWAY

by E. W. King, Jr.

The Virginian Railway was projected shortly after the turn of the century as the Deepwater Railway, a short line serving West Virginia coal mines in a district lying between the Chesapeake & Ohio on the north and the Norfolk & Western on the south. Westbound coal from the district would be given to C&O at Deepwater, W. Va., for forwarding, and the much greater eastbound volume of coal would be handed over to N&W at Matoaka, W. Va., for movement mainly to N&W's coal piers at Norfolk.

Neither C&O nor N&W was amused by the intrusion of the newcomer, and both refused to negotiate traffic and rate agreements with Deepwater's backers, who decided to build their own railroad, the Tidewater Railway, through Princeton, W. Va., and Roanoke and Victoria, Va., to Norfolk, and to construct their own coal piers. The Tidewater

and Deepwater were combined in 1907 to form the Virginian Railway; the railroad was completed to Norfolk in 1909.

In the 61 miles between the C&O and New York Central connections at Deepwater and the yard at Elmore the road traversed broken grades, with maximums of 1.65 percent westbound and 2 percent eastbound. But Virginian's major grade was east out of Elmore — Clark's Gap Mountain, thirteen miles of crooked 2 percent (maximum 2.07 percent) straight up to Algonquin. Every eastbound load of coal had to be dragged up this hill; it was double-tracked early in the road's history, and for sixteen years demanded the most potent power Alco and Baldwin could conceive: the region's first Mallets in 1909; monster 2-8-8-2s regarded as the world's largest locomotives in 1912; the only successful 2-10-10-2s; and what turned out to be the world's least successful Triplex. Because

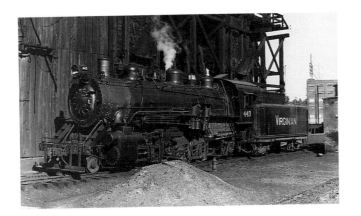

VGN's builders had the foresight to construct a heavy duty plant with liberal clearances, the road could accommodate big locomotives.

East of Clark's Gap, it was a different story. Trains dropped down a 1.5 percent grade from just east of the shop town of Princeton to the valley of the New River at Glen Lyn, crossing that river and the N&W main line on a steel bridge 2,155 feet long and 129 feet above the river. Where N&W's crossing of Alleghany Mountain was seven miles of 1.0 percent, Virginian got away with nine miles of 0.6 percent. East of Roanoke, the line followed the Roanoke River, and had a ruling grade of 0.2 percent compared with N&W's 1.2 percent; a class MC heavy 2-8-2 could get from Roanoke to Norfolk with a train of 100 loads of coal weighing 7500 tons.

For a railroad started in 1909 and thought to be the epitome of modernity, the Virginian showed a dogged loyalty to the slide valve. Where other roads had adopted piston valves a decade earlier, VGN insisted on the archaic slide valves for its new 4-4-0s and 4-6-0s, and for the low-pressure engines of some of its Mallets. Indeed, when the unfortunate Triplex was delivered from Baldwin, all three of its engines were

equipped with piston valves. When it was returned in ignominy for rebuilding — it was made into a Mallet and a Mikado — the resulting 2-8-8-0 had slide valves on its low-pressure cylinders.

By 1925 Virginian had decided that steam locomotives couldn't handle its traffic efficiently west of Roanoke, so the line from there to Elmore was electrified, using 3-unit jackshaft phase-converter locomotives capable of 6,000 horsepower and an astounding 231,000 pounds of starting tractive effort. The power plant — coal burning, naturally — was located at Narrows, Va., on the New River, and was connected to neighbor N&W's electrification; the two roads borrowed electric power from each other to cover peak demands and plant outages.

Virginian became noted for making huge profits by hauling huge trains consisting of huge cars (its 120-ton six-wheel truck coal gons were legendary) with huge locomotives. In 1959, two years after its steam-operated lines were dieselized, the road was merged into the N&W. No slouch at making money itself, N&W wanted the VGN's easier profile east of Princeton for its own coal traffic.

Freight locomotives

Deepwater's first locomotive, acquired in 1903, was an ancient 0-6-0 built at the Pennsylvania Railroad's Altoona Shop in 1873. It was joined by three light 2-8-0s (Nos. 2-4) from Richmond in 1904 and 1905; these were renumbered Virginian 300-302 in 1907 and classed CA. Two 51" drivered Mikados, 30 and 31, were delivered by Baldwin late in 1905; these became Virginian MAs 400 and 401.

The Tidewater obtained two little Consolidations similar to the Deepwater engines late in 1905; numbered 5 and 6, these became VGN CB class 303 and 304. Tidewater also ordered four light 2-8-2s similar to Deepwater 30 and 31, but these were delivered in 1907 as Virginian MAs 402-405. Consolidations 306 and 307 came to VGN from nearby short lines, and were classed CD. CC No. 305 wasn't delivered until 1909. All these 2-8-0s were used in building the roads, and were the 60-ton

2-10-10-2
By E. W. King, Jr.

The first 2-10-10-2s were ten locomotives rebuilt by the Atchison, Topeka and Santa Fe in 1911 from existing 2-10-2s. Baldwin supplied new front engines and tenders, and the boilers and fireboxes were modified at the road's Topeka shop. These monsters were intended for use on the 3 percent grades of Cajon Pass, but even their enlarged fireboxes and boilers were unable to supply the voracious 28" high-pressure cylinders. They lasted only seven years before being cut apart to make 20 2-10-2s.

While Santa Fe was giving up on its 2-10-10-2s, Alco's Schenectady works was fabricating ten of them for the Virginian Railway. These locomotives, class AE, were so huge they couldn't be shipped in one piece; even with cabs and low-pressure cylinders removed they had to be specially routed because of clearances. Huge is a mild term here — the 48" slide-valve low-pressure cylinders were the largest ever applied to a US locomotive and had to be canted to allow adequate clearance beneath them. The tender seemed ridiculously small (12 tons of coal and 13,000 gallons of water) but these monsters had to be turned on existing turntables; Virginian became an early user of auxiliary tenders.

There was a great difference between VGN's 1918 2-10-10-2s and their AT&SF predecessors — Alco's designers had provided a boiler that was up to the task of supplying the cylinders, so these engines could both develop their amazing 176,000-pound starting tractive effort and sustain it, and in compound operation could operate at full capacity, producing near their 147,200-pound rating for hours on end — at about 8 miles per hour.

In May 1921 engine 808 of this class handled 110 of Virginian's 120-ton 12-wheel coal gondolas — loaded — from Princeton, West Virginia, to the Sewalls Point Yard at Norfolk. This train weighed 17,050 tons, yet No. 808 was assisted only in starting at Princeton

The touring car was a large automobile by 1918 standards, but Virginian 802 dwarfs it. Note the dual sand domes. Alco photo.

(by a trio of 0-8-0 switchers) and on the 9.4 miles of 0.6 percent grade from Whitethorne, Virginia, up to Merrimac (by a 2-8-8-2). The rest of the way, 808 went it alone, slugging it out with the crooked miles east out of Roanoke and up the 0.3 percent grade into Abilene. This 2-10-10-2 was an effort at "ultimate" locomotive design that could back up its promise with performance, unlike its underboilered contemporaries, the Triplexes.

When the division from Elmore, W. Va., to Roanoke, Va., was electrified in 1925, the 2-10-10-2s found employment on lesser grades, and eventually shared coal train duties between Roanoke and Norfolk with more agile 2-8-8-2s. They remained in service until 1952, and with the exception of the application of Worthington BL feedwater heaters were never modified during their 34-year service lives.

Total built: 20
First: Santa Fe 3000, 1911
Last: Virginian 809, 1918
Longest lived: Virginian 805, July 1918-March 1958
Greatest number: Santa Fe and Virginian, 10 each
Heaviest: Virginian 800-809, 684,000 pounds
Lightest: Santa Fe 3000-3009, 616,000 pounds

20" × 24"-cylindered size popular 20 years before. All were scrapped in 1933, along with the MA Mikados.

Virginian's new mechanical engineering staff immediately set about devising a classification system for locomotives and cars and designing an all-purpose locomotive. The classification system for locomotives was simplicity itself, using the initial of the name of the wheel arrangement and a second letter for the group or series of engines; thus, the class MA 2-8-2s — M for Mikado, and A for the first series of them on the railroad.

The all-purpose locomotive was exactly that — a medium-size 2-8-2, class MB. Baldwin built 42 of these 56"-drivered machines (420-461) between May 1909 and August 1910, and they literally did everything on the Virginian: switching, pusher duty, coal drags, work trains, fast freights, mixed runs, and passenger trains. Built hand-fired and saturated, all were later equipped with stokers and superheaters.

VGN's first switchers also arrived in 1909, three large class SA (S for switcher, A for first series) 0-8-0s from Richmond numbered 1-3. They were followed a year later by two more from Baldwin, Nos. 4 and 5.

Virginian went right to work obtaining heavy power for Clark's Gap. The region's first Mallets were 2-6-6-0s 500-503, class AA (A for articulated, A for first series), delivered by Richmond in 1909. Hand-fired and non-superheated (all but No. 503 were later equipped with superheaters) the AAs were a challenge for their firemen, and the railroad stationed relief firemen at points along the line to help over the humps.

In 1910 Baldwin delivered a 2-8-8-2 (class AB, No. 600) that incorporated the separable boiler idea introduced on the two Southern Pacific engines of that type a year earlier. This concept was never satisfactory, and VGN's 600 was no exception. It was sent back to Baldwin to be re equipped with a conventional boiler in 1922, and lasted until 1937.

Eight more 2-6-6-0s came from Baldwin in 1910, making Virginian one of the largest owners of this type. ACs 510-517 were more powerful than many 2-6-6-2s and also required relief firemen (they were equipped with two firedoors); all were later equipped with stokers and superheaters

That eastbound 2.07 percent grade up out of Elmore was insatiable and VGN's first really big power came in the summer of 1912, when four 2-8-8-2s (ADs 601-604) arrived from Alco's Richmond Works. Possibly the largest locomotives in the world at the time, these 270-ton monsters had 56" drivers, 28" high pressure and whopping 44" low pressure cylinders, and, operating simple, could churn out 138,000 pounds of starting tractive effort. Compound tractive effort was 114,000 pounds. Two more (605 and 606) came in 1913.

Also in 1912 came 18 heavy Mikados, MCs 462-479. With bigger cylinders than the MBs, they bumped the tractive effort up over 60,000 pounds.

Trains of 58 loads with an AC on the head end and two ADs pushing could go from Elmore up Clark's Gap at 7 mph, the two pushers returning from the top of the hill and the AC taking the train on into Princeton. One MC could move 80 loads from Princeton to Roanoke with an MB pushing from Whitethorne over Merrimac Grade. From Roanoke to Norfolk one MC could handle 100 loads unassisted.

Virginian took delivery of a Triplex from Baldwin in 1916. Class XA (for eXperimental, first series) 2-8-8-8-4 No. 700 used six 34" × 32" cylinders to turn smaller drivers (56") than the original Erie Triplexes of a couple of years earlier. An inherent defect of the type was loss of adhesive weight on the tender engine as coal and water were depleted. More vexing was the necessity to exhaust the rear engine through its own stack at the rear of the tender; this meant that only half the exhaust was available to provide draft for combustion. VGN quickly found that the problems of the Erie prototypes were magnified in the XA. It often ran out of steam; the boiler was not capable of sustaining the engine's rated starting tractive effort, simple, of 199,560 pounds for more than a couple of revolutions of the drivers, and sustaining the compound tractive effort of 166,300 pounds was not a dependable proposition, either. Erie's 63" drivered 2-8-8-8-2s could be operated in compound at cutoffs short enough that steam demand was within the capabilities of their boilers (although they were no more powerful than a regular Mallet when run in that manner), but when No. 700 was hooked up that high, the draft from the exhaust was not adequate to burn the fire.

Baldwin had sent the 700 to VGN on a purely experimental basis, and factory personnel stayed with the engine to try to iron out the wrinkles, with frustrating results. But the locomotive was never accepted, and in 1920 returned to Baldwin. New 28" high-pressure and 44" low-pressure cylinders were installed, and the tender body was placed on a new frame and used behind the resulting 2-8-8-0. Classed AF and numbered 610, the rebuild was rated the same power as ADs 601-606. It was later equipped with a trailing truck, and worked as a 2-8-8-2 until 1953. The tender unit was given a pair of 26" cylinders and placed under a new boiler and tender. The resulting 2-8-2 was classed MD and numbered 410; rated at the same power as an MC, it soldiered on until 1953.

The unhappy experience with the Triplex did not deter Virginian in its search for big power. Alco's Schenectady Works built ten 2-10-10-2s in 1918 that represented the all-time high-water mark in usable tractive effort — 176,600 pounds simple, 147,200 pounds compound. Unlike the Triplexes, the AEs (800-809) could actually produce and sustain these outputs as long as operating conditions required. Although relieved of the heaviest duties by the electrics in 1925 — the 14 mph juice jacks doubled the AE's speed on the mountain — they performed well on less demanding grades until the early 1950s.

While under USRA control during World War I VGN was slated to receive five standard 2-8-8-2 Mallets from Schenectady in 1919. They were already lettered and numbered 900-904 when the railroad refused them; it was felt, probably with good cause, that they couldn't do the job of the AEs. The 900s were relettered and sold to N&W in 1919, where they became Y-3s 2000-2004, the first of 50 such engines.

Later in 1919 VGN and the USRA reached agreement and the road took delivery of 20 Richmond-built 2-8-8-2s, numbered 701-720 and classed USA. When additional power was needed in 1923, Richmond built fifteen class USB duplicates, Nos. 721-735.

The USRA 2-8-8-2s were all-purpose engines; while lacking the punch of the AEs for Clark's Gap, they could do everything else — mine runs, heavy switching, and helper service over Merrimac Grade. The older Mallets went into less-demanding service; all except No. 610 (the rebuilt Triplex) and the 2-10-10-2s were scrapped between 1933 and 1937.

In the mid 1930s Princeton Shop rebuilt six USBs, raising boiler pressure to 250 pounds and adding Worthington BL feedwater heaters. These engines — 721, 723, 726, 728, 729, and 733 — were reclassed USC.

Faster power was needed for Virginian's time freights by the late 1930s. The 1912-vintage MC 2-8-2s were still highly regarded, and five were upgraded at Princeton with disk drivers and lightweight rods. Between 1938 and 1941 MCs 472, 466, 470, 475, and 463 were rebuilt into MCAs 480-484. Major specifications were unchanged, and VGN obtained a satisfactory fast freight locomotive at a bargain price.

World War II brought the need for even faster power for the east end of the road. VGN obtained eight 2-6-6-6s from Lima in 1945. Duplicates of C&O's Alleghenies, AGs 900-907 were billed as the heaviest of the type, weighing in at 753,000 pounds; they held the title of heaviest 2-6-6-6s until it was discovered that C&O's original 2-6-6-6s weighed in at 778,000 pounds — the heaviest reciprocating steam locomotives ever built.

Even the rebuilt MCAs could not keep up with the need for fast freight power after the War. Five 2-8-4s, virtual duplicates of C&O's K-4 Kanawhas, were built by Lima in 1946. The 69"-drivered BAs, 505-509, had speed well beyond that required. The fastest known speed attained by a BA occurred on a detour move over neighbor N&W, where the 505 was said to have made 87 mph with a 3500-ton train.

In 1947 VGN bought seven USRA 2-8-8-2s from the Santa Fe. Originally N&W Y-3s 2014, 2015, 2021, 2022, 2026, 2029 and 2035, they had been bought by AT&SF for helper duty; they were numbered 1794, 1792, 1790, 1791, 1793, 1795 and 1796 (an eighth engine, 1797, was scrapped by AT&SF; it had originally been N&W 2042). Virginian numbered them 736-742 and classed them USE. They were readily identifiable with their characteristic N&W roll-top tenders and six-wheel Lewis trucks. The USEs had the distinction of having the highest boiler pressure ever used on the road — 270 pounds.

The 2-8-8-2s in coal service east of Roanoke were having trouble with broken low-pressure frames occurring while the engines were drifting. In 1947 and 1948 four USAs (701, 702, 703, and 705) and one USB (735) were rebuilt by Princeton with one-piece cast steel low-pressure engine beds and a bridge-pipe exhaust system similar to that used on N&W's modern 2-8-8-2s; Worthington feedwater heaters were also added. Although reclassed USD these engines were not renumbered, and major specifications remained unchanged.

Virginian bought its last steam locomotives in 1950, purchasing 15 secondhand 0-8-0s at a bargain price from C&O, which was dieselizing. These 1942 and 1943 Lima products retained their C&O numbers, 240-254, and were classed SB. They replaced aging MB Mikados that had been used in yard service.

Passenger Locomotives

Virginian's first passenger locomotives were six 67"-drivered 4-4-0s built by Baldwin in 1906 and 1907 as Tidewater Railway Nos. 11-16. They shortly became Virginian EAs (Eight-Wheeler, first series) 100-105, and were renumbered 294-299 in 1925 to avoid conflict with the new electric locomotives.

Class TA 4-6-0s 200-203 followed from Richmond in 1907; not as fast as the EAs, the 63"-drivered TAs were considerably more powerful for the steep grades west of Roanoke. Their original Stephenson valve gear was replaced with Southern in 1919 and 1920; they were the only Virginian locomotives to use this type.

Virginian's last and largest passenger locomotives were six PA 4-6-2s that came from Richmond in 1920. Equipped with Duplex Stokers, the 69"-drivered 210-215 were unusual for their two cross-compound air pumps under their left running boards and their switcher-like recessed tender coal bunkers. Originally built with 26" cylinders and 190 pounds pressure, their tractive effort was 44,300 pounds. When the pressure was raised to 200 pounds in the late 1930s, tractive effort increased to 46,634 pounds, putting them in a class with many larger and better known Pacifics and making them suitable for a considerable amount of freight duty during World War II.

Historical and technical society: Norfolk & Western Historical Society, P. O. Box 201, Forest, VA 24551-0201

Recommended reading: *The Virginian Railway*, by H. Reid, published in 1961 by Kalmbach Publishing Co., 21027 Crossroads Circle, P. O. Box 1612, Waukesha, WI 53187

Published rosters:
Railroad Magazine: April 1937, page 71; July 1951, page 106
Trains Magazine: January 1950, page 25

VIRGINIAN STEAM LOCOMOTIVES BUILT SINCE 1900

Type	Class	Numbers	Qty	Builder	Built	Scrapped	Notes
0-8-0	SA	1-5	5	Rich., Bald.	1909, 1910	1934, 1955	
0-8-0	SB	240-254	15	Lima	1942, 1943	1957-1959	
						Ex-Chesapeake & Ohio	
2-8-0	CA	300-302	3	Richmond	1904, 1905	1933	
2-8-0	CB	303, 304	2	Baldwin	1905	1933	
2-8-0	CC	305	1	Richmond	1909	1933	
2-8-0	CD	306, 307	2	Richmond	1907	1933	
2-8-2	MA	400-405	6	Baldwin	1905, 1907	1933	
2-8-2	MD	410	1	Baldwin	1921	1953	
						Rebuilt from No. 700	
2-8-2	MB	420-461	42	Baldwin	1909-1910	1938-1959	
2-8-2	MC	462-479	18	Baldwin	1912	1953-1960	
2-8-2	MCA	480-484	5	Baldwin	1912	1955	
						Rebuilt from 463, 466, 470, 472 and 475	
2-8-4	BA	505-509	5	Lima	1946	1960	

Type	Class	Numbers	Qty	Builder	Built	Scrapped	Notes
2-6-6-0	AA	500-503	4	Richmond	1909	1933	
2-6-6-0	AC	510-517	8	Baldwin	1910	1933	
2-6-6-6	AG	900-907	8	Lima	1945	1960	
2-8-8-0	AF	610	1	Baldwin	1921	1953	
						Rebuilt from No. 700; rebuilt to 2-8-8-2	
2-8-8-2	AB	600	1	Baldwin	1910	1937	
2-8-8-2	AD	601-606	6	Richmond	1912, 1913	1934	
2-8-8-2	USA	701-720	20	Richmond	1919	1953-1955	
2-8-8-2	USB	721-735	15	Richmond	1923	1954, 1955	
2-8-8-2	USE	736-742	7	Schenectady	1919	1954, 1955	Ex-Santa Fe
2-10-10-2	AE	800-809	10	Schenectady	1918	1948-1958	
2-8-8-8-4	XA	700	1	Baldwin	1916	1920	
4-4-0	EA	100-105	6	Baldwin	1906, 1907	1934-1953	
4-6-0	TA	200-203	4	Richmond	1907	1947, 1949	
4-6-2	PA	210-215	6	Richmond	1920	1957-1960	

WABASH RAILWAY

The Wabash of 1900 was part of the empire that George Gould inherited from his father Jay. Its lines linked Detroit, Toledo, Chicago, St. Louis, Kansas City, Omaha, and Des Moines, and formed major hubs at Decatur, Illinois, and Moberly, Missouri. It had just received trackage rights on the rails of the Grand Trunk from Detroit across southern Ontario to Buffalo. In 1902 Wabash opened a line that served Fort Wayne, Indiana, and in 1904 it reached Pittsburgh, Pennsylvania, over the rails of the Wheeling & Lake Erie and the Wabash Pittsburg Terminal. Financial difficulty overtook the road in 1911 and it lost the WPT; it reorganized in 1915. In 1928 Pennsylvania Railroad interests acquired control of the Wabash.

Only two Wabash 2-10-2s stayed home, Nos. 2503, shown in 1948, and 2507. The rest were dispersed across the Midwest to handle wartime traffic and move coal. Photo by R. J. Foster.

Within a few years the automobile industry in Detroit began to burgeon and Wabash found itself well situated with a fast route to the West that bypassed both Chicago and St. Louis. The road developed into a fast freight carrier.

In 1930 Wabash purchased 25 4-8-2s and 25 4-8-4s that were similar. The question "Why not 50 of one type?" remains unanswered. Baldwin photos.

On the passenger side Wabash was a regional carrier with little in the way of through trains or cars to points on other railroads. It furnished St. Louis connections for Union Pacific at Kansas City, it teamed up with Pennsy to offer Detroit-Chicago service, and in the early years of the 20th century it allied itself with West Shore and Boston & Maine to offer St. Louis-New York and St. Louis-Boston service in competition with the New York Central (West Shore was a secondary part of the NYC System).

Wabash purchased diesel switchers before and during World War II, and began to buy road diesels in quantity in 1949. Dieselization proceeded quickly and was complete by the end of 1953, except for the branch to Keokuk, Iowa, which continued to use ancient Moguls until 1955 because of bridge restrictions.

Freight locomotives

Wabash bought four groups of 2-6-0s between 1899 and 1904. All had 64" drivers. The F-5 and F-6 classes were compounds eventually rebuilt to simple engines; the F-4s and F-7s were built as simple engines. Four 1899 Moguls remained in service until 1955 because their 124,000 pound weight was the maximum that could be carried by the Illinois River bridge on the branch to Keokuk, Iowa. In common with several other Midwestern roads the Wabash had large numbers of 2-6-2s, all in a single class — the 90 G-1s. Like the Moguls they had 64" drivers; engine weight was 228,200 pounds. Between 1916 and 1926 Wabash rebuilt 23 Prairies to J-2-class Pacifics.

Both groups of 20th century 2-8-0s were secondhand, purchased in 1910 and 1911. The 17 I-2s were built in 1905 by Brooks for Detroit, Toledo & Ironton; and the 30 I-3s were 1930 Baldwin products built for the Wheeling & Lake Erie.

Wabash made up for its paucity of 2-8-0s with its 2-8-2s. The K-1s were built in 1912 by Richmond, Baldwin, and Pittsburgh. They had 64" drivers, $25\frac{1}{2}" \times 30"$ cylinders, and a weight of 266,840 pounds.

There was a six-year gap until the next group of Mikados arrived, and toward the end of that period Brooks delivered 25 2-10-2s weighing 395,000 pounds and rolling on 64" drivers, apparently Wabash's standard for freight locomotives.

In 1918 the USRA allocated 20 light Mikados to Wabash, which classed them K-2. Approximately a year after Schenectady delivered them, Nos. 2213, 2214, 2215, 2218, and 2219 were transferred to the Pere Marquette and five Baldwins were moved in from the Western Pacific to take their places. Curiously the USRA Mikes are shown in the roster with 64" drivers instead of the usual 63". Quite possibly thicker tires were substituted during repairs.

The K-3 and K-4 Mikados were built by Schenectady in 1923 and 1925. They had 64" drivers and 27" × 32" cylinders; engine weights ranged from 325,000 to 338,580 pounds. Five K-3s and 20 K-4s were built with boosters and classed K-3b and K-4b.

The five members of the K-5 class were built in 1925 immediately after the K-4b Mikados. They had 23" cylinders — two 23" × 32" cylinders in the usual positions and a 23" × 28" cylinder between them. They suffered the fate of most exotic and minority engines — storage. It proved to be a better fate than scrapping, because their boilers were used in 1943 and 1944 to make Hudsons.

In early 1930 Baldwin delivered 25 Mountains numbered 2800-2824 for dual service. They had 27" × 32" cylinders and 70" drivers; they weighed 406,400 pounds and had a tractive force of 67,400 pounds. Between August 1930 and January 1931 Baldwin built 25 Northerns, Nos. 2900-2924 — with the same size cylinders, same size drivers, same tenders, and many of the same details such as outside-journal lead trucks and vestibule cabs. The 4-8-2s were intended for freight service between Montpelier, Ohio, and Decatur, Ill., and when the 4-8-4s were delivered, *Railway Age* reported they were intended for the same duties. The 4-8-2s occasionally worked in passenger service.

Passenger locomotives

The J-1 Pacifics were built at the same time as the K-1 Mikados in 1912. Engines 660-669 were built by Alco's Richmond Works, and 670-675 by Baldwin. They were the last new steam passenger locomotives Wabash bought. Between 1916 and 1926 the road rebuilt 23 of its Prairies as J-2-class Pacifics. Numbers 1676-1681 were numbered for service between Windsor, Ont., and Buffalo, and Nos. 699-683 for service in the United States — the rebuilds were given successively lower numbers as they were completed, and 682/1682 remained vacant.

During World War II Wabash had plenty of locomotives but not the ones it needed. The 2-10-2s were unsuitable for Wabash's accelerated freight trains, but the road found ready buyers for 13 of them in 1941 and 1942 (Kansas City Southern, Missouri Pacific, and Chicago & Eastern Illinois) and after the war sold 10 to Chicago & Illinois Midland. Twenty-four K-1 Mikados were sold to Algers, Winslow & Western; Algoma Central & Hudson Bay; Alton & Southern; and Seaboard Air Line. (The first three railroads conjure up a picture of Wabash's chief of motive power with an alphabetical list of railroads in one hand and a telephone in the other.) The road also needed heavy passenger power. Unwilling to pull

During World War II Wabash rebuilt five three-cylinder Mikados into handsome blue-painted streamlined Hudsons like No. 703; two more followed after the war. Photo by R. J. Foster.

its 4-8-2s and 4-8-4s off freight, Wabash used the boilers of the unsuccessful three-cylinder Mikados as the basis for five 80"-drivered Hudsons in 1943 and 1944. They were successful enough that in 1946 and 1947 the road recalled the last two K-4 Mikados for similar rebuilding.

Switchers

The switcher fleet included a large group of 0-6-0s built between 1906 and 1912 and a group rebuilt from 2-6-0s. In the 1920s Wabash turned to an 0-8-0 with 25" × 28" cylinders, 52" drivers, and 55,781 pounds tractive effort, copies of the USRA 0-8-0. In 1923 Schenectady delivered 20 more 0-8-0s weighing 217,500 pounds, and in 1926 Lima delivered 25 that were slightly heavier — Wabash's only Lima locomotives.

Historical and technical society: Wabash Railroad Historical Society, c/o Vance Lischer, 535 Dielman Road, St. Louis, MO 63132

Recommended reading: *Wabash*, by Donald J. Heimburger, published in 1984 by Heimburger House Publishing Company, 310 Lathrop Avenue, River Forest, Illinois 60305 (ISBN 0-911581-02-2)

Published rosters: *Railroad History*, No. 133, page 36

WABASH STEAM LOCOMOTIVES BUILT SINCE 1900

Type	Class	Numbers	Qty	Builder	Built	Retired	Notes
0-6-0	B-6	509-524	16	BLW	1903-1904	1931-1947	
0-6-0	B-7	525-566	42	BLW, RI	1906-1912	1949-1954	
0-6-0	B-8	481-499	19	Wabash	1917-1923	1931-1938	Rebuilt from 2-6-0
0-8-0	C-1	1501, 1502	2	Rebuilt	1917	1947	
0-8-0	C-3	1525-1544	20	Schen	1923	1951-1954	
0-8-0	C-4	1545-1569	25	Lima	1926	1951-1954	
2-6-0	F-4	751-778	24	Richmond, RI	1899	1927-1955	Renumbered 569...599
2-6-0	F-5	752-755	4	RI, RIchmond	1899	1931-1953	Renumbered 571...586
2-6-0	F-6	801-866	66	Rich, BLW	1901-1903	1930-1952	
2-6-0	F-7	867-903	37	Baldwin	1904	1931-1947	
2-6-2	G-1	2001-2090	90	BLW, Rog	1906-1907	1934-1950	23 rebuilt to 4-6-2
2-8-0	I-2	2150-2166	17	Brooks	1905	1934-1951	Ex-Detroit, Toledo & Ironton
2-8-0	I-3	2301-2330	30	BLW	1906	1939-1947	Ex-Wheeling & Lake Erie
2-8-2	K-1	2401-2463	63	Rich,BLW,Pitt	1912	1939-1954	
2-8-2	K-2	2201-2220	20	Schen	1918	1949-1953	13,14,15,18,19 to Pere Marquette

Type	Class	Numbers	Qty	Builder	Built	Retired	Notes
2-8-2	K-2	2213...2219	5	BLW	1918	1951-1952	Ex-Western Pacific 321-325
2-8-2	K-3	2250-2274	25	Schen	1923		1944-1955
2-8-2	K-3b	2275-2279	5	Schen	1923	1951-1952	
2-8-2	K-4	2720-2744	25	Schen	1925	1951-1953	2743, 2744 rebuilt to 4-6-2
2-8-2	K-4b	2700-2719	20	Schen	1925	1951-1953	
2-8-2	K-5	2600-2604	5	Schen	1925		Rebuilt to 4-6-2
2-10-2	L-1	2501-2525	25	Brooks	1917	1950-1951	
4-4-2	E-2	606-611	6	Richmond	1901	1931, 1933	Renumbered 694-699, 624-629
4-4-2	E-3	612-623	12	Brooks	1903	1933-1945	
4-4-2	E-4	602-611	10	BLW	1904	1936-1949	
4-6-0	H-11	620-625	6	RIchmond	1901	1931	Renumbered 630-635, 1630-1635
4-6-0	H-12	636-645	10	BLW	1904	1931, 1933	
4-6-2	J-1	660-675	16	Rich, BLW	1912	1951-1954	
4-6-2	J-2	683-699	17	Wabash	1916-1926	1947-1952	Ex-G-1
4-6-2	J-2	1676-1681	6	Wabash	1916-1917	1951	Ex-G-1
4-6-4	P-1	700-706	7	Wabash	1943-1947	1956	
4-8-2	M-1	2800-2824	25	BLW	1930	1953	
4-8-4	O-1	2900-2924	25	BLW	1930	1955-1956	

WAR PRODUCTION BOARD

During World War I the United States Railroad Administration took over operation of U. S. railroads. It controlled the purchase and production of locomotives and cars and developed a set of standard locomotive designs that were used for nearly all locomotives built during the 26 months of USRA control. Before the war most railroads had their own designs for locomotives. After the war many railroads reverted to their own designs, even where the USRA design was better; other railroads enthusiastically adopted the standard designs.

During World War II the government did not take over the railroads, but two agencies were set up to regulate them: the Office of Defense Transportation, and the Transportation Equipment Division of the War Production Board.

A great shortage of locomotives was anticipated, but most railroads had come through the Depression with a surplus of locomotives. As the war progressed, railroads repaired and returned stored locomotives to service, and those railroads with surplus power leased locomotives to those needing it. The most severe shortage seemed to be the result of Electro-Motive overestimating the number of road freight diesels — FTs — it could produce. In 1942 Andrew Stevenson, who headed the Transportation Equipment Division, advocated limiting locomotive production to designs already in use, concentrating production of different types of locomotives — one builder would build 4-8-4s and another would build 4-6-6-4s, for example — and pooling orders for small batches of locomotives. The last policy was the most significant. Railroads that wanted fewer than ten locomotives of a type had to combine their orders and compromise on a design, a restriction that applied from June 1942 to January 1943.

Most of the combined orders were for Northerns. Southern Pacific, Western Pacific, and Central of Georgia got, respectively, ten, six, and eight 4-8-4s of a 73"-drivered SP design from Lima. They were a compromise — SP wanted 80" drivers; WP wanted copies of C&O's Greenbriers; CofG wanted Baldwin engines. Missouri Pacific and Northern Pacific got 4-8-4s that were copies of Rio Grande's second 4-8-4s.

The design restrictions did not endure long. Santa Fe insisted on its own 4-8-4 design, refused to accept any other, and ordered enough to ensure that its design would be used. Standardization of steam locomotives didn't catch on, even if the preponderance of 4-8-4s and 4-6-6-4s represented a kind of standardization. Consider the wheel arrangements produced during the latter part of the war and right after — everything from a Bangor & Aroostook 2-8-0 to Pennsylvania's 6-8-6 steam turbine. But locomotive standardization did occur eventually: 16 cylinders and four axles with a motor on each — and units of different manufacturers able to work together.

Recommended reading: "War Production Board," by Eugene L. Huddleston, in *Railfan & Railroad*, March 1985, page 41

During World War II Southern Pacific, Western Pacific, and Central of Georgia purchased 4-8-4s from Lima. They were built to the same basic design, and WP's engine differed from SP's in only minor details. The CofG engines lacked skyline casings and vestibule cabs; they were coal-burners and had short tenders. Lima photos.

WATER

Steam locomotives were both thirsty and hungry. They required water to turn into steam and fuel to boil the water. Water was easy to find in most places the rails ran, but water that could be used in a steam locomotive was a scarcer commodity. Most water — in rivers, lakes, and wells — contained minerals, which created problems. The minerals weren't carried off in the steam — some remained dissolved in the boiler water, gradually increasing in strength as fresh water was added; others precipitated out as sludge or formed a coating of scale on the outside of the flues, effectively insulating them and preventing heat transfer.

Railroads quickly learned the difference between good water and bad water and eventually built treatment plants to alleviate the problems of the bad water. They also developed procedures for washing out boilers between runs, and for "blowing down," briefly opening valves located at the lowest point of the boiler, where sludge and scale were likely to collect.

Two water problems were aggravated by increased boiler pressure and superheating. Dissolved minerals caused foaming or priming. When the water boiled, the minerals created tough-skinned bubbles, which increased the water level to the point that water could be carried through the throttle into the cylinders — and that could blow off a cylinder head. The other problem was caused by dissolved oxygen attacking the iron in the boiler — rust.

Railroads never completely solved the problem of bad water, or the bigger problem several railroads encountered in crossing the western deserts: no water. Sometimes the only answer was to bring in good water by the trainload, but that was an expensive proposition. A large steam locomotive might use as much as 6,000 gallons of water per hour, and a single tank car held 8,000 to 10,000 gallons. During World War II the

Santa Fe's pair of 203,000-gallon tanks at Yeso, New Mexico, contained enough water to fill the tenders of 17 big 2-10-4s. Photo by Stan Kistler.

Santa Fe was faced with an enormous increase in traffic across Arizona and California, bad-water and no-water country. Lack of water supply was the principal reason Santa Fe purchased freight diesels so eagerly to handle the traffic increase during World War II.

Railroads had to maintain extensive facilities to furnish water: pumps, treatment plants, storage tanks, heaters for the tanks, sometimes even the source itself. Tenders were usually filled from a spout on the tank or a water column or water crane connected to the tank by pipes. A few railroads had track pans between the rails from which water could be scooped up without stopping.

WESTERN MARYLAND RAILWAY

In 1900 Western Maryland was a rural affair that ambled northwest from Baltimore to York and Shippensburg, Pennsylvania, and west to a connection with Baltimore & Ohio west of Hagerstown, Md. The road was largely owned by the city of Baltimore, which sought a buyer for it — and found one in a syndicate representing George Gould.

WM became part of the Gould system, built a marine terminal in Baltimore, and extended its line west to Cumberland, Md., where it connected with the Cumberland & Piedmont, which in turn connected with the West Virginia Central & Pittsburg, down in coal country.

The Gould empire foundered in 1908. WM entered receivership and began building northwest from Cumberland to connect with Pittsburgh & Lake Erie at Connellsville, Pa. John D. Rockefeller acquired control of WM, and in 1927 B&O bought his holdings.

Western Maryland had a dual personality. It was a coal road, carrying prodigious quantities of coal from West Virginia to Baltimore. It was also a fast freight road. The Connellsville Extension connected not only with Pittsburgh & Lake Erie, giving the New York Central System an independent link to Baltimore, but also with Pittsburgh & West Virginia, which with Nickel Plate, Wheeling & Lake Erie, Reading, and Central of New Jersey formed a freight route between the Midwest and the Northeast (the Alphabet Route).

WM operated a few spotless local passenger trains behind immaculate Pacifics — that was the extent of passenger traffic.

The retirement dates of the steam locomotives document that dieselization was accomplished almost overnight in the early 1950s. WM's diesels continued a tradition of steam days — they were painted glossy black (and kept clean), and and they carried red-and-gold "fireball" heralds.

Freight locomotives

In common with several of the anthracite roads farther north, WM purchased ever-heavier 2-8-0s into the 1920s. The progression is easiest to show in tabular form (next page):

The H-8-class Consolidations had switcher-size drivers, 52", for use on steep branches out of Elkins, West Virginia. Photo by Russell L. Wilcox.

Western Maryland's I-2 Decapods were enormous engines, outweighing the Pennsylvania Railroad's 2-10-0s by more than 16 tons. Collection of H. K. Vollrath.

The low-drivered Pacifics that pulled WM's local passenger trains were the cleanest, shiniest 4-6-2s in North America. Photo by Philip R. Hastings.

Vestibule cabs gave Western Maryland's Potomacs something of a Rio Grande look. The front end, though, was pure WM: high headlight, small rectangular number plate, and rock-pusher pilot. Photo by Russell L. Wilcox.

Class	Nos.	Date	Cylinders	Drivers	Weight	Tractive Force
H-4, H-4A	401-416	1901, 1903	22" × 28"	56"	159,000	
H-5	501-518	1905	22" × 28"	51"	182,700	45,173
H-6	601-630	1906-1909	22" × 30"	57"	200,000	43,305
H-7	701-736	1910-1911	24" × 30"	60"	232,000	48,960
H-7B	750-764	1912	25" × 30"	60"	243,000	53,125
H-8	770-789	1914	25" × 30"	52"	244,500	61,398
H-9	801-850	1921-1923	27" × 32"	61"	285,600	71,500

The H-9 Consolidation weighed slightly less than a USRA light 2-8-2, but it had a tractive force equal to that of middle-size 2-10-2. WM had two groups of 2-10-0s. The I-1 class, Nos. 1101-1110, were Russian Decapods weighing 219,000 pounds. The I-2s weighed 419,280 pounds, and had 30" × 32" cylinders and 61" drivers; tractive force was 96,300 pounds, almost as much as a USRA 2-8-8-2.

A pair of 2-6-6-2s arrived from Baldwin in 1909 for pusher service, and seven more in 1911. By the late 1920s they had been superseded by larger engines — the H-9 Consolidations were capable of the same tractive effort and a little more speed — so between 1927 and 1931 WM converted them to 0-6-6-0s for yard service.

The Connellsville Extension, opened in 1912, required heavy power for 20 miles of 1.75 percent grade north out of Cumberland. Lima delivered ten 2-8-8-2s, its first Mallets, in 1915, then five more in 1916, two in 1917, and eight in 1918. They weighed 506,500 pounds, about 12 tons less than a USRA 2-8-8-2, but thanks to larger cylinders and smaller drivers (52", and the freight timetables must have listed days instead of hours and minutes) they could turn out 105,600 pounds of tractive effort, 4,000 more than the USRA engine.

The general acceleration of freight traffic in the 1930s prompted WM to order 12 4-6-6-4s, which were delivered by Baldwin in 1940 and 1941. They turned out to be the wrong engine for the job and spent most of their years in helper service.

WM pooled power with the Reading on the freight route to Shippensburg and admired Reading's home-built T-1 4-8-4s. For its contribution to the Hagerstown-Harrisburg-Allentown pool WM purchased 12 4-8-4s in 1947, making it the last road to acquire 4-8-4s for the first time. Since much of WM's track lay south of the Mason-Dixon Line, "Northern" wouldn't do — the 4-8-4s were called Potomacs.

Passenger locomotives

Baldwin built ten Pacifics for WM in 1909 and 1911. They were small, weighing 201,700 pounds, but their 68" drivers and 23" × 28" cylinders gave them 37,080 pounds tractive force. All ten were sold to Seaboard Air Line in 1943. In 1912 Baldwin followed up with nine larger 4-6-2s — 24" × 28" cylinders, 69" drivers, outside-journal trailing trucks, and 254,300 pounds total weight. Interestingly for a coal road, four of the K-2s were oil burners.

Switchers

WM had less than a dozen 0-6-0s: six built in 1905 and 1909 and five more-modern ones with slide valves and outside valve gear built in 1914. The latter group was sold in 1946 to the Conemaugh & Black Lick, a U. S. Steel switching road in Pennsylvania. WM converted 14 old 2-8-0s to eight-wheel switchers, and some were scrapped within two or three years of their conversion.

Oddities

Steep branches to coal mines occasioned several Shays on WM's roster, some acquired from coal companies and some purchased new. Three-truck Shay No. 6, built in 1945, was Lima's last Shay and the heaviest three-truck Shay built.

Historical and technical society: Western Maryland Railway Historical Society, Box 395, Union Bridge, MD 21791

Recommended reading: *Western Maryland Steam Album*, by William P. Price, published in 1985 by Potomac Chapter, National Railway Historical Society, P. O. Box 235, Kensington, MD 20895 (LCC 85-61150)

Published rosters:
Railroad Magazine: October 1933, page 88; October 1946, page 121; December 1952, page 106
Railroad History, No. 155, page 87

WM STEAM LOCOMOTIVES BUILT SINCE 1900

Type	Class	Numbers	Qty	Builder	Built	Retired	Notes
0-6-0	B-2	1003-1008	6	BLW	1905, 1909	1928-1947	
0-6-0	B-3	1009-1013	5	BLW	1914	1946	To Conemaugh & Black Lick
0-8-0	C-1	1051-1053	3	WM	1926-1927	1950-1951	Ex-H-6 2-8-0
0-8-0	C-2	1061-1068	8	WM	1928-1930	1931-1950	Ex-H-6 2-8-0
0-8-0	C-2A	1071-1073	3	WM	1928-1935	1930-1950	Ex-H-6 2-8-0
2-8-0	H-3G	357	1	BLW	1900	1925	Ex-West Virginia Central & Pittsburg
2-8-0	H-4B	451-454	4	BLW	1900-1901	1928-1950	Ex-WVC&P
2-8-0	H-4B	455-458	4	BLW	1903	1947-1953	Ex-WVC&P
2-8-0	H-5	501-518	18	BLW	1905	1927-1944	
2-8-0	H-6	601-630	30	BLW	1906-1909	1927-1950	
2-8-0	H-7	701-736	36	BLW	1910-1911	1936-1951	
2-8-0	H-7B	750-764	15	Richmond	1912	1954	
2-8-0	H-8	770-789	20	Schenectady	1914	1953-1954	
2-8-0	H-9	801-850	50	BLW	1921-1923	1952-1954	
2-10-0	I-1	1101-1110	10	BLW	1918	1950-1951	
2-10-0	I-2	1111-1130	20	BLW	1927	1954	
2-6-6-2	M-1	951-959	9	BLW	1909-1911	1944-1951	Rebuilt to 0-6-6-0
2-8-8-2	L-1	901-915	15	Lima	1915-1916	1939-1951	
2-8-8-2	L-2	916-925	10	Lima	1917-1918	1940-1951	
4-6-6-4	M-2	1201-1212	12	BLW	1940-1941	1952-1953	
4-4-0	D-8	51, 52	2	BLW	1902	1936, 1935	
4-6-0	G-5	90	1	BLW	1903	1926	
4-6-0	G-6	91, 92	2	BLW	1901	1924, 1927	Ex-WVC&P
4-6-2	K-1	151-160	10	BLW	1909, 1911	1943	To Seaboard Air Line
4-6-2	K-2	201-209	9	BLW	1912	1952-1954	
4-8-4	J-1	1401-1412	12	BLW	1947	1954	
Shay	2-truck 3		1	Lima	1912	1932	Ex-Lantz Coal Co.
Shay	3-truck 4		1	Lima	1918	1945	Ex-Chaffee Coal Co.
Shay	3-truck 6		1	Lima	1945	1953	
Shay	4-truck 5		1	Lima	1910	1954	Ex-Green C. & E.
Shay	4-truck 900		1	Lima	1906	1910	To Mexico North-Western

WESTERN PACIFIC RAILROAD

Western Pacific's steam roster was brutally straightforward: the road never indulged in renumbering or a major rebuilding program, and there is no pre-1900 locomotive development to account for — WP's first locomotives were Consolidations and Ten-Wheelers.

The WP was chartered in 1903 to build a line between San Francisco and Salt Lake City. The last spike was driven in 1909 on Spanish Creek trestle at Keddie, California. The line was almost 150 miles longer than the Southern Pacific route, but its crossing of the Sierra through Beckwourth Pass was 2,000 feet lower. It had a short climb over the Coast Range between Oakland and Stockton; a long run up the flat central valley of California from Stockton through Sacramento to Oroville; a steady climb at 1 percent through Feather River Canyon from Oroville to Portola; a short descent, then a long run across the desert of northwest Nevada; another short climb over the Pequop Mountains; then a 30-mile descent at 1 percent to the salt flats of Utah. The maximum grade was 1 percent, practically nothing compared to Southern Pacific's 2 to 2.4 percent over Donner Pass. (There was a penalty: the sides of Feather River Canyon are unstable and tend to slide down into the river, taking roadbed and track with them.)

The WP had a single main line and no branches — no feeder lines to contribute revenue. It entered bankruptcy in 1915 along with its financial backer, the Denver & Rio Grande. After reorganization WP set out to remedy its lack of feeders. It acquired the Tidewater Southern Railway, an interurban running south a few miles from Stockton, California, and fashioned a branch to Reno, Nevada, from part of the narrow gauge Nevada-California-Oregon Railway. In 1921 WP acquired the Sacramento Northern Railroad, an interurban between Sacramento and Chico, and in 1928 it bought the San Francisco-Sacramento Railroad, an interur-

Western Pacific's Mikados occasionally pulled passenger trains. Number 326 is at the head of train 39, the westbound *Exposition Flyer*, at Portola, Calif., on July 4, 1940. WP's Mikes all had Elesco feedwater heaters. Later classes were built with them; earlier classes received them during visits to the shops. Photo by Guy L. Dunscomb.

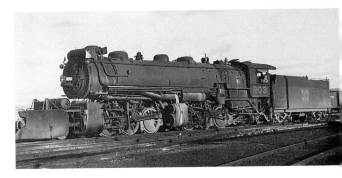

WP's 2-6-6-2s were somewhat lighter than the USRA 2-6-6-2 but had larger cylinders and could exert the same tractive effort. After 1931 they were assigned to the Keddie-Bieber line, where the snowplow pilot was a necessity in the winter. Photo by Philip C. Johnson.

The 2-8-8-2s were large, modern articulateds. Number 251 was the first of the 1931 batch. The second group, built in 1938, had disc drivers and welded tenders. Photo by Ed W. Bewley.

After the dieselized *California Zephyr* replaced the *Exposition Flyer*, Western Pacific's six 4-8-4s worked in freight service. The smoke deflectors and the enameled number plate on the cab and herald on the tender are the only non-Southern Pacific features on the engine. Photo by John C. Illman.

ban connecting Oakland with Sacramento. In 1926 WP came under the control of Arthur Curtiss James, who had large holdings in Great Northern, Northern Pacific, and Chicago, Burlington & Quincy. In 1931 it opened a line north from Keddie to a connection with GN at Bieber, California, creating a new north-south route through California and Oregon to compete with Southern Pacific. The new line had long 2.2 percent grades north from Keddie and 1.8 percent south from Bieber.

Dieselization began before World War II with a few switchers. The road noted that they could operate around the clock without stopping for water, they could be started and shut down quickly, and they were easy on fuel. As traffic increased during the war WP considered buying 4-8-8-4s to eliminate the use of helpers on the long grade west from Wendover, Utah, and reassigning the 4-6-6-4s farther west, but that would have required longer turntables at several locations. By then WP had tested Electro-Motive 103 and recognized that a four-unit FT would not require new turntables and would be quicker to purchase — the design work was already done. WP's first FTs arrived in 1941.

The road also wanted 4-8-4s about the size of Chesapeake & Ohio's 1942 Greenbriers, but their axle loading would have exceeded the limits Southern Pacific imposed on the paired track across Nevada. WP wound up with six medium-size 4-8-4s that were part of an SP order. By the end of 1948 management was committed to dieselization; most steam power was gone by the end of 1951. Mikado 329 was the last steam engine to operate in regular service, between Oroville and Stockton in June 1953.

Western Pacific never had a passenger locomotive built to its own specifications. For its freight locomotives it selected a basic design that exemplified the best current practice and stayed with the specifications for successive purchases — its Mikados are the best example. It was more usual to buy successively larger examples of a given type of locomotive.

WP classified by road number, and the lowest number in each group was the class designation. For example, Mikados 301-305 were class 301. WP also assigned a symbol, which was an abbreviation of the type plus the tractive effort in thousands of pounds. Some symbols had a second figure for tractive effort with the booster cut in. The "P" in the

symbols for the 4-6-0s and 4-8-2s in the roster below means passenger; a few 19th century low-drivered 4-6-0s inherited or acquired second-hand were TFs — freight Ten-Wheelers.

Freight locomotives

Western Pacific's first locomotives were 20 Consolidations built by Baldwin in 1906. They had 57" drivers, slide valves, and Stephenson valve gear; all but one were rebuilt eventually with piston valves. In 1909 Alco's Schenectady Works built 45 more 2-8-0s that were almost the same, except for having Walschaerts valve gear. Most were later superheated and equipped with piston valves.

WP had 41 2-8-2s, 31 of which were the same basic engine built over a period of 11 years. The first five, 301-305, came from Alco's Brooks Works in 1918. They were coal burners assigned to the east end of the railroad; two were converted to oil and moved west in 1950. In 1919 the United States Railroad Administration assigned five coal-burning light 2-8-2s to the WP. In anticipation of the purchase of more heavy 2-8-2s, WP assigned the numbers 321-325, well above its existing heavy Mikes. In 1920 WP sold them to the Wabash and bought five USRA heavy Mikes from the Elgin, Joliet & Eastern for $55,261 apiece, numbering them 306-310. They were also coal burners but were converted to oil in 1938 when the 4-6-6-4s arrived.

Brooks built five more coal burning Mikes, 311-315, in 1921 and delivered six oil burners, 316-321, in 1923. They were duplicates of 301-305, but somewhat heavier. Another five oil burners, 322-326, came from Brooks in 1924. The principal difference from previous classes was a booster-equipped Delta trailing truck. Schenectady built the final two batches of oil burners, 327-331 in 1926 and 332-336 in 1929. They were the same as the previous Mikes but looked bigger because of their 12-wheel tenders and Elesco feedwater heaters.

Articulateds

Western Pacific's first locomotives larger than a 2-8-0 were five 2-6-6-2s built by Brooks in 1917. They were oil burners intended for service through the Feather River Canyon between Oroville and Portola, Calif. Five more substantially identical Mallets came from Alco's Richmond Works in 1924. The ten 2-6-6-2s moved to the Northern California Extension between Keddie and Bieber upon its completion in 1931.

The 2-6-6-2s were replaced in the Feather River Canyon by six simple 2-8-8-2s from Baldwin in 1931 — WP's first Baldwins since the first 2-8-0s — and four more in 1938. They were unusual in having trailing truck boosters. During World War II they were equipped with steam heat and air signal lines for passenger service, probably on troop trains.

The seven Challengers built in 1938 were coal-burners for freight service across the desert between Elko, Nev., and Salt Lake City. They were replaced by diesels in 1950. In October of that year six were leased briefly to Union Pacific, and WP later offered to lease them to Rio Grande, Burlington, Great Northern, and Milwaukee Road, but found no takers.

Passenger locomotives

Western Pacific was not a major passenger carrier. The Oakland-Salt Lake City main line carried a daily first-class passenger train (successively the *Scenic Limited*, *Exposition Flyer*, and *California Zephyr*) and a secondary train that at times went only as far east as Gerlach or Reno,

Nev., or Portola, Calif. WP's running times between the Great Salt Lake and San Francisco Bay were five to ten hours longer than the competing Southern Pacific. Passengers rode the WP to go places SP didn't serve (and there weren't many of those) or to see different scenery.

WP's first passenger locomotives, and the only ones until 1936, were 36 Ten-Wheelers built by Alco's Brooks Works in 1908 and 1909. The only apparent difference between the 71 and 86 classes is delivery date. The 71 class was built for the Denver & Rio Grande but assigned to the WP before delivery. Although the Ten-Wheelers were built with piston valves and Walschaerts valve gear, they were not state-of-the-art passenger power — WP's California neighbors Southern Pacific and Santa Fe had already purchased Pacifics — but they were adequate for WP's needs for almost three decades. Very few photos show doubleheaded Ten-Wheelers on WP passenger trains.

When the Florida East Coast fell on hard times during the Depression, the bank holding the mortgage on some of its locomotives foreclosed and found itself in the locomotive business. In 1936 WP picked up 10 FEC 4-8-2s built in 1924 for the bargain price of $12,500 each. Three were rebuilt at the Rio Grande's shop in Salt Lake City, and WP's Jeffery Shops in Sacramento rebuilt the rest. Rebuilding cost about $33,000 each. They replaced 4-6-0s on the Oakland-Salt Lake City passenger trains. (That same year, Southern Pacific paid $133,547 apiece for six 4-8-4s for the new *Daylight* trains, and Detroit & Toledo Shore Line bought three Mikados for $84,196 each.)

WP's last steam engines were six 4-8-4s built by Lima in 1943 as part of a Southern Pacific order for unstreamlined, 73"-drivered 4-8-4s. They were allocated to WP by the War Production Board. They were identical to SP's GS-6 class. Before delivery some of SP's patented devices were removed, such as the oil burner. WP added smoke deflectors to the locomotives between 1946 and 1948. Three of them, 481, 484, and 485, were sold to SP for parts in 1953.

Switchers

WP had only 16 switchers, all 0-6-0s, mainly because the road had little work for switchers. The first dozen came from Alco's Pittsburgh Works in 1909. They had 51" drivers, slide valves, and slope-back tenders. Engines 151-158 were oil burners; 159-162 were built as coal burners and converted to oil in the 1920s. Engines 163-166 came from the United Verde Copper Company in 1927. They were built by Alco at Schenectady in 1915 and 1919. They were a little heavier than the earlier batches and had piston valves and Walschaerts valve gear. Two of the five surviving WP locomotives are from this group. A number of 2-8-0s were fitted with footboards and used for switching.

Historical and technical society: Feather River Rail Society, P. O. Box 608, Portola, CA 96122

Recommended reading: *Western Pacific Steam Locomotives, Passenger Cars and Trains*, by Guy L. Dunscomb and Fred A. Stindt, published in 1980 by Guy L. Dunscomb and Fred A. Stindt, 2502 Fremont Avenue, Modesto, CA 95350 (LCC 80-50321)

Published rosters:

Railroad Magazine: June 1932, page 330; December 1946, page 112; January 1953, page 100

Trains Magazine: May 1942, page 40

WP STEAM LOCOMOTIVES BUILT SINCE 1900

Type	Symbol	Numbers	Qty	Builder	Built	Retired	Notes
0-6-0	S-31	151-162	12	Pittsburgh	1909	1947-1953	
0-6-0	S-34	163-166	4	Schenectady	1915, 1919	1953	
							Ex-United Verde Copper
2-8-0	C-43	1-20	20	Baldwin	1906	1937-1950	
2-8-0	C-43	21-65	45	Schenectady	1909	1939-1954	
2-8-2	MK-60	301-321	21	Schen, Brks	1918-1923	1950-1953	
2-8-2	MK-55	321-325	5	Baldwin	1918		
							Acquired 1919, sold 1920
2-8-2	MK-60-71	322-336	15	Brks, Schen	1924-1929	1939-1953	
2-6-6-2	M-80	201-210	10	Brks, Rich	1917, 1924	1949-1953	
2-8-8-2	M-137-151	251-260	10	Baldwin	1931, 1938	1952	
4-6-0	TP-29	71-106	36	Brooks	1908-1909	1934-1950	
4-8-2	MTP-44	171-180	10	Schenectady	1924	1950-1952	Ex-FEC
4-8-4	GS-64-77	481-486	6	Lima	1943	1953-1957	
4-6-6-4	M-100	401-407	7	Alco	1938	1952	

APPENDIX

Compilation of this book consumed more than a year of research and writing, and its production — page layout, photo sizing, and typesetting — was begun before all the research was complete. The following five entries were originally to be omitted for lack of information, but enough material came to light late in the project to include them here, as an appendix.

BUFFALO, ROCHESTER & PITTSBURGH RAILWAY

Between 1869 and 1899 the Buffalo, Rochester & Pittsburgh developed into a coal carrier that extended from the coalfields of western Pennsylvania north to Buffalo, northeast to Rochester, New York, and west to a connection with the Baltimore & Ohio at Butler, Pennsylvania, about 50 miles north of Pittsburgh. The BR&P was a prosperous railroad, and the prosperity was reflected in its locomotives. The road appeared to wait until new technology had settled down, then it bought large batches of a single type of locomotive: 2-8-0s right after the turn of the century, 2-8-2s in the Teens, 2-6-6-2s in the late Teens and 1920s. Successive batches of each type were little different from the original group. Previous top-rank locomotives were bumped from mainline duties to local service; locomotives at the bottom of the heap were usually not scrapped but sold to short lines through dealers such as Southern Iron & Equipment of Atlanta.

Baltimore & Ohio acquired the BR&P at the beginning of 1932 and took over its operation. It is interesting to speculate how BR&P's motive power would have developed otherwise — in the late 1920s BR&P was investigating 4-8-4s and 2-10-4s.

Freight locomotives

The BR&P entered the 20th century using Consolidations as road freight engines. During the first decade of the century BR&P bought 133 2-8-0s, most of them 57"-drivered machines with only minor differences between successive batches. In 1912 BR&P got its first 2-8-2, and within 5 years had 48 of them. They represented a leap forward in locomotive design for the road: They were half again as heavy and powerful as the Consolidations, and their 63" drivers made them faster. The Mikados were hardly established when the road started buying 2-6-6-2s to eliminate doubleheading of the Mikados.

BR&P had a number of grades that required helper locomotives. At the turn of the century it used 4-8-0s for pusher service. They were replaced in part by eight Decapods built by Brooks in 1907 and 1909; the 2-10-0s were in turn replaced by 2-8-8-2s in 1918.

Passenger locomotives

The BR&P was not a major passenger carrier, but it was quick to adopt new technology. In 1901 the road ordered four Atlantics, two from Baldwin and two from Brooks. They had 72" drivers, inboard piston valves, and inside-bearing trailing trucks. Later Atlantics had 73" drivers and slide valves, and the last had Walschaerts valve gear. One curious characteristic of BR&P's Atlantics was the driver spacing, making the engines look as though the builder had intended to use 80" drivers, then changed his mind after the locomotive was under construction.

The 15 Atlantics the BR&P had acquired by 1909 were sufficient for the short trains the road operated, but they weren't powerful enough when steel cars replaced wood. Between 1912 and 1918 BR&P received

17 Pacifics from Brooks, medium-size machines with 73" drivers. Five more Pacifics came in 1923, smaller and lighter, surprisingly, than the first group — 241,200 pounds compared to 258,000 for the WW class.

In 1923, BR&P had 37 passenger locomotives, which seems like a lot, compared to the number of Amtrak F40s that today ply the rails on the Pittsburgh-Punxsutawney-Bradford-Buffalo run. Consider BR&P's passenger service in January 1930. Mainline passenger trains in each direction included day and night Buffalo-Pittsburgh expresses; two Buffalo-Springville, N. Y., locals; a Buffalo-Bradford, Pa., local; a Buffalo-Punxsutawney, Pa., local; a Bradford-Punxsutawney local; a Du Bois-Butler, Pa., local; a Du Bois-Pittsburgh local; two Rochester-East Salamanca, N. Y., trains; a Rochester-Perry, N. Y., local; and a Rochester-Le Roy, N. Y., local. Assuming engine runs of no more than 100 miles and allowing at least 2 hours to turn and service an engine, these mainline runs accounted for at least 17 locomotives, and the branches for at least another six. There were jobs for nearly all the Pacifics and Atlantics that were conveyed to B&O.

Baltimore & Ohio ownership

BR&P's locomotives were renumbered and reclassified into the B&O roster in 1932. BR&P had more locomotives than it needed, particularly during the Depression, so B&O retired the oldest and lightest — the Atlantics and the oldest Consolidations — by the mid-1930s. Other power remained in service until B&O dieselized in the early 1950s. Last to be scrapped were the 18 0-8-0s, which were considerably newer than any of B&O's own.

Historical and technical society: Baltimore & Ohio Railroad Historical Society, P. O. Box 13578, Baltimore, MD 21203-3578

Recommended reading: *The Buffalo, Rochester & Pittsburgh Railway*, by Paul Pietrak, published in 1979 by Paul Pietrak, North Boston, NY 14110

Published rosters:

Railway & Locomotive Historical Society Bulletin: No. 84, page 46; No. 119, page 34

Railroad Magazine: June 1934, page 90, and July 1934, page 82 (B&O)

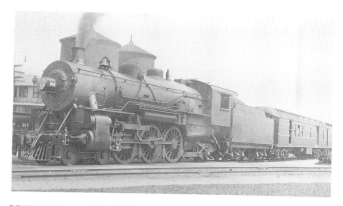

BR&P 616, shown at East Salamanca, New York, was the highest-numbered of the WW class of Pacifics. The piston-rod extensions and the undersized trailing truck frame are interesting features. Trains Collection.

BR&P had 18 eight-wheel switchers. They were similar to the USRA switcher in dimensions and tractive effort, but not in the shape of the tender. Photo by Carl E. Stolberg.

Baltimore & Ohio 7324, formerly Buffalo, Rochester & Pittsburgh 808, built by Brooks in 1923, drifts backward into the yard at Clarion Junction, Pennsylvania, after pushing a freight up Clarion Hill. The 2-8-8-2's low-pressure cylinders are 44" in diameter. It was common practice to use piston valves for high-pressure cylinders and slide valves for low-pressure cylinders on Mallets. Photo by W. G. Thornton.

BR&P STEAM LOCOMOTIVES ACQUIRED AFTER 1900

Type	Class	Numbers	Qty	Builder	Built	Retired	B&O class and number*
0-6-0	F3	152-156	5	Brooks	1904	-1954	D-44; 390-394
0-8-0	F4	520-537	18	Brooks	1918, 1923	1956-1958	L-4, L-4a; 772-789
2-8-0	V2	270-274	5	Baldwin	1902	-1935	4 to E-58; 3084-3087
2-8-0	V3	275-284	10	Baldwin	1903	-1936	9 to E-58a; 3088-3096
0-8-0	VR	285	1	Baldwin	1901	1934	E-58b; 3083
2-8-0	X	250-269	20	Brooks	1903		2 to E-53; 3011, 3012
2-8-0	X	300-319	20	Brooks	1903		3 to E-52; 3010, 3013, 3014
2-8-0	X2	320-334	15	Brooks	1904		6 to E-53, E-55; 3015-3017, 3025-3027
2-8-0	X4	335-354	20	Brooks	1905	-1950	17 to E56; 3051, 3054-3069
2-8-0	X3	355-384	30	Brooks	1906, 1907		29 to E-54, E-55; 3019-3024, 3028-3050
2-8-0	X6	385-396	12	Brooks	1909		12 to E-57; 3070-3081
2-8-2	Z	400-447	48	Brooks	1912-1917		Q-10; 4700-4747
2-10-0	Y	501-508	8	Brooks	1907, 1909	-1951	Y, 6500-6507
2-6-6-2	LL	700-754	55	Schen, Brks	1914-1923		KK-4; 7500-7554
2-8-8-2	XX	800-808	9	Brooks	1918, 1923		EE-2, 2a, 7316-7324
4-4-2	W	160, 161	2	Baldwin	1901		
4-4-2	W	168, 169	2	Baldwin	1905		
4-4-2	W2	162, 163	2	Brooks	1901	-1937	A-6; 1487, 1488
4-4-2	W3	164-167	4	Brooks	1903	-1936	A-7; 1489-1491 (165-167)
4-4-2	W4	170-173	4	Brooks	1906	-1937	A-8; 1492-1495
4-4-2	W5	174	1	Brooks	1909	1936	A-8a; 1496
4-6-0	T3	186-189	4	Brooks	1900		
4-6-2	WW	600-616	17	Brooks	1912-1918	-1953	P-17, 17a, 18, 18a; 5140-5148, 5185-5192
4-6-2	WW2	675-679	5	Brooks	1923	-1953	P-19; 5260-5264
4-8-0	S-2	200-228	29	Brooks	1898-1899		
4-8-0	S-3	229-245	17	Brooks	1900-1901		

* Most BR&P classes were given B&O numbers in sequence. The 2-8-0s were renumbered in all but random order, and B&O overclassified them — there was little difference among them. Not all subclasses are shown here, and the authorities disagree on those subclasses.

BUILDER'S PHOTOS

Many of the illustrations in this book are builder's photos, official portraits of locomotives made before they had rolled more than a few yards from the erecting floor. They show the new machines broadside in splendid isolation; often printed on the reverse side of the photo are complete specifications of the locomotive.

Usually one locomotive of an order was photographed. It was not necessarily the first or the last of the group built; selection depended on several factors such as work schedules. Since the engines in an order were usually identical, it didn't matter which one posed for the photographer.

The locomotive selected to be photographed was painted specially for the event: flat black paint on the side to be photographed (to minimize reflections and mask minor dents), white trim on the running boards and wheel tires, and polished rods. The engine was moved outdoors, and large white panels of wood and canvas were set up behind the engine to ease the task of blocking out the background on the negative. (This wasn't always done; photos taken at Alco's Schenectady Works often showed neighborhood buildings.)

The photographer used a large-format camera — usually 8" × 10" or larger — and aimed the camera at the side of the locomotive at some point between the pilot beam and the stack. The exact point depended on the photographer, and the side being photographed depended on the builder: Alco and Lima preferred the right (engineer's) side; Baldwin often showed the left.

In addition to the broadside view, builder's photographers often took three-quarter and head-on views and photos of the cab interior.

Recommended reading: "Super-power portraitist," by Eric E. Hirsimaki, in *Trains Magazine*, February 1977, pages 22-30

The official portrait of Boston & Maine P-4-a 3710 (Lima, 1934) shows the right side of the locomotive painted flat black. The running board and tires are trimmed in white and the rods have been painted white with the fluted areas filled in. Taken at the same time, the informal view of the left side shows glossy black paint and polished rods; the photographer's portable wood and canvas panels are visible behind the engine. Lima photos; lower photo, collection of Allen County (Ohio) Historical Society.

CHICAGO & ALTON RAILROAD

The Chicago & Alton was virtually full grown by 1878. It comprised a main line from Chicago to St. Louis, a second main line from Springfield, Illinois to Kansas City, Missouri, and a few branches in Illinois. It came under the control of E. H. Harriman in 1899 (the two major roads in his empire were Union Pacific and Southern Pacific). Control of the C&A passed briefly to the Toledo, St. Louis & Western (Clover Leaf) in 1907. Deficits began in 1912, and C&A entered receivership in 1922.

Baltimore & Ohio purchased the Chicago & Alton at a foreclosure sale in 1929, incorporated the Alton Railroad in January 1931, and in July 1931 sold the properties of the C&A to the Alton. The Alton was operated more or less as a portion of the B&O and was no more successful financially than the C&A had been.

In 1943 B&O cast off the Alton; the Gulf, Mobile & Ohio Railroad (created in 1940 from the Gulf, Mobile & Northern and Mobile & Ohio railroads) merged the Alton in 1947. By then both GM&O and Alton had begun dieselization in earnest. GM&O's last steam operation occurred on October 7, 1949.

Freight locomotives

The Chicago & Alton was still buying 2-6-0s as late as 1911. Its F-3 Moguls had 57" or 62" drivers (the latter likely a result of rebuilding); the F-4s, 62" drivers. The F-7 class of 1911 had 51" drivers, indicating they were probably intended for switching and transfer work. At the same time C&A was buying Moguls it also bought 2-8-0s with 57" or 62" drivers for road freight service.

The last Consolidations C&A received were three of a group of ten Buffalo & Susquehanna ordered, then canceled the order after Brooks had begun building them.

C&A purchased three 2-6-6-2s in 1910 for helper service and coal trains. One of the trio was sold almost immediately to the Chesapeake & Ohio. Baltimore & Ohio took the other two east in 1931 when it purchased the Alton, stored them, and scrapped them in 1938.

The road took delivery of its first Mikados, class L-1, in 1910. They had 26" × 30" cylinders and 62" drivers. In 1913 the road received 20 class L-2 Mikados, part of a group of 94 locomotives built by Baldwin to a Harriman design (other locomotives of that batch went to Union Pacific, Oregon Short Line, Southern Pacific, and Texas & New Orleans). The L-2, developed from the Harriman 1911 passenger-service 2-8-2, had 63" drivers, 20" × 28" cylinders, and a boiler pressure of 200 pounds. During World War II a number of L-2s were rebuilt extensively with new smokeboxes, new cylinders, feedwater heaters, and thermic syphons (a syphon is a water tube in the firebox from the bottom of the flue sheet to the crown sheet, providing additional heating surface and increasing circulation in the boiler). The five L-3s of 1918 were near-duplicates of the L-2s, the principal differences being cast trailing trucks and larger tenders.

In 1918 the USRA assigned ten light 2-8-2s to the C&A — they became class L-4. Three years later Standard Oil Company of Indiana bought five copies of the USRA light 2-8-2 (plus 500 coal cars) and leased them to the C&A, which used them to haul coal north from the mines to Standard Oil refineries. They eventually became railroad property.

C&A tested a pair of Santa Fe 2-8-4s in 1929, and considered buying that type in October 1929, but finances didn't permit new power, nor would Depression traffic have warranted it.

Passenger locomotives

C&A purchased a group of elegant maroon 4-4-0s in 1899 but soon recognized it needed something more powerful for its fast passenger trains. In 1901 it ordered 10 Vauclain compound Ten-Wheelers from Baldwin. Maintenance costs for the compounds were high, and between 1904 and 1908 C&A rebuilt them to single-expansion locomotives, at the same time changing the driver size from 68" to 73". They were retired when B&O took over in 1929.

In 1903 the road ordered four Atlantics, class E-1, and five Pacifics in three classes. The Atlantics had 80" drivers, Stephenson valve gear, inboard piston valves, and inboard-bearing trailing trucks. Class I-1

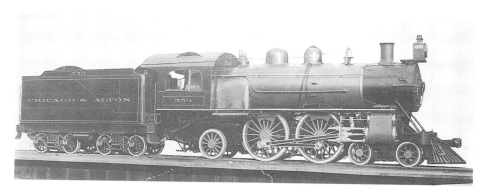

The eyebrow dormer in the cab roof of E-1 Atlantic 553 was found on most Alton engines built right after the turn of the century. Baldwin photo.

Pacific No. 600 had 73" drivers, and I-2 No. 601 had 80" drivers (plus 3" larger lead and trailing truck wheels) but were otherwise alike. Pacifics 602-604 were of Harriman design, with 77" drivers and slightly smaller fireboxes than the Atlantics and the previous two 4-6-2s. They were delivered as class P and were later reclassified I-3. All three classes of Pacifics had Stephenson valve gear and inboard-bearing trailing trucks, later replaced by Walschaerts valve gear (except on No. 600) and outboard-bearing trailing trucks.

Along with the Harriman Pacifics came a single Harriman-design Atlantic, No. 554, class A. It had been exhibited by Baldwin at the Louisiana Purchase Exposition in St. Louis in 1904. In 1906 it was sold to the Texas & New Orleans, and C&A received five more Atlantics, class E-2, numbered 554 (second 554) to 558. The E-2s were not of Harriman design (Harriman no longer controlled C&A) and had smaller fireboxes than their predecessors. Three Atlantics were scrapped before Baltimore & Ohio purchased the C&A; the others were scrapped soon afterward.

Twenty more Pacifics arrived on the property between 1908 and 1910 — five I-4s from Baldwin (22" × 28" cylinders, 73" drivers, and narrow fireboxes) and 15 from Brooks. The Brooks locomotives had cylinders an inch greater in diameter and 80" drivers for class I-5 (Nos. 620-624) and 77" for class I-5a (625-634). The I-6 Pacifics of 1913 were of Harriman design and were the same as Southern Pacific's P-6 class. The design combined the speed of earlier Harriman Pacifics and the boiler capacity of the 63"-drivered Harriman 2-8-2 that had been developed for passenger trains in the mountains. In 1943 and 1944, when new passenger locomotives were unavailable, the I-6s were modernized with Worthington feedwater heaters, Nicholson thermic syphons, and new superheaters. They were reclassified P-16b.

Baltimore & Ohio's two lightweight steam locomotives, 4-4-4 *Lady Baltimore* and 4-6-4 *Lord Baltimore*, worked on the Alton. The first few runs of the streamlined *Abraham Lincoln* in July 1935 were made with the 4-4-4, which proved too light for the job. The Hudson came to Illinois in July 1937 to power the *Ann Rutledge* and remained on the Alton until 1942.

Switchers

C&A's switchers were all 0-6-0s with 51" drivers and 20" × 26" cylinders, except for the B-9 class, built in 1913, which had 19" × 26" cylinders. By the mid-1930s only five of the B-9s and 11 of the other 0-6-0s remained in service.

Harriman characteristics of Chicago & Alton 4-6-2 658 include the extended smokebox, deeply arched cab roof, and a tapered boiler course between the steam dome and the sand dome. Alco photo.

Alton 5292 (formerly Chicago & Alton 652) has lost its extended smokebox and gained a shielded air pump above the pilot, a smaller cab, and a larger tender, but the taper of the boiler remains. Photo by Bruce Meyer.

Historical and technical society: Gulf, Mobile & Ohio Historical Society, P. O. Box 463, Fairfield, IL 62837.

Published rosters

Railroad History,: No. 156, page 55

Railroad Magazine: June 1934, page 90, and July 1934, page 82 (B&O) Baltimore & Ohio roster); October 1966, page 51 (1926 roster).

C&A STEAM LOCOMOTIVES ACQUIRED AFTER 1900

Type	Class	Numbers	Qty	Builder	Built	Alton class, numbers		Notes
0-6-0	B-3	67-71	5	Baldwin	1900	D-40	32-35	
0-6-0	B-3	77-94	18	Baldwin	1903	D-40	same (77 to 95)	
0-6-0	B-4	72-76	5	Baldwin	1901	D-41	46-49	
0-6-0	B-8	95-100	6	Brooks	1909	D-42	98 to 42	
0-6-0	B-9	57-66	10	Baldwin	1913	D-43	65, 66 to 59, 60	
0-6-0	B-10	42-56	15	C&A	1921-1928	D-39	300-314	
							Rebuilt from 2-6-0s	
2-6-0	F-3	300-349	50	Baldwin	1899-1900	K-18	2400-2422	
2-6-0	F-4	360-367	8	Baldwin	1902-1903	K-19	2423-2429	
2-6-0	F-7	390-399	10	Baldwin	1911	K-20	2430-2439	
2-8-0	H-1, a	400-409	10	Brooks	1900	E-46	2612-2615, 2660-2665	
2-8-0	H-2	450-459	10	Baldwin	1902	E-47, 47a	2957-2966	
2-8-0	H-3	410-429	20	Baldwin	1905-1906	E-48	2967-2986	
2-8-0	H-7	430-439	10	Brooks	1909	E-49	2987-2996	
2-8-0	H-8	440-442	3	Brooks	1910	E-50	2997-2999	
2-8-2	L-1, a	800-829	30	Brooks	1910	Q-5, Q-5a	4330-4359	
2-8-2	L-2	840-859	20	Baldwin	1913	Q-6	4360-4379	
2-8-2	L-3	860-864	5	Baldwin	1918	Q-7	4380-4384	
2-8-2	L-4	875-884	10	Schen	1918	Q-8	4385-4394	USRA
2-8-2	L-4a	885-889	5	Schen	1921	Q-8a	4395-4399	
2-6-6-2	K-1	700-702	3	Brooks	1910		Sold to C&O and B&O	
4-4-0	D-3b	116, 117	2	C&A	1905			
4-4-2	A	554	1	Baldwin	1903		Sold to Texas & New Orleans, 1906	
4-4-2	E-1	550-553	4	Baldwin	1903	A-4	Scrapped 1929, 1939	
4-4-2	E-2	554-558	5	Baldwin	1906	A-5	Scrapped 1929, 1939	
4-6-0	G-3A	250-259	10	Baldwin	1901			
4-6-2	I-1	600	1	Baldwin	1903	P-10	5265	
4-6-2	I-2	601	1	Baldwin	1903	P-11	5266	
4-6-2	I-3	602-604	3	Baldwin	1903-1904	P-12	5267-5269	
4-6-2	I-4	605-609	5	Baldwin	1908	P-13a	5270-5274	
4-6-2	I-5, a	620-634	15	Brooks	1909-1910	P-14, P-15	5275-5289	
4-6-2	I-6	650-659	10	Brooks	1913	P-16	5290-5299	

CHICAGO & EASTERN ILLINOIS RAILWAY

By Charles Kratz

In 1900 the Chicago & Eastern Illinois consisted of a main line from Chicago through Danville, Ill., to Terre Haute, Indiana; a line from Danville southwest to the Mississippi River at Thebes; a line from Wellsboro, Ind., south to Brazil (spun off in 1921 as the Chicago, Attica & Southern); and a few short branches and lines connecting the Wellsboro-Brazil route with the main line. In 1902 C&EI came under control of the St. Louis-San Francisco (Frisco) and extended its line to St Louis, mostly by trackage rights on the Big Four, part of the New York Central System. A few years later C&EI absorbed the Evansville & Terre Haute, which had two lines connecting the Indiana cities of its name (and which C&EI had controlled for some time). The Evansville route was essentially a Chicago extension of the Louisville & Nashville. The busiest section of the C&EI was from Danville north to Chicago, and double-tracking of that portion began in 1888.

Coal was C&EI's principal commodity, and its routes were located to feed Chicago's insatiable demand for bituminous. Its lines served four coal-mining areas; 350 of its 1,100 route miles were in the coalfields of Indiana and Illinois. C&EI inherited a nondescript assortment of locomotives from its predecessors, and its physical plant was ill suited to coal traffic. Dirt ballast, light bridges, and small locomotives all needed to be upgraded to move coal economically.

Control by the Frisco brought a change in motive power policy, from small orders placed with several builders to large orders of a single type from one or two builders. C&EI had favored Alco's predecessors; SLSF liked Baldwin. Between 1903 and 1913 C&EI retired aging Americans and Moguls and bought 252 locomotives — well over half the locomotives that were on the roster when Frisco control ended. SLSF control brought rationalization to the roster and a new numbering and classification system. Frisco's regimentation was precisely what C&EI's motive power department needed, but the price of the new power was a mountain of debt. The decline of the Indiana coalfields and the opening of the western Kentucky coalfields in the early years of the 20th century changed C&EI's traffic pattern. It no longer had a monopoly on Chicago coal and had to compete for bridge traffic. It turned from a strategy of running long, slow trains to one of running short, fast trains for high-value merchandise and perishables.

In 1912 SLSF entered bankruptcy, dragging the C&EI down with it. The primary reason for C&EI's bankruptcy was the Frisco-directed buying spree of the previous decade, during which C&EI acquired new locomotives and thousands of new cars. Resolution of the bankruptcy left C&EI a debt-ridden railroad with little hope for immediate improvement. As a consequence, the Frisco-era locomotives consti-

Atlantic 222 survived until 1947. Rebuilding has given the engine Walschaerts valve gear and a pair of cross-compound air pumps — a single pump would be enough for any train the 4-4-2 could pull — but wood cab and archbar tender trucks remain in this 1940 view. Photo by John B. Allen.

Pacific 1016 was one of a pair built by Schenectady in 1913, the road's only Alco 4-6-2s. Alco photo; collection of C. W. Witbeck.

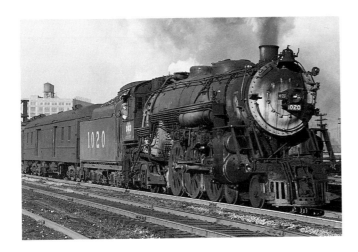

C&EI's best-known engines were the six Lima heavy Pacifics of 1923. Number 1020 displays latter-day improvements — a cast, drop-coupler pilot and a full set of Boxpok drivers — as it accelerates the *Dixie Limited* out of Chicago on a winter day in 1947. Photo by Donald R. Deneen.

tuted the major portion of C&EI's steam locomotive fleet until the end of steam. Bankruptcy also left C&EI with an extremely conservative mechanical department.

C&EI had a surplus of motive power in the 1920s and through the Depression. The road's shops at Danville, Illinois, upgraded the Pacifics and Mikes for performance rather than efficiency, with mechanical stokers and power reverses but not feedwater heaters. World War II was hard on the road, and by 1945 C&EI's locomotives were worn out. The road developed a preliminary design for a 4-8-4, but three Electro-Motive E7s delivered in 1946 for new streamliners changed management's mind. A steady stream of F3s began arriving from La Grange in 1948; steam was done. Mikado 1944 was the last steam locomotive to operate, at Vincennes, Ind., on May 5, 1950. No C&EI steam locomotives survive, but a set of drivers from one of the Atlantics is on operating display at Chicago's Museum of Science & Industry.

Freight locomotives

The largest group of locomotives bought during the era of Frisco control was the 120 Consolidations that arrived between 1903 and 1906, the H-2, H-3, H-5, and H-6 classes, Nos. 820-839 and 863-962. Driver size ranged from 54" to 58", and weight was about 175,000 pounds. They were significantly larger than Frisco's 2-8-0s, because C&EI's freight density — tons per mile — was about four times that of Frisco, and average train weight was more than twice as much. The Frisco-era Consolidations had long lives, although after the Mikados arrived they were limited to mine, transfer, and switching work. Even though the 2-8-0s were the most numerous type on the roster, only 16 of them were ever fitted with superheaters, an indication of their limited use in road service.

The most important group of locomotives were the 25 class N-1 Mikados, Nos. 1900-1924, delivered by Brooks in 1912. They had 63" drivers and 28" × 30" cylinders and were relatively heavy — 308,000 pounds, as rebuilt in later years with stokers and power reverses. They were fast and powerful, and they changed the way C&EI did business.

In 1918 Baldwin delivered seven heavy 2-10-2s with 63" drivers and

30" × 32" cylinders. They were classed O-1 and numbered 2000-2006. Soon afterward the USRA assigned five light 2-10-2s to C&EI. The road refused them, stating they were too heavy for their intended service — though they were lighter than the O-1 class. As it was, C&EI had difficulty finding work for its 2-10-2s; they eventually were relegated to Chicago transfer runs and southern Illinois coal drags.

C&EI accepted the USRA's other offering, 15 light 2-8-2s from Alco's Schenectady Works, classing them N-2 and numbering them 1925-1939. After World War I Alco delivered 20 2-8-2s of C&EI's N-1 design, Nos. 1940-1949 from Brooks in 1922, and 1950-1959 from Schenectady in 1923.

Passenger locomotives

The first five years of the 20th century brought an assortment of 4-6-0s to C&EI, some simple and some cross-compound, with drivers ranging from 63" to 78". They were soon either too light or too slow for passenger trains. The last Ten-Wheelers left the roster in 1936.

Except for Nos. 200 and 201, C&EI's Atlantics, built between 1903 and 1907, were of a New York Central design, with inside piston valves and 79" drivers. The two exceptions were 73"-drivered Evansville & Terre Haute engines that were considerably lighter. Most were too light for steel passenger trains and were retired in the 1930s, but two survived until 1947.

Pacifics 1000-1007 were delivered by Baldwin in 1910, relatively light machines with 73" drivers. Eight K-2 class Pacifics, Nos. 1008-1015, came from Baldwin in 1911 and 1912, and Alco's Schenectady Works delivered two more in 1913. They had the same 73" drivers but larger cylinders, 26½" × 28", and were about 15 to 20 tons heavier — a little heavier than a USRA light Pacific.

C&EI's best — and best-known — engines were six K-3 Pacifics, Nos. 1018-1023, built by Lima in 1923. They were based on the USRA heavy Pacific, and had cast trailing trucks and large tenders. Through the years C&EI's Pacifics underwent much improvement, the visible aspects being cast pilots and disk drivers. K-2 Pacific No. 1008 was streamlined in 1940 for the Chicago-Miami *Dixie Flagler*.

Switchers

Between 1903 and 1910 C&EI received 42 six-wheel switchers with 50" or 51" drivers and ranging in weight from 132,000 to 160,000 pounds. They lasted from 18 to 40 years; most were off the roster by the mid-1930s, replaced by 2-8-0s that had themselves been replaced by 2-8-2s.

Historical and technical society: Chicago & Eastern Illinois Railroad Historical Society, P. O. Box 606, Crestwood, IL 60445

Published rosters:

Railroad Magazine: June 1933, page 92

Trains Magazine: August 1949, page 20

C&EI STEAM LOCOMOTIVES BUILT SINCE 1900

Type	Class	Numbers	Qty	Builder	Built	Retired	Notes
0-6-0	M-1	1700-1704	5	C&EI		-1918	
						Rebuilt from M-1 Camelback compounds (Pittsburgh, 1900)	
0-6-0	B-2	3612-3614	3	Cooke	1903	-1921	
0-6-0	B-3	3615-3625	11	BLW	1906	1930-1946	
							3616 ex-E&TH, renumbered A962
0-6-0	B-3	3626-3634	9	Schenectady	1903, 1905	1930-1934	
0-6-0	B-4	3635-3653	19	BLW	1906, 1910	1934-1948	
0-6-0	B-5	3660-3675	16	C&EI	1916-1924	1934	
						Rebuilt from M-3 4-8-0s (Pittsburgh, 1897-1899)	
0-8-0	C-1	818	1	C&EI	1912	1921	
						Rebuilt from C&IC 2-8-0 (BLW, 1887)	
0-8-0	C-1	800-804	5	C&EI		1917-1921	
						Rebuilt from H-1 2-8-0s 800-804 (Schenectady, 1891)	
0-8-0	C-1	808	1	C&EI		1921	
						Rebuilt from H-1 2-8-0 808 (Schenectady, 1891)	
0-8-0	C-2	1800-1802	3	Baldwin	1906	1948-1949	
2-8-0	H-2	820-834	15	Schenectady	1905	1928-1930	
2-8-0	H-3	835-839	5	BLW, Pitt	1903	1930	Ex-E&TH
2-8-0	H-4	840-862	23	Schenectady	1901-1902	1934-1938	
						Compound, simpled 1907-1908	
2-8-0	H-4	963-965	3	Schenectady	1901-1902	1934-1949	
						Compound, simpled 1907-1908	
2-8-0	H-5	869-878	10	Schenectady	1903	1934-1938	
2-8-0	H-6	863-868	6	Baldwin	1906	1934-1944	Ex-E&TH
2-8-0	H-6	879-962	84	Baldwin	1904-1906	1934-1950	
2-8-2	N-4	1900-1924	25	Brooks	1912	1947-1950	Ex-N-1

Type	Class	Numbers	Qty	Builder	Built	Retired	Notes
2-8-2	N-2	1925-1939	15	Schenectady	1918	1940-1950	USRA light
2-8-2	N-3	1940-1959	20	Brks, Schen	1922, 1923	1949-1950	
							Rebuilt from N-1sa
2-10-2	O-1	2000-2006	7	Baldwin	1918	Sold to C&O and CofG, 1945	
2-10-2	O-2	4000, 4001	2	Brooks	1917		
						Ex-Wabash (1942), Sold to C&O, 1945	
2-10-2	O-2	2007-2011	5	Brooks	1919		
						USRA light, refused, transferred to PRR	
							Ex-E&TH
4-4-2	E-1	200, 201	2	Brooks	1903	1930	
4-4-2	E-2	202-215	14	Schenectady	1903-1905	1939-1941	
4-4-2	E-2	216-225	10	Baldwin	1906-1907	1934-1947	
4-6-0	G-3	611-615	5	Pittsburgh	1900	1929	

Type	Class	Numbers	Qty	Builder	Built	Retired	Notes
4-6-0	G-3	616	1	Pittsburgh	1902	1924	
						Cross-compound, later simpled	
4-6-0	G-6	621-625	5	Rhode Island	1902	1920-1924	
						Cross-compound	
4-6-0	G-7	626-639	14	Schenectady	1904	1920-1936	
4-6-0	G-4	617, 618	2	Baldwin	1905	1934	Compound
4-6-0	G-5	619, 620	2	Schenectady	1905	1924	Ex-E&TH
4-6-2	K-1	1000-1007	8	Baldwin	1910	1941-1949	
						1005-1007 were E&TH 535-537	
4-6-2	K-2	1008-1015	8	Baldwin	1911-1912	1948-1950	
4-6-2	K-2	1016, 1017	2	Schenectady	1913	1949	
4-6-2	K-3	1018-1023	6	Lima	1923	1949-1950	

MINNEAPOLIS & ST. LOUIS RAILROAD

The Minneapolis & St. Louis of 1900 had three lines: from Minneapolis south through Albert Lea, Minnesota, and Fort Dodge, Iowa, to Angus, a few miles north of Perry, Iowa; from Minneapolis west to Watertown, South Dakota; and from Winthrop, Minn., on the Watertown line, south to Storm Lake, Iowa. The Iowa Central, which had the same president, Edwin Hawley, consisted of a line from Albert Lea south through Hampton, Marshalltown, and Oskaloosa, Iowa, to Albia; and east from Oskaloosa to Peoria, Illinois, crossing the Mississippi River at Keithsburg, Ill.

In 1912 M&StL purchased the Iowa Central (it had leased it since 1903) and the Minnesota, Dakota & Pacific Railway, which extended west from Watertown to Akaska and Leola, S. D. In 1915 it purchased the Des Moines & Fort Dodge, which had a line from Des Moines northwest through Perry, Angus, and Fort Dodge to Ruthven, Iowa; a few miles of trackage rights on the Milwaukee Road provided a connection with the Storm Lake line at Spencer, Iowa.

M&StL's main line ran north and south, but most of the traffic in the area moved east and west. The traffic surge of World War I left the engines, cars, and track in poor condition, and the business recession of the early 1920s hurt the road's traffic. M&StL entered receivership in 1923, and its condition gradually worsened to the point where neighboring roads proposed carving it up.

Lucian Sprague became receiver in 1935 and undertook a thorough rehabilitation of the M&StL, developing it into a Chicago bypass. The road came out of receivership, healthy, in 1942. It completed dieselization in 1951. Chicago & North Western purchased M&StL in 1960 and subsequently abandoned large portions of it.

The newest steam locomotives on M&StL were 15 Mikados and five Pacifics delivered by Brooks in 1921 during a brief period of postwar prosperity. In the early 1940s the road sought bids on five 2-6-6-4s and went so far as to use photos of them in advertising — photos of Seaboard Air Line 2-6-6-4s with the lettering blanked out. The War Production Board assigned Electro-Motive FTs instead, and they proved a better choice for M&StL.

Iowa Central's locomotives were renumbered shortly after M&StL leased the road, and some of those numbers duplicated M&StL num-

Lucian Sprague's overhaul of the M&StL included rebuilding the best locomotives and scrapping the worst. The rebuilt Mikados were fitted with booster-equipped trailing trucks and running board skirts. Two Mikes got further beautification in the form of stainless-steel boiler jackets and concealed piping. M&StL photo.

bers. In 1912 the IaC locomotives were again renumbered, this time into M&StL series — and not usually in sequence. For example, IaC Ten-Wheelers 70-73 became IaC 224-227 in 1910 and M&StL 224, 225, 222, and 223 in 1912. Meanwhile, M&StL locomotives were renumbered in 1910. Classifications also changed, and digits were appended to indicate tonnage rating. The 2-8-2s, for example, were changed from M-1 to M1-46 to indicate 46,000 pounds tractive effort. The last numbers and classes are used here. Issue 154 of *Railroad History* gives the full story on renumbering.

Freight locomotives

M&StL and Iowa Central both favored the 2-6-0 for freight service. The most numerous class were the F-1s, with 63" drivers. The ex-Iowa Central 2-6-0s of the F2-33 class had 57" drivers. The F3-30, F4-33, and F5-32 Moguls had 51" drivers and were eventually numbered between two groups of 0-6-0s, a good indication they were assigned to switching duties.

Most of the 2-8-0s were purchased in parallel groups for M&StL and IaC. They had 59" drivers and 21" × 30" cylinders; the H5-39 class had 22" cylinders. The H2-38 engines were not superheated; the H6-38s were fitted with superheaters in 1915 and 1916. Number 451, an H5-39, was equipped with a tender booster. The H4-34 class was different — 55" drivers — and that difference probably accounts for its early retirement.

Alco's Schenectady Works delivered 15 Mikados in 1915. They had 24" × 30" cylinders and 59" drivers, and weighed 259,900 pounds — light as Mikados went. Brooks delivered five more in 1916 and 15 in 1921. The 1921 Mikes weighed less, 252,500 pounds, and were later upgraded with trailing truck boosters and 200-pound boiler pressure. Three earlier 2-8-2s also received boosters but remained at 185 pounds.

Pacific 502 was streamstyled and remained on the roster for special trains long after motor cars had taken over passenger service. The flat bar across the top of the bell prevented the bell from turning over when being rung vigorously. M&StL photo.

Some of the rebuilt Mikes were fitted with running board skirts, and two got stainless-steel boiler jackets.

Passenger locomotives

M&StL's 19th-century 4-4-0s were dual-service locomotives with drivers in the 60"-63" range. Engines 156 and 157, built by Schenectady in 1906, had 69" drivers, putting them in the passenger category. The G-3 and G-6 Ten-Wheelers, Nos. 214-217 and 226-229, were also passenger engines.

Iowa Central favored the 4-6-0 and in the 1890s purchased batches of them with 51", 55", and 62" drivers. Ten 4-6-0s were delivered in 1900, all with 63" drivers: four simple engines from Cooke (they became M&StL 222-225) and six Vauclain compounds from Baldwin (M&StL 230-235). The Baldwins were simpled between 1909 and 1911.

Brooks delivered five Pacifics along with the 15 Mikados in 1921. They were light, 225,000 pounds, and had 69" drivers. Gas-electric cars took over most M&StL passenger trains in the 1930s, and by the late 1940s the trains, all locals, consisted simply of mail-baggage motor cars and Budd-built streamlined coaches. Four Pacifics were scrapped in 1939 and 1940; No. 502, which had been dressed up with running board skirts and striping, remained on the roster until 1949.

Switchers

Six-wheel switchers 59 and 60 were the last of a series of eight built by Baldwin between 1896 and 1906. Ten good-sized modern 0-6-0s numbered 80-89 were delivered by Brooks in 1916. They had 57" drivers,

piston valves, and Walschaerts valve gear. They looked like USRA 0-6-0s but were 9,000 pounds heavier.

Historical and technical society: Chicago & North Western Historical Society, P. O. Box 1436, Elmhurst, IL 60126-9998

Published rosters:
Railroad Magazine, March 1935, page 81
Railroad History, No. 154

M&StL STEAM LOCOMOTIVES BUILT SINCE 1900

Type	Class	Numbers	Qty	Builder	Built	Retired	Notes
0-6-0	B2-27	59, 60	1	Baldwin	1906	1940, 1936	
0-6-0	B3-35	80-89	10	Brooks	1916	1949-1950	
2-6-0	F1-27	300-305	6	Schenectady	1902	1935-1950	Ex-Iowa Central
2-6-0	F1-28	306-328	23	Schenectady	1899-1906	1935-1951	
2-6-0	F2-33	329-334	6	Baldwin	1908	1936-1948	Ex-Iowa Central
2-6-0	F3-30	63, 64	2	Baldwin	1908	1942, 1938	Ex-Iowa Central
2-6-0	F4-33	65, 66	2	Baldwin	1910	1941, 1942	
2-6-0	F5-32	67-69	3	Baldwin	1909	1939-1946	
2-8-0	H2-38	400-406	7	Baldwin	1909	1936-1950	500-506
2-8-0	H2-38	408-419	12	Baldwin	1909	1935-1947	Ex-Iowa Central
2-8-0	H4-34	442-447	6	Schenectady	1902	1936-1939	Ex-Iowa Central
2-8-0	H5-39	450-461	12	Schenectady	1912	1944-1950	
2-8-0	H6-38	462-471	10	Baldwin	1910	1938-1946	Ex-Iowa Central
2-8-0	H6-38	472-481	10	Baldwin	1910	1938-1947	
2-8-2	M1-46	600-634	35	Schen, Brks	1915-1921	1940-1951	
4-4-0	D9-24	156, 157	2	Schenectady	1906	1938, 1937	
4-6-0	G3-22	214-217	4	Schenectady	1900-1901	1935-1938	
4-6-0	G5-25	222-225	4	Cooke	1900	1931, 1936	Ex-Iowa Central
4-6-0	G6-24	226-229	4	Baldwin	1909	1946-1950	
4-6-0	G7-25	230-235	6	Baldwin	1900	1935	Ex-Iowa Central
4-6-2	K1-32	500-504	5	Brooks	1921	1939-1949	

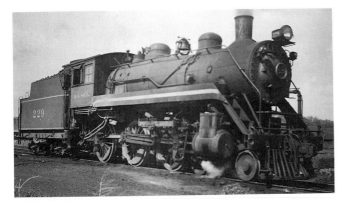

The G6-24 Ten-Wheelers were the last of their type on the roster, and at least one, No. 229, received running board skirts. Less obvious are piston valves retrofitted in the slide-valve steam chests. Photo by Robert Milner.

INDEX

Boldface type indicates the principal entry for a subject. *Italic type* indicates photographs of railroads' locomotives that are apart from the principal entry. Only the first appearance of a subject that appears throughout an entry is indexed.